Lecture Notes in Computer Science 2013

Edited by G. Goos, J. Hartmanis and J. van Leeuwen

W0107590

Springer

Berlin
Heidelberg
New York
Barcelona
Hong Kong
London
Milan
Paris
Singapore
Tokyo

Sameer Singh   Nabeel Murshed
Walter Kropatsch (Eds.)

Advances in Pattern Recognition – ICAPR 2001

Second International Conference
Rio de Janeiro, Brazil, March 11-14, 2001
Proceedings

 Springer

Series Editors

Gerhard Goos, Karlsruhe University, Germany
Juris Hartmanis, Cornell University, NY, USA
Jan van Leeuwen, Utrecht University, The Netherlands

Volume Editors

Sameer Singh
University of Exeter, Department of Computer Science
Exeter EX4 4PT, UK
E-mail: s.singh@ex.ac.uk

Nabeel Murshed
Tuiuti University of Parana, Computational Intelligence Group
Curitiba, Brazil
E-mail: nmurshed@cognus.eti.br

Walter Kropatsch
Vienna University of Technology
Institute of Computer Aided Automation, PRIP-Group 1832
Favoritenstr. 9/2/4, 1040 Wien, Austria
E-mail: krw@prip.tuwien.ac.at

Cataloging-in-Publication Data applied for

Die Deutsche Bibliothek - CIP-Einheitsaufnahme

Advances in pattern recognition : second international conference /
ICAPR 2001, Rio de Janeiro, Brazil, March 11 - 14, 2001. Sameer Singh
... (ed.). - Berlin ; Heidelberg ; New York ; Barcelona ; Hong Kong ;
London ; Milan ; Paris ; Singapore ; Tokyo : Springer, 2001
    (Lecture notes in computer science ; Vol. 2013)
    ISBN 3-540-41767-2

CR Subject Classification (1998): I.5, I.4, I.3, I.7.5

ISSN 0302-9743
ISBN 3-540-41767-2 Springer-Verlag Berlin Heidelberg New York

Springer-Verlag Berlin Heidelberg New York
a member of BertelsmannSpringer Science+Business Media GmbH

http://www.springer.de

© Springer-Verlag Berlin Heidelberg 2001
Printed in Germany

Typesetting: Camera-ready by author
Printed on acid-free paper   SPIN 10782141   06/3142   5 4 3 2 1 0

Preface

This volume of LNCS contains all of the papers that were presented at the Second International Conference on Advances in Pattern Recognition held in Rio, March 11-14, 2001. The conference was first organised in November 1998 in Plymouth UK as a platform to bring invited speakers to a key small-scale meeting where ideas could be shared in a scientific environment. Philosophically, the conference encourages papers that focus on the *advances* in the field of pattern recognition. As such, the emphasis has been on the open exchange of ideas. Paper presentation and discussion of technical issues is given more time and more focus using a single track for the conference. The conference encourages individuality and creativity in the scientific context with the aim of fostering new ideas that will lay the foundations for future scientific work in this area.

ICAPR 2001 was organised to bring together key plenary speeches by leading researchers in pattern recognition. The plenary speakers included Prof. Ruspini from SRI, USA, Prof. Pentland from MIT Media Lab, USA, Prof. Bunke from the University of Berne, Switzerland, Prof. Fukuda from Nagoya University, Japan, and Prof. Hlávač from the Czech Technical University, Czech Republic. Detailed knowledge of specific domains was made available through the tutorial program on the first day of the conference. The key themes under which the papers were submitted and accepted included neural networks and evolutionary computation, character recognition and document analysis, feature selection, pattern recognition, and image/signal processing theory and applications.

ICAPR 2001 was a fully reviewed conference and as such we are thankful to a number of people for their contribution to the review process. Also, thanks are due to the local arrangements committee for making the conference possible in Rio. The support from the International Association of Pattern Recognition has been key to generating good publicity in the pattern recognition community. The conference is also supported by the British Computer Society. Our thanks are due to the International University in Germany, Tuiuti University of Parana, and VARIG who have financially helped make this conference a success. We would like to thank Springer-Verlag for continuing to support this conference series. Springer London printed the previous proceedings of the UK conference in 1998 as a book. We hope that Springer will continue to support this conference series in the future.

For any conference, its success is determined by the quality of publications it has and the longevity of the research papers that appear in its proceedings. We hope that this LNCS volume will meet these expectations. For making this possible, the authors and attendees of the conference could not be thanked enough.

Sameer Singh
Nabeel Murshed
Walter Kropatsch

March 2001

ICAPR 2001 - List of Referees

We would like to thank the following referees for their valuable reviews and comments on submitted papers.

Adnan Amin, *University of New South Wales, Australia*
Horst Bischof, *Technical University of Vienna, Austria*
Dibio Borges, *Federal University of Goias, Brazil*
Guido Bugmann, *University of Plymouth, U.K.*
Horst Bunke, *Institut fur Informatik und angewandte Mathematik (IAM), Switzerland*
Andreas Dengel, *German Research Centre for AI GmbH, Germany*
Evgenia Dimitriadou, *Technical University of Vienna, Austria*
Nicolae Duta, *Michigan State University, U.S.A.*
Nick Efford, *University of Leeds, U.K.*
Richard Everson, *University of Exeter, U.K.*
Michael Fairhurst, *University of Kent, U.K.*
Luc Van Gool, *Katholieke Universitat Leuven, Belgium*
Marco Gori, *University of Siena, Italy*
John F. Haddon, *Defence Evaluation and Research Agency, U.K.*
Gregory Hager, *The Johns Hopkins University, U.S.A.*
Jean Michel Jolion, *INSA, France*
Gareth Jones, *University of Exeter, U.K.*
Joseph Kittler, *University of Surrey, U.K.*
Ales Leonardis, *University of Ljubljana, Slovenia*
Peter Meer, *Rutgers University, U.S.A.*
Nabeel Murshed, *Universidade Tuiuti do Parana, Brazil*
Ajit Narayanan, *University of Exeter, U.K.*
Derek Partridge, *University of Exeter, U.K.*
Maria Petrou, *University of Surrey, U.K.*
Nalini Ratha, *IBM Research, U.S.A.*
Sarunas Raudys, *Institute of Mathematics and Informatics, Lithuania*
Nasser Sherkat, *The Nottingham Trent University, U.K.*
Sameer Singh, *University of Exeter, U.K.*
Jasjit Suri, *Marconi Medical System, Inc., U.S.A.*
Jayaram K. Udupa, *Temple University, U.S.A.*
Zheng Yang, *University of Exeter, U.K.*

Tuiuti University of Paraná, Brazil
VARIG - The Brazilian Airlines
National Center for Information Management Development

Table of Contents

INVITED TALKS

NEURAL NETWORKS & COMPUTATIONAL INTELLIGENCE

CHARACTER RECOGNITION & DOCUMENT ANALYSIS

FEATURE SELECTION & ANALYSIS

PATTERN RECOGNITION & CLASSIFICATION

IMAGE & SIGNAL PROCESSING APPLICATIONS

IMAGE FEATURE ANALYSIS & RETRIEVAL

TUTORIALS

Towards Bridging the Gap between Statistical and Structural Pattern Recognition: Two New Concepts in Graph Matching

H. Bunke, S. Günter, X.Jiang

Dept. of Computer Science, Univ. of Bern, Switzerland

Email: {bunke,sguenter,jiang}@iam.unibe.ch

Abstract

Two novel concepts in structural pattern recognition are discussed in this paper. The first, median of a set of graphs, can be used to characterize a set of graphs by just a single prototype. Such a characterization is needed in various tasks, for example, in clustering. The second novel concept is weighted mean of a pair of graphs. It can be used to synthesize a graph that has a specified degree of similarity, or distance, to each of a pair of given graphs. Such an operation is needed in many machine learning tasks. It is argued that with these new concepts various well-established techniques from statistical pattern recognition become applicable in the structural domain, particularly to graph representations. Concrete examples include k-means clustering, vector quantization, and Kohonen maps.

Keywords: Graph matching, error-tolerant matching, edit distance, median graph, weighted mean

1 Introduction

The field of pattern recognition can be divided into the statistical and the structural approach. Statistical pattern recognition, including methods based on neural networks, is characterized by the use of feature vectors to represent patterns. A feature vector can be regarded as a point in an n-dimensional feature space, and classification is accomplished by dividing this space into disjoint regions, each of which represents a different pattern class. For a recent survey on statistical pattern recognition see [12]. In the structural approach, symbolic data structures, such as strings, trees, and graphs, are used for pattern representation and pattern recognition is achieved by either matching the data structure which represents an unknown input pattern with

S. Singh, N. Murshed, and W. Kropatsch (Eds.): ICAPR 2001, LNCS 2013, pp. 1–11, 2001.

a number of known prototypes, or by parsing it according to a given grammar [6, 10]. If grammars and syntactical parsing are involved, we usually refer to syntactic, rather than structural, pattern recognition.

A comparison of the statistical and the structural approach reveals that the latter is more powerful in terms of its representational capabilities, because any feature vector can be represented by a string, a tree, or a graph, but not vice versa. From the application oriented point of view, symbolic data structures are able to model structural relationships between the various parts of a complex pattern, while feature vectors are limited to the representation of the values of individual features, considered in isolation. On the other hand, the set of mathematical tools available in the statistical approach is much richer than in the structural domain. Basically, the vast majority of all structural and syntactic recognition methods rely on either nearest-neighbor classifiers using edit distance or some other similarity measure, or on some kind of parsing to determine class membership [1, 2, 8, 21]. By contrast, a large number of procedures have become available in statistical pattern recognition, including various types of neural networks, decision theoretic methods, and clustering techniques [12].

In this paper we present some novel work in the area of graph matching that aims at bridging the gap between statistical and structural pattern recognition in the sense that it may yield a basis for adapting various techniques from statistical pattern recognition to the structural domain. In particular, we consider the problem of computing the median and the weighted mean of a set of graphs. Computing the median of a set of numbers or vectors is a well understood problem. But for the symbolic domain it was only recently that this problem has been studied. In [19] median computation of a set of strings and its application to combining the results of several OCR devices has been studied. A similar idea based on the longest common subsequence of a set of strings was reported in [22]. As the complexity of mean string computation is exponential in the number of strings involved, its applicability is limited. To make it useful for large sets and long strings, several approximative procedures have been proposed [7, 18, 19, 22]. An application of the method proposed in [7] to the synthesis of shapes has been described in [16].

In this paper we consider an extension of median computation from the domain of strings to the domain of graphs. We first review recent work in this area [5, 14] and then introduce a second new concept, namely, the weighted mean of a pair of graphs. Given a set of patterns, each represented in terms of a graph, the median graph of the set is a concept to represent the whole set by just a single graph. Such a representation is needed, for example, in the well-known k-means clustering algorithm [12]. The weighted mean of a pair of graphs allows to interpolate between two given graphs. Such an interpolation is required, for example, in self-organizing maps [17].

This paper is organized as follow. First, we introduce our basic notation in Section 2. Then we review recent work on median graph computation in Section 3 [5, 14]. In Section 4, the weighted mean of a pair of graphs is proposed and related computational procedures are discussed. Examples and experimental results are given in Section 5. Finally, a discussion and conclusions will be presented in Section 6.

2 Basic concepts and notation

Graphs are a flexible and powerful data structure for the representation of objects and concepts. In a graph representation, the nodes typically represent objects or parts of objects, while the edges describe relations between objects or object parts. Formally, a graph is a 4-tuple, $g = (V, E, \mu, \nu)$ where V is the set of nodes, $E \subseteq V \times V$ is the set of edges, $\mu : V \to L_V$ is a function assigning labels to the nodes, and $\nu : E \to L_E$ is a function assigning labels to the edges. In this definition, L_V and L_E is the set of node and edge labels, respectively.

If we delete some nodes from a graph g, together with their incident edges, we obtain a *subgraph* $g' \subseteq g$. A graph *isomorphism* from a graph g to a graph g' is a bijective mapping from the nodes of g to the nodes of g' that preserves all labels and the structure of the edges. Similarly, a *subgraph isomorphism* from g' to g is an isomorphism from g' to a subgraph of g. Another important concept in graph matching is *maximum common subgraph*. A maximum common subgraph of two graphs, g and g', is a graph g'' that is a subgraph of both g and g' and has, among all possible subgraphs of g and g', the maximum number of nodes. Notice that the maximum common subgraph of two graphs is usually not unique.

Graph isomorphism is a useful concept to find out if two objects are the same, up to invariance properties inherent to the underlying graph representation. Similarly, subgraph isomorphism can be used to find out if one object is part of another object, or if one object is present in a group of objects. Maximum common subgraph can be used to measure the similarity of objects even if there exists no graph or subgraph isomorphism between the corresponding graphs. Clearly, the larger the maximum common subgraph of two graphs is, the greater is their similarity.

Real world objects are usually affected by noise such that the graph representation of identical objects may not exactly match. Therefore it is necessary to integrate some degree of error tolerance into the graph matching process. A powerful alternative to maximum common subgraph computation is *error-tolerant graph matching* using *graph edit distance*. In its most general form, a graph *edit operation* is either a deletion, insertion, or substitution (i.e. label change). Edit operations can be applied to nodes as well as to edges.

Formally, let $g_1 = (V_1, E_1, \mu_1, \nu_1)$ and $g_2 = (V_2, E_2, \mu_2, \nu_2)$ be two graphs. An error-correcting graph matching (*ecgm*) from g_1 to g_2 is a bijective function $f : \hat{V}_1 \to \hat{V}_2$, where $\hat{V}_1 \subseteq V_1$ and $\hat{V}_2 \subseteq V_2$. We say that node $x \in \hat{V}_1$ is *substituted* by node $y \in \hat{V}_2$ if $f(x) = y$. If $\mu_1(x) = \mu_2(f(x))$ then the substitution is called an *identical* substitution. Otherwise it is termed a *non-identical* substitution. Any node from $V_1 - \hat{V}_1$ is *deleted* from g_1, and any node from $V_2 - \hat{V}_2$ is *inserted* in g_2 under f.

The mapping f *directly* implies an edit operation on each node in g_1 and g_2. I.e., nodes are substituted, deleted, or inserted, as described above. Additionally, the mapping f *indirectly* implies edit operations on the edges of g_1 and g_2. If $f(x_1) = y_1$ and $f(x_2) = y_2$, then the following situations are possible:

- $(x_1, x_2) \in E_1$ and $(y_1, y_2) \notin E_2$: in this case (x_1, x_2) is deleted from g_1;

- $(x_1, x_2) \notin E_1$ and $(y_1, y_2) \in E_2$: here (y_1, y_2) is inserted in g_2;

- $(x_1, x_2) \in E_1$ and $(y_1, y_2) \in E_2$: in this situation (x_1, x_2) in g_1 is substituted by (y_1, y_2) in g_2; if $\nu_1(x_1, x_2) = \nu_2(y_1, y_2)$, the substitution is an identical substitution;

- $(x_1, x_2) \notin E_1$ and $(y_1, y_2) \notin E_2$: no edit operation is implied.

If a node x is deleted from g_1, then any edge incident to x is deleted, too. Similarly, if a node x' is inserted in g_2, then any edge incident to x' is inserted, too. Obviously, any *ecgm* f can be understood as a set of edit operations (substitutions, deletions, and insertions of both nodes and edges) that transform a given graph g_1 into another graph g_2.

By means of the edit operations implied by an *ecgm* differences between two graphs that are due to noise and distortions are modelled. In order to enhance the noise modelling capabilities, often a cost is assigned to each edit operation. The cost are real numbers greater than or equal to zero. They are application dependent. Typically, the more likely a certain distortion is to occur the lower is its costs. Some theoretical considerations about the influence of the costs on *ecgm* can be found in [3]. The cost $c(f)$ of an *ecgm* f from a graph g_1 to a graph g_2 is the sum of the costs of the individual edit operations implied by f. An *ecgm* f from graph g_1 to a graph g_2 is *optimal* if there is no other *ecgm* from g_1 to g_2 with a lower cost. The *edit distance*, $d(g_1, g_2)$, of two graphs is equal to the cost of an optimal *ecgm* from g_1 to g_2, i.e.

$$d(g_1, g_2) = min\{c(f) | f : \hat{V}_1 \rightarrow \hat{V}_2 \text{ is an ecgm}\} \qquad (1)$$

This means that $d(g_1, g_2)$ is equal to the minimum cost taken over all *ecgms* from g_1 to g_2. In other words, the edit distance is equal to the minimum costs that are required to transform one graph into the other.

Obviously graph edit distance is a generalization of the well-known concept of string edit distance [24].

3 Median of a set of graphs

Clustering is a key concept in pattern recognition. While a large number of clustering algorithms have become available in the domain of statistical pattern recognition, relatively little attention has been paid to the clustering of symbolic structures, such as strings, trees, or graphs [9, 20, 23]. In principle, however, given a suitable similarity (or dissimilarity) measure, for example, edit distance, many of the clustering algorithms originally developed in the context of statistical pattern recognition, can be applied in the symbolic domain.

In this section we review work on a particular problem in graph clustering, namely, the representation of a set of similar graphs through just a single prototype [5, 14]. This problem typically occurs after a set of graphs has been partitioned into clusters. Rather than storing all members of a cluster, only one, or a few, representative elements are being retained.

Assume that we are given a set $G = \{g_1, \cdots, g_n\}$ of graphs and some distance function $d(g_1, g_2)$ to measure the dissimilarity between graphs g_1 and g_2. A straightforward approach to capturing the essential information in set G is to find a graph $\bar{g}$ that minimizes the average distance to all graphs in G, i.e.,

$$\bar{g} = \arg \min_{g} \frac{1}{n} \sum_{i=1}^{n} d(g, g_i) \tag{2}$$

Let's call graph $\bar{g}$ the *median* of G. If we constrain g to be a member of the given set G, then the resultant graph

$$\hat{g} = \arg \min_{g \in G} \frac{1}{n} \sum_{i=1}^{n} d(g, g_i) \tag{3}$$

is called the *set median* of G.

Given set G, the computation of the set median is a straightforward task. It requires just $O(n^2)$ distance computations. (Notice, however, that each of these distance computations has a high computational complexity, in general.) But the set median is restricted in the sense that it can't really generalize from the given patterns represented by set G. Therefore, median is the more powerful and interesting concept. However, the actual computational procedure for finding a median of a given set of graphs is no longer obvious.

It was theoretically shown that for particular costs of the edit operations and the case where G consists of only two elements, any maximum common subgraph of the two graphs under consideration is a median [4]. Further theoretical properties of the median have been derived in [15]. These properties are useful to restrict the search space for median graph computation, which was shown to be exponential in the number of graphs in set G and their size.

A practical procedure for median graph computation using a genetic search algorithm was proposed in [14]. An interesting feature of this algorithm is the chromosome representation. This representation encodes both, a generalized median graph candidate, and the optimal mapping of the nodes of this candidate to the nodes of the given graphs. Hence, the computationally expensive step of computing the optimal mapping for each candidate arising during the genetic search is avoided. Nevertheless, because of the high computational

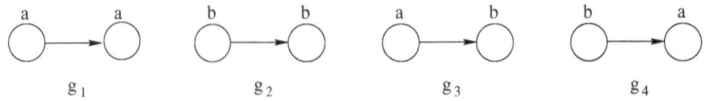

Figure 1: Both g_3 and g_4 are a mean of g_1 and g_2 (see text)

complexity inherent to the problem, the applicability of this procedure is still limited to rather small sets of graphs consisting of a few nodes each.

4 Weighted mean of a pair of graphs

Let g_1 and g_2 be graphs. The *mean* of g_1 and g_2 is a graph g such that

$$d(g_1, g) = d(g, g_2) \qquad (4)$$

and

$$d(g_1, g_2) = d(g_1, g) + d(g, g_2) \qquad (5)$$

Hence, g has the same distance to g_1 and g_2 and is, intuitively speaking, centred between g_1 and g_2. We call g a *weighted mean* of g_1 and g_2 if for some number α with $0 < \alpha < d(g_1, g_2)$ the following equations hold:

$$d(g_1, g) = \alpha \qquad (6)$$

and

$$d(g_1, g_2) = \alpha + d(g, g_2) \qquad (7)$$

Clearly, eqs. (4) and (5) are special cases of (6) and (7) if $d(g, g_2) = \alpha$ or, equivalently, $\alpha = 0.5 \cdot d(g_1, g_2)$.

Similarly to the median, the weighted mean of a pair of graphs isn't necessarily unique. Consider, for example, the graphs g_1 to g_4 in Fig. 1. Let the cost of each edit operation be equal to 1 (identical substitutions have cost 0). Then $d(g_1, g_2) = 2$, $d(g_1, g_3) = d(g_1, g_4) = d(g_2, g_3) = d(g_2, g_4) = 1$. Hence, both g_3 and g_4 are a mean of g_1 and g_2, or equivalently, both g_3 and g_4 are a weighted mean of g_1 and g_2 for $\alpha = 1$.

If $d(g_1, g_2)$ fulfills the triangular inequality[1], then any weighted mean of g_1 and g_2 is also a median. However, depending on the particular graphs and the cost of the edit operations, the weighted mean may not exist for arbitrary α. Therefore, not any median[2] of a pair of graphs is necessarily a mean. For the following considerations we assume that the costs associated with our edit operations fulfill the triangular inequality, i.e., if e_1, e_2 and e_3 are edit operations and the application of e_2 followed by e_3 has the same result as the application of e_1, then always

$$c(e_1) \leq c(e_2) + c(e_3) \qquad (8)$$

---

[1] This property holds if the costs of the individual edit operations fulfill the triangular equality, see eq. (8) below.
[2] Notice that a median of a pair of graphs always exists.

Notice that $d(g_1, g_2)$ is a metric, if additionally the costs are symmetric and strictly positive (i.e., $c(e_1) = c(e_2)$ if e_1 and e_2 are inverse to each other, and $c(e) > 0$ for any edit operation e different from a non-identical substitution).

We now turn to the question how to compute the weighted mean of a pair of given graphs, g_1 and g_2, and some α, $0 < \alpha < d(g_1, g_2)$. Assume that $f : \hat{V}_1 \to \hat{V}_2$ is an optimal $ecgm$ from g_1 to g_2. Furthermore, assume that there is a node $x \in \hat{V}_1$ which is non-identically substituted by $f(x) \in \hat{V}_2$, i.e. $\mu_1(x) \neq \mu_2(f(x))$. Let the cost of this substitution be γ. Apparently, if we replace the label of x by $\mu_2(f(x))$ we obtain a new graph, g, that is identical to g_1, up to the label of x. Clearly $d(g_1, g) = \gamma$ as one edit operation is needed to transform g_1 into g, and there can't be any other cheaper sequence of edit operations because of the triangular inequality (8) for edit costs. Now consider $d(g, g_2)$. Obviously, $d(g, g_2)$ can't be greater that $d(g_1, g_2) - \gamma$ because the $ecgm$ f from g_1 to g_2 can be used to map g to g_2. In other words, f may not only be regarded being an $ecgm$ from g_1 to g_2, but also one from g to g_2. In the second case, its cost is $d(g_1, g_2) - \gamma$. Can there exist another $ecgm$ f' from g to g_2 with a cost lower than $d(g_1, g_2) - \gamma$? The answer to this question is no, because the existence of such an $ecgm$ would contradict the optimality of f.

The considerations of the last paragraph hold not only for node substitutions, but also for any other edit operation. Furthermore, they can be extended form the case of a single edit operation to any sequence of edit operations induced by an optimal $ecgm$ (for details see [11].) This leads to the following scheme for computing the weighted mean of a pair of graphs. Given g_1 and g_2 we first compute an optimal $ecgm$ $f : \hat{V}_1 \to \hat{V}_2$. Then a subset $\{e_1, ..., e_n\}$ of the edit operations implied by f is taken and applied in any order to g, resulting in a new graph, g. If $\alpha = \sum_{i=1}^{n} c(e_i)$ then $d(g_1, g) = \alpha$ and $d(g, g_2) = d(g_1, g_2) - \alpha$, i.e., g is a weighted mean of g_1 and g_2. Depending on the cost of the edit operations, and on g_1 and g_2, there doesn't necessarily exist a weighted mean of any given value of α. However, given a fixed value of α, we first check for the existence of a subset $\{e_1, ..., e_n\}$ of edit operations such that $\alpha = \sum_{i=1}^{n} c(e_i)$. If such a subset doesn't exist, then we search for another subset the cost of which are as close to α as possible. A pseudo-code description of this procedure is shown in Fig. 2.

One step that is left unspecified in Fig. 2 is how to find the subsets of edit operations, E and E'. Actually, enumerating all possible subsets of the edit operations implied by the $ecgm$ f may be too expensive, as there exist 2^n such subsets for a total of n edit operations implied by f. In our implementation we have actually used a suboptimal procedure that is much more efficient. Under this procedure we first order all edit operations implied by the optimal $ecgm$ f according to their cost in descending order. Then we go sequentially through the resulting list, beginning with the most costly edit operation, and check the applicability of each edit operation. An edit operation e is applicable if $C + e \leq \alpha$, where C is the accumulated cost of all edit operations already applied on g_1. If the edit operation currently considered is applicable, we do

weighted_mean(g_1, g_2, α)
input: two graphs, g_1 and g_2 and a constant α with $0 < \alpha < d(g_1, g_2)$
output: a graph g such that $d(g_1, g) = \alpha$ and $d(g, g_2) = d(g_1, g_2) - \alpha$
begin
    compute an optimal *ecgm* $f : \hat{V}_1 \to \hat{V}_2$;
    if   there exists a subset $E = \{e_1, ..., e_n\}$ of edit operations implied by f
              such that $\alpha = \sum_{i=1}^{n} c(e_i)$
    then apply the edit operations of E in any order to g_1 to get graph g
    else choose a subset $E' = \{e'_1, ..., e'_m\}$ of edit operations such that $\alpha = \sum_{i=1}^{m} c(e_i)$ approximates α as closely as possible and apply them in any order to g_1 to get graph g.
    output g
end weighted_mean

Figure 2: Algorithm for computing the weighted mean

apply it to the current graph. Otherwise we skip it and continue with the next edit operation on the list. By means of this procedure, a sequence of edit operations is applied to g with a cost that is an approximation of α. It has been shown in practical experiments that very often the precise value of α is actually obtained [11].

The case of continuous labels and continuous substitution costs deserves special mentioning. This case occurs if the labels are real numbers, such as angles between line segments, or vectors in the 2-D plane, and the substitution cost is a linear function of the difference, i.e. the Euclidean distance, of the labels. Here we can apply *partial* substitutions in order to increase the similarity of g_1 and g_2 by any given degree. For example, if label $x \in R$ is to be changed into label $y \in R$ and the corresponding cost is $|x - y|$, but $|x - y| > \alpha$, we can choose label y' instead of y such that $|x - y'| = \alpha$. Hence, for this type of labels and cost functions, it is easier to find an exact weighted mean for a given value of α.

5 Applications and experiments

Concrete application examples of median graph computation involving graphical elements and hand-printed isolated characters have been given in [13, 14]. In the reminder of this section we describe a few experiments concerned with weighted mean graph computation. Two distorted versions of letter "F" are shown in Fig. 3a. In Fig. 3b various weighted means of these two line drawings resulting from different values of α are given. Apparently all of these weighted means capture our intuitive notion of shape similarity very well. With an increase of α, the original, left-most figure becomes gradually more similar to the right-most character.

The graph representation underlying Fig. 3 is quite simple. Each line segment is represented through a node with the coordinates of both endpoints

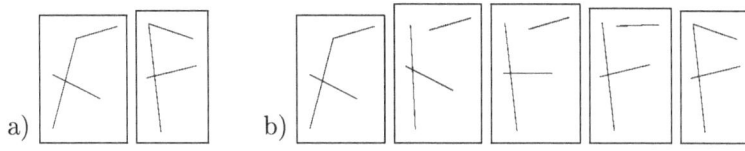

Figure 3: An example of weighted mean; a) source and target object, corresponding to g_1 and g_2, respectively; b) source and target object and three weighted means for $\alpha = 0.25$, $\alpha = 0.5$, $\alpha = 0.75$, resp.

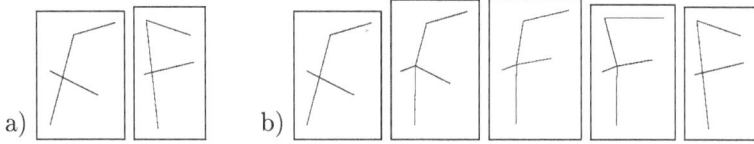

Figure 4: The same example as shown in Fig. 3 using a different graph representation; a) source and target object, corresponding to g_1 and g_2, respectively; b) source and target object and three weighted means for $\alpha = 0.25$, $\alpha = 0.5$, $\alpha = 0.75$, resp.

in the image plane as attributes. No edges are included in this kind of graph representation. The representation preserves all information of the underlying line drawing and is mathematically unique in the sense that two different line drawings will always have two different graphs associated with them and vice versa. Notice, however, that this representation explicitly includes only geometric, but no topological information, i.e., the connectivity of the lines is only implicitly represented in the node attributes.

The edit costs are defined as follows. The costs for deletion and insertion of a line segment is proportional to its length, while substitution costs are given by the summed distances of the end points of the considered line segments.

The experiment shown in Fig. 3 has been repeated for the same line drawing, but with a different graph representation. In the second graph representation the nodes represent locations where either a line segment ends, or where different line segments touch or overlap each other. The attributes of a node represent its location in the image. There is an edge between two nodes, if the corresponding locations are connected by a line in the image. No attributes are assigned to edges in this representation. Results for this type of graphs are shown in Fig. 4. Again our intuitive notion of shape similarity is well reflected in these figures. However, the connectivity of lines, which is not captured in the graph representation used in Fig. 3, is preserved in Fig. 4.

For the second type of graph representation the edit costs are defined as follows. The deletion and insertion cost of a node is constant, while the cost of a node substitution is proportional to the Euclidean distance of the corresponding points in the image plane. The deletion and insertion of an edge has also a constant cost. As there are no edge labels, edge substitutions can't occur with this type of graph representation.

For further experimental results with both graph representations see [11].

6   Conclusions

A rich set of tools have become available in the domain of statistical pattern recognition during the past years. On the other hand, structural approaches to pattern recognition are characterized by their high representational power. It appears that most methods from statistical pattern recognition aren't directly applicable to structural representations. Nevertheless their adaption to symbolic structures is highly desirable, resulting in a combination of sophisticated recognition techniques with enhanced representational power.

In this paper two novel concepts were introduced in the domain of structural pattern recognition. The first, median of a set of graphs, is useful to characterize a set of graphs by just one single prototype. Such a characterization is needed in various tasks. In clustering it is often necessary to represent a whole set of objects by just a single representative. An example is k-means clustering, where in each iteration step a new center for each cluster has to be computed. Median graphs as introduced in this paper can serve exactly this purpose. Hence, median graph together with graph edit distance allow to apply k-means clustering and related procedures in the domain of graphs. Furthermore, given the median and all original graphs of a set, the average distance of the set members to the median can be computed. This is similar to standard deviation in statistical pattern recognition. Hence the median of a set of graphs as defined in this paper is potentially useful to make concepts such as normal distribution or Mahalanobis distance [12] applicable to structural pattern recognition.

The second novel concept introduced in this paper is weighted mean of a pair of graphs. It is useful to interpolate between two given patterns in the sense that a new graph is constructed that has a given degree of similarity to each of the two given patterns. In other words, it allows to make one of the patterns more similar to the other. Weighted mean together with graph edit distance make it possible to apply methods such as Learning Vector Quantization and Kohonen Maps [17] in the domain of graphs. The crucial operation of these methods is to move one pattern closer to another by a given degree.

As strings and trees are special cases of graphs, median and weighted mean as introduced in this paper are applicable to these data structures as well. There are many more techniques in statistical pattern recognition that have been applied to vector representations only. Their adaption to the structural domain remains a challenge for future research.

References

[1] A. Admin, D. Dori, P. Pudil, and H. Freemann, editors. *Advances in Pattern Recognition.* Number 1451 in LNCS. Springer, 1998.

[2] H. Bunke, editor. *Advances in Structural and Syntactical Pattern Recognition.* World Scientific Publ. Co., 1992.

[3] H. Bunke. Error-tolerant graph matching: a formal framework and algorithms. In [1], pages 1–14. 1998.

[4] H. Bunke and A. Kandel. Mean and maximum common subgraph of two graphs. *Pattern Recognition Letters*, 21:163–168, 2000.

[5] H. Bunke, A. Münger, and X. Jiang. Combinatorial search versus genetic algorithms: a case study based on the generalized mean graph problem. *Pattern Recognition Letters*, 20:1271–1277, 1999.

[6] H. Bunke and A. Sanfeliu, editors. *Syntactic and Structural Pattern Recognition - Theory and Applications.* World Scientific Publ. Co., 1990.

[7] F. Casacuberta and M. Antonia. A greedy algorithm for computing approximate median strings. In *Proc. Nat. Symp. of Pattern Recognition and Image Analysis*, pages 193–198, Barcelona, Spain, 1996.

[8] D. Dori and A. Bruckstein, editors. *Shape, Structure and Pattern Recognition.* World Scientific Publ. Co., 1995.

[9] R. Englert and R. Glanz. Towards the clustering of graphs. In *Proc. 2nd IAPR-TC-15 Workshop on Graph Based Representations*, pages 125–133, 2000.

[10] K. Fu. *Syntactic Pattern Recognition and Applications.* Prentice Hall, 1982.

[11] S. Günter. Kohonen map for the domain of graphs. Master's thesis, University of Bern. In progress (in German).

[12] A. Jain, R. Duin, and J. Mao. Statistical Pattern Recognition: A Review. *IEEE Trans PAMI*, 22:4–37, 2000.

[13] X. Jiang, A. Münger, and H. Bunke. Synthesis of representative symbols by computing generalized median graphs. In *Proc. Int. Workshop on Graphics Recognition GREC '99*, pages 187–194, Jaipur, 1999.

[14] X. Jiang, A. Münger, and H. Bunke. Computing the generalized median of a set of graphs. In *Proc. 2nd IAPR-TC-15 Workshop on Graph Based Representations*, pages 115–124, 2000.

[15] X. Jiang, A. Münger, and H. Bunke. On median graphs: Properties, algorithms, and applications. *Submitted*, 2000.

[16] X. Jiang, L. Schiffmann, and H. Bunke. Computation of median shapes. In *4th Asian Conf. on Computer Vision*, pages 300–305, Taipei, Taiwan, 2000.

[17] T. Kohonen. *Self-Organizing Maps.* Springer Verlag, 1995.

[18] F. Kruzslicz. Improved greedy algorithm for computing approximate median strings. *Acta Cybernetica*, 14:331–339, 1999.

[19] D. Lopresti and J. Zhou. Using consensus voting to correct OCR errors. *Computer Vision and Image Understanding*, 67(1):39–47, 1997.

[20] S.-Y. Lu. A tree-to-tree distance and its application to cluster analysis. *IEEE Trans. PAMI*, 1:219–224, 1979.

[21] P. Perner, P. Wang, and A. Rosenfeld, editors. *Advances in Structural and Syntactical Pattern Recognition.* Number 1121 in LNCS. Springer, 1996.

[22] S. Rice, J. Kanai, and T. Nartker. A difference algorithm for OCR-generated text. In [2], pages 333–341, 1992.

[23] D. Seong, H. Kim, and K. Park. Incremental clustering of attributed graphs. *IEEE Trans. SMC*, 23:1399–1411, 1993.

[24] R. Wagner and M. Fischer. The string-to-string correction problem. *Journal of the Association for Computing Machinery*, 21(1):168–173, 1974.

Learning and Adaptation in Robotics

Toshio Fukuda[1] and Yasuhisa Hasegawa[2]

[1] Center for Cooperative Research in Advanced, Science and Technology, Nagoya
University, Furo-cho, Chikusa-ku, Nagoya 464-8603, Japan
[2] Dept. of Micro System Engineering, Nagoya University, Furo-cho, Chikusa-ku,
Nagoya 464-8603, Japan

Abstract. Intelligent systems are required in knowledge engineering,
computer science, mechatronics and robotics. This paper discusses the
machine (system) intelligence from the viewpoints of learning and adaptation of living things. Next, this paper introduces computational intelligence including neural network, fuzzy system, and genetic algorithm.
Finally, this paper shows some examples of intelligent robotic system:
brachiation robot and four-fingered robot hand.

1 Introduction

Intelligence for robot to grow and evolve can be observed both through growth
in computational power, and through the accumulation of knowledge of how
to sense, decide and act in a complex and dynamically changing world. There
are four elements of intelligence: sensory processing, world modeling, behavior
generation and value judgement. Input to, and output from, intelligent system
are via sensors and actuators. Recently, intelligent systems have been discussed
in knowledge engineering, computer science, mechatronics and robotics. Various
methodologies about intelligence have been successfully developed.

Artificial intelligence (AI) builds an intelligent agent, which perceives its environment by sensors, makes a decision and takes an action [1]. McCulloch and
Pitts suggested that suitably defined networks could learn [2], and furthermore,
Newell and Simon developed general problem solver [1]. Afterward, knowledge-
based system including expert systems has been developed [1]. In addition, language processing, reasoning, planning, and others have been discussed in AI so
far [1]. Human language enables the symbolic processing of information, and
is translate into numerical information according to an objective, that is, word
is classified into a certain attribute out of much information. In this way, the
symbolic information processing have resulted in success in AI. Further, The recent research fields concerning intelligence, include brain science, soft computing,
artificial life and computational intelligence [1]-[7].

Computational intelligence from the viewpoints of biology, evolution and self-
organization tries to construct intelligence by internal description, while classical
AI tries to construct intelligence by external (explicit) description. Therefore,
information and knowledge of a system in computational intelligence should be
learned or acquired by itself.

S. Singh, N. Murshed, and W. Kropatsch (Eds.): ICAPR 2001, LNCS 2013, pp. 12–23, 2001.

Robot is required to have intelligence and autonomous ability when it works far from an operator with large time delay, or when it works in a world containing ambiguous information. The robot collects or receives necessary information concerning its external environment, and takes actions to the environment. Both of them are often designed by human operators, but ideally, the robot should automatically perform the given task without human assistance. Computational intelligence methods including neural network (NN), fuzzy logic (FL) and evolutionary computation (EC), reinforcement learning, expert system and others, have been applied to realize intelligence on the robotic systems [2]-[14]. In addition, behavior-based AI has been discussed as learning methods dependent on environmental information [1],[15]. The behavior-based AI stresses the importance of the interaction between robot and environment, while classical AI is based on the representation and manipulation of explicit knowledge. Recently, behavior analysis and training as methodology for behavior engineering and model-based learning, have been proposed [15]-[18]. In this paper, we introduce a basic technique to build an intelligent system. After that, we introduce adaptation algorithm for brachiation robot and evolutionary computation for a four-fingered robot hand.

2   Intelligent System

Human being makes decision and takes actions based on the sensing information and internal state, when we consider human beings as an intelligent system. Furthermore, human beings can learn by acquiring or perceiving information concerning reward and penalty from the external environment. Thus, human beings perform the perception, decision making and action (Fig.1). In future, a robot will work out of a factory, in which an environment was simplified so that a robot could recognize it. The robot is required to have intelligence and autonomous capability when it works far from an operator with large time delay such as tele-operation, when sensing informations are contained ambiguous information. Key technologies for system intelligence and autonomous are knowledge representation, recognition, inference, search, planning, learning, prediction and so on [1].

The system intelligence emerges from the synthesis of various intelligent capabilities of the systems. Consequently, the whole intelligence of a system depends on the structure for processing information on hardware and software, and this means that the structure determines the potentiality of intelligence [20]. Therefore, we should consider a whole structure of intelligence for information process flow over the hardware and software.

3   Computational Intelligence

3.1   Neuro-Computing and Fuzzy Computing

Artificial neural network and fuzzy logic inference are based on the mechanism and information process of human brain. The human brain processes informa-

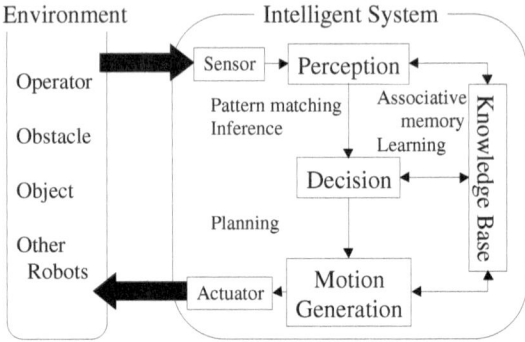

Fig. 1. Interaction between intelligent system and its environment

tion super-quickly. McCulloch and Pitts proposed that a suitably defined network could learn in 1943 [2]. After that, the rediscovery of back-propagation algorithm by Rumelhart, popularized artificial NN [2]. The artificial NN simulating the biological brain can be trained to recognize patterns and to identify incomplete patterns. The basic attributes of NN are the architecture and the functional properties; neurodynamics. The neurodynamics plays the role of nonlinear mapping from input to output. NN is composed of many interconnected neurons with input, output, synaptic strength and activation. The learning algorithms for adjusting weights of synaptic strength are classified into two types: supervised learning with target responses and unsupervised learning without explicit target responses. In general, a multi-layer NN is trained by a back propagation algorithm based on the error function between the output response and the target response. However, the back propagation algorithm, which is known as a gradient method, often misleads to local minimum. In addition, the learning capability of the NN depends on the structure of the NN and initial weights of the synaptic strength. Therefore, the optimization of the structure and the synaptic strength is very important for obtaining the desired target response. The other artificial NNs are Hopfield network, Boltzmann Machine, Adaptive Resonance Theory and Self-Organizing Map [2],[9]. The Hopfield network is regarded as an autoassociative fully connected network which has symmetrically weighted links [2]. The Boltzmann machine is based on the simulated annealing according to Metropolis dynamics [2]. The adaptive resonance theory model, which was developed by Grossberg and Carpenter, is composed of input/comparison layer and output/recognition layer [9],[21]. The self-organizing map, which was proposed by Kohonen, is a clustering algorithm creating a map of relationships among input and output patterns [9],[22].

While NN simulates physiological features of human brain, fuzzy logic inference simulates psychological features of human brain. Fuzzy logic provides us the linguistic representation such as 'slow' and 'fast' from numerical value. Fuzzy logic [5],[6],[9] expresses a degree of truth, which is represented as a grade of a membership function. It is a powerful tool for non-statistic and ill-defined structure. Fuzzy inference system is based on the concept of fuzzy set theory, fuzzy if-then rule, and fuzzy inference. The fuzzy inference derives conclusions from a set of fuzzy if-then rules. Fuzzy inference system implements mapping from its input space to output space by some fuzzy if-then rules. The widely used fuzzy inference systems are Mamdani fuzzy models and Takagi-Sugeno fuzzy models, which are used as a fuzzy controller. The feature of the fuzzy controller is the locality of control and the interpolation among local control laws. In the fuzzy controller, the state space of the system is divided into some regions as membership functions which are antecedent part, and the output (consequence) for the system control is designed as singletons, linear functions or membership functions. Next, the fuzzy rules are interpolated as a global controller. From the viewpoint of calculation in the inference, inference types are classified into min-max-gravity method, product-sum-gravity method, functional fuzzy inference method and simplified fuzzy inference method. In order to tune fuzzy rule, delta rule has been often applied to the functional fuzzy inference method and to the simplified fuzzy inference method like fuzzy-neural networks.

3.2   Evolutionary Computing

Evolutionary computation (EC) is a field of simulating evolution on a computer /citeFogel. From the historical point of view, the evolutionary optimization methods can be divided into three main categories, genetic algorithm (GA), evolutionary programming (EP) and evolution strategy (ES) [3],[4],[10]-[14]. These methods are fundamentally iterative generation and alternation processes operating on a set of candidate solutions, which is called a population. All the population evolves toward better candidate solutions by selection operation and genetic operators such as crossover and mutation. The selection operation picks up better solutions for the next generation, which limits the search space spanned by the candidate solutions. The crossover and mutation generate new candidates. EC methods can be divided into several categories from various points of view. This paper divides EC methods into genetic algorithm (GA) and evolutionary algorithm (EA) from the representation level.

GAs use simple symbolic operations from the viewpoint of genotype, and GAs are often applied to combinatorial optimization problems such as knapsack problems, traveling salesman problems and scheduling problems [10]-[14]. It is experimentally known that the GAs can obtain near or approximately optimal solutions with less computational cost. Other GAs are genetic programming and classifier system. The genetic programming, which was proposed by Koza [12],[13] can deal with the tree structure and have been applied for generating computer programs. The classifier system, which is known as a GA-based machine learning method, can learn syntactically simple string rules to guide its performance in an arbitrary environment.

On the other hand, EAs use numerical operations from the viewpoint of phenotype, but EAs also use symbolic operation such as mutation and crossover.

EAs including EP and ES, have been often applied for solving numerical optimization problems such as function optimization problems, weight optimization of NN [11]. The important feature of EAs is the self-adaptation, especially self-adaptive mutation is very useful operation. The search range can be adjustable according to its performance [11]. In the EAs, tournament selection and deterministic selection are often applied as the selection scheme.

In addition, the ECs provide the evolution mechanism for population dynamics, robot society and A-life [7]. From the viewpoint of simulated evolution, GAs can maintain the genetic diversity in a population to adapt to dynamic environment. Therefore, ECs are often called adaptive systems. However, the ECs eliminate worse individuals from the population only according to the evaluation from the current environment. As a result, it is difficult that the population adapts to a big change of the environment. Therefore the ECs often require methods to maintain genetic diversity in a population for the dynamically changing environment.

3.3 Synthesized Approach

To realize higher intelligent system, a synthesized algorithm of various techniques is required. Figure 2 shows the synthesis of NN, FL and EC. Each technique plays the peculiar role for intelligent function. There are not complete techniques for realizing all features of intelligence. Therefore, we should integrate and combine some techniques to compensate the disadvantages of each technique. The main characteristics of NN are to classify or recognize patterns, and to adapt itself to dynamic environments by learning, but the mapping structure of NN is a black box and incomprehensible. On the other hand, FL has been applied for representing human linguistic rules and classifying numerical information into symbolic class. It also has reasonable structure for inference, which is composed of if-then rules like human knowledge. However FL does not fundamentally have the learning capability. Fuzzy-neural networks have developed for overcoming their disadvantages [6]. In general, the neural network part is used for its learning, while the fuzzy logic part is used for representing knowledge. Learning capability is fundamentally performed as necessary change such as incremental learning, back propagation method and delta rule based on error functions. EC can also tune NN and FI. However, evolution can be defined as resultant or accidental change, not necessary change, since the EC can not predict and estimate the effect of the change. To summarize, an intelligent system can quickly adapt to dynamic environment by NN and FI with the back propagation method or delta rule, and furthermore, the structure of intelligent system can globally evolve by EC according to the objective problems. The capabilities concerning learning adaptation and evolution can construct more intelligent system. Intelligence arises from the information processing on the linkage of perception, decision making and action.

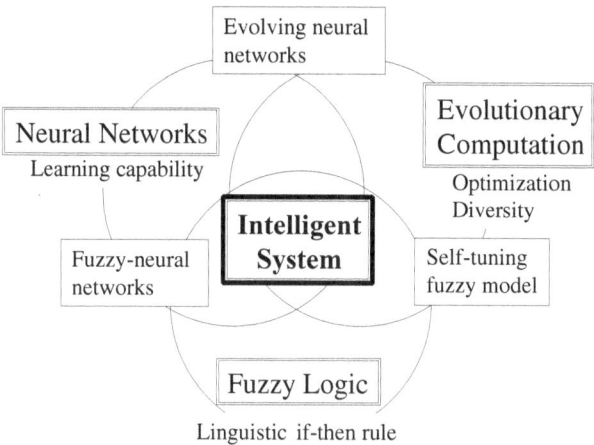

Fig. 2. Synthesis of NN, FL and EC

4   Intelligent Robotic System

4.1   Brachiation Robot

The brachiation robot is a mobile robot, which dynamically moves from branch
to branch like a gibbon, namely long-armed ape, swinging its body like a pen-
dulum [23],[24](Fig.3). A lot of research about a brachiation type locomotion
robot had been carried out. Saito et al [25]-[23] proposed the heuristic learning
method for generating feasible trajectory for two-link brachiation robot. Fukuda
et al [28] propose the self-scaling reinforcement learning algorithm to generate
feasible trajectory with robust property against some disturbances. The reinforcement learning method builds a fuzzy logic controller with four inputs and
one output. In these studies, the controller is acquired in a try-and-error learning
process and a dynamics model of the two-link brachiation robot is not used for
controller design. On the other hand, Nakanishi et al [31] took another approach,
using target dynamics, for controlling an underactuated system. The two-link
brachiation robot is an underactuated system with two degrees of freedom and
one actuator. As a two-dimensional extended model, seven-link brachiation robot
is studied by Hasegawa et al [30]. The seven-link brachiation robot has redundancy to locomote so that it is able to take a dexterous motion like a real ape
in plane, however a dynamical locomotion robot with multi-degree of freedoms
is difficult to be controlled. A hierarchical behavior architecture is adopted to
design the controller with multi-input and multi-output efficiently. The behavior controllers and their coordinators in the hierarchical structure are generated
using reinforcement learning method. The concept of the hierarchical behavior
controller is based on the behavior-based control, which has an advantage of
designing the controller for a higher-level behavior of the complex system from
simpler behaviors in reasonable process.

We developed 13-link brachiation robot shown in fig.4, that has almost same dimensions and weight as a real long-armed ape. The hierarchical behavior controller shown in fig.5 generates dynamical motion controlling 14 actuators. Hasegawa et al [31] proposed an adaptation algorithm for brachiation behavior in order to locomote on different branch intervals successfully(Fig.6) and achieve continuous locomotion(Fig.7). This adaptation algorithm adjusts four coefficients from behavior coordinator "locomotion" to four behavior controllers using Newton Raphson method when the branch intervals are extended from 90cm to 101cm. In order to achieve the continuous locomotion, the end posture of first swing should be useful for the second swing. We therefore applied the adaptation algorithm to tune the secondary swing motion controller with two parameters.

Fig. 3. Brachiation motion of a long-armed ape

Fig. 4. B13-link brachiation robot

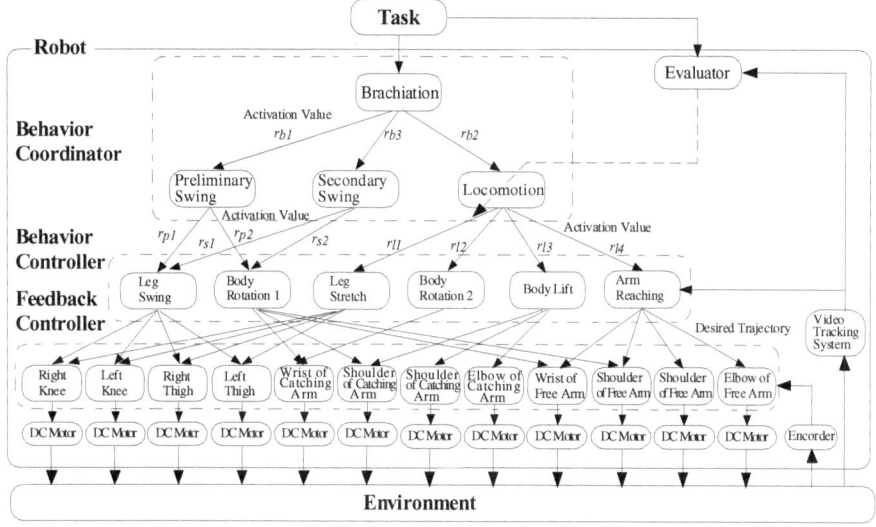

Fig. 5. Behavior-based controller for brachiation robot

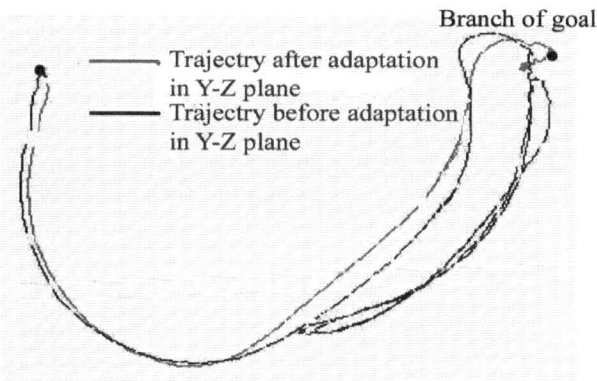

Fig. 6. Free hand's trajectories before and after adaptation

4.2 Regrasping Motion of Four-Fingered Robot Hand

Multi-fingered robot hand has an advantage to change the object posture during grasping as well as to grasp various shapes of objects. However, planing of this regrasping motion is hard task, because of a lot of parameters to be determined: grasping points, regrasping points, the object posture at regrasping moment, grasping force and grasping finger to be used.

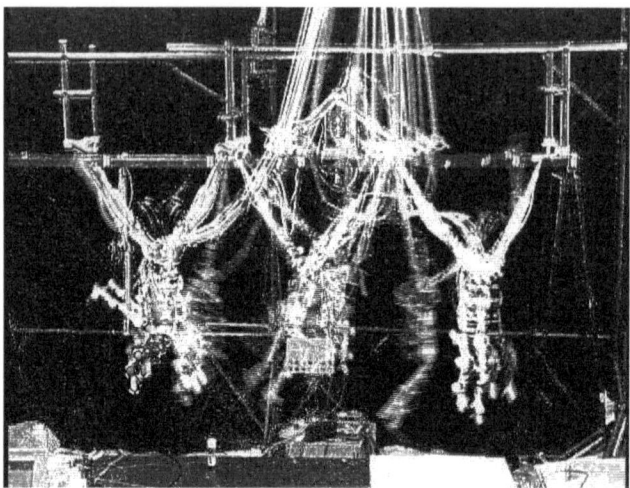

Fig. 7. Continuous locomotion

We proposed the algorithm to generate a regrasping motion using evolutionary programming(EP) [32]. EP is more effective to find a numerical solution like a grasping point than genetic algorithm. What we have to determine is the initial posture, the final posture of the grasping object and regrasping times. Evolutionary computation requires much iteration until it finds the solution, therefore, the regrasping motion is generated in numerical simulation. The obtained regrasping strategy is applied to the real robot system. Figure 8 shows the block diagram, in which planner means the desired grasping forces and the desired grasping points. The regrasping motion is shown in fig.9.

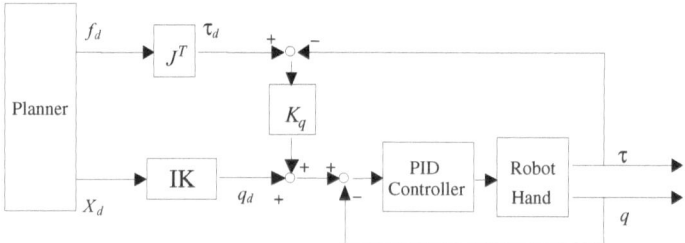

IK : Inverse Kinematics

Fig. 8. Block Diagram

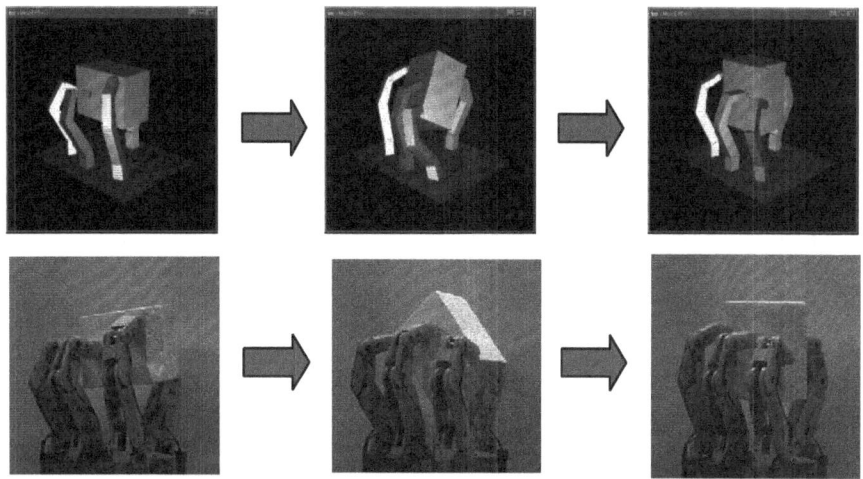

Fig. 9. Regrasping motions (Numerical simulation results and experimental results)

5   Summary

This paper presented recent research fields concerning computational intelligence. The computational intelligence is including neural network, fuzzy logic and evolutionary computation. The synthesis of neural network, fuzzy logic and evolutionary computation is important for advanced information processing and structure optimization. Furthermore, this paper showed the brachiation robot as an example of adaptation algorithm for hierarchical behavior-based control architecture, and the four-fingered robot hand as an application example of evolutionary computation. Intelligence of both robots is limited into motion generation capability. They do not deal with perception and of decision making. As future work, we should study about intelligent perception and decision algorithm from ambiguous information and stored knowledge.

References

1. S.J.Russell, P.Norvig, Artificial Intelligence, Prentice-Hall, Inc. (1995).
2. J.A.Anderson, E.Rosenfeld, Neurocomputing - Foundations of Research, The MIT Press (1988).
3. J.M.Zurada, R.J.Marks II, C.J.Robinson, Computational Intelligence - Imitating Life, IEEE Press (1994).
4. M.Palaniswami, Y.Attikiouzel, R.J.Marks II, D.Fogel, T.Fukuda, Computational Intelligence - A Dynamic System Perspective, IEEE Press (1995).
5. L.A.Zadeh, Fuzzy Sets, Information and Control, Vol.8, 338-353 (1965).
6. J.-S.R.Jang, C.-T.Sun, E.Mizutani, Neuro-Fuzzy and Soft Computing, New Jersey: Prentice Hall, Inc. (1997).
7. C.G.Langton, Artificial Life -An Overview, The MIT Press (1995).

8. R.J.Marks II, Intelligence: Computational Versus Artificial, IEEE Trans. on Neural Networks, Vol.4, No.5, 737-739 (1993).

9. S.V.Kartalopoulos, Understanding Neural Networks and Fuzzy Logic, IEEE Press (1996).

10. D.E.Goldberg, Genetic Algorithms in Search, Optimization, and Machine Learning, Addison Welsey (1989)

11. D.B.Fogel, Evolutionary Computation, IEEE Press (1995).

12. J.Koza, Genetic Programming, The Mit Press (1992).

13. J.Koza, Genetic Programming II, The Mit Press (1994).

14. J.Holland, Adaptation in Natural and Artificial Systems, Ann Arbor:University of Michigan Press, 1975.

15. R.Brooks, A Robust Layered Control System for a Mobile Robot, IEEE Journal of Robotics and Automation, RA-2-1, 14-23 (1986).

16. Marco Colombetti, Marco Dorigo, Giuseppe Borghi, Behavior Analysis and Training - A methodology for Behavior Engineering, IEEE Transaction on Systems, Man, And Cybernetics, Part B: Cybernetics, Vol.26, No.3, 365-380 (1996).

17. J.Y.Donnart, J.A.Meyer, Learning Reactive and Planning Rules in a Motivationally Autonomous Animat, IEEE Transaction on Systems, Man, And Cybernetics, Part B: Cybernetics, Vol.26, No.3, 381-395 (1996).

18. Jun Tani, Model-Based Learning for Mobile Robot Navigation from the Dynamical Systems Perspective, IEEE Transaction on Systems, Man, And Cybernetics, Part B: Cybernetics, Vol.26, No.3, 421-436 (1996).

19. G.A.Carpenter, S.Grossberg, The ART of Adaptive Pattern Recognition by a Self-Organizing Neural Network, Computer, Vol.21, 77-88 (1988).

20. T.Kohonen, Self-Organization and Associative Memory, Springer-Verlag (1984).

21. T.Fukuda, N.Kubota, Computational Intelligence in Robotics and Mechatronics, Proc. of The 23rd International Conference on Industrial Electronics, Control, and Instrumentation, 1517-1528 (1997).

22. T.Fukuda, N.Kubota, Intelligent Robotic System -Adaptation, Learning and Evolution, Proc. of The Third International Symposium on Artificial Life and Robotics 40-45 (1998).

23. T. Fukuda, H. Hosokai and Y. Kondo, Brachiation Type of Mobile Robot, Proc. IEEE Int. Conf. Advanced Robotics, pp. 915-920,(1991).

24. Spong, M. W., Swing Up Control of the Acrobot, Proc. 1994 IEEE International Conference on Robotics and Automation, pp. 2356-2361, (1994)

25. F. Saito, T. Fukuda, F. Arai, Swing and Locomotion Control for a Two-Link Brachiation Robot, IEEE Control Systems, Vol. 14, No. 1, pp. 5-12, (1994).

26. F. Saito, T. Fukuda, F. Arai, Swing and Locomotion Control for Two-Link Brachiation Robot, 1993 IEEE International Conference on Robotics and Automation, Atlanta, pp. II:719-724, (1993).

27. T. Fukuda, F. Saito and F. Arai, A Study on the Brachiation Type of Mobile Robot(Heuristic Creation of Driving Input and Control Using CMAC), Proc. IEEE/RSJ Int. Workshop on Intelligent Robots and Systems, pp. 478-483, (1991).

28. T. Fukuda Y. Hasegawa K. Shimojima and F. Saito, Self Scaling Reinforcement Learning for Fuzzy Logic Controller, IEEE International Conference on Evolutionary Computation, pp. 247-252, Japan, (1996)

29. J. Nakanishi, T. Fukuda and D.E. Koditschek, Experimental implementation of a Target dynamics controller on a two-link brachiating robot, IEEE International Conference on Robotics and Automation, pp. 787-792, (1998)

30. Y. Hasegawa and T. Fukuda, Learning Method for Hierarchical Behavior Controller, IEEE International Conference on Robotics and Automation, pp.2799-2804, (1999)
31. Y. Hasegawa, Y. Ito and T. Fukuda, Behavior Coordination and its Modification on Brachiation-type Mobile Robot, 2000 IEEE International Conference on Robotics and Automation, San Francisco, pp3984-3989, (2000)
32. Y.Hasegawa, J. Matsuno and T.Fukuda, Regrasping behavior generation for Rectangular Solid Object, 2000 IEEE International Conference on Robotics and Automation, San Francisco, pp3567-3572, (2000)

Image-based self-localization by means of zero phase representation in panoramic images[*]

Tomáš Pajdla and Václav Hlaváč

Center for Machine Perception, Faculty of Electrical Engineering
Czech Technical University
Karlovo náměstí 13, 121 35, Prague 2, Czech Republic
{pajdla,hlavac}@cmp.felk.cvut.cz, http://cmp.felk.cvut.cz

Abstract. The paradigm – image-based localization using panoramic images – is elaborated. Panoramic images provide complete views of an environment and their information content does not change if a panoramic camera is rotated. The "zero phase representation" of cylindrical panoramic images, an example of a rotation invariant representation, is constructed for the class of images which have non-zero first harmonic in column direction. It is an invariant and fully discriminative representation. The zero phase representation is demonstrated by an experiment with real data and it is shown that the alternative autocorrelation representation is outperformed.

Keywords omni-directional vision, self-localization from images, computer vision, robot navigation.

1 Introduction

The location of an observer is given by its position and orientation. The image based localization of an observer is a process in which the observer determines its location in an image map of the environment as the location in the image from the map which is the most similar to a momentary view. It is possible to do image based localization because images of an environment typically vary as a function of location.

Recently, it has been found that some species like bees or ants use vision extensively for localization and navigation [13, 14]. In contrary to techniques based on correspondence tracking, *they use whole images* to remember the way to food or nests [5, 3]. Attempts appeared to verify models explaining the behavior of animals by implementing mechanisms of ego-motion, localization, and navigation on mobile robots [12, 17, 16, 1].

Some animals like birds have developed eyes with a large field of view which allow them to see most of a surrounding environment and to use many cues

---

[*] This work was supported by the MSMT VS96049, J04/98:210000012 and GACR 102/00/1679 grants.

S. Singh, N. Murshed, and W. Kropatsch (Eds.): ICAPR 2001, LNCS 2013, pp. 24–31, 2001.

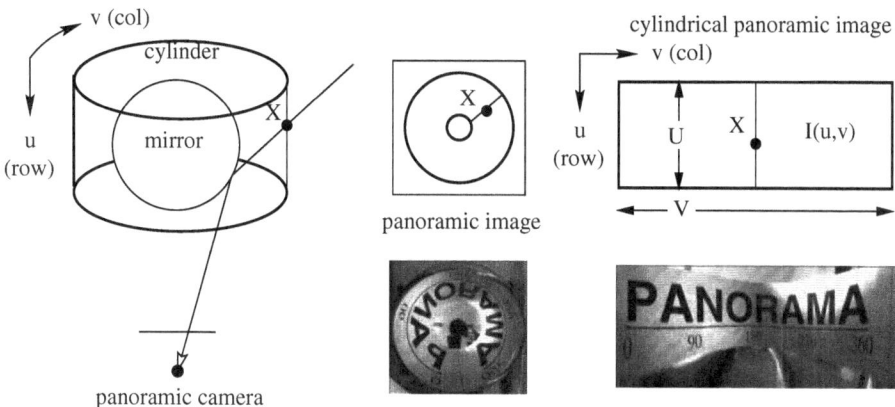

Fig. 1. A cylindrical panoramic image is obtained by projecting a panoramic image from the plane onto a cylinder and then by mapping the cylinder back to the plane by an isometry.

around them for localization and surveillance [6, 8]. Panoramic cameras, combining a curved convex mirror with an ordinary perspective camera [17, 2, 15], provide large field of view. The advantage of real time acquisition of images of whole environment suggests to use the panoramic camera for image based localization.

In this paper, we study image based localization using panoramic images. We concentrate on finding a proper representation of panoramic images in order to make the localization efficient. In contrary to approaches taken in [17, 16, 1], where rather straightforward methods were used to demonstrate image based localization, we develop the representation of panoramic images allowing an efficient storage of an image based map as well as fast localization while attaining the full discrimination between the positions.

2   Image based localization from cylindrical panoramic images

Cylindrical panoramic images are obtained by first projecting the panoramic image [15] from the plane onto a cylinder, Figure 1, and then mapped back into a plane by an isometry (cylinders are developable surfaces).

Cylindrical panoramic images can be modeled by a part of a cylinder $I(u, v)$ as shown in Figure 1. Function $I(u, v): R^2 \to R$ is defined on an interval $[0, U] \times R$. It is periodic with a period V, $I(u, v) = I(u, v + V)$, where U and V are called vertical and horizontal image size respectively.

The rotation of the panoramic camera around its vertical axis by an angle φ induces the rotation of the cylinder $I(u, v)$ to a cylinder $J(u, v)$ around the axis z so that $J(u, v) = I(u, v - \varphi)$. The set of all such transformations of $I(u, v)$ forms the Abelian group of 1D rotations $SO(1)$. We will call the above action "shift" to be compatible with the notation used in Fourier analysis.

How do the cylindrical panoramic images change when the observer moves?

Firstly, a cylindrical panoramic image shifts if the observer rotates (changes its orientation) at the same position. The images obtained at the same position with different orientations are same in the sense that there exists a shift (independent of the scene geometry) which maps images exactly onto each other. Secondly, the image changes when observer's motion involves a translation (observer changes its position). In this case, there is no image transform which transforms two images at different positions onto each other because images depend on depth variations and occlusions in the scene.

It is the advantage of using a panoramic camera to have a complete view so that image information content does not change when changing the orientation. Ordinary cameras lack this property. Image based maps are better to construct from panoramic images as it is sufficient to store only one panoramic image at each position to describe the environment seen from that position under any orientation.

Images taken at close locations are likely to be very similar. In fact, it has been found that they are quite linearly dependent [7]. In order to obtain an efficient representation of the image based map of an environment, close images have to be as similar as possible. If so, they can be compressed by using principal component analysis [9] or a similar technique. The linear dependence of panoramic images, however, is disturbed by the rotation of the observer. An efficient map cannot therefore be directly constructed from images acquired under different non-related orientations of the observer. Each cylindrical panoramic image has to be shifted before creating the map so that close images are similar.

Finding the most similar image in the map to the momentary image naturally calls for a correlation based technique that compares a momentary image with each image in the map and selects the one with the highest correlation. Each comparison is done again by a correlation along the column direction in order to find the best matching orientation of the momentary view.

The search for the orientation can be avoided by finding a *shift invariant representation* of each class of images taken at the same position. It means that there is a procedure which gives the same representation for all images taken at one position irrespectively of their orientations. The procedure of finding an invariant representation has to be able to transform each image into the invariant representation just by using the information contained in the image alone. It is required in order to get an invariant representation of individual momentary views. If images in the map, as well as momentary views, are transformed into an invariant representation, a simple squared image difference evaluates their similarity.

In Section 3, the *shift invariant representation* of panoramic images is introduced and limitations of its construction are discussed. In Section 4, the *zero phase representation* (ZPR) is constructed for the class of images with non-zero first harmonic in the column direction. Section 5 demonstrates the ZPR by an experiment. The paper concludes with comparison of the ZPR to an alternative representation given in [1].

3   Shift invariant representations of panoramic images

The set of all cylindrical panoramic images $I(u, v)$, as defined in Section 2, can be partitioned into equivalence classes $I\backslash\varphi$ so that each class contains all images which can be obtained by shifts from one image. The equivalence classes correspond to the orbits of $SO(1)$ in the image space.

If we single out one image I^* for each class, we may use it to represent the whole class $I\backslash\varphi$. The ability to find a fixed representative image $I^*(u, v)$ is equivalent to the ability of finding the shift φ for each image $I(u, v)$ so that $I^*(u, v) = I(u, v - \varphi)$.

There is no "natural" representative image of a shift equivalence class of cylindrical panoramic images in the sense that it would be an intrinsic property of all images in the class. If it was so, it would mean that we could find φ from any image alone to transform it into the intrinsic representative image. In other words, there had to be some preferred direction which one could detect in the image. However, there cannot be any direction anyhow fixed if the images can take any values.

On the other hand, a natural representative image is something what we would really need as it is important to be able to obtain a representative image from each image alone. Therefore, it is necessary to choose a "reference direction" so that it is "seen" in each image. It can be done in each shift equivalence class independently but we prefer doing it so that the images taken at close positions have similar representative images of their shift equivalence classes. Only then we can gain from approximating many close images by a few of their principal components.

We do not want to prefer any direction by introducing something which could be seen in the scene like a reference object because it needs to modify the scene.

In some cases, we may find (or force) images $I(u, v)$ to come from a class which allows us to define a reference direction without augmenting the scene, e.g. the images have non-zero first harmonic in v direction when expanded into the Fourier series. The way, the reference direction is chosen, depends mainly on the class of the images we can get. For practical reasons, we might want to broaden the equivalence class of images from the shift equivalence class to the class which allows also for all linear brightness transformations, some noise, certain occlusions, etc. It may, in some cases, be possible but need not in others.

4   Zero phase representation

Let us assume that all images $I(m, n)$ have non-zero first harmonic. Image $I(m, n)$ is acquired by a digital camera and therefore m and n are integers, not real numbers. However, there is some function $I(u, v)$ behind, for which u and v are real. We just sample it at discrete points. If the camera rotates by a real angle α, we obtain $J(m, n) = \text{sampled}[I(u, v - \varphi)]$, where $\varphi = \frac{N}{2\pi}\alpha$, and M and N are the row and the column sizes of the image respectively.

As the first harmonic of $I(m, n)$ is assumed to be nonzero, its phase is affected by shifting $I(u, v)$. We can eliminate any unknown shift by shifting the interpolation of $I(m, n)$ and re-sampling it so that the first harmonic of the the resulting representative image of each shift equivalence class $I^*(m, n)$ equals zero. Let us show how to compute I^* in 1D.

Definition 1 (Shift). *Let function $f(n): Z \to R$ be periodic on the interval $[0, \dots, N]$, i.e.*

$$f(n) = f(n + N) . \tag{1}$$

Mapping $\Phi_\varphi: R^Z \to R^Z$

$$\Phi_\varphi[f(n)] = \mathcal{F}^{-1}\{\mathcal{F}\{f(n)\} \, e^{-j\frac{2\pi}{N}\varphi k}\} , \tag{2}$$

where $F(k) = \mathcal{F}\{f(n)\}$ denotes the Discrete Fourier Transform of $f(n)$, and is called the shift of $f(n)$ by phase φ.

Definition 2 (Shift equivalence class). *Let function $f(n): Z \to R$ be periodic on interval $[0, \dots, N]$. Then, the set*

$$S[f(n)] = \{g(n) \mid g(n) = \Phi_\varphi[f(n)], \; \forall \, \varphi \in R\} \tag{3}$$

is called the shift equivalence class generated by $f(n)$.

Definition 3 (Representative function of a shift equivalence class). *Let function $f(n): Z \to R$ be periodic on interval $[0, \dots, N]$. Function $r(n)$ is a representative function of $S[f(n)]$ iff it generates $S[f(n)]$, i.e.*

$$S[f(n)] = \{g(n) \mid g(n) = \Phi_\varphi[r(n)], \; \forall \, \varphi \in R\} . \tag{4}$$

In other words, $r(n)$ is a representative function of an equivalence class iff it is its member, i.e. $r(n) \in S[f(n)]$.

Definition 4 (Shift invariant representation). *Let function $f(n): Z \to R$ be periodic on interval $[0, \dots, N]$. Let $\rho : R^Z \to R^Z$ assign to each $f(n)$ a function $s(n)$. The $s(n)$ is called the shift invariant representation of $f(n)$ iff*

$$s(n) = \rho[\Phi_\varphi[f(n)]], \; \forall \, \varphi \in R . \tag{5}$$

Observation 1 *There are shift invariant representations of $f(n)$ which are not representative functions of $S[f(n)]$.*

Autocorrelation of a function $f(n)$ is an example of a shift invariant representation which is not a representative function of a shift equivalence class $S[f(n)]$. By shifting the autocorrelation function we get a shifted autocorrelation function but certainly not the original $f(n)$. Moreover, all different functions which have the absolute value of their Fourier transform equal to the absolute value of the Fourier transform of $f(n)$ have the same autocorrelation representations. So, the autocorrelation representation is quite ambiguous.

Definition 5 (Zero phase representation (ZPR)). *Let function* $f(n): Z \rightarrow R$ *be periodic on interval* $[0, \ldots, N]$. *Function*

$$f^*(n) = \mathcal{F}^{-1}\{\mathcal{F}\{f(n)\} \; e^{-j\phi[F(1)]k}\} \, . \tag{6}$$

where $F(k) = \mathcal{F}\{f(n)\}$ *is the Discrete Fourier Transform of* $f(n)$ *and* $\mathcal{F}^{-1}$ *is its inverse, is called the* zero phase representation *of* $f(n)$.

Lemma 1. *Let functions* $f(n)$, $g(n): Z \rightarrow R$ *be periodic on interval* $[0, \ldots, N]$ *with non-zero first harmonic, i.e.* $|F(1)| \neq 0$, $|G(1)| \neq 0$, *and let* $f^*(n)$, $g^*(n)$ *be defined by (6). Then,*

$$\exists \varphi \in R, \; g(n) = \Phi_\varphi[f(n)] \iff g^*(n) = f^*(n) \, . \tag{7}$$

Proof. Lemma is verified by straightforward application of (2) and (6) on (7). See [10] for details.   **Q.E.D.**

Observation 2 $f^*(n)$ *defined by (6) is a representative function of* $\mathcal{S}[f(n)]$.

Observation 3 *If* $f(n)$ *has non-zero first harmonic then* $f^*(n)$ *defined by (6) is an invariant representation* $\mathcal{S}[f(n)]$.

Observations 2 and 3 show that the ZPR is a good representation of the class of images which have non-zero first harmonic in column direction. The ZPR assures that the images taken at different positions will be represented differently and the images taken at the same place will have the same representative image.

Observation 4 *The first harmonic of* $f^*(n)$ *defined by (6) equals zero, i.e.* $\phi[F^*(1)] = 0$.

Observation (4) explains why the name "zero phase representation" has been chosen.

A straightforward generalization of 1D ZPR for 2D cylindrical panoramic images can be achieved by replacing the 2D FFT by a 2D DFT so that (6) is replaced by

$$I^*(m, n) = \mathcal{F}^{-1}\{\mathcal{F}\{I(m, n)\} \; e^{-j\phi[F(0,1)]l}\} \, , \tag{8}$$

where $F(k, l) = \mathcal{F}\{I(m, n)\}$ is a Discrete Fourier Transform of $I(m, n)$.

5   Experiment

Figure 2 shows real images taken with different orientations (a, c) and position (a, e) of a panoramic camera. Ideally, the images (a, c) should be related by a shift but this is violated by the holder of the camera which stays at the same place in the image because it rotates with the camera and by occlusions and changes in the scene. Figures 2 (b), (d), (f) show the ZPR of the images. The images (b) and (d) are quite correctly shifted so that their relative shift is almost zero as expected even though there were changes in the scene. The relative shift of the ZPR of the images (d) and (f) which were taken at different positions differs quite a lot.

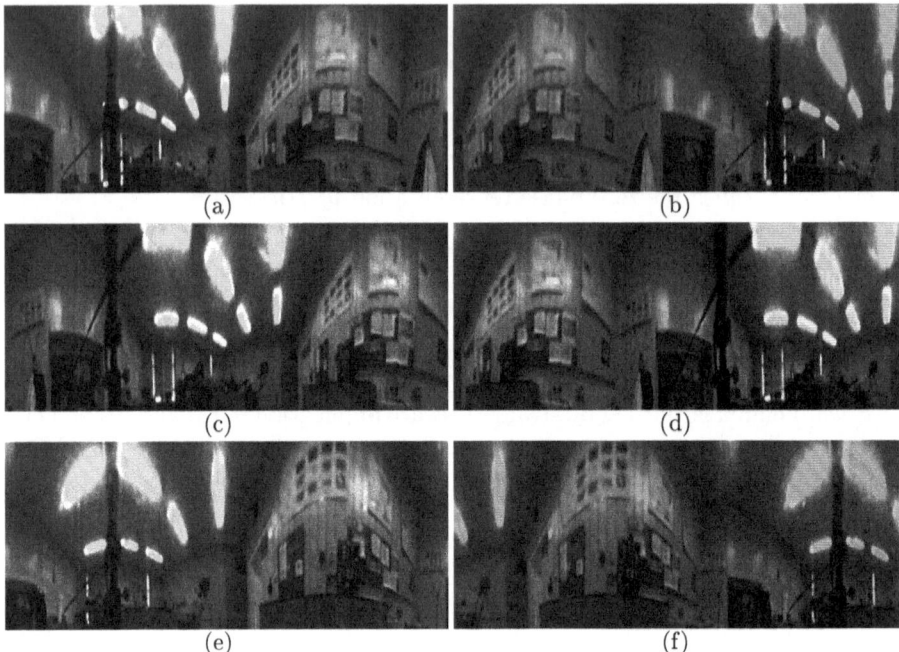

Fig. 2. (a) A panoramic image and its ZPR (b), (c) a panoramic image taken at the same position and different orientation and its ZPR (d), (e) a panoramic image taken at the different position and same orientation and its ZPR (f).

6   Conclusion

The fundamentals of image based robot localization have been given by providing the ZPR, an invariant and discriminative representation of cylindrical panoramic images with non-zero first harmonic in column direction. The idea of rotation invariant representation of panoramic images has independently been used by Aihara et. al [1] where independent autocorrelation of each row of a cylindrical panoramic image was used. The invariance for all images is achieved but it is not discriminative as images of many different scenes map into the same autocorrelation. In this respect, the ZPR is better suited for global localization as it is fully discriminative for the images with non-zero first harmonic in column direction.

In the future, we like to study a suitable representation of the images with zero first harmonic. The first experiments by Jogan and Leonardis [4] show that the ZPR provides images which can be compressed by principal component analysis. The question of further investigation is to find how smoothly the ZPR behaves when changing the position. More attention has to be paid to illumination changes and occlusions. Preliminary experiments [11] show that ZPR is not much affected by additive noise but it can strongly be affected by occlusions.

We thank to Tomáš Svoboda who acquired real panoramic images for the experiments, to Aleš Leonardis, Horst Bischof, and Radim Šára for discussions.

References

1. N. Aihara, H. Iwasa, N. Yokoya, and H. Takemura. Memory–based self–localization using omnidirectional images. In *14th Int. Conf. on Pattern Recognition, Brisbane, Australia*, volume II, pages 1799–1803. IEEE Computer Society Press, August 1998.
2. S. Baker and S.K. Nayar. A theory of catadioptric image formation. In *6th Int. Conf. on Computer Vision*, pages 35–42, India, January 1998. IEEE Computer Society, Narosa Publishing House.
3. T.S. Collet. Insect navigation en route to the goal: Multiple strategies for the use of landmarks. *J. Exp. Biol.*, 199.01:227–235, 1996.
4. M. Jogan and A. Leonardis. Mobile robot localization using panoramic eigen-images. In *4th Computer Vision Winter Workshop, Rastenfeld, Austria*. Pattern Recognition and Image Processing Group of the Vienna University of Technology, pages 13–23, February 1999.
5. S.P.D. Judd and T.S. Collet. Multiple stored views and landmark guidance in ants. *Nature*, 392:710–714, April 1998.
6. H.G. Krapp and R. Hengstenberg. Estimation of self-motion by optic flow processing in single visual interneurons. *Nature*, 384:463–466, 1996.
7. S.K. Nayar, S.A. Nene, and H. Murase. Subspace methods for robot vision. *RA*, 12(5):750–758, October 1996.
8. R.C. Nelson and J. Aloimonos. Finding motion parameters from spherical motion fields (or advantages of having eyes in the back of your head). *Biol. Cybern.*, 58:261–273, 1996.
9. E. Oja. *Subspace Methods of Patter Recognition*. Research Studies Press, Hertfordshire, 1983.
10. T. Pajdla. Robot localization using shift invariant representation of panoramic images. Tech. Rep. K335-CMP-1998-170, Czech Technical University, Dpt. of Cybernetics, Faculty of Electrical Engineering, Karlovo nám. 13, 12135 Praha, Czech Republic, November 1998. ftp://cmp.felk.cvut.cz/pub/cmp/articles/pajdla/Pajdla-TR-170.ps.gz.
11. T. Pajdla. Robot localization using panoramic images. In *4th Computer Vision Winter Workshop, Rastenfeld, Austria*. Pattern Recognition and Image Processing Group of the Vienna University of Technology, pages 1–12, February 1999.
12. M.V. Srinivasan. An image-interpolation technique for the computation of optical flow and egomotion. *Biol Cybern*, 71:401–415, 1994.
13. M.V. Srinivasan. Ants match as they march. *Nature*, 392:660–661, 1998.
14. M.V. Srinivasan and S.W. Zhang. Flies go with the flow. *Nature*, 384:411, 1996.
15. T. Svoboda, T. Pajdla, and V. Hlaváč. Epipolar geometry for panoramic cameras. In *5th European Conference on Computer Vision, Freiburg, Germany*, number 1406 in Lecture Notes in Computer Science, pages 218–232. Springer, June 1998.
16. K. Weber, S. Venkatesh, and M.V. Srinivasan. An insect–based approach to robotic homing. In *14th Int. Conf. on Pattern Recognition, Brisbane, Australia*, volume I, pages 297–299. IEEE Computer Society Press, August 1998.
17. Y. Yagi, K. Yamazawa, and M. Yachida. Rolling motion estimation for mobile robot by using omnidirectional image sensor hyperomnivision. In *13th Int. Conf. on Pattern Recognition, Vienna, Austria*, pages 946–950. IEEE Computer Society Press, September 1996.

A Cascaded Genetic Algorithm for efficient optimization and pattern matching

Gautam Garai
Computer Division
Saha Institute of Nuclear Physics
1/AF Bidhannagar
Calcutta-700064
India

B. B. Chaudhuri
Computer Vision & Pattern Recognition Unit
Indian Statistical Institute
203 B. T. Road
Calcutta-700035
India

Abstract

A modified Genetic Algorithm (GA) based search strategy is presented here that is computationally more efficient than the conventional GA. Here the idea is to start a GA with the chromosomes of small length. Such chromosomes represent possible solutions with coarse resolution. A finite space around the position of solution in the first stage is subject to the GA at the second stage. Since this space is much smaller than the original search space, chromosomes of same length now represent finer resolution. In this way, the search progresses from coarse to fine solution in a cascaded manner. Since chromosomes of small size are used at each stage, the overall approach becomes computationally more efficient than a single stage algorithm with the same degree of final resolution. Also, since at the lower stage we work on low resolution, the algorithm can avoid local spurious extrema. The effectiveness of the proposed GA has been demonstrated for the optimization of some synthetic functions and on pattern recognition problems namely dot pattern matching and object matching with edge map.

Keywords: Genetic algorithm, search technique, chromosome, mutation, optimization, dot pattern matching.

1 Introduction

Genetic Algorithms (GAs) belong to a class of stochastic search method inspired by natural population genetics. They represent a highly parallel adaptive search process. Central to the idea of GA is a population where individuals in the population represent possible solutions. An individual is called *chromosome*, in analogy with the genetic chromosome. New population is generated from old population with three basic genetic operators namely selection/reproduction, crossover and mutation [1] which complete one cycle of operation. The process is explained in a more algorithmic way in section 2.

The GAs have been employed in a wide variety of problems related to pattern recognition and image processing among others. Some of the studies involving medical image registration, image segmentation and contour recognition are available in [2-4]. Other practical applications like normalization of Chinese handwriting, classification of endothelial cells are also reported in literature [5-6]. Moreover, GAs have been used in optimization of feature extraction chain and dot pattern matching [7-8]. Some variants of GA are also reported in the literature [9-10].

Usually, GAs need a large number of cycles to converge to a solution. In a pattern recognition or related problems, generally one starts with chromosomes of length dependent on the accuracy of the solution required. The length remains constant throughout the execution of the algorithm. Thus, if more accurate solution is required, the chromosome length should be larger, thereby increasing the execution time of the GA. It is the purpose of this paper to show that the speed of the search process can be improved if a coarse to fine search strategy is employed in a cascaded GA framework, where the chromosome size can be kept small at each stage.

In the proposed approach, we have otherwise employed conventional genetic method with constant chromosome size at each stage. The chromosomes of small length in the first stage represents coarse resolution. A small space

S. Singh, N. Murshed, and W. Kropatsch (Eds.): ICAPR 2001, LNCS 2013, pp. 32–39, 2001.
© Springer-Verlag Berlin Heidelberg 2001

around the solution position in the first stage is considered for the next stage. Thus, at a higher stage the search space is reduced and hence a chromosome of small length effectively represents higher resolution. This leads to an overall speed up of the algorithm. Moreover, since we use coarse resolution at lower stage, the chance of getting trapped at a spurious local optima is greatly reduced because of a kind of low-pass effect due to course resolution.

We have divided the paper as follows. The basic Genetic Algorithm for optimization is described in section 2. The proposed CAscaded GA (CAGA) approach has been narrated in section 3. Section 4 deals with the experimental results and the conclusion is in section 5.

2   Conventional GA Approach

Central to the idea of GA is a set of chromosomes, each representing a particular solution to the optimization problem. The chromosome is usually represented as a string of 0's and 1's of fixed length. However, the chromosomes of variable length [11] can also be maintained in the population. Initially, the set of chromosomes in the population are chosen randomly.

An impotant parameter of GA is the fitness function that describes how well a chromosome represents the solution to the problem. The genetic algorithm is an iterative approach with three basic operators called selection, crossover and mutation. For the selection process the fitness values of the chromosomes are computed. There exist several approaches of selection based on the fitness value [1],[9]. In the classical roulette wheel method, two mates are selected for reproduction with probability directly proportional to their fitness. Thus, fitter chromosomes will contribute a large number of offsprings to the next generation.

In crossover operation (illustrated below with chromosome pair C_1, C_2) the new chromosomes are formed due to crossover i.e., interchange of a gene (bit) at a particular position of the two existing chromosomes. The value of crossover probability, p_c is usually maintained between 0.5 and 0.9. The algorithm may not generate new solution for very small value of p_c and can be unstable for too large value.

C_1 : x_1 x_2 x_3 x_4 x_5 x_6 x_7 x_8 C_2 : y_1 y_2 y_3 y_4 y_5 y_6 y_7 y_8
        Chromosome pair before crossover operation.

C_1' : x_1 x_2 x_3 | y_4 y_5 y_6 y_7 y_8 C_2' : y_1 y_2 y_3 | x_4 x_5 x_6 x_7 x_8
        Chromosome pair after crossover operation in 1 position.
            (crossover operation is performed after | line)

The mutation operation shown below, is used to introduce new genetic materials to the chromosomes. The value of mutation probability, p_m usually lies between 0.001 and 0.03 [11] and reflects the progress of search method. The algorithm cannot easily converge for too high value of p_m but converges to a spurious local optimum for very low value. However, it is usually better to consider small value of p_m initially and increase the value with the advancement of search cycles.

C_{1m}' : x_1 $\overline{x_2}$ x_3 y_4 y_5 $\overline{y_6}$ y_7 y_8
        Mutation operation over chromosome, C_1' (given above).
            (upper bar indicates bit complementation)

The performance and effectiveness of GA largely depend on the population size. The size is generally maintained between 30 and 100. If it is small then the algorithm leads to a premature convergenge which is unacceptable for searching a global optimum but the higher value of the population size increases the evaluation cost per iteration which results in slow convergenge. However, the proper choice of the population size is mostly related to the problem in hand.

Thus, the conventional GA called CGA works as follows.

Step 1: Initialize the crossover probability, p_c and the mutation probability, p_m. Set $G=0$.
Step 2: Randomly create the initial population $P(G)$.
Step 3: Evaluate fitness of each individual (chromosome) in $P(G)$.
Step 4: Increment G by 1.
Step 5: Select chromosome pairs randomly from $P(G)$.
Step 6: Crossover two parents randomly to generate offsprings.
Step 7: Mutate randomly the chosen bits of the crossovered individuals in $P(G)$.
Step 8: Evaluate fitness of each individual (chromosome) of $P(G)$.
Step 9: Repeat Step 4 to Step 8 until G exceeds a predefined integer (say, N) or there exists a chromosome, C_{fit}

whose fitness satisfies a prespecified criterion. In the former case C_{fit} is the fittest chromosome in the population and the solution.

3   Proposed CAscaded GA Approach

In the conventional GA the area of the entire solution space is divided depending on the final resolution or the accuracy of the solution. The size of the chromosome is, therefore, set accordingly and remains constant till the termination of the algorithm which eventually slows down the convergence if highly accurate solution is needed. To overcome the drawbacks we have proposed an algorithm called CAscaded GA (CAGA), employing coarse to fine search strategy where the search space is exponentially reduced. At the first stage, small length chromosomes (say, l) are used to get an approximate location of solution. A small space around this solution is considered as search space for the second stage GA. Since the search space is reduced, a chromosome of length, l represents higher resolution. After a few stages the solution is obtained at the desired resolution.

This cascading approach has two advantages. First, it increases the overall speed of achieving a solution due to small chromosome size. Second, it reduces the risk of being trapped in a local optimum for employing the search in coarse to fine resolution.

The cascading process is illustrated in 2-D by Figure 1. Suppose an optimization problem should be solved by the GA in a space bounded by the largest square of Fig.1. Here we show a three stage procedure. The chromosome size is 4 bits at each stage, two bits for each x and y-axis to partition the solution space into smaller sixteen squares. Suppose the solution at the first stage is obtained at the hatched square marked by a dark line. Then at the next stage, this square along with the surrounding hashed region are considered as the search region and the GA is again invoked. Thus, the search space is reduced at each subsequent stage and the chromosome of the same length (4 bits) represents higher resolution. Since the spurious local optima are avoided, the algorithm converges faster and works more efficiently than the CGA.

Let us now address the choice of other remaining parameters for CAGA. The chromosome length in general depends on the search space size and the degree of freedom as well as the required solution accuracy. Consider, for example, the problem of pattern matching in 2-D where an unknown pattern is matched with some known patterns and the best matching pattern is to be found. For this purpose the unknown pattern is to be translated and then rotated in the known pattern space. If the space has a rectangular area with length L_x in x-direction and L_y in y-direction and the resolutions are r_x and r_y in those directions respectively and also the angular resolution, r_θ, then for the CGA we should have the chromosome length, l_n given by

$$l = n + m + k \tag{1}$$

where $n = \lceil \frac{L_x}{r_x} \rceil$, $m = \lceil \frac{L_y}{r_y} \rceil$ and $k = \lceil \frac{2\pi}{r_\theta} \rceil$. A chromosome, C may be written as $C = p_1\, p_2\, p_3\, \cdots\, p_n\, q_1\, q_2\, q_3\, \cdots\, q_m$ $\theta_1\, \theta_2\, \theta_3\, \ldots\, \theta_k$ where p_i's and q_i's represent chromosome bit for x-direction and y-direction, respectively and p_i, q_i and θ_i can take values in $(0,1)$.

A set of randomly chosen chromosomes constitutes the initial population in the first stage. In the following stages the initial population is generated using the same procedure except the solution chromosome which is picked up from the population of the previous stage. A population, P is represented as $P = \{C_i \mid i = 1, 2, 3, ..., M\}$ where M=population size.

The intermediate populations are created using the basic genetic operators namely selection, crossover and mutation. In CAGA the operations of the three operators are performed using the same method as described in section 2. The selection operation selects a chromosome pair using roulette wheel method.

The crossover operation accepts the chromosome pair and produces two offsprings using either one-point or multi-point crossover to interchange information between them. The type of operation (one-point or multi-point crossover) depends on the number of parameters which are represented by a single chromosome and the cohesive nature of the parameters. Two-point crossover operation in CAGA and CGA is illustrated below.

$$C_i = x_{i1}\, x_{i2}\, x_{i3}\, x_{i4}\, x_{i5}\, x_{i6}\, y_{i1}\, y_{i2}\, y_{i3}\, y_{i4}\, y_{i5}\, y_{i6}\quad \theta_{i1}\, \theta_{i2}\, \theta_{i3}\, \theta_{i4}\, \theta_{i5}\, \theta_{i6}$$
$$C_j = x_{j1}\, x_{j2}\, x_{j3}\, x_{j4}\, x_{j5}\, x_{j6}\, y_{j1}\, y_{j2}\, y_{j3}\, y_{j4}\, y_{j5}\, y_{j6}\quad \theta_{j1}\, \theta_{j2}\, \theta_{j3}\, \theta_{j4}\, \theta_{j5}\, \theta_{j6}$$

Multi-parameter chromosome pair before two-point crossover operation

$$C_i' = x_{i1}\, x_{i2}\, x_{i3}\, x_{i4}\, x_{i5} \mid x_{j6}\, y_{j1}\, y_{j2}\, y_{j3}\, y_{j4}\, y_{j5}\, y_{j6}\quad \theta_{i1}\, \theta_{i2} \mid \theta_{j3}\, \theta_{j4}\, \theta_{j5}\, \theta_{j6}$$
$$C_j' = x_{j1}\, x_{j2}\, x_{j3}\, x_{j4}\, x_{j5} \mid x_{i6}\, y_{i1}\, y_{i2}\, y_{i3}\, y_{i4}\, y_{i5}\, y_{i6}\quad \theta_{j1}\, \theta_{j2} \mid \theta_{i3}\, \theta_{i4}\, \theta_{i5}\, \theta_{i6}$$

Multi-parameter chromosome pair after two-point crossover operation

As described before, the mutation operator is used to maintain the heterogeneity in a population. As the number of cycles increases and the system goes towards convergence, it is better to increase the value of p_m. In CAGA we have redefined the rate at the starting of each stage. Now if $(L_c)_1$ and $(L_c)_t$ are the total length of the chromosome initially and in the t-th step, respectively and $(p_m)_t$ is the mutation probability in the t-th stage, then we can define p_m in each step as follows.

$$(p_m)_t = (p_m)_{t-1} \ X \ \frac{(L_c)_t}{(L_c)_1} \ X \ t \tag{2}$$

Therefore, the CAGA can be described by the following steps.

Step 1: Initialize p_c and p_m. Set generation, $G=0$ and step, $t=1$.

Step 2: Randomly create the initial population $P(G,t)$.

Step 3: Evaluate fitness of each individual (chromosome) in $P(G,t)$.

Step 4: Increment G by 1.

Step 5: Select chromosome pairs randomly from $P(G,t)$.

Step 6: Crossover two parents randomly from $P(G,t)$ to generate offsprings.

Step 7: Mutate randomly the chosen bits of the crossovered individuals in $P(G,t)$.

Step 8: Evaluate fitness of each individual (chromosome) of $P(G,t)$.

Step 9: Repeat Step 4 to Step 8 until a solution is obtained for the t-th step.

Step 10: Redefine the solution space for fine resolution (as this is a coarse to fine resolution approach) and p_m using equation 2.

Step 11: Increment t by 1.

Step 12: Again randomly create the population $P(G,t)$ and propagate the elite chromosome from $(t-1)$-th stage.

Step 13: Go to Step 4 if $t \leq t_{max}$ and G does not exceed a predefined integer (say, N) or $t \leq t_{max}$ and there does not exist a chromosome, C_{fit} whose fitness satisfies a prespecified criterion. C_{fit} is the fittest chromosome in the population.

Step 14: C_{fit} represents the solution.

The value of t_{max} depends on the problem in hand. Usually, it does not exceed 4.

4   Experimental Results

We have demonstrated the effectiveness of the CAGA on some classical functions in one or more dimensions. Moreover, in our experiment we have considered pattern recognition problems of object matching from edge map as well as dot pattern matching.

The mathematical functions (f_1 to f_8) contain various types of unimodal and multimodal functions for optimization. We tried to evaluate maximum value for f_1 to f_4 and minimum value for f_5 to f_8. The functions (f_1-f_4) are defined in Table 1 along with their global maximum value, the search range and dimensionality. Among these functions, f_1 and f_2 have several local maxima but only one global maximum. However, the monotonic function, f_3 and the bell-shaped function, f_4 have only one maximum. The schematic diagrams of some functions are depicted in Figure 2(a)-(c).

Similarly, the functions (f_5-f_8) are defined in Table 2. Of them, f_5-f_7 are high-dimensional, while f_8 is a low-dimensional one. Also, f_5 is a unimodal function, while f_6 and f_7 are multimodal where the number of local minima increases exponentially with the problem dimension. f_8 has only a few local minima. We have chosen various classes of functions to make the experiment unbiased and to test the robustness of the proposed technique.

TABLE 1: Mathematical Functions for Maximization

Function	Dimension (n)	Range	Maximum Value
$f_1(x) = \begin{cases} 2 + e^{x-10}cos(x-10) & \text{if } x \leq 10 \\ 2 + e^{10-x}cos(10-x) & \text{if } x > 10 \end{cases}$	1	$0 \leq x \leq 20$	3.00
$f_2(\mathbf{x}) = \sum_{i=1}^{n}\{x_i e^{1-x_i} + (1-x_i)e^{x_i}\}$	5	$0 \leq x_i \leq 1$	8.30
$f_3(\mathbf{x}) = \sum_{i=1}^{n} x_i^2$	3	$0 \leq x_i \leq 10$	300.0
$f_4(\mathbf{x}) = 1 + \sum_{j=1}^{n} \frac{1}{1+\sum_{i=1}^{4}(x_i-1)^6}$	4	$0 \leq x_i \leq 10$	5.00

TABLE 2: Mathematical Functions for Minimization

Function	Dimension (n)	Range	Minimum Value
$f_5(\mathbf{x}) = \sum_{i=1}^{n} \|x_i\| + \prod_{i=1}^{n} \|x_i\|$	15	$-10 \leq x \leq 10$	0.00
$f_6(\mathbf{x}) = \frac{1}{4000} \sum_{i=1}^{n} x_i{}^2 - \prod_{i=1}^{n} cos(\frac{x_i}{\sqrt{i}}) + 1$	15	$-15 \leq x_i \leq 15$	0.00
$f_7(\mathbf{x}) = -20exp\left(-0.2\sqrt{\frac{1}{n}\sum_{i=1}^{n}}\right)$	15	$-32 \leq x_i \leq 32$	0.00
$\quad - exp\left(\frac{1}{n}cos(2\pi x_i)\right) + 20 + e$			
$f_8(\mathbf{x}) = 4x_1^2 - 2.1x_1^4 + \frac{1}{3}x_1^6 + x_1 x_2$	2	$-5 \leq x_i \leq 5$	-1.031628
$\quad - 4x_2^2 + 4x_2^4$			

In the experiment we have evaluated the efficiency of CAGA compared to CGA. In both cases the same initial population, initial mutation probability (p_m) and initial crossover probability (p_c) have been considered as starting inputs of the algorithms. The mutation rate (p_m) remains constant in CGA throughout the entire search process but in CAGA the input, p_m (according to equation 2) and the search space are altered at each stage. For all the functions the starting input value of p_c is taken in the range [0.5-0.9], that of p_m is in the range [0.001-0.008] and the population size is set to 30 with the same initial population for both methods. The chromosome size in CGA is larger since the initial and final resolutions of the search domain are unaltered. On the other hand, the chromosome length is small in CAGA since the resolution is gradually increased at each stage due to the reduction of search space. The fitness value of a chromosome for each mathematical function is its functional value.

The first set of experimental results which are the average of 30 independent runs is shown in Table 3. It is noted that CAGA performs better than or equal to CGA for $f_1 - f_4$. The performance of both methods is identical for f_2. In CAGA f_1 and f_4 can attain the exact global maximum. f_1 and f_4 reach close to the global maximum value in CGA with an oscillation for f_4. The functional value of f_3 in CGA is close to the global maximum but in CAGA it is more closer to the solution.

TABLE 3: Results of the functions considered for maximization

Function	Number of Generations	CAGA		CGA	
		Mean Best	Std. Dev.	Mean Best	Std. Dev.
$f_1(x)$	100	3.00	0.00	2.99	2.98
$f_2(\mathbf{x})$	1000	8.24	0.00	8.24	0.00
$f_3(\mathbf{x})$	400	299.99	0.00	299.41	0.00
$f_4(\mathbf{x})$	100	5.00	0.00	4.97	$1.4 X 10^{-2}$

TABLE 4: Results of the functions considered for minimization

Function	Number of Generations	CAGA		CGA	
		Mean Best	Std. Dev.	Mean Best	Std. Dev.
$f_5(\mathbf{x})$	1000	$2.8 X 10^{-4}$	0.00	$7.0 X 10^{-1}$	$1.6 X 10^{-1}$
$f_6(\mathbf{x})$	2000	0.00	0.00	$1.1 X 10^{-1}$	$9.0 X 10^{-3}$
$f_7(\mathbf{x})$	3500	$5.1 X 10^{-5}$	0.00	1.46	1.00
$f_8(\mathbf{x})$	200	-1.03	0.00	-1.07	$6.4 X 10^{-2}$

Similarly, the results of $f_5 - f_8$ is shown in Table 4 considering the average of 30 independent runs. Here, $f_5 - f_8$ perform much better in CAGA compared to CGA and there is a uniformity in convergence in all individual runs. Among them, f_6 and f_8 can attain the exact global minimum value. However, the uniformity is not maintained for $f_5 - f_8$ in all individual runs in CGA. Such oscillation is maximum for f_7 and minimum for f_6. However, f_5, f_6 and f_8 can reach close to the global minimum value compared to f_7 which is far from the solution.

The convergence speed of CAGA is faster than or equal to that of CGA except for f_2. The speed of CAGA is 2.5 times faster than that of CGA for f_1. However, CGA converges faster than CAGA for f_2 (with dimension 5) although none of the two methods can attain the exact global maximum value in this case.

As mentioned before, we have also performed our experiment on dot pattern matching and object matching from edge map. A dot pattern is a set of dots or points in 2-D or 3-D space arranged to represent some physical object or class of objects in a feature space. In the multidimensional space the dot patterns are located either wide apart or overlapped with each other. We encounter dot patterns in astronomy and astrophysics, geographic and cartographic data, remote sensing, spatial information system, biomedical imaging, image texture analysis and many other deciplines of computer science. The studies involving dot pattern includes shape identification and set estimation, classification and clustering, and point process parameter identification.

The dot pattern matching problem has been performed in the following way. We have taken S as a set of dot patterns of different shapes shown in Figure 3. Let one of them be a test pattern, T and matched it with S. Usually CAGA performs better than CGA in speed. However, in both the methods sometimes T does not match with the correct pattern of S.

Figure 3: A scene of multiple dot patterns in 2-D

The matching score of two dot patterns, T and S are computed as follows. T is translated to a point, P and rotated by an angle, θ with respect to the origin, O. Now the distance, $d(t_i, s_j)$ between a point, t_i of T and each of the points, s_j of S is measured and the minimum distance is taken into consideration. If the number of points of T is α, then the sum of minimum distances, D_{min} for all α points is

$$D_{min} \;=\; \sum_{i=1}^{\alpha} Min[d(t_i, s_j)]_{j=1, \beta} \tag{3}$$

where $t_1, t_2, \dots t_\alpha$ and $s_1, s_2, \dots s_\beta$ are the points of T and S, respectively and in our test $\alpha \leq \beta$. The value of D_{min} is the best matching score of two dot patterns for a solution chromosome in a population.

In our experiment the number of dots in patterns of S shown in Figure 3 is 2215. Let T be the test pattern which can be one of the four patterns in Fig. 3. The best matching scores of T and S are shown in Table 5 for CAGA and CGA methods. The patterns are either *matched* or *unmatched*. We can consider two types of matching namely *perfect matching* and *imperfect* but *visual matching*. For visually matched patterns we see that T is superimposed over S without any visible error although the error of the matching is computationally reasonable. On the other hand, in perfectly matched situation the error of the matching between T and S is very close to zero. Naturally, the patterns are also visually matched.

TABLE 5: Results of CAGA and CGA Methods on Dot Patterns

	CAGA			CGA		
	Success Rate		*Unsuccess Rate*	*Success Rate*		*Unsuccess Rate*
Dot	*Perfectly*	*Visually*	*Not*	*Perfectly*	*Visually*	*Not*
Patterns	*Matched*	*Matched*	*Matched*	*Matched*	*Matched*	*Matched*
DP1	33%	47%	20%	0%	20%	80%
DP2	53%	20%	27%	0%	7%	93%
DP3	66%	27%	7%	7%	40%	53%
DP4	27%	66%	7%	0%	33%	67%

For each dot pattern we have performed our experiment for 15 independent runs. The population size is 30, the value of p_c lies between 0.6 and 0.8, the value of p_m is in the range [0.004-0.008] and the maximum number of iterations required is 100. It is noticed that in CGA the search stuck to a local optimum for most cases. The chromosome size is always considered 50% longer in CGA to provide equal resolution of solution space with CAGA. The results of Table 5 show that the performance of CAGA is much better than that of CGA. The rate of failure in CAGA is less than 30% at most while in CGA it is at least 50%. In CGA the dot patterns did not exactly match except for DP3.

The other pattern recognition experiment is matching with edge map. Initially, the object was a *gray-tone* digital image in the space of *256X256* pixels with *256* possible gray levels. It is then converted into a two tone edge map using *Sobel Operator* [12]. The edge map may be considered as a discrete dot pattern where a dot is represented by *1* and a blank (white space) is by *0*. See Fig. 4(a)-4(b).

The number of pixels in the edge map is 6856. The object, S is the original one and T is the test pattern (a distorted form of S). We have distorted the original object by rorating it with a certain angle. The angle may be between 0 and 360 degrees. In the experiment the parameters are p_c =[0.6-0.9], p_m =[0.005-0.008], the population size is 30 and the maximum number of iterations allowed is 100 for both methods. We have considered several independent runs to perform the experiment for both methods. The patterns are matched in the same way as described before. In CGA the chromosome length is always 60% larger. Fig. 4(c) and Fig. 4(d) show the position of the dot patterns after the convergence of the search in CAGA and CGA, respectively.

From the experiment it is observed that the performance of CAGA is better than that of CGA. The success rate is also encouraging but not 100%. The rate of successful matching (visually matched) of CAGA is at least 70% whereas in CGA it is 60%. Moreover, the convergence speed of CGA is slower than that of CAGA when the object is visually matched.

In pattern recognition problems we have considered the fitness function as sum of shortest distances between the points of S and T. The fitness value at a single point is defined as follows.

$$F = D_{min} \tag{4}$$

5   Conclusion

We have proposed the cascaded GA method to enhance the computation efficiencey of the conventional GA. Here, the genetic search starts with small chromosome size. The choice of chromosome length is determined by the search space dimensionality and size, the degree of freedom as well as the required solution accuracy. Initially, the small chromosome size represents the solution space with coarse resolution. However, since in successive stages the search space is reduced and the chromosome size remains constant, the resolution is eventually increased. Thus, the small chromosome size saves the computation cost per iteration as well as the memory space, and restricts the search from falling in the spurious local extrema.

We have demonstrated our approach on a number of synthetic functions for optimization as well as on the pattern recognition problems. We have considered two pattern recognition problems, one on dot pattern matching and the other on object matching from edge map.

Two sets of experiments have been performed on eight mathematical functions in single or multi-dimensional space. All functions contain either one or multiple local optimum. However, there are some functions for which the number of local optima increases exponentially with the problem dimension. The CAGA method can attain the exact global optimum for most of the functions and there is a uniformity in convergence.

Next, we have taken the matching problem between two dot patterns. The match between two dot patterns is obtained by first translating the test pattern to a point, P and then rotating by an angle, θ with respect to the mean point, O as origin. From the test results it is observed that CAGA makes the search efficient with a success rate between 70% and 90% for smaller chromosome length compared to the chromosome size in CGA.

In object matching with edge map the object is a digital image with 256 possible gray levels in a space of $256X256$ pixels. It is then converted to a two-tone edge map using *Sobel Operator* [12] and transformed to a dot pattern where the edge is indicated by a series of dots. The match between two objects is performed similar to the dot pattern matching problem. Here the test object is considered as a distorted form of the sample object. In the experiment CAGA proforms better with a success rate of at least 70%.

Acknowledgements

The authors would like to thank Dr. U. Pal, Mr. A. Roy Chaudhuri and others of the CVPR unit, ISI for their helpful support.

References

1. D. E. Goldberg. Genetic Algorithms in Search, Optimization and Machine Learning. Addison-Wesley, New York, 1989.
2. B. Bhanu, S. Lee and J. Ming. Self-optimizing image segmentation system using a genetic algorithm. Proc. of 4th Int. Conf. on Genetic Algorithms. San Diego, CA. 1991; 362-369.
3. A. Hill and C. J. Taylor. Model-based image interpretation using genetic algorithm. Image and Vision Comput. 1992; 10:295-300.
4. A. Toet and W. P. Hajema. Genetic contour matching. Pattern Recognition Letters 1995; 16:849-856.
5. D. S. Lin and J. J. Leou. A Genetic Algorithm approach to Chinese handwriting normalization. IEEE Trans. Systems, Man and Cybernetics-Part B 1997; 27(6):999-1007.
6. S. M. Yamany, K. J. Khiani and A. A. Farag. Application of neural networks and genetic algorithms in the classification of endothelial cells. Pattern Recognition Letters 1997; 18:1205-1210.
7. Nirwan Ansari, M. H. Chen abd E. S. H. Hou. Point pattern matching by a Genetic Algorithm. Proc. of the 16th Annual Conf. of IEEE Industrial Electronic Society (IECON'90), Vol. II. Pacific Grove, 1990; 1233-1238.
8. M. Mirmehdi, P. L. Palmer and J. Kittler. Genetic optimization of the image feature extraction process. Pattern Recognition Letters 1997; 18:355-365.
9. D.E. Goldberg, K. Deb and B. Korb. Messy genetic algorithms: Motivation, analysis and first results. Complex Systems 1989; 3:493-530.
10. S. Rizzi. Genetic operators for hierarchical graph clustering. Pattern Recognition Letters 1998; 19:1293-1300.
11. T. Back and F. Hoffmeister. Extended selection mechanisms in genetic algorithms. Proc. 4th Int. Conf. Genetic Algorithms. Univ. California, San Diego 1991; 92-99.
12. A.K. Jain. Fundamentals of Digital Image Processing. Prentice-Hall, Englewood Cliffs, N.J., 1989.

Using Unlabelled Data to Train a Multilayer Perceptron

Antanas Verikas[1,2], Adas Gelzinis[2], Kerstin Malmqvist[1], Marija Bacauskiene[2]

[1]Intelligent Systems Laboratory, Halmstad University,
Box 823, S-301 18 Halmstad, Sweden
Email: antanas.verikas@ide.hh.se

[2]Kaunas University of Technology, Studentu 50, 3031, Kaunas, Lithuania

Abstract

This paper presents an approach to using both labelled and unlabelled data to train a multilayer perceptron. The unlabelled data are iteratively pre-processed by a perceptron being trained to obtain the soft class label estimates. It is demonstrated that substantial gains in classification performance may be achieved from the use of the approach when the labelled data do not represent adequately the entire class distributions. The experimental investigations performed have shown that the approach proposed may be successfully used to train neural networks for learning different classification problems.

Keywords: Classification, Multilayer Perceptron, Neural Networks, Unlabelled Data

1 Introduction

Artificial neural networks proved themselves very useful in various applications. Many of the neural network applications concern classification. One of the most important features of neural networks is learning from examples. There are three main types of learning: supervised, unsupervised, and reinforcement. In the supervised learning case, the decision function sought is learned from training pairs: input vector, class label. Numerous classifiers and associated learning algorithms have been developed. A common feature of nearly all the approaches is the assumption that class labels are known for each input data vector used for training. The training for such classifiers typically involves dividing the training data into subsets by class and then using the maximum likelihood estimation to separately learn each class density.

It has been recently recognised the value of the use of both labelled and unlabelled data for learning classification problems [1,2,3,4,5]. Labelled data can be plentiful for some applications. For others, such as medical imaging, quality control in halftone multicoloured printing, the correct class labels can not be easily obtained for a significant part of the vast amount of training data available. The difficulty in obtaining class labels may arise due to incomplete knowledge or limited resources. An expensive expertise is often required to derive class labels. Besides, labelling of the data is often a very tedious and time-consuming procedure.

S. Singh, N. Murshed, W. Kropatsch (Eds.): ICAPR 2001, LNCS 2013, pp. 40–49, 2001.

The practical significance of training with labelled and unlabelled data was recognised in [2]. Towell [5], Shashahani and Landgrebe [4], Miller and Uyar [3] have obtained substantial gains in classification performance when using both labelled and unlabelled data. However, despite the promising results, there has been little work done on using both labelled and unlabelled data for learning classification problems. One reason is that conventional supervised learning approaches such as the error back propagation have no direct way to incorporate unlabelled data and, therefore, discard them. In this paper, we propose an approach to using both labelled and unlabelled data to train a multilayer perceptron. The unlabelled data are iteratively pre-processed by a perceptron being trained to obtain the soft class label estimates.

2 Related Work

It has been shown that the MLP trained by minimising the mean squared error can be viewed as a tool to estimate the posteriori class probability from the set of input data:

$$P(c_j / \mathbf{x}) = \frac{\exp\left(o_j^{(L)}(\mathbf{x}, \mathbf{w})\right)}{\sum_{i=1}^{Q} \exp\left(o_i^{(L)}(\mathbf{x}, \mathbf{w})\right)} \tag{1}$$

where $o_j^{(L)}(\mathbf{x}, \mathbf{w})$ is the output signal of the j th output node, Q stands for the number of output nodes of the perceptron, and L is the number of layers in the network. In [6], this estimate of the posteriori class probability obtained for an unlabelled data point served as target value when learning the point. In [7], the decision classes are treated as fuzzy sets. The membership degrees to the fuzzy sets are estimated for each data point and used as target values to train a multilayer perceptron. The learning algorithm proposed by Towell uses a conventional supervised training technique except that it occasionally replaces a labelled sample with a synthetic one [5]. The synthetic sample is the centroid of labelled and unlabelled samples in the neighbourhood of the labelled sample. Therefore, the algorithm uses both labelled and unlabelled samples to make local variances estimates.

Another approach to using unlabelled data for learning classification problems relies on probability mixture models. A mixture-based probability model [3,4] is the key to incorporate unlabelled data in the learning process. In [4], the conditional likelihood is maximised, while Miller and Uyar [3] maximise the joint data likelihood given by

$$\log L = \sum_{\mathbf{x}_i \in \mathbf{X}^u} \log \sum_{l=1}^{L} \alpha_l f(\mathbf{x}_i / \theta_l) + \sum_{\mathbf{x}_i \in \mathbf{X}^l} \log \sum_{l=1}^{L} \alpha_l P\big[c_i / \mathbf{x}_i, m_i = l\big] f(\mathbf{x}_i / \theta_l) \tag{2}$$

where $f(\mathbf{x}_i / \theta_l)$ is one of L component densities, with non-negative mixing parameters α_l, such that $\sum_{l=1}^{L} \alpha_l = 1$, θ_l is the set of parameters of the component density, $\mathbf{X}^u$ is the unlabelled data set and $\mathbf{X}^l$ is the labelled data set. The class labels are also assumed to be random quantities and are chosen according to the probabilities $P[c_i / \mathbf{x}_i, m_i]$, i.e. conditioned on the selected mixture component $m_i \in \{1, 2, ..., L\}$ and on the feature values. The optimal classification rule for this model is given by the following selector function with range in the class label set:

$$S(\mathbf{x}) = arg \max_k \sum_j P[c_i = k / m_i = j, \mathbf{x}_i] P[m_i = j / \mathbf{x}_i] \qquad (3)$$

where

$$P[m_i = j / \mathbf{x}_i] = \frac{\alpha_j f(\mathbf{x}_i / \theta_j)}{\sum_{l=1}^{L} \alpha_l f(\mathbf{x}_i / \theta_l)} \qquad (4)$$

The expectation maximisation (EM) algorithm [8] is used to maximise the likelihood. The EM algorithm iteratively guesses the value of missing information. The algorithm uses global information in this process and, therefore, it may not perform well on some problems. We use the approach chosen by Miller and Uyar [3] for our comparisons.

3 Training the Network

3.1 The Network

The network used is a multilayer perceptron. Let $o_j^{(q)}$ denote the output signal of the j th neuron in the q th layer induced by presentation of an input pattern $\mathbf{x}$, and $w_{ij}^{(q)}$ the connection weight coming from the i th neuron in the $(q-1)$ layer to the j th neuron in the q th layer. Assume that $\mathbf{x}$ is an augmented vector, i.e. $x_0 = 1$. Then $o_j^{(0)} = x_j$, $o_j^{(q)} = f(net_j^{(q)})$, and

$$net_j^{(q)} = \sum_{i=0}^{n_{q-1}} w_{ij}^{(q)} o_i^{(q-1)} \qquad (5)$$

where $net_j^{(q)}$ stands for the activation level of the neuron, n_{q-1} is the number of neurons in the $q-1$ layer and $f(net)$ is a sigmoid activation function.

3.2 Learning Set

We assume that the learning set $\mathbf{X}$ consists of two subsets $\mathbf{X} = \{\mathbf{X}_l, \mathbf{X}_u\}$, where $\mathbf{X}^u = \{\mathbf{x}^{N_l+1}, ..., \mathbf{x}^{N_l+N_u}\}$ is the unlabelled data subset and $\mathbf{X}^l = \{(\mathbf{x}^1, c^1), (\mathbf{x}^2, c^2)...(\mathbf{x}^{N_l}, c^{N_l})\}$ is the labelled data subset, $\mathbf{x}^n \in R^K$ is the n th data vector, $c^n \in I = \{1, 2, ..., Q\}$ is the class label, Q is the number of classes, N_l and N_u are the number of labelled and unlabelled data points, respectively; $N = N_l + N_u$. The target values for the labelled data subset $\mathbf{t}^1, ..., \mathbf{t}^{N_l}$ are encoded according to the scheme 1-of-Q, i.e. $t_k^n = 1$, if $c^n = k$ and $t_k^n = 0$, otherwise.

3.2.1 Target values for unlabelled data

In this study, we treat the decision classes as fuzzy sets and assume that the neural network's output values provide membership degrees to the fuzzy sets. Suppose that the n th input pattern $\mathbf{x}''$ is presented to the network. The membership degree $\mu_{C_j}(\mathbf{x}'')$ of the n th input pattern $\mathbf{x}''$ to the j th fuzzy set is then given by the output signal $o_j^{(L)}(\mathbf{x}'', \mathbf{w})$ of the j th output node of the network. Next, the contrast within the set of membership values $\mu_{C_j}(\mathbf{x}'')$ is increased:

$$\eta_{C_j}(\mathbf{x}'') = \begin{cases} 2[\mu_{C_j}(\mathbf{x}'')]^2, & \text{for } 0 \le \mu_{C_j}(\mathbf{x}'') \le 0.5 \\ 1 - 2[1 - \mu_{C_j}(\mathbf{x}'')]^2 & \text{otherwise.} \end{cases}, \quad j = 1, 2, ..., Q \qquad (6)$$

This implies that the membership assignment is possibilistic. Let M'' be the set of indices of the k_{nn} nearest neighbours of the unlabelled data point $\mathbf{x}''$, i.e.

$$\left\| \mathbf{x}'' - \mathbf{x}^k \right\| < \left\| \mathbf{x}'' - \mathbf{x}^i \right\|, \quad \forall k \in M'' \text{ and } \forall i \notin M''; \; N_l + 1 \le n \le N; \; 1 \le k, i \le N \quad (7)$$

Then, the target vector $\mathbf{t}''$ for the unlabelled data point $\mathbf{x}''$ is given by

$$\mathbf{t}'' = \sum_{l \in M^n} \mathbf{t}^l / k_{nn}, \qquad (8)$$

where

$$t_j^l = \eta_{C_j}(\mathbf{x}^l), \; \forall j = 1, ..., Q, \forall n = N_{l+1}, ..., N \qquad (9)$$

if $N_l + 1 \le l \le N$, and $t_j^l = 1 \text{ or } 0$, if $1 \le l \le N_l$.

The problem of an optimum choice for the value of k_{nn} is equivalent to the problem of finding the optimum value of K in the K-nearest-neighbours based probability density estimation task.

3.3 Learning Algorithm

We assume that regions of lower pattern density usually separate data classes. Therefore, decision boundary between the classes should be located in such low pattern density regions. First, the network is trained using labelled data only. The target values for unlabelled data are then estimated using (8). Next, the network is retrained using both the labelled and unlabelled data and the target values for the unlabelled data are re-estimated. In the following, the training and re-estimation steps are iterated until the classification results obtained from the network in a predetermined number of subsequent iterations stop changing or the number of iterations exceeds some given number. We use the error backpropagation algorithm to train the network. The network is trained by minimising the sum-squared error augmented with the additional regularisation term

$$E(\mathbf{w}) = \frac{1}{2} \sum_{n=1}^{N} \sum_{j=1}^{Q} \left(o_j^{(L)n}(\mathbf{w}) - t_j^n \right)^2 + \beta \sum_{i=1}^{N_W} w_i^2 \tag{10}$$

where N_W is the number of weights in the network and β is the regularisation coefficient. The learning algorithm is encapsulated in the following four steps.

1. Train the network using labelled data only.
2. Calculate target values for the unlabelled data using (8).
3. Train the network using both the labelled and unlabelled data.
4. Stop, if the classification results obtained from the network in a predetermined number of subsequent iterations stop changing or the number of iterations exceeds some given number; otherwise go to Step 2.

4 Experimental testing

The learning approach developed was compared with the EM algorithm based approach proposed in [3] and the conventional error backpropagation learning when only labelled data are exploited. We used data of two types to test the approach: the 2D artificial data, and the data from three real applications.

4.1 Tests for Artificial Data

We performed two series of experiments with artificial data. In the first series, a two-class separation problem that requires a linear decision boundary was considered. In the second series, the network had to develop highly non-linear decision boundaries for classifying two-dimensional data into three classes.

4.1.1 A two class problem

The data set is shown in Fig. 1. The data classes are Gaussian with the same covariance matrix. The optimal decision boundary for the data is linear. There are 2000 data points in the class 'o' and 400 in the class '+'. The black dots illustrate the labelled data. Only 40 data points from each class are labelled. As it often happens in practice, the labelled data do not adequately represent the entire class distributions. A single layer perceptron can yield the optimal solution. However, to have some redundancy in the model, we used a one hidden layer perceptron with two nodes in the hidden layer.

Fig. 1 (left) illustrates the typical classification result obtained from the MLP trained on the labelled data only. The classification errors are shown in black '+' and 'o'. As can be seen from the figure, the labelled data are classified correctly. However, the average classification error for the unlabelled data is 8.98%.

The classification result obtained using the proposed training approach is shown in Fig. 1 (right). The number of nearest neighbours used in the experiment is $k_{nn} = 8$. The improvement obtained from the use of both the labelled and unlabelled data in the learning process should be obvious. In this experiment, the EM based approach yielded a very similar solution. The error rate obtained was 1.77% for the approach proposed and 1.89% for the EM based approach.

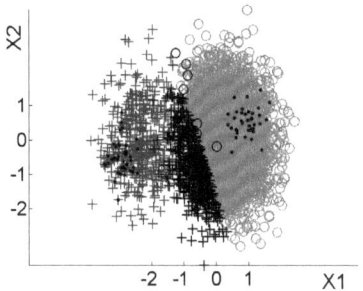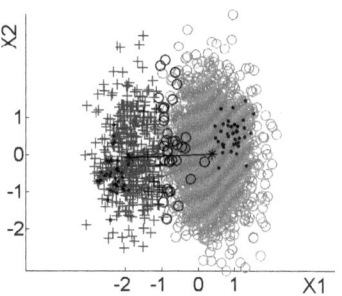

Fig. 1. A two-class ('+' and 'o') classification problem. Classification result obtained from the MLP trained on: (left) labelled data only, (right) both labelled and unlabelled data.

4.1.2 Location of the decision boundary

The next experiment aims to justify that the decision boundary found is situated in a place sparse in data points. First, we uniformly distribute some number of data points, let say 100, on the line connecting centres of the classes. The connecting line is shown in Fig. 1 (right). The asterisks stand for the centres of the classes. For each data point on the line we then evaluate the average distance to the k_{nn} nearest neighbours in the data set. To evaluate the distance we always used the same number of the nearest neighbours as for the target value estimate when training the network. The average distance evaluated for all the data points on the line reflects the density of the data points in the neighbourhood of the line. Fig. 2 (left) illustrates the distribution of the average distance obtained using eight nearest neighbours ($k_{nn} = 8$). The characters '+' and 'o' show to which class the points of the line are assigned. As can be seen from Fig. 2 (left), the class label changes in the place of the lowest pattern density. A more accurate estimate of the average distance, the generalised average distance, is obtained by averaging the estimates conveyed by several lines drawn in parallel to the line connecting the centres of the classes. The end points of the i th line are given by

$$\mathbf{p}_c^i = \mathbf{p}_c^* + \{0, [((N_{lin} + 1)/2) - i]\Delta h\}, \quad c = 1,2; \quad i = 1,2,...,N_{lin} \qquad (11)$$

where c is the class index, $\mathbf{p}_c^*$ is the centre of the class c, N_{lin} stands for the number of the lines, and Δh is a constant. The generalised average distance from the j th point on the generalised line to the k_{nn} nearest neighbours is given by

$$d_j = \frac{1}{N_{lin}} \sum_{i=1}^{N_{lin}} d_j^i \qquad (12)$$

where d_j^i is the average distance from the j th point on the i th line. Fig. 2 (right) illustrates the distribution of the generalised average distance evaluated using $N_{lin} = 15$, $\Delta h = 0.1$, and $k_{nn} = 50$. As we can see, the class label changes in the place of the lowest pattern density.

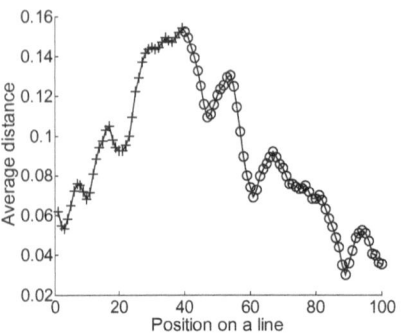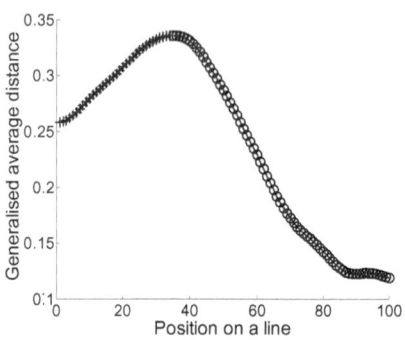

Fig. 2. Distribution of the average distance (left). Distribution of the generalised average distance for $k_{nn} = 50$ (right).

4.1.3 A three class problem

The data set used in this experiment is shown in Fig. 3. There are three classes in the set: 'o', '+', and '□' containing 1683, 1739, and 1735 data points, respectively. Only 40 data points from each class, shown as black dots, are labelled. The labelled data extremely badly represent the class distributions. The one hidden layer perceptron used in this experiment contained ten nodes in the hidden layer.

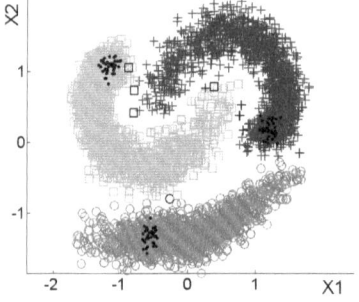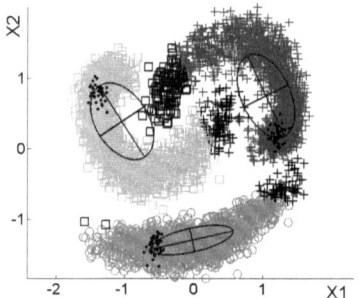

Fig. 3. A three-class ('o', '+', and '□') classification problem. Classification result obtained: (left) from the network trained according the approach proposed, (right) from the EM based approach for $L = 3$ mixture components.

Fig. 3 (left) shows a typical classification result of the data set obtained from the network trained according to the approach proposed. The black dots illustrate the labelled data. The unlabelled data points shown in grey are correctly classified. The classification errors are shown in black 'o', '+', and '□'.

We have experimented with the EM based approach using different number of mixture components. In all the trials, the obtained classification accuracy was far bellow the accuracy depicted in Fig. 3 (left). Fig. 3 (right) displays the best outcome from the EM based approach, which was obtained for $L = 3$. It is obvious that it is not enough to use three mixture components for modelling the class distributions properly. Using more mixture components, however, causes errors in the estimate of the probabilities $P[c_i / \mathbf{x}_i, m_i]$. The ellipses shown in the figure illustrate the constant density contours at the level given by the standard deviation equal to one.

4.2 Experiments with real data

4.2.1 Colour classification

Nowadays, multi-coloured pictures in newspapers, books, journals and many other places are most often created by printing dots of cyan (C), magenta (M), yellow (Y), and black (K) inks upon each other through screens having different raster angles. Fig. 4 (left) illustrates an example of an enlarged view of a small area of a newspaper picture that contains dots of all the four inks.

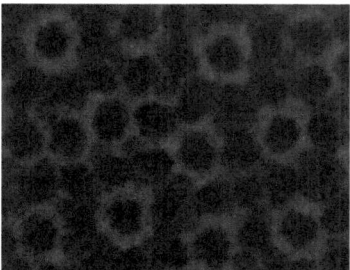 

Fig. 4. An enlarged view of a part of a newspaper picture that was created by printing dots of cyan, magenta, yellow, and black inks (left) and magenta ink (right).

In graphic arts, it is important to accurately measure the size of halftone printing dots. Such a need arises when studying interaction between different types of ink, paper and printing devices. It is not an easy task if we have to deal with very small or very large tonal values. Fig. 4 (right) represents an example of such a task. Approximately 96% of the area of the picture the image was taken from is covered by the magenta ink. The task is to determine the percentage of the "white" areas. Fig. 5 and Fig. 6 visualise two solutions to the problem. The same set of labelled data has been used in both experiments. The result obtained from the MLP trained on labelled data only is shown in Fig. 5. Fig. 6 illustrates the result obtained from the approach proposed. The results are presented in both the *ijk* and the image spaces. Comparing Fig. 5 and Fig. 6, we find that an obvious improvement in classification accuracy has been obtained when using the proposed training approach.

In this experiment, every pixel was described by the normalised variables $i=R+G+B$, $j=R-B$, and $k=R-2G+B$. These variables are obtained by performing a linear transformation of the $\{R,G,B\}$ vector by eigenvectors of the covariance matrix of the R, G and B variables (under the assumption that the variables are of equal variances and covariances).

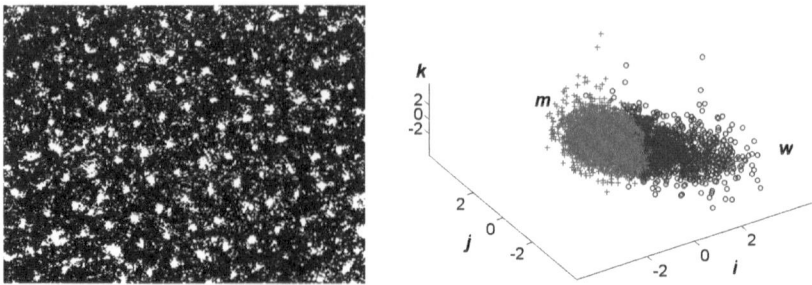

Fig. 5. Classification result obtained from the MLP trained on labelled data only. The result presented: (left) in the image space, (right) in the *ijk* colour space.

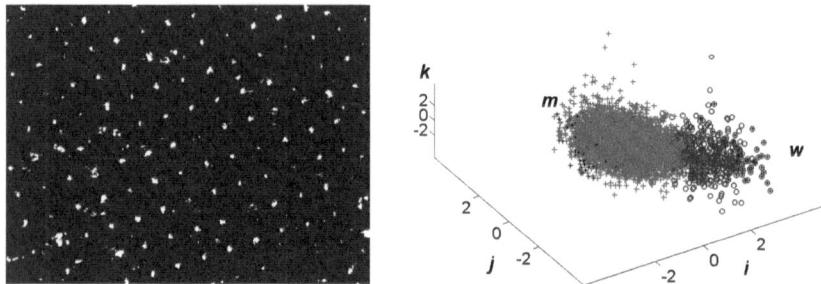

Fig. 6. Classification result obtained from the MLP trained on both labelled and unlabelled data. The result presented: (left) in the image space, (right) in the *ijk* colour space.

4.2.1 Classification tasks from the ELENA project

The *ESPRIT* Basic Research Project Number 6891 *(ELENA)* provides databases and technical reports designed for testing both conventional and neural classifiers. All the databases and technical reports are available via anonymous ftp: *ftp.dice.ucl.ac.be* in the directory *pub/neural/ELENA/databases*. From the *ELENA* project we have chosen two data sets representing real applications, *Phoneme* and *Satimage*.

The *Satimage* database was generated from Landsat Multi-Spectral Scanner image data. The database contains 6435 36-dimensional patterns. There are six classes in the database. The database also contains the five-dimensional description of the data. The five dimensions were obtained by using discriminat factorial analysis. In this study, we used the 5-dimensional description of the *Satimage* data.

The *Phoneme* database. The aim of this database is to distinguish between nasal and oral vowels. Thus, there are two different classes: the *Nasals* in class ω_0 and the *Orals* in class ω_1. There are 3818 patterns from class ω_0 and 1586 patterns from class ω_1.

For both databases, the data available were divided into training and testing sets of the same size. Fig. 7 visualises the classification performance as a function of the number of the labelled training data exploited in the training process. The superiority of the training approach proposed should be obvious from the figure.

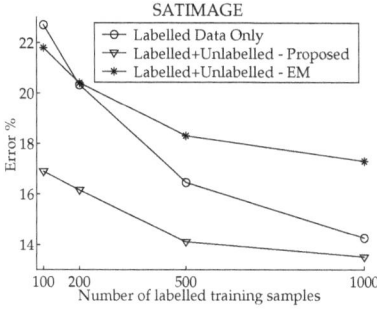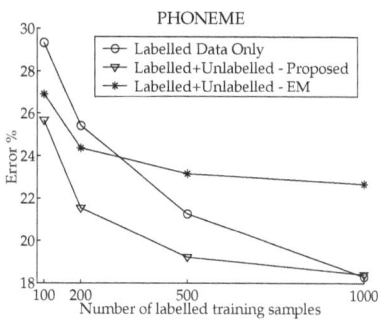

Fig. 7. Classification performance as a function of the number of the labelled training data.

5 Conclusions

We have presented an approach to using both labelled and unlabelled data to train a multilayer perceptron. The approach banks on the assumption that regions of low pattern density usually separate data classes. Decision boundaries developed during training according to the approach proposed are positioned in such low pattern density regions. We have demonstrated experimentally that substantial gains in classification performance may be achieved from the use of the approach when the labelled data do not adequately represent the entire class distributions. In all the tests performed, we found superiority of the proposed training approach over the EM based approach and the MLP trained on labelled data only.

References

1. Cataltepe Z, Magdon-Ismail M. Incorporating test inputs into learning. In: Jordan MI, Kearns MJ, Solla SA.(eds). NIPS 10, MIT Press, 1998, pp 437-443
2. Lippman RP. Pattern Classification Using Neural Networks. IEEE Communications Magazine 1989; 27: 47-64
3. Miller DJ, Uyar HS. Combined learning and use for a mixture model equivalent to the RBF classifier. Neural Computation 1998; 10: 281-293
4. Shashahani B, Landgrebe D. The Effect on Unlabelled Samples in Reducing the Small Sample Size Problem and Mitigating the Huges Phenomenon. IEEE Transactions on Geoscience and Remote Sensing 1994; 32: 1087-1095
5. Towell G. Using unlabeled data for supervised learning. In: Mozer MC, Jordan MI, Petsche T. (eds). NIPS 9, MIT Press, 1997, pp 647-653
6. Verikas A, Gelzinis A, Malmqvist K. Using labelled and unlabelled data to train a multilayer perceptron for colour classification in graphic arts. In: Imam L, Kodratoff Y, El-Dessouki A, Ali M. (eds). Lecture Notes in Artificial Intelligence 1611, Multiple Approaches to Intelligent Systems, Springer-Verlag Heidelberg, 1999, pp 550-559
7. Verikas A, Malmqvist K, Bacauskiene M, Bergman L. Monitoring the De-Inking Process through Neural Network Based Colour Image Analysis. Neural Computing & Applications 2000; 9(2): 142-151
8. Dempster AP, Laird NM, Rubin DB. Maximum-likelihood from incomplete data via the EM algorithm. Journal of the Royal Statistical Society, Series B, 39: 1977, 1-38

A Neural Multi -Expert Classification System for MPEG Audio Segmentation

M. De Santo*, G. Percannella*, C. Sansone°, M.Vento°

(*) Dipart. di Ingegneria dell'Informazione e di Ingegneria Elettrica
Università di Salerno - Via P.te Don Melillo,1 I-84084, Fisciano (SA), Italy.
(°) Dipart. di Informatica e Sistemistica Università di Napoli "Federico II"
Via Claudio, 21 I-80125 Napoli, Italy.

Abstract

The current research efforts in the field of video parsing and analysis are mainly focused on the use of pictorial information, while neglecting an important supplementary source of content information such as the embedded audio or soundtrack. In contrast, in this paper we address the issue of exploiting audio information that can be jointly used with video information for scene changes detection. The proposed method directly works on MPEG encoded sequences so to avoid computationally intensive decoding procedures. It is based on a multi-expert classification system made up of a hierarchical ensemble of neural networks.

Finally, after presentation of a large audio database, suitably designed for assessing the performance of the approach, preliminary experimental results are discussed.

Keywords: Audio segmentation, MPEG audio stream, Scene changes detection, Neural Networks, Multi-Expert Systems, Hierarchical classification.

1 Introduction

It is part of common life experience that a video can be defined as a combination of images and sounds. Soundtracks have a very significant role in defining the essence of a video footage; so the video can completely change its meaning if embedded into different soundtracks. Despite of these considerations, the current efforts for content characterization are mainly focused on the use of pictorial information [1-3], while only a modest number of research works related with the use of audio for video analysis is present in the literature [4-6].

A problem in this kind of applications is that the input audio stream is composed of different audio types (speech, music, silence, noise) which should be processed in

S. Singh, N. Murshed, and W. Kropatsch (Eds.): ICAPR 2001, LNCS 2013, pp. 50–59, 2001.
© Springer-Verlag Berlin Heidelberg 2001

different ways depending on the particular application considered. As an example, in speech recognition only intervals containing a speaker are considered [7], while distinguishing between music and speech sequences is necessary for recognizing different types of TV programs [6]. Techniques for partitioning the audio stream into homogeneous segments of different audio types are thus required as a necessary preliminary step for a reliable interpretation of an audio signal.

While the silence detection is a simple task, generally performed by thresholding the energy of the signal, the speech and music detection represents a quite complicated task. The typical approach used to distinguish between the two classes is based on the computation of a suitable set of features from the PCM samples of the audio stream [8-10]. Anyway, video sources are more often provided in compressed form, according to standards like MPEG. Only few papers [11,12] have faced the problem of audio classification by using features directly computed in the MPEG coded domain, so avoiding the computationally intensive task of decoding audio. In particular, in [11] Patel et al. in order to distinguish among silent, dialog and non-dialog segments propose a method based on features (pitch, pause rate, bandwidth) computed without performing any MPEG decoding step. The classification is performed by using such features in a rule based framework. In [12], Nakajima et al. detect silent, speech, music and applause segments using temporal density, bandwidth and center frequency of subband energy.

In this paper, the proposed classification system also works directly on MPEG encoded sequences. It is based on a hierarchy of neural networks suitably cooperating so as to face the classification task at different levels. Each classifier belonging to the multi-expert system provides, together with the classification decision, a reliability parameter which is used, in the final classification stage, to weight the decision of each classifier. So, classifiers exhibiting higher values of the reliability parameters receive more credit in the final classification decision.

Another relevant point is the experimental assessment of the system performance. To this aim, a very large database of audio is built and used for extensively verifying the performance of the system either in real situations or even in more crucial conditions, occurring fi. when speech and music overlap.

2 The Audio Classification System

The adopted classification strategy is based on a multi-expert system. Multi-expert systems have recently gained more and more popularity within the field of Pattern Recognition. The rationale of a multi-expert system lies in the fact that facing complex classification problems with a single classifier typically leads to crucial choices both in the process of selecting the features and in the determination of the classification paradigm, and again in the design of suitable training strategies of the classifier.

Anyway, no matter how complex the single classifier is, the whole system will be particularly strong in recognizing a large amount of input patterns, but unavoidably some other pattern will be wrongly classified. It is widely recognized by people working on Pattern Recognition that the effort in reducing the error rate, by iteratively intervening on the different parts of the system, grows more and more. After a certain number of successive improvements in the classifier performance, a lot of efforts are necessary for further decrease the error rate of a bit.

This problem has been addressed by making an ensemble, according to different architectures (parallel, serial and hierarchical topologies are the most common ones), of a set (typically under 10) of simple classifiers, as much as possible "complementary" each other; complementariness lies in the feature set, in the classification model, in the learning strategies, and so on. This way, the lack of a classifier can be, at least partially, recovered by the strength of the other classifiers participating to the multi-expert system. The approach experimented in various areas of Pattern Recognition, within different applications, revealed to be very promising, and the number of papers reporting related researches increased significantly [13-15].

The problem we are dealing with, can be profitably faced by using a multi-expert system, as the segmentation of audio within an MPEG stream is undoubtedly a very hard classification problem: the audio contains speech, music, silence, being each of them widely variable. Speech comes from people of different age, nationality, culture, can be slow or rather speedy, can vary in tone, volume and so on. Moreover, it is trivial to recognize that music is even more variable.

The detection of the instants in which an audio break can occur it is not a simple task, due to the fact that the interval in which a break happens is not constant and because of the high number of different break types. Typically, it is very difficult to choose an observation interval in such a way to ensure the presence of a break inside it. All these reasons make particularly difficult the design of a recognition system devoted to detect audio breaks.

So, an alternative solution can be given. Let us consider a system which does not try to directly detect audio breaks, but is able to recognize if a portion of an audio stream belongs to one of the classes introduced above. If it is possible to define a reliability measure for the decisions that this system performs, we could use this kind of information to detect audio breaks. In fact, if the decision of the system about a given audio portion is very reliable, it can be inferred that the audio portion examined is made of a unique audio type. Vice versa, if the classification act is not reliable enough, this unreliable decision could be due to the contemporary presence of more than one audio type and thus a break inside the audio portion considered could be present.

Neural networks can be used to implement such a recognition system efficiently. The design of a system for the detection of audio breaks could be made by employing the audio type recognition system described in a multi-expert system. In particular, the first level could be composed by a neural network devoted to classify a frame of the audio stream into one of four possible classes (silence, voice, music and noise). If the classification act of the network is judged reliable, it will be assumed that in the audio frame considered there are no breaks (and the system will consider the next audio frame). On the contrary, the audio frame considered is split into n subparts, each of which is classified by another neural network belonging to the second level of the whole system. On the basis of the responses supplied by these networks it is possible to use a combination module devoted to detect if there is really a break into the original audio frame or not. The combined decision will be supplied on the basis of the decisions of the second level classifier and of the reliability associated to them.

In figure 1 the whole system architecture is presented, while in the next section the features extracted from the MPEG audio stream are discussed in detail.

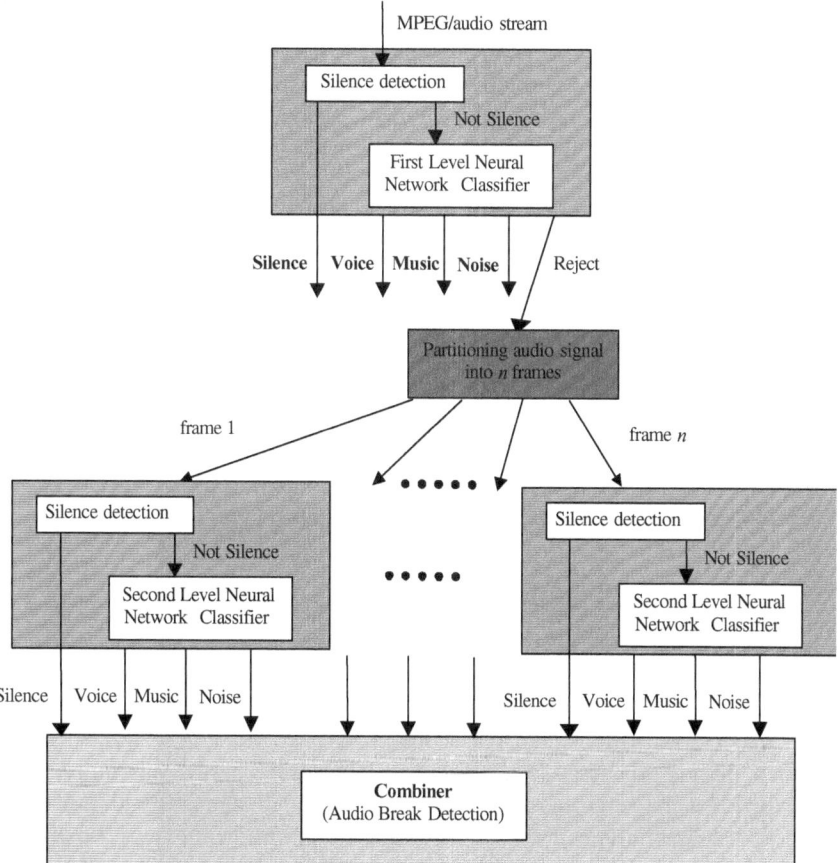

Fig. 1: The architecture of the proposed multi-expert classification scheme.

3 The Proposed Features

Before describing the proposed features let us introduce some useful notations:
- T is the duration of the observation interval expressed in seconds or the observation interval itself; the meaning is clear from the context; its value can be 5 or 1;
- $x_{s,i}$ is the i-th sample in T of the s-th sub-band;
- N is the number of samples for each sub-band in T.

Each of the following features is computed with respect to intervals of five or one seconds, depending on which level of the multistage classifier the computation is performed. As a consequence, the features extracted from the MPEG audio stream and used for classification by the first level neural network are 14, while the second level neural classifiers has, as input, a feature vector based only on the first 13 features.

Energy (E_0, E_1, E_2, E_3, E_4): this group of five features models the different energy profiles of speech and music signals. In particular, we compute the energy of audio signals by dividing the whole range of audible frequencies in five bands, each containing an increasing number of MPEG/audio sub-bands. In this way, we try to model the decreasing sensibility of the human auditive system to the increasing frequencies. We aggregate the MPEG/audio sub-band in energy bands according to the following table:

Band	MPEG/audio sub-bands
1	0-1
2	2-4
3	5-8
4	9-16
5	17-31

Then, computation of the energy profile of the signal in T is performed on the basis of the following formulas:

$$E_0 = \sum_{s=0}^{1} \sum_{i=1}^{N} \frac{x_{s,i}^2}{N}, \quad E_1 = \sum_{s=2}^{4} \sum_{i=1}^{N} \frac{x_{s,i}^2}{N}, \quad E_2 = \sum_{s=5}^{8} \sum_{i=1}^{N} \frac{x_{s,i}^2}{N},$$

$$E_3 = \sum_{s=9}^{16} \sum_{i=1}^{N} \frac{x_{s,i}^2}{N}, \quad E_4 = \sum_{s=17}^{31} \sum_{i=1}^{N} \frac{x_{s,i}^2}{N}.$$

Temporal Energy Variability (TEV): considering generic speech and music waveforms it is possible to observe that speech has an intermittent energy behavior due to the alternation between voiced and unvoiced speech; differently music is usually characterized by a more continuous behavior. Modeling such behavior is performed through the feature that we call temporal energy variability, which simply computes the variance of the duration of the short segments with low energy and whose calculation is carried out according to the following steps. Firstly, it is computed:

$$y_i = \sum_{s=0}^{31} x_{s,i}^2, \quad \text{with } s = 1, \dots, N \cdot$$

Then, a new series $\{y'_i\}$ is constructed by binarizing the $\{y_i\}$ series with a predetermined threshold Th_{TEV}:

$$y'_i = \begin{cases} 1 & \text{if } y_i > Th_{TEV} \\ 0 & \text{otherwise} \end{cases}, \quad \text{with } i = 1, \dots, N \cdot$$

The $\{y'_i\}$ series results to be constituted by alternating groups of 0s and 1s.

Starting from $\{y'_i\}$ it is constructed the $\{r_j\}$ series, whose generic element r_j represents the number of element in the j-th group of 0s in $\{y'_i\}$. Finally, we compute the temporal energy distribution as:

$$TEV = \frac{1}{M}\sum_{i=1}^{M}\left(r_i - \bar{r}\right)^2$$

where M is the number of groups of $0s$.

Average and Variance of the Number of Significant Bands (ASB, VSB): other characteristics of speech and music are that the bandwidth of speech is usually narrower than that of music. In fact the spectrum of speech signals is generally concentrated in the first 5-6 kHz. This property can be modeled through the average and the variance of the number of sub-band with significant energy level. In fact if the audio signal in T is characterized by a broad bandwidth, this number becomes large. The computation of these features is performed respectively according to the following formulas:

$$ASB = \frac{1}{N}\sum_{i=1}^{N}SB_i \quad \text{and} \quad VSB = \frac{1}{N}\sum_{i=1}^{N}\left(SB_i - ASB\right)^2$$

where SB_i is the number of significant bands in the i-th group of sub-band samples, for $i = 1,\ldots,N$, defined as:

$$SB_i = \sum_{s=0}^{31}x'_{s,i} \quad \text{and} \quad x'_{s,i} = \begin{cases} 1 & \text{if } x^2_{s,i} > Th_{SBs} \\ 0 & \text{otherwise} \end{cases}.$$

Sub-band centroid mean and variance (SC_M, SC_V, SC_T, D_{SC}): the spectral centroid represents the "balancing point" of the spectral power distribution. We estimate it by calculating the sub-band centroid for each MPEG audio group of sub-band samples. The sub-band centroid is given by:

$$SC_i = \frac{\sum_{s=0}^{31}s\cdot x^2_{s,i}}{\sum_{s=0}^{31}x^2_{s,i}}$$

When computed on music, the values of SC_i are usually larger than when computed on speech because of the different spectral distributions. This behavior can be modeled considering the mean value of the sub-band centroid on T, as:

$$SC_M = \frac{1}{N}\sum_{i=1}^{N}SC_i$$

Furthermore, SC_i has different values for voiced and unvoiced speech; on the contrary when computed on music SC_i tends to be more stable. Hence, we compute the variance and the third order central moment of SC_i in T, respectively as:

$$SC_V = \frac{1}{N}\sum_{i=1}^{N}\left(SC_i - SC_M\right)^2 \quad \text{and} \quad SC_T = \frac{1}{N}\sum_{i=1}^{N}\left(SC_i - SC_M\right)^3$$

and the difference between the number of SC_i greater (G_{CF}) and lower (L_{CF}) than SC_M in T, as:

$D_{SC} = G_{CF} - L_{CF}$.

Pause rate (PR): continuity of the signal is another major property found in non-speech signals, differently from speech that is characterized by stops due to separation of words and sentences. The pause rate measures the rate of stop in speech signals and can be computed by counting the number of silent segments in a talk. Let us denote with S_T the number of silent segments in T; then S_T is given by:

$$S_T = \sum_{j=0}^{k} \begin{cases} 1 & \text{if } (E_j < Th_S) AND (E_{j-1} > Th_S) \\ 0 & \text{otherwise} \end{cases}, \tag{1}$$

meaning that if energy E_j of the j-th segment in T is lower than the silent threshold Th_S, and the previous window is non-silence, S_T is incremented by 1 otherwise 0. Then the pause rate is given by:

$$PR = \frac{S_T}{T}.$$

It is worth noting that in (1), the energy E_j is given by: $E_j = \sum_{s=0}^{31} \sum_{i=1}^{K} \frac{x_{s,i}^2}{K}$, where K

is the number of sub-band samples in the j-th segment in T. The duration of the segments is 0,2 seconds.

Energy sub-band ratio (E_{SR}): the speech signals are characterized by the fact that the energy is mostly accumulated in the first 1,5 kHz; differently from music which is characterized by a spectrum usually spread on all the audible frequencies. This characteristic can be easily modeled in the sub-band domain by the energy sub-band ratio given by:

$$E_{SR} = \frac{\sum_{s=0}^{1} \sum_{i=0}^{N} \frac{x_{S_i}^2}{N}}{\sum_{s=2}^{31} \sum_{i=0}^{N} \frac{x_{S_i}^2}{N}}$$

after considering that the bandwidth of each MPEG audio sub-band is about 650 Hz, more or less depending on the sampling rate.

4 Experimental Results

In this paper we report a preliminary experimental analysis of the proposed system. In particular results obtained by the first level classifier (based on features evaluated with reference to intervals of five seconds) are reported with reference to a large audio database.

This database contains speech, music and noise: all the audio components have been sampled at a 44,1 kHz rate digitized in MPEG/audio Layer 2 stereo format with a bit rate ranging from 96 to 192 kbit/s. Particular care in the construction of the database has been adopted to include a large representative of major genres of speech and music. Speech material includes examples extracted from movies with male, female and child voices alone or mixed, while music material includes examples of the most representative genres as blues, classical, pop, rock, etc. The total duration of each class in the database is about twelve hours. In the following table a complete review of the speech and music audio track types included in our audio database is presented. It is worth noting that the different size of the various classes in the database also tries to reflect their real distribution in videos. For instance, the size of the child one-voice class is smaller than that of the man one-voice class since in general is more probable to watch a man as a character of a movie, or as an anchor in TV-news, than a child.

From the above described database three sets have been extracted: one for training the neural network (the training set, in the following TRS) made up of about 5700 samples (40% of the whole database), one for evaluating the training performance of the neural network (the so-called training-test set – in the following TTS) made up of about 4300 samples (30% of the whole database), and one for testing the neural network (the test set, in the following TS) made up of the remaining 30% (about 4300 samples).

Speech			Music	
Type of voice	Number of voices	Duration (total sec.)	Music genre	Duration (total sec.)
Child	1	9′ 54″ - (594)	Alternative	55′ 19″ - (3319)
Female	1	27′ 49″ - (1669)	Blues	1h. 39′ 49″ - (5989)
Male	1	1h. 36′ 45″ - (5805)	Children	58′ 40″ - (3520)
Child + Adult	2	39′ 01″ - (2341)	Classical	1h. 25′ 27″ - (5127)
Child	2	19′ 28″ - (1168)	Country	1h. 39′ 41″ - (5981)
Female	2	50′ 55″ - (3055)	Dance	1h. 44′ 53″ - (6293)
Male	2	1h. 13′ 30″ - (4410)	Folk	54′ 39″ - (3279)
Male + Female	2	54′ 28″ - (3268)	Gospel	59′ 18″ - (3558)
Child + Adult	> 2	33′ 55″ - (2035)	Jazz	2h. 11′ 04″ - (7864)
Child	> 2	17′ 12″ - (1032)	Latin	1h. 37′ 12″ - (5832)
Female	> 2	30′ 33″ - (1833)	Metal	50′ 26″ - (3026)
Male	> 2	40′ 37″ - (2437)	New Age	1h. 58′ 01″ - (7081)
Male + Female	> 2	42′ 42″ - (2562)	Pop	2h. 20′ 27″ - (8427)
			Punk	1h. 03′ 35″ - (3815)
			Rap	2h. 09′ 40″ - (7780)
			Reggae	1h. 41′ 38″ - (6098)
			Religious	1h. 11′ 34″ - (4294)
			Rock	1h. 12′ 08″ - (4328)
Total		8h. 56′ 49″ (32209)	Total	26h. 33′ 40″ (99611)

Table 1: A description of the audio database used.

The chosen network architecture was a Multi-Layer Perceptron with a single hidden layer. The learning algorithm was the standard Back-Propagation one, with a constant learning rate equal to 0.5. The sigmoidal activation function was chosen for all the neurons. The input and the output layer were made up of 14 and 2 neurons respectively.

Before using this classifier, we perform the silence detection separately on each audio segment. This is due to the fact that silence signals are characterized by a very low energy level, so that they can be simply detected on the basis of an energy thresholding. We compute the total energy of the signal in T according to the following formula: $E_{TOT} = \sum_{s=0}^{31} \sum_{i=1}^{N} \frac{x_{s,i}^2}{N}$, where the meaning of the symbols is that introduced in Section 3. The value E_{TOT} is compared with a predefined threshold (Th_{SIL}): if $E_{TOT} < Th_{SIL}$, then the considered audio segment is classified as silence, otherwise it is forwarded to the neural classifier.

On the database used about 93% of correct silence detection has been obtained.

In table 2 results obtained on TTS and TS by neural classifiers with different values of hidden neurons are reported.

# of hidden neurons	TTS	TS
10	95.87	94.22
15	97.17	93.56
20	98.03	94.59
25	97.80	94.43
30	97.89	93.96

Table 2: Results obtained on the considered database as a function of the number of neurons.

In order to test the ability of the neural classifier in rejecting transitions, the method proposed in [16] for selecting a reject threshold ensuring the best trade-off between error and reject rates has been applied. In table 3 the results relative to the use of the reject option on a set of samples not containing only speech or music are reported. As it is evident, almost all of these samples are correctly rejected, confirming the effectiveness of using such a technique for detecting transitions.

# of hidden neurons	Error Rate	Reject Rate
10	0.99	99.01
15	1.33	98.67
20	3.33	96.67
25	2.67	97.33
30	2.67	97.33

Table 3: Results obtained on a set of samples not containing only speech or music, as a function of the number of neurons.

Conclusions

In this paper a multi-expert system for the segmentation of audio MPEG stream is proposed.

The proposed method works directly on MPEG encoded sequences so as to avoid computationally intensive decoding procedures.

Preliminary results on a large audio database, specifically constructed for the performance assessment of the method, confirming the effectiveness of the proposed approach.

References

1. Hanjalic A, Lagendijk RL, Biemond J. Automated High-Level Movie Segmentation for Advanced Video-Retrieval Systems. IEEE Trans. on Circuits and Systems for Video Technology 1999, 9:580-588.
2. Yeung M, Yeo BL, Liu B. Extracting Story Units from Long Programs for Video Browsing and navigation. In: IEEE International Conference on Multimedia Computing and Systems, 1996, pp 296-305.
3. Kender JR, Yeo BL. Video Scene Segmentation Via Continuous Video Coherence. In: IEEE International Conference on Computer Vision and Pattern Recognition, 1998, pp 367-373.
4. Saraceno C, Leonardi R. Audio as a Support to Scene Change Detection and Characterization of Video Sequences. In: Proc. ICASSP'97, Munich, 1997.
5. Nam J, Cetin E, Tewfik H. Speaker Identification and Video Analysis for Hierarchical Video Shot Classification. In: Proc. ICIP '97, S. Barbara, 1997.
6. Boreczky JS, Wilcox LD. A Hidden Markov Model Framework for Video Segmentation Using Audio and Image Features. In: Proc. ICASSP '98, Seattle, 1998.
7. Jang PJ, Hauptmann AG. Improving acoustic models with captioned multimedia speech. In: Proc. of IEEE Intl. Conf. on Multimedia Computing and Systems, vol. 2, 1999, pp 767-771.
8. Scheirer E, Slaney M. Construction and Evaluation of a Robust Multifeature Speech/Music Discriminator. In: IEEE International Conference on Acoustics, Speech, and Signal Processing, vol. 2 , 1997, pp 1331-1334.
9. Saunders J. Real-Time Discrimination of Broadcast Speech/Music. In: IEEE Intern. Conf. on Acoustics, Speech, and Signal Processing, vol. 2, 1996, pp 993-996.
10. Liu Z, Wang Y, Chen T. Audio Feature Extraction and Analysis for Scene Segmentation and Classification. Journal of VLSI Signal Processing Systems for Signal, Image and Video Technology 1998, 20.
11. Patel NV, Sethi IK. Audio Characterization for Video Indexing. In: IS&T SPIE Proc. Storage and Retrieval for Image and Video Databases IV, 1996.
12. Nakajima Y, Lu Y, Sugano M, Yoneyama A, Yanagihara H, Kurematsu A. A Fast Audio Classification from MPEG Coded Data. In: IEEE Intern. Conf. on Acoustics, Speech, and Signal Processing, vol. 6, 1999, pp 3005-3008.
13. Ackermann B, Bunke H. Combination of Classifiers on the Decision Level for Face Recognition. Technical Report IAM-96-002, Institut für Informatik und angewandte Mathematik, Universität Bern, 1996.
14. Kittler J, Hatef M,. Duin RPW, Matas J. On Combining Classifiers. IEEE Trans. on Pattern Analysis and Machine Intelligence 1998; 20:226-239.
15. Rahman AFR, Fairhurst MC. An Evaluation of Multi-expert Configurations for the Recognition of Handwritten Numerals. Pattern Recognition 1998, 31:1255-1273.
16. Cordella LP, Sansone C, Tortorella F, Vento M, De Stefano C. Neural Network Classification Reliability: Problems and Application. In: Image Processing and Pattern Recognition, Academic Press, San Diego, CA, 1998, pp 161-200.

Pattern Recognition
with Quantum Neural Networks

A.A.Ezhov

Troitsk Institute of Innovation and Fusion Researches

Troitsk, Moscow region, Russia

Abstract.

New model of quantum neural nework able to solve classification problems is presented. It is based on the extention of the model of quantum associative memory [1] and also utilizes Everett's interpretation of quantum mechanics [2-4]. For presented model not neural weights but quantum entanglement is responsible for associations between input and output patterns. Distributed form of queries permits the system to generalize. Spurious memory trick is used to control the number of Grover's iterations which is necessary to transform initial quantum state into the state which can give correct classification in most measurements. Numerical modelling of counting problem illustrates model's behavior and its potential benefits.

Keywords quantum neural networks, entanglement, many universes interpretation, pattern recognition, counting problem

1. Quantum neural networks

The study of quantum neural networks (QNN) combines neurocomputing with quantum computations. Therefore, QNN models share main features both of quantum computers and of artificial neural networks. Pre-history of quantum computations started with works of R.Feynman [5], D.Deutsch [6] and Yu.Manin [7] in 80-s. Great break-through in this field is connected with the invention of factoring algorithm by P.Shor [8] in 1994 and also with the development of Grover's algorithm for the search in unsorted database in 1996 [9].The main advantages of quantum computing are connected with the use of quantum phenomena, which are not inherent to classical computations. These phenomena are as follows:

• *quantum superposition*, which suggests that n-bit register can in some sense exist in all its possible 2^n states in a moment;

• *quantum interference* gives the possibility for multiple decisions of given problem to compete each other in such a manner, that wrong decisions disappear in destructive interference, while correct decision survives and a probability to detect it grows due to the constructive interference;

• *quantum entanglement* – this purely quantum phenomenon has no classical analog and sometimes is characterized as super-correlation which can cause the appearance of classical correlations.

S. Singh, N. Murshed, and W. Kropatsch (Eds.): ICAPR 2001, LNCS 2013, pp. 60–71, 2001.

Quantum computations promise to solve problems untractable on classical computers. For some of them they can give exponential acceleration for the time of the solution and also permit to create memory with exponential capacity. It is well known that power of artificial neural networks is due to:

- ability to process wide-band signals (patterns);
- non-algorithmicity (neural networks can be trained using restricted set of examples, not programmed);
- generalization ability – neural networks can classify novel patterns;

There are many approaches to the development of QNN models, proposed by M.Peruš [10], D.Ventura and T.Martinez [1], R.Chrisley [11], T.Menneer [2-4], E.Behrman [12], S. Kak[13] et al. These models focuse on different aspects of quantum computations and neural processing. M.Peruš outlined some similarities existing between formalisms of quantum mechanics and also of neural networks. E.Behrman et al. [12] clarified a role of nonlinearity using Feynman pass integral approach and proposed possible physical implementation of their model. D.Ventura showed how quantum superposition can be used to develop associative memory with exponential capacity. R.Chrisley described how quantum neural networks with continuous weights able to process gradual signals can be implemented. It is suggested that quantum neural network can have many advantages such as exponential aceleration of computations, smaller number of hidden units and, as the consequence, better generalization [14]. Many features of classical neural networks seem to be hardly realized in quantum analogs. For example, processing of wide-band signals is complicated because it demands maintainence of coherence of the system consisting of many qubits. However, one of the most important problem which have to be decided for quantum neural networks to be effective pattern recognition systems is *generalization*. T.Menneer investigated this questions in her thesis [3]. Together with D.Deutsch [15] A.Naraynan and T.Menneer argued a necessity to use Everett interpretation of quantum mechanics for clear undestanding of the source of power of quantum computations.

In this presentation we outline some new approach to the generalization problem, considering QNN model based on Grover's algorithm.

2. Menneer's approach

T. Menneer defines quantum neural network as a superposition of single component networks each trained on *only one pattern*. Everett's interpretation of quantum theory suggests that each component network exists in separate universe. T.Menneer has performed computer simulations to show that her model is more effective in classification than classical neural networks.

First reason for this effectiveness is that training of component network using single pattern is very fast. Second reason is that, because of the absence of pattern's interference, the model escapes the problem of "catastrophic forgetting", which is typical for networks trained on many patterns. Third reason is that QNNs can learn more complicated classification problems' than their classical analogs. It was also found that there is no loss of generalization and scheme is independent on quantum hardware. However, this approach has some other advantages and shortcomings which would be briefly outlined.

First, training of component neural network using only one pattern is very rasonable approach which can be considered as natural extention of the tendency in neurocomputing to use modular systems consisting of single-class modules (neural networks trained using only patterns belonging to particular class [16,17]). But it seems unreasonable to use backpropagation to train single-pattern networks because weights of corresponding network can be directly *calculated* either for simple linear neuron-associator or for Hopfield network with Hebbian interconnections. Below we shall argue that there is no need to associate input and output values using weights of component neural networks, because suitable mechanism of association of qubit's states already exists in quantum mechanics. Corresponding phenomenon is known as *entanglement*, which can be considered as super-correlation generating ordinary correlations or, in other words, *associations*.

Seconds, catastrophic forgetting does a real problem for *passive* memory systems which try to memorize *all training patterns*. But this problem disappears if neural networks are considered as the models of *active* memory which suggests just *nontrivial mapping* of the set of learned patterns onto the set of attractors which leads to prototype-based classification and emergency of predictive abilities [16] .

Third, it seems preferable to outline how QNN model can be implemented. From this point of view the Menneer's model seems to be questionable, because it suggests unphysical mechanisms of wave-function collapse [3]. At last, her approach classifies patterns according to minimal Hamming distance.

It is also necessary to comment the problem of generalization. Apart of evident practical achivements, the theoretical belief in effectiveness of neural networks is based on some principal results. Among of them are: ability of perceptrons with single hidden layer to approximate any multivariable and multivalue function; existence of effective training algorithms for multilayered systems, and the ability of neural networks to generalize data, which is expressed in finitness of VC-dimension. It means that given neural network with restricted number of hidden neurons should not realize any patterns dichotomy. On the other hand, the exponential capacity of quantum associative memory [1] can be considered as argument in favor to infinite VC-dimension for considered quantum systems. Indeed, the ability of network to memorize any set of patterns means that any Boolean function can be realized using Grover scheme for the search of item in a "phone book", if "number" field is used to represent argument and "name" field – value of this function. It seems that to obtain quantum systems with finite VC-dimension it is necessary to restrict a number of iterations in Grover algorithm or, in general, to restrict a number of transformations (steps) in given quantum computational process. In any case, problem of generalization has not been clarified yet for quantum neural systems. For quantum associative memory the attempt to treat this problem using notion of distributed queries has been done in [18]. Below we shall show, how promising Menener's approach can be used in schemes based on powerful Grover algorithm, which has been already implemented in NMR systems [19] .

3. Quantum associative memory

We use some extention [18] of the model of quantum associative memory proposed by D.Ventura [1] as the prototype of quantum pattern recognition system able to classify novel patterns, e.g. to generalize. Ventura's model is based on the use of Grover's algorithm, which is treated as prototype for other effective quantum algorithms [20]. In simplest form it starts with the initiation of quantum memory $|\psi\rangle = \sum_{x=0}^{2^d-1} a_x|x\rangle$ in a form of uniform superposition[1] of the states belonging to the prescribed subset M (these states will be refered to as memory states) of the complete set of basic states (the last one includes all possible states of d-qubit register $|x_1\rangle \otimes |x_2\rangle \otimes ... \otimes |x_d\rangle$, where $\otimes$ denotes tensor product):

$$|\psi\rangle = |m\rangle = |M|^{-1/2} \sum_{x\in M} |x\rangle. \tag{1}$$

In (1) M denotes memory set, and $|M|$ – number of patterns in it. It is assumed that we know only a part of qubit's states of external stimulus $|p\rangle$. The problem is *to complete* it to one of the memory states[2]. To solve this problem Grover's iterations can be applied [9]. Each iteration is performed in two steps:

1. *Oracle* inverts the phase of such memory state which has a part coinciding with known part of presented stimulus $|p\rangle$ (let us denote this situation as $x \supset p$) :

$$a_x \to \begin{cases} -a_x, x \supset p \\ a_x, otherwise \end{cases} \tag{2}$$

2. *NameFinder-in-Memory* inverts amplitudes of all memory states around their average value

$$a_x \to 2\langle a\rangle_M - a_x, \tag{3}$$

leaving zero amplitudes of basic states which do not belong to memory.

After sufficient number of iterations module of amplitude of memory state having part coinciding with known part of $|p\rangle$ takes value near 1, while amplitude modules of other memories vanish. If measurement process is performed after proper number of iterations, then completed version of stimulus $|p\rangle$ can be detected in quantum register. There is a problem connected with this scheme: it fails if known part of presented stimulus coincide with no part of any memory state. Moreover, this approach cannot realize associative memory of general type, when no exact part of memory is known and arbitrary noised version of it is presented. Some extention of

---

[1] The algorithm of this initializing is rather complicated and has been comprehensively described in [20].

[2] It is assumed that only one memory state has a part which exactly coincides with known part of stimulus.

described model, which can find memory state nearest to the stimulus has been presented in [18]. According to this approach distributed query $|b^p\rangle$ should be used. Distributed query is a quantum superpositional state having maximal amplitude in a central basic state, defined by true query $|p\rangle$, and non-zero amplitudes of other basic states, decreasing with the Hamming distance from this center. For example it can be chosen in the form

$$|b^p\rangle = \sum_{x=0}^{2^{d-1}} b_x^p |x\rangle, \qquad b_x^p = q^{\frac{|p-x|}{2}} (1-q)^{\frac{d-h|p-x|}{2}}. \qquad (4)$$

In (4) $|p-x|$ denotes Hamming distance between binary strings p and x and q tunes a width of distribution $(0 < q < 0.5)$. It has been shown, that using distributed queries it is possible to model *correcting* associative memory [18]. The problem connected with this memory is a necessity to estimate needed number of Grover's iteration. The difficulty arizes from the fact that the number of iterations depends on a number of stored memories and on their distribution in configurational space. To solve this problem "spurious memory" trick can be used. It can be shown, that amplitudes of basic states, which do not reperesent memories, oscillate with the same phase value in Grover's iterations. So, if instead of formation of memory using desired basic states we shall use only *all other possible states*, than effectively, desired memories states will become "spurious" one and, therefore, will be in-phase in iterations. This situation facilitates the control of memories detection because if the number of desired memory states is relatively small, then it is possible *to calculate* approximate number of iteration steps, for probability of detection of memories states be maximal [18][3]. Only restriction of this trick seems to be the neccessity to have small memory sets. It can be considered as disadvatnage because just high capacity is the most important feature of quantum memory.

However, for the case of real pattern recognition systems[4], it is preferable and only possible to train them using *small part* of <pattern,class> associations. Of course, corresponding system should *generalize* data in order to be able to classify novel patterns. Below, we shall outline an approach to this problem, using as the basis the model of correcting quantum associative memory.

4. Quantum pattern recognition

Consider a register consisting of $d+1$ qubits. Let first d qubits contain classified binary pattern x, while last qubit contains pattern's binary classification index $C_x \in \{0,1\}$. So, this register has a form $|x\rangle\otimes|C_x\rangle$. We shall call first d qubits *input register* and last $(d+1)$-th qubit – *class qubit*. Let T be a training set,

---

[3] We shall further give a formal expression for this number of steps for the case of pattern classification

[4] It is true in general for any neural system processing many component patterns.

$T = T^+ \bigcup T^-$, where $T^\pm$ – training subsets corresponding to two object classes $C_\pm$ and $|T|$ – number of elements in T). Consider quantum superposition

$$|m\rangle = \frac{1}{\sqrt{2^{d+1}-|T|}}\left\{\sum_{x \in T}|x\rangle \otimes |\neg C_x\rangle + \sum_{x \notin T}|x\rangle \otimes (|0\rangle + |1\rangle)\right\} \qquad (5)$$

According to "spurious memory" trick all basic states are included in this superposition apart of those belonging to training set: $\{|x\rangle \otimes |C_x\rangle, x \in T\}$. It can be seen from the expression above that in superposition $|m\rangle$ only the inputs $|x\rangle \in T$ are *entangled* with the (wrong) state of class qubit.   Let $|p\rangle$ be a d-bit pattern we want to classify. Consider $(d+1)$-qubits distributed query of the form:

$$|b^p\rangle = \sum_{x=0}^{2^d-1}b_x^p|x\rangle \otimes(|0\rangle + |1\rangle)/\sqrt{2} \qquad (6)$$

for which b_x^p are given by expression (4).   Introduce quantum system $|\psi\rangle$ consisting of $d+1$ qubits and let its initial state be given by (5), so $\forall x\, a_x^{(0)} \equiv m_x$, where $|\psi\rangle = \sum_{x=0}^{2^d-1}a_x|x\rangle$.   Let us iterate the state $|\psi\rangle$ using Grover's scheme generalized to the case of distributed queries [18]:

$$a_x^{(\tau+1/2)} \rightarrow a_x^{(\tau)} - 2\langle a^{(\tau)}|b^p\rangle b_x^p \quad ,$$

$$a_x^{(\tau)} \rightarrow 2\langle a^{(\tau+1/2)}|m\rangle m_x - a_x^{(\tau+1/2)}, \qquad (7)$$

where τ counts interation step. It is possible to find a number of iterations for which amplitudes of "spurious" states take their equal maximal values:

$$T_{\max} = \pi/2\omega \quad , \qquad \omega = 2\arcsin(\langle b^p|m\rangle) \qquad (8)$$

If a number of associations in training set is small comparing to full number of $(d+1)$-bit binary patterns, $|T| \ll 2^{d+1}$, then we can approximately set

$$\omega \cong \bar{\omega} = 2\arcsin\left(2^{-d/2}\sum_{x=0}^{2^d-1}b_x^p\right), \quad T_{\max} = \pi/2\bar{\omega} \qquad (9)$$

The last approximation for the number of iterations will be used in all examples considered below.

Counting problem

This problem has been investigated by T.Menneer for the case $d=4$. Average number of items in training sets equals to 10, so 60% of all possible patterns were used for training. Note that, in opposite to our approach, this training set was not small. We start with simpler symmetrical problem: in this case $d=3$, and 3-bit string is classified as belonging to the class C_- if number of zeros is less or equal to 1, otherwise it is classified as belonging to C_+. We use training set consisting of only 2 patterns: (000) (C_-) and (111) (C_+). Note, that exact number of Grover's iterations depends on the stimulus to be recognized (center of presented query). It is not difficult to show that it is the same (T_{max}^{train}) for two chosen training patterns and also the same (T_{max}^{test}) for all test patterns. It is interesting to note, that approximate value of iteration number T_{max} is closer to T_{max}^{train} rather than to T_{max}^{train} and is near to T_{max}^{train} for $q = 0.2 - 0.3$ (see Table 1).   So, approximation for iteration number is more suitable for **novel** stimuli, which are not presented in training set. Therefore, our scheme is well-suited for generalization.

Table 1. Angular frequences and corresponding maximal numbers of Grover's iterations calculated using (8) for training and test patterns together with their approximated values (9) calculated for different value of parameter q. Zone of close correspondence between approximate frequence and ones for test patterns is greyed.

q	ω^{train}	ω^{test}	ω	T_{max}^{train}	T_{max}^{test}	T_{max}
0	0.190	0.388	0.361	8	4	4
0.05	0.493	0.645	0.654	3	2	2
0.1	0.641	0.766	0.797	2	2	1
0.15	0.760	0.863	0.916	2	1	1
0.2	0.864	0.946	1.023	1	1	1
0.25	0.956	1.019	1.123	1	1	1
0.3	1.037	1.082	1.217	1	1	1
0.35	1.107	1.135	1.308	1	1	1
0.4	1.161	1.175	1.397	1	1	1
0.45	1.197	1.201	1.484	1	1	1
0.5	1.209	1.209	1.571	1	1	1

The results of application of described scheme for different widths of distributed query are summarized in Table 2.
1. Compare the second and the third columns in Table 2. In the second one modules of amplitude corresponding to the probablility to find query's center $|p\rangle$ in the first d qubits together with the correct value of class $(d+1)$-th qubit are presented. It is evident, that for $q=0.2-0.35$ probability to check just query's center (clasified pattern) is high enough (0.4-0.6), and ones to classify it correctly is very near to 1.
2. *If we ignore what state of input register is measured*, then correct classification can be obtained by performing multiple classification trials for the same values of $q=0.2-0.35$. It is not expensive procedure because each trial demands only one Grover's iteration. Comparing these two approaches we can reveal those stimuli (input patterns) which really have been used in training. Indeed, if we fix some

pattern measured in input register, and if this pattern was not used for training, then measured state of class qubit will be completely random. It is due to the amplitudes of the pairs of novel (not used for training) states, which differ only by the state of class qubit, retain equal values because they have equal initial values m_x and also have equal b_x^p values. Taking into account the form of equation (7) we are convinced that amplitudes of these states are equal at any iteration's step. It follows from this fact, that our quantum system can operate *as novelty detector*.   Unfortunately, this equality of amplitudes of novel states corresponding to two basic values of class qubit give no possibility to classify them for fixed value of input register. So, *we must ignore its value if we want to have generalization!* Really, in this case correct classification of presented pattern (it defines query' center) also can be obtained statistically (see 6th and 7th columns of Table 2) though it should be reacher than for the case of trained patterns. It can be qualitatively explained.

Table 2. Final parameters of quantum system for different values of parameter q (1st column) are presented (zone with best recognition parameters is greyed)
For training set:
- 2nd and 3rd columns: probabilities to find center of query in input register together with correct (incorrect) value of class qubit;
- 4th and 5th columns: probabilities to find correct (incorrect) class qubit for *any* state in input register;
For test set:
- 6th and 7th columns: probabilities to find correct (incorrect) class qubit for *any* state in input register;
- 8th and 9th columns: Recognition rate for training (test) sets.

q	$|a(C_x)|^2$ (train)	$|a(\neg C_x)|$ (train)	$\langle|a(C_x)|^2\rangle$ (train)	$\langle|a(\neg C_x)|^2$ (train)	$\langle|a(C_x)|^2\rangle$ (test)	$\langle|a(\neg C_x)|^2$ (test)	R_{train}	R_{test}
0	0.517	0.464	0.527	0.473	0.500	0.500	100	50
0.05	0.468	0.200	0.660	0.340	0.526	0.474	100	100
0.1	0.521	0.369	0.580	0.420	0.546	0.454	100	100
0.15	0.582	0.274	0.670	0.330	0.572	0.428	100	100
0.2	0.592	0.175	0.737	0.263	0.590	0.410	100	100
0.25	0.563	0.092	0.771	0.229	0.597	0.403	100	100
0.3	0.509	0.035	0.770	0.230	0.594	0.406	100	100
0.35	0.439	0.006	0.735	0.265	0.580	0.420	100	100
0.4	0.363	0.001	0.674	0.326	0.558	0.442	100	100
0.45	0.288	0.015	0.592	0.408	0.531	0.469	100	100
0.5	0. 219	0.040	0.500	0.500	0.500	0.500	50	50

Indeed, taking into account a form of iteration scheme (7), and remembering that $a_x^0 = m_x$, we can obtain after single iteration (which is sufficient for intermediate q values):

$$a_x^{(1)} = (1-4\langle m|b^p \rangle^2)m_x + 2\langle m|b^p \rangle b_x^p \tag{10}$$

Here it is crucial, that first factor in the first term of right side is as a rule negative. Actually, because we use for training only small set of patterns,

$$\langle m|b^p \rangle \cong 2^{(1-d)/2} \sum_{x=0}^{2^d-1} b_x^p = F(q). \tag{11}$$

It is easy to see that for our problem for $q>0.05$ $F(q) > 0.25$, so this factor is really negative. It follows from the expression (10), that for training patterns after one iteration the associations between states of input register and correct value of classifiaction qubit have higher amplitudes, than associations with incorrect value of this qubit. This is because of only for training state $m_x = 0$ and the first term does not reduce the sum in right side in (10). What about inputs which were not used in training? Despite of we ignore the state of input register it sometimes will collapse to novel or also training pattern. In the first case the state of class qubit will be *completely random* for given detected state of input register. In the second case, when input register is detected in training pattern, class qubit will take both values *with different probabilities*. So, for the input pattern $|p\rangle \notin T$ class qubit will attribute it to both classes with the probabilities:

$$\Pr(C_\pm) = \sum_{x \in T^\pm} |a_x|^2 + \sum_{x \notin T} |a_x|^2 \tag{12}$$

From (12) it follows that

$$\Pr(C_+) - \Pr(C_-) = \sum_{x \in T^+} |a_x|^2 - \sum_{x \in T^-} |a_x|^2 \tag{13}$$

Taking into account that for training pairs $m_x = 0$, after first iteration we have:

$$\Pr(C_+) - \Pr(C_-) \propto \sum_{x \in T^+} |b_x^p|^2 - \sum_{x \in T^-} |b_x^p|^2 \propto \langle |b_x^p|^2 \rangle_{x \in T^+} - \langle |b_x^p|^2 \rangle_{x \in T^-}$$

The brackets in the right side ofthe last expression means averaging by patterns of training set belonging to given set. It is evident, that vector $|p\rangle \notin T$ will be presumably classified as belonging to that class, for which averaged   by class states module of query's amplitudes $|b_x^p|^2$ is maximal. Because of amplitude modules decrease with the Hamming distance from the query's center, those states which are nearest to one of trained pattern will be classified just as the last one.   In our case only two patters form training set. Therefore, pattern classification is directly performed according to the class label of nearest (in the sense of Hamming distance) training pattern. So, described quantum system will be used for statistical decision of simplest counting problem. We conclude, that because *all patterns* are correctly classified by our quantum system, then, at least for this variant of counting problem, generalization is possible. General situation corresponds to the case when fixed number of ones in a string plays a role of classificational threshold. Assume that it is just 2 for any string's length and consider counting problem corresponding

to the case $d = 6$. In this case there is no symmetry between number of ones and zeroes in a pattern. Consider the training set consisting of 9 patterns:
$C_+ = \{000000, 010000, 011000, 100010\};$ $C_- = \{001111, 010111, 111011, 111101, 111111\}.$

Note, that it containes only about 14% of 64 6-bit patterns. Simulations shows, that for $q>0.22$ approximate number of Grover's iterations coincides with ones given by (8) and equals to 1. In this region probability to find correct class bit for *any* detected argument-register (x-value) has well-defined maximum located near $q \cong 0.67$ both for training and also for test sets – about 0.61 and 0.55 correspondingly (Figure 1). In this region generalization ability of the system is about 75%. Higher values (87%) can be reached for $q \cong 0.16$ after two iterations (this correct value is also given by (9)). But for this q value probabilities to find correct class bit for any detected argument-register are lower (0.55 and 0.51 correspondindly). It means that reacher statistics is needed for the training set, while for the test set statistical estimation is extremely difficult. Note, that for training set perfect recognition is observed for almost all q-values ($q < 0.49$). Moreover, for fixed state of argument's register, corresponding to trained pattern, probability of correct classification exceeds 75%.

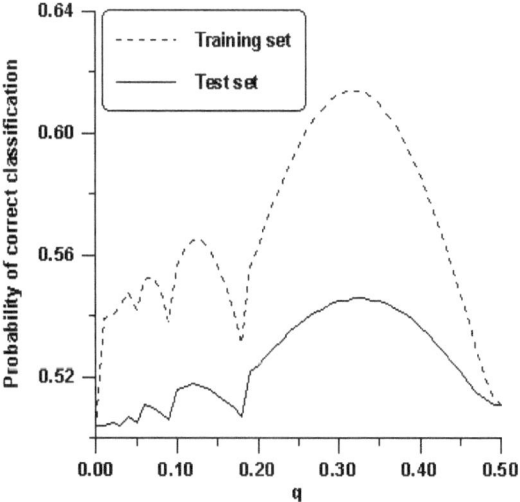

Figure 1. Probability of correct pattern classification for training and test sets.

Conclusions

We present quantum neural network model which uses not weights but entanglement of qubit's states to provide associations. Therefore, this model is similar to "weightless" neural networks [22]. Some examples are presented to show that the system can generalize data, though generalization is not high enough. It can be happened that quantum systems are too flexible to generalize well without using special means. Nevertheless, presented approach seems to be promissing because the system can be trained using small number of examples, it can be physically implemented, and also can be used as novelty detector.

Acknowledgements

Professor S.Singh is gratefully acknowledged for invitation to participate in ICAPR'2001. I wish to express my considerable gratitude to professor N. Murshed to the interest to our research, and also to R. Chrisley for the fruightful discussion.

References

1. Ventura D, Martinez M. A quantum associative memory based on Grover's algorithm. In: Proceedings of the International Conference on Artificial Neural Networks and Genetics Algorithms, April 1999; pp 22-27.
2. Menneer T, Narayanan A. Quantum inspired neural networks. Department of Computer Sciences, University of Exeter, UK 1995. http:/www.dcs.ex.ac.uk/reports/reports.html
3. Menneer T. Quantum artificial neural networks. PhD thesis, Faculty of Science, University of Exeter, UK, 1998.
4. Menneer T & Narayanan A. Quantum artificial neural networks vs. Classical artificial neural networks: Experiments in Simulation. Proceedings of the Fifth Joint Conference on Information Sciences, Atlantic City, 2000; 1: 757-759.
5. Feynman R. Quantum mechanical computers. Foundations of Physics 1986; 16: 507-531.
6. Deutsch D. Quantum theory, the Church-Turing principle and the universal quantum computer. Proceedings of the Royal Society of London 1985; A400:.97-117.
7. Manin Yu. Computable and uncomputable (in Russian). Sovetskoye Radio, Moscow, 1980.
8. Shor PW. Polynomial-time algorithm for prime factorization and discrete logarithms on a quantum computer, SIAM Journal on Computing 1997; 26: 1484 -1509.
9. Grover LK. A fast quantum mechanical algorithm for database search. In: Proceedings of the 28th Annual ACM Symposium on the Theory of Computation, 1996, pp.212-219.
10. Peruš M. Neuro-Quantum parallelism in brain-mind and computers, Informatica 1996; 20: 173-183.
11. Chrisley RL. Learning in Non-superpositional Quantum Neurocomputers. In: Pylkkänen, P., and Pylkkö, P. (eds.) Brain, Mind and Physics, IOS Press, Amsterdam, 1997, pp. 127-139.
12. Behrman EC, Niemel J, Steck JE et al. A quantum dot neural network. In: Proceedings of the 4th Workshop on Physics of Computation, Boston, 1996, pp.22-24.
13. S.Kak. The initialization problem in quantum computing, Foundations of Physics 1999; 29: 267-279.
14. Cutting D. Would quantum neural networks be subject to the decidability constraints of the Church-Turing thesis? Discussion on Neurocomputers after ten years, Frolov AA, Ezhov AA (eds), Neural Network World 1999; 9: 163-168.
15. Deutsch D. The fabric of reality. Alen Lane: The Penguin Press, 1997.

16. Ezhov AA, Vvedensky VL (1996) Object generation with neural networks (when spurious memories are useful), Neural Networks 1996; 9: 1491-1495.
17. Ezhov AA, Ventura D. Quantum neural networks. In: Future directions for Intelligent Information Systems and Information Sciences. Kasabov N (ed), Physica-Verlag, Heidelberg, 2000, pp 213-235 (Studies in Fuzziness and Soft Computing, vol.45).
18. Ezhov AA, Nifanova AV, Ventura D. Quantum associative memory with distributed queries. Information Science 2000 (in press).
19. Gershenfeld N, Chuang IL. Bulk spin-resonance quantum computation. Science 1997; 275: 350-355.
20. Preskill J. Quantum computers: pro and con. CALT 68-2113, QUIC 97-031. 1997, Pasadena.
21. Ventura D. Initializing the amplitude distribution of a quantum state, Foundations of Physics Letters 1999; 12 :547-559.
22. Alexander I. Connectionism or weightless neurocomputing? In: Artificial Neural Networks, (Kohonen et al., eds) North-Holland, Amsterdam, 1991.

Pattern Matching and Neural Networks based Hybrid Forecasting System

Sameer Singh and Jonathan Fieldsend

PANN Research, Department of Computer Science, University of Exeter, Exeter, UK

Abstract. In this paper we propose a Neural Net-PMRS hybrid for forecasting time-series data. The neural network model uses the traditional MLP architecture and backpropagation method of training. Rather than using the last *n* lags for prediction, the input to the network is determined by the output of the PMRS (Pattern Modelling and Recognition System). PMRS matches current patterns in the time-series with historic data and generates input for the neural network that consists of both current and historic information. The results of the hybrid model are compared with those of neural networks and PMRS on their own. In general, there is no outright winner on all performance measures, however, the hybrid model is a better choice for certain types of data, or on certain error measures.

1. Hybrid Forecasting System

The science of forecasting relies heavily on the models used for forecasting, quantity and quality of data, and the ability to pick the right models for a given data. A number of past publications on pattern matching have argued the need for using historic information through pattern matching for forecasting. A number of these pattern matching techniques, such as our previous PMRS model, have been very successful on a range of economic and financial data. The main philosophy behind these pattern matching techniques is to identify the best matching past trends to current ones and use the knowledge of how the time series behaved in the past in those situations to make predictions for the future. A range of nearest neighbour strategies can be adopted for this matching such as the fuzzy Single Nearest Neighbour (SNN) approach.

Neural networks do not normally use historic matches for forecasting. Instead, their inputs are taken as recent lags [2]. However, their ability to formulate a non-linear relationship between inputs and output has a considerable advantage for producing accurate forecasts [3].

S. Singh, N. Murshed, and W. Kropatsch (Eds.): ICAPR 2001, LNCS 2013, pp. 72–82, 2001.

In this paper we combine the pattern matching ability with the determination of non-linear relationship between inputs and output by generating a hybrid model for forecasting. The hybrid model uses the PMRS model [6,7] for determining historic matches used as inputs to a neural network model. The results are shown on a range of scientific time series data and financial market data. We first describe our PMRS and neural network models on a stand-alone basis, and then their combination.

1.1 PMRS Component

If we choose to represent a time-series as $y = \{y_1, y_2, \dots y_n\}$, then the current state of size one of the time-series is represented by its current value y_n. One simple method of prediction can be based on identifying the closest neighbour of y_n in the past data, say y_j, and predicting y_{n+1} on the basis of y_{j+1}. Calculating an average prediction based on more than one nearest neighbour can modify this approach. The definition of the current state of a time-series can be extended to include more than one value, e.g. the current state s_c of size two may be defined as $\{y_{n-1}, y_n\}$. For such a current state, the prediction will depend on the past state s_p $\{y_{j-1}, y_j\}$ and next series value y^+_p given by y_{j+1}, provided that we establish that the state $\{y_{j-1}, y_j\}$ is the nearest neighbour of the state $\{y_{n-1}, y_n\}$ using some similarity measurement. In this paper, we also refer to *states* as *patterns*. In theory, we can have a current state of any size but in practice only matching current states of optimal size to past states of the same size yields accurate forecasts since too small or too large neighbourhoods do not generalise well. The optimal state size must be determined experimentally on the basis of achieving minimal errors on standard measures through an iterative procedure.

We can formalise the prediction procedure as follows:

$$\ddot{y} = \phi(s_c, s_p, y^+_p, k, c)$$

where $\ddot{y}$ is the prediction for the next time step, s_c is the current state, s_p is the nearest past state, y^+_p is the series value following past state s_p, k is the state size and c is the matching constraint. Here $\ddot{y}$ is a real value, s_c or s_p can be represented as a set of real values, k is a constant representing the number of values in each state, i.e. size of the set, and c is a constraint which is user defined for the matching process. We define c as the condition of matching operation that series direction change for each member in s_c and s_p is the same.

In order to illustrate the matching process for series prediction further, consider the time series as a vector $y = \{y_1, y_2, \dots y_n\}$ where n is the total number of points in the series. Often, we also represent such a series as a function of time, e.g. $y_n = y_t$, $y_{n-1} = y_{t-1}$, and so on. A segment in the series is defined as a difference vector $\delta = (\delta_1, \delta_2, \dots \delta_{n-1})$ where $\delta_i = y_{i+1} - y_i$, $\forall i$, $1 \leq i \leq n-1$. A pattern contains one or more segments and it can be visualised as a string of segments $\rho = (\delta_i, \delta_{i+1}, \dots \delta_h)$ for given values of i and h, $1 \leq i, h \leq n-1$, provided that h>i. In order to define any pattern mathematically, we choose to tag the time series y with a vector of change in direction. For this purpose, a value y_i is tagged with a 0 if $y_{i+1} < y_i$, and as a 1 if $y_{i+1} \geq y_i$. Formally, a pattern in the time-series is represented as $\rho = (b_i, b_{i+1}, \ldots b_h)$ where b is a binary value.

The complete time-series is tagged as $(b_1, \ldots b_{n-1})$. For a total of k segments in a pattern, it is tagged with a string of k b values. For a pattern of size k, the total number of binary patterns (shapes) possible is 2^k. The technique of matching structural primitives is based on the premise that the past repeats itself. It has been noted in previous studies that the dynamic behaviour of time-series can be efficiently predicted by using local approximation. For this purpose, a map between current states and the nearest neighbour past states can be generated for forecasting.

Pattern matching in the context of time-series forecasting refers to the process of matching current state of the time series with its past states. Consider the tagged time series $(b_1, b_i, \ldots b_{n-1})$. Suppose that we are at time n (y_n) trying to predict y_{n+1}. A pattern of size k is first formulated from the last k tag values in the series, $\rho' = (b_{n-k}, \ldots b_{n-1})$. The size k of the structural primitive (pattern) used for matching has a direct effect on the prediction accuracy. Thus the pattern size k must be optimised for obtaining the best results. For this k is increased in every trial by one unit till it reaches a predefined maximum allowed for the experiment and the error measures are noted; the value of k that gives the least error is finally selected. The aim of a pattern matching algorithm is to find the closest match of ρ' in the historical data (estimation period) and use this for predicting y_{n+1}. The magnitude and direction of prediction depend on the match found. The success in correctly predicting series depends directly on the pattern matching algorithm.

The first step is to select a state/pattern of minimal size (k=2). A nearest neighbour of this pattern is determined from historical data on the basis of smallest offset ∇. There are two cases for prediction: either we predict high or we predict low. The prediction $\ddot{y}_{n+1}$ is scaled on the basis of the similarity of the match found. We use a number of widely applied error measures for estimating the accuracy of the forecast and selecting optimal k size for minimal error. The forecasting process is repeated with a given test data for states/patterns of size greater than two and a model with smallest k giving minimal error is selected. In our experiments k is iterated between $2 \leq k \leq 5$.

1.2 Neural Network Component

In this paper we use the standard MLP architecture with backpropagation mode of learning. In order to enable consistency between the Neural Network model and the PMRS model, the Neural Network inputs are the 6 most recent lags of the time series (i.e. Y_{t-1}, Y_{t-2}, Y_{t-3}, Y_{t-4}, Y_{t-5} & Y_{t-6}, when the value to be predicted is the actual Y_t). This mimics the PMRS approach of pattern matching of up to 5 historic differences (δ values) which therefore uses the information contained in the most recent 6 lags. (In other circumstances the 6 lags chosen would be those with the highest partial autocorrelation function value when correlated with the actual [5]).

In our study, neural networks have two hidden layers with 5 sigmoidal nodes in each and the networks are fully connected.

The learning rate was set at 0.05 with a momentum of 0.5. The Neural Networks training was stopped when the combined RMSE on the test and training set had fallen by less than 0.025% of their value 5 epochs ago. The inclusion of the validation error prevents over- fitting, however by summing the two errors (as opposed to strictly using the test error on its own), a slight trade-off is permitted between the errors while pushing through local minima. In addition this stopping operator was only used after at least 1000 epochs had passed during training.

1.3 Neural Net-PMRS

Neural Networks with PMRS generated inputs have the same stopping regime as the standard neural network described above with only topological difference in the form of number of inputs. Two hybrid models were trained. The first was training on the matched deltas δ found by the PMRS algorithm, the predicted delta and the lags used to find them, i.e. a PMRS model fitting two historic deltas would use 3 lags. A single asterisk in Table 2 denotes this model (NNPMRS*). The second model used the matched deltas δ found by the PMRS algorithm, the predicted delta and the most recent lag (this model is denoted by a double asterisk in Table 2 - NNPMRS**).

2. Experimental Details

Each data set was partitioned into consecutive segments of 75% (training data) 15% (test data) and 10% (validation data). The Neural Network model weights are adjusted using the Backpropagation algorithm on the training set and stopped (using the stopping method described later) using the root mean square errors on the training set and test set. In the case of PMRS, four different PMRS models with pattern sizes of 2,3,4,and 5 were fitted to the training set and compared on the test set data. The best performing PMRS model on the test set was then chosen for use on the validation set and as the input to the NN-PMRS model. The 'best performing' model was judged as the PMRS lagged model which had the highest number of 'best' error statistics out of the six statistics used: R^2, Percentage direction success, Root Mean Square Error (RMSE), Geometric Mean Relative Absolute Error (GMRAE), Mean Average Percentage Error (MAPE) and Percentage better than random walk (BRW). When two PMRS models performed equally well using this criteria, two NN-PMRS models were fitted.

As the PMRS model needs a store of historical data before it can make predictions (and therefore be of use as an input to a non-linear system such as a Neural Network), the data split is slightly different for the NN-PMRS models. The end 10% of the data is again set aside as an 'unseen' validation set, and of the remaining 90% data, the first 40% is used as the estimation data for the PMRS model to be fitted to. The remaining 50% is split such that the neural network is fitted to the next 40% and tested on the following 10%. This results in a 40/40/10/10 split as opposed to the 75/15/10 split used in the other models.

3. Results

The results for the performance of the two hybrid models, PMRS and Neural networks is shown in Table 2 on a range of error measures recommended by Armstrong and Collopy [1]. It is evident that no single model performs the best on all error measures. In this table, we have picked the best performing PMRS models on the basis of how it performs on test data. For PMRS, we vary the parameter k (pattern size for matching) between 2 and 5 and select those models that perform the best on most number of error measures. In some cases, more than one model is chosen as the best performer as two models can perform equally well on different error measures. Out of the two hybrid models, we find that NNPMRS* model consistently outperforms the second model and therefore we use this as our base hybrid model for comparison with other methods. It is difficult to visualise an overall winner on each measure. In order to interpret results we simplify this process in Figure 1. We find that on most time-series, the hybrid model is the best for generating the lowest GMRAE error and is significantly good on generating high direction rate success. It outperforms the two other models on all error measures in a small proportion of cases, and there is no generic trend to comment on. From these experiments it is abundantly clear that the hybrid model has a considerable future in the forecasting domain. Some of the improvement in results is small, however any improvement is of considerable importance in financial domains, where the capital involved can be extremely large.

4. Conclusions

In this paper we have proposed a novel method of combing pattern matching techniques with neural networks. This hybrid strategy has the advantage that it becomes possible to use historic information efficiently, which is not possible in traditional neural network models. In general, the hybrid model is a better choice in situations where the model selection process relies heavily on low error on GMRAE and high direction success. On other error measures, the hybrid model does not, in the majority of time series, outperform the PMRS and neural net stand-alone models. Our understanding is that the hybrid strategy is of considerable use in a range of prediction domains and it is only through empirical analysis, we can interpret its advantages.

References

1. Armstrong S. and Collopy F. Error measures for generalizing about forecasting methods: Empirical comparisons. International Journal of Forecasting 1992; 8:69-80.
2. Azoff M.E. Neural Network Time Series Forecasting of Financial Markets. John Wiley, 1994.
3. Gately E. Neural Networks for Financial Forecasting. John Wiley, 1996.
4. Peters E. Fractal Market Hypothesis: Applying Chaos Theory to Investment and Economics. John Wiley, 1994.

5. Refenes A.N., Burgess N. and Bentz Y. Neural networks in financial engineering: A study in methodology. IEEE Transactions on Neural Networks 1997; 8:6:1222-1267.
6. Singh S. A long memory pattern modelling and recognition system for financial time-series forecasting. Pattern Analysis and Applications 1999; 2:3:264-273.
7. Singh S. and Fieldsend J.E. Financial Time Series Forecasts using Fuzzy and Long Memory Pattern Recognition Systems. IEEE International Conference on Computational Intelligence for Financial Engineering, New York, (26-28 March, 2000). IEEE Press, 2000.

Table 1. 1991 Santa Fe Competition data & exchange rate data

Data set	Description	Observations
A	Laser generated data	1000
B1, B2, B3	Physiological data, spaced by 0.5 second intervals. The first set is the heart rate, the second is the chest volume (respiration force), and the third is the blood oxygen concentration (measured by ear oximetry).	34000 each
C	tickwise bids for the exchange rate from Swiss francs to US dollars; they were recorded by a currency trading group from August 7, 1990 to April 18, 1991	30000
D1, D2	Computer generated series	50000
E	Astrophysical data. This is a set of measurements of the light curve (time variation of the intensity) of the variable white dwarf star PG1159-035 during March 1989, 10 second intervals.	27204
USDBRL	Daily Exchange Rate of Brazilian Reals to the US Dollar (4 & ¾ years) 22nd Oct 95 to 2nd August 2000	1747
USDCAN	Daily Exchange Rate of Canadian Dollars to the US Dollar (8 years) 3rd August 1992 to 2nd August 2000	2722
USDDEM	Daily Exchange Rate of German Marks to the US Dollar (8 years) 3rd August 1992 to 2nd August 2000	2722
USDJPY	Daily Exchange Rate of Japanese Yen to the US Dollar (8 years) 3rd August 1992 to 2nd August 2000	2722
USDCHF	Daily Exchange Rate of Swiss Francs to the US Dollar (8 years) 3rd August 1992 to 2nd August 2000	2722
USDGBP	Daily Exchange Rate of Pounds Sterling to the US Dollar (8 years) 3rd August 1992 to 2nd August 2000	2722

Exchange Rates are daily average Interbank rates (where the average is calculated as the mid point of the low and the high of that day), 14 Data sets in all, longest being 50,000 points, shortest 1,000 points.

Table 2. Table of results for each time series.

Dataset	Model	k	R^2	% Dir. Suc	RMSE	GMRAE $(\times 10^{-3})$	MAPE	BRW
A	PMRS	4	0.98326	**97.000**	0.98933	1.635	10.28	**95.000**
	NN (bp)	-	**0.99707**	94.949	**0.39313**	**1.2764**	**7.0041**	92.929
	nn-pmrs*	4	0.9845	93.137	0.86214	1.6978	11.287	93.137
	nn-pmrs**	4	0.9826	95.098	0.90955	1.7974	12.146	88.235
B1	PMRS	2	**0.99366**	70.647	**0.077997**	0.29556	**11.024**	35.794
	PMRS	5	0.98997	63.471	0.098606	0.26968	14.356	44.735
	NN (bp)	-	0.98204	**78.464**	0.131870	0.25546	847.26	38.364
	nn-pmrs*	2	0.97110	78.182	0.15517	**0.25512**	10011	47.636
	nn-pmrs*	5	0.94505	76.125	0.21848	0.2678	1446.6	**50.346**
	nn-pmrs**	2	0.98657	75.577	0.10449	0.26309	646.56	22.405
	nn-pmrs**	5	0.97112	76.009	0.15474	0.26463	1007.6	38.322
B2	PMRS	2	0.83335	60.147	72.295	0.50022	67.339	41.647
	PMRS	5	0.77703	67.412	90.893	**0.44723**	81.976	49.324
	NN (bp)	-	**0.91510**	**70.315**	44.175	0.84700	**58.310**	**56.899**
	nn-pmrs*	2	0.90470	65.542	44.439	1.09990	59.607	52.422
	nn-pmrs*	5	0.91469	67.734	**42.434**	0.88111	59.270	53.749
	nn-pmrs**	2	0.89625	60.438	46.421	0.94134	64.565	44.867
	nn-pmrs**	5	0.9028	64.475	44.652	0.95816	61.165	50.865
B3	PMRS	3	0.98993	51.029	21.219	0.43080	1.3969	30.882
	PMRS	4	0.99009	54.529	21.052	0.40880	**1.3522**	33.735
	PMRS	5	0.98993	54.647	21.229	0.39971	1.4022	35.588
	NN (bp)	-	0.98660	55.075	23.318	4.16300	4.6472	51.368
	nn-pmrs*	3	0.82640	49.683	69.114	1.9272	7.1579	41.522
	nn-pmrs*	4	0.989100	65.484	22.449	1.4900	2.5309	**60.467**
	nn-pmrs*	5	0.989100	65.484	22.449	1.4900	2.5309	**60.467**
	nn-pmrs**	3	0.021970	**69.550**	**5.9163**	**0.2390**	4.51 $\times 10^{13}$	49.510
	nn-pmrs**	4	**0.99040**	48.875	20.420	1.2641	2.1728	43.080
	nn-pmrs**	5	0.99033	48.320	20.25	1.4067	2.2562	42.762
C	PMRS	2	**1.00000**	47.800	2.15×10^{-5}	0.19019	**0.0485**	36.333
	NN (bp)	-	0.99950	43.481	0.000524	0.19000	1.9894	**43.481**
	nn-pmrs*	2	0.99820	43.399	0.000873	**0.18932**	3.3581	43.431
	nn-pmrs**	2	0.99829	43.399	0.000854	**0.18932**	3.2846	43.431

Dataset	Model	k	R^2	% Dir. Suc	RMSE	GMRAE $(\times 10^{-3})$	MAPE	BRW
D1	PMRS	4	0.98671	77.660	0.000931	0.19888	10.457	63.400
	PMRS	5	0.98787	79.540	0.000894	0.19884	10.069	66.120
	NN (bp)	-	**0.99640**	**86.737**	**0.000489**	0.19900	**6.3906**	**70.454**
	nn-pmrs*	4	0.98973	80.804	0.000709	0.19485	8.3753	64.804
	nn-pmrs*	5	0.99416	85.275	0.000549	**0.19477**	6.7570	69.647
	nn-pmrs**	4	0.99204	81.961	0.000647	0.19486	7.7160	61.941
	nn-pmrs**	5	0.99287	82.627	0.000617	0.19483	7.5616	63.882
D2	PMRS	4	0.98535	79.680	0.000929	0.19885	11.869	64.500
	NN (bp)	-	0.99230	83.957	0.000644	0.19900	8.8072	65.913
	nn-pmrs*	4	**0.99440**	**86.863**	0.000542	**0.19469**	8.2082	72.314
	nn-pmrs**	4	0.99173	83.980	0.000654	0.19481	9.2745	63.49
E	PMRS	4	0.57996	56.487	0.003196	0.36995	7.929×10^{17}	**41.455**
	NN (bp)	-	**0.59060**	**67.929**	0.001641	0.36600	$\mathbf{2.076 \times 10^{13}}$	39.757
	nn-pmrs*	4	0.58428	67.916	**0.001628**	**0.35847**	2.343×10^{13}	40.159
	nn-pmrs**	4	0.51360	65.321	0.001759	0.35890	2.283×10^{13}	35.400
USD BRL	PMRS	2	0.99988	56.000	0.001336	**2.8258**	**0.5106**	17.143
	NN (bp)	-	**0.99994**	46.552	**0.000943**	2.8445	0.5700	33.333
	nn-pmrs*	2	0.99989	**64.423**	0.001690	4.7359	0.8820	**39.423**
	nn-pmrs**	2	0.99989	**64.423**	0.001656	4.7359	0.8581	**39.423**
USD CAD	PMRS	2	**0.99998**	47.44	**0.000324**	1.9101	**0.2729**	27.645
	NN (bp)	-	**0.99998**	**54.983**	0.000328	1.9211	0.3115	40.893
	nn-pmrs*	2	**0.99998**	54.027	0.000352	**1.8900**	0.3411	**42.953**
	nn-pmrs**	2	**0.99998**	54.362	0.000354	**1.8900**	0.3425	42.617
USD CHF	PMRS	2	**0.99991**	**48.805**	**0.000817**	1.9384	**0.6265**	27.645
	NN (bp)	-	0.99856	44.674	0.003165	1.9493	2.8534	**43.299**
	nn-pmrs*	2	0.9979	41.275	0.003481	1.8639	3.2294	40.604
	nn-pmrs**	2	0.9976	42.282	0.003727	**1.8638**	3.4605	40.940
USD DEM	PMRS	2	**0.99993**	**50.853**	**0.000898**	1.6618	**0.5617**	26.621
	NN (bp)	-	0.99730	40.550	0.005284	1.6771	3.7971	40.550
	nn-pmrs*	2	0.99622	40.604	0.005600	1.6064	4.1274	40.604
	nn-pmrs**	2	0.99641	41.611	0.005539	**1.6062**	3.9973	**41.611**

Dataset	Model	k	R^2	% Dir. Suc	RMSE	GMRAE $(\times 10^{-3})$	MAPE	BRW
USD GBP	PMRS	2	0.99995	**52.218**	0.000229	2.9284	0.4277	29.693
	NN (bp)	-	**0.99997**	51.890	**0.000189**	2.9496	**0.3805**	**30.584**
	nn-pmrs*	2	0.99996	45.973	0.000199	**2.8721**	0.3839	29.866
	nn-pmrs**	2	0.99995	46.309	0.000206	**2.8721**	0.3934	29.866
USD JPY	PMRS	2	0.99988	47.440	0.060916	3.7303	0.6552	24.915
	NN (bp)	-	**0.99993**	51.890	**0.047101**	**3.6057**	**0.5727**	31.271
	nn-pmrs*	2	0.99987	55.034	0.058962	3.7064	0.7538	37.919
	nn-pmrs**	2	0.99985	**56.376**	0.063695	3.7870	0.8195	**38.255**

The results are on the performance of the chosen PMRS model, NN model and the two fitted NN models using PMRS inputs on the test set. Results in bold indicate the best result for that error term.

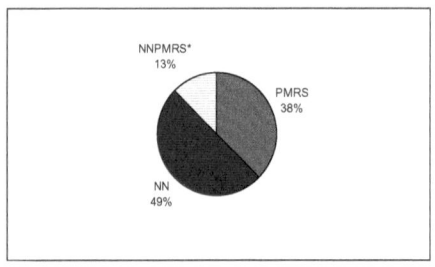

1 (a) Highest R-Squared value

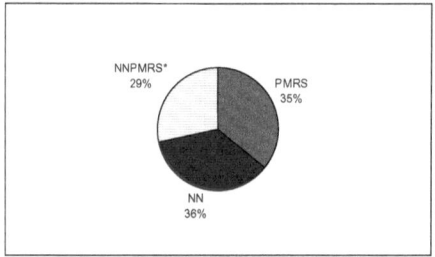

1 (b) Highest direction success

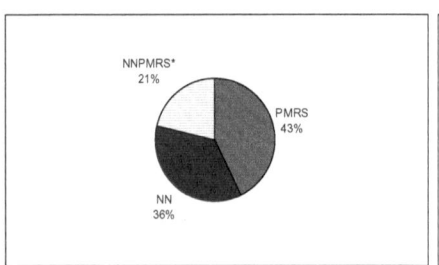

1 (c) Lowest RMSE

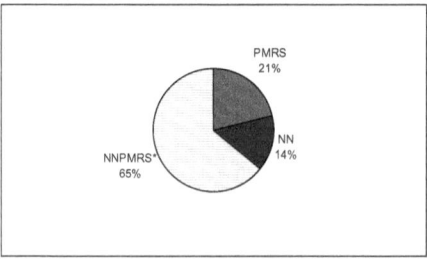

1 (d) Lowest GMRAE

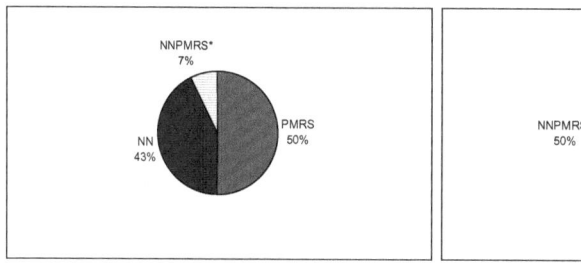
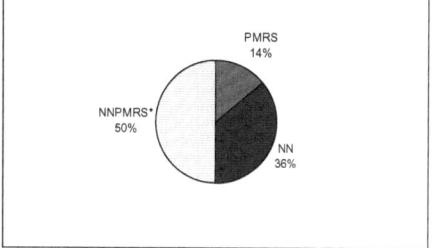

1 (e) Lowest MAPE   1 (f) Highest BRW

Fig. 1. (a)-(f) Proportion of models with the best performance on the error measures averaged across all data tested.

APPENDIX: DATA SETS

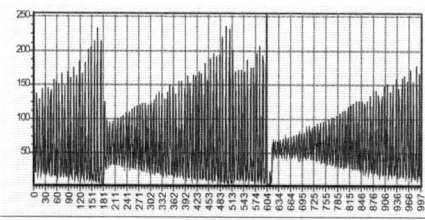

Data Set A

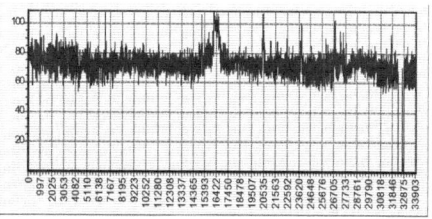

Data Set B1

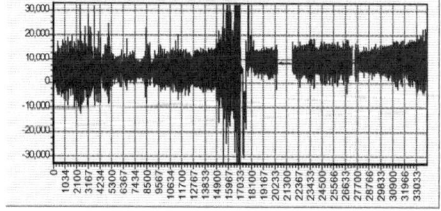

Data Set B2

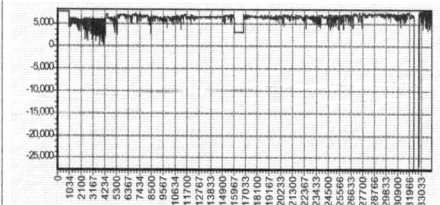

Data Set B3

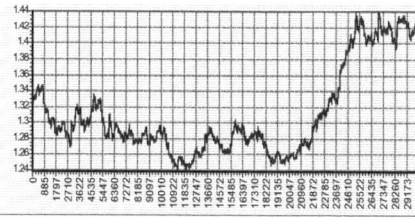

Data Set C

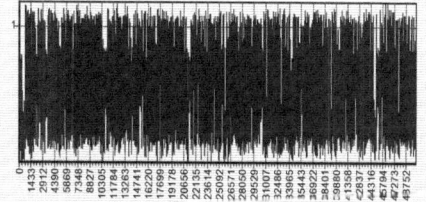

Data Set D1

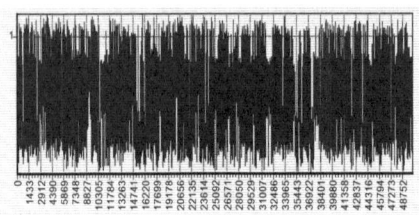

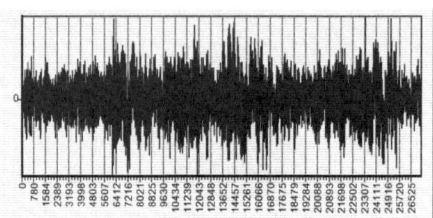

Data Set D2   Data Set E

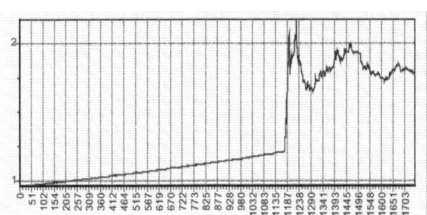

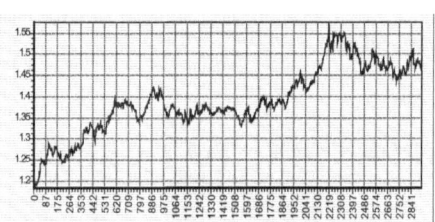

Data Set USDBRL   Data Set USDCAD

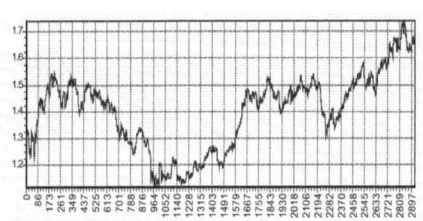

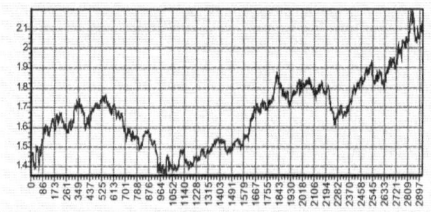

Data Set USDCHF   Data Set USDDEM

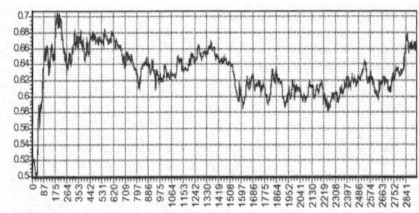

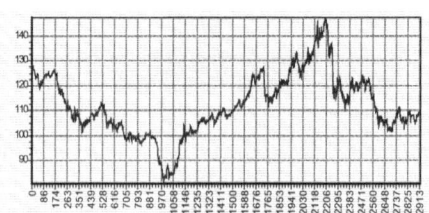

Data Set USDGBP   Data Set USDJPY

Invariant Face Detection in Color Images Using Orthogonal Fourier-Mellin Moments and Support Vector Machines

Jean-Christophe Terrillon [†], Mahdad N. Shirazi [‡], Daniel McReynolds*,
Mohamed Sadek**, Yunlong Sheng*, Shigeru Akamatsu**
and Kazuhiko Yamamoto[†]

[†] Office of Regional Intensive Research Project,
Softopia Japan Foundation, Ogaki-City, Gifu, Japan
[‡] Kansai Advanced Research Center,
Communications Research Laboratory, Kobe, Japan
* Centre d'Optique, Photonique et Laser, Département de Physique,
Université Laval, ste-Foy, P.Q., Canada
**ATR Human Information Processing Research Laboratories,
Kyoto, Japan

Abstract

This paper proposes an automatic face detection system that combines two novel methods to achieve invariant face detection and a high discrimination between faces and distractors in static color images of complex scenes. The system applies Orthogonal Fourier-Mellin Moments (OFMMs), recently developed by one of the authors [1], to achieve fully translation-, scale- and in-plane rotation-invariant face detection. Support Vector Machines (SVMs), a binary classifier based on a novel statistical learning technique that has been developed in recent years by Vapnik [2], are applied for face/non-face classification. The face detection system first performs a skin color-based image segmentation by modeling the skin chrominance distribution for several different chrominance spaces. Feature extraction of each face candidate in the segmented images is then implemented by calculating a selected number of OFMMs. Finally, the OFMMs form the input vector to the SVMs. The comparative face detection performance of the SVMs and of a multilayer perceptron Neural Network (NN) is analyzed for a set of 100 test images. For all the chrominance spaces that are used, the application of SVMs to the OFMMs yields a higher detection performance than when applying the NN. Normalized chrominance spaces produce the best segmentation results, and subsequently the highest rate of detection of faces with a large variety of poses, of skin tones and against complex backgrounds. The combination of the OFMMs and of the SVMs, and of the skin color-based image

S. Singh, N. Murshed, and W. Kropatsch (Eds.): ICAPR 2001, LNCS 2013, pp. 83–92, 2001.
© Springer-Verlag Berlin Heidelberg 2001

segmentation using normalized chrominance spaces, constitutes a promising approach to achieve robustness in the task of face detection.
Keywords: Automatic face detection; Skin color-based image segmentation; Invariant moments; Support vector machines; Multilayer perceptron

1   Introduction

Images of human faces play a central role in intelligent human-computer interaction. As a result, in recent years, automatic face detection has been receiving increasing attention in the pattern recognition community [3]. Face detection, as a first step for higher-level face recognition tasks, is a challenging task, because human faces are highly non-rigid objects, and real-world applications require that they be detected regardless of their positions, scales, orientations, poses, of the illumination conditions and of the complexity of the scene backgrounds. In fact, in [4], Jain *et al.* consider that face recognition is an emerging application at the frontier of pattern recognition and stress the desirability of invariant pattern recognition in applications such as face recognition. Therefore, two important issues that must be addressed in order to build a robust face detection system are invariance and also a high discrimination between faces and distractors (other objects with similar attributes as faces in terms of color and shape).

Invariant face detection has not been explored until recently [5,6,7]. In [6], partial in-plane rotation invariance is achieved by use of a neural network-based, template-based algorithm. In [7], we proposed to use non-orthogonal Fourier-Mellin moments (FMMs) in combination with a multilayer perceptron NN for fully translation-, scale- and in-plane rotation-invariant face detection in color images. In this paper, we use Orthogonal Fourier-Mellin Moments (OFMMs), that have been recently developed by one of the authors [1]. In addition to the same invariant properties as the FMMs and owing to their orthogonality, the OFMMs have the advantages that they do not suffer from information redundancy, are more robust with respect to noise, and they can be used to reconstruct the original object [1]. We recently applied the OFMMs to face detection in combination with the same NN architecture as in [7] for face/non-face classification, and found the OFMMs to yield a slightly superior face detection performance than the FMMs [8].

In order to achieve a high discrimination between faces and distractors in a complex scene image, we propose to use Support Vector Machines (SVMs), with the OFMMs as the input features. The application of SVMs to real-life pattern recognition problems is very recent and is receiving rapidly growing attention. SVMs are a new type of classifier which is a generalization of a large class of NNs, Radial Basis Functions (RBFs) and polynomial classifiers for solving binary classification problems [2]. To our knowledge, the only work published until now on the application of SVMs to the specific task of face detection is that of Osuna *et al.* [9], where they used grey-level images.

As a first step in the face detection process, we propose a skin color-based image segmentation. Color is a powerful fundamental cue that can be used at an early stage to detect objects in complex scene images. Robustness of image segmentation is achieved if a color space efficiently separating the chrominance from the luminance in the original color image and a plausible model of the chrominance distribution of human skin are used for thresholding. This requires a suitable transformation from a 3-D RGB color space into a 2-D chrominance space (and into a separate luminance component). In this work, we segment images for seven different chrominance spaces and by use of two skin chrominance models, namely the single Gaussian model and a Gaussian mixture model. A selected number of OFMMs are calculated for each cluster representing a face candidate that remains in the segmented binary images after a connected-component analysis, and the resulting feature vector is used to train or test the SVM.

The paper is organized as follows : in section 2, we briefly examine the chrominance distribution of human skin for each of the seven chrominance spaces, and summarize the calibration method used to find a suitable threshold for image segmentation. In section 3, we present a brief description of the mathematical formulation of the OFMMs, based on the analysis in [1], and of the selection of an appropriate combination of OFMMs, which is presented in details in [8]. Section 4 summarizes the theoretical foundations and the properties of SVMs. Experimental results of face detection with the SVMs are presented and discussed in section 5. A comparison is made with the corresponding results obtained with a multilayer perceptron NN, and that we presented in [8]. Conclusions are drawn in section 6.

2   Skin Color-based Image Segmentation

Original color images are segmented by use of the seven following color spaces : the standard normalized r-g and CIE-xy spaces, where $r=R/(R+G+B)$ and $g=G/(R+G+B)$, the perceptually plausible CIE-DSH and HSV spaces, the perceptually uniform CIE-L*u*v* and CIE-L*a*b* spaces, and finally a normalized, perceptually plausible Tint-Saturation (T-S) space, which is defined in [8]. Images of 11 Asian and 19 Caucasian subjects were recorded under slowly varying illumination conditions in an office environment with a single video camera mounted on an SGI computer. 110 skin sample images were manually selected to calculate the cumulative skin pixel histogram in each of the chrominance spaces and to calibrate the camera for color segmentation. The histograms are shown in figure 1. Visually, the skin distribution in the normalized chrominance spaces (T-S, r-g and CIE-xy) fits well to the single Gaussian model whereas in the un-normalized spaces, it is complex and cannot be described well by a simple model. In the simplest case where the skin chrominance distribution for both Asians and Caucasians is modeled by a single Gaussian, the Mahalanobis metric is used for skin color calibration and for thesholding of test images. The calibration requires finding a "standard" threshold value of the Mahalanobis metric for each chrominance space such that the proportion of true positives TP over the ensemble of skin pixels in the 110 skin sample images is equal to the proportion of true negatives TN over an ensemble of "non-skin" pixels in 5 large images not containing skin [7]. The single Gaussian model is a particular case of a Gaussian mixture model. The latter model is flexible enough to describe complex-shaped distributions. The estimation of the skin distribution is then performed by use of the Expectation-Maximization (EM) algorithm. For each chrominance space where the skin distribution is estimated with the Gaussian mixture model, we chose to use

8 Gaussian components, which yield visually plausible estimates even for complex-shaped distributions. The color calibration and the thresholding of the original color images are based on the same method as for the single Gaussian model, but use the likelihood [10]. Together with the accuracy of estimation of the skin chrominance distribution, the degree of overlap between skin and non-skin distributions in a given chrominance space ultimately limits the quality of segmentation, and subsequently the performance of face detection [10].

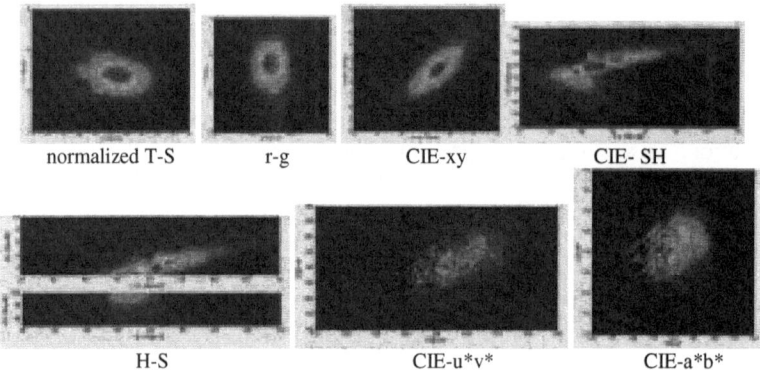

Figure 1. 2-D top view of the cumulative histograms in seven different chrominance spaces of 110 skin sample images (N_s = 1.5 x 10E + 05 skin pixels) of 11 Asian and 19 Caucasian subjects used to calibrate the SGI camera. Total histogram dimensions are 100 x 100 bins in all spaces except in CIE-u*v* and CIE-a*b* spaces where the dimensions are 200x200 bins.

3   Orthogonal Fourier-Mellin Moments

The OFMMs are defined in polar coordinates (r,θ) as ([1]) :

$$\Phi_{n,m} = \frac{1}{2\pi\,a_n} \int_0^{2\pi} \int_0^1 f(r,\theta)\, Q_n(r)\, \exp(-im\theta)\, r\, dr\, d\theta \tag{1}$$

where $f(r,\theta)$ is the object or image to be analyzed, $a_n = 1/[2(n+1)]$ is a normalization constant, $Q_n(r)$ is a polynomial in r of degree n, and where $i^2 = -1$. The radial order n = 0, 1, 2, ..., and the circular harmonic order m = 0, ±1, ±2, ... The set of $Q_n(r)$ is orthogonal over the range $0 \le r \le 1$. Hence the basis functions $Q_n(r)\exp(-im\theta)$ of the OFMMs are orthogonal over the interior of the unit circle. The polynomials $Q_n(r)$ are defined as

$$Q_n(r) = \sum_{s=0}^{n} \alpha_{ns}\, r^s \tag{2}$$

where $\alpha_{ns} = (-1)^{n+s}(n+s+1)! \, / [(n-s)!\, s!\, (s+1)!\,]$. The basis functions $Q_n(r)\exp(-im\theta)$ can be expressed as complex polynomials in $(x+iy)$ and $(x-iy)$. After a transformation from polar to cartesian coordinates, the translation- and scale-invariant OFMMs are given by

$$\Phi_{n,m} = \exp(im\alpha)\frac{n+1}{\pi} \sum_{s=0}^{n} \frac{\alpha_{ns}}{M'_{0,0}{}^{s/2+1}} \int \int_{-\infty}^{\infty} (x+iy)^{(s-m)/2} (x-iy)^{(s+m)/2} f(x,y)\, dx\, dy \tag{3}$$

where $M'_{0,0}$ is the zero-order geometric moment of the object to be analyzed $f(x,y)$ (the area of the object in a binary image) and where α is an arbitrary angle. The modulus of the OFMMs, $|\Phi_{n,m}|$, is rotation invariant. Also, in the case of binary images, the moments are independent of illumination.

The selection of an appropriate combination of OFMMs to be used in the face detection system is an important task. It is based on the object reconstruction capability of the set of OFMMs that is considered, but most importantly, as we showed in [8], on the underlying assumption that frontal views of faces are approximately elliptical, with holes at the location of the eyes and of the mouth in the segmented images. If we use a pure ellipse as a model to describe segmented frontal views of faces, the modulus of every OFMM depends only on the aspect ratio a/b of the ellipse, where a and b are respectively the semi-major axis and the semi-minor axis of the ellipse. The value of $|\Phi_{n,m}|$ as a function of a/b should have a small variability, at least in the range of values of a/b that characterizes human faces, in order to obtain a small intra-class variability. This range was assumed to be $1/2 \leq a/b \leq 2.0$. Also, in order not to amplify the effects of noise, only a small number of the lowest-order OFMMs, in particular the lowest radial orders n, should be used for face detection [1]. In [9], we selected 11 OFMMs from an ensemble of 27 low-order OFMMs, with an upper bound for n of n=2 and for the circular harmonic order m of m=8. As an example, Figure 2 show the graphs of $|\Phi_{1,0}|$, $|\Phi_{1,2}|$, $|\Phi_{2,0}|$, and $|\Phi_{2,2}|$ as a function of a/b. We note that $|\Phi_{1,0}|$ and $|\Phi_{2,0}|$ have a small variability over the desired range of a/b, while $|\Phi_{1,2}|$ and $|\Phi_{2,2}|$ exhibit a high variability and were considered unsuitable for face detection. On the basis of the analysis of the OFMMs for an ellipse and of object reconstruction experiments (of faces and non-faces), the following combination of OFMMs was selected for the face detection task : $|\Phi_{0,1}|$, $|\Phi_{0,3}|$, $|\Phi_{0,4}|$, $|\Phi_{0,6}|$, $|\Phi_{1,0}|$, $|\Phi_{1,1}|$, $|\Phi_{1,3}|$, $|\Phi_{1,4}|$, $|\Phi_{2,0}|$, $|\Phi_{2,1}|$, and $|\Phi_{2,6}|$. When a face is detected, either by use of an SVM or of a NN, it is marked by an ellipse, as described in [7].

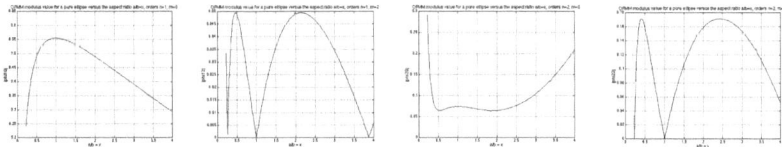

Figure 2. Graphs of the moduli of four low-order OFMMs for a pure ellipse versus a/b=x, From left to right : n=1, 2 and m=0, 2 ($|\Phi_{1,0}|$, $|\Phi_{1,2}|$, $|\Phi_{2,0}|$ and $|\Phi_{2,2}|$).respectively).

4 Support Vector Machines

In a binary classification problem where feature extraction is initially performed, a Support Vector Machine (SVM) determines, among the infinite number of possible hyperplanes in R^n that separate two classes described by l feature vectors $x_i \in R^n$, i =1, ..., l , which hyperplane yields the smallest generalization error. As is shown in [11], such an optimal hyperplane is the one with the maximum margin of separation between the two classes, where the margin is the sum of the distances from the hyperplane to the closest data points) of each of the two classes, which are called support vectors. In practical applications, two classes are not completely separable, so that a hyperplane that maximizes the margin while minimizing a quantity proportional to the misclassification error is determined. Just as for the separable case, this is a Quadratic Programming (QP) problem [11]. When training an SVM, the training data always appear as a dot product $\mathbf{x}_i \cdot \mathbf{x}_j$. It is also unlikely that real-life classification problems can be solved by a linear classifier, so that an extension to non-linear decision functions (or surfaces) is necessary. In order to do this, an initial mapping $\mathbf{\Phi}$ of the data into a (usually significantly higher dimensional) Euclidean space H is performed as $\mathbf{\Phi} : R^n \rightarrow H$, and the linear classification problem is formulated in the new space with dimension d. The training algorithm then only depends on the data through dot products in H of the form $\mathbf{\Phi}(\mathbf{x}_i) \cdot \mathbf{\Phi}(\mathbf{x}_j)$. Since the computation of the dot products is prohibitive if the number l of training vectors $\mathbf{\Phi}(\mathbf{x}_i)$ is very large, and since $\mathbf{\Phi}$ is not known a priori, the Mercer-Hilbert-Schmidt theorem ([11]) for positive definite functions allows to replace $\mathbf{\Phi}(\mathbf{x}_i) \cdot \mathbf{\Phi}(\mathbf{x}_j)$ by a positive definite symmetric kernel function $K(\mathbf{x}_i, \mathbf{x}_j)$, that is, $K(\mathbf{x}_i, \mathbf{x}_j) = \mathbf{\Phi}(\mathbf{x}_i) \cdot \mathbf{\Phi}(\mathbf{x}_j)$. Only K is needed in the training algorithm and we do not need to know $\mathbf{\Phi}$ explicitly. The QP problem to be solved is exactly the same as before. Some examples of possible $K(\mathbf{x}_i, \mathbf{x}_j)$ that lead to well-known classifiers are : $K(\mathbf{x}_i, \mathbf{x}_j) = (\mathbf{x}_i \cdot \mathbf{x}_j + 1)^p$, a simple polynomial of degree p ; $K(\mathbf{x}_i, \mathbf{x}_j) = \exp(-\gamma \| \mathbf{x}_i - \mathbf{x}_j \|^2)$, a Gaussian RBF with real parameter γ (with $d \rightarrow \infty$) ; and $K(\mathbf{x}_i, \mathbf{x}_j) = \tanh(\kappa \mathbf{x}_i \cdot \mathbf{x}_j - \delta)$, a multilayer perceptron NN with real parameters κ and δ.

A great advantage of the SVMs over other classifiers such as a multilayer perceptron NN is that they use structural risk minimization which minimizes a bound on the generalization error, and therefore they should perform better on novel test data [11], whereas the other classifiers use empirical risk minimization and only guarantee a minimum error over the training data set. The solution found by the SVM classifier is always global, because it originates from a convex QP problem [11]. The mapping to a higher dimensional space significantly increases the discriminative power of the classifier. The requirement of maximum margin hyperplanes in H obviates the "curse of dimensionality", and thus ensures the generalization performance of the SVM [11]. Finally, the SVM approach is better founded theoretically and more general than that for the other classifiers, so that less training (and testing) are needed to achieve good results. Two limitations of the SVMs are the selection of a suitable kernel and of the associated parameter(s) to solve a given problem, and the size of the training data sets [9], [11]. A detailed analysis of the SVMs is presented in [11].

5   Experimental Results of Face Detection

The face detection system is implemented on a SGI Indigo computer. All images were captured by use of an inexpensive SGI camera. As when we applied a multilayer perceptron NN in [8], the training file consists here of a total of 227 feature vectors (or clusters), obtained from 108 segmented images of 9 Asian and 20 Caucasian subjects. The segmentation was performed with the normalized T-S chrominance space when using both the SVMs and the NN. The T-S space produces the best results in the chrominance analysis and the color calibration when using the single Gaussian chrominance model [10]. Considering then that the faces in the training set are well segmented, it is reasoned that the training need not be performed for each chrominance space separately, so that the same trained SVM (or NN weights) may be applied to test images segmented by use of the other chrominance spaces. The test file (for both the SVM and the NN) consists of 100 images with 144 faces and 65 subjects (30 Asians, 34 Caucasians and one subject of African descent), with a large variety of poses and against various complex backgrounds. All the kernels defined in Section 4, as well as a kernel consisting of linear splines with an infinite number of points, were used to train and test the SVM, and several different values were selected for the associated parameter(s). The NN is a feed-forward 3-layer perceptron, with one hidden layer containing 6 nodes and with one output unit [8]. All the units take on continuous bipolar-sigmoid activation values in the range [-1.0;1.0]. The NN is trained by use of the backpropagation algorithm. The face detection performance is measured in terms of the rate of correct face detection CD and of the rate of correct rejection of distractors CR. When comparing the performance of the SVM with that of the NN, the selection of the kernel and of the value of its associated parameter(s) can be based on two different criteria : one might favor a higher detection rate CD to the detriment of CR, or one might try to find the best tradeoff between CD and CR. Figure 3a) shows the general results of face detection with both the SVM and the NN for the single Gaussian model and for five chrominance spaces, while Figure 3b) shows the results for the Gaussian mixture model and for the CIE-L*u*v* and CIE-L*a*b* spaces. The total number of blobs is the cumulative number of face candidates in the test file remaining after the connected-component analysis. The shaded areas emphasize the best comparative results. Here the results reflect the best tradeoff between CD and CR. In the case of the single Gaussian model, the kernel yielding the best performance was found to be the Gaussian RBF for all five chrominance spaces, and generally for intermediate values of γ (0.5<γ<2.0). CD is significantly higher with the SVM than with the NN for almost all chrominance spaces, while CR is slightly higher for most spaces. Independently of the type of classifier that is used, the face detection performance is generally reduced for the un-normalized CIE-DSH and HSV spaces, owing to a lower goodness of fit of the corresponding skin chrominance distributions to the single Gaussian model. However, the SVM partially compensates the detrimental effects of a lower quality of segmentation because it always finds a global solution to a binary classification problem. In the case of the Gaussian mixture model, three different types of kernels have been found to yield a suitable tradeoff between CD and CR, as compared to the performance of the NN : they are, once again, a Gaussian RBF, with γ = 1.0, a simple polynomial with degree p=3, and linear splines with an infinite number of points, for both color spaces. CD is less significantly higher than when applying a NN, because the overlap between the skin and non-skin distributions in both color spaces is higher than in the other spaces [10]. Overall, whatever the skin chrominance model that is used, the performance of the SVM is superior to that of the NN. Figure 4 shows the variation of CD and of CR as a

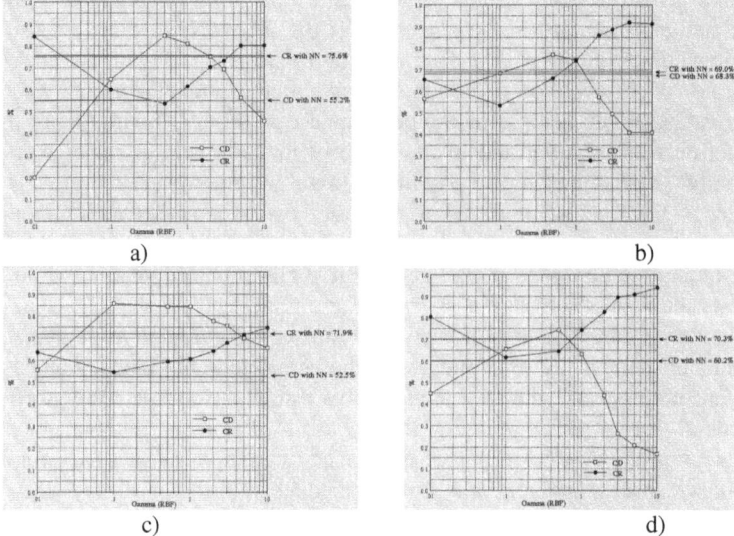

Figure 3. General results of face detection with the SVM and with a 3-layer perceptron NN for the single Gaussian skin chrominance model and for five different chrominance spaces, and for the Gaussian mixture density model and for the CIE-L*u*v* and CIE-L*a*b* color spaces. In the left table, the kernel used to train the SVM is a Gaussian RBF with parameter $\gamma = 0.5, 1.0, 2.0, 1.0$ and 10.0 respectively ; In the right table, the kernels are a Gaussian RBF (with $\gamma = 1.0$ for both spaces), a simple polynomial (with degree p=3 for both spaces) and linear splines with an infinite number of points .

Figure 4. Graphs of CD and of CR as a function of the parameter γ when applying a Gaussian RBF kernel to train an SVM for face detection in binary images segmented by use of the single Gaussian chrominance model in the CIE-xy (a), CIE-DSH (b) and HSV (c) color spaces, and by use of the Gaussian mixture model in the CIE-L*a*b* color space (d) . The CD and CR obtained with the NN are shown for comparison in each graph .

function of the parameter γ when applying a Gaussian RBF kernel for the single Gaussian model (in the CIE-xy, DSH and HSV spaces) and for the Gaussian mixture model (in the CIE-L*a*b* space). The CD and CR obtained with the NN are shown for comparison. A strong negative correlation between CD and CR is observed in all cases. If one favors CD to the detriment of CR, a value of CD=84.8% is obtained for the CIE-xy space for γ=0.5 (against 55.2% with the NN), compared to 75.2% if a tradeoff between CD and CR is favored (as shown in Figure 3a), with γ=2.0), but the value of CR is then low (CR=53.5%, against CR=75.6% with the NN). The same significantly higher value of CD than with the NN is produced for the HSV space, which is again strongly detrimental to CR. The best tradeoff between CD and CR produces values of CD and CR that are both higher than the corresponding values obtained with the NN for the CIE-DSH, HSV and CIE-L*a*b* spaces (Figures 4b), c) and d)), but this is clearly not the case for the CIE-xy space (Figure 4a)). In the latter case, it is therefore not easy to find a suitable tradeoff. Figure 5 shows a graph of the experimental value of the OFMM $|\Phi_{1,0}|$ versus the aspect ratio a/b calculated for a subset of the detected faces. The graph shows also the non-face data points with the same ordinate as the face data points from the same image, and the theoretical curve of $|\Phi_{1,0}|$ for an ellipse. The distribution of moment values for faces clusters reasonably well near the theoretical curve, thus validating the analysis of the modulus of the OFMMs for an ellipse in the selection process of the OFMMs for face detection. Non-face data points are diffusely distributed and have a relatively small intersection with the face distribution.

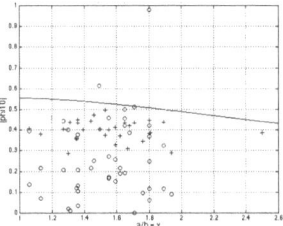

Figure 5.   Experimental values of $|\Phi_{1,0}|$ for 30 faces (+) and 44 distractors (o) for 30 images selected from the test file . The solid line is $|\Phi_{1,0}|$ versus a/b for an ellipse .

Finally, Figures 6 and 7 show examples of the successful detection of faces as well as of errors occurring with the present face detection system. The examples of Figure 6 show that faces of Asian, Caucasian and Indo-Caucasian subjects are equally well detected, with a large variety of poses that include small out-of-plane rotations. They show also that the general performance in terms of CR (Figure 3) can be considered to be high given the variety and complexity of the scene backgrounds. Figure 7 shows examples of different types of detection errors : face localization errors, false positives (in part due to the invariant properties of the OFMMs), and false negatives.

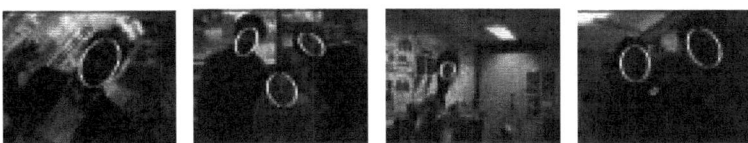

Figure 6. Examples of the detection of faces with different poses and different skin colors against various complex backgrounds (normalized T-S space, single Gaussian model).

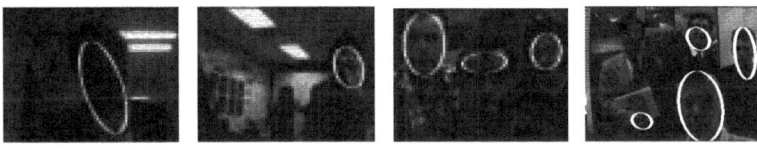

Figure 7. Examples of errors occurring with the present face detection system

6 Conclusions

In conclusion, for all chrominance spaces and for both skin chrominance models that were used, the most robust face detection system when applying SVMs to invariant OFMMs for binary face/non-face classification in segmented images is obtained by use of a Gaussian RBF kernel and generally for intermediate values of the associated parameter γ. A simple polynomial with degree p=3 and linear splines with an infinite number of points also produce good results with the Gaussian mixture model. One might favor the face detection rate CD to the detriment of the rate of correct rejection of distractors CR if a suitable post-processing of detected face candidates, using the luminance for example, reduces the proportion of false positives FP. Overall, the performance of the SVMs is superior to that of a 3-layer perceptron NN, if a suitable kernel function used to train the SVMs and a suitable value of the associated parameter are selected. However, the SVMs require much less training and tuning than a NN, and always find a global solution. Owing to their invariant properties and to their better capability to describe an object than other types of moments such as the FMMs [1], the OFMMs are powerful new features for face detection and for pattern recognition in general. The best choice of kernel and of the value of the associated parameter for a given problem is an important issue that requires further research.

Acknowledgements

The work presented in this paper was entirely performed at ATR Human Information Processing Research Laboratories while the first author was an invited researcher at ATR, and the authors gratefully acknowledge the support of ATR.

References

[1] Sheng Y and Shen L, Orthogonal Fourier-Mellin moments for invariant pattern recognition, Journal of the Optical Society of America-A, 1994; 11(6):1748-1757.

[2] Vapnik V, The Nature of statistical learning theory, Springer Verlag, New York, 1995.

[3] I. C. S. Press. Proc. of the 4th Int. Conf. on Face and Gesture Recog., Grenoble, France, March 2000.

[4] Jain AK, Duin RPW, and Mao J, Statistical pattern recognition : a review, IEEE Transactions on Pattern Analysis and Machine Intelligence, January 2000; 22(1):4-37.

[5] Hotta K, Kurita T, and Mishima T, Scale invariant face detection method using higher-order local autocorrelation features extracted from log-polar images. In Proceedings of the Third International Conference on Automatic Face and Gesture Recognition, Nara, Japan, April 1998, pp. 70-75.

[6] Rowley HA, Baluja S, and Kanade T, Rotation invariant neural network-based face detection. In Proceedings of the CVPR, Santa Barbara, California, June 1998. pp. 38-44.

[7] Terrillon JC, David M, and Akamatsu A, Automatic detection of human faces in natural scene images by use of a skin color model and of invariant moments. In Proceedings of the Third International Conference on Automatic Face and Gesture Recognition, Nara, Japan, April 1998, pp. 112-117.

[8] Terrillon JC, McReynolds D, Sadek M, Sheng Y, and Akamatsu S, Invariant neural network-based face detection.with orthogonal Fourier-Mellin Moments, in Proceedings of the 15th International Conference on Pattern Recognition, Barcelona, Spain, September 2000. Vol. 2, pp. 997-1004.

[9] Osuna E, Freund R, and Girosi F, Training support vector machines : an application to face detection. In Proceedings of the CVPR, Puerto Rico, 1997. pp. 130-136.

[10] Terrillon JC, Shirazi MN, Fukamachi H, and Akamatsu S, Comparative performance of different skin chrominance models and chrominance spaces for the automatic detection of human faces in color images. In Proceedings of the 4th International Conference on Automatic Face and Gesture Recognition, Grenoble, France, March 2000, pp. 54-61.

[11] Burges CJC, A tutorial on support vector machines for pattern recognition, Data Mining and Knowledge Discovery, 1998; 2(2):121-167.

Character Extraction from Interfering Background – Analysis of Double-sided Handwritten Archival Documents

Chew Lim Tan, Ruini Cao, Qian Wang, Peiyi Shen
School of Computing, National University of Singapore,
Lower Kent Ridge Crescent, Singapore, 119260
{tancl, caoruini, shenpy}@comp.nus.edu.sg
citwangq@nus.edu.sg

Abstract

The sipping of ink through the pages of certain double-sided handwritten documents after long periods of storage poses a serious problem to human readers or OCR systems. This paper addresses this problem through the recovery of content on the front side of a page from the interfering image caused by the handwriting on the reverse side. First, by adapting the Gaussian stochastic model, the interfering model based on norm-orientation-discontinuity is proposed in analyzing the properties of the interfering strokes. Secondly, an improved canny edge detector with edge norm-orientation similarity constraint is applied. At the same time, two low thresholds are used to detect edges instead of a single low threshold. This improvement could link weaker foreground edges without introducing noises in the overlapping/overshadowed area. The proposed algorithms perform well regardless of the intensity differences between the image on the front side and the interfering image from the reverse side. The segmentation results of real images are shown and evaluated

Keywords.   Document image analysis, historical documents, double-sided interfering images, text extraction, Canny edge detector, orientation constraint

1. Introduction

Document image analysis is an important research area of image processing and pattern recognition. As an essential step, traditionally, text extraction is the segmentation of text from the background. But this paper introduces a rather different problem, that is, how to extract clear text strings on the front side from the seriously sipping, dominating, overlapping and interfering images originating from the reverse side.

The motivation of this paper comes from a request from the National Archives of Singapore. Two original images are shown in Figure 1. We can see that reading of the contents is often difficult and sometimes even impossible. Thus, there is a request to find some way to remove such interfering noises to produce readable copies for public viewers in a digital library or on the internet.

Many segmentation and binary approaches have been reported in the literature [1]. In considering help for researchers in humanities to compare old manuscripts with printed matters on the internet, Negishi et al.[2] presented several automatic thresholding algorithms based on Otsu's [3] method in extracting the character bodies from the noisy background. Also, for complex background, Liu and Srihari [4] presented a thresholding algorithm based on texture features to extract characters from the run-length featured texture background, in that, the characters normally occupy a separable gray-level range in the gray-scale histogram and that the text images contain highly structured-stroke units. Similar works could be seen in Liang and Ahmadi's algorithm [5] which adopts a morphological approach to extract text strings from regular periodic overlapping text/background images. In their work different typical geometric background patterns were used as the mathematical morphological masks. White and Rohrer's [6] method may be more traditional. It is basically an image thresholding technique based on boundary characteristics to suppress unwanted background patterns.

Since the interfering strokes appear in varying intensities relative to the foreground text in different documents, it is difficult to apply the above methods directly to solve this problem [10]. It is observed that the edges of the strokes that sipped from the reverse side are not as sharp as those on the front side (cf Figure 1, Figure 2). This prompts us to adopt an edge detection algorithm followed by the use of boundary characteristics to suppress unwanted interfering strokes. The edge detection algorithm chosen here is an improved Canny edge detector [7] as its double-threshold method could provide us with the selection of the front stroke edges and its candidates.

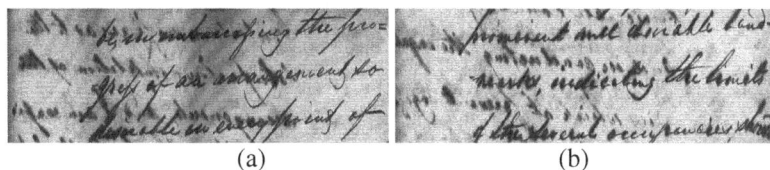

Figure 1. Two samples of the original archival documents, (interfering, dimming and overlapping)

The paper is organized as follows: In section 2, we describe the norm-orientation-discontinuity interfering model based on a Gaussian stochastic model in analyzing the properties of the interfering strokes. In section 3, we describe the improved canny edge detector with an edge-orientation constraint to detect the edges and recover the weak ones of the foreground words and characters; In section 4, we illustrate, discuss and evaluate the experimental results of the proposed method, demonstrating that our algorithm significantly improves the segmentation quality; Section 5 concludes this paper.

2. The norm-orientation-discontinuity interfering stroke model

Figure 2 shows three typical samples of original image segments from the original documents and their magnitude of the detected edges

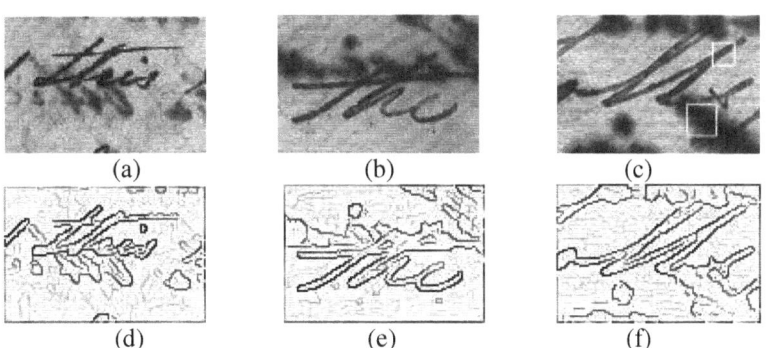

Figure 2. Sample images with different properties: (a) ~ (c) the original images; (d) ~ (f) the magnitude of all detected edges;

Assume that the pixels in background strokes are scattered on the foreground. For each noise spot at position (i, j), a Gaussian-shaped respectively. The magnitude of the gradient is converted into the gray level value. The darker the edge is, the larger is the gradient magnitude. It is obvious that the topmost strong edges correspond to foreground edges. It should be noted that, while usually, the foreground writing appears darker than the background image, as shown in sample image Figure 2(a), there are cases where the foreground and background have similar intensities as shown in Figure 2(b), or worst still, the background is more prominent than the foreground as in Figure 2(c). So using only the intensity value is not enough to differentiate the foreground from the background.

Assume that the pixels in background strokes are scattered on the foreground. For each noise spot at position (i, j), a Gaussian-shaped function is assumed to be superimposed on the foreground image, then $N(m,n)$, the neighbor pixels of (i, j) could be modeled as [8] :

$$N(m,n) = x(i, j)e^{\frac{-((m-i)^2+(n-j)^2)}{2\sigma^2}} \tag{1}$$

The intensity x is a random variable which is assumed to have a Gaussian distribution with zero mean and variance σ_1^2, that is [8]:

$$p_X(x) = \frac{1}{\sigma_1^2 \sqrt{2\pi}} e^{\frac{-x^2}{2\sigma_1^2}} \tag{2}$$

The interaction of the adjacent pixels of the scattering of the background stroke pixels could be modeled as:

$$I_i(i, j) = \sum_{(m,n) \in Neighbour\ (i,j)} x(m,n)G * I(i-m, j-n) \tag{3}$$

where $I(i, j)$ is the background stroke pixel, G denotes $Gaussian(0, \sigma^2)$, $I_i(i, j)$ is the interfering stroke pixel which appears as noise in the foreground..

Due to the anisotropy of the absorption/dispersion properties of the paper materials, $x(m,n)$ differs greatly even in the adjacent pixels, usually $\sigma_1 >> \sigma$ [8], which means that the high frequency of x is induced into the interfering image. And this results in the ripples appearing in the interfering strokes, such that the edges become "wandering" and the norm-orientation becomes a discontinuity when applying Canny's non-maximum suppression. Figure 3 (a) and (b) show the 3D surfaces of the interfering background and foreground strokes respectively, while Figure 4 (a) and (b) show the numerical values of their norm orientation along

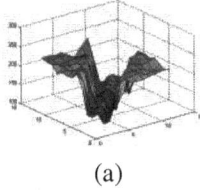

(a)

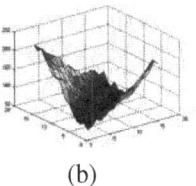

(b)

Figure 3. Three-dimensional illustration of dark strokes written on a light background, obtained from Figure 2(c) marked by the two white boxes respectively: (a) a normal stroke on the front side; (b) an interfering stroke from the reverse

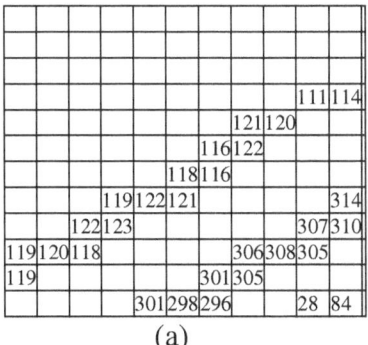

(a)

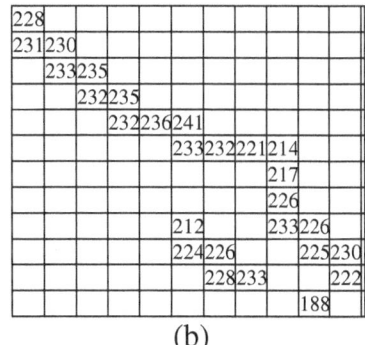

(b)

Figure 4. The norm-orientation (in degree unit) of the detected strokes (Gaussian filtering in Canny edge detector: 5x5 mask, $G(0,1.414)$) that are shown in Figure 3 respectively: (a) the front stroke in diagonal direction, standard deviation is 3.88, (b) the interfering stroke in diagonal direction, standard deviation is 6.73

the detected edges respectively. From Figure 3 and Figure 4, we could see clearly that the standard deviation between the norm-orientation of the front stroke and that of the interfering stroke differs greatly. This means that for the edges in the interfering stokes, the norm-orientation between the connected pixels will not be modeled as a smooth function in contrast with that of the front strokes [11]. And this performance between the foreground and interfering strokes, which we call the norm-orientation-discontinuity, will be favored in picking up the weak foreground strokes as discussed in the next section

3. Improved canny edge detector: the norm-orientation similarity constraint

Traditional canny edge detector [7] works in detecting most of the foreground edges. The detected edges for the samples in Figure 2 are shown in Figure 5. Note that the algorithm fails when the interfering edges are present nearby and edge tracing is misled along the interfering edges. In the overlapping area, the foreground edges are often broken and the resultant boundary is not complete [9]. For the existing broken foreground edges in the overlapping area, it is necessary to pick them up in recovering the complete edges of the foreground characters. In many cases, in order to detect the "weak" foreground strokes in the seriously overlapping/overshadowed area, the low-level threshold often has to be traded off in favor of the foreground edges over the interfering stroke. In the case that interfering strokes are "strong" enough to be detected in the low-threshold stage and adjacent with the seeds of the front edges, these "strong" interfering strokes would be regarded as the foreground edges in the final results. Thus, in practice, the low-threshold (*denoted as low-threshold1*) is often selected a little higher so as not to introduce too much "strong" interfering strokes and the result is that some "weak" foreground edges, especially in the overlapping area, are often lost.

In order to connect more of the weak foreground edges and reduce the risk of linking noisy edges detected in the low-level threshold stage, we lower the low-threshold (*denoted as low-threshold2*) and superimpose

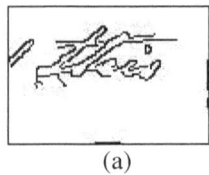   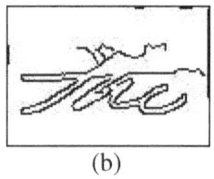   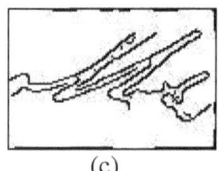

(a)   (b)   (c)

Figure 5 Traditional canny edge detection, (a) detected edges for the image shown in Figure 2(a), high-level threshold = 0.980, low-level threshold = 0.900; (b) detected edges for the image shown in Figure. 2(b), high-level threshold = 0.973, low-level threshold = 0.820; (c) detected edges for the image shown in Figure 2(c), high-level threshold = 0.972, low-level threshold = 0.820.

the norm-orientation-discontinuity of the interfering strokes in picking up the faint foreground strokes.

Let σ_f be the standard deviation of norm-orientation of the foreground strokes selected manually. Thus the traditional canny edge detector is revised like this: adding two more steps into the traditional canny edge detection algorithm (cf Figure 6).

---

1. New low-level threshold (*low-threshold2*) edge detection.
2. Edge linking: with the linked edges in *low-threshold1* being "seeds", from the position of each seed, if the norm difference between the seed and its candidate is smaller than $3*\sigma_f$ or $\pi/4$, then the candidate could be linked as the foreground stroke.

Figure 6 Improved linking strategy in canny edge detection algorithm

The above constraint is what we call the norm-orientation similarity constraint, which facilitates selecting the appropriate candidate fragment of the foreground edges in a smooth stroke, and at the same time prevents introducing the interfering strokes. It should be noted that, in the interfering cases, the maximum gradient intensity reflects the strength of the strokes, sharper or blurred; the norm-orientation similarity reflects the smoothness property of a stroke. With this improvement, we could raise *low-threshold1* a little in the traditional Canny edge detector. Accordingly, some of the interfering strokes will be successfully filtered out. And *low-threshold2* could be set at a rather low value in practice. In this way, more details of the front strokes will be recovered without introducing noises in the dimming area (cf Figure 7).

Since the essential aim of our project is to obtain clean and readable copies for public viewing of the archival documents, after the edge detection, the image recovery stage is that the neighboring pixels within the statically 7x7 window centered on each edge are recovered. The restored front side images for the above three samples are shown in Figure 8.

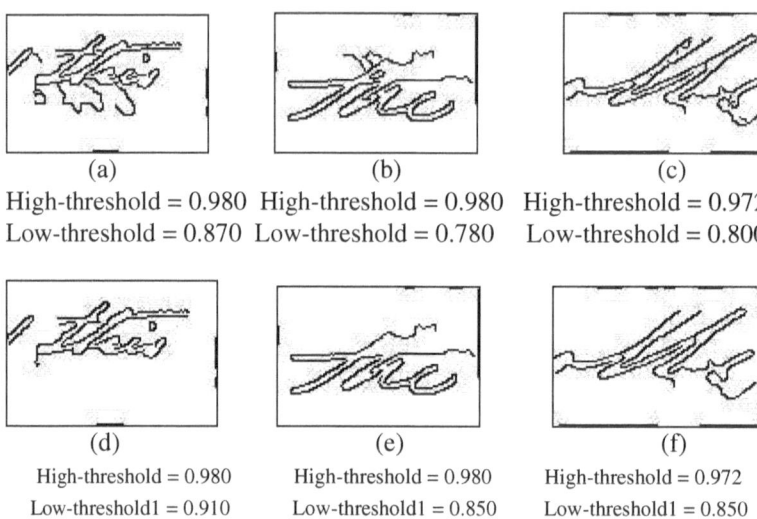

(a)   (b)   (c)

High-threshold = 0.980 High-threshold = 0.980 High-threshold = 0.972
Low-threshold = 0.870 Low-threshold = 0.780   Low-threshold = 0.800

(d)   (e)   (f)

High-threshold = 0.980   High-threshold = 0.980   High-threshold = 0.972
Low-threshold1 = 0.910   Low-threshold1 = 0.850   Low-threshold1 = 0.850
Low-threshold2 = 0.870   Low-threshold2 = 0.780   Low-threshold2 = 0.800

Figure 7 (a), (b) and (c): traditional Canny edge detection results; (d), (e) and (f): improved Canny edge detection results: orientation constraint.

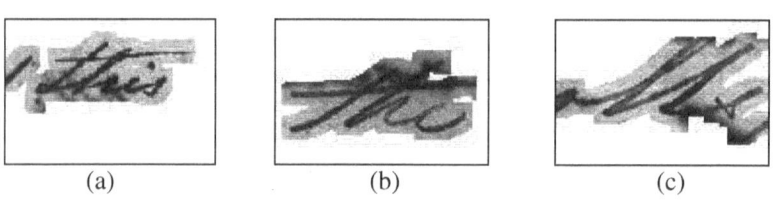

(a)   (b)   (c)

Figure 8 Restored foreground text images: (a), (b) and (c) segmented result for the images Fig. 2(a), (b)and (c) respectively

4. Experiment observation and discussion

The performance of our approach has been evaluated based on the scanned images of historical handwritten documents provided by the National Archives of Singapore. The cleaned up images were visually inspected to assess the readability of the words extracted. Here, 12 typical images are adopted in illustrating the performance of the system. The two evaluation metrics: precision and recall (defined below) are used to measure the performance of the system.

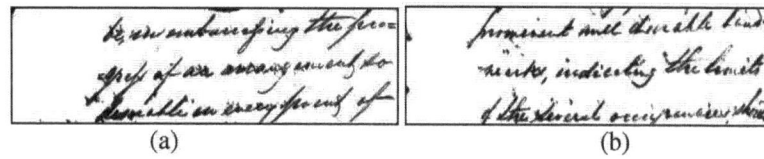

(a)   (b)

Figure 9 Segmentation results of the test images shown in Figure 1(a)
and (c)

Precision =

Number of Detected Correct Words / Total Number of Detected Words,   (4)

Recall = Number of Detected Correct Words / Total Number of Words.   (5)

where *total number of words* includes all the words in the foreground
image, while the *total number of detected words* means the sum of the
detected correct words and incorrect words (interfering words).

If some characters in a foreground word are lost or not recovered
properly, the whole word is considered lost. If parts of characters coming
from the back are detected, the total number of incorrect words will be
increased by 1. Precision reflects the performance of removing the
interfering strokes of the system and recall reflects the performance of
restoring the foreground words of the system. The higher the precision,
the lesser is the number of detected interfering strokes. The higher the
recall, the more the foreground words are detected.

Table 1 shows the evaluation of the segmentation results of the 12
typical testing images. The average precision and recall are 81% and
94% respectively. The proposed algorithms are not image-dependent, and
thus the high precision and recall are achieved for varying degrees of
interference among these images. The final extracted and binarized text
image for the original image in Figure 1 is shown in Figure 9. Since most
of the interfering area could be removed successfully, the Ostu's
threshold is adopted to binarize the segmentation images. The binary
images of other segmentation results are shown in Figure 10. And we can
see that the appearance of the binary images is much cleaner and the
foreground strokes are more readable.

In fact, sometimes the interfering is so serious that the edges of the
interfering strokes are even stronger than that of the foreground edges.
As a result, the edges of the interfering strokes would be erroneously
regarded as the front "seed" and would remain in the resultant text image.
In this case, the precision decreases. Therefore, how to separate the front

Table1. Evaluation of the system in 12 testing images

Image number	1	2	3	4	5	6	7
Total no. of words	132	124	103	125	125	123	121
Precision	91%	86%	51%	94%	87%	77%	79%
Recall	98%	100%	89%	94%	82%	92%	89%
Image number	8	9	10	11	12		Average
Total no. of words	128	112	113	114	114		
Precision	75%	84%	82%	91%	78%		81%
Recall	97%	97%	98%	96%	96%		94%

(a)

(b)

(c)

(d)

(e)

(f)

(g)

(h)

Figure 10 (a), (b), (e), (f): original test images; (c), (d), (g), (h): the   binary images of segmentation results by the proposed algorithm of (a), (b), (e), (f) respectively, Ostu's threshold method [4].

"seed" from all the high thresholded edges is still a problem in our further work.

5. Conclusion and further work

The paper describes a method for the removal of interfering images. This method is especially designed for old handwritten documents by using the fact that the edges of the interfering images caused by interfering sipping from the reverse side are not as sharp as those of the foreground images. The algorithm performs well and can improve the appearance of the original documents greatly.

With the norm-orientation similarity constraint, the parameters of hi-threshold, low-threshold1 and low-threshold2 have their robustness in handling different types of original images. But there is still one problem, that is how to judge the standard deviation σ_f locally or adaptively. And this is the reason, in practice, that we use $\pi / 4$ as another threshold in the norm-similarity constraint. A different approach will be also attempted. That is to superimpose the mirror-image rendition of the reverse page image with the front page image. In this way, corresponding mapping of the strokes of the two superimposed images will aid in identifying characters from either side of the paper.

References

1. Oivind Due Trier, Anil K. Jain: *Goal-directed evaluation of binarization methods,* IEEE Trans. on PAMI, Vol. 17, No. 12, Dec. 1995, pp1191-1201
2. Hideyuki Negishi, Jien Kato, Hiroyuki Hase, Toyohide Watanabe: *Character extraction from noisy background for an automatic reference system,* Proceedings of the 5th Int. Conf. on Document Analysis and Recognition, ICDAR, Sep. 1999, Bangalore, India, pp143-146
3. N.Otsu: *A threshold selection method from gray-level histograms,* IEEE Trans. System, Man, and Cybernetics, Vol. 9, No. 1, 1979, pp 62-66
4. Ying Liu, Sargur N. Srihari: *Document image binarization based on texture features,* IEEE Trans. on PAMI, Vol. 19, No. 5, May 1997, pp 540-544
5. Su Liang, M. Ahmadi: *A morphological approach to text string extraction from regular periodic overlapping text/background images,* Graphical Models and Image Processing, CVGIP, Vol. 56, No. 5, Sep. 1994, pp 402-413

6. J.M. White, G.D. Rohrer: *Image thresholding for optical character recognition and other applications requiring character image extraction*, IBM J. Res. Dev. 27(4), 1983, pp 400–410

7. Canny J.: *A computational approach to edge detection*, IEEE Trans. on PAMI, Vol. 8, No. 6, Nov. 1986, pp 679-689

8. Hon-Son Don: A noise attribute thresholding method for document image binarization, Proceedings of the 3rd Int. Conf. on Document Analysis and Recognition, ICDAR'95, pp231-234

9. Stefano Casadei, Sanjoy K. Mitter: A hierarchical approach to high resolution edge contour reconstruction, CVPR'96, June 18-20, 1996, San Francisco, California, IEEE Computer Society Press, pp149-154

10. George Nagy: Twenty years of document image analysis in PAMI, IEEE Trans. on PAMI, Vol. 22, No. 1, Jan. 2000, pp38-62

11. Warren M. Krueger, Keith Phillips: The geometry of differential operators with application to image processing, IEEE Trans. on PAMI, Vol.11, No.12, Dec. 1989, pp1252-1264.

An Enhanced HMM Topology in an LBA Framework for the Recognition of Handwritten Numeral Strings

Alceu de S. Britto Jr.[1,2], Robert Sabourin[1,3,4], Flavio Bortolozzi[1]
and Ching Y. Suen[4]

[1] Pontifícia Universidade Católica do Paraná (PUCPR), Curitiba, Brazil
[2] Universidade Estadual de Ponta Grossa (UEPG), Ponta Grossa, Brazil
[3] École de Technologie Supérieure (ETS), Montreal, Canada
[4] Centre for Pattern Recognition and Machine Intelligence (CENPARMI) Montreal, Canada

Abstract. In this study we evaluate different HMM topologies in terms of recognition of handwritten numeral strings by considering the framework of the Level Building Algorithm (LBA). By including an end-state in a left-to-right HMM structure we observe a significant improvement in the string recognition performance since it provides a better definition of the segmentation cuts by the LBA. In addition, this end-state allows us the use of a two-step training mechanism with the objective of integrating handwriting-specific knowledge into the numeral models to obtain a more accurate representation of numeral strings. The contextual information regarding the interaction between adjacent numerals in strings (spaces, overlapping and touching) is modeled in a pause model built into the numeral HMMs. This has shown to be a promising approach even though it is really dependent on the training database.

Keywords: HMM topology, LBA framework, pause model, handwritten numeral string recognition

1. Introduction

Hidden Markov models have been successfully applied to various pattern recognition environments. Specially to handwriting recognition, in which the HMM approach provides a way of avoiding the prior segmentation of words into characters usually found in OCR systems. This has shown to be a promising strategy, since often word segmentation without the help of a recognizer is difficult or impossible. In this context, the Level Building Algorithm (LBA) [1] is fundamental, since it allows to match models against an observation sequence, without having to first segment the sequence into subsequences that may have been produced by different models.

In this study the LBA is used to recognize handwritten numeral strings using an implicit segmentation-based approach. In this framework we focus on the HMM topology, which is very important in providing a precise matching of the numeral models against the observation sequence representing a numeral string. In addition,

S. Singh, N. Murshed, and W. Kropatsch (Eds.): ICAPR 2001, LNCS 2013, pp. 105–114, 2001.

we investigate a way of integrating in the numeral models some contextual information regarding the interaction between adjacent numerals in strings. For this purpose, we use a two-step training mechanism, in which numeral models previously trained on isolated digits are submitted to a string-based training. In the second step of this training mechanism a pause model is built into the numeral models. Cho, Lee and Kim [2] also use pauses in off-line word recognition and show some significant improvement on the recognition accuracy depending on the dictionary size. They use a number of pause models in order to describe categories of character transitions depending on the neighboring characters. In contrast to their approach, Dolfing [3] assumes that the number of ligatures is limited and models all ligatures with the same pause model. In our work we evaluate two strategies: 1) constructing one pause model by numeral class; 2) constructing one pause model representing all numeral classes.

This work is organized into 6 sections. Section 2 describes our system for the recognition of handwritten numeral strings. Section 3 presents the HMM topologies evaluated in this work. The experiments and discussions are summarized, respectively, in Section 4 and 5. Finally, we draw a conclusion in Section 6.

2. System Outline

The system architecture is shown in Figure 1. In the first module, a word slant normalization method has been modified by considering the slant and contour length of each connected component to estimate the slant of handwritten numeral strings. A detailed description of this process is presented in [4].

In the Segmentation-Recognition module, the string recognition is carried out using an implicit segmentation-based method. This module matches numeral HMMs against the string using LBA. To this end, the numeral string is scanned from left-to-right, while local and global features are extracted from each column. The local features are based on transitions from background to foreground pixels and *vice versa*. For each transition, the mean direction and corresponding variance are obtained by means of the statistic estimators defined in [5].

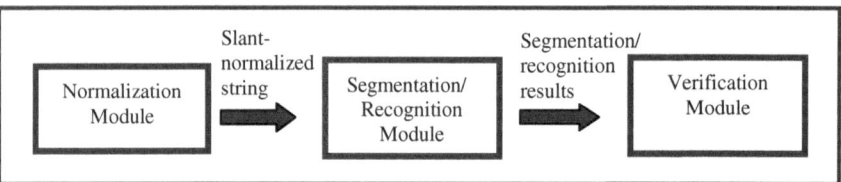

Figure 1. System architecture

These estimators are more suitable for directional observations, since they are based on a circular scale. For instance, given the directional observations $\alpha_1 = 1°$ and $\alpha_2 = 359°$, they provide a mean direction ($\overline{\alpha}$) of $0°$ instead of $180°$ calculated by conventional estimators.

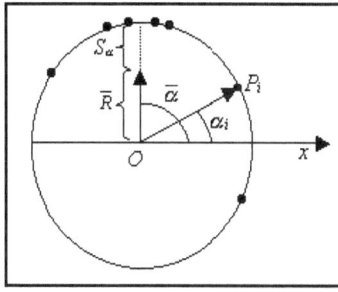

Figure 2. Circular mean direction $\overline{\alpha}$ and variance S_α for a distribution $F(\alpha_i)$

Let $\alpha_1, \ldots, \alpha_i, \ldots, \alpha_N$ be a set of directional observations with distribution $F(\alpha_i)$ and size N. Figure 2 shows that α_i represents the angle between the unit vector $\overline{OP_i}$ and the horizontal axis, while P_i is the intersection point between $\overline{OP_i}$ and the unit circle. The cartesian coordinates of P_i are defined as:

$$(cos(\alpha_i),\ sin(\alpha_i)) \tag{5}$$

The circular mean direction $\overline{\alpha}$ of the N directional observations on the unit circle corresponds to the direction of the resulting vector $(\overline{R})$ obtained by the sum of the unit vectors $(\overline{OP_1}, \ldots, \overline{OP_i}, \ldots, \overline{OP_N})$. The center of gravity $(\overline{C}, \overline{S})$ of the N coordinates $(cos(\alpha_i),\ sin(\alpha_i))$ is defined as:

$$\overline{C} = \frac{1}{N} \sum_{i=1}^{N} cos(\alpha_i) \tag{6}$$

$$\overline{S} = \frac{1}{N} \sum_{i=1}^{N} sin(\alpha_i) \tag{7}$$

These coordinates are used to estimate the mean size of $\overline{R}$, as:

$$\overline{R} = \sqrt{\left(\overline{C}^2 + \overline{S}^2\right)} \tag{8}$$

Then, the circular mean direction can be obtained by solving one of the following equations:

$$sin(\overline{\alpha}) = \frac{\overline{S}}{\overline{R}} \quad \text{or} \quad cos(\overline{\alpha}) = \frac{\overline{C}}{\overline{R}} \tag{9}$$

Finally, the circular variance of $\overline{\alpha}$ is calculated as:

$$S_\alpha = 1 - \overline{R} \qquad 0 \leq S_\alpha \leq 1 \tag{10}$$

To estimate $\overline{\alpha}$ and S_α for each transition of a numeral image, we have considered $\{0°,\ 45°,\ 90°,\ 135°,\ 180°,\ 225°,\ 270°,\ 315°\}$ as the set of directional observations, while $F(\alpha_i)$ is computed by counting the number of successive black pixels over the direction α_i from a transition until the encounter of a white pixel. In Figure 3 the transitions in a column of numeral 5 are enumerated from 1 to 6, and the possible directional observations from transitions 3 and 6 are shown.

In addition to this directional information, we have calculated two other local features: a) relative position of each transition [6], taking into account the top of the digit bounding box, and b) whether the transition belongs to the outer or inner contour, which shows the presence of loops in the numeral image. Since for each column we consider 8 possible transitions, at this point our feature vector is composed of 32 features. The global features are based on horizontal projection (HP) of black pixels for each column, and the derivative of HP between adjacent columns. This constitutes a total of 34 features extracted from each column image and normalized between 0-1. A codebook with 128 entries is created using the LBG algorithm [7].

The last system module is based on an isolated digit classifier, which is under construction. This verification module was not used in the experiments described in this paper.

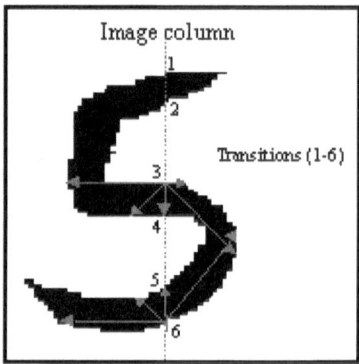

Figure 3. Transitions in a column image of numeral 5, and the directional observations used to estimate the mean direction for transitions 3 and 6

3. Topology of the Numeral HMMs

The topology of the numeral models is defined taking into account the feature extraction method and considering the use of the LBA. The number of states is experimentally defined based on the recognition of isolated numerals. The HMM topology used in the baseline system is shown in Figure 4.

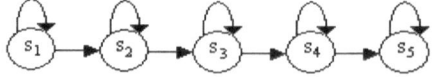

Figure 4. Left-to-right HMM model with 5 states

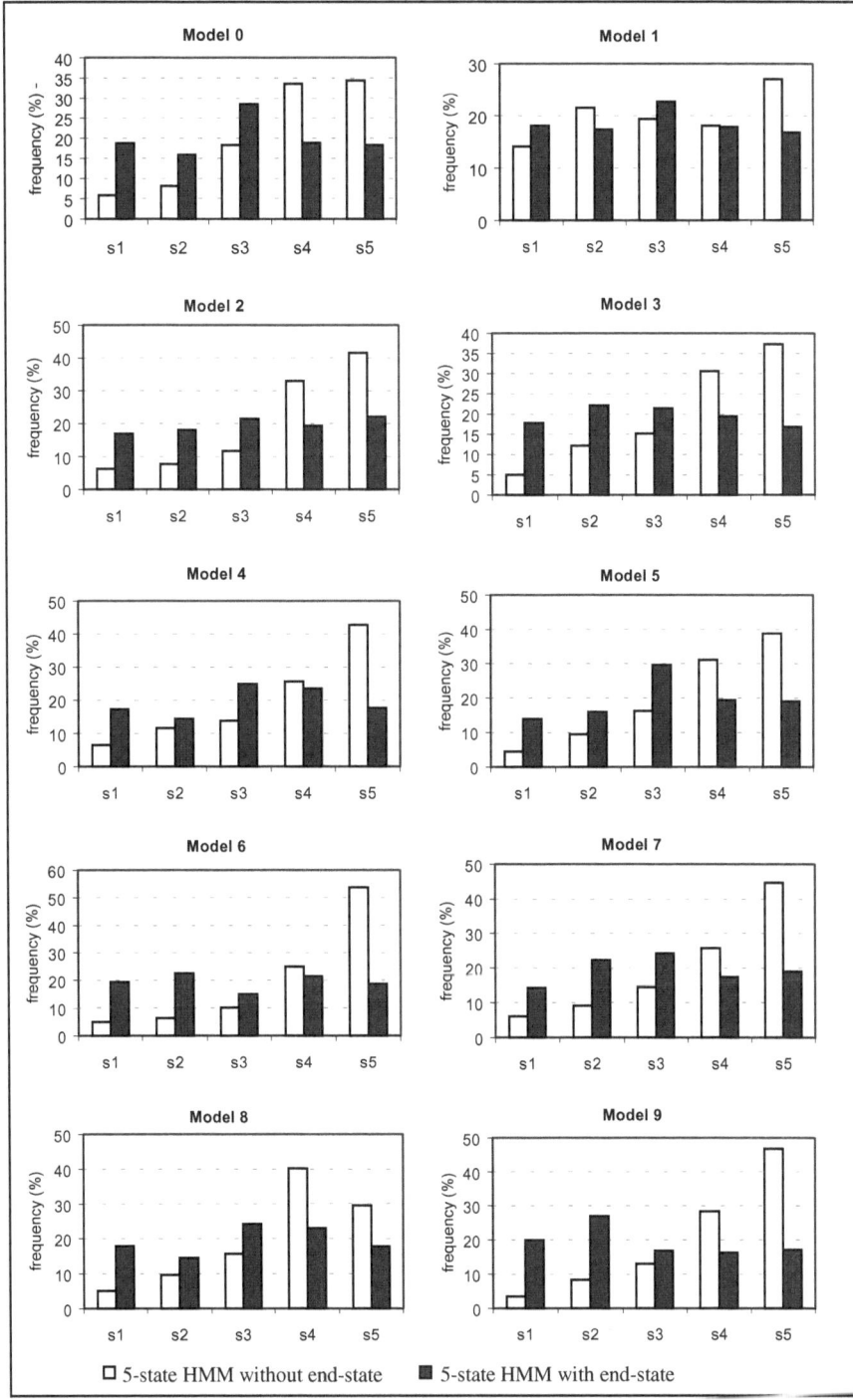

Figure 5. Distributions of observations among the HMM states computed during model training

The same or similar topology can be found in related works. In [8] the authors use it to model character classes to recognize fax printed words. The same structure is used for modeling numeral classes to recognize handwritten numeral strings in [9]. Similar HMM topology, with additional skip transitions, is used for modeling airlines vocabulary in [10]. In all these works the LBA is used as a recognition algorithm.

As we can see the HMM topology used in our baseline system does not present additional states or transitions to allow the concatenation of numeral models, since they are not necessary in the LBA framework. In this system 10 numeral models independently trained on isolated numerals are used to recognize strings, and the LBA is responsible for finding the best sequence of these models for a given numeral string. However, this kind of topology does not allow us to model the interaction between adjacent numerals in strings. Moreover, in the experiments on numeral strings we have observed a significant loss in terms of recognition performance as the string length increases. In order to better understand the behavior of these numeral models, we compute the distribution of observations among the HMM states during the training of them on 50,000 isolated numerals (5,000 samples per class).

We can see the corresponding distributions in Figure 5 as *5-state HMM without end-state*. These unbalanced distributions of observations among the states, associated with the presence of a self-transition with probability value equal to 1.0 in the last state (s_5), have a negative impact on the system segmentation performance. To better explain, let us consider the paths A and B in the LBA trellis in Figure 6, which share the same way until time t=4. Path A reaches the state 5 (s_5) first (at time t=6). From this time path B may not reach the last state even being a promising path. This may happen because the transition probability from state 4 to 5 (a_{45}) (a small value because of the nature of the distributions observed), must compete with the self-transition probability on state 5 (equal to 1.0 since there is no transition going out of this state). Under this condition the numeral recognition at this level may succeed, however without representing the best segmentation path. This non-optimum matching can bring problems to the next levels. This explains why, in the baseline system, the recognition of numeral strings drops drastically as their length increases (see Section 4).

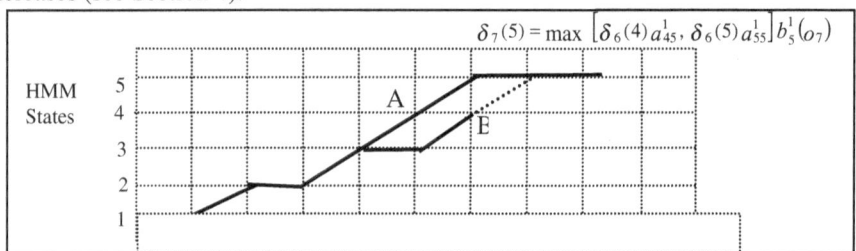

Figure 6. Paths A and B in an LBA level considering model λ_1

To deal with this problem and also adapt the numeral models to a string-based training, we include an end-state in the HMM topology (see Figure 7). The new models show a better distribution of the observations among their states, as we can see in Figure 5 (*5-state HMM with end-sta*te), and avoid a self-transition with probability value equal to 1.0 in the state 5 (s_5). The end-state does not absorb any observation and it is useful to concatenate the numeral models during a string-based training. The positive impact of this modification on the HMM topology to the string recognition is shown in Section 4.

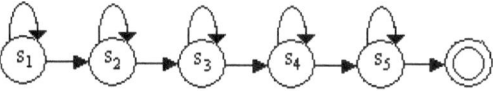

Figure 7. 5-state HMM with an end-state

Based on this new topology, we can pay some attention to the possibility of integrating handwriting-specific knowledge into the model structure to obtain a more accurate representation of numeral strings. We believe that as the knowledge learned from ligatures and spaces between adjacent characters have shown to be very important to increase the word recognition performance, the knowledge about overlapping, touching and spaces between adjacent numerals may play the same role for numeral strings.

Similar to [2,3], we investigate the use of a pause model. The objective is to model inter-digit spaces and local interactions (overlapping, touching) between adjacent numerals in strings. However, our pause model is built-in the numeral models. This strategy allows us to keep the L parameter of the LBA fixed. The pause model is trained on digit-pairs extracted from the NIST database. In this training, for a given digit-pair the corresponding numeral models are concatenated by using the end-state. In fact, the end-state of the first model is replaced with the first state of the second (see Figure 8). The strategy used to train this pause model is presented in the next section.

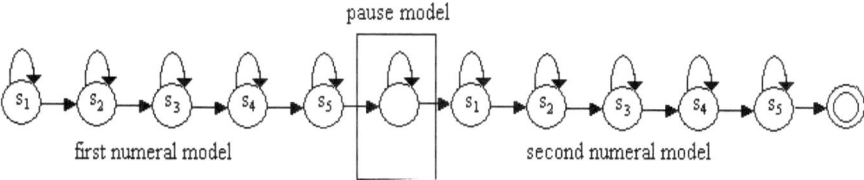

Figure 8. Concatenation of numeral models during string-based training

4. Experiments

The isolated numerals used in these experiments come from the NIST SD19 database. In order to construct 10 numeral models we use 50,000 numeral samples for training, 10,000 for validation and 10,000 for testing. The slant normalization of these numerals is done taking into account contextual information regarding the slant of their original strings, and the feature extraction is performed considering the intra-string size variation. All this process is detailed in [4].

The experiments using numeral strings are based on 12,802 numeral strings extracted from NIST SD19 and distributed into 6 classes: 2_digit (2,370), 3_digit (2385), 4_digit (2,345) and 5_digit (2,316), 6_digit(2,169) and 10_digit(1,217) strings respectively. These strings exhibit different problems, such as touching, overlapping and fragmentation.

During the comparison of the HMM topology with and without the end-state, we did not consider the inter-digit spaces in order to evaluate the LBA in terms of segmentation performance. For each string, features have been extracted considering just foreground pixels (black pixels). There is no symbol to represent inter-digit spaces. This also may give us some idea about the real contribution of the pause model in our system.

Class	HMM without end-state	HMM with end-state	Pause model (1 by class)	Pause model (1 for all classes)
Isolated numerals	91.10	91.73	91.60	91.60
2_digit (2,370)	85.32	87.72	88.23	88.40
3_digit (2,385)	78.19	82.43	83.31	83.61
4_digit (2,345)	71.34	78.17	78.55	78.72
5_digit (2,316)	66.32	75.65	75.35	76.21
2,3,4 and 5_digit (9,416)	**75.32**	**81.00**	**81.40**	**81.77**
6_digit (2,169)	63.85	71.69	71.37	72.01
10_digit (1,217)	44.04	60.64	57.68	61.05
Global (All classes)	**70.43**	**77.51**	**77.45**	**78.15**

Table 1. String recognition results on the test database

For the pause model experiment, we use a two step-training mechanism: 1) 10 numeral models are trained first on isolated digits, 2) the numeral models are submitted to a string-based training using digit pairs (DPs) extracted from the NIST database. The DP database is balanced in terms of number of naturally segmented, overlapping and touching numerals. The NIST series *hsf_0 to hsf_3* were used for providing 15,000 training samples, while *hsf_7* was used for providing 3,500 validation samples.

We use the two-step training mechanism described above to evaluate the following strategies: 1) the use of one pause model for each numeral class; and 2) the use of one pause model representing all numeral classes. In both just the pause model parameters are estimated during the second-step training. The parameters corresponding to the numeral models are kept the same as estimated during the first training step based on isolated numerals. Table 1 resumes all the experiment results, in which a zero-rejection level is used.

5. Discussion

The HMM topology with end-state does not bring a significant improvement to the recognition of isolated numerals (about 0.6%). On the other hand, this brought 7.08% of improvement to the global string recognition rate. This is due the better distribution of the observations between the states, and a better estimation of the self-transition probability in the last HMM-state (s_5). Consequently, the LBA provides a better match of numeral models against the observation sequence. This means a better definition of string segmentation cuts. Maybe, this can also explain the importance given by the authors to space model in [8,9], and the use of durational constraints in [10].

Figure 9 shows an example in which the segmentation cuts at top and bottom were provided respectively by the models with and without end-state. To confirm the improvement on segmentation cuts, we made an error analysis considering the

10_digit strings misrecognized using the models without end-state, which were recognized with the models with end-state. A total of 245 samples were manually checked.

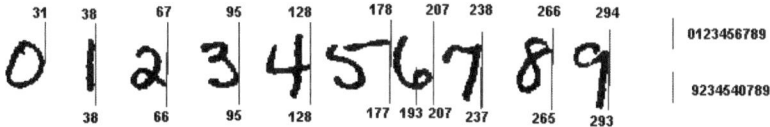

Figure 9: Segmentation points and recognition result produced by the LBA using 5-state HMMs with end-state (top) and without end-state (bottom).

Figure 10(a) shows that 72.2% of these misrecognitions are related to mis-segmentation problems. Moreover, we compute the difference of location of the segmentation points provided by these two HMM-structures in terms of the number of observations. Figure 10(b) shows that the frequencies of location differences equal to 1, 2 and more than 2 observations are respectively 47.3%, 18% and 6.9%.

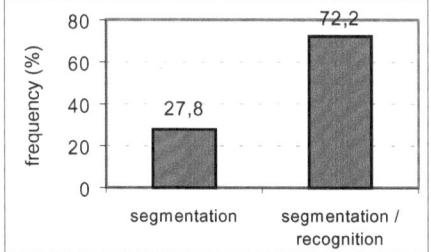 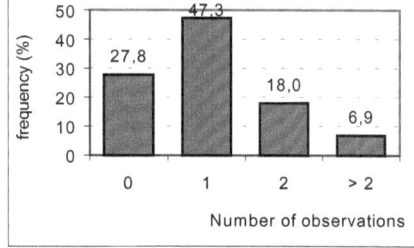

Figure 10: a) Frequency of recognition and recognition/segmentation mistakes; b) Difference between the location of segmentation points considering the number of observations

In the pause model experiments we consider all the spaces (white columns) between adjacent digits in strings. In fact, the pause model is used to absorb all interactions between adjacent numerals including inter-digit spaces, overlapping and touching. The experiment considering one pause model for each numeral class does not show improvements for all numeral string classes. We observe a small loss in terms of recognition rate of numeral strings composed of more than 4 numerals. This is due the lack of training samples of specific digit-pair classes in the database. In fact, the database used for the second-step training is well balanced in terms of natural segmented, overlapping and touching numerals, but it needs also be balanced in terms of isolated numeral classes and digit-pair classes. This experiment also shows that the interaction between adjacent digits varies as the string length. We can see some improvement for all string classes when we use all the database to model just one pause model.

The small improvement obtained by considering the pause model also confirms the nice string segmentation performance provided by the LBA by using the 5-state HMM with end-state. In fact, this shows that even without considering the inter-digit spaces, the models based on this topology can provide a good string segmentation.

6. Conclusions

In this work we have evaluated different HMM topologies on the LBA framework. The inclusion of an end-state in numeral HMM structure allowed us to balance the importance between their states. Under this condition, the LBA finds a more precise match of the numeral models against the observation sequence representing a numeral string. This new HMM structure improves the LBA string segmentation performance. In addition, the end-state provides a way of concatenating the numeral models to evaluate the use of a pause model built-in the numeral models.

The preliminary results on the pause model show us that integrating handwriting-specific knowledge into the model structure to obtain a more accurate representation of numeral strings is a promising approach. However, this approach is strongly dependent on a representative database.

Acknowledgements: The authors wish to thank the Pontifícia Universidade Católica do Paraná (PUC-PR, Brazil), the Universidade Estadual de Ponta Grossa (UEPG, Brazil), the École de Technologie Supérieure (ETS, Canada) and the Centre for Pattern Recognition and Machine Intelligence (CENPARMI, Canada), which have supported this work.

References

1. Rabiner L. and Juang B.H., Fundamentals of Speech Recognition. Prentice Hall, New Jersey, 1993
2. Cho W., Lee S.W., and Kim, J.H. Modeling and Recognition of Cursive Words with Hidden Markov Models, Pattern Recognition 1995; 28:1941-1953
3. Dolfing J.G.A. Handwriting recognition and verification: A hidden Markov approach. PhD. thesis, Eindhoven University of Technology, Netherlands, 1998
4. Britto A. S., Sabourin R., Lethelier E., Bortolozzi F., Suen C.Y. Improvement in handwritten numeral string recognition by slant normalization and contextual information. In: Proceedings of the 7th International Workshop on Frontiers of Handwriting Recognition (7th IWFHR), Netherlands, 2000, pp 323-332
5. Sabourin R., 1990. Une Approache de Type Compréhension de Scène Appliquée au Probleme de la Vérification Automatique de L'Identité par L'Image de la Signature Manuscrite. Thèse de Doctorat, École Polytechnique, Université de Montréal, 1990
6. Mohamed M. and Gader P. Handwritten word recognition using segmentation-free hidden Markov modeling and segmentation-based dynamic programming techniques. IEEE Transactions on Pattern Analysis and Machine Intelligence, 1996;18 548-554
7. Linde Y., Buzo A., and Gray R.M. An algorithm for Vector Quantizer Design. IEEE Transactions on Communications, 1980; COM-28: 84-95
8. Elms A.J., Procter S. and Illingworth J. The Advantage of using an HMM-bases Approach for Faxed Word Recognition. International Journal on Document Analysis and Recognition (IJDAR). 1998; 18-36
9. Procter S., Illingworth J. and Elms A.J., The recognition of handwritten digit strings of unknown length using hidden Markov models, In: Proceedings of the Fourteenth International Conference on Pattern Recognition, 1998, pp 1515-1517
10. Rabiner L. and Levinson L. A speak-independent, syntax-directed, connected word recognition system based on hidden Markov models and Level Building. Transactions on Acoustics, Speech, and Signal Processing, 1985;Vol. ASSP-33, N°. 3.

Segmentation of Printed Arabic Text

Adnan Amin

School of Computer Science and Engineering
University of New South Wales
Sydney 2052, NSW, Australia

Abstract: This paper proposes a new technique to segment Printed Arabic words into characters using Explicit Segmentation. The technique can be divided into several steps: (1) Digitization and preprocessing (2) binary tree construction; and (3) Segmentation. The advantage of this technique is that its execution does depend on either the font or size of character.

Keywords: Segmentation, Construction binary tree, Parallel Thinning, Smoothing, Arabic Characters, Pattern Recognition.

1.   Introduction

Machine recognition of both printed and handwritten characters, has been intensively and extensively researched by scientists in different countries around the world. Characters written in many different languages have been recognized, e.g. from numerals to alphanumeric, and from Roman languages to Oriental languages. However, the infinite varieties of qualities and character shapes produced by handwriting and by modern printing machines have posed a major challenge to researchers in the field of pattern recognition. But the urgent need is there, and it has become increasingly evident that satisfactory solutions to this problem would be very useful in applications where it is necessary to process large volumes of printed and handwritten data,   e.g. in automatic sorting of mail and cheques, payment slips, signature verification, and machine recognition and analysis of engineering drawings.

Many papers have been concerned with Latin, Chinese and Japanese characters, However, although almost a third of a billion people worldwide, in several different languages, use Arabic characters for writing, little research progress, in both on-line and off-line has been   achieved   towards the automatic recognition of Arabic characters. This is a result of the lack of adequate support in terms of funding, and other utilities such as Arabic text database, dictionaries, etc.

S. Singh, N. Murshed, and W. Kropatsch (Eds.): ICAPR 2001, LNCS 2013, pp. 115–126, 2001.

Two techniques have been applied for segmenting machine printed and handwritten Arabic words into individual characters: implicit and explicit segmentations.

(i)   Implicit segmentation (straight segmentation): In this technique, words are segmented directly into letters. This type of segmentation is usually designed with rules that attempt to identify all the character's segmentation points [1, 2].

(ii)   Explicit segmentation: In this case, words are externally segmented into pseudo-letters which are then recognized individually. This approach is usually more expensive due to the increased complexity of finding optimum word hypotheses [3-5].

This paper describes the design and implement of a new technique to segment an Arabic word into characters using explicit segmentation. The technique can be divide into three steps: First, is digitization and Preprocessing step in which the original image is transformed into binary image utilizing a scanner 300 dpi with some cleaning. Then the binary image is thinned using one of the existing thinning algorithms. Second, the skeleton of the image is traced from right to left and a binary tree is constructed. Finally, a segmentation algorithm is used to segment the binary tree into subtrees such that each subtree describes a character in the image.

2.   General Characteristics of the Arabic Writing System

A comparison of the various characteristics of Arabic, Latin, Hebrew and Hindi scripts are outlined in Table 1. Arabic, like Hebrew, is written from right to left. Arabic text (machine printed or handwritten) is cursive in general and Arabic letters are normally connected on the base line. This feature of connectivity will be shown to be important in the segmentation process. Some machine printed and handwritten texts are not cursive, but most Arabic texts are, and thus it is not surprising that the recognition rate of Arabic characters is lower than that of disconnected characters such as printed English.

Table 1. Comparison of various scripts.

Characteristics	Arabic	Latin	Hebrew	Hindi
Justification	R-to-L	L-to-R	R-to-L	L-to-R
Cursive	Yes	No	No	Yes
Diacritics	Yes	No	No	Yes
Number of vowels	2	5	11	–
Letters shapes	1 – 4	2	1	1
Number of letters	28	26	22	40
Complementary characters	3	–	–	–

Arabic writing is similar to English in that it uses letters (which consist of 28 basic letters), numerals, punctuation marks, as well as spaces and special symbols. It differs from English, however, in its representation of vowels since Arabic utilizes various diacritical markings. The presence and absence of vowel diacritics indicates different meanings in what would otherwise be the same word. For example, □ □ □ □ □ is the Arabic word for both "school" and "teacher". If the word is isolated, diacritics are essential to distinguish between the two possible meanings. If it occurs in a sentence, contextual information inherent in the sentence can be used to infer the appropriate meaning.

The Arabic alphabet is represented numerically by a standard communication interchange code approved by the Arab Standard and Metrology Organization (ASMO). Similar to the American Standard Code for Information Interchange (ASCII), each character in the ASMO code is represented by one byte. An English letter has two possible shapes, capital and small. The ASCII code provides separate representations for both of these shapes, whereas an Arabic letter has only one representation in the ASMO table. This is not to say, however, that the Arabic letter has only one shape. On the contrary, an Arabic letter might have up to four different shapes, depending on its relative position in the text. For instance, the letter (□ A'in) has four different shapes: at the beginning of the word (preceded by a space), in the middle of the word (no space around it), at the end of the word (followed by a space), and in isolation (preceded by an unconnected letter and followed by a space). These four possibilities are exemplified in Fig.1.

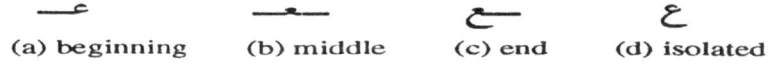

(a) beginning   (b) middle   (c) end   (d) isolated

Fig. 1. Different shapes of the Arabic letter " • A'in "

In addition, different Arabic characters may have exactly the same shape, and are distinguished from each other only by the addition of a complementary character (see Appendix). Complementary characters are positioned differently, for instance, above, below or within the confines of the character. Figure 2 depicts two sets of characters, the first set having five characters and the other set three characters. Clearly, each set contains characters which differ only by the position and/or the number of dots associated with it. It is worth noting that any erosion or deletion of these complementary characters results in a misrepresentation of the character. Hence, any thinning algorithm needs to efficiently deal with these dots so as not to change the identity of the character.

Arabic writing is cursive and is such that words are separated by spaces. However, a word can be divided into smaller units called subwords (see Appendix). Some Arabic characters are not connectable with the succeeding character. Therefore, if one of these characters exists in a word, it divides that word into two subwords. These characters appear only at the tail of a subword, and the succeeding character forms the head of the next subword. Figure 3 shows three Arabic words with one, two, and three subwords. The first word consists of one subword which has nine letters; the second has two subwords with three and one letter, respectively. The last word contains three subwords, each consisting of only one letter.

Fig. 2. Arabic characters differing only with regard to the position and number of associated dots.

قسطنطينية   مقدس   أوردت
(a)   (b)   (c)

Fig. 3.. Arabic words with constituent subwords.

Arabic writing is similar to Latin in that it contains many fonts and writing styles. The letters are overlaid in some of these fonts and styles. As a result, word segmentation using the baseline, which is the line on which all Arabic characters are connected, is not possible. Furthermore, characters of the same font have different sizes (i.e. characters may have different widths even though the two characters have the same font and point size). Hence, word segmentation based on a fixed size width cannot be applied to Arabic.

3.   Digitization and Preprocessing

3. 1.   Digitization

The first phase in our character recognition system is digitization. Documents to be processed are first scanned and digitized. A 300 dpi scanner is used to digitize the image. This generates a TIFF file which is then converted to 1-bit plane PBM file. The PBM format contains a small header which incorporates a file stamp followed by the dimensions of the image in pixels. The remainder of the file contains the image data.

3.2.   Pre-thinning and Thinning

This step aims to reduce the noise due to the binarization process. The pre-thinning algorithm used in this paper is as follows:

Input. A digitized image I in PBM format.

Output. A pre-thinned image I', also in PBM format.

begin

1.   For each pixel P in image I, let $P0$ to $P7$ be its 8 neighbors, starting from the east neighbor and counted in an anti-clockwise fashion.

2.   Let $B(P) = P0 + P2 + P4 + P6$. Let P' be the corresponding pixel of P in the pre-thinned image I'.

3.   **If** B (P) < 2 **then** set P' to white

> **Else If** $B(P) > 2$ then set P' to black

> **Else** set P' to the value of P;

end

3. 3.   Thinning

The thinning of elongated objects is a fundamental preprocessing operation in image analysis, defined as the process of reducing the width of a line-like object from several pixels to a single pixel. The resultant image is called "the skeleton".

This paper adopts Jang and Chin's one pass parallel thinning algorithm [6] because it gives skeletons with fewer spurious branches. Figure 4 illustrates an original scanned image and the resulting skeleton after applying the thinning.

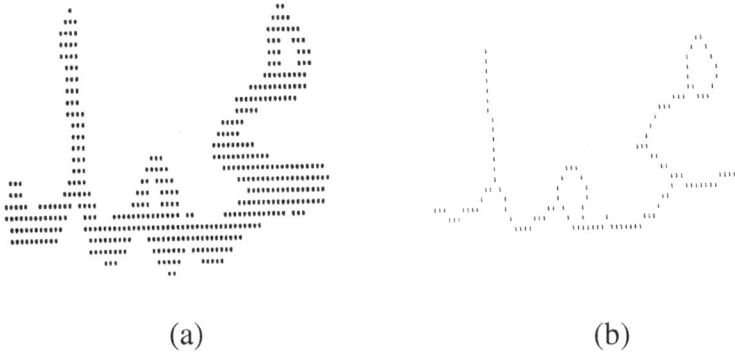

(a)   (b)

Fig. 4. An example for an Arabic word before and after thinning.

After the thinning of the binary image, the structure of the image can be recorded by tracing the skeleton. However, the thinning process might alter the shape of the character, which in turn makes difficult to be recognized. Some of the common problems encountered during the thinning process include the elimination of vertical notches in some characters and elimination or erosion of complimentary characters. These modification make the recognition of the thinned image a difficult task even for nature human visual processing.

4.   Thinned Image Tracing

The objective of this step in the process is to build a binary tree with all the information describing the structure of the image. The technique used involves tracing the thinned image using 3 x 3 window, and recording the structure of the traced parts. The image structure is written using some primitives such as lines, loop, and double loops etc.. This approach has a number of advantages:

(a). *Generality*: The technique can be applied to any font or size of Arabic text. In addition, it can be applied to hand printed text. Furthermore, the technique can be used in processing other language data such as Latin or Chinese.

(b). *Simple Segmentation:* The technique will simplify the segmentation process. The examination of the subword structure from right to left will identify potential points for segmentation. Some of these points are false segmentation points (i.e. they are within one character). However, all of the segmentation points (i.e. points between two consecutive characters) are part of these potential points.

The binary tree consists of several nodes. Each node describes the shape of the corresponding part of the subword. The structure of the node in the binary tree is show in Figure 5:

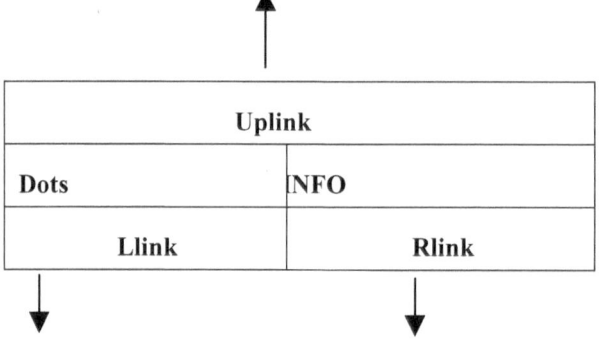

Fig. 5. The node of the binary tree.

Where Uplink is pointing to the parent node, the Rlink is pointed to the right son of that node, and Llink is pointed to the left son of that node. The Dots field signals the existence of complimentary characters in this part of the subword. The INFO field contains the primitive description of the corresponding part in the subword.

The following points are taken into consideration when building the binary tree:

1.   The primitives used in the INFO field of the subtree node are the eight Freeman codes [7], 0 through 7; the Loop (L); and Double loop (LL).

2.   The INFO field contains a description of the structure of the binary image which corresponds to a part of the subword. This description will terminates if a junction point is reached (the junction point is described as the point at which tracing can follow more than one possible path).

3.   The L (Loop) and LL (Double loop) primitives are identified if the junction points force a looping connection within the binary tree. In other words, every time there is a pointer from a node in the ith level of the tree to another node not in the $I + 1^{st}$ level of the tree, it is regarded as either an L or LL primitive.

4.   The tracing of the complimentary characters takes place after the termination of subword tracing. The complimentary characters, if they exust in the subword, can exist in any one of the following cases:

One.   One dot above the subword baseline.
Two.   One dot below the subword baseline.
Three.   One dot within the subword baseline.
Four.   Two dots above the subword baseline.
Five.   Two dots below the subword baseline.
Six. Three dots above the subword baseline.
Seven.   Zig-zag shape above the subword baseline.
Eight.   Zig-zag shape within the subword baseline.
Nine.   Vertical bar on some of the characters, in the case that the bar is separated from the main body of the character.

The image of the complimentary character can be identified as an image which fits into a small window. The size of the window is a parameter of the font point size. In the experiments performed, the window used was 45 pixels in perimeter. Certain features of the image within the window such as the length, width and density of the image, can be used to identify the type of complimentary character.

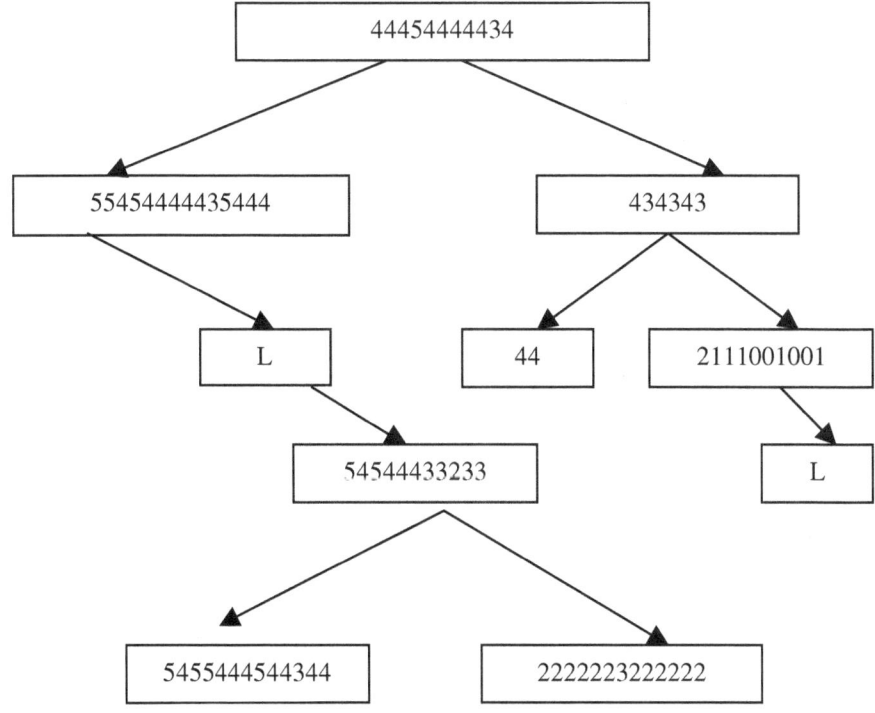

Fig. 6. Binary tree of the image in Figure 4(b)

The binary tree of the image of Figure 4(b) is depicted in Figure 6 above. After the construction of the binary tree takes place according to the above rules, the smoothing of the tree is performed. The smoothing of the binary tree is designed to;

(a). Minimize the number of the node in the tree.

(b). Minimize the Freeman code string in the INFO field of the nodes, and

(c). Eliminate or minimize any noise in the thinned image.

The smoothing phase of the binary tree can be summarized as follows:

(a). *Eliminated the empty nodes:* All the nodes which have an empty INFO field are eliminated. The only exception is the root node which can retain an empty INFO field. An empty INFO field is defined as the field with the null string or one Freeman code character.

(b): *Smooth the Freeman Code:*   In this study,   we use simple but effective smoothing algorithm, illustrated in Figure 7 for direction 0 only. The patterns and codes are rotated for other directions. Any pattern in the first column is replaced by the pattern in the second column. Thus, the string 070010 is replaced by 000000.

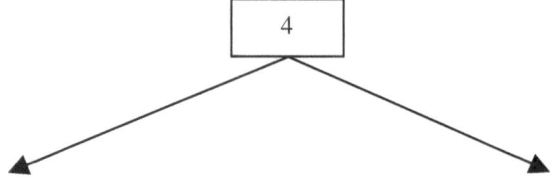

Fig. 7. Smoothing algorithm.

(c). *Compact the string in the INFO field:* Note that the string of Freeman code can be compacted by replacing it by a shorter string without any lose in information. The shorter form is the Freeman code character and its length. Therefore, if the INFO field in a node contains the following string:

$$2222 \quad 4444444444 \quad 6666666$$

it will be replaced by

$$2_4 \quad 4_{10} \quad 6_7$$

The length of the Freeman code can be used later in the recognition process to remove any ambiguities if necessary.

The smoothed binary tree of the image in Figure 4 (b) is depicted in Figure 8.

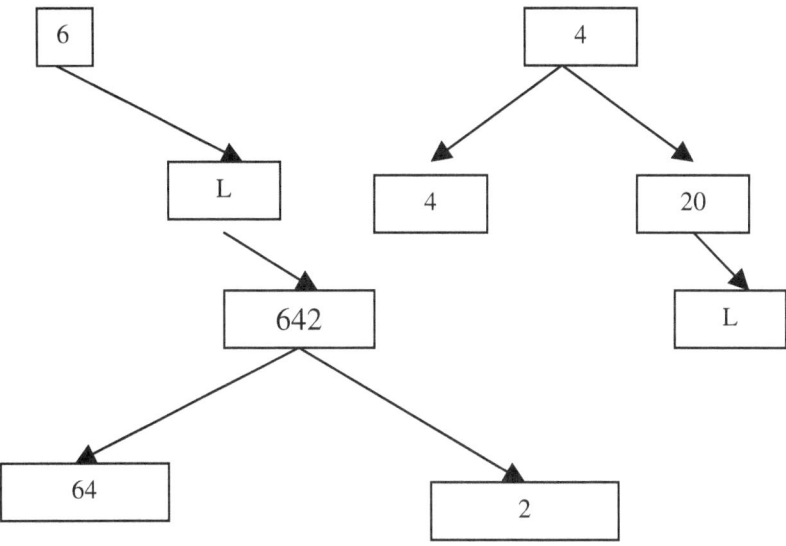

Fig. 8. The smoothed binary tree of the image in Figure 4 (b).

5. Segmentation of the Subword

Segmentation is defined as the process of dividing a subword into characters. This phase is a necessary and crucial step in recognizing printed Arabic text. To segment an Arabic subword into characters, the fundamental property of connectivity is decomposed. Segmentation techniques can be classified

There are two major problems with the traditional segmentation method which depends on the baseline:

(i)   Overlapping of adjacent Arabic characters occurs naturally, see Fig. 9 (a). Hence, no baseline exists. This phenomenon is common in both typed and handwritten Arabic text.

(ii)   The connection between two characters is often short. Therefore, placing the segmentation points is a difficult task. In many cases, the potential segmentation points will be placed within a character rather than between characters.

The word in Fig. 9 (a) was segmented utilizing a baseline technique. Figure 9 (b) shows the proper segmentation and the result of the new segmentation method is shown in Fig. 9 (c).

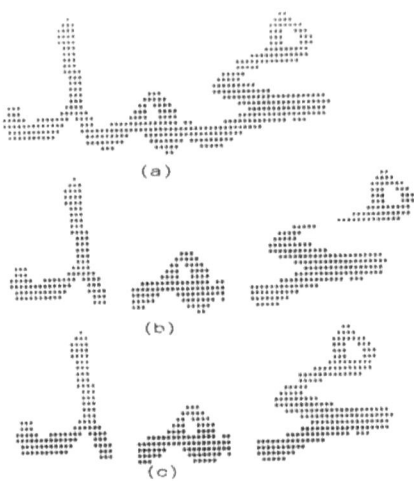

Fig. 9. Example of an Arabic word • • • • and different techniques of the segmentation.

The basic idea in the segmentation process, in this case, can be summarized in the following points:

Neun. The binary tree can be traversed in an order such that first node in the traversal process contains the beginning of the first character. However, this node is not necessarily the root node.

ii.   A character description is then spread in one or more of the tree node INFO field. Nevertheless, these nodes are placed such that their traversal is undertaken one after the other depending on the shape of the character. Hence, the node which processes the beginning of a character is traversed first while the node which has the end of the character is traversed last.

iii. Some of the characters which are non-connectable from left may be contained in one node, in addition to the end of the proceeding character. In such a case, the node must be the last node traversed in the subword.

iv. A binary tree with one node indicates that the subword corresponding to that tree contains one or two characters.

During the traversal process, the subword is segmented into characters. The segmentation process can be viewed as the way to identified the beginning of the next character or realize the end of the current character. Whenever the start of a character is identified, the character "@" is concatenated to the string in the INFO field of the node. In a similar manner the character "*" is concatenated to the string in the INFO field of the node that contains the end of a character.

The process produces several subtrees each containing the Freeman code description of a character in the subword. Figure 11 depicts the tree corresponding to the subword shown in Figure 5(b). the word contains four characters. The four characters of the sunword are describes as:

1st character : in the nodes 1, 2.

2nd character: in the nodes 3, 4, 5, 6.

3rd character: in the nodes 7, 8.

4th character: in the nodes 9, 10.

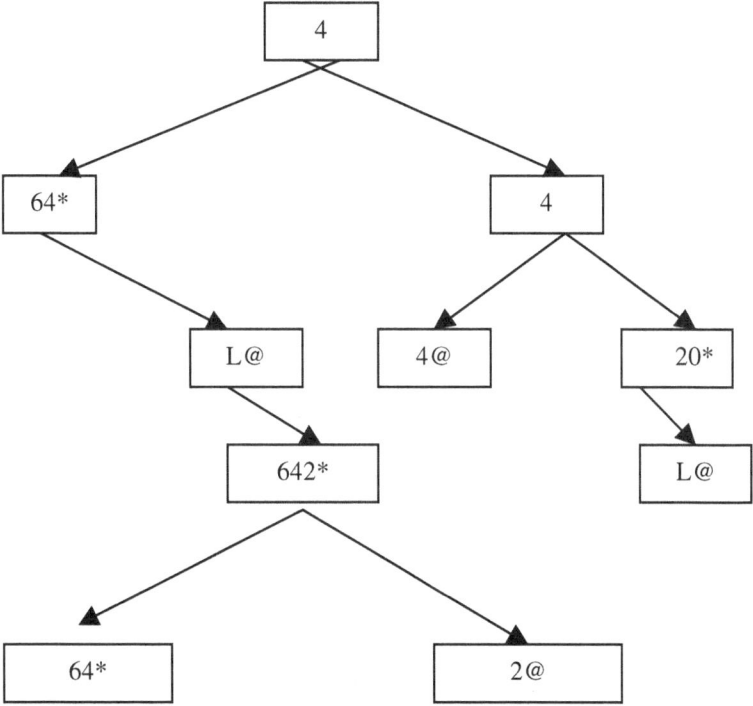

Fig. 10. Segmentation of the Binary tree shown in Figure 9.

6. Conclusion

This paper presents a new algorithm to segment Arabic word into characters. The algorithm can be applied to any font and it permits the overlay of characters. The algorithm was tested by many different fonts and size for the Arabic alphabet which ranged from excellent print to poor quality and the results was satisfactory.

The thinning of the binary image was used in order to produce a correct representation of the structure of the image by tracing the skeleton. However, due to the erosion experienced in the image, some of the characters were not segmented properly.

This is still an open research area and this is because of the segmentation problem, which is in fact similar to the segmentation of cursive script in many languages, and because of the complexity of Arabic characters.

References

1. A. Amin and G. Masini, Machine recognition of muti-fonts printed Arabic texts, 8th *International Conf. on Pattern Recognition,* Paris, 392–395, 1986.
2. A. Amin, Arabic Character Recognition. Handbook of Character Recognition and Document Image Analysis edited by H Bunke and P S P Wang, May 1997.
3. H. Almuallim and S. Yamaguchi, A method of recognition of Arabic cursive handwriting, *IEEE, Trans. Pattern Anal. and Machine Intell.* PAMI-9, 715–722, 1987.
4. V. Margner, SARAT- A system for the recognition of Arabic printed text, *11th Int. Conf. on Pattern Recognition*, 1992, 561–564.
5. B. Al-Badr and R. Haralick, Segmentation-free word recognition with application to Arabic, *3rd Int. Conf. on Document Analysis and Recognition*, Montreal, 1995, 355–359.
6. B.K. Jang and R.T. Chin, One-pass parallel thinning: analysis, properties, and quantitative evaluation, *IEEE Trans. Pattern Anal. Mach. Intell.* PAMI-14, 1129-1140 (1992).
7.   H. Freeman, On the encoding of arbitrary geometric configuration, *IEEE. Trans. Electronic Comp. EC-10 (1968)* 260–268.

A Time–Length Constrained Level Building Algorithm for Large Vocabulary Handwritten Word Recognition

Alessandro L. Koerich[1,2], Robert Sabourin[1,2], and Ching Y. Suen[2]

[1]Laboratoire d'Imagerie, de Vision et d'Intelligence Artificielle
École de Technologie Supérieure
Montréal, QC, Canada

[2]Centre for Pattern Recognition and Machine Intelligence
Concordia University
Montréal, QC, Canada

Abstract

In this paper we introduce a constrained Level Building Algorithm (LBA) in order to reduce the search space of a Large Vocabulary Handwritten Word Recognition (LVHWR) system. A time and a length constraint are introduced to limit the number of frames and the number of levels of the LBA respectively. A regression model that fits the response variables, namely, accuracy and speed, to a non–linear function of the constraints is proposed and a statistical experimental design technique is employed to analyse the effects of the two constraints on the responses. Experimental results prove that the inclusion of these constraints improve the recognition speed of the LVHWR system without changing the recognition rate significantly.

1 Introduction

In spite of recent advances in the field of handwriting recognition, few early studies have addressed the problem of large vocabulary off–line handwritten word recognition [1] [2] [3]. The most frequent simplification has been a pre–selection of possible candidate words before the recognition based on other sources of knowledge [4]. The majority of works have focused on improving the accuracy of small vocabulary systems while the speed is not taken into account.

In HMM–based systems, to handle the huge search space and keep search effort as small as possible, generally beam search is used together with the Viterbi algorithm. Beam search finds locally, i.e. at the current frame, best state hypothesis and discard

S. Singh, N. Murshed, and W. Kropatsch (Eds.): ICAPR 2001, LNCS 2013, pp. 127–136, 2001.

all other state hypotheses that are less probable than the locally best hypothesis by a fixed threshold [5]. The conventional LBA does not incorporate any kind of time or length constraint. Rabiner and Levinson [7] introduced global duration constraints built into the algorithm to limit the duration of the models.

In this work, we introduce two constraints to the LBA, one to limit the number of frames at each level and another to limit the number of levels of the LBA. Furthermore, we characterize the performance of the system by two responses, recognition rate (RR) and recognition speed (RS), and we assume that these responses are governed by the two constraints. A statistical experimental design technique [8] is employed to better characterize the behaviour of the LVHWR system as well as to optimise its performance as a function of these two constraints.

This paper is organized as follows. Section 2 gives an overview of the LVHWR system. Section 3 introduces the two constraints to the LBA. Section 4 describes the experimental plan, the statistical analysis of the experimental data and the results of the verification experiment over another database. Finally, some conclusions are drawn in the last section.

2 The LVHWR System

This section presents a brief overview of the structure and the main components of the LVHWR system. The system is composed of several modules: pre–processing, segmentation, feature extraction, training and recognition. The pre–processing normalizes the word images in terms of slant and size. After, the images are segmented into graphemes and the sequence of segments is transformed into a sequence of symbols (or features). There is a set of 69 models among characters, digits and special characters that are modelled by a 10–state–arc–based HMM [4]. Training of the HMMs is done by using the Maximum Likelihood criterion and through the Baum–Welch algorithm. Recognition is based on a syntax–directed level building algorithm (SDLBA) using a tree–structured lexicon generated from a 36,100–word vocabulary.

The lexicon is organized as a character tree (Fig. 1). If the spelling of two or more words contains the same n initial characters, they share a single sequence of n character HMMs representing that initial portion of their spelling. The recognition engine works in such a way that for a certain lexicon size (from 10 to 30,000) made up of words randomly chosen from the global vocabulary, the corresponding word HMMs are made up by the concatenation of character HMMs. All words are matched against the sequence of observations extracted from the word image and the probability that such word HMMs have generated that sequence of observations are computed. The word candidate is that one that provides the highest likelihood.

A crucial problem of such a system is the recognition speed. Since we do not know a priori the case of the characters we need to test both uppercase and lowercase characters at each level of the LBA and that increase the size of the search space. For digits and symbols, only a single model is tested at each level of the LBA. This approach provides good recognition rates but at the cost of low speed for lexicons that contain more than 1,000 entries. Therefore, our goal is to find a best compromise between the recognition rate and the recognition speed when considering large vocabularies.

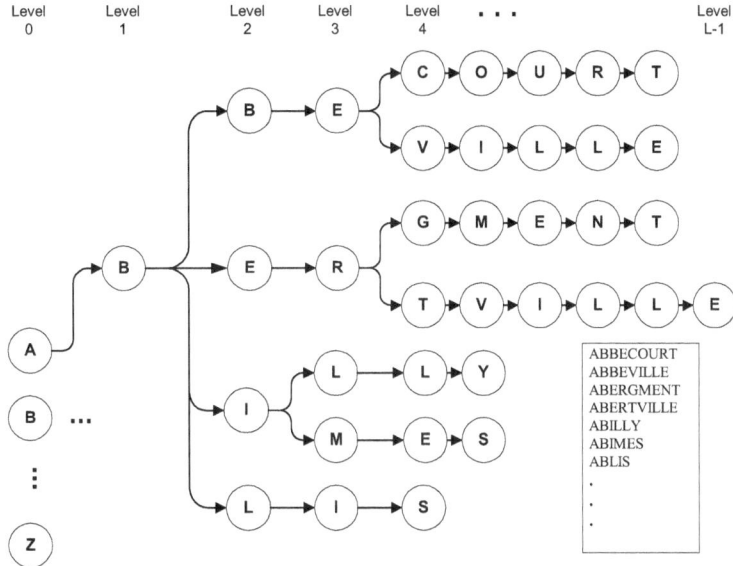

Figure 1: Tree–structured lexicon

2.1 Level Building Algorithm (LBA)

The LBA has been used for a long time in speech recognition [7], and more recently on handwriting recognition. Given a set of individual character models $c = \{c_0, c_1, c_2, ..., c_{K-1}\}$ where K denotes the number of models and a sequence of observations $O = \{o_0, o_1, ..., o_{T-1}\}$, where T denotes the length of the sequence, recognition means decoding O into the sequence of models. Namely, it is to match the observation sequence to a state sequence of models with maximum joint likelihood. The LBA jointly optimises the segmentation of the sequence into subsequences produced by different models, and the matching of the subsequences to particular models.

In the LVHWR system, we have adapted the LBA to take into account some particular characteristics of our character model since it is modelled by a 10–state–left–right–arc–based HMM, and also to take into account some contextual information. Since the lexical tree guides the recognition process, the LBA incorporates some constraints to handle the language syntax provided by the lexical tree as well as the contextual information related to the character class transition probabilities. Different from an open vocabulary problem where all character HMMs are permitted in all levels of the LBA, here the character HMMs that will be tested in each level depend on the sequence of nodes of the lexical tree. Furthermore, since only two character models compete in each level of the LBA, one corresponding to the uppercase and other corresponding to the lowercase character, it will be only necessary to compute the likelihood of two character HMMs at each level of the LBA. For digits and special characters, only one model is computed by level.

3 Incorporating Time and Length Constraints to the LBA

The SDLBA presented by Koerich *et al.* [3] is constrained only by the HMM topology and the lexical tree. The SDLBA implies the testing of the whole sequence of observations at each level. Due to the fact that our HMMs do not include self–transitions, we know that such a model can emit a limited number of observations. In other words, we have a priori knowledge of the model duration since it is implicitly modelled by the HMM topology [9]. Furthermore, it seems to be wasteful to align the whole observation sequence at all levels of the LBA, since it is expected that in average four observations be emitted at each level of the LBA. Therefore, limiting the number of observations at each level could reduce the size of the search space.

If we take into account again the topology of our HMM, it is easy to verify that short observation sequences are more likely to be generated by short words. Therefore, it seems useless to align the observation sequences with nodes of high levels if the sequence is short. Nevertheless, we know in advance the length of the sequence of features and considering that each character model can emit 0, 2, 4 or 6 observations, we can estimate from the length of the sequence of features the length of the words that could have generated such a sequence and use such information to limit the search to words with appropriate lengths. Therefore, it is expected that the performance of the system will be improved by constraining the LBA both in time and in length without changing the accuracy significantly.

3.1 Time Constraint

The time constraint concerns the limitation of the number of frames aligned at each level of LBA. We introduce two variables: $FL_{IT}(l)$ and $FL_{FT}(l)$. The first one denotes the index of the first frame while the second one denotes the index of the last observation frame that will be aligned at each level of the LBA. Both variables are functions of the level (l). Figure 2 shows how these two constraints are incorporated to the LBA.

To incorporate these two constraints into the LBA, the equations of the LBA are not modified, but just the range of the variable t that denotes the frame index. The variable t, that originally ranges from 0 to $T-1$, now, its range will be given by equation (1).

$$t = FL_{IT}(l), FL_{IT}(l)+1, FL_{IT}(l)+2,..., FL_{FT}(l) \tag{1}$$

where $FL_{IT}(l)$ and $FL_{FT}(l)$ must be integers and they are given by equations (2) and (3) respectively. The lower and upper limits for $FL_{IT}(l)$ and $FL_{FT}(l)$ are 0 to $T-1$ respectively.

$$FL_{IT}(l) = \begin{cases} 0 & \text{if } l = 0 \\ l - FL_I & \text{if } l > 0 \end{cases} \tag{2}$$

$$FL_{FT}(l) = 6.(l + FL_F)$$ (3)

where FL_I and FL_F are the two control factors to be determined.

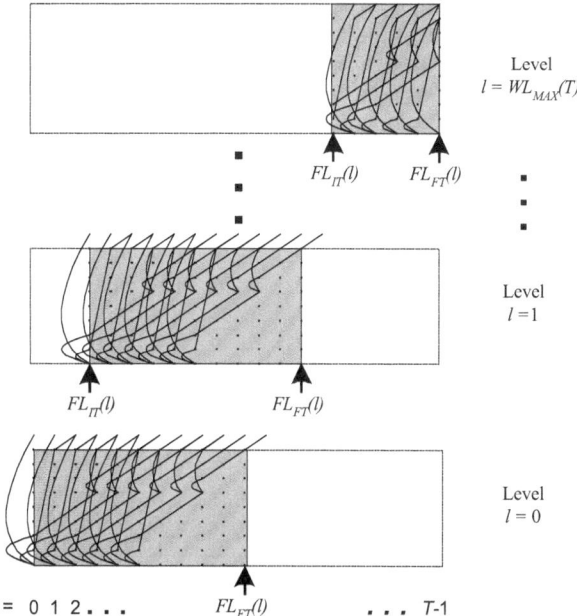

Figure 2: LBA incorporating time and length constraints

3.2 Length Constraint

As we have discussed in the first paragraphs of section 3, the length constraint concerns the limitation of the number of levels of the LBA. We introduce the variable $WL_{MAX}(T)$ which denotes the maximum number of levels of the LBA for a given observation sequence with length T. To incorporate this constraint to the LBA, the equations of the LBA are preserved, but the range of the variable l that denotes the level index, is modified slightly. Now, instead of ranging from levels 0 to $L-1$, the range will be given by equation (4).

$$l = 0,1,2,...,WL_{MAX}(T)$$ (4)

where $WL_{MAX}(T)$ is an integer given by equation (5) and its lower and upper limits are given by the shortest and the longest word in the lexicon respectively.

$$WL_{MAX}(T) = \frac{T}{WL}$$ (5)

where WL is the control factor to be determined.

4 Factorial Analysis

Here we introduce a formal method to determine the values of the control factors (FL_I, FL_F, and WL) based on a statistical experimental design technique that optimises the performance of the LVHWR system. In order to simplify our analysis, we take into account only two control factors, FL_I and WL. The value of the other control factor, FL_F, is fixed equal to 1.

First, we derive two regression models where the independent variables are FL_I, and WL, and the dependent variables are the responses of the system: recognition rate (RR) and recognition speed (RS). Afterwards, a complete factorial plan is employed to gain information on the control factors and to determine the coefficients of the regression models. Based on these regression models, the optimal values of the control factors that jointly optimise both RR and RS can be determined.

4.1 Multiple Regression Model

We need to establish a multiple regression model before carrying out any experiment. We assume that the responses RR and RS are approximated by the mean (M), the two control factors (FL_I and WL), the square of the control factors (FL_I^2 and WL^2), and the interaction between them ($FL_I.WL$). We assume that equation (6) gives the regression model for the recognition rate (RR) while equation (7) gives the regression model for the recognition speed (RS).

$$RR \cong M_{RR} + a_1 FL_I + a_2 WL + a_3 FL_I^2 + a_4 WL^2 + a_5 FL_I.WL \qquad (6)$$

$$RS \cong M_{RS} + b_1 FL_I + b_2 WL + b_3 FL_I^2 + b_4 WL^2 + b_5 FL_I.WL \qquad (7)$$

By analysing RS and RR for different values of WL and FL_I, it is possible to determine the means M_{RR} and M_{RS} and estimate the coefficients $a_1, ..., a_5$ and $b_1, ..., b_5$ for the control factors and the interactions.

4.2 Experimental Design

Since we have only two control factors, we can use a complete factorial plan, assigning three levels to each factor to capture the linear and the quadratic effects of both constraints over the responses. For this plan we have only 9 treatment combinations and 8 degrees of freedom (df's) to estimate the effects in the process we are investigating. However, to accommodate the non–linear effects and the interactions, we replicate the experiments by using a different random lexicon. Therefore, we will have 18 treatment combinations from which we lose 1 df due to finding the mean of the data and other 17 df's to estimate the effects.

Eighteen experimental runs were conducted, corresponding to the 18 combinations of the two control factors (9 for each random lexicon) and both RR and RS were measured. In these experiments, we have used a validation set that has been taken from the Service de Recherche Technique de la Poste (*SRTP*) database. The *SRTP* database is composed of digitised images of French postal envelopes. The information written on the envelopes is labelled and segmented. This dataset is composed of 3,475 images of French city names. The experiments were carried out for lexicons with 10, 100, 1,000, 5,000, 10,000, 20,000 and 30,000 entries.

4.3 Analysis of Results

In order to perform a multifactor analysis of variance for *RR* and *RS*, we have constructed various tests and graphs to determine which factors have a statistically significant effect on both responses for different lexicon sizes. Figure 3 shows an example of the effects of the linear and quadratic terms of both *WL* and FL_l in both responses for a 100–entry lexicon. The control factor *WL* has the most pronounced effect on *RR*. The effect of this control factor is approximately quadratic. The other control factor has less effect and it seems to be approximately linear. On the other hand, the control factor *WL* has the most pronounced effect on *RS*, but the effect due to the control factor FL_l is also pronounced. The effect of both factors is approximately quadratic.

For each lexicon size, the sum of squares, the mean of squares, and the Fischer coefficients were computed. All Fischer coefficients were based on the mean square error. For the different lexicon sizes, both *WL* and FL_l have a statistically significant effect on *RR*. For the control factor FL_l, the quadratic effect can be neglected. On the other hand, both the linear and the quadratic effects of the factor *WL* are significant. These results confirm what we have seen in Figure 3. Both constraints have a statistically significant effect on *RS* and the linear and quadratic effects of both constraints are significant. The effects of the interaction of the two control factors are not significant and they can be neglected. The same behaviour was observed for the different lexicon sizes.

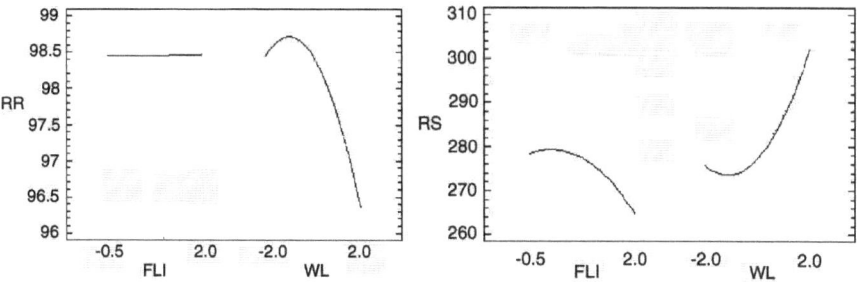

Figure 3: Main effects of the control factors on *RR* and *RS* for a 100–entry lexicon

The coefficients of the regression models can be determined by using a least–square procedure [11]. For each lexicon size, we will have different multiple regression equations that have been fitted to the experimental data.

4.4 Optimisation of Parameters

Optimisation involves estimating the relationship between *RR* and *RS*, and the two control factors. Once the form of this relationship is known approximately, the constraints may be adjusted to jointly optimise the system performance.

In our system an optimal response means maximizing both *RR* and *RS*. Therefore, we need to determine the combination of experimental factors that simultaneously optimise both response variables. We do so by maximizing equations (6) and (7) for each lexicon size. The combination of control factor levels that achieves the overall optimum responses for each lexicon size is given in Figure 4.

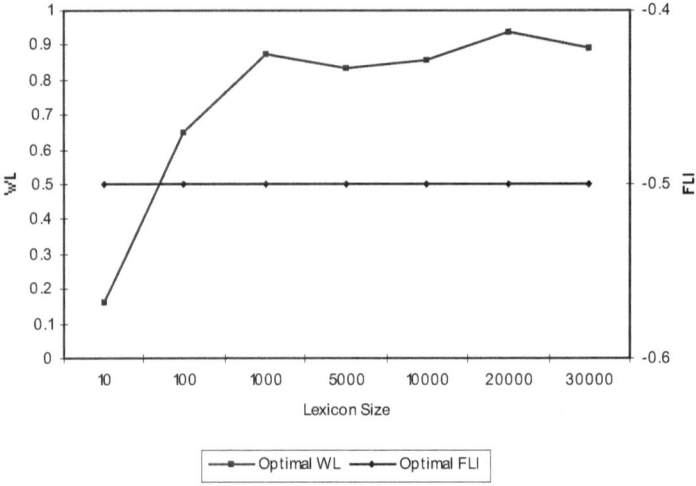

Figure 4: Optimal control factor values for each lexicon size

4.5 Experimental Results

In order to demonstrate the applicability of these constraints in the reduction of the search space and to verify the effects of the control factors in the responses of the LVHWR system, we have run a confirmation experiment. We have used a different dataset. This testing dataset contains 4,674 samples of city name images also taken from the *SRTP* database. Figure 5 shows the results obtained by the standard LBA (*STD*) and the constrained LBA (*TLC*). By comparing the results for recognition speed we can verify that by using the two constraints and setting them up to the optimal values given by the statistical experimental design technique, we improved the recognition speed significantly while keeping almost the same recognition rate.

It should be notice that, in spite of the values of the control factors are dependent on the lexicon size the improvement in speed is almost independent. Table 1 shows the approximate individual contribution of the constraints in speeding up the system. The number of character is related to *WL* while the number of frames is related to FL_l but it is also dependent on the *WL*.

5 Discussion and Conclusion

In this study, we have presented a constrained LBA where two control factors were chosen and analysed through a complete factorial plan. The effects of these two factors in the outputs of a LVHWR system were investigated. We have seen that limiting the number of observations according to the level of the LBA as well as limiting the number of levels of the LBA by taking into account the length of the observation sequences lead to an improvement of 24.4–30.3% in the recognition speed with a slight reduction of 0.28–0.77% in the recognition rate for lexicons with 10–30,000 entries respectively. If we compare with the results of a previous version of the system based on a Viterbi–flat–lexicon scheme [3] [4], the improvement in speed is more expressive (627–1,010%) with a reasonable reduction in the recognition rate (0.45–1.8%). Furthermore, the experimental design technique used for adjusting the values of the control factors provides us a robust framework where the responses of the system are non–linear functions of the control factors. Our future work will focus on the pruning the number of characters by using a beam search technique.

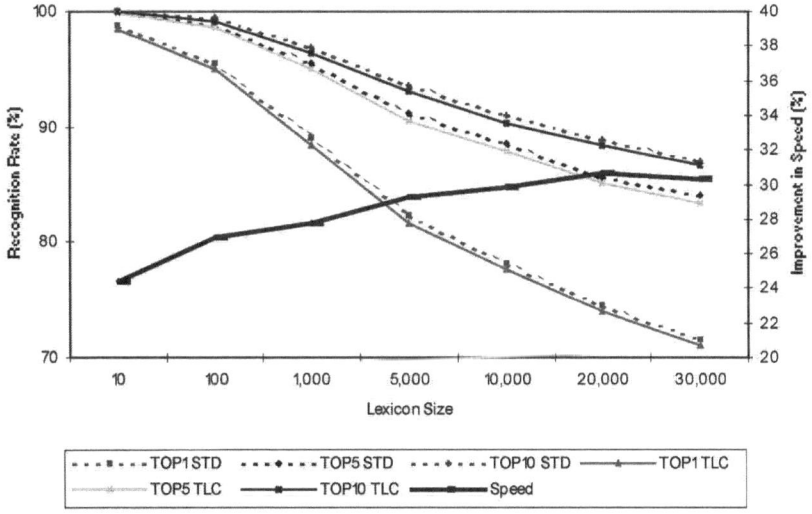

Figure 5: *RR* and *RS* for the standard LBA (*STD*) and the constrained LBA (*TLC*)

Table 1: Reduction in the number of frames and characters

Lexicon Size	Characters (%)	Frames (%)	Speed (%)
10	0	29.41	24.38
100	0.632	31.58	26.90
1,000	2.542	33.47	27.77
5,000	2.568	35.06	29.25
10,000	2.855	35.90	29.79
20,000	4.357	36.88	30.63
30,000	3.879	37.46	30.28

Acknowledgements

The authors wish to thank the CNPq–Brazil, and the MEQ–Canada, which have supported this work and the SRTP–France for supplying the baseline system and the database.

References

1. Kaltenmeier A, Caesar T, Gloger J M, Mandler E. Sophisticated topology of hidden Markov models for cursive script recognition. 2nd ICDAR, Tsukuba Science City, Japan, 1993, pp 139–142.

2. Koga M, Mine R, Sako H., Fujisawa H. Lexical search approach for character–string recognition. 3rd IWDAS, Nagano, Japan, 1998, pp 237–251.

3. Koerich A L, Sabourin R, Suen C Y, El–Yacoubi A. A syntax–directed level building algorithm for large vocabulary handwritten word recognition. 4th IWDAS, 2000, Rio de Janeiro, Brazil.

4. El–Yacoubi A, Gilloux M, Sabourin R, Suen C Y. An HMM based approach for off–line unconstrained handwritten word modelling and recognition. IEEE Trans on PAMI 1999; 21: 752–760.

5. Umbach R H, Ney H. Improvements in beam search for 10,000–word continuous–speech recognition. IEEE Trans on SAP 1984; 2: 353–356.

6. Ney H. The use of a one–stage dynamic programming algorithm for connected word recognition. IEEE Trans on ASSP 1984; 32: 263–271.

7. Rabiner L R, Levinson S E. A speaker–independent, syntax–directed, connected word recognition system based on hidden Markov models and level building. IEEE Trans on ASSP 1985; 33: 561–573.

8. Barker T B. Quality by experimental design. Marcel Dekker, NY, 1994.

9. Grandidier F, Sabourin R, El–Yacoubi A, Gilloux M, Suen C Y. Influence of word length on handwriting recognition. 5th ICDAR, 1999, Bangalore, India, pp 777–780.

10. Manke S, Finke M, Waibel A. A fast search technique for large vocabulary on–line handwriting recognition. In: Progress in handwriting recognition. World Scientific, Singapore, 1996, pp 437–444.

11. Dowdy S, Wearden S. Statistics for research. John Wiley & Sons, NY, 1991.

Preventing Overfitting in Learning Text Patterns for Document Categorization

Markus Junker and Andreas Dengel

German Research Center for Artificial Intelligence (DFKI) GmbH, P.O. 2080,
D-67608 Kaiserslautern, Germany

Abstract. There is an increasing interest in categorizing texts using learning algorithms. While the majority of approaches rely on learning linear classifiers, there is also some interest in describing document categories by text patterns. We introduce a model for learning patterns for text categorization (the LPT-model) that does not rely on an attribute-value representation of documents but represents documents essentially "as they are". Based on the LPT-model, we focus on learning patterns within a relatively simple pattern language. We compare different search heuristics and pruning methods known from various symbolic rule learners on a set of representative text categorization problems. The best results were obtained using the m-estimate as search heuristics combined with the likelihood-ratio-statics for pruning. Even better results can be obtained, when replacing the likelihood-ratio-statics by a new measure for pruning; this we call l-measure. In contrast to conventional measures for pruning, the l-measure takes into account properties of the search space.

Key Words: Text Categorization, Rule Learning, Overfitting, Pruning, Application

1 Introduction

Assigning text documents to content specific categories is an important task in document analysis. In office automation, systems for document categorization are used to categorize documents into categories such as invoices, confirmation of order [4]. These assignments can be used to distribute mail in the house, but they are also used for triggering document-specific information extraction tools, extracting, e.g, the total amount from an invoice. Automatic categorization systems rely on hand-crafted categorization rules of the form "**if** text pattern p_c occurs in document d **then** document d belongs to category c". Typical pattern languages rely on the boolean combination of tests on word occurrences. Within this language, the pattern (**or** (**and** gold jewelry) (**and** silver jewelry)) can be used to find documents which deal with gold or silver jewelry. More elaborated pattern constructs generally also allow tests on word sequences and word properties. The most prominent example for a rule-based automatic categorization system is *TCS* [6].

Since hand-crafting categorization rules is labor intensive, there is interest in automatic document categorization based on example documents. The majority of these algorithms rely on linear classifiers [12]. Until now, only a

S. Singh, N. Murshed, and W. Kropatsch (Eds.): ICAPR 2001, LNCS 2013, pp. 137–146, 2001.

few rule learners have been applied to text categorization [1,3]. Nevertheless, rule learners offer some practical advantages:

- they produce *very compact classifiers*,
- the classifiers are *easy to understand and to modify* by humans (if, e.g., manual fine tuning is needed), and
- the classifiers are *portable* in the sense that the classifier can be used to query nearly any IR search engine.

In the remainder of the paper we first introduce our model for learning patterns for text categorization (Section 2). Based on a set of text categorization problems (described in Section 3) we then investigate different search heuristics to avoid overfitted pattern (Section 4), standard pruning techniques (Section 5), and a new pruning method relying on a measure we call *l*-measure (Section 6). A summary is is given in Section 7.

2   The LPT-Mo del

A text categorization problem in our sense is characterized as follows: Given

- an (in general infinite) set $\mathcal{D}$, the *text domain*;
- a category $\mathcal{K} \subset \mathcal{D}$, the *target category*
- positives $\mathcal{B}^{\oplus}$ and negatives examples $\mathcal{B}^{\ominus}$ for $\mathcal{K} \subset \mathcal{D}$, i.e. $\mathcal{B}^{\oplus} \subseteq \mathcal{K}$ and $\mathcal{B}^{\ominus} \subseteq \mathcal{D} \setminus \mathcal{K}$
- a representation language T_{LPT} for documents and a transformation $t_{LPT} : \mathcal{D} \to T_{LPT}$
- a pattern language $\mathcal{P}$ with an associated function $m : \mathcal{P} \times T_{LPT} \to \{0,1\}$

We search for an algorithm that computes a pattern $p_{\mathcal{K}} \in \mathcal{P}$ from $\mathcal{B}^{\oplus}$ and $\mathcal{B}^{\ominus}$ which approximates

$$m(p_{\mathcal{K}}, t_{LPT}(\delta)) = \begin{cases} 1 : \delta \in \mathcal{K} \\ 0 : \delta \in \mathcal{D} \setminus \mathcal{K} \end{cases}, \text{ the } match\ function.$$

In our model, real world documents (usually given as character sequences) are transformed via the transformation function t_{LPT} into the LPT document representation language. Within this language a document d is represented as a word sequence $(w_1 \ldots w_n)$ while a word w_i is represented as a character sequence. It is important to note that the transformation preserves almost all information in the original document. This allows us to, e.g. define pattern language constructs that rely on word sequences or complex word properties.

We did not commit to a specific pattern language $\mathcal{P}$ but only give a general frame for simplifying the construction of pattern languages. Here, we only introduce one very simple instance of possible pattern languages. This instance relies on a set of so-called *word tests* with $w \in \mathcal{P}$ iff w is a word. The semantics of word tests is given by

$$m(w, (w_1, \ldots, w_n)) = \begin{cases} 1 : \exists_i w = w_i \\ 0 : else \end{cases}$$

Based on word tests we define the simple pattern language used in the following by $k_1 \vee k_2 \vee \cdots \vee k_n$ with $k_i = w_{i,1} \wedge \cdots \wedge w_{i,m_i}$ and $w_{i,j}$ word test The LPT-document representation also allows much more complex pattern languages which rely on word orderings and word properties [7].

Learning Algorithm The search for patterns is done using a separate-and-conquer algorithm as used in the well-known rule learner $CN2$ [2]. To simplify the representation we use $\oplus$ (respectively $\ominus$) as a unary operator that returns the set of all positives (respectively negatives) example documents for a given example document set. The inputs of the algorithm are example documents B for the target category, a search heuristics sh and a pruning method sig (figure 1). It first initializes the document set R by B and the pattern p by false. Using the function s the algorithm then chooses the "best" conjunction of words c_{best} for describing a subset of the positives examples in R. All documents of R covered by c_{best} are then removed from R and the algorithm iterates until the best conjunction of words results in true. The disjunction of all conjunctions given by s is the pattern p which is returned as learning result.

Input: Example documents B for target category
Output: "best" pattern p for target category
$\quad R \leftarrow B, p \leftarrow$ false
$\quad$**repeat**
$\quad\quad S = s\,(B, R, \{\text{true}\}) \cup \{\text{true}\}$
$\quad\quad c_{best} \leftarrow$ "best" conjunction in R
$\quad\quad R \leftarrow R \setminus \{d \in R^{\oplus} \mid m(c_{best}, d) = 1\}$
$\quad\quad p \leftarrow p \vee c_{best}$
$\quad$**until** $(c_{best} = \text{true})$

Fig. 1. Algorithm for finding the best pattern

Finding the best conjunction c_{best} is done using the algorithm shown in figure 2. The algorithm starts with the empty conjunction as the best conjunction c_{best}. Within a loop this conjunction is refined by word tests. From those refinements that are significant with respect to sig, the best one according to the search heuristics sh is taken as the new best conjunction. The loop ends if no better significant refinement than the current c_{best} can be found anymore.

3   Methods and Material

For the experimental evaluation we rely on four text collections with positive and negative examples for 98 different categories: a collection of German technical abstracts with categories such as "computer science and modeling"

Input: Example documents R, search heuristic sh, significance criterion sig
Output: "best" conjunction c_{best} in R for target category
    $c_{best} \leftarrow$ true, $c \leftarrow c_{best}$
    repeat
        $S = \{c_{best} \wedge w \mid w$ word occurring in $R\}$
        $S_{pruned} = \{c \in S \mid \mathrm{sig}(B, R, c_{best}, c)\}$
        $c \leftarrow c' \in S_{pruned}$ with best value of $\mathrm{sh}(R, c')$
    until $c_{best} = c$

Fig. 2. Algorithm for finding the best conjunction

and "classification, document analysis and recognition", a collection of office documents which consists of OCR'ed German business letters and with
categories such as "invoice" and "offer" and two freely available English collections: the *Reuters*-collection[1] and a collection of newsgroups articles [2]. For
the evaluation we split each collection 1:1 in a learning and a test set.

For the evaluation of learned patterns on the test set, we use the effectiveness measures recall and precision which are widespread in information
retrieval [9]. Recall and precision correspond to the characteristic requirements on patterns: They should cover a category as completely as possible
(measured by the recall) and they should cover it as correctly as possible
(measured by the precision). For each learned pattern $p = k_1 \vee \cdots \vee k_n$ a range
of recall/precision values corresponding to $p_i = k_1 \vee \cdots \vee k_i$ for $i = 0 \ldots n$
was computed. Averaging over the categories was done at predefined recall
points by averaging the approximated precision for all patterns at these recall points. The resulting range of recall/precision points will be graphically
shown in recall/precision diagrams. The little arrows in the diagrams shown
later indicate the minimum increase in recall or effectiveness needed at certain recall/precision points for significance according to the p-Test as used in
[12] (error probability 5%).

4   Search Heuristics

In literature in different rule learners various search heuristics for complexes
are used [5] of which some of the most prominent ones are (we use the ab-
breviations $p = |m(k, R^{\oplus})|$, $n = |m(k, R^{\ominus})|$, $P = |R^{\oplus}|$, and $N = |R^{\ominus}|$):
Precision $(\frac{p}{p+n})$, *Information Content* $(-\log(\frac{p}{p+n}))$, *Entropy* $(-\log(\frac{p}{p+n}))$,
Laplace Estimate $(\frac{n+1}{n+p+2})$, *Accuracy* $(\frac{p+(N-n)}{P+N})$, and *m-Estimate* $(\frac{p+m\frac{P}{P+N}}{p+n+m})$.
Figure 3 compares the effectiveness we obtained on our text categorization
problems with the search heuristics. To alleviate problems arising with small
coverages when using precision, information content and entropy the order

---

[1] available via `http://www.research.att.com/~lewis`
[2] available   via   `http://www.cs.cmu.edu/afs/cs/project/theo-11/www/`
`naive-bayes.html`

given by these function were refined as follows: If two complexes obtain the same weight, the one which covered more documents was preferred (i.e. the one with $p + n$ maximal). In addition, for the entropy, complexes with $\frac{p}{p+n} < \frac{1}{2}$ were excluded. For the m-estimate we evaluated the parameters $m \in \{0.01, 1, 10, 20, 50, 100\}$.

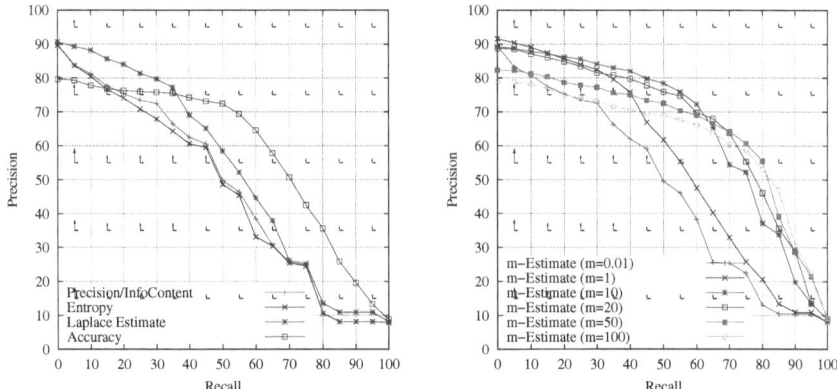

Fig. 3. Influence of the search heuristics on the effectiveness

It can be observed that the effectiveness of precision/information content and entropy do not differ much. This can be explained by the equivalence of precision/informations content and entropy for $\frac{p}{p+n} > \frac{1}{2}$. Compared to precision/information content and entropy the Laplace estimate performs better. This can be explained by the weighting of complexes with small coverages close to $\frac{1}{2}$. The rather pessimistic estimate gives, e.g., a better weight to a complex with $p = 100$ and $n = 1$ than for a complex with $p = 2$ and $n = 0$. The accuracy shows a lower precision on a lower recall, but obtains a higher precision at higher recalls than the other search heuristics. In general by going from precision/information content and entropy to the Laplace-estimate and from the Laplace-Estimate to the accuracy a high precision at low recalls is replaced by a high precision at higher recalls. The same also holds for the m-estimate with increasing m. Choosing the right value for m for each recall, a precision can be obtained that is better than the one of all other search heuristics on this recall.

5   Pruning Methods

Table 1 shows the pruning methods we have evaluated on our text categorization problems. The method *syntactic constraints* restricts conjunctions to a maximal number of arguments n_{max}. The intention for this method is the belief that complexes with more arguments are more likely to obtain a good rating by the search heuristics just by chance. Another pruning method, *minimum coverages*, requires complexes to cover at least c positive examples in the remaining learning set R. It follows the belief that the values of the search heuristic are more reliable if more (positive) examples can be used for its computation. Furthermore, we considered two pruning methods relying on the likelihood ratio statics (lrs). This measure gives high significance to complexes whose distribution of covered positive and negative example differs much from the distribution on some reference set. The variants of the lrs differ in what set it used as reference set. In the *CN2* variant used in the rule learner *CN2* the whole example set B is used as reference, i.e. $P' = |B^\oplus|$ and $N' = |B^\ominus|$. The *BEXA* variant (used in *BEXA* [11]) uses the predecessor complex k_{pre} of the complex to be judged, i.e. $P' = |m(k_{\text{pre}}, R^\oplus)|, N' = |m(k_{\text{pre}}, R^\ominus)|$.

syntactic constraints	$\mathrm{sig}(B, R, k_{\text{pre}}, w_1 \wedge \cdots \wedge w_n) = \begin{cases} 1 : n \leq n_{\max}, n_{\max} \in I\!N \\ 0 : \text{else} \end{cases}$
minimum coverages	$\mathrm{sig}() = \begin{cases} 1 : |m(k, R^\oplus)| \geq c \\ 0 : \text{else} \end{cases}$
lrs	$\mathrm{sig}() = \begin{cases} 1 : -2 \left(p \log \left(\frac{p}{(p+n)\frac{P'}{P'+N'}} \right) + n \log \left(\frac{n}{(p+n)\frac{N'}{P'+N'}} \right) \right) \geq \vartheta \\ 0 : \text{else} \end{cases}$

Table 1. Pruning methods and their definitions

Figure 4 summarizes the results obtained with the different pruning methods (the diagram showed in the lower right will be subject of the next section). The results of the *CN2* and *BEXA* variants are practically indistinguishable. It can be observed that:

- The method *minimum coverages* (upper right) has practically no positive influence on the effectiveness over the whole recall range. Increasing the minimal number of documents in $R^\oplus$ even decreases the precision.
- The effect of the other pruning methods *syntactic constraints* (upper left) and *likelihood ratio statics* (lower left) depends on the respective parameter and is very similar. By varying the parameter, high precision at low recall levels is traded for high precision at high recall levels.
- Pruning with the *likelihood ratio statistics* (lower left) slightly outperforms *syntactic constraints* (upper left). While with the lrs and $\vartheta = 20$ the precision is higher at the high recall level, the corresponding decrease in precision at lower recall levers is less dramatic than when using *syntactic constraints*.

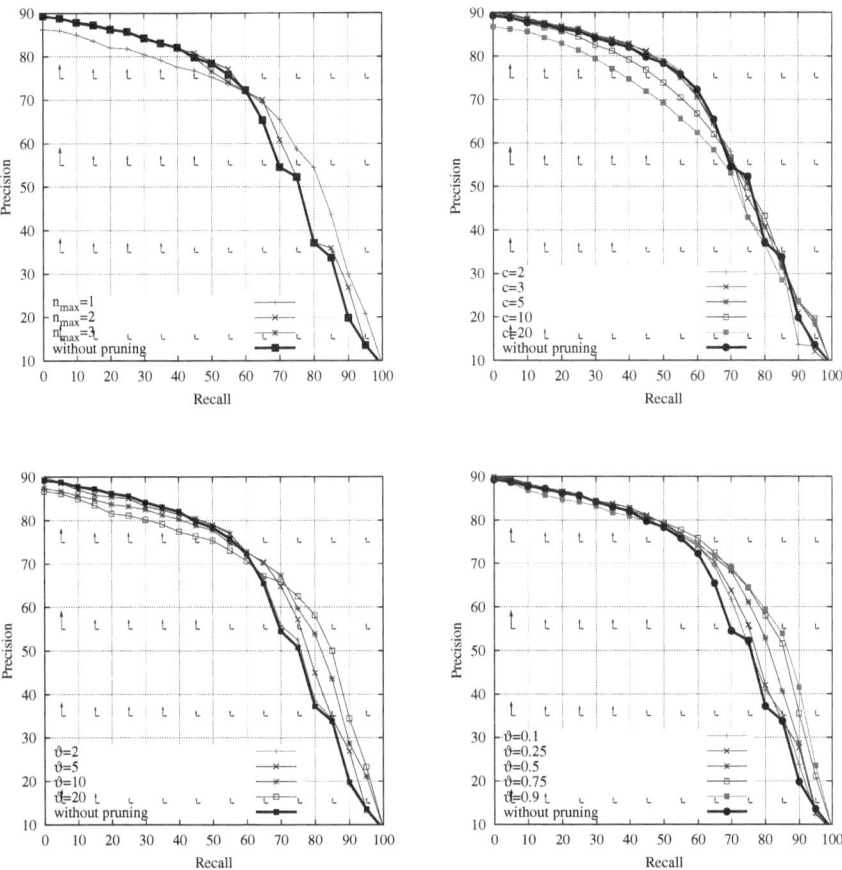

Fig. 4. Influence of pruning methods on the effectiveness: *syntactic constraints* (upper left), *minimum coverages* (upper right), *lrs (BEXA)* (lower left), *l-measure* (lower right)

6   A New Pruning Method

In this section we propose a new pruning method that does —in contrast to the methods listed in table 1— takes the size of the search space into account. In order to motivate the new significance measure, table 2 shows a part of the learning process for the category *invoice* in the German office document collection[3]. The first column contains the i-th iteration in the separate-and-conquer algorithms according to figure 1. For each iteration step the following two columns contain the number of remaining positives ($|R^{\oplus}|$) and negatives

---

[3] The words in the table translate as follows: rechnung(s) – invoice, zahlung – payment, angeben – specify

documents ($|R^\ominus|$). The following columns show the best conjunctions built within the algorithm to find the best conjunction (cmp. figure 2) as well as the number of positives and negatives examples $p = |m(c_{i,j}, R^\oplus)|$ respectively $n = |m(c_{i,j}, R^\ominus)|$ they cover in R. The column $\mathrm{sh}(R, c_{i,j})$ shows the value of the m-estimate for $c_{i,j}$ ($m = 10$). Finally, the last column contains the value $l = \left|\left\{c \in S \mid |m(c, R)| = |m(c_{i,j}, R)|\right\}\right|$ with $S = \{c_{i,j-1} \wedge w \mid w \in \mathrm{words}(R)\}$ the *local search space*. According to this definition l is the number of refinements of $c_{i,j-1}$ that covers the same number of documents in R as the conjunction $c_{i,j}$.

i	$\|R^\oplus\|$	$\|R^\ominus\|$	j	conjunction $c_{i,j}$	p	n	$\mathrm{sh}(R, c_{i,j})$	l
1	357	513	0	true	357	513	0.41	
			1	rechnung	203	54	0.78	2
			2	rechnung $\wedge$ rechnungs	37	1	0.87	5
2	320	513	0	true	320	513	0.38	
			1	rechnung	166	54	0.74	4
			2	rechnung $\wedge$ zahlung	57	2	0.78	3
			3	rechnung $\wedge$ zahlung $\wedge$ angeben	28	2	0.80	2
.	.	.	.	.	.	.	.	.
10	171	513	0	true	171	513	0.25	
			1	rechnung	60	54	0.50	5
			2	rechnung $\wedge$ 10060	8	0	0.58	64
.	.	.	.	.	.	.	.	.
19	119	513	0	true	119	513	0.19	
			1	1157	4	1	0.39	506

Table 2. Capture of the learning process for the category *Rechnung*

In order to motivate the l-measure we first consider the refinement step from $c_{19,0}$ to $c_{19,1}$. The conjunction $c_{19,0}$ covers 119 positives and 513 negatives examples. The probability of an example being a positive one can thus be estimated with $\frac{119}{119+513} \approx 0.19$. This probability can be interpreted as the a-priori probability for covering a positive example by a refinement of $c_{19,0}$.

The value of the m-estimate for $c_{19,0}$ is $\frac{4+10\frac{119}{119+513}}{4+1+10} \approx 0.39$. Each refinement of $c_{19,0}$ that covers exactly 5 documents (as does $c_{19,1}$) has a weighting at least as good as 0.39 iff the refinement covers at least as many positives examples as $c_{19,1}$: 4. The probability for covering randomly at least 4 positive examples can be computed using the a-priori probability estimated by $c_{19,0}$ with $\binom{5}{4}0.19^4(1 - 0.19)^1 + \binom{5}{5}0.19^5(1 - 0.19)^0 \approx 0.0055$ The low value indicates that the observed good coverage of $c_{19,1}$ has not occurred by chance. Thus, we would not prune $c_{19,1}$.

If we take into account how many refinements of $c_{19,0}$ exist that also cover exactly 5 documents, the result changes. This number is given as l in table 2 with 506. If we assume that the coverage of all 506 words that cover exactly 5 documents is random, the probability of covering 4 or more positive examples by chance (and thus the probability of getting a better weight than 0.39) increases drastically. It can be approximated by $\sum_{i=1}^{509} \binom{509}{i} 0.0055^i (1 - 0.0063)^{(509-i)} = 1 - (1 - 0.0055)^{509} \approx 0.94$. In this way, the consideration of the value l computed by the local search space would suggest we should prune $k_{19,1}$.

Without going into the details of the general derivation, the idea given by the above example can be used to formulate a new significance measure as follows. Using

$$\text{Bin}\,(p+n, w, p) = \sum_{i=p}^{p+n} \binom{p+n}{i} w^i (1 - w)^{p+n-i}$$

and

$$l = \left| \left\{ c' \in S \mid |m(c', R)| = |m(c, R)| \right\} \right|,$$

the new pruning method can be formulated as

$$\text{sig}(B, R, c_{\text{pre}}, S, k) = \begin{cases} 1 : \text{sigm}(B, R, c_{\text{pre}}, S, c) \geq \vartheta \\ 0 : \text{else} \end{cases} \quad \text{with}$$

$$\text{sigm}(B, R, c_{\text{pre}}, S, c) = 1 - (1 - \text{Bin}\,(p+n, w, p))^{\left| \left\{ c' \in S \mid |m(c',R)|=|m(c,R)| \right\} \right|}$$

The results of the new pruning method using the l-measure are shown in the lower right corner of figure 4 for $\vartheta \in \{0.25, 0.5, 0.75, 0.9\}$. It can observed that with increasing ϑ the precision for higher recall values can be increased without harming the precision at lower recall as much as the likelihood-ratio-statistics does. Thus, the new pruning method — taking account of the local search space— outperforms the previously investigated pruning methods for our text categorization problems.

7   Summary

In this paper we have shown our model for learning patterns for text categorization. In contrast to the conventional models we do not use an attribute value representation of documents but represent documents as they are, i.e. as a sequence of words which again are represented by a sequence of words. This enables us to introduce complex pattern languages with patterns relying on word orders and word properties. Within the model, in this paper, we focused on preventing from overfitting in a simple pattern language, in which pattern are disjunctions of conjuncted word tests. We proposed and evaluated different methods for optimizing the effectiveness of patterns within this language. Of all search heuristics we evaluated the best results on our set of text categorization methods was obtained with the m-estimate. In addition to search heuristics we investigated pruning methods for text categorization. The best pruning method we found was the likelihood-ratio-statistics. We proposed a pruning method relying new measure we call l-measure. To our knowledge this is the only pruning method that takes into account the size of the search space. An experimental comparison of the new methods showed that the new pruning method gives better effectiveness than the likelihood-ratio-statistics.

References

1. C. Apté, F. Damerau and S. Weiss. Towards Language Independent Automated Learning of Text Categorization Models. In: *Proceedings of the 17th Annual International ACM/SIGIR Conference on Research and Development in Information Retrieval (SIGIR 94)*, page: 23–30, Dublin, Ireland, July 3-6 1994.
2. P. Clark and T. Niblett. The CN2 Algorithm. *Machine Learning*, 3(4) Seite: 261–283, 1989.
3. W.W. Cohen. Learning to Classify English Text with ILP Methods. In: *Advances in Inductive Logic Programming*, page: 124–143. IOS Press, 1996.
4. A. Dengel und K. Hinkelmann. The Specialist Board — A Technology Workbench for Document Analysis and Understanding. In: *Proceedings of the 2nd World Conference on Integrated Design and Process Technology (IDPT '96)*, page: 36–47, Austin, TX, USA, December 1996.
5. J. Fürnkranz. Separate-and-Conquer Rule Learning. *Artificial Intelligence Review*, 13(1) Seite: 3–54, 1999.
6. P.J. Hayes, P.M. Anderson, I.B. Nirenburg und L.M. Schmandt. TCS: A Shell for Content-Based Text Categorization. In: *Proceedings of 6th Conference on Artificial Intelligence Applications*, page: 320–326, Santa Barbara, CA, USA, May 5-9 1990.
7. M. Junker. *Heuristisches Lernen von Regeln für die Textkategorisierung*. Dissertation, University of Kaiserslautern, Germany, 2000 (in German).
8. J.R. Quinlan. Introduction of Decision Trees. *Machine Learning*, 3 Seite: 81–106, 1986.
9. C. van Rijsbergen. *Information Retrieval*. Butterworth, London, England, 1979.
10. C. Schaffer. Overfitting Avoidance as Bias. *Machine Learning*, 10(2) Seite: 233–241, February 1993.
11. H. Theron und I. Cloete. BEXA: A Covering Algorithm for Learning Propositional Concept Descriptions. *Machine Learning*, 24 Seite: 5–40, 1996.
12. Y. Yang und X. Liu. A Re-Examination of Text Categorization Methods. In: *Proceedings of the 22th Annual International ACM/SIGIR Conference on Research and Development in Information Retrieval (SIGIR 94)*, page: 42–49, Berkeley, CA, USA, August 15-19 1999.

Image Document Categorization using Hidden Tree Markov Models and Structured Representations

Michelangelo Diligenti[1], Paolo Frasconi[2], and Marco Gori[1]

[1] Dept. of Information Engineering, Università di Siena, Italy
[2] Dept. of Systems and Computer Science, Università di Firenze, Italy

Abstract. Categorization is an important problem in image document processing and is often a preliminary step for solving subsequent tasks such as recognition, understanding, and information extraction. In this paper the problem is formulated in the framework of concept learning and each category corresponds to the set of image documents with similar physical structure. We propose a solution based on two algorithmic ideas. First, we transform the image document into a structured representation based on X-Y trees. Compared to "flat" or vector-based feature extraction techniques, structured representations allow us to preserve important relationships between image sub-constituents. Second, we introduce a novel probabilistic architecture that extends hidden Markov models for learning probability distributions defined on spaces of labeled trees.

1 Introduction

Despite the explosive increase of electronic intercommunication in recent years, a significant amount of documents is still printed on paper. Image document processing aims at automating operations normally carried out by individuals on printed documents, such as reading, understanding, extracting useful information, and organizing documents according to given criteria. In its general form, this task is formidable in absence of information about the physical layout of the document. Layout classification is therefore an important preliminary step for guiding the subsequent recognition task [3]. For example, in a commercial domain involving recognition of invoices, a classifier can be employed to determine which company invoice form is being analyzed. In the case of electronic libraries, classification can partition scanned pages according to useful criteria such as presence of title, advertisement, number of columns, etc.

   In [3] documents are represented as structured patterns (allowing to preserve relationships among the components) and then classified by special decision trees which are able to deal with structured patterns. In [2] both the physical and the logical structure are used to recognize documents. In this paper we formulate layout classification as a concept learning problem. Our approach is based on a generalization of hidden Markov models (HMMs), which have been introduced several years ago as a tool for modeling probability distributions defined on sets of strings. The interest on probabilistic

S. Singh, N. Murshed, and W. Kropatsch (Eds.): ICAPR 2001, LNCS 2013, pp. 147–156, 2001.

sequence modeling developed particularly in the Seventies, within the speech recognition research community. The basic model was very simple, yet so flexible and effective that it rapidly became extremely popular. During the last years a large number of variants and improvements over the standard HMM have been proposed and applied. Undoubtedly, Markovian models are now regarded as one of the most significant state-of-the-art approaches for sequence learning. The recent view of the HMM as a particular case of Bayesian networks [1,12] has helped the theoretical understanding and the ability to conceive extensions to the standard model in a sound and formally elegant framework.

In this paper, we propose an extension of the model for learning probability distributions defined on sets of labeled trees. We call this architecture Hidden Tree Markov Model (HTMM). This extension was first suggested in [5] as one of the possible architectures for connectionist learning of data structures, but it has never been employed in a real application. In the case of document classification, instances are obtained by an X-Y tree extraction algorithm as a preprocessing step.

2   The X-Y trees extraction algorithm

The physical layouts of documents are represented by XY-trees, which allow to preserve relationships among the components. Structured representations, like XY-trees, are more suitable then vector-based representations to describe complex patterns (like documents), which are composed by many sub-parts with different semantic meanings. XY-trees are commonly used to segment an input document [9]. Each node of an XY-tree is associated to a region of the document. Nodes nearer the leaves are associated to smaller areas of the document (see Fig. 1). The root of the XY-tree is associated to the whole document. The document is then split into regions that are separated by white horizontal spaces. Each region corresponds to a node, child of the root node. The algorithm is applied recursively over each subregion detected at the previous step. Horizontal and vertical white spaces are alternatively used to further divide a region. A region is not further subdivided if: (1) neither a horizontal or vertical white space can be found, and (2) the area of a region is smaller of the selected resolution of the algorithm. Since each node is associated to a region of the document, children are ordered left-to-right for vertical cuts and top-to-bottom for horizontal cuts. If a horizontal (or vertical) white space can not be found and then the region can not be divided, a dummy node is inserted and the algorithm tries to split the region searching vertical (or horizontal) white spaces. Pseudo-code is given in Algorithm 1.

A drawback of this algorithm is that it is not able to represent a document properly if it contains lines across the formatted area. For example a rectangular box can not be split and the information inside the box can not be represented using traditional XY-trees. In order to deal with documents containing lines, a modified XY-tree algorithm has been used: at each step

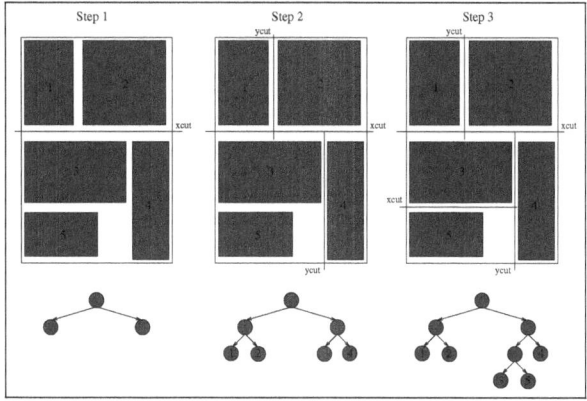

Fig. 1. Extraction of a XY-tree representing a document. The final tree is shown at the bottom of the figure

---

Algorithm 1 xyExtract (region, cut_direction, cut_dir_at_previous_step)
    if *region.area < resolution*   **return**;
    lines ← **FindLines**(region, cut_direction);
    sub_regions ← **LineCut**(region, lines);
    if cut_direction = Horizontal   cut_direction ← Vertical;
    else   cut_direction ← Horizontal;
    if sub_regions = ∅
        spaces ← **FindSpaces**(region,cut_direction);
        sub_regions ← **SpaceCut**(region,spaces);
    if sub_regions ≠ ∅
        go ← 0;
        foreach region ∈ sub_regions
            XY-Extract(region, cut_direction, cut_dir_at_previous_step);
    else
        if cut_dir_at_previous_step ← 1   **return**;
        else   **XY-Extract**(region, cut_direction, 1);

---

the region can be subdivided using either white spaces or a lines. A line has priority over space, when both a line and a space split a region. Each node of the XY-tree contains a real vector of features describing the region associated to the node.

3   Hidden tree-Markov models

In this section we develop a general theoretical framework for modeling probability distributions defined over spaces of trees. An m-ary tree T is a recursive structure that either empty, or it is comprised of an ordered sequence $T = < r, T_1, T_2, \ldots, T_m >$ where r is a node called root and T_i is the i-th subtree of T. Information is associated to trees by means of *labels* attached to their nodes. Each label is a tuple of features (or attributes) extracted from the pattern being represented and will be uniquely associated to one node. Features are modeled by discrete or continuous random variables. 1Since different kinds of features can be extracted, it is convenient to distinguish variables according to their *type*. In this way, the universe of discourse (that comprises all the features in a given domain) can be partitioned into K equivalence classes $\mathcal{Y}^{(1)}, \ldots, \mathcal{Y}^{(K)}$ so that each class contains variables of the same type. Parenthesized superscripts will be used to refer to a particular type. We denote by $\mathcal{O}^{(k)}$ the set of admissible realizations for variables of type k. The label attached to node v will be denoted as $Y(v)$. If each label is a k-tuple containing exactly one variable for each equivalence class we say that the tree is *uniformly labeled*. In this case each label can be denoted as $Y(v) = \{Y^{(1)}(v), \ldots, Y^{(K)}(v)\} \in \mathcal{Y}$, being $\mathcal{Y} \doteq \mathcal{Y}^{(1)} \times \cdots \mathcal{Y}^{(K)}$. Correspondingly, an observed label can be denoted as $y(v) = \{y^{(1)}(v), \cdots, y^{(K)}(v)\} \in \mathcal{O}$ being $\mathcal{O} \doteq \mathcal{O}^{(1)} \times \cdots \times \mathcal{O}^{(K)}$.

Model definition

According to the previous definitions, let us consider a generic tree $\boldsymbol{Y}$. We are interested in the specification of a probabilistic model λ that satisfies the following desiderata:

1. The model should be *generative*, i.e. it should specify the probability distribution $P(\boldsymbol{Y}|\lambda)$ thus enabling two basic operations: sampling (i.e. picking up a tree according to the distribution) and evaluation, i.e. given an observed tree $\boldsymbol{y}$ computing the probability $P(\boldsymbol{Y} = \boldsymbol{y}|\lambda)$.
2. The model should be *trainable*, i.e. given a set of observed trees it should be possible to estimate the "optimal" parameters of the model according to some well assessed statistical criterion.
3. The model should be *compositional* in order to allow computations to be performed efficiently. Given the recursive nature of the data, it seems natural to seek a divide-and-conquer approach that carries out computations on the whole tree by taking advantage of partial results obtained on subtrees.

Points 1 and 2 are rather generic and there are several generative adaptive models in the literature for dealing with vector-based and sequential data. However, these models cannot deal with rich recursive representations such as trees. Point 3 is specific for model intended to exploit the hierarchical structure of the data. Stochastic structural grammars [6] are able to satisfy desiderata 1 and 3. However, no statistically sound learning methods are available in the literature. Desiderata 2 and 3 are satisfied by a recent class of artificial neural networks especially designed for adaptive processing of directed acyclic graphs [5]. However, these networks are conceived as

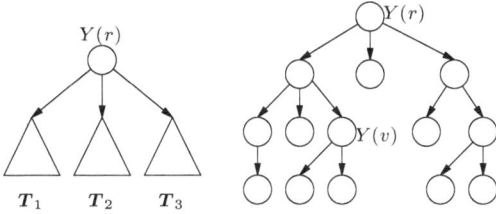

Fig. 2. Belief network representing the first-order tree-Markov property

discriminant rather than generative models: they allow to estimate the conditional probability of a dependent output variable given a graph as input, but they do not support the estimation of generative probabilities.

Composionality in a stochastic model can be achieved using probabilistic independence. For each tree $\mathbf{Y}$ we can write $P(\mathbf{Y}) = P(Y(r), \mathbf{Y}_1, \ldots, \mathbf{Y}_m)$ where $Y(r)$ is the label at the root node r and $\mathbf{Y}_i$ are random subtrees. Ideally we would like to combine in a simple way $P(\mathbf{Y}_1), \ldots, P(\mathbf{Y}_m)$ in order to compute $P(\mathbf{Y})$, thus enabling an efficient recursive procedure. The following decomposition always holds true and can be trivially obtained by repeated applications of the chain rule of probabilities:

$$P(\mathbf{Y}) = P(\mathbf{Y}_1|Y(r), \mathbf{Y}_2, \ldots, \mathbf{Y}_m) \cdot P(\mathbf{Y}_2|Y(r), \mathbf{Y}_3, \ldots, \mathbf{Y}_m) \cdots$$
$$\cdot P(\mathbf{Y}_m|Y(r))P(Y(r))$$

At this point one might introduce a rather drastic conditional independence assumption, namely that all the subtrees of $\mathbf{Y}$ are mutually independent given the label $Y(r)$ at the root:

$$P(\mathbf{Y}_i|\mathbf{Y}_j, Y(r)) = P(\mathbf{Y}_i|Y(r)) \quad \forall i, j = 1, \ldots, m. \tag{1}$$

If Equation (1) holds true we say that the *first-order* tree-Markov property is satisfied for $\mathbf{Y}$. An immediate consequence is that

$$P(\mathbf{Y}) = P(Y(r)) \prod_{j=1}^{m} P(\mathbf{Y}_j|Y(r))$$

and from this equation one can easily show that

$$P(\mathbf{Y}) = P(Y(r)) \prod_{v \in V \setminus \{r\}} P(Y(v)|Y(\mathrm{pa}[v])), \tag{2}$$

where V denotes the set of nodes of $\mathbf{Y}$ and pa[v] denotes the parent of v (proof by mathematical induction using a tree comprised by a single node as a base step). The factorization formula (2) can be graphically depicted using either a Markov or a Bayesian network [10], as shown in Fig. 2. Interestingly, if the first-order tree-Markov property holds for $\mathbf{Y}$, then the standard first-order Markov property also holds for each sequence of nodes constructed by following a path in the tree. This follows by direct inspection of Fig. 2. Although the approach just described would introduce the desirable compositionality property in the model, there are at least two main disadvantages. First, the conditional independence assumption (1) is very unrealistic in many practical cases. In facts, it implies that the label of each node v is independent of the rest of the tree given the label attached to v's parent. This does not allow the model to capture correlations that might exist between any two non adjacent nodes. Second, the parameterization of $P(Y(v)|Y(\text{pa}[v]))$ might be problematic if each label contains several variables. For example if each label is formed by 5 integer variables in the range $[1, 10]$, $P(Y(v)|Y(\text{pa}[v]))$ is a table containing 10 billions of parameters. One possibility for removing the first limitation might consist of extending the "memory depth" of the model, defining a higher-order tree-Markov property (in some way that extends the notion of higher-order Markov chains for sequential data). However this would further increase the number of parameters in the model. Instead, following the idea of hidden Markov models for sequences, we opt for the introduction of hidden state variables in charge of "storing" and "summarizing" distant information. More precisely, let $\mathcal{X} = \{x_1, \ldots, x_n\}$ be a *finite* set of states. We assume that each tree $\mathbf{Y}$ is generated by an underlying *hidden tree* $\mathbf{X}$, a data structure defined as follows. The skeleton of $\mathbf{X}$ is identical to the skeleton of $\mathbf{Y}$. Nodes of $\mathbf{X}$ are labeled by hidden state variables, denoted $X(v)$. Finally, realizations of state variables take values on $\mathcal{X}$. In this way, $P(\mathbf{Y}) = \sum_{\mathbf{X}} P(\mathbf{Y}, \mathbf{X})$, where the sum over $\mathbf{X}$ indicates the marginalization over all the hidden trees. The first-order tree-Markov property in the case of hidden tree models is formulated as follows.

1. First, the first-order tree-Markov property (as defined above – see Equation (1)) must hold for the hidden tree:

$$P(\mathbf{X}_i|\mathbf{X}_j, X(r)) = P(\mathbf{X}_i|X(r)) \quad \forall i, j = 1, \ldots, m. \tag{3}$$

   As a consequence

$$P(\mathbf{X}) = P(X(r)) \prod_{v \in V \setminus \{r\}} P(X(v)|X(\text{pa}[v])), \tag{4}$$

2. Second, for each node v the observed label $Y(v)$ is independent of the rest given $X(v)$:

$$P(Y(v)|\mathbf{Y}, \mathbf{X}) = P(Y(v)|X(v)) \tag{5}$$

From the two above conditional independence assumptions it is easy to derive the following global factorization formula:

$$P(BY, \mathbf{X}) = P(X(r))P(Y(r)|X(r))$$
$$\cdot \prod_{v \in V \setminus \{r\}} P(Y(v)|X(v))P(X(v)|X(\text{pa}[v])) \tag{6}$$

that can be graphically represented by a belief networks as shown in Fig. 3. The associated stochastic model will be called hidden tree-Markov model (HTMM). Note that in the degenerate case of trees reducing to sequences, HTMMs are identical to standard HMMs.

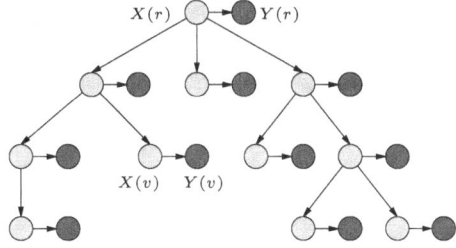

Fig. 3. Belief network for a hidden tree-Markov model. White nodes belong to the underlying hidden tree **X**. Shaded nodes are observations

Parameterization and model's properties

According to Equation (6) we see that parameters for the HTMM are $P(X(r))$, a prior on the root hidden state, $P(Y(v)|X(v))$, the *emission* parameters, and $P(X(v)|X(\text{pa}[v]))$, the *transition* parameters. For simplicity, in the remainder of the paper we shall assume categorical labels only since the extension to numerical variables is rather trivial.

In this initial setting parameters are permitted to vary with the particular node being considered. In this way, however, it is very likely to obtain a large total number of parameters, especially when dealing with large graphs. Obviously this may quickly lead to overfitting problems when one attempts to learn the model from data. A similar difficulty would arise with standard HMMs if one allowed emission and transition parameters to depend on the time index t. Typically, HMMs parameters do not depend on t, a property called *stationarity* [11]. In the case of trees, the notion of "time" is replaced by the notion of "node." Therefore, a similar parameter sharing property can be introduced for HTMMs. In particular, we say that an HTMM is *fully stationary* if the CPTs attached to network nodes $X(v)$ and $X(w)$ are the same for each pair of tree nodes v and w, and the CPTs attached to network nodes $Y^{(k)}(v)$ and $Y^{(k)}(w)$ are the same for each pair of tree nodes v and w and for each $k = 1, \ldots, m$.

Inference and learning algorithms

Since the model is a special case of Bayesian network, the two main algorithms (inference and parameter estimation) can be derived as special cases of corresponding algorithms for Bayesian networks. Inference consists of computing all the conditional probabilities of hidden states, given the evidence entered into the observation nodes (i.e. the labels of the tree). Since the network is singly connected, the inference problem can be solved either by π-λ propagation [10] or by the more general junction tree algorithm [8]. In our experiments we implemented a specialized version of the junction tree algorithm. Given the special structure of the HTMM network (see Fig. 3), no moralization is required and cliques forming the junction tree are of two kinds: one containing $X(v)$ and $X(\mathrm{pa}[v])$, the other one containing $Y(v)$ and $X(v)$. In both cases, only two variables are contained into a clique. It should be remarked that $P(\mathbf{Y})$ is simply obtained as the normalization factor in any clique after propagation in the junction tree. Inference in HTMMs is very efficient and runs in time proportional to the number of nodes in $\mathbf{Y}$ and to the number of states in $\mathcal{X}$.

Each model is trained using positive examples from the class associated to that model. Learning can be formulated in the maximum likelihood framework and the model can be trained using the Expectation-Maximization (EM) algorithm as described in [7].

4   Dataset preparation

We have collected 889 commercial invoices, issued by 9 different companies. The class of an invoice corresponds to the issuing company. The number of available instances of different classes in our dataset is rather imbalanced and varies between 46 and 191. At a first step, all the XY-trees representations of the documents in the dataset are extracted. The minimum area of a region associated to a node of an XY-tree is set to 1% of the total area of the document. This means that the recursive splitting of the document, is stopped when a further splitting would end up only with regions featuring an area smaller then 1% of the whole image. Using this resolution yelded an average tree size of 28 nodes. Each region of a document is represented by a vector of six features:

1. a flag indicating whether the parent was cut using a line or a space;
2. the normalized document space coordinates of the 4 boundaries of the region associated with the node;
3. the average grey level of the region associated with the node.

Since the HTMM model is formulated for discrete variables only, real variables lebeling each node (the last 5 attributes described above) must be quantized. This was accomplished by running the maximum entropy discretization algorithm described in [4], obtaining 5 discrete attributes with 10 values each. It must be remarked that this discretization algorithm collects statistics over the available data and, therefore, it was run using the documents belonging to the training set.

5   Implementation and results

We have used one HTMM, λ_k, for each class, and each HTMM had 10 states $x_1, \ldots, x_{10}$. At each step only a small number of transitions were allowed, typically the model can jump only to the previous or to the next state or to remain in the actual state, i.e. we forced $P(X(v) = x_i | X(\mathrm{pa}[v]) = x_j) = 0$ if $|i - j| > 1$. This helps to reduce the number of parameters to estimate. We have used a fully stationary model (CPTs attached to network nodes are the same for each pair of tree nodes).

Algorithm 2 `Cross-validation` (number_of_groups M, dataset L)

$\quad Model \leftarrow Create\_Random\_Model$

$\quad L_1 \ldots L_M = Divide\_The\_dataset(M, L)$

$\quad$ **for** $i \leftarrow 1, \cdots, M$ **do**

$\qquad$ Compute the permutations of i groups over M sets with the sets L_i,

$\qquad$ Create $\binom{M}{i}$ couples of learning and test set $\left((L_1, T_1), \ldots, (L_{\binom{M}{i}}, T_{\binom{M}{i}})\right)$

$\qquad I_j = Compute\_Maximum\_Entropy\_Quantization\_Intervals(L_j)$

$\qquad$ **for** $j \leftarrow 1, \cdots, \binom{M}{i}$ **do**

$\qquad\quad L_j' = quantize(L_j, I_j)$

$\qquad\quad T_j' = quantize(T_j, I_j)$

$\qquad\quad TrainedModel = train(Model, L_j')$

$\qquad\quad testResults += (TrainedModel, T_j')$

$\qquad Flush\_out(i, testResults)$

Since the number of available documents is small, cross-validation has been used to validate the results. We aim to demonstrate that the proposed approach can be successful even if a small number of learning invoices is available. The dataset was divided into M groups, N groups $(N < M)$ form the learning set and the remaining $M - N$ groups compose the test one. The maximum entropy quantization intervals were computed and the set of HTMMs was trained on the learning set. The trained models are then tested by classifying the documents in the test set. A document is classified as belonging to class i if $P(\boldsymbol{Y}|\lambda_k) > P(\boldsymbol{Y}|\lambda_j)$ for $j \neq k$. These operations are iterated with N varying between 1 and $M - 1$ and each time all the $\binom{M}{N}$ permutations of groups are used to carry out an experiment on a new test and training set. In Algorithm 2 we give a pseudo-code for our cross-validation procedure. The number of single experiments which are carried out, depends on M:

$$\text{NUM\_EXPERIMENTS} = \sum_{N=1}^{M-1} \binom{M}{N} = 2^M - 2 \tag{7}$$

Two experiments sessions have been performed, in the first one we set $M = 7$ while in the second one we set $M = 10$. The proposed technique performs well on the classification task. Using 800 examples (about 90 examples for class) to the train the hidden Markov models, the correct recognition percentage is equal to 99.28%. Accuracy does not rapidly decrease when a smaller number of examples are used to train the models. Table 1 shows that, even when 20% of the examples are used to train the hidden Markov models (80% of examples are included in the test set), the accuracy is still equal to 95%.

6   Conclusions

In this paper we have presented a novel automatic document categorization system in which the documents are represented by X-Y trees. The documents are classified by special Hidden Markov Models which are able to deal

Table 1. Test set accuracy as a function of the percentage of examples, which are included in the training set (test is performed on the remaining documents).

CV-7		CV-10	
training examples	accuracy	training examples	accuracy
86%	99.16%	90%	99.28%
71%	98.72%	70%	97.89%
57%	98.20%	50%	97.83%
43%	97.44%	40%	97.28%
29%	95.53%	30%	96.79%
14%	88.87%	20%	94.99%

with labeled trees. Some preliminary experiments have been carried out on a dataset of commercial invoices with very promising results. We plan to carry out more systematic experiments on a larger dataset and to use the information provided by the intermediate states of the HTMMs to perform a logical labeling of the documents.

References

1. Y. Bengio and P. Frasconi, "An input output HMM architecture," in *Advances in Neural Information Processing Systems 7*, (G. Tesauro, D. Touretzky, and T. Leen, eds.), pp. 427–434, The MIT Press, 1995.
2. R. Brugger, A. Zramdini, and R. Ingold, "Modeling documents for structure recognition using generalized n-grams," in *Proceedings of ICDAR*, 1997.
3. A. Dengel, "Initial learning of document structure," in *Proceedings of ICDAR*, pp. 86–90, 1993.
4. U. M. Fayyad and K. B. Irani, "Multi-interval discretization of continuous-valued attributes for classification learning," in *Proc. 13th Int. Joint Conf. on Artificial Intelligence*, pp. 1022–1027, Morgan Kaufmann, 1993.
5. P. Frasconi, M. Gori, and A. Sperduti, "A general framework for adaptive processing of data structures," *IEEE Trans. on Neural Networks*, vol. 9, no. 5, pp. 768–786, 1998.
6. R. C. Gonzalez and M. G. Thomason, *Syntactic Pattern Recognition*. Reading, Massachusettes: Addison Wesley, 1978.
7. D. Heckerman, "Bayesian networks dor data mining," *Data Mining and Knowledge Discovery*, vol. 1, no. 1, pp. 79–120, 1997.
8. F. V. Jensen, S. L. Lauritzen, and K. G. Olosen, "Bayesian updating in recursive graphical models by local computations," *Computational Statistical Quarterly*, vol. 4, pp. 269–282, 1990.
9. G. Nagy and S. Seth, "Hierarchical representation of optically scanned documents," in *Proc. Int. Conf. on Pattern Recognition*, pp. 347–349, 1984.
10. J. Pearl, *Probabilistic Reasoning in Intelligent Systems : Networks of Plausible Inference*. Morgan Kaufmann, 1988.
11. L. R. Rabiner, "A tutorial on hidden Markov models and selected applications in speech recognition," *Proc. of the IEEE*, vol. 77, no. 2, pp. 257–286, 1989.
12. P. Smyth, D. Heckerman, and M. I. Jordan, "Probabilistic independence networks for hidden markov probability models," *Neural Computation*, vol. 9, no. 2, pp. 227–269, 1997.

Handwriting Quality Evaluation

Victor Kulesh *Oakland University,*
Kevin Schaffer *Mandala Sciences, Inc.,*
Ishwar Sethi *Oakland University,*
Mark Schwartz *Mandala Sciences, Inc.*
Rochester, MI 48309, USA

Abstract

This paper presents an approach to evaluate the quality of handwritten letters based on the set of features that are used by human handwriting experts. The use of these attributes allows very intuitive interpretation of the results and as a consequence provides solid foundation for feedback to the end user of the system. A combination of an artificial neural network and an expert system is used to evaluate and grade each handwritten letter, as well as to provide feedback to the student. The application of such a system would be in the educational field for handwriting teaching and repair.

Keywords: digital ink, handwriting teaching

1. Introduction

It is not a secret that handwriting is one of the major activities in everybody's life (those that doubt this should just try to spend a day without writing anything). However, it does not necessarily mean that everything we write is always useful, simply because in many cases the handwritten text is often of such a poor quality that it can not be understood either by people or computers. This has been our motivation for creating a tool that would be able to help a person learn the proper way of writing.

In order to automate the whole process we have decided to go with so called "digital ink" which is produced by any pen-based device such as WACOM tablet and is composed of strokes that contain sequences of points as well as the timing information. Many researchers for handwriting recognition have used digital ink extensively; however, there has not been any noticeable activity in terms of handwriting quality evaluation. Most of the handwriting instruction systems are based on template matching that teach handwriting using drilling without providing the end-user with any meaningful feedback. Taking into consideration that we know what is supposed to be written, our task is to evaluate that text using several criteria and let the user know how good he or she performs in each category and what can be done for improvement.

Since a lot of research has been conducted in the area of handwriting recognition our work relies on the achievements as far as the extraction of low-level features is concerned, see [1] – [4]. These low-level features are used for

S. Singh, N. Murshed, and W. Kropatsch (Eds.): ICAPR 2001, LNCS 2013, pp. 157–165, 2001.

generating a set of high-level attributes that are drawn from the research area of handwriting teaching and repair; see [5] for example. Given a set of high-level attributes the decision about the quality of the handwritten text is made and feedback is provided for the user.

The proposed approach is flexible in terms of accommodating various languages (for instance the algorithms can be easily trained to work not only with English but also with Spanish or Russian). Also we will show that different approaches to teaching handwriting can also be incorporated into the system. This will of course mean that the algorithms can be adapted to emulate handwriting experts even though the latter may use different methods in their work.

2. From Digital Ink to Grades

The problem of handwriting quality evaluation can be stated as follows: given a sequence of known handwritten letters grade each letter on a scale from 1 to 5 by estimating the following 4 criteria: shape, size, slant and position. It is necessary to note that these criteria can be changed depending on our handwriting instruction approach. In order to solve this problem we utilize the following approach consisting of 4 stages: data acquisition, feature extraction, attribute evaluation and feedback generation. The whole process is depicted in Figure 1. Enrollment Process and Letter Database are used during the training stage of the system.

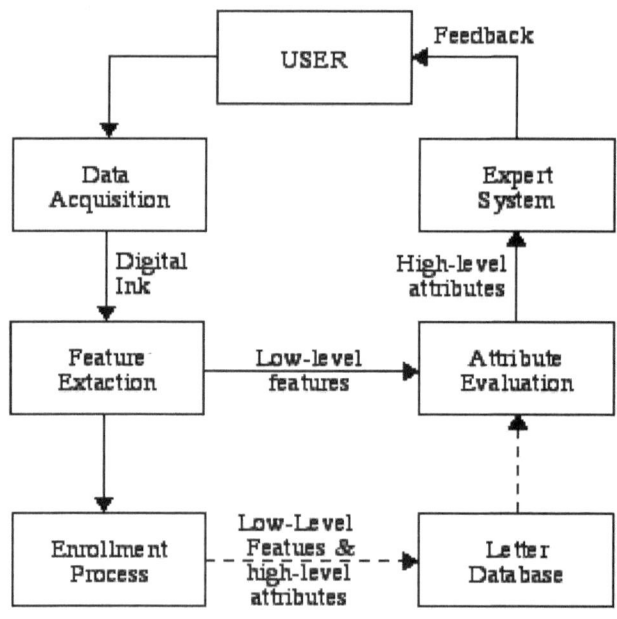

Figure 1

2.1 Data acquisition

Since we know the sequence of letters that the user is writing, data acquisition has to deal only with formation of separate letters from strokes of the input device, i.e. tablet. Each letter consists of one or more strokes that are composed of a sequence of points with timing information. After a "digital letter" is acquired and matched with the expected letter, it is sent to the feature extraction block. As of today we have a choice of hardware devices that could be used as the data acquisition tool: from a classical tablet to PDA to touch-screen monitors. Touch-screen tablets are still very expensive even though they provide the best user experience. Personal Digital Assistants (PDA) are very common and cheap, however, they are so small that the user does not get the same feeling compared to writing on ordinary paper. That left us with the choice of a tablet that allows the use of a pen with ordinary ink. Also, even though the user is stuck with the computer when using the tablet, it has the advantage of providing an instantaneous feedback.

2.2 Feature Extraction

The feature extraction algorithms that we used are based on the results described in [2] and [3]. For each letter a set of features is extracted that includes a subset of slants, min, max and average zero-crossings, and width profiles for 4 zones of the letter as well as number of rows and columns, their ratio, area and the distance between the expected and actual starting points of the letter. Since we want to evaluate the handwriting using the same criteria as the real teacher would use, the following high-level attributes are utilized: shape, slant, size and (super)position of the letter. The low-level features serve as input to the neural network during both training and testing phases. High level attributes are the output of the neural net that is sent as input to the expert system that grades each letter and provides the feedback to the user. While size and (super)position are easily quantifiable using the number of rows, columns, area of the letter and the distance from the starting point, shape and slant require somewhat more complex data.

For shape the following low-level features are utilized:
1. Aspect ratio of height to width
2. Distributions of zero-crossings that deal with the number of times letter-boundaries are crossed while scanning from left to right; see Figure 2.
3. Width distributions across the height of the character.

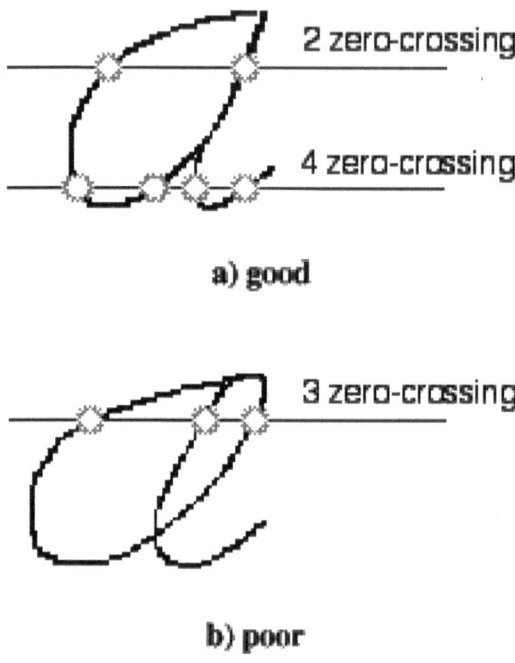

a) good

b) poor

Figure 2

From Figure 2 one can see why the number of zero-crossings is so important when dealing with the shape of the letter. Figure 2(a) is an example of a well-written lower-case letter 'a', and the top part of the letter has 2 zero-crossings. The picture of the same letter in Figure 2(b) shows a poorly written sample, because the strokes on the right side of the letter form two curves instead of one. This is easily detected by the number of zero-crossings which is 3 for this sample.

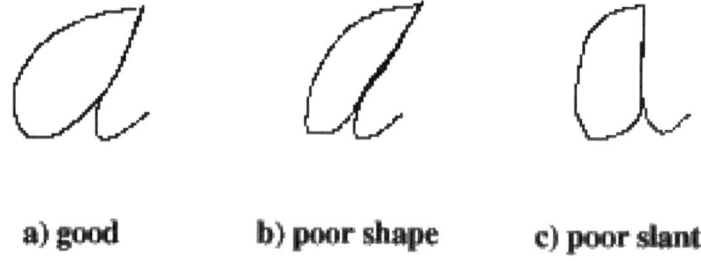

a) good   **b) poor shape**   **c) poor slant**

Figure 3

Another important feature is width distribution of the height of the letter. Handwriting experts define several classes of letters that have similar width distributions; for instance, letters 'c' and 'o' will belong to the same class, while letters 'n' and 'i' will belong to different classes. Figure 3 shows examples of good and bad letters in terms of width distribution.

One very important characteristic of good handwriting as defined by Donald Thurber [5] is the slant of the written letters. For our system we used average slants at angles of 0, 45 and 90 degrees that were computed using chain-codes for letters. Figure 3(c) gives an example of a bad slanted letter 'a'. Studies show that in case of cursive handwriting the slant angle of 25 to 28 degrees from the vertical axis is the easiest to read, therefore these numbers were taken into consideration when grading the training set of letters.

2.3 Attribute Evaluator

Given a vector of low-level features the job of the attribute evaluation block is to map the low-level features into a smaller set of high-level features that we call attributes to distinguish between the two sets. In our approach, we use an artificial neural network to perform this task.

An artificial neural network is a weighted directed graph in which artificial neurons serve as nodes and directed edges with the corresponding weights are used to connect the neuron outputs to neuron inputs, see for instance [6]. There are many properties, such as learning and generalization ability, adaptability, and fault tolerance that made a neural network a very attractive choice for our system. Learning in the context of artificial neural networks means the ability to adjust the network connections and /or the weights on each edge so that the network is able to make a decision or solve a specific problem over and over again. In our case supervised learning technique was used because the classes of high-level attributes were known a priori.

We used a fully connected backpropagation artificial neural network which adjusts the weights according to the following formula:

$$\Delta w_{ij} = \eta \delta_j o_i$$

$$\delta_j = \begin{cases} f_j'(net_j)(t_j - o_j) & \text{if unit } j \text{ is an output unit} \\ f_j'(net_j)\sum_k \delta_k w_{jk} & \text{if unit } j \text{ is a hidden unit} \end{cases}$$

Our goal was to estimate 4 high-level attributes using 19 low-level features. After experimenting with different models we decided in favor of having a dedicated ANN for each high-level attribute, thus resulting in 4 separately trained neural networks for each letter. All neural networks had the same structure. The input layer consisted of 19 neurons, the hidden layer had 4 neurons and the output layer had only one neuron. The 19 features of the input vector were normalized so that their values were in the range from 0 to +1. Similarly, the output vector elements that were used in the training phase were scaled from their original values to the interval of 0 to 1. Further details of using this set of neural networks and the results we obtained are given in Section 3.

2.4 Grading Expert System

A rule-based specialized expert system was created using the knowledge and expertise of the handwriting experts that accepts the four criteria from the attribute evaluator and generates the feedback along with confidence levels for each letter. Expert system can be loosely defined as a computer system that is capable of giving an advice in some particular domain by the virtue of the fact that it possesses the knowledge provided by a human expert. Following this definition the following must be present in the expert system: *knowledge base,* which is created by the expert through the *expert interface, inference engine* and *user interface.* Knowledge base is a subsystem capable of accepting and storing knowledge in the form of cause and effect information. Inference engine provides the means of using the knowledge to provide the end user with results based on the presented facts and questions.

The knowledge base of our expert system incorporates two major sets of rule. The first set contains rules that allow a grading of each letter based on the 4 high-level attributes described above. The second set includes the rules that incorporate the knowledge of a teacher about the process of teaching handwriting. The function of these rules in our system is to provide a feedback to the user for improving handwriting. The rules that we used were similar to the following example:

The size and superposition are good (confidence level 9 out of 10), the slant is satisfactory (confidence level 7 out of 10), shape is poor (confidence level 8 out of 10), and therefore you need to work on the shape of letters in class A, i.e. letters that belong to the same cluster. Please take remedial lesson i.

As of today we only have a small number of rules. For instance, for lowercase letter 'a' there are 10 rules of type one and 4 rules of type two. However, we are in the process of building our expert system and many more rules are expected. The major difficulty here is that of converting the knowledge of a human expert into the rules that the computer can utilize consistently.

This module seems to have a very useful side effect for real life application of teaching handwriting. In cases when different criteria must be used for grading (say for first graders and second graders), instead of training a separate neural net for each of those we can use the same net but plug-in a different expert system that utilizes rules tailored for specific audience. Another reason for having a separate module for attribute evaluation is its ease of customization for use with different languages, even though the neural network has to be retrained in this case.

3. Experimental Results

We conducted our experiments on the data that was collected using a tablet, however, we did not use any timing information as of now. A total of 19 individual features were computed and normalized for each letter. The sample letters were graded by a human expert on a scale from 1 to 5 in terms of the 4 criteria mentioned above. We used a combination of 4 neural networks described above to train and test our grading system. The numbers below were obtained using a neural network that was trained on a training set of 252 samples of letter 'a' and then tested on a set of 48 samples. The two tables below give the numbers that show in how many cases that grades given by the neural network agree with the grades given by the teacher. The normalized values of the grades were 0.9, 0.7, 0.5, 0.3 and 0.1 for 5, 4, 3, 2 and 1 accordingly. We consider the system to agree with the human expert if the difference between the expert's and system's grades differ no more than 0.1. We ranked the differences for the test data and put them into Table 3.

Table 1 shows the results for the training phase.

	Agreement %	Disagreement %
Shape	89.29%	10.71%
Size	84.52%	15.48%
Slant	84.52%	15.48%
Superposition	98.02%	1.98%

Table 1

Table 2 shows the test results on unseen (test) data.

	Agreement %	Disagreement %
Shape	75%	25%
Size	91.7%	8.3%
Slant	86%	14%
Superposition	99.8%	0.2%

Table 2

We also experimented with a neural network that had the same number of neurons in the input and hidden layers, and 4 neurons for each of the high-level attributes in the output layer. The results were slightly worse but still comparable to those in Table 2.

Table 3 shows how much the grades given by the human expert differ from those given by the computer for our test data set.

Rank	0	1	2	3	4
Shape	34	10	1	2	1
Size	40	6	1	1	0
Slant	39	7	1	1	0
Superposition	47	0	0	1	0

Table 3

Table 3 gives an idea about the actual performance of the system. The rank values determine the amount of disagreement on the grade between the human expert and the computer. Rank = 0 implies that both gave the same grade to the letter, rank = 1 means that one gave a grade of say 5 while the other gave a grade of 4 (1 point difference) and so on. The numbers inside the table cells tell us the number of times the human expert and the computer system agree (in case of rank 0) or disagree (for all other values of the rank) for a total of 48 letters. As one can see the highest count of disagreement is of rank=1 which implies that most of the differences are 1 point only on a 5 point scale.

From the numbers in Table 2 we can see that there is a high percentage of misclassification for the shape attribute, which in our opinion occurs because of two reasons: 1) the set of low-level features that influence the shape representation that we used is robust enough to differentiate well among different letters; however it is not sensitive to variations of the same letter, and 2) the data used for training was collected from 2 writers only which can not possibly represent the entire universe of people. While 2) is a trivial problem we are working on 1) in order to improve the performance of the system.

The use of the neural network achieves the goal of determining how good or bad the shape, size, slant and position of each letter are on a scale from 1 to 5. Instead of simply grading each letter we decided to add one more block to the system that is intelligent enough to not only give a grade to the student but also provide certain feedback in the form of advice as to what is wrong and what lesson might help to improve the handwriting. This is achieved by means of a handwriting expert system.

4. Conclusions and future work

We have presented an approach to quantitatively evaluate handwritten text and our experimental results prove that this could be a fairly accurate method in terms of grading and consistency. In several cases we found out that the computer was more consistent than the human when grading a lot of letters, which is clearly good when it comes to evaluating the work of different people. We, however, still have a lot of research in front of us in the area of shape evaluation to further improve the feedback to the user. The timing information and direction of pen movement is currently under investigation. We believe that this can improve out approach tremendously because this will provide the same advantage of following every movement of the pen and immediately recognizing the wrong practices that students might use when learning how to write. Another area of research that we are planning to do is adapting out approach for handwriting teaching techniques that use joined cursive letters instead of separate letters, as used by D'Nealian handwriting system [5].

References

[1] F.Kimura, M. Shridhar, N. Narasimhamurthi, "Lexicon Directed Segmentation-recognition Procedure for Unconstrained Handwritten Words," Proceedings of the Thirds Int'l workshop on Frontiers Handwriting Recognition, SUNY Buffalo, May 25-27, 1993, pp.122-131.

[2] F.Kimura, S. Tsuruoka, M. Shridhar, and Z. Chen, "Context Directed Handwritten Word Recognition for Postal Service Applications," Proc. of Fifth Advanced Technology Conference, Wash. DC, 1992, pp. 199-213.

[3] F.Kimura, M. Shridhar, "Segmentation-Recognition Algorithm for ZIP Code Field Recognition," Machine Vision and Apoplications (1992) 5:199-210.

[4] M. Belkasim, M. Shridhar, M. Ahmadi, "Pattern Recognition Using Moment Invariants: A Comparative Study," Pattern Recognition. Vol. 24, No. 12, pp.1117-1138, 1991.

[5] Handwriting Research and Information, An Administrator's Handbook, ScottForesman, 1993.

[6] Anil K. Jain, Jianchang Mao, and K.M Mohiuddin, "Artificial Neural Networks: A Tutorial," IEEE Computer Society, Volume 29, Number 3, March 1996.

Texture Based Look-Ahead for Decision-Tree Induction

Ming Dong and Ravi Kothari

Artificial Neural Systems Laboratory
Department of Electrical & Computer Engineering & Computer Science
University of Cincinnati, Cincinnati, OH 45221-0030, USA

Abstract. Decision tree induction corresponds to partitioning the input space through the use of internal nodes. A node attempts to classify the instances misclassified by upper level nodes using a greedy search strategy, i.e. to maximize the number of instances correctly classified at the node. However, in so doing it is possible that the distribution of the remaining (misclassified) instances is complex thereby requiring a large number of additional nodes for classification. The so-called look-ahead method was proposed to examine the classifiability of the remaining instances. Typically, this is done using a classifier parameterized identically (e.g. hyperplane) to the one used for partitioning. The number of correct classification achieved in the look-ahead stage is factored in choosing the partition established at a node. This has led to mixed results. In this paper we argue that 1-step (or a few step) look-ahead amounts to an approximate estimate of the classifiability of the remaining instances. In many cases, it is gross approximation and hence the results are mixed. We present an alternative approach to look-ahead which uses the joint probability of occurrence of the classes as a way of characterizing the classifiability of the remaining instances. We present the algorithm and some experimental results.

Keywords: Decision tree, Look-ahead, Classification, Texture

1 Introduction

Each node of the decision tree partitions a region of the input space in an attempt to classify the remaining instances (or patterns). Differences between the approaches to decision tree induction arise based on whether,

(C1) The partition at each node is established based on a single attribute or all the attributes. When based on a single attribute, the partition boundary is orthogonal to the chosen attribute. When all the attributes are used, the partition is typically based on a linear discriminant, i.e. the partitioning is achieved using a hyperplane though higher order parameterizations are possible. In the following we assume that the partition is established using a hyperplane.

S. Singh, N. Murshed, and W. Kropatsch (Eds.): ICAPR 2001, LNCS 2013, pp. 166–175, 2001.
© Springer-Verlag Berlin Heidelberg 2001

(**C2**) The node splitting criteria that is used. Some of the popular node splitting criteria include entropy or its variants [1], the chi-square statistic [2,3], the G statistic [3], and the GINI index of diversity [4]. There appears to be no single node splitting that performs the best in all cases [5,6]; however there is little doubt that random splitting performs the worst.

The different node splitting criteria are united by their goal of seeking a split that maximizes the number of instances correctly classified at the node so as to arriving at smaller decision trees. However, the partition created by a node corresponds to a locally optimum and irrevocable decision. Consequently, it is possible that a (locally optimum) partition at node i leaves incorrectly classified patterns that further require a large number of nodes for classification.

To illustrate, consider the following 2-class classification scenario. In the top panel of Figure 1, there is only 1 instance that remains misclassified after the first partition (identified with '(1)') is induced. This single remaining pattern however, requires two additional partitions (nodes) to achieve correct classification. The reason being that this remaining instance (incorrectly classified) was surrounded by instances of other classes – a complex distribution (or low classifiability) of the remaining instances. On the other hand, consider the bottom panel of Figure 1 in which the first partition leaves two instances misclassified. However, a single additional partition (node) is sufficient to classify all instances correctly. The reason being that the distribution of the remaining instances was simpler than in the first case.

Motivated by the above, we propose an *accurate and inexpensive* node splitting criteria that not only attempts to maximize the number of correctly classified instances but also tries to produce a distribution of incorrectly classified instances that facilitates easy classification. In Section 2, we discuss prior work on look-ahead, discuss why these past efforts have resulted in mixed results, and motivate the use of joint probabilities for characterizing the complexity of the distribution of the remaining instances[1]. In Section 3, we present the complete objective function based on joint probability and derive an algorithm for obtaining the decision tree. In Section 4 we present our experimental results and in Section 5 our conclusions.

2   Characterizing the Distribution of Remaining Instances

There are a handful of earlier efforts which attempt to characterize the distribution of the remaining instances based on look-ahead [7–9]. Look-ahead at node i factors in the number of correct classifications that would result with the patterns misclassified at node ii. Mixed results are reported (ranging from look-ahead makes no difference to look-ahead produces larger trees [9]).

We believe these mixed results (or more strongly, the lack of consistently favorable results despite using look-ahead), arise because of the following considerations [10],

---

[1] In other words, the classifiability of the remaining instances.

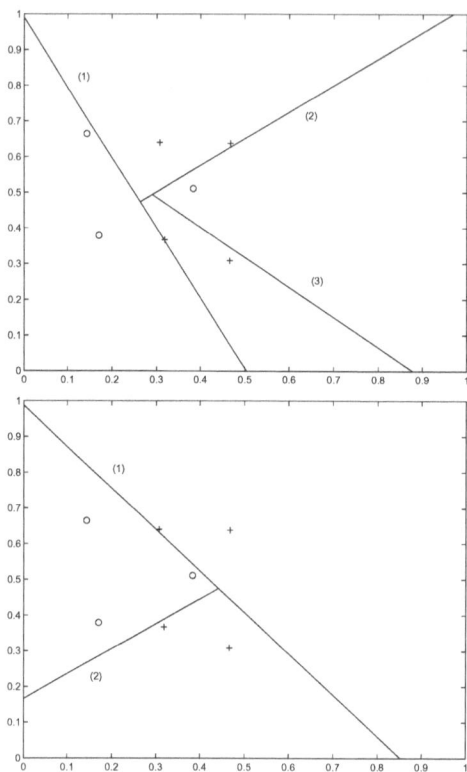

Fig. 1. The distribution of the incorrectly classified patterns is important. The distribution of the remaining instances after the first partition is established is more complex in the top panel than in the bottom panel. Consequently, more additional partitions (nodes) are required to achieve correct classification.

- Ideally, the look-ahead should be multi-step corresponding to an exhaustive search. This multi-step look-ahead is computationally not feasible for all but the most trivial of problems. Consequently, single- or at most a few-step look-ahead is commonly used.
- The partitions (hyperplane) in the look-ahead stage are based on a classifier that is identically parameterized as the one used for node splitting. Typically, at each node, a hyperplane (or other lower order curve) is used.
- A single-step look-ahead with a hyperplane corresponds to an approximation of the *true* decision boundary in the space of remaining patterns with a hyperplane. This single-step look-ahead results in an incorrect estimate of the classifiability of the remaining instances. An illustrative situation is depicted in Figure 2. If single-step look-ahead is used, then the classifiability of the remaining instances is poor even though the remaining instances can be accurately classified using two additional nodes, i.e. the look-ahead should

have been a 3-step one. Of course, if a d step look-ahead is used, then a $(d + 1)$ or more-step look-ahead might have been more appropriate. Thus when look-ahead is used with a *parameterized decision boundary* the results are approximate. The accuracy of the approximation varies with the problem and hence the results are mixed.

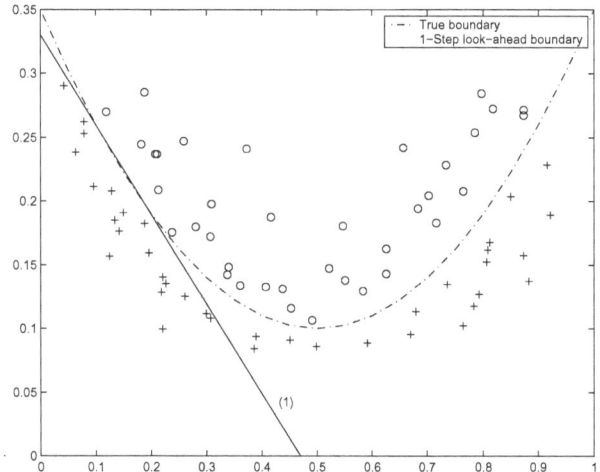

Fig. 2. 1-step look-ahead corresponds to an approximation of the true decision boundary. In the above case, the 1-step look-ahead indicates poor classifiability even though the instances are classifiable using three hyperplanes.

Because of the above considerations, we propose the use of a non-parametric approach for determining the classifiability of the remaining instances. Due to the fact that the decision boundary is not parameterized (linearly or non-linearly), classifiability results obtained by our proposed approach better reflects the complexity of the true decision boundary required to classify the remaining instances. We discuss our approach in greater detail in the next section.

3   Texture Based Decision Tree Induction

We consider a classification problem in which there are a total of C classes characterized by the set $\Omega = \{\omega_1, \omega_2, \ldots, \omega_C\}$. We represent the number of instances (or patterns) remaining at node i by $N^{(i)}$ and the number of instances of class ω_k at node i by $N_{\omega_k}^{(i)}$. $\sum_k N_{\omega_k}^{(i)} = N^{(i)}$. The hyperplane established at node i is identified by $\mathcal{H}^{(i)}(W)$ where W represents the parameters of the hyperplane. We propose to identify the hyperplane $\mathcal{H}^{(i)}$ by maximizing the following objective function [10],

$$J^{(i)} = G^{(i)} + \lambda L^{(i)} \tag{1}$$

where, $G^{(i)}$ represents the information gain, $L^{(i)}$ the classifiability of the remaining (incorrectly classified) instances, and λ represents the relative weighting of $G^{(i)}$ and $L^{(i)}$. In what follows, we discuss each of these terms in greater detail.

- The information gain term in equation (1) attempts to establish a partition so as to maximize the number of correct classifications [1]. More specifically, representing the two child nodes of node i as node $(i + 1)$ and $(i + 2)$ we obtain,

$$G^{(i)} = \sum_{k=1}^{C} -\frac{N_{\omega_k}^{(i)}}{N^{(i)}} \log \frac{N_{\omega_k}^{(i)}}{N^{(i)}} - \sum_{j=i+1}^{i+2} \sum_{k=1}^{C} -\frac{N^{(j)}}{N^{(i)}} \left[\frac{N_{\omega_k}^{(j)}}{N^{(j)}} \log \frac{N_{\omega_k}^{(j)}}{N^{(j)}} \right] \quad (2)$$

Note that in equation (2), the number of instances of each class on a given side of the hyperplane is expressed in terms of the number of instances of the next node.
- The classifiability term attempts to evaluate the distribution of the incorrectly classified instances. A distribution of these remaining instances which can be partitioned using few additional nodes is favored over one requiring a larger number of additional nodes to classify. We evaluate the classifiability of the remaining instances using the concept of texture (or roughness). Observe that we can visualize the $(n + 1)$ variables of the classification problem (n input variables and 1 variable indicating the class label) as a surface. For example, when there are 2 inputs, the class label can be plotted on the z axis and the inputs in the $x - y$ plane. If nearby instances belong to different classes, then this surface is rough. However, when local patches belong to single class, the surface is smooth. Hence, our usage of *texture* as an indicator of classifiability. The joint-probability of occurrence of the classes captures the notion of texture or the roughness of the class-label surface[2].
We propose computing this classifiability as follows. From one side of the partition established at node i, we obtain a matrix of joint probabilities $P^{(i)}$ of size $C \times C$ (recall that C is the number of classes). Elements of $P_{jk}^{(i)}$ are the total number of remaining instances (i.e. instances misclassified at node i) of class ω_k that occur within a circular neighborhood of radius r of an instance of class ω_j, i.e.,

$$P_{jk}^{(i)} = \sum_{l=1}^{N_{\omega_j}^{(i+1)}} \sum_{m=1}^{N_{\omega_k}^{(i+1)}} f(x_l, x_m) \quad (3)$$

where, x_l denotes an instance of class ω_j and x_m denotes an instance of class ω_k, and $f(\cdot)$ is an indicator function which is 1 if $\| x_l - x_m \| \leq r$. Similarly, we can obtain a matrix of joint probabilities, say $Q^{(i)}$ from the other side of the partition, i.e.

$$A^{(i)} = P^{(i)} + Q^{(i)} \quad (4)$$

---

[2] This has a parallel in image processing where the co-occurrence matrix, a matrix of joint gray level probabilities, is commonly used for quantifying texture[11, 12].

One can normalize $A^{(i)}$ such that the sum of the elements of $A^{(i)}$ is 1. Note that in the ideal case (perfect classifiability) matrix $A^{(i)}$ becomes a diagonal matrix. In the general case, the off-diagonal terms correspond to instances of different classes that occur with a neighborhood of radius r^3. We thus obtain $L^{(i)}$ as,

$$L^{(i)} = \sum_{j=1}^{C} A_{jj}^{(i)} - \sum_{j=1}^{C} \sum_{\substack{k=1 \\ k \neq j}}^{C} A_{jk}^{(i)} \tag{5}$$

The partition induced at node i is thus based on maximization of equation (1). However, $J^{(i)}$ in equation (1) is not a continuous function of the parameters of $\mathcal{H}^{(i)}$. We thus use a Genetic Algorithm (GA) [13, 14] to obtain the parameters of the hyperplane $\mathcal{H}^{(i)}$.

In the next section, we present some experimental results obtained using the proposed texture based look-ahead approach described above.

4   Experimental Results

We present the results of four simulations to illustrate the efficacy of the proposed texture based look-ahead algorithm. The following applies to all the simulations. The GA was run for a maximum of 600 generations or until the fitness value (equation (1)) stopped increasing. In the GA, parameters were represented as real values between -1 and $+1$ and quantized to a resolution of 10^{-6}. Arithmetic crossover and non-uniform mutation [14] were used. The total number of nodes reported for the simulations are based on the number of decisions (leaf nodes are not included).

In general, there is no way of knowing an appropriate value to use for λ in equation (1) or the value of the Neighborhood (r). For the latter three simulations, we thus show the results shown below are thus over a range of λ and r. For these latter three simulations, we also report the results obtained when the look-ahead is done using a classifier parameterized identically to the one used for partitioning. This situation corresponds to the way look-ahead has typically been implemented by other authors.

4.1   Data Set I: Synthetic Data

For the first simulation, we use a synthetic data set designed to illustrate the effect of including texture based look-ahead. The left panel of Figure 3 shows the results when look-ahead was not used. The information gain at the root node was 0.3113. The right panel of Figure 3 shows the results when look-ahead was used. The information gain at the root node was 0.2543 with $\lambda = 3$ and $r = 0.5$. This lower information gain based first partition however leads to a more compact decision tree.

---

[3] Controlling r corresponds to adjusting the bias and the variance [10].

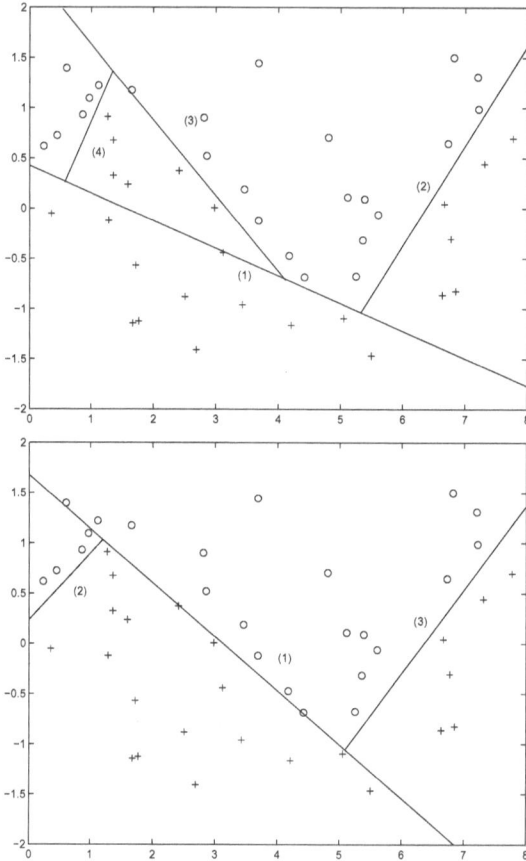

Fig. 3. Look-ahead results in more compact decision trees as shown through this example. The left panel is without the use of look-ahead (i.e. a greedy strategy, $\lambda = 0$ is equation (1). The right panel is with the use of look-ahead.

4.2   Data Set II: Iris Data

For the second simulation, we consider the well known Iris data set. The data set consists of 3 classes (types of Iris plants — Setosa, Versicolor, and Virginica) with 50 instances of each class. There are a total of 4 features (the sepal length and width, and the petal length and width). It is also well known that one class (Setosa) is linearly separable from the other two (Versicolor and Viriginica) and that the latter two are not linearly separable from each other.

Initial population size for the GA was 200. As there is no separate testing data in this case, we added internal nodes to achieve an accuracy of 100%, i.e. correct classification of the 150 instances.

Table 1 summarizes the results obtained. The first row in the table ($r = 0$, $\lambda = 0$) corresponds to no look-ahead. The second row corresponds to a single step look-ahead using the a classifier parameterized identically to that used for partitioning (a hyperplane in this case) and the remaining rows reflect the results obtained with the proposed texture based look-ahead. It is clear from observing the other rows that the use of the proposed texture based look-ahead results in better performance. For example, without the use of the texture based look-ahead we obtain a total of 6 nodes while the number is consistently less if texture based look-ahead is used. For reference, ID3[4] requires 8 nodes to achieve an accuracy of 100% on the training data.

Neighborhood (r)	λ	Number of Nodes
0	0	6
0	1	6
0.6	1	5
0.8	1	5
0.6	3	4
0.6	4	5

Table 1. Results obtained for the Iris data set.

4.3   Data Set III: Breast Cancer Data

For the third simulation, we used the Wisconsin Breast Cancer data set available at the UCI Machine Learning Repository [15]. Each pattern has 9 inputs and an associated class label (benign or malignant). The two classes are known to be linearly inseparable. The total number of instances are 699 (458 benign, and 241 malignant), of which 16 instances have a single missing feature. We removed those 16 instances and used the remaining 683 instances. A total of 200 benign and 200 malignant instances were used for training and the rest were used for testing.

Initial population size for the GA was 600. Internal nodes were added until the error on the training patterns was 0.

Table 2 shows the results obtained with the Wisconsin Breast Cancer data set with varying values of the parameter. The first row in the table ($r = 0$, $\lambda = 0$) corresponds to no look-ahead. The second row corresponds to a single step look-ahead using the a classifier parameterized identically to that used for partitioning (a hyperplane in this case) and the remaining rows reflect the results obtained with the proposed texture based look-ahead. It is clear from observing the other rows that the use of the proposed texture based look-ahead results in better performance. For reference, ID3 requires 19 nodes to achieve an accuracy of 100% on the training data. The testing accuracy of ID3 was 95.40%.

---

[4] This is provided for reference and should not be used for a direct comparison. Recall that ID3 does not uses a linear discriminant but rather a single attribute at each node.

Neighborhood (r)	λ	Testing Accuracy (%)	Number of Nodes
0	0	94.3	17
0	1	94.3	18
8	1	96.3	14
15	1	95.8	15
10	2	95.3	16

Table 2. Results obtained for the Wisconsin Breast Cancer data set.

4.4   Data Set IV: Balance Data

For the fourth simulation, we used the Balance Scale Weight and Distance data set available at the UCI Machine Learning Repository [15]. Each pattern is described by 4 inputs: the left weight, the left distance, the right weight, and the right distance. There are three classes: balance scale "tip to the right", "tip to the left", and "balanced". The underlying concept is to compare (left distance × left weight) and (right distance × right weight). If they are equal, it is balanced. If the "left term" is larger then the class is "tip to the left" and so on.

The total number of instances are 625 (49 balanced, 288 tip to the left, and 288 tip to the right) with no missing values. We used the entire data set and kept adding nodes until all the 625 training patterns are correctly classified.

Neighborhood (r)	λ	Number of Nodes
0	0	27
0	1	26
6	1	20
10	1	19

Table 3. Results obtained with the Balance Scale Weight and Distance data set.

Table 3 shows the results obtained with the Balance Scale Weight and Distance data set. The first row in the table ($r = 0$, $\lambda = 0$) corresponds to no look-ahead. The second row corresponds to a single step look-ahead using the a classifier parameterized identically to that used for partitioning (a hyperplane in this case) and the remaining rows reflect the results obtained with the proposed texture based look-ahead. It is clear from observing the other rows that the use of the proposed texture based look-ahead results in better performance.

5   Conclusion

Towards establishing compact decision trees, we presented a look-ahead method which utilizes the concept of joint probability of occurrence of classes (texture) to establish partitions at internal nodes of a decision tree. The rationale for looking at texture is to establish partitions which maximize the number of instances correctly classified at a node and ensuring high classifiability of the remaining (misclassified) instances. The algorithm proposed herein shows superior results on test problems.

References

1. J. R. Quinlan, "Induction of decision trees," *Machine Learning*, vol. 1, pp. 81–106, 1986.
2. A. Hart, "Experience in the use of inductive system in knowledge engineering," in *Research and Developments in Expert Systems*, M. Bramer, Ed., Cambridge, 1984, Cambridge University Press.
3. J. Mingers, "Expert systems - experiments with rule induction," *Journal of the Operational Research Society*, vol. 38, pp. 39–47, 1987.
4. L. Breiman, J. H. Friedman, J. A. Olshen, and C. J. Stone, *Classification and Regression Trees*, Wadsworth International Group, Belmont, CA, 1984.
5. J. Mingers, "An empirical comparison of selection measures for decision-tree induction," *Machine Learning*, vol. 3, pp. 319–342, 1989.
6. W. Buntine and T. Niblett, "A further comparison of splitting rules for decision-tree induction," *Machine Learning*, vol. 8, pp. 75–85, 1989.
7. J. R. Quinlan and R. M. Cameron-Jones, "Oversearching and layered search in empirical learning," in *Proc. 14th International Conference on Artificial Intelligence*, San Manteo, California, 1995, pp. 1019–1024, Morgan Kaufman.
8. J. F. Elder, "Heuristic search for model structure," in *Learning from Data: Artificial Intelligence and Statistics V, Lecture Notes in Statistics*, D. Fischer and H-J. Lenz, Eds. 1995, vol. 112, pp. 131–142, Springer-Verlag.
9. S. K. Murthy and S. Salzberg, "Lookahead and pathology in decision tree induction," in *Proc. 14th International Conference on Artificial Intelligence*, San Manteo, California, 1995, pp. 1025–1031, Morgan Kaufman.
10. R. Kothari and M. Dong, "Decision trees for classification: A review and some new results," in *Lecture Notes in Pattern Recognition*, S. K. Pal and A. Pal, Eds., Singapore, 2000, World Scientific Publishing Company.
11. R. M. Haralick and L. G. Shapiro, *Computer and Robot Vision*, Addison-Wesley, Reading, Massachusetts, 1992.
12. R. Kothari, "Image segmentation," in *Encyclopedia of Electrical and Electronics Engineering*, J. Webster, Ed., New York, 1999, vol. 9, pp. 642–652, John Wiley.
13. D. Goldberg, *Genetic Algorithms in Search, Optimization, and Machine Learning*, Addison-Wesley, Reading, Massachusetts, 1989.
14. Z. Michalewicz, *Genetic Algorithms + Data Structures = Evolution Programs*, Springer-Verlag, New York, 1994.
15. C. J. Merz and P. M. Murphy, "UCI repository of machine learning databases," Tech. Rep., Department of Information and Computer Science, University of California at Irvine, [http:// www.ics.uci.edu/~mlearn/MLRepository.html], 1996.

Acknowledgment: The breast cancer database is available at the UCI Repository of Machine Learning Databases [http:// www.ics.uci.edu/~mlearn/ML-Repository.html] where it was obtained from the University of Wisconsin Hospitals, Madison from Dr. William H. Wolberg. Part of this work was done when RK was on a sabbatical leave from the University of Cincinnati.

Feature Based Decision Fusion

Nayer M. Wanas and Mohamed S. Kamel

Pattern Analysis and Machine Intelligence lab,
Department of Systems Design Engineering,
University of Waterloo, Waterloo, Ontario, Canada, N2L-3G1
{nwanas,mkamel}@pami.uwaterloo.ca

Abstract. In this paper we present a new architecture for combining classifiers. This approach integrates learning into the voting scheme used to aggregate individual classifiers decisions. This overcomes the drawbacks of having static voting techniques. The focus of this work is to make the decision fusion a more *adaptive* process. This approach makes use of feature *detectors* responsible for gathering information about the input to perform adaptive decision aggregation. Test results show improvement in the overall classification rates over any individual classifier, as well as different static classifier-combining schemes.

Keywords: *Decision Fusion, Multiple Classifiers, Adaptive, Architecture, Neural Networks*

1 Introduction

Combining classifiers for classification has been recently an extensively researched topic. This is due to the fact that classification accuracy can be improved using a multiple classifier paradigm. The fact that the patterns that are misclassified by the different classifiers are not necessarily the same [1], suggests that the use of multiple classifiers can complement the decision about the patterns under classification. This will improve the reliability of the overall classification process. However, the issue of *efficiently* combing the individual decisions to provide an aggregated decision is a very crucial issue in making such systems worthwhile [2].

A variety of schemes have been proposed in the literature for classifier combining. Perhaps the most often used schemes are the majority vote [3], average vote [4], and weighted average [5]. Other techniques include Borda count [6], Bayes approach and probabilistic schemes [3], Dempster Shafer theory [7], and fuzzy integrals [8]. These different approaches can be viewed as a means by which relative weights are assigned to each classifier. These weights can be data dependent. Woods [9], presents methods of combining classifiers that use estimates of each individual classifier's local accuracy in small regions of the feature space surrounding the unknown test sample. The Behavior-Knowledge Space (BKS) approach [10] is a similar approach. The output of the individual classifier represent a decision space where every dimension corresponds to the decision of one classifier. An unknown test

S. Singh, N. Murshed, and W. Kropatsch (Eds.): ICAPR 2001, LNCS 2013, pp. 176–185, 2001.
© Springer-Verlag Berlin Heidelberg 2001

sample is assigned a class with the most training samples in the same BKS proximity.

The aggregations phase of a classifier combining approach can also be viewed as a mapping between the input and out put of the combiner. Linear combining is perhaps the most widely used techniques because of its simplicity. In this case the final output is a linear function of expert outputs $Y(x) = \sum_{i=1}^{n} W_i(x).Y_i(x)$, where $Y_i(x)$ is the output of the i-th classifier and W_i is the weight assigned to this classifier.Non-linear mapping include methods such as stacked generalization [11]. In this approach classifiers are used to correct the errors of one another. Order statistics combining, in which the output of each classifier is considered an approximation of the a posteriori probability of class membership. These probabilities are ordered and either the maximum, minimum or media probability is considered as the final output. Rank based combining [6] in which classifiers using different representations are used. These different classifiers provide outputs such as, *distance to prototypes, Values of an arbitrary discriminant, estimates of posterior probabilities and confidence measures.* The rank of the classes in the output vector of each classifier has a meaningful interpretation in this case. Belief-based methods, where the output of each classifier represents a *belief* that the classifier has in it's answer. Dempster Shafer theory [7] decouples the classifier output from the confidence it has for this output. Both these values are used in combining for the final output.

Another way of categorizing these different classifier combining techniques is based on architecture. While parallel architectures are the most popular. In this case each classifier operates independently and only the output of these classifiers is used in the final combining phase. In this approach modular design is possible. On the other hand non-parallel cases the individual classifiers are not independent, such as binary decision making. In this case the classification procedure is sequential. The main objective it to transform a multi-class problem to a set of two-class problems that are easier to solve.

Combining methods can be divided into two different classes depending on the representation methodology. The classifiers can all use the same representation, and hence the classifiers themselves should be different. In multi-representation approaches [1] the different classifiers us different representations of the same inputs. This can be due to the use of different sensors or different features extracted from the same data set. Another, and final categorization of classifier combining methods are if they encourage specialization [12] in certain areas of the feature space. On the other hand, ensemble of classifiers [2] have classifiers that do not encourage such specialization and hence the classifiers themselves must have different classification powers.

The Cooperative Modular Neural Network (CMNN) [13] and the Ensembles Voting OnLine (EVOL) [14] have presented techniques that make the individual classifiers more involved in the final decision making process. However, even in these setups, the aggregation schemes implemented are totally isolated from the problem being considered. This fact makes the aggregation procedure a predefined scheme, i.e., determined prior to the actual use of the overall system. This work will focus on making the decision fusion a more *adaptive* process. Local classification decisions are combined in a way similar to the parallel suite in decision fusion models [15]. This approach requires the aggregation procedure to gather information about the input beyond what individual classifiers provide. The gathered information (i.e., the extracted additional features) is used to tune the aggregation procedure.

This strategy will automatically guide the modules, during the development phase to adapt more about the learning samples that are not correctly classified, on the global level. This makes the efficiency of the global fusion scheme related to the learning efficiency of all of the input samples, not the local modular efficiency.

2 Feature Based Decision Aggregation

Figure 1 shows the block diagram of a proposed architecture that incorporates these requirements. In the following subsections, we address each component of this architecture in some detail.

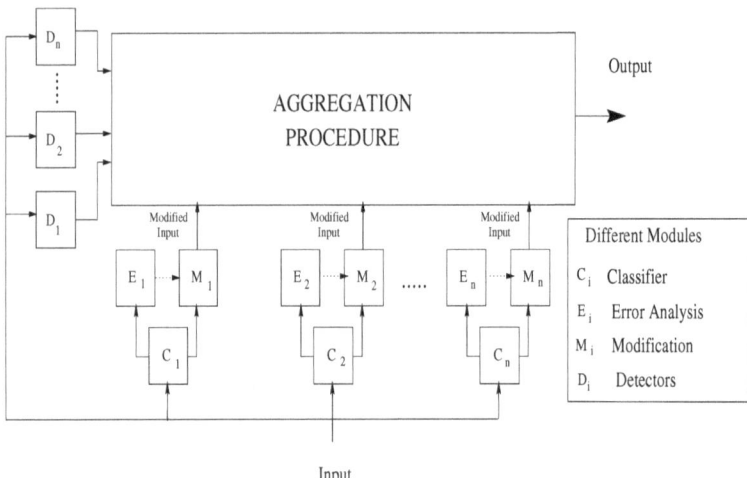

Fig. 1. Block Diagram for the Proposed Architecture.

2.1 Classifiers

Each individual classifier, C_i, produces some output representing its interpretation of the input. In the context of this paper, we are more interested in using the output of these classifiers to help in the aggregation procedure rather than the methodology of classification. Another goal is to utilize suboptimal classifiers in the proposed architecture, to make the development overhead of such a system worthwhile.

2.2   Error Analysis

These modules $\{E_i\}$ use the previously studied error analysis of the individual output and produce means to modify the output so as to overcome possible errors. These modules must be dynamic as well as comprehensive to adequately suit their purpose. Relevant information only is passed to the modifying module.

The accuracy of a pattern recognizer depends upon the intrinsic overlap of the class distributions and the estimation error due to the finite size of the set of learning objects. Errors can be classified into two categories: classification errors and systematic errors. The classification error, defined as the probability of error in classifying new objects, is used as a measure for the accuracy. The classification error depends on the characteristics of the features chosen, the number of features, the size of the learning set, and on the procedure used for the estimation of the discriminant function. A number of these items are influenced or determined by a priori knowledge. Systematic errors may be constant or may vary in a regular way [18]. Eliminating those errors would help in achieving better performance. This is the main role of this module. The techniques and approaches used are totally dependent on the nature of the problem and the classification technique implemented in the classification module.

2.3   Modification Modules

These modules $\{M_i\}$ use the information from the error analysis modules and operate on the classifier input to produce a modified output that is normalized to be within a common representation with all other inputs fed to the aggregation procedure. Hence, the comparison between the different inputs then is meaningful. Similar to the error analysis modules, these modules are dependent on the nature of the problem and the classifier used. In these modules, a confidence index is associated to each classifier. This index can be interpreted as the conditional probability that the classifier experienced success given a certain input, or $P(x_i$ correct | Input), where x_i is the output vector of classifier i. The confidence in the output can be interpreted in different ways. In this work, the difference between the two top output values of each classifier is used as the confidence in the output of that classifier.

2.4   Detectors

Each detector, D_i, takes the input space and tries to extract useful information for the aggregation procedure, rather than aiming to solve the classification problem. In other words, it tries to understand and collect information that might be helpful in the aggregation procedure. For instance, in a character recognition problem, the goal is to identify a given character. While the individual classifiers try to determine the character, the detectors try to identify the category of the character. This helps the aggregation scheme in determining how to combine the different classification outputs to achieve a better performance.

2.5   The Aggregation Procedure

The aggregation procedure represents the fusion layer of all the different outputs to generate a more competent output. The aggregation procedure uses detectors' outputs to guide the means of combining different classification results. The aggregation scheme can be divided into two phases: a learning phase and a decision making phase. The learning phase assigns a weight factor to each input to support each decision maker. This weighting factor represents a confidence in the output of each classifier. These confidences are then aggregated using standard classifier-combining methods.

A neural network approach is selected to perform the weighting of the individual classifier. The neural network would take the inputs from both individual classifiers and detectors and presents a newly modified probability of success of each classifier. Implementation details are given in the following section.

3   Combining methods

The majority vote, maximum vote, average vote, Borda count and Nash vote are the combining methods used in comparision to the feature-based aggreagtion procedure. In the following we will berifly decribe each of these combining schemes.

3.1   Majority Vote

The correct class is the one most often chosen by different classifiers. If all the classifiers indicate different classes, then the one with the highest overall output is selected to be the correct class.

3.2   Maximum Vote

The class with the highest overall output is selected as the correct class. $q(x) = \arg\max_{i=1}^{n} Y_i(x)$ where n is the number of classifiers, $Y_i(x)$ represents the output of the ith classifier for the input vector x.

3.3   Average Vote

This approach averages the individual classifier outputs across all the ensemble. The output yielding the highest average value is chosen to be the correct class. $q(x) = \arg\max_{k=1}^{K} \left(Y_k(x) = \frac{1}{n} \sum_{i=1}^{n} y_{i,k}(x) \right)$ where K is the number of classes, $y_{ik}(x)$ represents the output of the ith classifier for the kth class for the input x.

3.4   Borda Count

For any class k, the Borda count is the sum of the number of classes ranked below k by each classifier. If $B_i(k)$ is the number of classes ranked below class k by the ith classifier, then the Borda count for class k is $B(k) = \sum_{i=1}^{n} B_i(k)$ The output is the class with the largest Borda count.

3.5   Nash Vote

Each voter assigns a number between zero and one for each candidate. Compare the product of the voter's values for all the candidates. The higher is the winner. $q(x) = \arg\max_{k=1}^{K} \prod_{i=1}^{n} V_{ik}$

4   Results

This architecture was tested using two data sets. In both cases the data was divided into three sections, training, verification and testing. The individual classifiers were implemented as backpropagation neural networks[1]. The stopping criteria was to save the best network, with respect to the verification set, over 10,000 iterations. A test for the best performance was performed every 1000 iterations. All network used as part of the ensemble had 10 hidden nodes. The utilized learning schemes is Backprop with Delta-Bar-Delta, *tanh* transfer function and *softmax* outputs. The momentum and learning coefficient were set to 0.4 and 0.5 respectivily. Each classifier is trained 10 times, the best performance module is chosen. The ensemble of networks created had partially disjointed training data.

4.1   Gaussian 20-class problem

This problem is basically a two dimensional recognition problem. It contains 20 different classes that have equal probability presented by Auda and Kamel[2]. Each class had a total number of 100 samples generated to follow a Gaussian distribution around a random class mean. The classes also assumed the same standard deviation. The complexity, and in this case what makes the presented results more general, lies in the "non-homogeneous"

---

[1] Implementation was performed on Neural Works II/Plus©NeuralWare Inc. 1993

regions in the feature space and the overlapping boundaries between them. The data set was divided into three sets, training, validation and testing sets; 1000/300/700 entries were used for training, validation and testing, respectively.

Five individual backpropagation neural networks with 10 hidden nodes composed the set of individual modules. The training set used was divided into five parts. Each module was trained by four parts of these sets. This partially disjointed training set between the modules allowed for different training within these modules. Table 1 shows the performance of one module across different training instances.

Table 1. Performance of an individual module on the Gaussian 20-Class problem.

Data set	Training	Verification	Testing
Maximum performance	76.88	67.33	72.43
Minimum performance	66.88	62.00	66.14
Average performance	69.50	64.73	68.69
STD	4.27	1.96	2.45

The detector was a Self organizing map that divides the feature space into 3 groups. These 3 groups contained classes {1,2,3,4,5,6,7}, {8,9}, and {10,11,12,13,14,15,16,17, 18,19,20} respectively. The aggregation procedure was another backpropagation neural network, taking the confidence output of each classifier and the output of the detectors. The confidence was evaluated using the confusion matrix of each classifier. The training of the aggregation network is performed by running the training data through all the individual classifiers and then using the outputs as the training data for the aggregating neural network.

Table 2 shows the performance of the different techniques implemented.

Table 2. Performance of the Gaussian 20-Class problem.

	Maximum	Majority	Average	Borda Count	Nash	Feature Based
Testing	78.71	80.71	84.86	79.43	84.85	85.57
Group 1	81.63	84.90	88.16	88.57	88.98	91.83
Group 3	73.25	74.55	80.00	69.87	79.48	78.96

All the different classifier combination schemes did succeed in recognizing data from classes 8 and 9 (group 2) perfectly; therefore it is not included in the table. It can be noted that the static classifier combination procedures did improve on the single classifier case, however, the feature based procedure proposed improved the performance further. Furthermore, it was consistent with all the data subsets in producing high classification results and did not suffer from high fluctuations in the reported output. This robustness is due to its adaptability to the input data through the detectors.

4.2   Arabic Caps Problem

Handwritten Arabic character recognition data is a reasonably complex classification problem due to the similarities among many groups of its characters [16]. This introduces different levels of overlap among the different characters in the input-space, and hence complicates the job of the classifier due to the resulting internal interference.

The structure used in this problem was an ensemble of networks. Four different back-propagation neural networks were implemented. These networks had 10 hidden nodes and 28 output nodes. Training was perfromed using partially disjoint training sets for 100k iterations. In this case the data set was divided into three sets, training, validation and testing sets; 704/100/696 entries were used for training, validation and testing, respectively. The validation set was used to evaluate the best performance network

A self organizing feature map neural network dividing the characters into 6 groups was implemented as a detector. The output of this self organizing feature map was used to assist the aggregation procedure. The final aggregation procedure was a back-propagation neural network. The training procedure is performed by running the training data through all the individual classifiers and then using the outputs as the training data for the aggregating neural network.

Table 3 shows the recognition rates achieved by the individual classifiers on the testing data. The proposed architecture showed a higher performance than any of the individual classifiers. It successfully reduces the number of classification errors by at least 14%. Moreover, it also produces better results than some of the other architectures proposed in the literature to solve this problem [13]. The results were also compared to different static combining schemes. These schemes are the majority vote, Borda count, and average vote. The proposed architecture outperformed all these schemes. The short-come of the static combining schemes is due to the lack of consistency between the output of the individual classifiers. The aggregation neural network overcomes this problem. Table 4 shows the results of applying both the feature based and static classifier combining schemes to the Arabic problem set.

To demonstrate the adaptive ability of the feature based architecture we presented the system with different parts of the data set and observed how each combining technique performs. The testing set was divided into six groups based on the grouping proposed in [17]. Each group had a certain set of characters. The Self Organizing Map used as a detector that classifies the different characters into these six groups. Table 5 shows the results obtained. If we observe the performance of the different static combining methods we

Table 3. Performance of individual classifiers.

	Classifier 1	Classifier 2	Classifier 3	Classifier 4
Performance	74.86	77.44	75.57	76.15

Table 4. Comparison of recognition rate between the new approach and static classifier-combining techniques for the Arabic Caps problem.

	Maximum	Majority	Average	Borda Count	Nash	Feature Based
Type of CT	static	static	static	static	static	adaptive
Performance	88.36	88.94	88.36	88.07	88.65	90.52

find that, in some groups one technique outperforms the others, while the same combining scheme is outmatched in a different test group. The feature-based technique consistently provides the best performance across all the different testing groups.

Table 5. Comparison of recognition rate between the new approach and static classifier-combining techniques for different testing groups.

Combination Technique	Group 1	Group 2	Group 3	Group 4	Group 5	Group 6
Maximum	80.26	89.58	90.63	87.18	90.29	92.31
Majority	81.58	89.59	92.97	86.15	90.85	96.15
Average	80.26	89.59	92.19	85.12	90.85	96.15
Borda Count	80.26	87.50	91.41	86.67	90.29	92.31
Nash	77.63	90.63	90.63	87.18	91.43	96.15
Feature Based	86.84	91.67	92.97	86.15	92.57	100.00

5   Conclusion

A new architecture was proposed to allow for dynamic decision fusion of classifiers. In this architecture, the aggregation procedure has the flexibility to adapt to changes in the input and output in order to improve on the final output. The main idea behind this architecture is that it tries to understand changes in the input, by means of extracting features using the detectors, to direct the way it performs the aggregation. The aggregation learns how to combine the different decisions in order to improve the overall performance of classification. This approach also aims at reducing the cost and time of designing individual classifiers by allowing collaborate work. The empirical results were satisfactory. Both of the test problems showed improvement in the performance over static combiners. The architecture proposed here provides a robust and adaptive scheme for combining classifiers.

References

1. Kittler J., Hatef M., Robert D., Matas J. (1998) On Combining Classifiers. IEEE Transactions on Pattern Analysis and Machine Intelligence, **20(3)**, pp. 226-239
2. Auda, G., Kamel M. (1998) Modular Neural Network Classifiers: A Compartive Study. Journal of Intelligent and Robotic Systems, **21**, pp. 117-129.
3. Lam, L., Suen, C. (1995), Optimal combination of pattern classifiers, Pattern recognition Letters, **16**, pp. 945-954.
4. Munro, P., Parmanto, B. (1997), Competition Among Networks Improves Committee Performance, In: Mozer, M., Jordon, M., Petsche, T. (Eds.), Advances in Neural Information Processing Systems 9, MIT Press, Cambridge, pp. 592-598.
5. Hashem, S. (1997), Optimal Linear Combinations of Neural Networks, Neural Networks **10(4)**, pp. 599-614.
6. Ho, T., Hull, J., Srihari, S. (1994), Decision Combination in Multiple Classifier Systems, IEEE Transactions on Pattern Analysis and Machine Intelligence, **16(1)**, pp. 66-75.
7. Rogova, G. (1994). Combining the Results of Several Neural Network Classifiers. Neural Networks **7(5)**, pp. 777-781.
8. Gader, P., Mohamed, M, Keller, J. (1996), Fusion of Handwritten Word Classifiers, Pattern Recognition Letters, **17**, pp. 577-584.
9. Woods, K., Kegelmeyer, W., Bowyer, K. (1997), Combining of Multiple Classifiers Using Local Accuracy Estimates, IEEE Transactions on Pattern Analysis and Machine Intelligence, **19(4)**, pp. 405-410.
10. Huang, Y., Suen, C. (1995), A Method of Combining Multiple Experts for the Recognition of Unconstrained Handwritten Numerals, IEEE Transactions on Pattern Analysis and Machine Intelligence, **17(1)**, pp. 90-94.
11. Wolpert, D. (1992), Stacked Generalization, Neural Networks, **5**, pp. 241-259.
12. Jacobs, R., Jordan, S., Nowlan, M., Hinton, G. (1991), Adaptive Mixture of Local Experts, Neural Computations **3**, pp. 78-88.
13. Auda, G., Kamel M. (1997). CMNN: Cooperative Modular Neural Networks for Pattern Recognition. Pattern Recognition Letters, **18**, pp. 1391-1398.
14. Hodge, L., Auda, G., Kamel, M. (1999), Learning Decision Fusion in Cooperative Modular Neural Networks, In: Proceedings of the International Joint Conference on Neural Networks, Washington D.C..
15. Dasarthy, B. (1994). Decision Fusion. IEEE Computer Society Press.
16. Drawish, A., Auda, G. (1994). New Composite Feature Vector for Arabic Handwritten Signature Recognition. In: Proceedings of the 1994 Intern ational Conference on Acoustics, Speech and Signal Processing, Australia.
17. Auda, G., Kamel, M., Raafat, H. (1995). Voting Schemes for Cooperative Neural Network Classifiers. In: Proceedings of the 1995 International Conference on Neural Networks, Perth, Australia, pp. 1240-1243.
18. Topping, J. (1962). Errors of Observation and their Treatment. Chapman and Hall Ltd., London.

Feature Selection
Based on Fuzzy Distances Between Clusters:
First Results on Simulated Data

Teófilo E. Campos[1], Isabelle Bloch[2], and Roberto M. Cesar Jr.[1]

[1] Computer Science Department - IME - USP
   Rua do Matão, 1010, 05508-900 São Paulo - SP - Brazil
   {teo,cesar}@ime.usp.br
   http://www.vision.ime.usp.br/~creativision
[2] Ecole Nationale Supérieure des Télécommunications
   Département Traitement du Signal et des Images
   CNRS - URA 820 - 46 rue Barrault - 75013 Paris - France
   Isabelle.Bloch@enst.fr
   http://www.tsi.enst.fr/~bloch/

Abstract. Automatic feature selection methods are important in many situations where a large set of possible features are available from which a subset should be selected in order to compose suitable feature vectors. Several methods for automatic feature selection are based on two main points: a selection algorithm and a criterion function. Many criterion functions usually adopted depend on a distance between the clusters, being extremely important to the final result. Most distances between clusters are more suitable to convex sets, and do not produce good results for concave clusters, or for clusters presenting overlapping areas. In order to circumvent these problems, this paper presents a new approach using a criterion function based on a fuzzy distance. In our approach, each cluster is fuzzified and a fuzzy distance is applied to the fuzzy sets. Experimental results illustrating the advantages of the new approach are discussed.

Keywords: feature selection, floating search methods, and fuzzy distance.

1 Introduction

Most methods for pattern recognition, both for statistical and for neural networks paradigms, are based on extraction of a feature vector followed by classification. Generally, there is a very large set of possible features to compose the feature vectors, and it is desirable to choose a minimal subset among it. Although using "as many features as possible" could be intuitively attractive, it is well-known that this naive approach normally leads to worse results because the training set size should increase exponentially with the feature vector size [7,2].

Despite the importance of such features, there are no definitive rules or procedures to select which should be used for each particular application [2]. Some generic tips to choose a good feature set include the facts that they should discriminate as much as possible the pattern classes and that they should not be

S. Singh, N. Murshed, and W. Kropatsch (Eds.): ICAPR 2001, LNCS 2013, pp. 186–195, 2001.
© Springer-Verlag Berlin Heidelberg 2001

correlated/redundant. Expert knowledge about each specific problem is also frequently important when designing a feature set for a classifier. Finally, it is highly desirable to have feature clusters with small variance, meaning that the measures do not vary a lot for similar patterns.

Besides these generic rules, which are difficult to apply when a large set of possible features has to be handled, several automatic feature selection algorithms have been proposed, and the reader is referred to [1] for a brief review with taxonomy of this topic. Among the many different approaches, there is a large class of algorithms based on two main points: a decision criterion and an algorithm to search for feature sub-sets that are better with respect to the chosen decision criterion. Among the search algorithms, it is worth mentioning those based on search trees or on genetic algorithms.

As far as the decision criterion is concerned, there are two basic approaches: (1) those based on classification results; and (2) those based on a distance between clusters. In the former, each possible feature subset is used to train and to test a classifier, and the recognition rates are used as a decision criterion: the higher the recognition rate, the better is the feature subset. The main disadvantage of this approach is that choosing a classifier is a critical problem on its own, and that the final selected subset clearly depends on the classifier [7]. On the other hand, the latter depends on defining a distance between sets (i.e. the clusters), and some possibilities are Mahalanobis, Bhattacharyya and the class separation distance [2,4]. In this work, we present a comparison between these approaches by performing feature selection using, as decision criterion, the results of a classifier and a measure of distance between clusters.

The large majority of distances between clusters are more suitable to convex sets, tending to privilege linearly separable sets. The problem is that they fail to detect good clusters with near means. As an example refer to the feature space shown in Figures 3. Although the two clusters are well defined and would achieve nice recognition rates e.g. with a k-nearest neighbor classifier, they would hardly be recognized as good clusters by the majority of the standard distances.

In order to circumvent this problem, a new approach to calculate the distance between clusters based on fuzzy sets and fuzzy distances is proposed. The underlying idea of our approach is to consider the clusters as fuzzy sets (through fuzzification of the original clusters) and to apply fuzzy distances [6] between them as the criterion decision.

The idea is to consider that all points in a cluster do not play the same role. Some points are more typical of the cluster than others, and should have a higher degree of membership to the cluster. This typicality, and the fuzzy membership to the cluster, is defined as a function of the distance to the cluster prototypes, which are considered as the most typical samples. This step is described in Section 3.1. Once fuzzy clusters are defined, the quality of the clustering is derived from a distance between fuzzy clusters. This distance aims at evaluating if the clusters are compact and well separated. This is described in Section 3.2, while the search algorithm, based on the work of Pudil [5], is described in Section 2. At this level of development, the proposed approach has been applied only on simulated data, with the only aim of illustration and first evaluation. In the experimental results (Section 4), some tests are performed on a set of 6 features (generated by normal distributions) from two classes. The samples are labeled a priori (supervised learning), and the experiments aim at selecting a feature vector with 2 features. Once the feature vector has been selected, its performance is evaluated by classifying the samples using two statistical classifiers: a minimum-distance to the prototype and a k-nearest neighbors classifier. As expected, the new distance is more suitable for selecting feature vectors for the k-nearest neighbors classifier, leading to the best results.

2 Feature Selection: The Algorithm

Automatic feature selection is an optimization technique that, given a set of m features, attempts to select a subset of size n that leads to the maximization of some criterion function, with $n \leq m$. Feature selection algorithms are important to recognition and classification systems because, if a feature space with a large dimension is used, the performance of the classifier will decrease with respect to execution time and to recognition rate. The execution time increases with the number of features because of the measurement cost. The recognition rate can decrease because of redundant features and of the fact that small number of features can alleviate the course of dimensionality when the training samples set is limited. On the other hand, a reduction in the number of features may lead to a loss in the discrimination power and thereby lower the accuracy of the recognition system [7].

In order to determine the best feature subset for some criterion, some automatic feature selection algorithm can be applied to the complete feature space, varying the number of selected features (n) from 1 to m.

According to Jain and Zongker [1], probably the most effective feature selection technique is the sequential floating search methods (SFSM) [5]. There are two main categories of floating search methods: forward (SFFS) and backward (SFBS). Basically, in the case of forward search (SFFS), the algorithm starts with a null feature set and, for each step, the best feature that satisfies some criterion function is included with the current feature set, i. e., one step of the sequential forward selection (SFS) is performed. The algorithm also verifies the possibility of improvement of the criterion if some feature is excluded. In this case, the worst feature (concerning the criterion) is eliminated from the set through one step of sequential backward selection (SBS). Therefore, the SFFS proceeds dynamically increasing and decreasing the number of features until the desired n is reached.

The backward search (SFBS) works analogously, but starting with the full feature set (of size m) and performing the search until the desired dimension n is reached, using SBS and SFS steps. The time complexity of these methods is proportional to n for SFFS and to $m - n$ for SFBS. See [5] for further details.

These algorithms have been improved in [4], leading to the adaptive floating search methods (AFSM). The main difference between this new approach and the previous one (SFSM) is on the number of features that can be inserted or excluded from the feature set on each step. The new algorithms can determine dynamically this number, while the earlier tests just one feature per step. This characteristic is possible because AFSM applies, in each iteration, one step of the generalized sequential forward selection (GSFS) or generalized sequential backward selection (GSBS), instead of one step of the SFS or of the SBS.

The AFSM's results are closer to the optimum solution than the results of SFSM. In fact, in the worst case, ASFM give the same results of SFSM. However, for large values of n, AFFS (adaptive floating forward search) is very slow, the same for large values of $m - n$ in the case of AFBS (adaptive floating backward search).

In [8], we did some tests comparing different feature selection methods in terms of performance of the minimum distance to the prototype classifier, concluding that the performance of AFSM was very similar to the performance of SFSM. But in some cases, the AFSM spent more than four hours, while the SFSM spent just two seconds for the same feature space and n.

For these reasons, we chose to test the criterion function with automatic feature selection based on SFSM.

3   Feature Selection: The Distance

3.1   Fuzzy clusters

Let A and B be two pattern classes, and let f_1, f_2, ..., f_m, be the set of possible features. The features $f_1(x)$, $f_2(x)$, ..., $f_m(x)$ can be calculated for each $x \in A$ or $x \in B$. The problem is to find a subset F of $\{f_i, i \in [1...m]\}$ with $|F| = n$ $(n < m)$ that defines two good clusters for A and B. Let F_A and F_B be these clusters for A and B, respectively. The concept of "good clusters" is taken under the sense of distance between clusters $d(F_A, F_B)$. As discussed in Section 2, it is desirable to find F_A and F_B such that $d(F_A, F_B)$ is as large as possible.

Generally clusters may be spread around some prototypes. Samples in cluster that are close to its prototypes are very typical of the cluster, while further samples are less representatives. Crisp clusters are too restrictive to account for this, and therefore we propose to perform their fuzzification. Now if we consider the overlapping areas between clusters, intuitively we would like to judge this overlap as strong if it contains typical samples, and weak if it contains not typical samples (by strong overlap we mean not well separated clusters). This is another reason why we propose to define fuzzy clusters, where the membership function of each sample to a cluster is a function of its typicality. We use for this a distance d_{SP} between samples in the feature space (Euclidean or Mahalanobis distance can be typically used). Let P_A be the set of prototypes of cluster A (it may contain only one sample). Then the membership of any sample x to the cluster A is defined as:

$$\mu_A(x) = f(\min_{y \in P_A, x \in A} d_{SP}(x, y)), \tag{1}$$

where f is a decreasing function from $\mathbb{R}^+$ into $[0, 1]$, with $f(0) = 1$. This guarantees that prototypes completely belong to the fuzzy cluster, samples that are closed to the prototypes have a high membership function, and samples that are far have a low membership function. In our experiments, we have taken for f the following function:

$$f(w) = \frac{1}{1 + w} \tag{2}$$

We have adopted just one prototype per cluster (e.g. p_A for cluster A). Therefore, our membership function can be simplified to:

$$\mu_A(x) = \frac{1}{1 + d_{SP}(x, p_A)} \tag{3}$$

where d_E is the Euclidean distance between points of the feature space. It is important to note that we also set $\mu_A(x) = 0$ if $x \notin A$.

3.2   Fuzzy Distance

Distances between fuzzy sets have lead to several works in the literature. Many definitions exist, differing in several aspects, such as the type of information they convey, their formal properties, and the underlying mathematical approaches. Classifications of these distances have been proposed e.g. in [9,6]. Most distances are concerned only by the point-wise comparison of the membership functions, while other distances introduce also metrics in the considered space. Distances of the first type are easy to compute, and complexity is linear in the cardinality of the space. Typically, this type is well adapted when the two fuzzy sets to be compared represent the same structure or a structure and a model. They are also closely related to the notion of fuzzy similarity (if s is a similarity measure between fuzzy sets, then $1 - s$ is a distance, see e.g. [10] for a review on fuzzy comparison measures). For instance, applications in model-based or case-based pattern recognition can make use of such distances. On the other hand, the definitions which combine spatial distance and fuzzy membership comparison allow for a more general analysis of structures in the considered space, for applications where topological and spatial arrangement of the structures is important. This is permitted by the fact that these distances combine membership values at different points in the space, therefore taking into account their proximity or distance in this space. The price to pay is an increased complexity, generally quadratic in the cardinality of the space. This is discussed in more detail in [6], and several examples of both classes are given.

Here we are interested in the overlapping part of two clusters, and in the evaluation of this overlap. In most problems of clustering, the samples are not necessarily dense in the feature space. If this space is considered to be $\mathbb{R}^n$ for instance, a point x of this space may be a sample of one cluster but not of the other one. So comparing membership values only point-wise does not really make sense. The spatial information in the feature space has therefore to be taken into account, at least locally around each sample. The idea is to check if in a neighborhood of a sample of one cluster, there are samples of the other cluster. A fuzzy distance which is well appropriate for this task is the tolerance-based approach, proposed in [11], which combines comparison between membership values and local distances in the space. In this sense, it can be considered as intermediate between the two classes mentioned before. The basic idea is to combine spatial information and membership values by assuming a tolerance value τ, indicating the differences that can occur without saying that the objects are no more similar. The authors in [11] first define a local difference between μ_A and μ_B at a point x of the space as:

$$d_x^\tau(\mu_A, \mu_B) = \inf_{y,z \in B(x,\tau)} |\mu_A(y) - \mu_B(z)|, \tag{4}$$

where $B(x,\tau)$ denotes the (spatial) closed ball centered at x of radius τ.

Then the functions d_p, d_∞ and d_{EssSup} are defined up to a tolerance τ as:

$$d_p^\tau(\mu_A, \mu_B) = [\int_S [d_x^\tau(\mu_A, \nu_B)]^p dx]^{1/p}, \tag{5a}$$

$$d_\infty^\tau(\mu_A, \mu_B) = \sup_{x \in S} d_x^\tau(\mu_A, \mu_B), \tag{5b}$$

$$d_{EssSup}^\tau(\mu, \nu) = \inf\{k \in \mathbb{R}, \lambda(\{x \in S, d_x^\tau(\mu, \nu) > k\}) = 0\}. \tag{5c}$$

Several results are proved in [11], in particular about convergence: $d_p^\tau(\mu, \nu)$ converges towards $d_{EssSup}^\tau(\mu, \nu)$ when p goes to infinity, all pseudo-metrics are decreasing with respect to τ, and converge towards d_p, d_∞ and d_{EssSup}[1] when τ becomes infinitely small, for continuous fuzzy sets. This approach can been extended by allowing the neighborhood around each point to depend on the point.

Note that this approach has strong links with morphological approaches as described in [6], since the neighborhood considered around each point can be considered as a structuring element. In our experiments, we have used $d_2^\tau(\mu_A, \mu_B)$ as the criterion function for the feature selection algorithm discussed in Section 2.

4   Experiments

In order to test the performance of our feature selection system, some tests have been done comparing SFSM [5] associated with two criterion functions: the tolerance-based fuzzy distance [11] and the performance of a classifier based on minimum distance to the prototype [3].

Two classifiers are used to evaluate the performance of our system: k-nearest neighbor (for k=3) and minimum distance to the prototype [3]. Two kinds of tests have been done: one using the complete database to train and test the classifiers, and other using 2/3 of the database to train and 1/3 to test.

4.1   Simulated data

The selection algorithm has been evaluated with an artificial data set. This data set is 6-dimensional, being composed of 2-classes, and each class has 100 samples. For each class, the data set was generated using, for each dimension, a mixture of Gaussian distributions. The feature sets are shown in pairs in Figures 1, 2, and 3, in which (*) represents class A, and (o) class B.

The characteristics of this data set allow us to perform the feature selection tests for $n = 2$ and visualize the results. From the pictures, it is possible to infer that the feature space defined by dimensions 5 and 6 is the one in which the pattern distribution presents the least overlapping areas. Therefore, this feature space is the best one for classifiers such as k-nearest neighbors.

4.2   Feature space normalization

Before performing the tests, it is important to normalize the feature space. This normalization avoids problems with statistical classification based on the Euclidean distance, like the k-nearest neighbor and the minimum distance to the prototype classifiers.

Another advantage of using this normalization is that the tolerance-based fuzzy distance depends on a ball $B(x, \tau)$ (see Equation 4), thus depending on a distance in the feature space. The whole feature space has been normalized to have 0 mean and unitary variance for each dimension.

The plots in Figures 1, 2, and 3 show the data set after the normalization.

---

[1] d_p denotes the L^p-metric between μ_A and μ_B, i.e. corresponds to d_x^0, computed for $y = z = x$ in Equation 4, and d_∞ and d_{EssSup} are defined similarly.

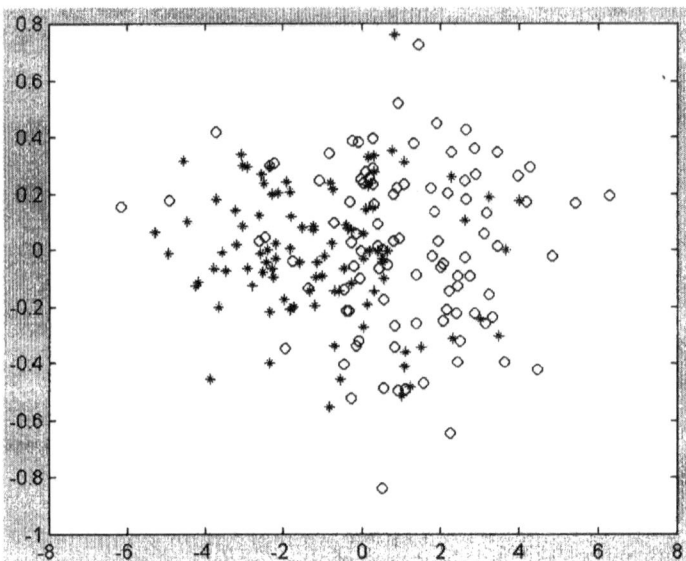

Fig. 1. Gaussian distributions for features 1 and 2

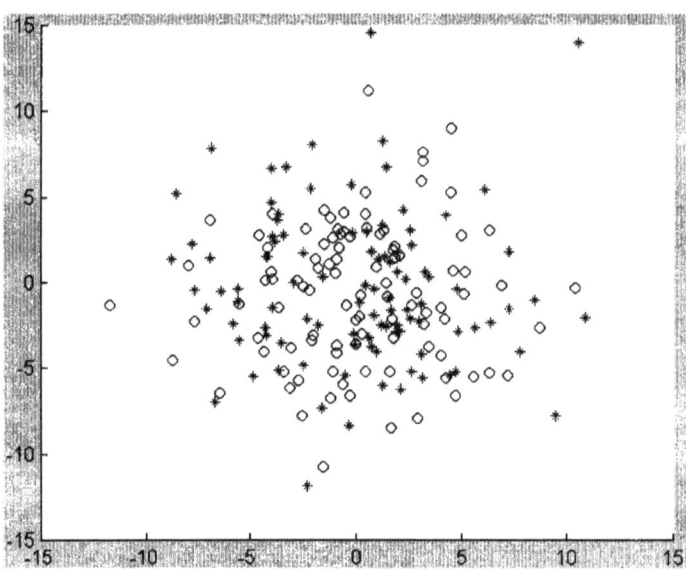

Fig. 2. Noisy data for features 3 and 4

4.3   Experimental results

We performed tests with 100 sets of class A and class B generated using the same statistical distributions as in Figures 1, 2, and 3. For each set 100 samples are generated, resulting in 20000 patterns. Table 1 shows the correct classification rates

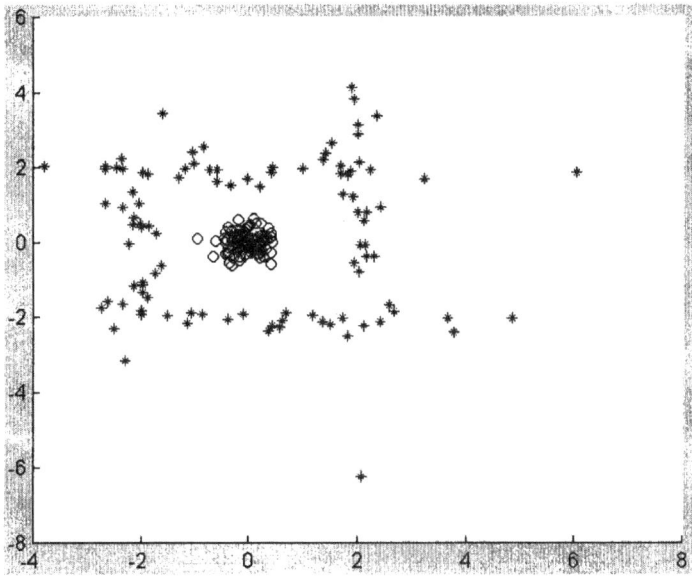

Fig. 3. Class B "inside" class A according to the mixture of Gaussian distributions of features 5 and 6

that have been determined as the average among all the experiments. The two classifiers are tested over feature subsets selected using the two criterion functions. For the tolerance-based fuzzy distance criterion, the tests have been performed using $\tau = 0.5$. All the tests with the k-nearest neighbor classifier have been done using $k = 3$. The results reflect the correct classification rate. In order to better describe the accuracy of our results, the standard deviation of the results in Table 1 are shown in Table 2.

Table 1. Correct classification rate of two classifiers under feature subsets selected using two criteria

	DP^1	DP^2	Knn^1	Knn^2
CR	63.15 %	83.71 %	95.56 %	89.47 %
FD	63.43 %	81.26 %	100.00 %	95.07 %

DP: distance to the prototype classifier
Knn: K-nearest neighbors classifier
[1]: $\alpha = \beta$
[2]: $\alpha \cap \beta = \emptyset$, $|\alpha| = 2|\beta|$, for α = training set and β = testing set
CR: correct classification rate criterion function
FD: fuzzy distance criterion function

Table 2. Standard deviation of the results showed in Table 1

	DP^1	DP^2	Knn^1	Knn^2
CR	8.40 %	8.69 %	6.67 %	11.25 %
FD	7.46 %	10.47 %	0.05 %	3.14 %

As we can see, tolerance-based fuzzy distance performs significantly better than the classification rate criterion for the k-nearest neighbor classifier. This can be explained by the fact that, when the tolerance-based fuzzy distance is applied, the feature selection algorithm chooses dimensions 5 and 6 (Figure 3). Therefore, although one cluster is "inside" the other one, they are well-separated, and the tolerance τ of the distance can be chosen quite large without any intersection with the samples of the other cluster. This is typically a case where classical distances between clusters or minimum distance to prototypes would not perform well, while the fuzzy distance based on tolerance is appropriate, and even robust with respect to the choice of τ. On the contrary, using, as criterion function, the performance of a classifier based on minimum distance to the prototype, in the majority of the cases, the algorithm chooses dimensions 1 and 2 (Figure 1), because in these dimensions, the distance between prototypes is larger.

This shows the advantage of the tolerance-based fuzzy distance. It is obvious that the feature space of Figure 3 is better than the features of Figure 1 for a k-nearest neighbors classifier.

5   Concluding Remarks

We have presented a new approach to perform feature selection using an efficient search algorithm associated with a tolerance-based fuzzy distance as criterion function. It is worth emphasizing that the criterion function results depend on how much the clusters overlap, on the shape of the clusters and on the spatial distance between them. Our system was compared with another one that uses the performance of a classifier as the criterion function. The obtained results show that our system performs better than the other one on feature spaces having concave clusters or for clusters presenting overlapping areas.

As a future work, we intend to test the influence of τ in the results and to automatically tune the best value from the data sets. We also plan to apply this feature selection technique on real data sets and to evaluate the selected features using others classifiers, such as multi-layer neural networks, or varying the parameter k of the k-nearest neighbor classifier.

Acknowledgments

Roberto M. Cesar Junior is grateful to FAPESP for the financial support (98/07722-0 and 99/1276-2), to "pró-reitoria de pesquisa" and to "pró-reitoria de pós-graduação" - USP, as well as to CNPq (300722/ 98-2). Teofilo E. Campos is grateful to FAPESP

(99/01488-8). We are grateful to Dr. Pudil for providing some source code and for discussions.

References

1. Jain, A. K., Zongker, D. (1997) Feature selection: evaluation, application, and small sample performance. IEEE Trans. on Pattern Analysis and Machine Intelligence. **19(2)**, 153–158.
2. Castleman, K. R. (1996) Digital image processing. Prentice-Hall, Englewood Cliffs, NJ.
3. Duda, R., Hart, P. (1973) Pattern classification and scene analysis. Wiley, New-York.
4. Somol,P. et al. (1999) Adaptive floating search methods in feature selection. Pattern Recognition Letters. **20**, 1157–1163.
5. Pudil, P. et al. (1994) Floating search methods in feature selection. Pattern Recognition Letters. **15**, 1119–1125.
6. Bloch, I. (1999) On fuzzy distances and their use in image processing under imprecision. Pattern Recognition. **11(32)**, 1873–1895.
7. Jain, A. et al. (2000) Statistical pattern recognition: a review. IEEE Trans. on Pattern Analysis and Machine Intelligence. **22(1)**, 4–37.
8. Campos, T. E. et al. (2000) Impoved face x non-face discrimination using Fourier descriptors through feature selection, 13th Brasilian Symposium on Computer Graphics and Image Processing, Gramado, RS, Brazil. IEEE Computer Society Press.
9. Zwick, R. et al. (1987) Measures of similarity among fuzzy concepts: a comparative analysis. International Journal of Approximate Reasoning. **1**, 221–242.
10. Bouchon–Meunier, B. et al. (1986) Towards general measures of comparison of objects. Fuzzy Sets and Sytems. **84(2)**, 143–153.
11. Lowen, R., Peeters, W. (1998) Distances between fuzzy sets representing grey level images. Fuzzy Sets and Systems. **99(2)**, 135–150.

Efficient and Effective Feature Selection in the Presence of Feature Interaction and Noise

D. Partridge, W. Wang[*] and P. Jones

Department of Computer Science
University of Exeter, UK

Abstract. This paper addresses the problem of feature subset selection for classification tasks. In particular, it focuses on the initial stages of complex real-world classification tasks when feature interaction is expected but ill-understood, and noise contaminating actual feature vectors must be expected to further complicate the classification problem. A neural-network based feature-ranking technique, the `clamping' technique, is proposed as a robust and effective basis for feature selection that is more efficient than the established comparable techniques of sequential floating searches. The efficiency gain is that of an Order(n) algorithm over the Order(n^2) floating search techniques. These claims are supported by an empirical study of a complex classification task.

1. Introduction

The problem of feature selection has been defined as follows: given a set of candidate features, select a subset that performs the best under some classification system [1]. Thus the term `feature selection' refers to procedures that output a subset of the input feature set. These are distinguished from `feature extraction' procedures which create new features based on transformations or combinations of the input feature set. This paper addresses the problems of feature selection in the context of complex real-world classification problems — i.e., problems for which the available features may be mutually correlated, redundant or simply irrelevant (and hence effectively `noise' to the classification process). In addition, individual feature values are liable to be contaminated with errors (from observation, measurement or transcription inaccuracies) — a further source of noise.

The term `best' in the above definition can be viewed as composed of three elements: effectiveness, efficiency and robustness. Robustness is essentially the ability of the procedure to produce useful guidance from a noisy and ill-understood feature set. If a feature-selection procedure crashes when dealing with noisy and complex feature sets then it will be of little practical use unless preliminary preprocessing can be applied to clean up and simplify the input feature set. An example of the robustness problem can be found in the Automatic Relevance Determination (ARD) technique which is an impeccably grounded neural-network technique for assessing the relative importance of features for a classification task [2]. It has been shown to produce optimal results when it completes its processing, but it has also been shown to be highly vulnerable to failure to complete in which case it produces no result [3].

Efficiency is essentially cost of classifier system construction. It involves the computational complexity of the feature-selection algorithm used. Thus, the simple exhaustive algorithm for optimal subset selection (i.e., evaluate all possible feature subsets) is generally excluded as a practical possibility on efficiency grounds. However, there may be other important efficiency concerns — an early reduction in feature-set size will result in subsequent savings in feature collection or computation, and certain classifier strategies may be significantly less efficient in execution than others. Multiple classifier systems, such as that of [4], that dynamically compute partition membership for each feature vector input in order to assign the vector to the appropriate specialized classifier will introduce significant execution overhead which must be set against effectiveness gains. This efficiency concern may seem to lie outside the declared remit of this paper as its impact would seem to be subsequent to, and independent of, the feature subset selected. However, if classifier performance is the basis for feature selection then classifier efficiency must impact on feature-selection efficiency.

---

[*] now with Department of Computer Science, University of Bradford, UK

Classifier effectiveness is usually the main concern — i.e., how accurately does the classifier perform once the input feature set has been determined? In the context of prohibitively large feature sets or prohibitively costly individual features efficiency concerns may dictate that some feature reduction will be necessary. Then the goal will be to minimize the loss of effectiveness while maximizing efficiency or achieving acceptable cost.   But feature selection may also lead to improved effectiveness. Jain and Zongker [1] point out that effectiveness may be improved through ``sample size effect'' [5]. In addition, when working with complex real-world problems there are several reasons why effectiveness might be improved:

1.   Some features may be redundant, and therefore their omission removes unnecessary complexity and inevitably some noise from the classification problem.
2.   Some features may be irrelevant, and their removal removes complexity that is all noise.
3.   The degree of noise associated with values of a feature may be such as to nullify the positive classificatory information of the feature, and so removal of the noisy feature will improve classifier effectiveness.

2.   Feature Subset Selection

The variety of approaches to the problem of feature subset selection have been variously classified. Theodoridis and Koutroumbas [6] present a two-way split into methods that treat features individually and those that do not, i.e., those that focus on techniques measuring classification capabilities of feature vectors. As they point out: treating features individually has the advantage of computational simplicity but may not be effective for complex problems and for features with high mutual correlation. If we add the possibility of noise (as described above) then we have a characterization of the sort of pattern recognition task that we wish to focus on. Thus it is the latter category of feature subset selection methods that are of interest.

Within this category, [6] focus on suboptimal techniques as the alternative of assessing all possible vector combinations is impractical for all but the most trivial problems.   Two well established suboptimal techniques are Sequential Forward Selection (SFS) and Sequential Backward Selection (SBS) both of which select features, and accept or reject them one at a time in an attempt to minimize the number of feature vectors evaluated whilst accommodating some aspects of mutual correlation between features. But both techniques suffer from the so-called 'nesting effect' — once a feature has been accepted or rejected it cannot be reconsidered in the context of a different feature vector.

An improvement, which increases computational cost, uses a `floating search' [7] — this encompasses the flexibility to reconsider previously accepted or rejected features. It can be added to either SFS to give Sequential Floating Forward Selection (SFFS) or to SBS to give Sequential Floating Backward Selection (SFBS).

Jain and Dongker [1] present a taxonomy of feature selection algorithms which bifurcates at the root to cluster ``statistical pattern recognition'' (SPR) techniques on one branch and those using ``artificial neural networks'' (ANN) on the other. They further divide the SPR techniques into ``optimal'' and ``suboptimal'', and this latter branch encompasses SFFS and SFBS under the heading ``deterministic single-solution suboptimal'' techniques.

Under the ANN branch only a node-pruning technique [8] is mentioned.   This technique uses a multilayer perceptron (MLP) with the standard backpropagation learning algorithm [9].   They define ``node saliency'' and successively : train a network, remove the least salient node (either input node or hidden node), retrain the reduced network, remove the least salient node, etc. until the desired tradeoff between classification error and size of the network is achieved. Removal, or pruning, of input nodes removes a feature from the feature set.

The feature-selection technique that we have developed, the clamping technique, is also an ANN technique. It does not encompass network complexity reduction through the removal of hidden nodes but neither does it require repeated retraining of networks.

A number of other ANN-based feature-selection techniques have been developed and are surveyed in [3]. The intent of the current study is to explore the possibility that one such ANN-based technique (described below) may, by virtue of the non-linear feature interaction accommodated by ANNs, support a particularly simple, effective and efficient method of feature selection in the presence of noise and mutual correlation between features. The basis for this exploration is direct comparison with the standard floating sequential search techniques, SFFS and SFBS.

3. Feature Selection by Ranked-List Partitioning

The foundation for the ranked-list partitioning (RLP) technique is a clamping procedure for determining the relative importance of a feature, or subset of features. The relative importance, or ``salience'', of an input feature with respect to some classification task, is reflected in the relative decrease in accuracy of a classifier when the feature is rendered informationless. This idea has been implemented, tested and evaluated in competition with other similar feature-selection techniques [3,10] using MLP classifiers together with the standard backpropagation training algorithm [9].

The essential elements of feature selection by node clamping are:

1. train an MLP network with n input nodes, one for each potential feature;
2. test the trained network to obtain the baseline measure of classification accuracy, $g(x)$;
3. successively retest the network with each of the input features reset to be informationless (e.g. set to the mean value in all test vectors) to obtain classification accuracies, $g(x/x_i=mean\_value)$ where $i=1,2, \ldots n$; such an informationless feature is said to be `clamped';
4. compute **salience** of each feature, $S(x_i)$,

$$\text{where } S(x_i) = 1 - (g(x/x_i=mean\_value)/g(x));$$

5. rank the features in order of descending salience values;
6. select the first l features as the best subset size l, where $l <= n$.

It is step (1) that is both the most problematic and the most computationally expensive aspect of the technique. The potential difficulties centre on the fact that a properly trained neural network is not always readily obtainable from the data available. On the positive side we note that the training does not have to converge on an optimal classifier. For the clamping technique to succeed, convergence on a reasonably good local optimum is sufficient. In addition, the process of MLP training is robust to the presence of noise in the training vector set which is of course crucial to our goal of early feature selection on ill-understood classification problems.

Within the two floating search techniques subsets of features are simultaneously clamped to obtain a salience for that clamped subset; this we term subset salience.

4. Computational Cost of Feature Selection

The computational cost of MLP training can be considerable, but for the necessary salience ranking training does not have to be pushed beyond a crude local optimum which may be all that noisy, redundant and irrelevant features may permit in the very first stages of feature-set exploration. Backpropagation training cannot be quantified solely in terms of feature vector length for it is also dependent upon the inherent complexity of the classification task, and number of features is only one factor that contributes to complexity. Neural network training is, however, an equal fixed cost overhead on all of the three feature-selection techniques to be compared.

Once network training has been completed, the complexity of the clamping technique for feature selection is linearly dependent upon the number of features to be surveyed. Each feature is clamped in turn to obtain its salience value (steps 3 and 4). Feature selection is then no more than a partitioning of the ranked list (step 6). Because neural net training is a process of finding a (probably suboptimal) classifier that accommodates all feature interdependencies and noise that happen to be present in the set of training vectors, the final salience ranking might be expected to reflect these aspects of the total feature set. It is thus reasonable to anticipate that the salience ranking is an estimate of the importance of each feature in the context of all the other features considered. This observation suggests the following hypothesis:

The sublist of highest-salience features as ranked by the clamping technique is also the optimal subset of that size whatever the feature interaction present.

In other words, a `non-selection' process of simply partitioning a rank order may deliver the same `best' , or equally good, feature subsets as the SFFS and SFBS heuristics, and do it with significantly increased efficiency — a linear, or $Order(n)$ technique performing as well as (or possibly better than) either of two $Order(n^2)$ heuristics, where n is the total number of candidate features. It is this possibility that the following empirical study explores.

5. Empirical Investigation

A real-world problem that we used to explore the feature interaction hypothesis is one of classifying flight patterns of descending aircraft (radar trajectory, physical attributes of the plane and the airspace) as patterns for which the aircraft will level-off or not at the next flight level. This level-off or non-level-off classification problem forms part of a larger study of the Short-Term Conflict Alert system developed by National Air Traffic Services in the UK.

Preliminary feature extraction delivers 28 potentially useful features. These range from features extracted from the radar track, such as $d34$ which is the vertical distance travelled between radar time points 3 and 4, and $v5$ which is the vertical velocity at radar time point 5. Other features are the flight level being approached, such as the 7000ft or 8000ft levels, which are $FL07000$ and $FL08000$ respectively. Further features are the name of the particular stack at Heathrow Airport (there are 4 different stacks), and the category of the aircraft, such as *heavy* or *light* (there are 5 of these categories). This classification problem thus involves both continuous and discrete features, noise (particularly in the radar track data), significant feature interaction (e.g. $d34$ is causally dependent upon $d45$), and redundancy (e.g. the vertical distances travelled between radar points carry some of the same information as the vertical velocities at the radar points).

The full set of 28 features used was: five vertical velocities ($v1$ through $v5$); four vertical distances travelled ($d12$ through $d45$); nine distinct flight levels ($FL07000$ through $FL15000$); four stack names (*Lambourne, Biggin, Ockham* and *Boving*); five aircraft size categories (*Light, Small, Lo-Medium, Up-Medium* and *Heavy*); and altitude at radar time point 5 ($h5$).

Empirical support for the existence of mutual correlation between features comes from the observation that the simple (i.e., non-floating) sequential searches do reveal evidence of the nesting effect.

The 'natural' data (i.e. as supplied to us by NATS) has approximately twice as many level-off outcomes as non-level-offs. This was adjusted to a 50:50 point of balance in the data used for the experiments described below so that classification accuracy becomes a simple measure of performance.

Nine different multilayer perceptron (MLP) networks were trained using the standard backpropagation algorithm [9] and approximately 30,000 feature vectors. Each network was only trained for 20 epochs. The raw value of the single output node (a value between 0.0 and 1.0)was thresholded at 0.5 so that an output greater than or equal to 0.5 was coded as 'level-off' and output less than 0.5 was coded as 'non-level-off'.

These trained networks were then used for clamping both individual features and feature subsets in order to obtain saliences for individual features and for feature subsets as a whole, respectively. Three feature selection techniques were explored:

- Partitioning a ranked list of individual feature saliences
- Feature subset saliences using the SFFS technique
- Feature subset saliences using the SFBS technique

The average result and standard deviations obtained are shown in Figure 1, where the saliences recorded are defined in step 4 of the 'clamping' algorithm given earlier. The standard deviations computed are illustrated as error bars on the salience values.

As the SFFS and the SFBS techniques generated identical feature subsets on all occasions, further experiment was reduced to a comparison of effectively two techniques — RLP and SFFS/SFBS.

As the 'best' feature subset is the subset that produces the most accurate classifier, we can assess the relative merits of the various subsets chosen by constructing and testing classifiers based on each feature subset. The subsets of size 5, 10, 15, 20 and the full 28 were each used to train a further nine MLP networks on the same data sets as were used for the original salience determinations. However, each network was now trained on 12,000 data vectors with a further 12,000 data vectors used for cross-validation to determine when the training was optimal (a validation set is used to test the classification accuracy of the network periodically during training; training may be considered optimal when the validation test set delivers a maximum value). Under this regime training took 200-500 epochs. As with the prior clamping the output threshold was set at 0.5. Such a set of 45 trained networks (nine variations times five feature set sizes) was generated for each of the two selection techniques.

All of the trained networks were then tested for classification accuracy on an unseen test set of 15,000 further vectors that had been adjusted to exhibit a 50:50 distribution of level-off and non-level-off targets. Average percentage classification accuracies (over nine networks) and the standard deviations are given in Table 1 where classification accuracy is percentage of test cases correctly classified. The top row of figures give the accuracy of MLP classifiers when constructed with feature subsets selected by the RLP heuristic and the lower row gives the comparable data when the feature subsets were selected with the SFFS/SBFS heuristic. The final two columns contain only one entry each because when all 28 features are used there is no subset selection.

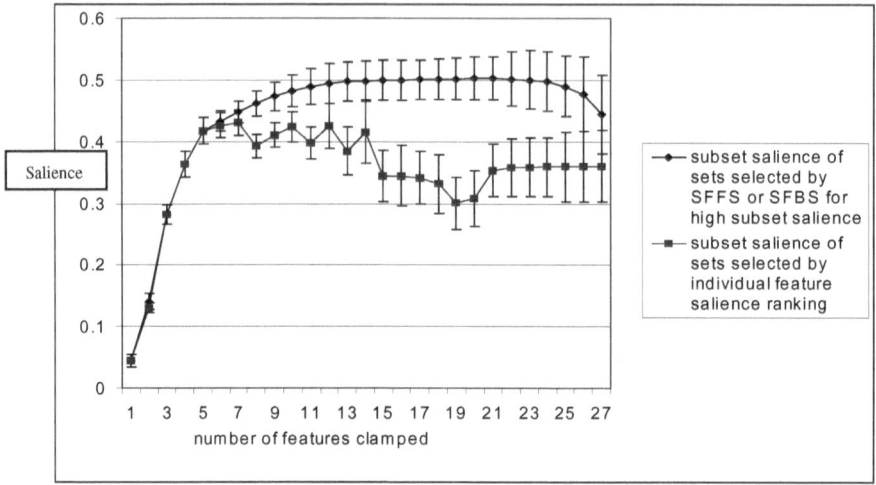

Fig. 1. Saliences for feature subsets of the level-off problem

Table 1: accuracy of classifiers constructed using feature subsets selected by alternative selection methods

	number of features used for training:									
	5		10		15		20		all 28	
features selected by:	average	sd	average	sd	average	sd	average	sd	average	sd
RLP	73.9%	0.7%	75.6%	0.7%	76.4%	0.4%	76.5%	0.5%	76.3%	0.7%
SFFS/ SFBS	73.9%	0.7%	75.2%	0.4%	75.9%	0.6%	75.9%	0.7%		

6. Discussion

The first point to note is that (on the data sets used) the SFFS and SFBS techniques always produced identical feature subsets which implies that these are the optimal groups under a group clamping procedure. In Figure 1, the single salience value associated which each feature subset selected using either SFFS or SFBS is in fact exactly the same subset of feature in all instances (which it need not necessarily be, of course). In fact, on all instances in Figure 1 where more than one technique generates a feature subset with the same salience value, they are also identical feature subsets. Thus RLP, SFFS and SFBS all generate exactly the same feature subset for subsets of 1, 3, 4 and 5 features.

From feature subsets of size 6 upwards the RLP heuristic generates different subsets to the floating search techniques. In addition, the floating search subsets are always of higher total salience than the RLP alternative, and the differences generally exceed the standard deviation error bars illustrated. However, they are not better feature subsets in the sense that they do not produce more accurate classifier systems. Table 1 shows that the feature subsets selected using the floating search techniques are no better than those chosen by simple ranked list partitioning. It also indicates that the best 10 features, however generated, produce a better classifier than the best 5 features, and that the best 15 features, however generated, produce a further small improvement in classification accuracy. But then the increases to the best 20 features and the full 28 features yield no significant improvement on the best 15.

It is somewhat curious that feature subsets consistently returning significantly higher salience values (i.e. the SFFS/SFBS features subsets compared to those of the same size selected by the RLP heuristic when set size is greater than 7, Figure 1) do not translate into more accurate classifiers (i.e. no significant differences between the two rows of results in Table 1). Why this should be the case remains to be explained.

In addition, it should be noted that the salience rankings were based on networks that were trained for only 20 epochs which supports the contention that rough and ready neural-net training is sufficient for the RLP heuristic. The optimal training used to construct classifiers to test the classification accuracy of the various feature subsets selected required an order of magnitude increase in training time.

7. Conclusions

Our hypothesis that the clamping technique for feature selection through salience ranking does accommodate feature interaction gained support from the empirical study. This study (which must be treated cautiously as it is only one study) showed that a `non-search' partitioning of the ranked list of individual saliences performed as well as the floating search techniques, and therefore it delivers a considerable saving in computational cost. Moreover, this efficiency gain is made in the face of noisy and mutually correlated features. The very nature of such problems, especially at the initial stages which is when the real savings are to be made as a result of feature selection, precludes the possibility of knowing exactly what feature interactions are present and the structure of the noise in the available feature vectors. However, the study provided a variety of indicators to support the supposition that the chosen classification problem was significantly complicated by feature interaction and noise. We note particularly, maximum classification accuracy was obtained with just 15 of the original 28 features. This is a result that supports the earlier contention that feature subset selection has important implications for noisy and complex classification tasks beyond the traditional objective of dimensionality reduction to reduce complexity.

Acknowledgements

Support for this research from Engineering and Physical Sciences Research Council of the UK (grant GR/K78607) is gratefully acknowledged as well as from National Air-Traffic Services, particularly Julia Sonander and Harri Howells.

References

1. Jain, A. and Zongker, D Feature selection: evaluation, application, and small sample performance, *IEEE Trans. on Pattern Analysis and Machine Intelligence*, 1997, **19**(2), 153-158
2. MacKay D. A practical bayesian framework for backpropagation networks. Neural Computation 1992; 4:448-472
3. Wang, W., Jones, P., and Partridge, D. A comparative study of feature salience ranking techniques, *Neural Computation* , 2000 (in press).
4. Giacinto G, Roli F. Dynamic classifier selection. In: Kittler J, Roli F (eds) Multiple classifier systems. Springer, Berlin, 2000, pp. 177-189 (Lecture notes in computer science no. 1857)
5.   Jain A, Chandrasekaran B. Dimensionality and sample size considerations. In: Krishnaiah P R, Kanal L N (eds.) *Pattern Recognition in Practice*. North Holland, 1982, vol. 2, chap. 39, pp. 835-855
6. Theodoridis S, Koutroumbas K. *Pattern Recognition*, Academic Press, San Diego, 1999
7. Pudil P, Novovicova J, Kittler J. Floating search methods in feature selection, *Pattern Recognition Letters* 1994, 15: 1119-1125
8. Mao J, Mohiuddin K, Jain A K. Parsimonious network design and feature selection through node pruning, Proc. 12th ICPR, Jerusalem, pp. 622-624, 1994
9. Rumelhart D E, Hinton G E, Williams R J. Learning internal representations by error propagation. In: Rumelhart D E, McClelland J L (eds) Parallel Distributed Processing: Explorations in the Microstructure of Cognition. MIT Press, Cambridge, Mass., 1986, pp. 318-362
10. Wang, W., Jones, P., and Partridge, D. Assessing the impact of input features in a feedforward neural network. *Neural Computing & Applications* 2000: 9(2): 101-112.

Integrating Recognition Paradigms in a Multiple-path Architecture

G. Sagerer, C. Bauckhage, E. Braun, G. Heidemann, F. Kummert,
H. Ritter, D. Schlüter

Faculty of Technology, Bielefeld University, Germany

Abstract Four decades of intensive research in computer vision have lead to numerous computational paradigms. This fact is comprehensible since problems like object recognition or scene descriptions are of high complexity, have different aspects and can be attacked by processing various features. In this paper we propose an architecture that combines the advantages of different paradigms in pattern recognition. Voting and Bayesian networks provide a computational framework to integrate approaches to knowledge based and probabilistic reasoning as well as neural computations.

Keywords: object recognition, localization, various classifiers, architecture, voting

1 Introduction

Most pattern recognition systems are organized as hierarchical processes. The classical architecture takes an input pattern and sequentially combines preprocessing, feature extraction, and a classification unit. Although many different approaches to each of the processing units exist, all paradigms realize such multi layer systems. As a result systems may either assign the input pattern to a certain abstract class or to a pattern within a given data base of individual objects. Distinguishing these two tasks, we denote the first one as *symbolizing* and the latter one as *indexing*. In the fields of image understanding or computer vision detection and classification of objects are still challenging problems. Depending on the task to be solved symbolizing or indexing of objects or patterns may be required. Another important question is whether it is sufficient to get information on symbol or index only or are location and elongation of an object required as well. In order to answer the second question, the *segmentation* problem must be addressed. By selecting interest points or small regions of fixed size the *recognition* task can be solved without segmentation. Besides these two dimensions, a third one must be taken into account. Is the *classification*, i.e. the symbol or index of an object sufficient, or is there a need for a detailed individual *description* of the objects? In addition, systems are characterized according to the technical approaches they follow. Besides *data driven* attempts, *model driven* processing is proposed in two manners. Domain dependent knowledge is used by means of constraints in knowledge based systems. For geometrical purposes object models are applied in order to reconstruct the location and the model of an object based on the visual data. At least since [1] it is widely agreed that for tasks which require the recognition and description of

* This work has been supported by the German Research Foundation within SFB 360.

S. Singh, N. Murshed, and W. Kropatsch (Eds.): ICAPR 2001, LNCS 2013, pp. 202–211, 2001.

complex objects, some kind of object models as well as powerful image processing and reasoning algorithms are necessary.

In this contribution, we present a system, which is developed to achieve individual descriptions of complex objects and scenes. The approach will be demonstrated for the recognition, location, and description of a special type of complex objects. An example of this "Baufix-Scenario" is shown in Fig. 3. In this domain localizing and describing isolated and assembled wooden toy pieces must be solved embedded in a human-machine-dialog concerning mechanical construction [2]. Due to the overall task segmentation and classification must be addressed. Furthermore, any description must deliver symbols in order to support the dialog and the construction capabilities of the system.

We propose an architecture which extends an earlier system [4]. It integrates different data driven and model driven processing steps. The integration of knowledge based and probabilistic reasoning is done by a Bayesian network and applying a voting scheme within the individual nodes. As we have to solve both the segmentation and classification task, different processing paths are necessary. They cover aspects of shapes and interest points. Object hypotheses must be grounded on regions and contours. The competition of algorithms as well as mutual support is of interest for the overall task. The combination of fast algorithms with slower but more reliable ones yields an any-time object recognition system.

2 Architecture

The proposed system architecture is characterized by a combination of various processing paths (Fig. 1). The pathways deliver different kinds of results with different information content as well as varying reliability and robustness. Moreover, the modules differ in the amount of task specific knowledge. The overall result benefits from combining the complete and fast results of task specific modules with the robustness of more general approaches. The results of the recognition system, denoted *object descriptions* in Fig. 1, are hypotheses for Baufix elements corresponding to certain image regions. For assemblies a structural description is generated in addition.

The first data driven processing path (1) is built up by a hybrid recognition module specialized

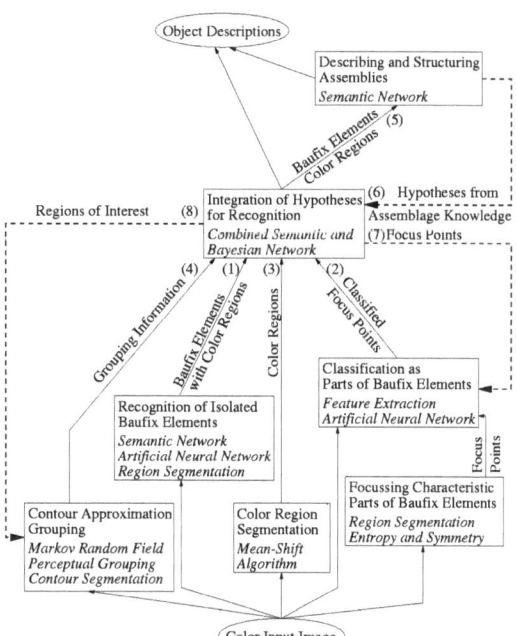

Figure 1. Outline of the system architecture and the processing paths.

in isolated Baufix elements [8]. However, perspective occlusions occur frequently, thus, often only subparts of the elements are visible. Within the second pathway (2) small windows around interesting points in the image, called *focus points* in the following, are classified using a suitable set of classes of subparts of Baufix elements [7]. Following the algorithm of [6] the color region segmentation (3) calculates regions by using only problem-independent general color properties. Analogously, the contour-based perceptual grouping (4) calculates closure groups on the basis of Gestalt laws independent of the concrete scenario [11].

The assembly unit (5) generates model based descriptions of the structure of assemblies consisting of Baufix elements [3]. It also determines whether a recognition result complies with a feasible assembly structure or not (6). All these modules are described more detailedly in section 3. In order to combine the different data driven results on the basis of the associated region information, a voting scheme is applied. To get additional information, the central recognition tool marks supplementary focus points for the neural classifier (7) and regions of interest for an efficient perceptual grouping. In case of competing interpretations knowledge based and probabilistic reasoning is done using a Bayesian network.

3   Processing Paths and Modules

In this section, the modules of the different pathways are outlined more detailedly. The structure of the integration module which combines the results of the various paths is described in section 4.

Hybrid object recognition: The first working path (1) provides hypotheses based on models for isolated Baufix elements [8].

With regard to region segmentation a polynomial classifier is used to assign one of the Baufix colors to each pixel. Afterwards, regions are established as areas of identical color class. The center of gravity of each region serves as a point of interest.

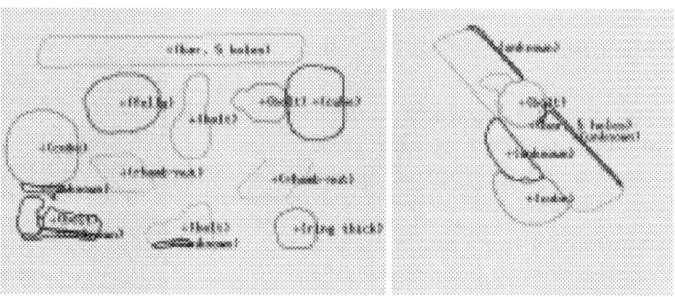

Figure2. Result from the recognition unit specialized for isolated objects.

Centered at each such point, a 16-dimensional feature vector is extracted by 16 Gabor filters. These feature vectors are processed by an artificial neural network specialized in classification of isolated objects. These point based results initialize the instantiation process of a semantic network exploiting knowledge of the fixed set of Baufix elements and of the features of the color regions. This process yields an assignment of hypotheses for Baufix elements to image regions. As this module is optimized for the detection of isolated Baufix elements, its results are reliable if elements are totally visible or just slightly occluded (Fig. 2).

Holistic detection of object parts: The second pathway (2) is designed for recognizing the occluded elements of complex objects by detecting characteristic parts of the elements [7].

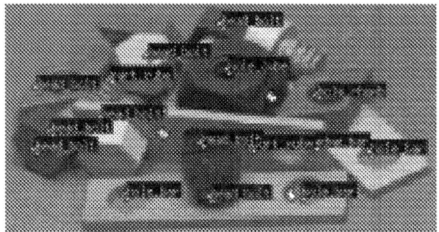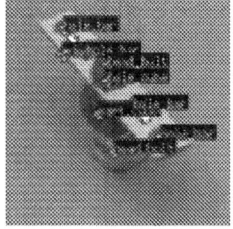

Figure3. Example input image showing the scenario with data driven focus points and classification results.

Focusing these parts is done following two separate approaches. One way is to do a rough segmentation of the image by calculating the entropy map and mask those areas with high entropy or information content. Within these areas, a symmetry value is calculated for each pixel following the method of [15]. This symmetry measure judges the amount of symmetry of the gray value gradients within the surroundings of a pixel. From the symmetry values of each pixel a symmetry map arises, the maxima of which are taken as focus points. The second way of detecting interesting points bases on the segmentation results of the color structure code approach developed in [14]. This algorithm detects areas of homogeneous color. The centers of gravity of regions with high contrast at their boundary are taken as interesting points. Both focusing approaches follow general ideas of detecting interesting areas without modeling task specific knowledge. Adaptation to our domain is done by means of just a few parameters which specify the scale of interest and color contrast. After focusing a point in the image, a window around this point has to be classified as a part of a Baufix element (see Fig. 3). A set of labeled data is used to train the feature extraction and the neural classifier of the type Local Linear Map.

Color-based region segmentation: This module (3) uses the Mean-Shift algorithm and pixel colors within the Luv color space for segmentation [6].

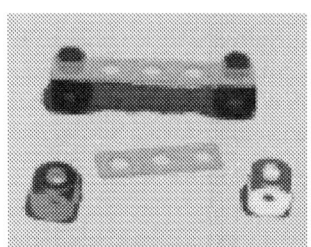

Figure4. Results of Mean-Shift Color Segmentation.

The algorithm first reduces the number of colors occurring in the image by clustering within the color space. The number of clusters is not required as a parameter, but the threshold for the color distance is deduced from a segmentation parameter and the global variance matrix of the image. Afterwards pixels are associated to color classes. The result is optimized by eliminating color classes that only occur within small regions and finally re-sorting the corresponding pixels to spatial adjacent classes. This kind of region information uses general color properties and mediates between the object regions hypothesized by the recognition module for the isolated elements and the point based information of the focus points. Fig. 4 shows an example of the segmentation results.

Contour-based Perceptual Grouping:

The initial contour segmentation uses a standard Sobel operator and a subsequent thinning with non maximum suppression and hysteresis threshold. The resulting edge elements are approximated with straight line segments and elliptical arcs with the method due

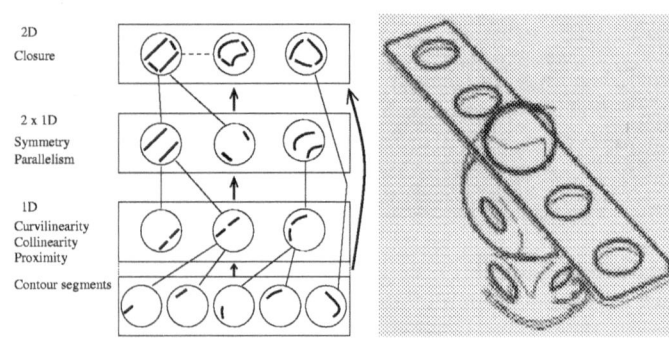

Figure 5. Left: Grouping hierarchy with groups depicted as circles and arrows showing the data flow of the grouping process. Right: Results of contour approximation and grouping.

to Leonardis [9]. Afterwards, these contour segments are organized within a hierarchy of grouping hypotheses (Fig. 5) using various Gestalt laws to overcome fragmentation and to obtain more abstract image primitives. In the lowest 1D level contour segments are combined to form collinear and curvilinear groups which again are approximated with straight line segments or elliptical arcs. These groups as well as the initial contour segments are called *linear groups* subsequently. In addition, pairs of linear groups may form a proximity grouping within the 1D level if their endpoints are spatially close. The next 2×1D level deals with pairs of symmetric or parallel linear groups. To generate hypotheses within the 1D and 2×1D level of the hierarchy we employ the concept of *Areas of Perceptual Attentiveness* which are derived from a hand labeled training set [10]. In the highest level linear groups are organized into closed contours. To this end we construct an undirected graph from all linear groups. The endpoints of the groups represent the nodes in the graph, and the edges of the graph are distinguished into *contour edges*, modeling the underlying contours of a group, and *proximity edges*, connecting two linear groups at their endpoints due to a proximity group. In this graph a closed contour corresponds to a simple cycle with an alternating sequence of contour and proximity edges, which do not intersect.

The generation of grouping hypotheses within the hierarchy relies on local evidence of the image data only. Therefore, subsequently all hypotheses are judged in a more global context using a Markov Random Field. This results in a subset of significant groups yielding a globally consistent contour-based interpretation of the image data [11,13] (Fig. 5). Along with results of the region segmentation process (8) these groups are used to enhance the object recognition module [16].

Models of assemblies for recognition and contextual inference: The very nature of the construction-kit's elementary parts implies that rigid connections yield *bolted assemblies*, i.e. mechanical structures where a bolt and a nut hold together a series of parts [5].

Studying these assemblies reveals that the bolt, the nut, and the parts between bolt and nut may be elementary or assembled objects. This leads to a recursive model capable to generate structural descriptions for every possible toy-assembly. Implemented as a semantic network this model enables to detect assemblies by analyzing clusters of recognized objects [3]. Furthermore, the recursive model of bolted assemblies provides additional information for the recognition of elementary objects. Contextual knowledge gathered during an assembly detection process allows to generate hypotheses for unknown objects. Figure 6 illustrates this inference mechanism. On the left, an assembly and the corresponding object recognition results are shown. Note that besides the shadowy regions there is a cube which was not recognized. The second image shows the assembly detection result. The sequential analysis of the cluster of object regions and unlabeled regions started with the bolt, continued with an adjacent object (i.e. the bar) and then found two adjacent objects. Since the unlabeled one is closer to the bolt it was chosen to be examined next. In order to complete the description of a feasible assembly and according to the model, unexamined objects near a bar are expected to represent further bolted objects or a nut. This restricts the type of the unknown object. As it is blue and has a certain extension it is hypothezised to represent a cube (see the rightmost image). Since there was another cube visually adjacent to the bar the analysis continued and incorrectly yielded that the bolt, the bar and the lower cube form an assembly.

Figure6. Left: recognition results for assembled objects. Middle: complex structure resulting from an object cluster. Right: object hypothesis including contextual information.

4   The recognition scheme

Based on a hierarchy of region segmentation results the central recognition unit integrates the different sources of information and resolves competing interpretations by knowledge-based and probabilistic reasoning within a Bayesian network.

Hierarchy of region segmentation results: Generally, segmentation algorithms are not able to yield a single segment for each object that has to be identified. Object regions are rather split into several segments or adjacent objects are covered by just one segment. In order to detect and evaluate such situations (Fig. 7) we integrate the results from different segmentation algorithms within a unified representation described in the following.

The results of the segmentation algorithms are characterized by line approximations of the chain of those pixels that form the outer border of each segment.

In this representation the resulting areas of a segmentation process either include each other or they are independent from each other. Due to the approximation of the border adjacent areas may slightly overlap. Furthermore, taking into account different segmentation processes additional situations occur. If for a certain area only small parts are not contained in another one the areas are said to be similar. Finally, areas might not be similar but overlap each other in greater parts.

Following this in defining the relations *contains*, *independent*, *similar* and *partially overlapping*, between the areas, the results from different segmentation algorithms are integrated

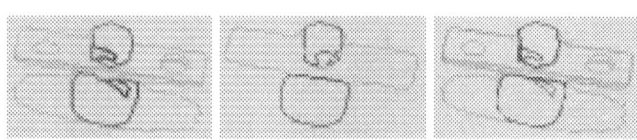

Figure7. Results from two different segmentation algorithms (left, middle), integrated results (right)

in a unified hierarchical representation (Fig. 8).

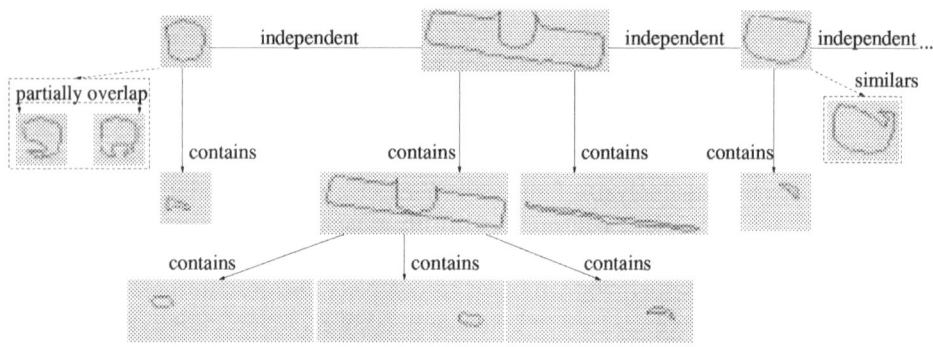

Figure8. Hierarchy of segmentation results built from areas and their relations. Relations that are dashed within the figure are not considered in evaluation. See text for explanation.

The decision for one of these relations between two areas is made by correlating the overlapping area with the original areas and applying a threshold that has proven to yield good results when set to 0.85.

In case of similar areas only one of them is considered further. Partially overlapping areas result from uncertain segment borders caused by shadows or slight color changes. In these cases there is no information about the borderline and therefore partially overlapping areas are summarized to a new one, covering the union of the original ones and are handled as a single area further on. In future work other sources of information like contours or knowledge from models or history shall be exploited during interpretation to evaluate whether reorganizing these unified areas is necessary.

Integrated object recognition: Object labels resulting from different recognition modules are attached to the region hierarchy. Those delivered with region information are attached to the corresponding areas or to similar ones, respectively. Hypotheses from the focus point classification module are point based, thus, they are attached to all areas that contain the corresponding focus point. Given this, deriving hypotheses from the region hierarchy means to coherently label those areas that probably correspond to object elements. Competing alternatives that are generated during this procedure are evaluated by the assembly module later on.

The procedure interpreting the hierarchy sequentially examines the independent areas starting with their innermost parts, respectively. For these parts hypotheses are generated according to the attached object labels. If there is no object label, the area is labeled *unknown*. In case of more than one label the most probable label is chosen by applying the plurality voting strategy [12] within the system of object element classes. Subsequently, the next level of the hierarchy, i.e. the level preceding the just interpreted one, is evaluated. For each area in this higher level the results from the lower level and the object labels already attached to it are taken into account.

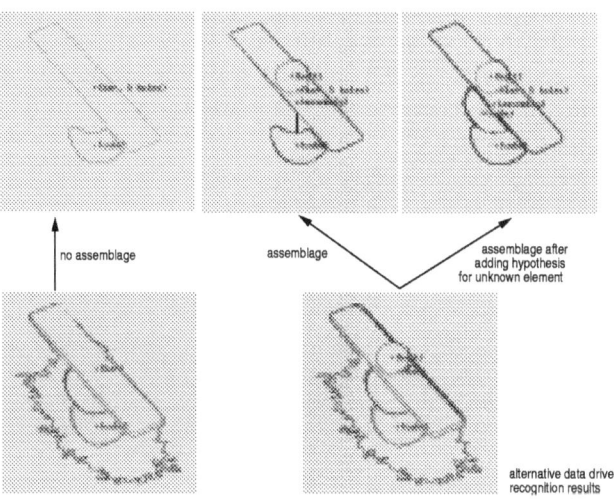

Figure9. Alternative data driven hypotheses (bottom) are analyzed using assemblage knowledge. In the first case (left) no assemblage of the recognized elements is possible. In the second case (right) the assembly module generates different assembly structures one based on the data driven recognition results and another after hypothesizing and integrating the missing cube.

In processing higher levels the question arises, if an area and all the included ones belong to one object or if there are several elements represented by this area. In the latter case it has to be decided which areas correspond to which objects. This is explained best by means of an example: let a focus point contained in the hole area of a bar be classified as the *head of a bolt*. Thus, without contextual knowledge the region containing this focus point is interpreted as a bolt. In the next hierarchical level, however, this interpretation has to be brought in accordance with the fact that the bolt area is contained in another area which is labeled bar due to other strong evidence. Two possibilities can explain this situation. Either, there is a bolt sticking in a bar or classifying the contained area as a bolt was wrong and it actually represents a bar. Consequently, both hypotheses are generated, the voting strategy attaches the corresponding labels to the areas and the hypotheses are marked as possible alternatives. While processing the hierarchy such alternatives may be generated at all levels and serve as input for the next hierarchical level. Alternatives are pruned if they contradict a set of geometry rules. In the Baufix scenario, for instance, a bolt cannot contain another element or a hole of a bar cannot contain more than one bolt.

At the highest level image regions corresponding to objects may be split into more than one segment. Therefore, further alternatives result from merging adjacent independent areas that form a group according

Figure10. Analyzed assemblies where contour and assemblage information is necessary for a correct result

to the grouping module. These alternatives are verified by the assembly module. It exploits structural and contextual knowledge to analyze assemblies as well as to generate hypotheses for unlabeled regions (see Fig. 9). Finally, all alternatives are ordered according to the complexity of the detected assembly structures. The labeling scheme corresponding to the most complex structure is decided to be the best interpretation of the region hierarchy.

5 Conclusion

In this paper, we presented a system achieving individual descriptions of complex objects by integrating various processing paths. This approach is necessary to interpret complex scenes typical for our construction

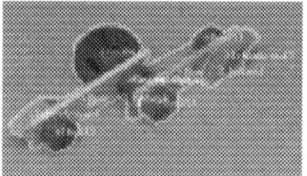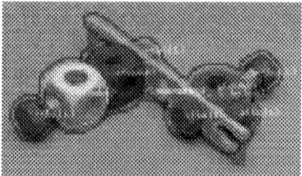

Figure11. Complex assemblies analyzed by the integrated object recognition system

scenario. Figure 10, e.g., shows assemblies where the integrated use of contour information and assemblage knowledge is essential to achieve a correct recognition result. Further results for rather complex assemblies are shown in Fig. 11.

The system was tested on a sample of 26 assemblies including 119 Baufix elements. For the results presented here we did not make use of pathway (8). Compared to the recognition module specialized in isolated objects (pathway (1)) which yields a performance of 56% the integrated approach increases the recognition rate for Baufix elements to 66%. In fact, this reflects the system's decision for one of the automatically generated scene interpretations. Choosing from all alternatives by hand would have lead to a rate of 70%. Thus, the automatic evaluation of alternatives works well. Furthermore, the integrated approach yields 13% of partially correct results where the object hypothesis is correct but the associated color region coincides with the object's proper image by less than 80%. For 20% of the 119 objects the system does not produce an interpretation, so that there are only very few misclassifications.

In summary, we state that the integration of different segmentation and classification paradigms in a multi-path architecture leads to an effective object recognition system. Although the pathways yield various kinds of results differing in their information content, their reliability, and robustness the voting scheme of the combination process produces reliable recognition results. Therefore, we are convinced that this architecture suggests an avenue towards more robust and reliable recognition modules in computer vision.

References

1. D.H. Ballard and C.M. Brown. *Computer Vision*. Prentice Hall, 1982.
2. C. Bauckhage, G.A. Fink, G. Heidemann, N. Jungclaus, F. Kummert, S. Posch, H. Ritter, G. Sagerer, and D. Schlüter. Towards an image understanding architecture for a situated artificial communicator. *Int. J. of Pattern Recognition and Image Analysis*, 9(4):542–, 1999.
3. C. Bauckhage, F. Kummert, and G. Sagerer. Modeling and recognition of assembled objects. In *Proc. IEEE Conf. IECON 98*, pages 2051–2056, 1998.
4. E. Braun, G. Heidemann, H. Ritter, and G. Sagerer. A multi-directional multiple path recognition scheme for complex objects applied to the domain of a wooden toy kit. *Pattern Recognition Letters*, 20:1085–1091, 1999.
5. S. Chakrabarty and J. Wolter. A Structure-Oriented Approach to Assembly Sequence Planning. *IEEE Trans. on Robotics and Automation*, 13(1):14–29, 1997.
6. D. Comaniciu and P. Meer. Robust analysis of feature space: Color image segmentation. In *Proc. IEEE Conf. CVPR*, pages 750–755, 1997.
7. G. Heidemann. *Ein flexibel einsetzbares Objekterkennungssystem auf der Basis neuronaler Netze*. PhD thesis, Universität Bielefeld, 1998.
8. G. Heidemann, F. Kummert, H. Ritter, and G. Sagerer. A hybrid object recognition architecture. In *Proc. ICANN 96*, pages 305–310, 1996.
9. A. Leonardis. *Image Analysis Using Parametric Models*. PhD thesis, University of Ljubljana, 1993.
10. A. Maßmann and S. Posch. Mask-oriented grouping operations in a contour-based approach. In *Proc. IEEE 2nd Asian Conf. on Computer Vision*, volume III, pages 58–61, 1995.
11. A. Maßmann, S. Posch, G. Sagerer, and D. Schlüter. Using markov random fields for contour-based grouping. In *Proc. IEEE Int. Conf. on Image Processing*, volume II, pages 207–210, 1997.
12. B. Parhami. Voting algorithm. *IEEE Trans. on Reliability*, 43(4):617–629, 1994.
13. S. Posch and D. Schlüter. Perceptual grouping using markov random fields and cue integration of contour and region information. TR 98/10, SFB 360, Univ. of Bielefeld, 1998.
14. L. Priese and V. Rehrmann. A fast hybrid color segmentation method. In S. Pöppel and H. Handels, editors, *Mustererkennung 93*, pages 297–304, 1993.
15. D. Reisfeld, H. Wolfson, and Y. Yeshurun. Context-free attentional operators: The generalized symmetry transform. *Int. J. of Computer Vision*, 14:119–130, 1995.
16. D. Schlüter, F. Kummert, G. Sagerer, and S. Posch. Integration of regions and contours for object recognition. In *Proc. 15th Int. Conf. on Pattern Recognition*, volume I, pages 944–947, 2000.

A New Geometric Tool for Pattern Recognition - An Algorithm for Real Time Insertion of Layered Segment Trees

Gopal Racherla[*][1], Sridhar Radhakrishnan[*][1], and
B. John Oommen[**][2]

[1] University of Oklahoma, Norman, OK 73019, USA
[2] Carleton University, Ottawa, ON K1S 5B6, Canada

Abstract. The data structure that is probably most used in the pattern recognition and image processing of geometric objects is the segment tree and its optimized variant, the "layered segment tree". In all the versions currently known except the work in [8], these structures do not operate in real time. Even in the best known scheme [8], although the structure can be implemented in real time and in an on-line fashion, the operation of "insertion" involves the *sorting* of the data representations of the line segments in the tree. In essence, for all the reported algorithms, there is no known strategy to insert the segments one by one, other than the trivial strategy of processing them all together as in a batched-mode. In this paper we present a strategy by which all the operations done on the tree can be done efficiently, Indeed, by improving the bottle-neck, we prove that an arbitrary horizontal segment can be inserted into this data structure *without* invoking an expensive sorting process. We show that while this is accomplished by maintaining the same space and query complexity of the best-known algorithm, the version presented here is applicable to on-line real-time processing of line segments. The paper thus has applications in all areas of pattern recognition and image processing involving geometric objects.

Key words: pattern recognition of geometric objects, segment trees, layered segment trees.

1 Introduction

1.1 Problem Statement and Applications

It can be argued that the "art" of pattern recognition and image processing involves data representation. The "science" involves the underlying mathematics behind the techniques themselves. In statistical

---

[*] e:mail : {gopalr, sridhar}@cs.ou.edu.
[**] Author to whom all correspondence should be sent. Senior Member, IEEE. School of Computer Science, Carleton University, Ottawa, ON, K1S 5B6, Canada. e-mail: oommen@scs.carleton.ca. Partially supported by NSERC, the Natural Science and Engineering Research Council of Canada.

S. Singh, N. Murshed, and W. Kropatsch (Eds.): ICAPR 2001, LNCS 2013, pp. 212–221, 2001.

pattern recognition this is really of question of determining what numerical features can be used to completely or adequately represent the pattern being recognized. Thus, it is typical that the time series coefficients or the LPC coefficients are used to represent a speech signal. The same issue arises in image processing, where the objects in the image are represented geometrically. The question here is one of whether we should represent the objects using lines, arcs, polygons etc. or as pixel-based shapes themselves.

The data structure that is probably most used in the pattern recognition and image processing of *geometric objects* is the segment tree and its optimized variant, the "layered segment tree". In this paper we present a refined version of this structure that can be used for real-time on-line applications. A brief catalog of the many areas where segment trees and layered segment trees have been utilized [2,6] including those in pattern recognition, and image processing is included in [4]. Also included in [4] are the particular features of the insertion operation in pattern recognition, editing processes, and in the field of data structures.

By designing a superior variant of the "layered segment tree", we believe that we will be presenting a solution that can be used to improve the existing solutions for *all the* problems discussed in [4].

2   Formal Problem Statement

In this short paper we present an enhancement on the "layered segment tree" (an optimized variant of the segment tree) which can be used in real-time and in an on-line manner. Even for the best of the reported algorithms [8], the only one that can be used in a real-time mode, the scheme inserts the segments one by one, by invoking the expensive operation of sorting. Since this operation is the only time consuming operation on this structure, we shall achieve our goal by designing a fast strategy for it. As we shall see, this will be a strategy that does not require the sorting of the line segments, and which can consequently process the segments more efficiently "as they come" in real-time.

A line segment is rectilinear if it is parallel to either the x-axis or the y-axis. A line segment L is presented as an ordered pair (l, r) where if L is horizontal then l and r are the leftmost and right most endpoints of L. Alternatively, L is vertical then l and r are the bottom most and topmost endpoints of L. Layered segment trees have been used to store rectilinear segments and solve the *true intersection problem*[8]. The latter problem can be specified as follows : Given a set of n horizontal segments S_{hor} and a query vertical segment V, the layered segment tree can determine all the line segments in S_{hor} that intersect with V. We assume that the number of line segments stored in the layered segment tree is n.

The insertion algorithm for a layered segment tree due to Vaishnavi and Wood requires the n horizontal segments in S_{hor} to be sorted by their y-values. The insertion takes $O(n \log n)$ time and requires $O(n \log n)$ space. The query requires $O(\log n + k)$ time where k is the number of segments in S_{hor} that satisfy the query. Thus, the amortized cost of insertion of a segment requires $O(\log n)$ time and $O(\log n)$ space. The primary result of this *present* paper can be stated as follows : We prove that the insertion of an *arbitrary* horizontal segment can be done $O(\log n)$ time. The insertion procedure adds $O(\log n)$ additional space and thus the space complexity remains $O(n \log n)$. The query time complexity also remains unaffected.

3   Layered Segment Trees

Vaishnavi and Wood [8] developed the layered segment tree based on the concept of "layering" originally proposed for the range tree by Willard and Leuker [9]. This idea is referred to in the literature by the phrase *iterated search*. The layering approach of Vaishnavi and Wood has been generalized by Chazelle and Guibas. This generalized approach called *fractional cascading* has been used by several researchers [1,7]. The dynamic version of fractional-cascading was proposed by Mehlhorn and Näher [3].

The traditional segment tree stores segments that span over a single dimension. Without any loss of generality, we assume that the line segments are in the x-dimension, and that they all share the same y-value. The layered segment tree stores line segments that have different y-values when considered from a two-dimensional perspective. More formally, given n horizontal line segments S_h and an arbitrary query consisting of a vertical line segment V, we determine all intersections of V with the line segments in S_h, using the layered segment tree.

The layered segment tree enables us to solve the above intersection problem with $O(n \log n)$ time and space, and takes $O(\log n + k)$ time to answer search queries, where k is the number of segments reported [8].

If we assume that V is a vertical line that is a double infinite line segment, we can solve the intersection problem by representing the elements of the set S_{hor} using the segment tree, as the y-value associated with the line segment is of no consequence with regard to the intersection. If we also assume that V is only infinite in the negative direction (that is, y can extend to $-\infty$ but not to ∞), then S_{hor} can still be represented by a segment tree. However, in order to avoid searching each node list for line segments that lie below the topmost point of V, we need to sort the node lists. We sort the elements of S_{hor} in descending order of their y-values before constructing the segment tree. This ordering of the segments ensures that the line segments in each node lists are sorted in an ascending order of their y-values. The search query remains the same as that of the traditional segment tree, except that only that the initial portion of each node list is reported each of whose line segments lie below the topmost point of V. We get a $O(\log n + k)$ time for search operations where k is the number of intersections reported by the query.

The layered segment tree proposed by Vaishnavi and Wood [8] maintains $O(n \log n)$ space and pre-processing time and $O(\log n + k)$ search time. Let $L(u)$ denote the segment represented by a node u in a segment tree T. The segment tree with sorted node lists is augmented by adding a line segment H to a node u whenever $L(u) \cap H \neq \Phi$ during insertion. In case $L(u) \subseteq H$ then the node is marked as a white node, while if $L(u) \not\subseteq H$ or $L(u) \cap H \neq \Phi$ then the node is marked as a black node. Each node in the list is linked to its successor and a w-link is added from each node to the next white node in the list in one exists (See [4] for figures which explain how insertions are done in the layered segment tree, and which explain how the nodes list are maintained for the black and white nodes). Also, let u_λ and u_ρ be defined as the left and the right children of the node u in the segment tree.

The insertion algorithm of a line segment for this augmented tree is described as follows:

If the line segments are added in S_{hor} to this skeletal segment tree in descending order of y-values using this insertion algorithm, it again takes $O(n \log n)$ time and $O(n \log n)$ space. The information at each node can be used to improve the time and space complexities of structure.

Layering is added in the tree by adding pointers (or bridges) for each node in every node list of a tree node u, with left and right suc-

INSERT(H, T)
Input: The augmented segment tree T and the segment to be inserted – H.
Output: Updated augmented segment tree T.
Begin

```
1        u = root(T)
2.       If L(u) ⊆ H Then
3.           Add H to the node list of u using a white node, linking it not
             only to the next node in the list but also to the next white node.
4.       End If
5.       If L(u) ⊄ H Then
6.           Add H to the node list of u using a black node, linking it not
             only to the next node in the list but also to the next white node.
7.                   If L(u_λ) ∩ H ≠ Φ Then Repeat the algorithm with u = u_λ
8.                   If L(u_ρ) ∩ H ≠ Φ Then Repeat the algorithm with u = u_ρ.
         End If
End
```

cessor in the node lists u_λ and u_ρ respectively. These pointers/bridges point to the corresponding successors [8,9]. We now describe the procedure to find these successors. If v is a node, let its left and right successors be defined as u_λ and u_ρ respectively. We first state the scheme to find the successors v_λ and v_ρ of a node v in the node list corresponding to the node u in the augmented segment tree.

Let w be the first node of the node list of u_λ whose y-value is greater than or equal to the y-value of v. Let this be v_λ. If no such w exists, then v_λ is empty. The process is similar for v_ρ. For the augmented segment tree, the layered tree structure can be obtained by carrying out a pre-order traversal of T [8]. On visiting each node u, find the v_λ (resp. v_ρ) for each node v in the node list of u by a single scan of node list of u and that of u_λ (resp. v_ρ) .

Since the node lists of u_λ and u_ρ are no larger than that of u, this means that the time taken for all nodes in the tree is $O(n \log n)$. Since for each entry in each node list we are adding a constant amount of space, the total space is still $O(n \log n)$ for this layered segment tree.

Now, $O(n)$ root entries for the node list of the root are added. A simple form of this is a sorted array of q distinct y-values of the line segments in S_{hor}. We shall use this fact to prove the theorem involving the insertion of an arbitrary segment into the layered segment tree. Each element y_l in the array is linked to the first appearance of a line segment in the node list of the root with that y-value. This structure is the layered segment tree.

We observe that the entry at any one of the root values in the node list of the root, determines a segment tree via the left and right successors. The node lists of this tree only contain line segments whose y-value is greater than or equal to the y-value of the root node. Moreover, there are no other node list entries in the layered segment tree, which satisfy this condition.

The above discussion leads to the query algorithm formally given in [8,?] which takes $O(\log n + k)$ time. In summary, the layered segment tree enables us to solve the true intersection problem between a vertical segment and a collection of horizontal segments with $O(n \log n)$ preprocessing time and space. The query time for the structure is $O(\log n + k)$.

4   Insertion of an Arbitrary Segment into a Layered Segment Tree

The insertion algorithm described in the previous section assumes that the line segments to be inserted are sorted by their y-values. We shall now show that an arbitrary horizontal line segment H can be inserted in the layered segment tree in $O(\log n)$ time[5]. Furthermore, as will be clear presently, the proposed scheme also permits the on-line insertion of the nodes in real time.

Consider the layered segment tree T. Let the segment to be inserted be of the form $H = (x_1, x_2, y)$. To enhance the basic algorithm, we opt to use the binary search in the node list of the root – $NL(\text{root})$ – to insert a node corresponding to the segment H. This takes $O(\log n)$ time. To accomplish this we need to modify the traditional insertion algorithm because it assumes that the segments being inserted are given in a sorted sequence of their y values.

In order to accomplish our goal, we shall add a node h corresponding to the segment H to the node list (NL) of the root node using a white node. Without loss of generality, we assume that all the y-values in the NL are distinct. In case they are not, we can trivially (i.e., without adding to the complexity) augment the NL nodes to have an associated counter with each distinct y-value which counts and keeps track of the number of segments with that y-value. The insertion of

h in the $NL(\text{root})$ after locating the proper location using a slightly modified (in case of non-distinct y-values) binary search requires $O(1)$ time. Thus, the total time taken for the insertion of h in $NL(\text{root})$ is $O(\log n)$.

We now state and prove the main result of this paper.

Theorem 1. *Insertion of an arbitrary segment H into a layered segment tree can be achieved in $O(\log n)$ time and $O(\log n)$. The space complexity of the structure is $O(n \log n)$ and the query complexity is $O(\log n + k)$ where k is the number of segments satisfying the query and n is the number of segments stored in the layered segment tree.*

Sketch of Proof. On inserting h to the $NL(\text{root})$, maintenance and update of the left and right bridges can be done in $O(1)$ time as it only involves constant number of bridge pointer updates.

If h is a black node, it is possible that it is added to the node list of the (left and/or right) child of the corresponding node in the segment tree. As explained in the insertion algorithm in section 3, if the node is white, it is not inserted in the node lists of its left and right children.

Consider a node u and its left child u_λ and their node list $NL(u)$ and $NL(u_\lambda)$ respectively (shown in greater detail in a figure in [4] and omitted here for space limitations). We can extend this approach to the right bridge of h.

Assume that a node h has been inserted between nodes a and b, where a and b are adjacent to each other in the node list with no nodes between them. Let $a_{\lambda'} = LB(a)$, and $b_{\lambda'} = LB(b)$ be the left bridges of a and b respectively. As explained earlier, we assume that a and b have distinct y-values. Without any loss of generality, we assume that the y-value of a is less than or equal to the y-value of b.

By the definition of the left bridge,

$$y\text{-value}(a_{\lambda'}) \geq y\text{-value}(a) \tag{1}$$

$$y\text{-value}(b_{\lambda'}) \geq y\text{-value}(b) \tag{2}$$

The insertion of h involves two different cases, namely when h is white, and when h is black.

We consider both these case separately for the purpose of analysis and discussion.

Case 1: h is a white node. If h is white, h would not be inserted in any node lists in the subtree of u. We note that u was the root initially. We thus need to find LB and RB – the left and the right bridges of h.

Since the entries a and b are distinct and adjacent in the node list, we know that y-value $(a) < y$-value(b). Let $a_{\lambda'} = LB(a)$ and $b_{\lambda'} = LB(b)$ be the left bridges of a and b respectively. We shall now prove that $a_{\lambda'}$ and $b_{\lambda'}$ are adjacent to each other *if and only if* they are distinct.

The sufficiency condition follows directly from our assumptions. The necessary condition will be proved by contradiction. Let us assume that there exists a node $P_{\lambda'}$ between $a_{\lambda'}$ and $b_{\lambda'}$ in the node list $NL(u_\lambda)$. So, by our assumption of the distinctness of y-values of nodes

$$y\text{-value}(a_{\lambda'}) < y\text{-value}(P_{\lambda'}) < y\text{-value}(b_{\lambda'}). \qquad (3)$$

From the equations 1, 2, 3, we get

$$y\text{-value}(a) \leq y\text{-value}(P_{\lambda'}) \leq y\text{-value}(b) \qquad (4)$$

This can hold true if either y-value$(a) = y$-value$(P_{\lambda'})$ and/or y-value$(b) = y$-value$(P_{\lambda'})$ because y-value$(a) < y$-value $(P_{\lambda'}) < y$-value(b) is not possible because of our initial assumption of the adjacency of nodes a and b without any elements in between them. Hence, our assumption that $P_{\lambda'}$ is positioned between $a_{\lambda'}$ and $b_{\lambda'}$ is false. This leads to the proof of the necessary condition.

So, the left bridge of h - $LB(h)$ is the same as $LB(b)$. Therefore, $LB(h) = LB(b)$. Similarly, we can also determine the right bridge of h. Consequently, the maintenance and update of the layering structure involves constant number of pointer manipulations which takes $O(1)$ time.

Case 2: h is a black node. This means that h may or may not be added to $NL(u_\lambda)$. If h is added to $NL(u_\lambda)$ as h_λ, then $LB(h) = h_\lambda$. Thus, the left bridge LB can be found in $O(1)$ time if the location of h_λ is known in $NL(u_\lambda)$.

Since $a_{\lambda'}$ and $b_{\lambda'}$ are adjacent and $h_{\lambda'}$ is to be inserted in $NL(u_\lambda)$, we know that,

$$y\text{-value}(a) < y\text{-value}(h) < y\text{-value}(b) \qquad (5)$$

$$y\text{-value}(a_{\lambda'}) \geq y\text{-value}(a) \qquad (6)$$

$$y\text{-value}(b_{\lambda'}) \geq y\text{-value}(b). \tag{7}$$

From the above it follows that

$$y\text{-value}(h) \leq y\text{-value}(b_{\lambda'}). \tag{8}$$

It is clear from the discussion above that the insertion of node h as h_λ has to be done to the immediate left of $b_{\lambda'}$ which requires $O(1)$ time. We can similarly find the right bridge of h is $O(1)$ time. Thus, if h_λ has to be added to $NL(u_\lambda)$, the bridges can be found in $O(1)$ time. If h is not to be inserted, we can follow the same approach as in Case 1.

Thus, the total time required for the insertion of the segment is the sum of the time required for inserting the node in $NL(\text{root})$ $(O(\log n))$ and the time required for adjusting the left and right bridges of the inserted nodes $(O(1))$. Clearly, the complete insertion operation takes $O(\log n)$.

In addition, as a result of the insertion of the node, only $O(\log n)$ space is added. This is because the node can be inserted at most $(\log n)$ time and the space associated with the node and its corresponding links is $O(1)$.

Hence the theorem.   ∎

Since the time required for this operation is $O(\log n)$ and since it does not require that the elements be sorted *a priori*, it is clear that all the essential operations associated with the layered segment tree can be done efficiently, and the primary goals of the paper have been met.

We are currently investigating how these principles can be utilized in the contour processing of maps and in geographic information systems.

5   Conclusion

The data structure that is probably most used in the pattern recognition and image processing of geometric objects is the segment tree and its optimized variant, the "layered segment tree". In the versions currently known, the bottleneck on this structure is the operation of "insertion". The best reported scheme for this is the one due to Vaishnavi and Wood where the insertion of n horizontal segments in a layered segment tree is achieved in $O(n \log n)$ time and $O(n \log n)$ space.

Their insertion algorithm requires that the horizontal segments that are inserted be sorted by their y-values.

In this paper we have proved that the insertion of an arbitrary interval in the layered segment tree can be done in $O(\log n)$ time. We have thus demonstrated that even *without sorting* the line segments based on their y-values prior to insertion (as proposed by Vaishnavi and Wood [8]), we can maintain the same amortized time complexity for insertion. Thus, the enhanced structure can be effectively used in real-time, on-line applications very powerfully.

References

1. Bernard Chazelle and Leonidas J. Guibas. Fractional cascading: I. A data structuring technique. *Algorithmica*, 1:133–162, 1986.
2. K. Mehlhorn. *Data Structures and Algorithms 3: Multidimensional Searching and Computational Geometry*. Springer-Verlag, Germany, 1984.
3. K. Mehlhorn and S. Näher. Dynamic fractional cascading. *Algorithmica*, 5:215–241, 1990.
4. Gopal Racherla, Sridhar Radhakrishnan, and B. John Oommen. Layered segment trees applicable for real-time pattern recognition and image processing of geometric objects. *Submitted for Publication.*, Unabridged Version of this Paper.
5. Venkatagopal Racherla. Parallelization and concurrent access of dynamic segment trees based on 2-3 trees. Master's thesis, School of Computer Science, University of Oklahoma, Norman, Oklahoma, USA, 1995.
6. H. Samet. *The Design and Analysis of Spatial Data Structures*. Addison-Wesley, 1989.
7. S. Sen. Fractional cascading simplified. In *Proc. 3rd Scand. Workshop Algorithm Theory*, volume 621 of *Lecture Notes Comput. Sci.*, pages 212–220. Springer-Verlag, 1992.
8. V. K. Vaishnavi and D. Wood. Rectilinear line segment intersection, layered segment trees and dynamization. *Journal of Algorithms*, 3:160–176, 1982.
9. D. Willard. New data structures for orthogonal queries. Technical Report 22, Harvard University, 1978.

Improvements in K-Nearest Neighbor Classification

Yingquan Wu, Krasimir G. Ianakiev, and Venu Govindaraju*
CEDAR, Department of Computer Science and Engineering
State University of New York at Buffalo
Buffalo, NY 14228

Abstract

We have developed two novel methods to improve K-nearest neighbor (K-NN) classifications. First, we introduce a new technique to greatly reduce the template size. This significantly improves classification time with no accuracy drop. Secondly, we introduce a preprocessing procedure to preclude a large part of prototype patterns which are unlikely to match the unknown pattern. This again accelerates the classification procedure considerably. The simulation results on the GSC digit recognizer [1] show that the accommodation of two procedures to K-NN search achieves 7 times faster than the original one without any decay in classification accuracy.

1 Introduction

The K nearest neighbor (K-NN) rule [2]–[6] is a well-known decision rule used extensively in pattern classification problems. The misclassification rate of the K-NN rule approaches the optimal Bayes error rate asymptotically as K increases [7]. The K-NN rule is particularly effective, when probability distributions of the feature variable are not known, and therefore, rendering the Bayes decision rule [7] is not useful. To perform template matching, each matching requires complexity $O(n)$, where n is the dimension of a pattern. When n is a large number, such as $n = 512$ in GSC recognizer [1], it takes enormous time to match the whole template set. There are two effective algorithmic techniques for reducing the computational burden: template condensing and preprocessing.

Selection of templates is an important part of the nearest neighbor (1-NN) rule [8]–[11]. Templates are selected so that classifications obtained using any proper subset of the initial template set leads to gradual degradation in

---

*Corresponding author: E-Mail: govind@cedar.buffalo.edu

S. Singh, N. Murshed, and W. Kropatsch (Eds.): ICAPR 2001, LNCS 2013, pp. 222–229, 2001.

recognition accuracy. This greatly decreases the number of prototypes that an unknown pattern must be compared to. In this paper, we develop a novel method of selecting the subsets. The idea behind comes from the fact that, if many prototypes are assembled in an area but without any prototypes from any other classes, then a number much larger than sufficient number K of patterns in this area could happen to be nearest to an unknown pattern as long as it is in this area. Our approach is to reduce redundant prototypes from such area. It not only reduces the template size greatly but also maintains the classification accuracy.

We also describe a preprocessing stage wherein an unknown pattern is matched to a prototype in two stages. In the first stage a quick assessment of the potential of match is made. Using the number of ones in the binary prototype. In order for a match to occur in the first stage, the difference in the number of ones in the prototype and the unknown pattern must be less than a predetermined threshold. Prototypes that fail in the first stage of matching are not considered any further, and thus dynamically preclude a big part of prototypes. Since the proposed preprocessing just take one step, i.e., the complexity is $O(1)$, it considerably reduces the time of processing. Furthermore, such preprocessing does not sacrifice the accuracy for it only rejects prototypes which are not close enough, if properly used.

2   Preliminary: Weighted K-NN Classification

Let p be the number of classes, and $c \triangleq \{c^{(i)}, i = 1, 2, \dots, p\}$ be the set of class labels. Let Φ be a set of labeled prototype patterns, called templates. A labeled pattern $\mathbf{y} \in \{0, 1\}^n$ in the template set is called a prototype, where n denotes the pattern dimension, . The class label of a prototype $\mathbf{y}$ is denoted by $c(\mathbf{y})$.

Let $H(\mathbf{x}, \mathbf{y})$ be the matching measure between pattern $\mathbf{x}$ and $\mathbf{y}$, where H is supposed to be a nonnegative and symmetric function. The larger the value $H(\mathbf{x}, \mathbf{y})$ shows the nearer between $\mathbf{y}$ and $\mathbf{x}$. A well-known matching measure is the reciprocal of Hamming distance, i.e.,

$$H(\mathbf{x}, \mathbf{y}) = (\sum_{i=1}^{n} |x_i - y_i|)^{-1} \tag{1}$$

Let $\mathbf{y}^{(1)}, \mathbf{y}^{(2)}, \dots, \mathbf{y}^{(K)}$ be the K prototypes which are nearest to $\mathbf{x}$, in sense of H among all the prototypes in the template set Φ. A weighted voting for each class is computed as follows:

$$w_i \triangleq \sum_{k=1}^{K} H(\mathbf{x}, \mathbf{y}^{(k)}) \cdot \delta(\mathbf{y}^{(k)}, c^{(i)}), \quad i = 1, 2, \dots, p, \tag{2}$$

where $\delta(\cdot, \cdot)$ satisfies

$$\delta(\mathbf{y}^{(k)}, c^{(i)}) \triangleq \begin{cases} 1, & \text{if } c^{(i)} \text{ is the class label of } \mathbf{y}^{(k)}; \\ 0, & \text{otherwise.} \end{cases} \tag{3}$$

Let w_i, w_j be the largest and second largest values over $\{w_1, w_2, \ldots, w_p\}$, respectively. The pattern $\mathbf{x}$ is classified to the class $c^{(i)}$ and its confidence (reliability) is defined as

$$\eta \triangleq \frac{w_i}{\sum_{k=1}^{p} w_k}(1 - \frac{w_j}{w_i}). \tag{4}$$

It is worth noting that:
(b) $\eta \in [0, 1]$.
(b) $\eta = 0$, iff $w_j = w_i$.
(c) $\eta = 1$, iff $w_j = 0$ or $w_i = \infty$.

3   Template Reduction

We note that, in the K-NN classification, given an unknown pattern $\mathbf{x}$, the $(K+1)$-th, $(K+2)$-th $\ldots$, prototypes in the template set nearest to $\mathbf{x}$, in the sense of $H(\mathbf{x}, \cdot)$, do not affect the classification of pattern $\mathbf{x}$. In fact, K is supposed to be a quite small number. Otherwise, Sorting K nearest patterns over a template with size of N, after all matching measures $H(\mathbf{x}, \cdot)$ are calculated, needs the complexity $O(KN)$ and hence takes a great part of the overall complexity, therefore it is not desirable. It frequently happens that the number of prototypes, which come from a class and nearer to $\mathbf{x}$ than any other prototypes from different class, is much larger than sufficient number K, according to our confidence measure. Specifically, we imagine an area such that it includes very many patterns of same class in template set but has no any patterns of other class. If $\mathbf{x}$ is located in such area, then the number of patterns in this area which are nearer to the unknown pattern than any other patterns of other classes, could be much greater than K. This fact motivates us to come up with a method to reduce the template set but hold the accuracy.

We describe the training process whereby we decide on the set Φ. We start with a training set $\mathfrak{R}$ that is very large, and then iteratively refine this training set using the algorithm developed below.

We assume that all p classes are equally probable. The training set is initially created by extracting feature vectors from a very large set of images of interest, among which each class has equal representation. We assume the feature extraction algorithm is perfect so that the any two images in different classes generate different features (patterns). However, different images representing the same class may have identical feature vectors. First, we

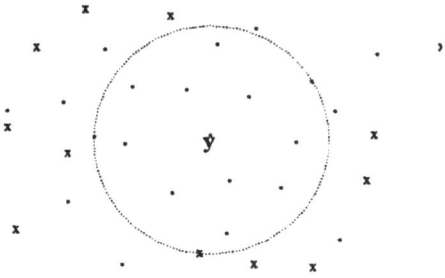

Figure 1: Pictorial plane representation of the attractive capacity.

eliminate all redundant patterns from the set $\Re$ such as those that correspond to different images of the same class. For simplicity, let us continue to denote the new set by $\Re$.

In a given set of binary patterns, we define the attractive capacity s_y of a pattern y as the number of patterns that match more than any other patterns in different classes from y. Analytically, the attractive capacity of the pattern $y \in A$ is defined as follows

$$s_y \triangleq |\{x \in A : H(y, x) > H(y, x'), \forall x' \in A \text{ such that } c(x') \neq c(y)\}|. \quad (5)$$

We note that the prototypes accounted in s_y have same class label as y. Figure 1 illustrates the concept of attractive capacity. In the figure, "." stands for the prototypes in the same class as y, and "x" stands for the prototypes in the class different from y. In the example, the attractive capacity of y is $s_y = 11$.

We note that the patterns that have high capacities are in the center of dense areas. Thus a reasonable approach is to remove some prototypes with high attractive capacity from the training set $\Re$. However, if we eliminate all patterns whose attractive capacity over certain threshold, we over-sparsify the dense area, and thus inevitably lower down the accuracy. Let us give an example to illustrate the disadvantage of this method.
Supposing the patterns of each class are very close to each other but are very far from the patterns of any other class in the template set. So the capacity of each patterns are equally high. Then we would remove all training patterns according the above method. Of course this is not reasonable.
The reason is that the capacity of a prototype is determined by other patterns, instead of it own. When some patterns are eliminated from the template set, some of the remaining patterns which initially have high capacities no longer hold, on the other hand, some of the remaining patterns which initially have low capacity turn to have high capacity.
An efficient way to overcome this obstruction is to eliminate the prototypes with high capacities gradually. Specifically, we gradually eliminate the $\zeta(t), t = 0, 1, \ldots$, portion of patterns which have higher attractive capacity than those of the rest prototypes in the class $c^{(i)}$, $i = 1, 2, \ldots, p$,

respectively, where t represents the iteration number and $\xi(t)$ is a decreasing function of t. We stop iterating when t is greater than certain number N. We present the detail procedure as follows.

Template Reduction Procedure

Step 1: Set $\Phi \leftarrow \Re$ and $t = 1$.

Step 2: Calculate the attractive capacity for each prototype in the updated template set Φ.

Step 3: Eliminate the $\xi(t)$ portion of patterns which have higher attractive capacity than those of the rest prototypes in the class $c^{(i)}$, $i = 1, 2, \ldots, p$, respectively.

Step 4: Set $t \leftarrow t + 1$. If $t > N$ then stop; else go to Step 2.

4   Preprocessing

We observe that the computational complexity of the matching measure H is $O(n)$. When n is rather large, this is very time-consuming if each prototype pattern is to be matched once to classify an unknown pattern. In the previous Section we have introduced a method to reduce the template size. However, to maintain the accuracy, the template size is not able to be infinitely reduced. We imagine that we must be able to reject a large part of prototypes at the first sight if we are required to find out K nearest prototypes manually. In the following we give an interpretation of "first sight" for classification process.

We observe that the numbers of ones (or equivalently the number of zeros) of prototype y is a special characteristic of that prototype, such that

$$\lambda_{\mathbf{y}} = \sum_{i=1}^{n} y_i. \tag{6}$$

An unknown pattern x can be considered to be a distorted version of y if the difference of their numbers of ones, $|\lambda_{\mathbf{x}} - \lambda_{\mathbf{y}}|$, is within certain threshold $\theta_{\mathbf{y}}$. It is worth noting that $|\lambda_{\mathbf{x}} - \lambda_{\mathbf{y}}| = 0$ if $y = x$.

The crucial point is to give an appropriate threshold for each prototype. Here we give a straight-forward method. We consider τ prototypes $\mathbf{y}^{(1)}, \mathbf{y}^{(2)}, \ldots, \mathbf{y}^{(\tau)}$ which are nearest to y, in the sense of $H(\mathbf{y}, \cdot)$, among all prototypes in the same class as y. In fact, we can regard $\mathbf{y}^{(1)}, \mathbf{y}^{(2)}, \ldots, \mathbf{y}^{(\tau)}$ as the distorted versions of y. Therefore we determine the threshold by

$$\theta_{\mathbf{y}} \stackrel{\triangle}{=} \max\{|\lambda_{\mathbf{y}} - \lambda_{\mathbf{y}}^{(i)}| : i = 1, 2, \ldots, \tau\}. \tag{7}$$

To classify an unknown pattern x, we first check whether $|\lambda_{\mathbf{x}} - \lambda_{\mathbf{y}}| \leq \theta_{\mathbf{y}}$. If the check fails, we simply do not consider y any further. Figure 2 shows

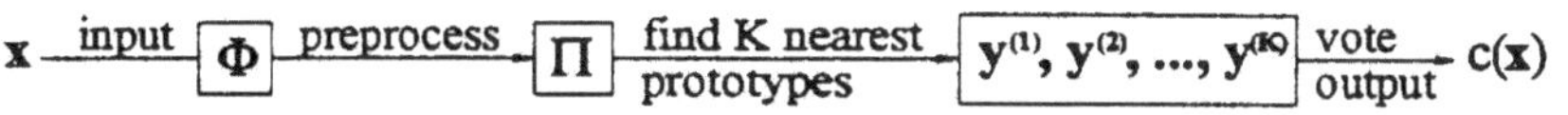

Figure 2: Classification process

two stages of classification, where Π denotes the set of prototypes $\mathbf{y}$ which are qualified as candidate prototypes of $\mathbf{x}$, that is, $|\lambda_{\mathbf{x}} - \lambda_{\mathbf{y}}| \leq \theta_{\mathbf{y}}$, and $c(\mathbf{x})$ denotes the label that $\mathbf{x}$ is classified to.

Since $\lambda_{\mathbf{y}}$ and $\theta_{\mathbf{y}}$ for each prototype can be pre-calculated in the training procedure. We just need to calculate $\lambda_{\mathbf{x}}$ once. The complexity of preprocessing for each prototype is $O(1)$, especially, it is independent of the pattern dimension n. However, to obtain the matching measure $H(\mathbf{y}, \mathbf{x})$ the complexity is $O(n)$. Thus, the larger the value n, the more powerful the preprocessing. We observe that, the smaller the value τ, the smaller the threshold, therefore, the more prototypes are precluded in the preprocessing. However, with the threshold smaller and smaller, the preprocessing even rejects the truly close prototypes, which is not desirable.

5   Experimental Results

In this Section we accommodate the above two methods to a well-known digit recognizer, GSC [1]. A GSC feature vector is a 512-dimensional binary vector, i.e., $n = 512$. In GSC recognizer the matching measure is defined as

$$H(\mathbf{x}, \mathbf{y}) = 2 * |\{1 \leq i \leq n : x_i = y_i = 1\}| + |\{1 \leq i \leq n : x_i = y_i = 0\}|, \quad (8)$$

and the parameter $K = 6$.

For digital recognition, there are 10 classes, i.e., $p = 10$. The given training set $\Re$ of 126,000 patterns has equal number of patterns in each class. The given testing set has 25,300 patterns and again equal number in each class. We simulate on a SPARC 400 MHZ computer.

Experiment 1:
In this experiment we apply the proposed approach of template reduction to the GSC recognizer. We simulate on 4 classifiers. Classifier I uses the training set of 126,000 patterns as template and original scheme as in [1]. In the template reduction procedure, we set $\xi(t) = 0.4 \times (t+1)^{-0.5}$. Classifier II uses the reduced template of 23,900 patterns ($N = 5$). Classifier III uses the reduced template of 33,320 patterns ($N = 4$), Classifier IV uses the reduced template of 46,470 patterns ($N = 3$). The results are listed in Table I.

By applying the proposed template reduction, Classifier III reveals the similar accuracy as Classifier I, however, the classification procedure of Classifier III takes almost 1/4 of that of Classifier I.

Table I

Simulation Comparisons for Different Classifiers

Classifier	Time (ms)	Accuracy (%)
I	307.1	97.62
II	58.2	96.86
III	80.9	97.58
IV	113.0	97.63

Table II

Simulation Comparisons for Different Classifiers

Classifier	Time (ms)	Accuracy (%)
I	307.1	97.62
III	80.9	97.58
V	35.2	95.83
VI	44.8	97.56
VII	61.2	97.61

Experiment 2:

In this experiment we apply the proposed preprocessing to accommodate Classifier III. Classifier V, VI, VII are generated by combining Classifier III and preprocessing with parameter $\tau = 10, 15, 20$, respectively. We show the simulation results along with those of Classifier I and Classifier III as in Table II.

We observe that the preprocessing reduces classification time by almost one time while maintaining similar accuracy. Totally, the combination of two techniques makes the classification time almost 7 times less than the original one but sacrifices no accuracy.

6   Conclusion and Future Work

We have presented two approaches to improve the efficacy of K-NN classifications. Differing from the template reduction methods in literature, which reduced the template size also lowered down the classification accuracy, we implement the template reduction by gradually eliminating the prototypes with high capacity. This method allow us to cease a lot of redundant prototypes. Consequently it is able to notably reduce the template size but maintain the accuracy. We also developed an efficient preprocessing. It took just one step, i.e., the complexity is $O(1)$, which is much less than full matching complexity of $O(n)$. It precluded a large part of prototypes which were not close to the unknown pattern, thus significantly reduced the classification time, especially when n is rather large, at same time kept the classification accuracy.

We have not proposed any rules for optimal selection of template prototypes. We are confident that it should result better performance if parameter

ξ depends on both class label and iteration times. Furthermore, the proposed stopping rule is heuristic and nothing to do with optimality. This aspect is worthwhile to be further studied.

In the proposed preprocessing, the optimal selection rule of parameter τ is to be studied. In a broader view, it is worthwhile to study on the optimal selection of threshold for each prototype, which is unnecessary to be based on the proposed scheme. Furthermore, it is worth working on some other interpretations of "first sight", or more broadly, "finite sights".

References

[1] S. W. Lam, G. Srikantan, and S. N. Srihari, "Gradient-based contour encoding for character recognition", *Pattern Recognition*, vol. 29, no. 7, pp. 1147–1160, 1996.

[2] K. Hattori and M. Takahashi, "A new nearest-neighbor rule in the pattern classification problem", *Pattern Recognition*, vol. 32, no. 3, pp. 425-432, Mar. 1999.

[3] S. A. Dudani, *The distance-weighted k-nearest neighbor rule, neighbor neighbor norms: NN pattern classification techniques*, IEEE Comp. Soc. Press, Los Alamitos, California, pp. 92–94, 1991.

[4] J. M. Keller, M. R. Gray, and J. A. Givens, Jr., "A fuzzy k-nearest neighbor algorithm", *IEEE Trans. on Systems, Man, and Cybernetics*, vol. 15, pp. 580–585, 1985.

[5] R. O. Duda and P. E. Hart, "Pattern Classification and Scene Analysis", Wiley, New York, 1973.

[6] T. M. Cover, and P. E. Hart, "Nearest neighbor pattern classification", *IEEE Trans. on Inform. Theory*, vol. 13, pp. 21–27, 1967

[7] K. Fukunaga and L. D. Hostetler, "K-nearest-neighbor Bayes-risk estimation", *IEEE Trans. Inform. Theory*, vol. 21, pp. 285–293, 1975.

[8] P. E. Hart, "The condensed neatest neighbor rule", *IEEE Trans. Inform. Theory*, vol. 14, pp. 515-516, 1968.

[9] G. W. Gates, "The reduced nearest neighbor rule", *IEEE Trans. Inform. Theory*, pp. 431-433, May 1972.

[10] C. L. Chang, "Finding prototypes for nearest neighbor classifiers", *IEEE Trans. Comput.*, vol. 23, no. 11, pp. 1179–1184, Nov. 1974.

[11] G. L. Ritter, H. B. Woodruff, S. R. Lowry, and T. L. Isenhour, "An algorithm for a selective nearest neighbor decision rule", *IEEE Trans. Inform. Theory*, pp. 665–669, 1975.

Branch & Bound Algorithm with Partial Prediction for Use with Recursive and Non-Recursive Criterion Forms

Petr Somol, Pavel Pudil, and Jiří Grim

Dept. of Pattern Recognition, Inst. of Information Theory and Automation, Academy of Sciences of the Czech Republic, 182 08 Prague 8, Czech Republic
{somol, pudil, grim}@utia.cas.cz

Abstract. We introduce a novel algorithm for optimal feature selection. As opposed to our recent *Fast Branch & Bound* (FBB) algorithm [5] the new algorithm is well suitable for use with recursive criterion forms. Even if the new algorithm does not operate as effectively as the FBB algorithm, it is able to find the optimum significantly faster than any other Branch & Bound [1,3] algorithm.

Keywords: subset search, feature selection, search tree, recursive criteria, optimal search, subset selection.

1 Introduction

The problem of optimal feature selection (or more generally of subset selection) is difficult especially because of its time complexity. Any known optimal search algorithm has an exponential nature. The only alternative to the exhaustive search is the *Branch & Bound* (BB) algorithm [1,3] and ancestor algorithms based on a similar principle. Any BB algorithm requires the criterion function fulfilling the *monotonicity condition*. Let $\bar{\chi}_j$ be the set of features obtained by removing j features $y_1, y_2, \cdots, y_j$ from the set Y of all D features, i.e.

$$\bar{\chi}_j = \{\xi_i | \xi_i \in Y, 1 \leq i \leq D; \xi_i \neq y_k, \forall k\} \tag{1}$$

The *monotonicity condition* assumes that for feature subsets $\bar{\chi}_1, \bar{\chi}_2, \cdots, \bar{\chi}_j$, where

$$\bar{\chi}_1 \supset \bar{\chi}_2 \supset \cdots \supset \bar{\chi}_j$$

the criterion function J fulfills

$$J(\bar{\chi}_1) \geq J(\bar{\chi}_2) \geq \cdots \geq J(\bar{\chi}_j). \tag{2}$$

By a straightforward application of this property many feature subset evaluations may be omitted.

Before discussing the new algorithm, let us summarize the BB principle briefly. The algorithm constructs a search tree where the root represents the

S. Singh, N. Murshed, and W. Kropatsch (Eds.): ICAPR 2001, LNCS 2013, pp. 230–239, 2001.

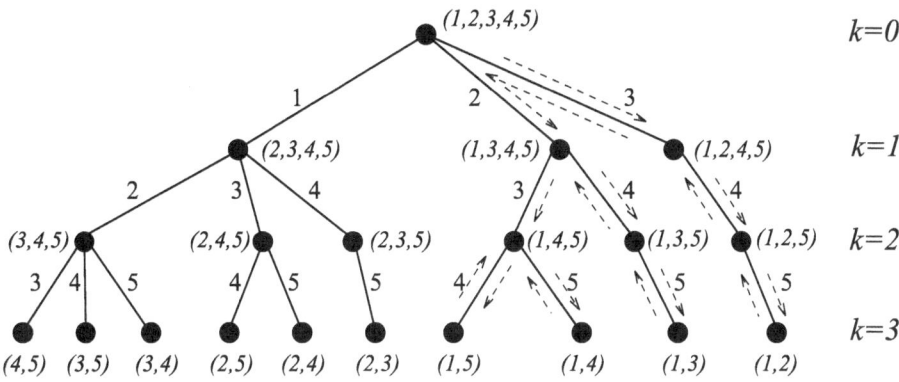

Fig. 1. Example of "branch & bound" problem solution, where $d = 2$ features are to be selected from the set of $D = 5$ features. The dashed arrows illustrate the way of tracking the search tree.

set of all D features and leaves represent target subsets of d features. While tracking the tree down to leaves the algorithm removes successively single features from the current set of "candidates" ($\bar{\chi}_k$ in the k-th level). The algorithm keeps the information about both the till-now best subset $\mathcal{X}$ and the criterion value X^* it yields (we denote this value the *bound*). Anytime the criterion value in some internal node is found to be lower than the current *bound*, due to the condition (2) the whole sub-tree may be cut-off and many computations may be omitted. The course of the BB algorithm is illustrated on Fig. 1. For details see [1,3,2].

Several improvements of this scheme are known: the "Improved" BB algorithm [3] utilizes a heuristic for ordering tree branches so as to find the optimum faster and therefore to allow more sub-tree cut-offs. The "Fast" BB algorithm [5] introduces a prediction mechanism being able to predict impossibility of cutting-off a sub-tree and therefore to save a significant number of computations.

2   Drawbacks of the Traditional Branch & Bound Algorithm

When compared to the exhaustive search, every BB algorithm requires additional computations. Not only the target subsets of d features $\bar{\chi}_{D-d}$, but also their supersets $\bar{\chi}_{D-d-j}$, $j = 1, 2, \cdots, D - d$ have to be evaluated.

The BB principle does not guarantee that enough sub-trees will be cut-off to keep the total number of criterion computations lower than their number in exhaustive search. The worst theoretical case would arise when we defined a criterion function $J(\bar{\chi}_k) = |\bar{\chi}_k| \equiv D - k$; the criterion function would be computed not only in every leaf (the same number of computations as in exhaustive search), but additionally also in every other node inside the tree.

Weak BB performance in certain situations may result from simple facts that nearer to the root: a) criterion value computation is usually slower (evaluated feature subsets are larger), b) sub-tree cut-offs are less frequent nearer the root (higher criterion values may be expected for larger subsets, which reduces the chance of the criterion value to remain under the *bound*, which is updated in leaves). The BB algorithm usually spends most of time by tedious, but less promising evaluation of tree nodes near the root. This effect is to be expected especially for $d \ll D$. In case of the "Improved" BB algorithm a significant number of additional computations is needed for ordering internal search tree node descendants. The advantage following from these computations may become questionable, because a slightly better heuristic organization of the search tree is often outweighted by the additional computational time.

A very effective way of resolving BB disadvantages offers the FBB algorithm, which is able to replace a large number of computations by means of prediction. Although the FBB algorithm requires usually several times less criterion computations than any other BB algorithm, its suitability for many practical problems is limited if the recursive criterion forms are to be used. To resolve this limitation we define a new, more universal algorithm.

3   Improving the "Improved" Algorithm

Let's focus on the "Improved" BB algorithm heuristics for ordering the internal tree node descendants. Let the *criterion value decrease* be the difference between the current criterion value and the value after the removal of a particular feature. Let *bad* features be those features, whose removal from the current candidate set causes only a slight *criterion value decrease*. Let *good* features be those ones, whose removal from the current candidate set causes a significant *criterion value decrease*. (At this stage there is no need to quantify what a slight or significant decrease is).

In this explanation we assume that the BB algorithm constructs a search tree with a given topology (e.g. the "minimum solution tree" described by Yu and Yuan [4]). It is apparent that given the search tree topology, different feature assignments to the tree edges may be defined. The "Improved" algorithm aims to position *bad* features to the right, less dense part of the tree and *good* features to its left, more dense part . Based on such ordering we may expect faster *bound* increase, because preferred removal of *bad* features should keep the candidate criterion value higher. Consequently, removing *good* features from later candidate sets in the left, dense part of the tree gives better chance to decrease the criterion value under the *bound* and therefore to allow more effective sub-tree cut-offs.

The "Improved" BB algorithm operates approximately twice as fast as the "Basic" BB algorithm in most practical problems. However, the ordering heuristic requires a significant number of additional computations. Let's illustrate this drawback on Fig. 1 – when constructing the first level, i.e. when specifying the ordering of root descendants, the "Improved" algorithm evaluates the *criterion*

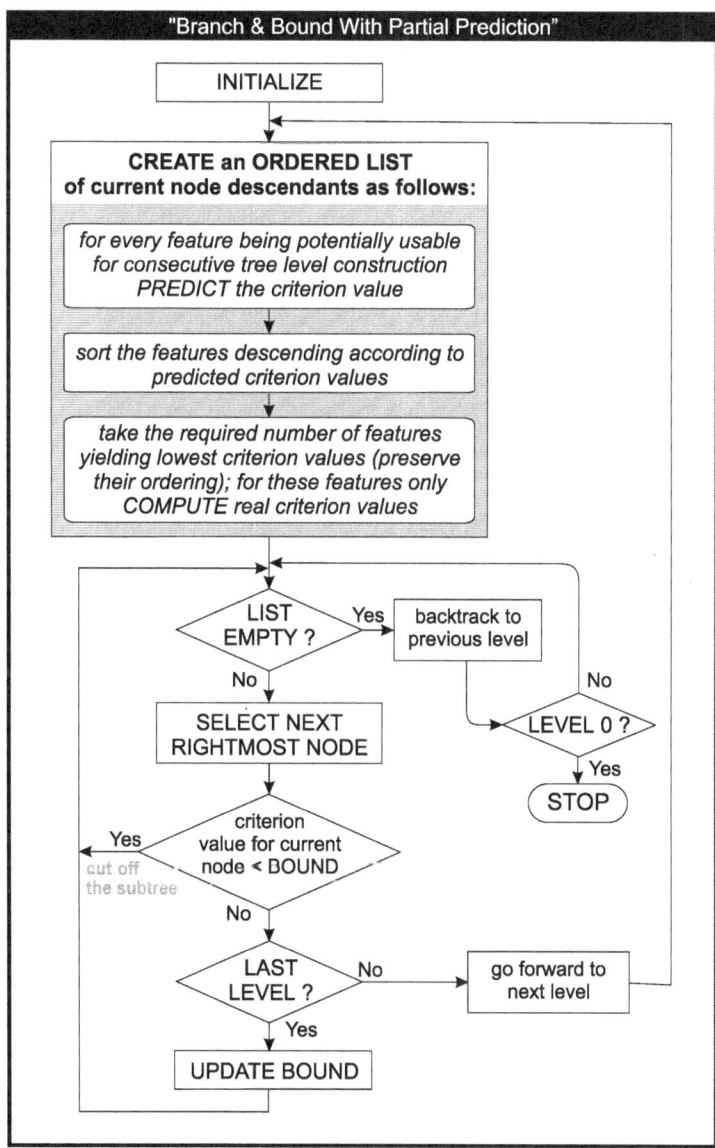

Fig. 2. Simplified diagram of the new algorithm

value decrease for every available feature (all 5 features), although only 3 features are to be assigned to first level edges.

Our intention is to find the same (or very similar) ordering of tree nodes as given by means of the "Improved" BB algorithm with reduced number of criterion evaluations. To achieve this goal we utilize the prediction mechanism as defined for purposes of the FBB algorithm. The new algorithm will construct the consecutive tree levels in several phases. First the *criterion value decrease* will be *predicted* for every feature being currently available for the tree construction. The features will be sorted descending according to the *predicted criterion value decreases*. Then, the required number of features (beginning from the feature with highest *predicted criterion value decrease*) will be taken to form the consecutive tree level.

Different features appear in different search tree construction stages, therefore we need to collect the prediction information separately for every feature. First we introduce a *vector of feature contributions to criterion value* for storing the individual information about average *criterion value decrease* caused by removing single features from current "candidate" subsets. Next we introduce a *counter vector* recording the number of *criterion value decrease* evaluations for every individual feature.

4   Branch & Bound with Partial Prediction (BBPP)

Our algorithm description is based on the notion from book [2]. We will use following symbols:

constants:

D – number of all features,

d – required number of selected features,

other symbols:

Y – set of all D features,

$J(.)$ – criterion function,

k – tree level ($k = 0$ denotes the root),

$\bar{X}_k = \{\xi_j \mid j = 1, 2, \cdots, D - k\}$ – current "candidate" feature subset in k-th tree level,

q_k – number of current node descendants (in consecutive tree level),

$\mathcal{Q}_k = \{Q_{k,1}, Q_{k,2}, \ldots, Q_{k,q_k}\}$ – ordered set of features assigned to edges leading to the current node descendants (note that "candidate" subsets $\bar{X}_{k+1}$ corresponding to the current node descendants are fully determined by features $Q_{k,i}$ for $i = 1, \cdots q_k$),

$\mathbf{J}_k = [J_{k,1}, J_{k,2}, \ldots, J_{k,q_k}]^{\mathrm{T}}$ – vector of criterion values corresponding to the current node descendants in consecutive tree level ($J_{k,i} = J(\bar{X}_k \setminus \{Q_{k,i}\})$ for $i = 1, \cdots, q_k$),

$\Psi = \{\psi_j \mid j = 1, 2, \cdots, r\}$ – control set of r features being currently available for search-tree construction, i.e. for building consecutive descendant vector $\mathcal{Q}_k$; the Ψ set serves for maintaining the search tree topology,

$X = \{x_j \mid j = 1, 2, \cdots, d\}$ – current best subset of d features

X^* – current *bound* (criterion value corresponding to $\mathcal{X}$),
$\mathbf{A} = [A_1, A_2, \ldots, A_D]^\mathrm{T}$ – *vector of feature contributions to criterion value,*
$\mathbf{S} = [S_1, S_2, \ldots, S_D]^\mathrm{T}$ – *counter vector* (together with $\mathbf{A}$ serves for prediction)

Remark: it is necessary to store all values q_j, ordered sets $\mathcal{Q}_j$ and vectors $\mathbf{J}_j$ for $j = 0, \cdots, k$ during the algorithm course to allow backtracking.

The algorithm is to be initialized as follows:
$k = 0$ (starting in the root),
$\bar{\chi}_0 = Y$,
$\Psi = Y, r = D$
X^* – lowest possible value (computer dependent)
$S_i = 0$ for all $i = 1, \cdots, D$.

──────────────── **The BBPP Algorithm** ────────────────

Whenever the algorithm removes some feature y_i from the current "candidate" subset and computes the corresponding real criterion value $J(\bar{\chi}_k \setminus \{y_i\})$ in k-th tree level, use the difference $J(\bar{\chi}_k) - J(\bar{\chi}_k \setminus \{y_i\})$ for updating the *prediction information*. Let

$$A_{y_i} = \frac{A_{y_i} \cdot S_{y_i} + J(\bar{\chi}_k) - J(\bar{\chi}_k \setminus \{y_i\})}{S_{y_i} + 1} \tag{3}$$

and let

$$S_{y_i} = S_{y_i} + 1 \tag{4}$$

STEP 1: *Select descendants of the current node to form the consecutive tree level:* first set their number to $q_k = r - (D - d - k - 1)$. Construct an ordered set $\mathcal{Q}_k$ and vector $\mathbf{J}_k$ specifying the current node descendants as follows: sort all features $\psi_j \in \Psi, j = 1, \cdots, r$ descending according to their $A_{\psi_j}, j = 1, \cdots, r$ values, i.e.

$$A_{\psi_{j_1}} \geq A_{\psi_{j_1}} \geq \cdots \geq A_{\psi_{j_r}}$$

and choose successively first q_k features among them, i.e. let
$Q_{k,i} = \psi_{j_i}$ for $i = 1, \cdots, q_k$
$J_{k,i} = J(\bar{\chi}_k \setminus \{\psi_{j_i}\})$ for $i = 1, \cdots, q_k$
To avoid future duplicate testing, features ψ_{j_i} cannot be used for construction of consecutive tree levels, so let $\Psi = \Psi \setminus Q_k$ and $r = r - q_k$

STEP 2: *Test the right-most descendant node (connected by the Q_{k,q_k}-edge):* if $q_k = 0$, all descendants were tested, go to **Step 4** (backtracking). If $J_{k,q_k} < X^*$, then go to **Step 3**. Else let $\bar{\chi}_{k+1} = \bar{\chi}_k \setminus \{Q_{k,q_k}\}$. If $k + 1 = D - d$, then you have reached a leaf, go to **Step 5**. Otherwise go to the consecutive level: let $k = k + 1$ and go to **Step 1**.

STEP 3: *Descendant node connected by the Q_{k,q_k}-edge (and its possible sub-tree) may be cut-off:* return feature Q_{k,q_k} to the set of features available for tree construction, i.e. let $\Psi = \Psi \cup \{Q_{k,q_k}\}$ and $r = r + 1$, $\mathcal{Q}_k = \mathcal{Q}_k \setminus \{Q_{k,q_k}\}$ and $q_k = q_k - 1$ and continue with its left neighbor; go to **Step 2**.

STEP 4: *Backtracking:* Let $k = k - 1$. If $k = -1$, then the complete tree had been searched through; stop the algorithm. Otherwise return feature Q_{k,q_k} to the set of "candidates": let $\bar{\chi}_k = \bar{\chi}_{k+1} \cup \{Q_{k,q_k}\}$ and go to **Step 3**.

STEP 5: *Actualize the bound value:* Let $X^* = J_{k,q_k}$. Store the currently best feature subset $\mathcal{X} = \bar{\chi}_{k+1}$ and go to **Step 2**.

Remark: In Step 1 for $k = 0$ the term $J_{-1,q-1}$ denotes the criterion value on a set of all features, $J(Y)$.

5   New Algorithm Properties

The algorithm may be expected to be most effective, if the individual feature contribution to the criterion value does not change strongly in relation to different subsets. Practical tests on real data fulfilled this property in most of cases. Moreover, the BBPP algorithm proved to be effective even in cases, when due to difficult statistical dependencies individual feature contributions failed to remain stable.

When compared to the FBB algorithm, the BBPP may be expected to be more robust. A potential failure of the prediction mechanism would have only indirect influence on the overall algorithm performance. A potentially wrong ordering of internal tree nodes (i.e. assigning of features to edges) would eventually decrease the efficiency of sub-tree cut-offs, but on the other hand the basic advantage over the "Improved BB" algorithm – reducing the number of additional computations – remains preserved.

When compared to both "Basic" and "Improved" algorithms the BBPP always spends some additional time for maintaining the prediction mechanism. However, this time proved not to be important in case of non-recursive criterion forms, while in case of faster recursive criterion forms it still proved to be short enough to ensure overall algorithm speedup. Moreover, especially for use with recursive criterion forms attempts to define even simpler prediction mechanisms to save computational time (e.g. to utilize the last known feature contribution to criterion value only) have been made with promising results.

Remark: To ensure good results we recommend to evaluate the *individual feature contributions to criterion value* once for all features in the initial algorithm phase. This will ensure a correct start of the prediction mechanism. Moreover, the first search tree level may then be constructed in the same way as in the "Improved" BB, what may prove to be advantageous for later algorithm phases.

6   Experiments

The algorithms were tested on a number of different data sets. Here we present representative results computed on 30-dimensional mammogram data (2 classes – 357 benign and 212 malignant samples) obtained from Wisconsin Diagnostic Breast Center via the UCI repository - ftp.ics.uci.edu. We used both the recursive and non-recursive Bhattacharyya distance as the criterion function. Performance of different methods is illustrated on Fig. 3 and Fig. 4 by a graph of total computational time and a graph of criterion evaluation numbers. We did not include the graph of criterion values, because all the methods yield the same optimum values.

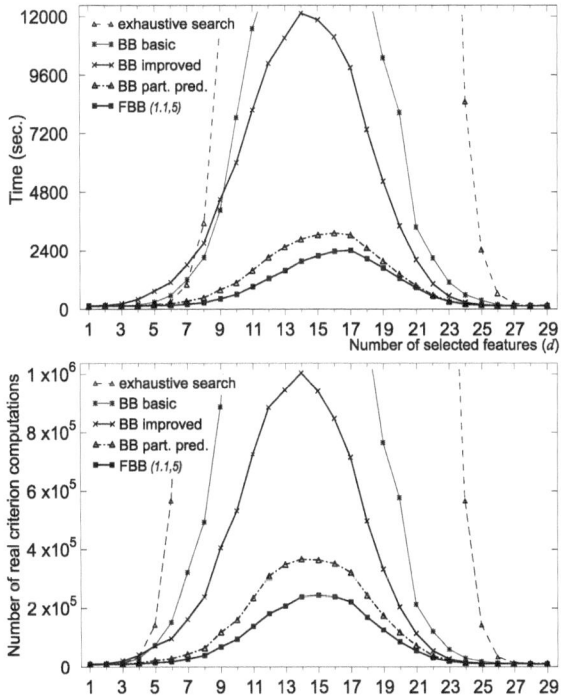

Fig. 3. Example: Optimal subset search methods performance when maximizing the **non-recursive** Bhattacharyya distance on 30-dimensional data (Wisconsin Diagnostic Breast Center). Results computed on a Pentium II-350 MHz computer.

We compare all the results especially with the results of the "Improved" BB algorithm [3,2], because this algorithm is generally accepted to be the most effective optimal subset search strategy. In case of non-recursive criterion functions we compare the new algorithm also with our recent FBB algorithm. Note that in case of non recursive criterion computations we implemented all BB algorithms so as they construct the "minimum solution tree" [4].

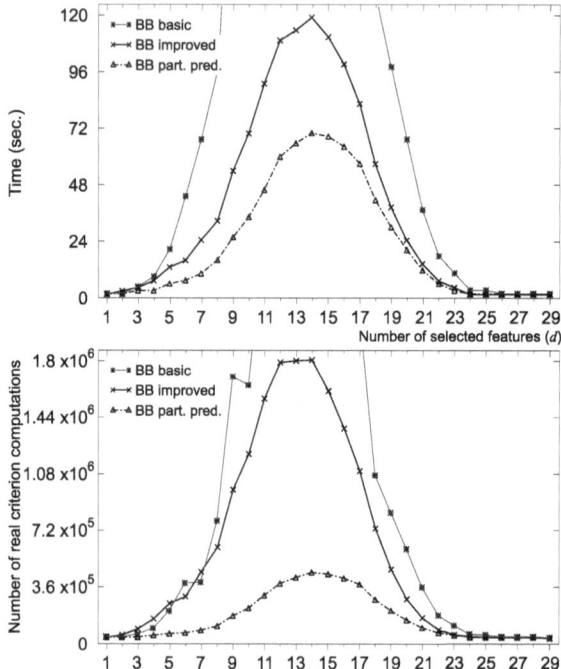

Fig. 4. Example: Optimal subset search methods performance when maximizing the **recursive** Bhattacharyya distance on 30-dimensional data (Wisconsin Diagnostic Breast Center). Results computed on a Pentium II-350 MHz computer.

Although the FBB algorithm usually finds the optimum after the smallest number of computations, its principle prevents it to be used with recursive criterion functions. The graphs on Fig. 3 and Fig. 4 illustrate that the BBPP operates faster than the "Improved" BB when used both with non-recursive or recursive criterion forms. According to expectations, being used with recursive criterion forms the new algorithm brings a less significant speedup; the computational complexity of recursive criterion forms is usually significantly lower than in non-recursive case, although the computational time spend by the prediction mechanism remains the same.

Remark: When used with recursive criterion form, no BB algorithm may utilize the "minimum solution tree" [4] due to the necessity to preserve criterion value computation sequence. The minimum solution tree assumes shortening of straight paths to leaves, what breaks the criterion computation sequence. Because of this reason numbers of computations differ in recursive and non-recursive case.

Both for the FBB and BBPP a slight shift of their graphs to the right may be observed when compared to the "Improved" BB algorithm. The prediction mechanism based algorithm acceleration relates to the number of criterion evaluation savings in internal search tree nodes, therefore with decreasing d the search tree depth increases and allows more effective operation of the prediction mechanism.

The majority of experiments produced results similar to those on Fig. 3 and Fig. 4. In one isolated worst case the speed of the BBPP used with recursive criterion form remained comparable to the speed of "Improved" BB. Theoretically we can not exclude the prediction mechanism failure – if the individual feature contributions to criterion value were unstable, i.e. changed too often and too strongly, the BBPP operation could become comparable with the "Basic BB" algorithm. However, we have not met such situation in our experiments.

7   Conclusion

We defined a new algorithm for optimal subset search. Its prediction mechanism allows significant time savings when compared to "Basic" or "Improved" Branch & Bound algorithms [3]. The algorithm was experimentally proved to be robust and well suitable for use with different criterion functions, both in recursive and non-recursive form.

Acknowledgement: The work has been supported by the grants of Czech Ministry of Education MŠMT No.VS96063, ME187, CEZ:J18/98:311600001 and Academy of Sciences K1075601.

References

1. Narendra P. M., Fukunaga K. (1977) A branch and bound algorithm for feature subset selection. IEEE Transactions on Computers, C-**26**, 917–922
2. Devijver P. A., Kittler J. (1982) Pattern Recognition: A Statistical Approach. Prentice-Hall
3. Fukunaga K. (1990) Introduction to Statistical Pattern Recognition: 2nd edition. Academic Press, Inc.
4. Yu B., Yuan B. (1993) A more efficient branch and bound algorithm for feature selection. Pattern Recognition, **26**, 883–889
5. Somol P., Pudil P., Ferri F. J., Kittler J. (2000) Fast Branch & Bound Algorithm in Feature Selection. Proc 4th World Multiconference on Systemics, Cybernetics and Informatics SCI 2000, Orlando, Florida, Vol VII, Part 1, 646–651

Model Validation for Model Selection

Josef Kittler, Kieron Messer, and Mohammed Sadeghi

University of Surrey, Guildford, Surrey. UK. GU2 7XH.

Abstract. Gaussian mixture modelling is used to provide a semi-parametric density description for a given data set. The fundamental problem with this approach is that the number of mixtures required to adequately describe the data is not known in advance. In our previous work [12] we introduced a new concept, termed `Predictive Validation` as a basis for an automatic method to select the number of components. In this paper we investigate the influence of the various parameters in our model selection method in order to develop it into an operational tool. We also demonstrate the utility of our model validation method to two applications in which the selected models are used for supervised classification and outlier detection tasks.

Keywords: model selection, gaussian mixtures, predictive validation.

1 Introduction

In this paper we are concerned with the problem of density estimation using mixture modelling. Consider a finite set of data points $X = \{\mathbf{x}_1, \mathbf{x}_2, \dots \mathbf{x}_N\}$, that are independent and identically distributed samples of the random variable $\mathbf{x}$. We wish to find the function that describes the data, i.e. its pdf $p(\mathbf{x})$. Building such a model has many potential applications, especially in pattern classification.

In this work the density is estimated using a semi-parametric technique based on Gaussian mixture distribution modelling. This offers a compromise between parametric and non-parametric methods. A Gaussian mixture has a functional form, but the free parameters in the model are allowed to vary which facilitates a more concise and adaptable model of the data to be built. The number of free parameters does not depend upon the size of the data set. In here we are particularly concerned with the problem of model selection, i.e. determining the number of mixture components required to successfully model the data.

A simple method of model selection would be to choose the model which gives the highest likelihood of the data given that model. Schwarz [13] stated that, in the limit of an infinitely large training set, the log-likelihood selects the optimal model. In practice, very large data sets are rarely available and this criterion is biased to selecting more complex models than actually required. This bias can be reduced by the use of re-sampling plans such as cross validation, bootstrapping or jackkniving [4].

S. Singh, N. Murshed, and W. Kropatsch (Eds.): ICAPR 2001, LNCS 2013, pp. 240–249, 2001.

Information criteria work on the principal that the model to be preferred is the simplest one. All work on the product of the likelihood of the data with a prior imposed over the different models. Many information criteria have been suggested including, [1], [13], [11], [10] and[2]. The main advantage of information criteria are their simplicity and hence low computational cost. The downside is that the chosen penalty term depends on the problem analysed. If the function is complex and the penalty is too strong the model will be under-fitted.

Other approaches to model selection include total kurtosis [14] and multiscale clustering [6].

The work in this paper is an extension of a conceptually novel approach to model selection based on the idea of *model validation* [12]. Predictive validation works on the assumption that a good model will predict the data. In the case of an under-fitted model the model will not predict the data and the model will be rejected. We investigate the influence of the various parameters of the model validation method in order to develop it into an operational tool: The dependence of the algorithm on the estimation errors of the empirical probilities; the sensitivity to training data set sample size and the problem of window size selection have all been investigated. As a result of the work reported in here and in [8], several modifications to the algorithm are proposed. Finally, the proposed effectiveness of the modified algorithm is demonstrated on several real world applications.

The rest of this paper is organised as follows. In the next section our `Predictive Validation` algorithm is detailed in full. In section 3 experiments are performed on real data sets. Finally, some conclusions are given and possible directions for future research are suggested in section 4.

2   Mixture Modelling

A mixture model is defined by equation 1.

$$p(\mathbf{x}) = \sum_{j=1}^{M} p(\mathbf{x}|j)P(j) \tag{1}$$

The coefficients $P(j)$ are called the mixing parameters and are chosen such that

$$\sum_{j=1}^{M} P(j) = 1 \quad \text{and} \quad 0 \le P(j) \le 1 \tag{2}$$

Also note that the component functions satisfy the axiomatic properties of probility density functions

$$\int p(\mathbf{x}|j)d\mathbf{x} = 1 \tag{3}$$

In this work we use the normal distribution with a diagonal covariance matrix for the individual component density functions. The estimation of the parameters governing the Gaussian mixture model is done via the Expectation Maximisation (EM) algorithm [3].

Unfortunately, the EM algorithm suffers from a few major flaws. Firstly, even-though the EM increases the likelihood of the observations, it does not guarantee a global maximum and it can easily get confined to a local maximum or saddle point. For this reason, different initialisations of the algorithm have to be considered which may give rise to different models being obtained. Secondly, there exist parameter values for which the likelihood goes to infinity. This happens when one of the components collapses onto one of the data points. Finally, the most difficult problem is that the number of components k, required as an input, is very rarely known in advance.

Ideally, when setting k, the goal is to find the least complex model (fewer components) that gives a satisfactory fit to the data. In practice, this usually involves computing a set of models with a different number of components and selecting the model according to some other optimality criteria. This process is often referred to as model selection.

2.1   Predictive Validation

Suppose we have a model that predicts an event $A = x_L \leq x \leq x_U$ with probability $p(A) = 0.9$. If in the dataset X there is no such value for x that lies in this range, i.e. the observed probability is zero, the model computed must be a bad one. This is irrespective of any classification performance the model might have, how many data samples are in the data set and how many parameters describe the model.

Suppose that a model M_j with j components has been estimated for data set X. The empirical probability p_{emp} in a hyper-cubic window W placed at random in the observation space is defined as

$$p_{emp}(\mathbf{x}) = \frac{k(W)}{N} \tag{4}$$

where $k(W)$ is the number of training points falling within window W.

The predicted probability of the data in the window based on the same model M_j is computed using

$$p_{pred}(\mathbf{x}) = \int_W p(\mathbf{x})d\mathbf{x} \tag{5}$$

If the model is good the empirical and predicted frequencies should be approximately equal. Making repeated observations of p_{emp} and p_{pred}, for different window sizes and random placements, permits a weighted linear least square fit of p_{pred} versus p_{diff} to be formed, where $p_{diff} = p_{pred} - p_{emp}$.

$$P_{pred} = a \cdot (P_{emp} - P_{pred}) + b \qquad (6)$$

where a is the gradient and b the intercept.

If the model is good then the fitted line in equation 6 should lie close to the line $y = 0$. This can easily be checked via a statistical test. Performing this test allows a model to be self-calibrated.

In summary, the predictive validation algorithm is as follows,

---

Algorithm 1: Predictive validation

---

1 Obtain the candidate Gaussian mixture model M_j that has been computed on data set X which contains j components.
2 For each training point x_i in X choose a window W of random size and compute p_{emp} and p_{pred}.
3 Find the weighted least squares fit for $P_{pred} = a \cdot (P_{emp} - P_{pred}) + b$.
4 Check the (p_{pred}, p_{diff}) data can be fitted to a linear model. If it can, then proceed to step 5. Else model is not validated.
5 Statistically test whether the fitted line is close to the line $y = 0$. If it is then accept the model. Else the model is rejected.

In our previous work, the calculation of p_{emp} was selected randomly in such a way that p_{cmp} spanned the interval $[0, 1]$. Through experimentation [8], we have found that this is not the best strategy and more control over the window size and range of p_{emp} needs to be made.

The procedure that is employed to select a window, for each data sample in the data set, in which p_{emp} and p_{pred} are computed is given by algorithm 2.

Algorithm 2: Calculation of p_{emp} and p_{pred}

---

1 For all points in data set X_N compute the Euclidean distance to all other points and form a distance matrix. Set $i = 1$.
2 Select point x_i from X_N and sort the $(N - 1)$ remaining points in the order of Euclidean distance from this point.

3 Randomly choose the desired level of probability, p_{ran}, from the chosen range, e.g. $[0, 1]$

4 Compute the corresponding number of points k that would be required to give this level of probability, i.e. $k = p_{ran} \times N$.

5 Find the minimum bounding window, centred on x_i which includes the k nearest points. This window is used to compute p^i_{emp} and p^i_{pred}.

6 If $i = N$ then stop. Else set $i = i + 1$ and goto step 2.

Weighted least squares is used to fit the line to the computed p_{emp} and p_{pred} data. For this step, it is important that the associated error on the p_{emp} measurement is calculated correctly. In practice we estimate this error from the binomial distribution. Experimental results [8] suggest that this assumption is valid.

Another critical issue in weighted least squares fitting is that the errors should be uncorrelated. Experimental results [8] indicate that the correlation effects present are minimal and can be safely ignored.

2.2 Model Selection

The predictive validation measure, used by algorithm 1, detects underfitting models. If this measure is performed on the same data that has been used for training, there is no hope of detecting overfitting. In this scenario, the obvious choice is to select the model that validates with the lowest number of parameters.

The model selection algorithm we utilise is similar in principal to the SFS algorithm used in feature selection [9]. It is a bottom up procedure which keeps adding components until the model is validated , M_{val}. Using this procedure ensures that an overfitted model is never computed.

Algorithm 3: Model Selection

B.1 Set $j = 1$.

B.2 Using the EM algorithm compute model M_j on data set X with j components.

B.3 Using algorithm 1 perform the model validation step.

B.4 If the model does not validate, set $j = j + 1$ and goto step 2.

B.5 Else if the model validates terminate the algorithm and set $M_{val} = M_j$.

3   Experiments

In this section we demonstrate how the models selected can be used in two real world applications.

3.1   Automatic Target Recognition

Automatic Target Recognition (ATR) is concerned with the detection, tracking and recognition of small targets using input data obtained from a multitude of sensor types such as forward looking infrared (FLIR), synthetic aperture radar (SAR) and laser radar (LADAR). Applications of ATR are numerous and include the assessment of battlefield situations, monitoring of possible targets over land, sea and air and the re-evaluation of target position during unmanned missiles weapon firing.

We are designing an adaptive ATR system which is suitable for scenes with strong clutter that can be spatially and temporally highly structured, such as sea glint and atmospheric scintillation.

For this application we view target detection as an outlier detection problem. That is, anything that does not normally occur in the background is viewed as a potential target. Our target detection algorithm has three basic steps:

Model Generation The background is described using a Gaussian mixture model.

Model Optimisation The model and model size are optimised using training data (if available).

Target Detection Outliers are found by deciding, per pixel, whether it is consistent with the model.

The background is represented by computing a feature vector, $\mathbf{f} = [y_0, y_1, \cdots, y_n]$, for every pixel in the training image. Each y_k represents a measurement obtained by the kth filter. The distribution of these feature vectors is modelled by a mixture of Gaussians. The number of mixture components is found using the model selection algorithm, algorithm 3.

To detect possible targets in test frames the same set of n features is generated for every pixel in the image. Each feature vector, $\mathbf{f}_{test}$, is tested in turn to see whether it belongs to the same distribution as the background or is an outlier (i.e. possible target). This is done by computing the density function value for that pixel, based on the mixture model. If this value falls below a threshold, the pixel is considered an outlier and treated as a possible target. This threshold can be automatically determined from the training data.

There is also a problem of knowing which features to use to ensure the targets and background vectors are well separated in the feature space. For this reason a feature selection stage was added which selects features using the *sequential forward selection* algorithm [9].

The background regions of an image are described adaptively using Principal Component Analysis (PCA, also known as the Karhunen-Loeve transform). More on this method can be found in [7].

The proposed target detection technique has been applied to several sequences made available by DERA Farnborough and compared to the results obtained on the same sequence using the multivariate conditional probability (MCP) methods described in [15]. Typical results are shown in this section on sequence SEASIM.

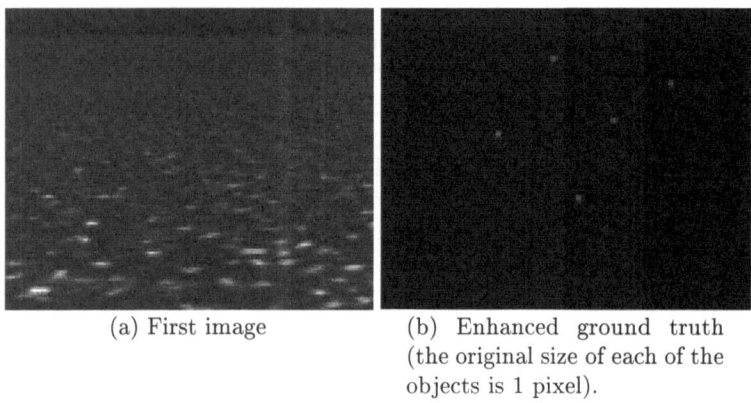

(a) First image   (b) Enhanced ground truth (the original size of each of the objects is 1 pixel).

Fig. 1. Sequence SEASIM.

The SEASIM sequence contains about twenty frames which have been artificially generated using a standard ray-tracing package. It represents the scenario of a sensor attached to a ship looking out over the ocean. Figure 1(a) shows the first frame of this sequence. Five targets have been inserted into this sequence; whose locations are given by the ground truth image of figure 1(b). These targets are very small (typically one pixel) and represent missiles moving towards the observer. The intensity of these targets are lower than the maximum intensity of the image and as the targets are moving slowly its pixel intensity will vary in time due to aliasing effects. A human observer will find it extremely difficult to identify all targets in this sequence. The two methods of target detection were then applied to this sequence.

The top ten most likely targets using multivariate conditional probability are shown in figure 2(a). The results obtained using mixture modelling are shown in figure 2(b). As one can see only four of the five targets have been recognised and two false positives have been identified in the top five for MCP. Using the proposed adaptive method, all five targets have been selected as the five most likely.

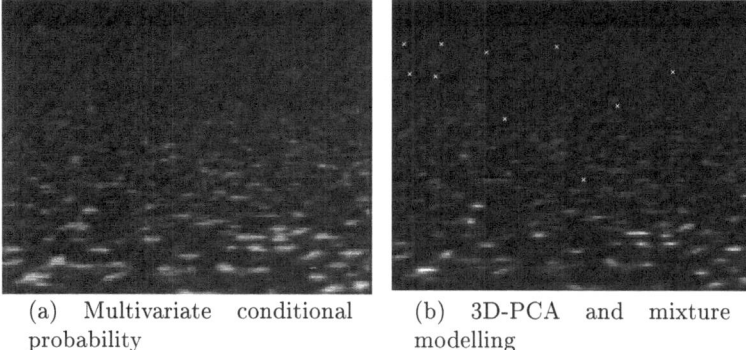

(a) Multivariate conditional probability

(b) 3D-PCA and mixture modelling

Fig. 2. SEASIM: Top 10 detections using both methods

3.2   Humber Bridge Data

A sequence of 280 consecutive grey-scale frames was captured from a plane flying over the `Humber` bridge. Each frame was then automatically segmented into homogeneous textured regions. If the segmented region was bigger than a pre-defined size it was manually classified as belonging to one of the ten classes. A total of 2,663 regions were identified. Each region then had a 121-dimensional feature vector computed on it where each value in the vector described a property of that region. Using principal component analysis the dimensionality of these vectors was reduced to just two.

Half the samples from the labelled `Humber` data set were then randomly selected. For each labelled class, a Gaussian mixture model model was selected using Predictive Validation. These models were then used to perform a maximum likelihood classification on the remaining half of the `Humber` data set. This process was repeated 10 times using different sets of training and test samples (cross-validation). The average probability of miss-classification (PMC) rate was computed. This process was also repeated using a 3-nearest neighbour classifier.

The PMC rate for the k-nearest neighbour classifier was 0.2022(0.013). The corresponding PMC rate for the PDF classifier was PDF 0.1564(0.013).

4   Conclusions

In this paper we have developed our proposed `Predictive Validation` algorithm into an operational tool that automatically selects the number of components for Gaussian mixture models. It was demonstrated that the selected models could be used in real world applications, including

	GD	RS	GM	VM	G	T	GS	M	S	SM
Grass Distant	130	0	0	0	18	0	0	0	0	0
River Sky	0	540	1	0	3	0	49	0	0	1
Grass Mixed	3	0	47	1	0	1	10	3	28	0
Veg Mixed	1	0	12	105	3	13	2	38	16	10
Grass	11	0	8	0	71	0	5	0	1	0
Trees	0	0	2	4	0	79	5	0	2	2
Grass Shadow	2	0	2	0	1	0	10	0	0	0
Mixed	0	0	0	12	0	0	0	29	0	1
Shadow	3	0	4	1	0	1	2	0	26	0
Structured Mixed	0	0	0	0	0	0	0	6	0	3

Table 1. Example confusion matrix for Humber data set using kNN classifier.

	GD	RS	GM	VM	G	T	GS	M	S	SM
Grass Distant	135	0	1	0	12	0	0	0	0	0
River Sky	0	591	1	0	1	0	1	0	0	0
Grass Mixed	2	0	63	6	1	2	0	0	19	0
Veg Mixed	1	0	19	106	3	14	0	39	10	8
Grass	11	1	8	4	69	0	3	0	0	0
Trees	0	0	3	5	0	83	0	2	1	0
Grass Shadow	2	0	6	0	0	0	7	0	0	0
Mixed	0	0	0	6	0	0	0	27	0	9
Shadow	2	0	4	2	0	1	0	0	28	0
Structured Mixed	0	0	1	2	0	0	0	5	0	1

Table 2. Example confusion matrix for Humber data set using PDF classifier.

Outlier Detection A Gaussian mixture model was used to describe the background region in an image. Anything that was not described by this model, i.e. an outlier, was consider a target. This modelling approach performed well in detecting targets and compared to a baseline, state of the art, ATR system in the literature.

Supervised classification A Gaussian mixture model was generated for each labelled class in a ground-truth annotated data set. These models were then used to build a Bayes classifier. It was demonstrated that this classifier produced a lower PMC rate than a k-nearest neighbour classifier on a test data set.

In the future we intend to investigate the possibility of using this technique with full covariance matrices for each component. This should enable more flexible models to be built. However, this would rely upon the estimation of the integration of the mixture-model in a window, through numerical Monte-Carlo techniques, see [5]. The error in this estimation and its effects on the accuracy of our algorithm needs to be addressed. It would also be interesting to investigate the effect of different window shapes, such as hyper-spheric, on the algorithm.

Acknowledgements This research was funded by the MoD under the Corporate Research Program by Technology Group 10: Information Processing and Technology Group 3: Aerodynamics, Propulsion, Guidance and Control. ©British Crown copyright 2000. Published with the permission of the Defence Evaluation and Research Agency on behalf of the Controller of HMSO.

References

1. H. Akaike. A new look at the statistical model identification. *IEEE trans. on Automatic Control*, AC-19(6):716–723, 1974.
2. A. Barron and T. Cover. Minimum complexity density-estimation. *IEEE trans. on Information Theory*, 37(4):1034–1054, 1991.
3. A Dempster, N Laird, and D Rubin. Maximum likelihood from incomplete data via the em algorithm. *Journal of the Royal Statistical Society*, 39(1):1–38, 1977.
4. K Fukunaga. *Introduction to Statistical Pattern Recognition*. Academic Press, 1990.
5. A. Genz. Comparison of methods for computation of multi-variate normal probabilities. *Computing Science and Statistics*, 25:400–405, 1993.
6. N Kehtarnavaz and E Nakamura. Generalization of the em algorithm for mixture density estimation. *Pattern recognition letters*, 19:133–140, February 1998.
7. K Messer, D. de Ridder, and J Kittler. Adaptive texture representation methods for automatic target recognition. In *Proc British Machine Vision Conference BMVC99*, September 1999.
8. K Messer, J Kittler, and M Sadeghi. Predicitive validation. Technical report, University of Surrey, 2000.
9. P Pudil, J Novovicova, and J Kittler. Floating search methods in feature selection. *Pattern Recognition Letters*, 15:1119–1125, 1994.
10. J. Rissanen. Stochastic complexity. *Journal of The Royal Statistical Society, Series B*, 49(3):223–239 and 252–265, 1987.
11. L. Sardo and J. Kittler. Complexity analysis of rbf networks for pattern recognition. In *Proceedings of CVPR96 (Computer Vision and Pattern Recognition Conference), San Francisco*, pages 574–579, 18-20 June 1996.
12. L Sardo and J Kittler. Model complexity validation for pdf estimation using gaussian mixtures. In S Venkatesh A K Jain and B C Lovell, editors, *International Conference on Pattern Recognition*, pages 195–197, 1998.
13. G. Schwarz. Estimating the dimension of a model. *The Annals of Statistics*, 6(2):461–464, 1978.
14. N. Vlassis, G. Papakonstantinou, and P. Tsanakas. Mixture density estimation on maximum likelihood and sequential test statistics. *Neural Processing Letters*, 1999.
15. G. Watson and S. Watson. Detection and clutter rejection in image sequences based on multivariate conditional probability. In *SPIE: Signal and Data Processing of Small Targets*, volume 3809, pages 107–118, 1999.

Grouping via the Matching of Repeated Patterns

Andreas Turina[1], Tinne Tuytelaars[2], Theo Moons[2], and Luc Van Gool[1,2]

[1] Computer Vision Group, ETH Zürich, Switzerland;
aturina,vangool@vision.ee.ethz.ch
[2] ESAT / VISICS, Kath. Univ. Leuven, Belgium;
Tinne.Tuytelaars,Theo.Moons,Luc.VanGool@esat.kuleuven.ac.be

Abstract. In this contribution, a novel and robust, geometry-based grouping strategy is proposed. Repeated, planar patterns in special relative positions are detected. The grouping is based on the idea of fixed structures. These are structures such as lines or points that remain fixed under the transformations mapping the patterns onto each other. As they define subgroups of the general group of projectivities, they significantly reduce the complexity of the problem. First, some initial matches are found by comparing local, affinely invariant regions. Then, possible fixed structure candidates are hypothesized using a cascaded Hough transform. In a further step, these candidates are verified. In this paper, we concentrate on planar homologies, i.e. subgroups that have a line of fixed points and a pencil of fixed lines.

Keywords: Grouping, Planar Homologies, Projective Geometry, Affinely Invariant Regions, Fixed Structures, Cascaded Hough Transform

1 Grouping from a Geometric Perspective

'Grouping' is an important step in vision that combines features into higher-order perceptual entities, more amenable to semantic interpretation. Many grouping types boil down to the repetition of one or more basic patterns. Different grouping types are distinguished by the specific nature of this repetition, i.e. the relative placements of the patterns, rather than the nature of the patterns themselves. In many cases the patterns are planar or even coplanar. Here we will assume repeated, planar but not necessarily coplanar patterns.

Although the repetition often is of a simple nature, image projection complicates its appearance through the perspective skew that it induces. Even if a pattern is for instance mirror symmetric, its images are usually not. What survives projection are the structures that remain fixed. Structures like points and lines that are their own image under the repetition also remain fixed under the special projectivity that exists between the projected patterns in the image. As an example, mirror symmetric point pairs remain fixed as a pair, all points on the (projected) symmetry axis are their own symmetric image – i.e. form a line of fixed points – and the joins (lines) connecting symmetric points are also mapped onto themselves, forming a pencil of fixed lines [1].

S. Singh, N. Murshed, and W. Kropatsch (Eds.): ICAPR 2001, LNCS 2013, pp. 250–259, 2001.
© Springer-Verlag Berlin Heidelberg 2001

This property that fixed structures under the original symmetry also remain fixed under the transformation between the repeated patterns in the image is valid in general. The eigenvalues of the transformation that represents the original repetition are not changed through conjugation with a perspectivity. Hence, the same kind of fixed structures are found after the perspective skew. We conclude that fixed structures form a good basis to build a grouping strategy. This idea, propounded in more detail in [8], lies at the heart of our grouping strategy.

One can build a hierarchy of grouping types based on their fixed structures [8]. Taking all projectivities that keep a specific structure fixed yields a subgroup of the projectivities. The subgroups that have a line of fixed points or a pencil of fixed lines are of particular interest. These fixed structures both lift 5 degrees of freedom, yet only require two parameters to specify them. This eases the detection of these grouping types, as their subgroups have invariants that are strictly simpler than general, projective invariants. Also, these are the types of fixed structures that are easiest to find, as they correspond to non-accidental configurations. In this paper we will restrict the discussion to the detection of these cases, and more in particular to repetitions that amount to *planar homologies* in the images. If a projectivity has a line of fixed points it automatically also has a pencil of fixed lines and v.v. Such transformations are called planar homologies [5,9]. A special case are the homologies that have the vertex of the pencil on the axis. These are called *elations* [5,4]. Planar homologies occur often in images, e.g. as the transformation between a planar shape and its shadow, between identical patterns in parallel planes, between the two halves of a mirror symmetric pattern (harmonic planar homologies), between identical patterns under a point symmetry or between coplanar, periodic patterns (elations).

2   A Grouping Strategy

Our strategy towards geometry-based grouping, dedicated to finding repeated patterns that are related by planar homologies, is the following:

step 1: find small regions of interest, that remain invariant under changing viewpoint and illumination
step 2: find matches between these regions, i.e. repeated patterns
step 3: use region matches as input to a cascaded Hough transform, which yields candidate fixed structures (non-accidental alignments)
step 4: test the validity of the fixed structures and find out the extent of the image regions that can be mapped onto each other by the corresponding transformation

The work that comes closest to our approach is that by Schaffalitzky and Zisserman [4]. They detect coplanar, periodic structures by picking up elations that bring multiple basic features into correspondence. Our work differs in a number of respects. First, we widen the class of groupings that can be detected to repetitions characterized by the more general class of planar homologies. Secondly, the features for which matches are searched in the initial steps of our algorithm are more general than the lines, line intersections and parallelograms present in the images that they use. Thirdly, the way in which these matches are used also differs. Schaffalitzky and Zisserman use a RANSAC approach to elicit a specific elation, whereas we first hypothesize fixed structures, a process to which matches under different transformations can contribute. This process entails less search and smoothes out noise on the position of the individual features.

In the sequel of the paper, the different steps mentioned above are discussed in somewhat more detail, although for some we mainly refer to earlier work.

3   Selecting Affinely Invariant Regions (Step 1)

The first step consists of finding small regions of interest. The regions are those propounded by Tuytelaars *et al.* [6,10]. They are invariant under changing viewpoint in that they change their shape in the image in order to systematically keep covering identical physical parts of surfaces. A limitation of the regions proposed by Tuytelaars *et al.* is that they require a corner that lies next to a well-textured region for one type of such regions and variations of intensity around a local extremum for another. We propose to also extract parallelogram shaped regions of a constant colour as an additional type of invariant region. Such regions often appear in practice, e.g. as tilings on a wall or floor, or as windows in a building.

Starting from corner points with straight edges at both sides, two points are moved away from the corner, one on each edge. But first, the two edges are brought into normalized position, with one is the horizontal x-axis and the other is the vertical y-axis. With each position of these points corresponds a parallelogram defined by the corner and the points. Positions of the points are selected where a function calculated over the parallelogram's edges opposite to the corner reaches its local extrema:

$$f(x,y) = \frac{1}{xy} \left[\sum_{j=0}^{y} D_x I(x, y_j) \cdot \sum_{i=0}^{x} D_y I(x_i, y) \right]$$

where $D_x I$, $D_y I$ denote differences of the intensity $I(x,y)$ between horizontally and vertically neighbouring pixels, resp. It is assumed that the borders of the homogeneous areas consist of step discontinuities. This decision function reaches its extrema when the edges opposite to the corner coincide with the boundaries of the homogeneous region (which is mentioned to have a parallelogram shape). It is invariant under affine deformations and changes of illumination. This construction is illustrated in Fig. 1.

Fig. 1. Extraction of homogeneous, parallelogram-shaped regions, for example floor tiles. (**a**) The filled area is the two-dimensional search space where $f(x, y)$ reaches its extrema at the opposite corner. (**b**) The result when applied to an image with a large number of homogeneous areas

4 Finding Region Matches (Step 2)

Matching proceeds according to two different principles. The regions proposed by Tuytelaars *et al.* [6] are matched on the basis of the geometric-photometric moment invariants presented in the same reference. Matching for these regions amounts to the calculation of a Mahalanobis distance between the corresponding invariant feature vectors (18 moment invariants are used).

The homogeneous regions proposed in the previous section cannot be matched like that, however. Such regions only supply us with three colour values. Three measurements do not suffice to build invariants under the combination of affine distortions and photometric changes consisting of independent scalings and offsets for the three colour bands. Fortunately, in the case of grouping we are not interested in matching regions between different images as was the case in the original work by Tuytelaars *et al.*. Here we want to group regions within a single image. The chance that similar regions are subject to a completely different illumination is smaller in such case. Hence, matching the homogeneous regions is based on the clustering of the average red, green, and blue colour values within the regions.

5 Generating Fixed Structure Hypotheses (Step 3)

The matches between these invariant regions are then fed into the Cascaded Hough Transform (CHT) [7] that allows to detect collinear points and pencils of lines. The CHT amounts to an iterated application of the Hough transform, where straight lines are parameterized as $ax + y + b = 0$, a parameterization that brings out the projective duality between points and lines explicitly. We refer to [7] for a more detailed discussion of the CHT and examples of its output.

The positions of matching regions (e.g. the corresponding corners or intensity extrema) are fed into the first level of the CHT, if there are at least three that match each other. This level detects collinear arrangements. Also the second and third level of the CHT are of direct interest. We feed lines that connect the positions of matching pairs of regions into the second level (and not if there is more than a pair of such matching regions). Pencils of fixed lines can be detected that way, when lines connecting corresponding points all intersect in a single point, the vertex of the pencil. Intersections of corresponding edges connected to matching region pairs are fed into the third level of the CHT. The edges of the parallelogram shaped regions are a good case in point. For the elliptical regions [10], lines through the region center with corresponding orientations are used. This allows to detect lines of fixed points, as corresponding lines all have their intersection on this axis. Also the vertices of the pencils that come out of the second level are fed into the Hough. This allows for instance to find horizon lines from collinear vanishing points.

This CHT based strategy allows different transformations of the subgroup characterized by a line of fixed points or a pencil of fixed lines to contribute all to its extraction. In fact, the CHT draws on the invariants of these subgroups.

6   Validating Fixed Structures (Step 4)

Non-accidental structures like pencils of fixed lines or axes of fixed points are selected based on the CHT's output. We start with the structures that obtain the most votes at its second and third level. They represent good candidates for the possible center of a pencil of fixed lines or a line of fixed points, resp.

Even if structures obtain good scores by the CHT, they still don't need to be fixed structures though. Further tests are needed, and this is the task of this step. It also produces a more precise delineation of the extent of the grouping. Matches between the local, affinely invariant regions are extended to matches between larger areas, while taking perspective effects fully into account. To this end, the image is divided into a quadrilateral tessellation with cells that can be mapped onto each other by the planar homology defined by the hypothesized fixed structures and some individual matches.

We are most interested in pairs of an hypothesized axis and pencil that are supported by the same invariant regions in the CHT voting process. Once a pencil and an axis have been selected, a single match will in principle fix the planar homology (it fixes the cross ratio of the vertex, the first feature position, the second feature position and the intersection of the join with the axis) [9]. Suppose $\mathbf{m}$ and $\mathbf{m}'$ are such a pair of matching positions.

Once the homology is fully fixed, a tessellation of the image is built. How this tessellation is constructed is explained in Fig. 2 (**a**). The axis is labeled A, while the vertex v is at the intersection of lines B, C and D. The lines of the pencil, such as B, C and D yield a first set of lines in the construction of the tessellation's quadrangles. These lines are their own corresponding lines. For the transversal lines such as E and E' which are chosen parallel to the axis, we use the fact that their intersections with the lines through the vertex such as B and D give the same cross ratio as the known match $\mathbf{m}$ and $\mathbf{m}'$:

$$\mathcal{C}(\mathbf{b}', \mathbf{a_b}, \mathbf{b}, \mathbf{v}) = \mathcal{C}(\mathbf{c}', \mathbf{a_c}, \mathbf{c}, \mathbf{v}) = \mathcal{C}(\mathbf{m}', \mathbf{a_m}, \mathbf{m}, \mathbf{v})$$

So given the line E, the position of E' can be derived.

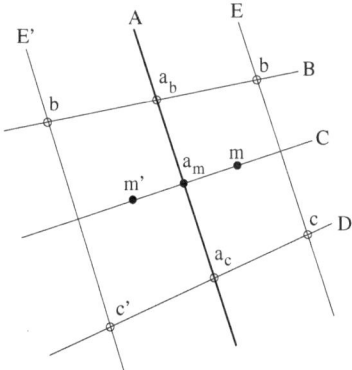

Fig. 2. Tessellation based on a hypothesized axis and pencil

It is also interesting to look at cases where the CHT has only detected an axis or pencil. Indeed, it is not always guaranteed that both fixed structures appear equally strong in the CHT. Then a construction method based on a hypothesized pencil of fixed lines or line of fixed points only should be used instead, in combination with point correspondences to fix the other structure. If the axis is available a pair of matches yields the pencil. If the pencil is available, three point matches yield the axis (or a pair of matching lines, according to the projective duality between points and lines).

Once the tessellation has been constructed, we can proceed with the actual validation of the hypothesized fixed structures and the corresponding planar homology. To this end, each cell of the tessellation is compared with its corresponding counterpart. If several matching cells can be found, this supplies sufficient evidence that the planar homology under scrutiny is actually present in the image. At the same time, the extent of the image regions that can be mapped onto each other by the transformation is found. This results in the segmentation of the image part that is symmetric under the tested homology.

For the comparison of the patterns within corresponding cells, the normalized cross correlation between the intensities of corresponding pixels within the cells is computed. Since the cross correlation is rather sensitive to even small misalignments if the image contains high spatial frequencies, we locally adjust the corner points of one of the two cells using a nonlinear optimization technique that tries to maximize the cross correlation. If the final cross correlation is above a certain threshold, the two cells are identified as being symmetric. If not, we do not immediately discard the whole cell, but subdivide it into smaller subcells and repeat the same procedure on each of the subcells.

7   Experimental Results

As a first example, the method is used to extract the mirror symmetric region in fig. 3 that corresponds to the butterfly. By comparing corresponding cells, the validity of the hypothesized fixed structures is checked and at the same time we find out the spatial extent of the grouping. The final result is shown in Fig. 4, where the image is segmented into the grouping and the background. Clearly, our initial hypothesis was correct. As a second example, consider

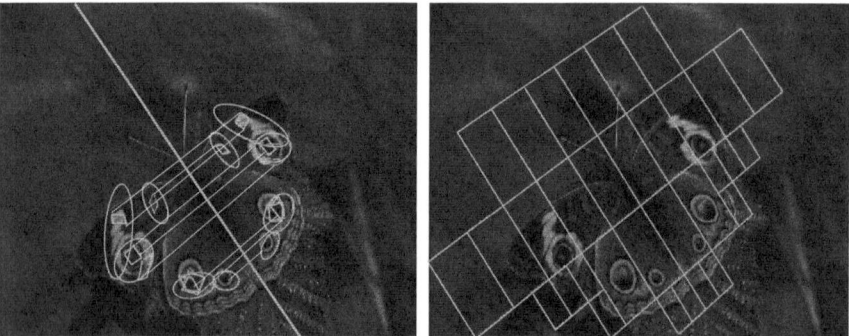

Fig. 3. (a) The image of a butterfly, with the hypothesized axis (line of fixed points) and the matching regions that contributed to this hypothesis. (b) Based on the hypothesized axis and vertex, the image is divided in two quadrilateral tessellations

the image of a carpet, shown in Fig. 5. As this is a hand-woven carpet, the symmetry is not perfect. Also, this example shows a much stronger perspective skew than the one with the butterfly. Nevertheless, again the symmetry could be detected in the image. The hypothesized axis, together with the matching regions that contributed to it in the CHT, are shown superimposed on Fig. 5 (b).

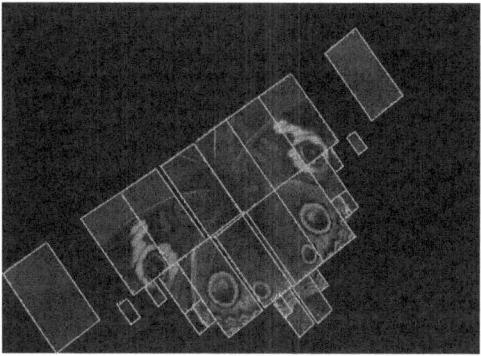

Fig. 4. Segmentation of the image based on the hypothesized planar homology. Clearly the initial hypothesis was correct

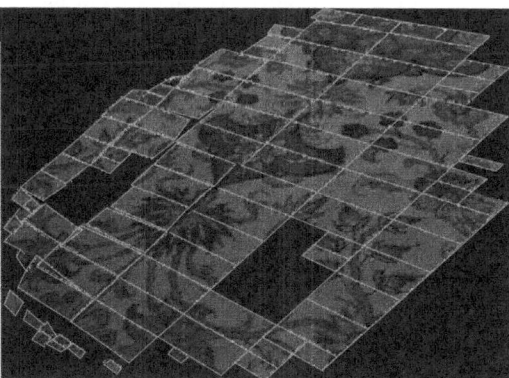

Fig. 5. (a) The image of a detail of a carpet, with the hypothesized axis (line of fixed points) and the matching regions that contributed to this hypothesis. (b) Segmentation of the image based on the hypothesized planar homology. Clearly the initial hypothesis was correct

8 Conclusions

We have presented a method for grouping repeated planar (but not necessarily coplanar) patterns in an image based on the idea of fixed structures. It offers a principled, powerful, and efficient approach for the cases where the grouping amounts to a planar homology, which is more general than the elation oriented approach proposed by Shaffalitzky and Zisserman [4]. It is principled in that it presents a single mathematical framework in which all planar homologies are encapsulated. It is powerful as it takes perspective distortions into account. It is efficient as it eliminates much of the search by which grouping strategies are so often plagued, through the combination of invariant-based indexing and the Hough transform. It also avoids the use of RANSAC, which is less efficient for general planar homologies, as 3 correspondences have to be hypothesized in order to fix the transformation (in the case of elations this is less of a problem as two correspondences suffice).

Acknowledgements: The authors gratefully acknowledge support from ETH's research council, European Project CIWOS, and the Flemish Fund for Scientific Research FWO.

References

1. M. Dhome, R. Glachet and J. Lapreste, Locating and Modeling a flat Symmetric Object from a single Projective Image, *Computer Vision, Graphics, and Image Processing: Image Understanding*, Vol. 57, 1993, pp. 219–266
2. F. Mindru, T. Moons and L. Van Gool, Color-based moment Invariants for Viewpoint and Illumination independent Recognition of planar Color Patterns, *International Conference on Advances in Pattern Recognition*, ICAPR'98, 1998, pp. 113–122
3. F. Mindru, T. Moons and L. Van Gool, Recognizing Color Patterns irrespective of Viewpoint and Illumination, *IEEE Conference on Computer Vision and Pattern Recognition*, CVPR'99, Vol. 1, 1999, pp. 368–373
4. F. Schaffalitzky and A. Zisserman, Geometric Grouping of repeated Elements within Images, *Shape, Contour and Grouping in Computer Vision*, 1999, pp. 165–181
5. J. Semple and G. Kneebone, Algebraic Projective Geometry, *Oxford University Press*, 1979
6. T. Tuytelaars, L. Van Gool, L. D'haene and R. Koch, Matching Affinely Invariant Regions for Visual Servoing, *IEEE Conference on Robotics and Automation*, ICRA'99, 1999, pp. 1601–1606
7. T. Tuytelaars, L. Van Gool, M. Proesmans and T. Moons, The Cascaded Hough Transform as an Aid in aerial Image Interpretation, *International Conference on Computer Vision*, ICCV'98, 1998, pp. 67–72
8. L. Van Gool, Projective Subgroups for Grouping, *Phil. Trans. Royal Society London A*, Vol. 356, 1998, pp. 1251–1266

9. L. Van Gool, M. Proesmans and A. Zisserman, Planar Homologies as a Basis for Grouping and Recognition, *Image and Vision Computing*, Vol. 16, No. 1, 1998, pp. 21–26
10. T. Tuytelaars and L. Van Gool, Wide Baseline Stereo based on Local, Affinely invariant Regions, *British Machine Vision Conference*, BMVC'2000, 2000

Complex Fittings

Thomas Kämpke

Forschungsinstitut für anwendungsorientierte Wissensverarbeitung FAW

Helmholtzstr. 16, 89081 Ulm, Germany

kaempke@faw.uni-ulm.de

Abstract

Fitting models with several components to data consists of the two operations of identifying components with subsets of the data and of fine tuning. These operations are elaborated for polygon fitting as a sample case. The frequently used iterative closest point ICP algorithm is replaced by an iterative best point IBP algorithm.

Key words: correspondence problem, global optimization, relaxation.

1 Introduction

Due to the increasing variety and availability of data collecting and storage devices, methods for estimation, fitting, and matching between data and models are of increasing importance. Models that consist of several components may easily lead to complex, challanging estimation issues. A pragmatic approach to complex estimation is to break down the estimation to all components and then merge individual estimates. While the former typically leads to mathematically clean operations, the latter may become an uncontrolled process.

Whenenver models consist of several components, estimation consists of the interrelated operations of fitting and matching. While fitting typically adheres to continuous methods and appeals to "fine tuning", matching adheres to discrete methods by devicing the data into subsets and deciding for each subset on the model component that should be considered for fitting.

Estimations will be assessed by least squares which are chosen for their algorithmic implications being comparatively simple. Computation of *the* zero of the gradient may lead to *the* best estimate. Complex models may lead to quadratic non-convex fitting objectives having multipe minima. Then, optimiziation techniques often rely critically on initial conditions so that final estimates tend to be good if initial estimates are good but they tend to run out of control for bad initial estimates. Fitting procedures may run into local minima which are not global and the underlying notion of locality is not always

S. Singh, N. Murshed, and W. Kropatsch (Eds.): ICAPR 2001, LNCS 2013, pp. 260–269, 2001.
© Springer-Verlag Berlin Heidelberg 2001

clear. This work aims at making estimation procedures robust against (bad) initial estimates by globally convergent optimization procedures.

The concept is illustrated by polygons. They are to be aligned to a finite data set that typically stems from an image. Instead of using edge detectors from computer vision for locating individual lines and then somehow aggregating individual findings, positions of polygons will be estimated holistically. Besides image interpretation and image registration, the interest in this problem originates from position estimation of a robot moving in a mapped environment and taking distance measurements.

Global optimization here relies on lower bounding by geometric relaxation. Polygonal segments are allowed to vary individually which appeals to the notion of elasticity of a polygon. This is eventually combined with Lipschitz techniques leading to certain restrictions for elasticity.

Permitting the matchings to vary involves a precise neighbourhood notion. The celebrated iterative closest point ICP algorithm need not result in a local minimum. Variations of the matchings will be organized within a general assignment problem. This comprises various combinatorial problems and leads to the notion of k-optimality to replace the ICP by the a computation scheme that is called iterative best point IBP algorithm.

2 Problem

2.1 The general problem

A polygon of μ segments lying on the lines $H_1, \ldots, H_\mu \subseteq \mathbb{R}^2$ is to be aligned with the finite point set $X = \{p_1, \ldots, p_n\} \subseteq \mathbb{R}^2$. The alignment adheres to translation and rotation. The objective is to minimize the sum of squared Euclidean distances between the points and their assigned lines, comp. figure 1. An assignment $C = \{X_1, \ldots, X_\mu\}$ with all points of X_i being matched to H_i is called correspondence. The set of all correspondences is denoted $\mathcal{C}$.

In case $\mu = 1$, the correspondence trivially assigns all points of X to a single line and the alignment problem restricts to the classical problem of finding a line of minimum inertia. The polygon alignment problem hence is called minimum inertia polygon. Minimum inertia lines can be computed in closed form either algebraically or trigonometrically [9].

The two cases of fixed correspondences and variable correspondences are considered. For any correspondence the polygon fitting problem with given and known consecutive intersection angles $\beta_1, \ldots, \beta_{\mu-1}$ between H_1 and H_2, H_2 and H_3, $\ldots$, $H_{\mu-1}$ and H_μ respectively is formally given by

$$\min_{\varphi \in [0, 2\pi), \vartheta \in \mathbb{R}^2} \sum_{j=1}^{\mu} \sum_{p_i \in X_j} \left((\cos(\Omega_j + \varphi), \sin(\Omega_j \mid \varphi)) \cdot (p_i - \vartheta) - c_j \right)^2,$$

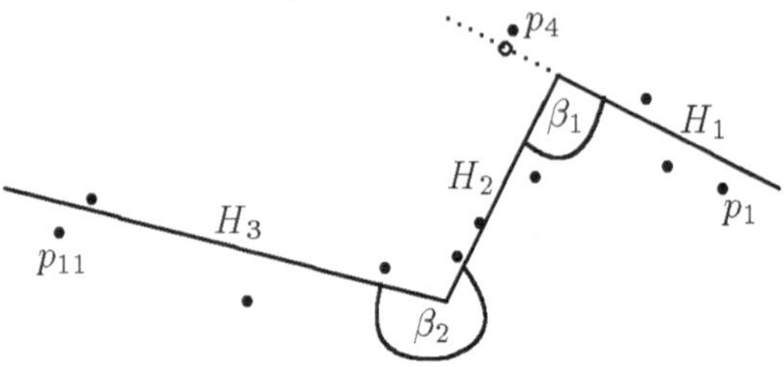

Figure 1: Polygon with $\mu = 3$. Point p_4 corresponding to H_1 has closest distance to H_1 on the "extension" rather than on the proper polygonal segment.

where $\Omega_1 := 0$ and $\Omega_j := \beta_1 + \ldots + \beta_{j-1}$ for $j = 2, \ldots, \mu$. The lines $H_j = \{x \mid (\cos \Omega_j, \sin \Omega_j)x = c_j\}$ describe the initial position of the polygon which is translated by $\vartheta = (\vartheta_1, \vartheta_2)^T$ and rotated by φ about the origin.

2.2   Related approaches

Closed form solutions of matching two finite point sets have been stated for fixed correspondences in two-dimensional problems [11] and for three-dimensional problems by linear algebraic methods [6] and by the use of quaternions by [4], [2].

Correspondences are typically determined by the nearest neighbours, clustering [1], minimum weighted distances embodying features like colour [12], and restrictions to particular search regions like cones [11]. All these require estimates for rotation and translation prior to fitting. Both the determination of a correspondence and the fitting operation can be merged to form a two step procedure in which a new correspondence is found based on the current fit. Whenever the new correspondence results from nearest neighbours, the procedure is called iterative closest point ICP algorithm. It has been investigated in theoretical settings [2], for self-localization of autonomous robots [3], and for registration in computer vision problems [13]. In any of these cases the ICP need not lead to a global optimum.

2.3   Properties of polygonal fits

The objective of polygon fitting is convex and quadratic in ϑ for fixed φ. This allows to explicitly compute optimal translations. Solutions of the restricted problem $\min_{\vartheta \in \mathbb{R}^2} \sum_{j=1}^{\mu} \sum_{p_i \in X_j} ((\cos(\Omega_j + \varphi), \sin(\Omega_j + \varphi)) \cdot (p_i - \vartheta) - c_j)^2$ are computable by solving a linear 2×2 system. The solutions, denoted by $\vartheta = \vartheta(\varphi)$, are unique if and only if two nonparallel lines are each assigned at least one point of X. This gives an underpinning of an observation from [4, p. 42] that "lines should not be parallel".

A closed form solution of the polygon fitting problem does not appear to exist. An iterative solution will be obtained by substituting $\vartheta = \vartheta(\varphi)$ in the objective leading to the univariate objective

$$\min_{\varphi \in [0, 2\pi)} \sum_{j=1}^{\mu} \sum_{p_i \in X_j} \Big((\cos(\Omega_j + \varphi), \sin(\Omega_j + \varphi)) \cdot (p_i - \vartheta(\varphi)) - c_j \Big)^2.$$

3   Fixed correspondence solutions

Even for fixed correspondences, the fitting problem can have local minima which are not global. Polygonal fitting thus falls into the category of so-called multiextremal global optimization problems [8, p. 6].

Example 1 *Let four line segments be arranged in a square bounded by the lines $H_1, \ldots H_4$. These are assumed to correspond to singletons $X_1 = \{p_1 = (1,0)^T\}$, $X_2 = \{p_2 = (0,1)^T\}$, $X_3 = \{p_3 = (-1,0)^T\}$, and $X_4 = \{p_4 = (0,-1)^T\}$, comp. figure 2. Optimal rotations are $\varphi_{opt} = \pi/2$ and $\varphi_{opt} = 3\pi/2$*

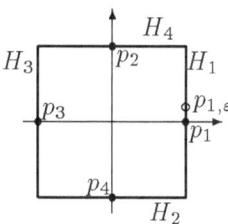

Figure 2: Square with corresponding measurement set.

with $F(\varphi_{opt}) = 4$. Perturbing p_1 to become $p_{1,\varepsilon} = (1,\varepsilon)^T$ for $0 < \varepsilon < 1/2$ results in $F(\pi/2) = 3 + (1 - \varepsilon)^2 < 3 + (1 + \varepsilon)^2 = F(3\pi/2)$ making the smaller minimum unique and hence global. ◇

A local minimum of the fitting objective can be approximated by bisection i.e. by iterated subdivision of a search interval into those halves that are guaranteed to contain a zero of the derivative.

3.1   Geometrical relaxation

Global minimization of the fitting objective can be based on lower bounds. Such can be obtained for any fixed rotation by translating each line individually to its corresponding partial point cloud. All angles between lines being preserved motivates to call such an arrangement of lines an elastic polygon [9], comp. figure 3. The optimal fit of an elastic polygon can be computed explicitly and efficiently based on independent minimum inertia line computations.

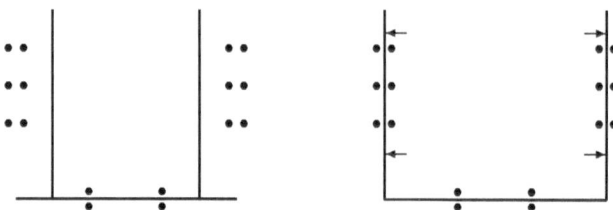

Figure 3: Line arrangement (left) and elastic relaxation (right).

3.2   Lipschitz bounds and bound improvement

Another bounding strategy is so-called Lipschitz bounding which uses linear functions whose absolute slope is guaranteed to be smaller than that of the objective function. Computations of Lipschitz bounds are quite intricate here and the result is sketched in figure 4. The Lipschitz bounds and the geometrical bounds can be overlayed to the bounding function H as sketched in figure 5.

This allows for the subsequent, so-called saw tooth cover algorithm employing ideas from Piavskii and Pinter [8]. The algorithm follows a branch and bound approach over the set $\mathcal{U}$ of unexplored subintervals of $[0, 2\pi]$. An interval is explored if its length falls below a threshold δ_0 or if it cannot contain the global minimum due to lower bounding. All other intervals are unexplored.

Afixcor

1. $\mathcal{U} = \{[0, 2\pi]\}$, Select $\varphi_{init} \in (0, 2\pi)$, $M = F(\varphi_{init})$, $Li = \{\varphi_{init}\}$, $\delta_0 > 0$.

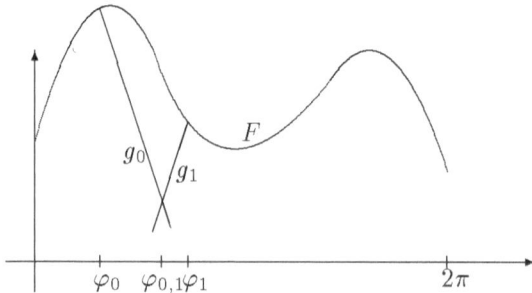

Figure 4: Fitting objective with lower linear bounds over the interval $[\varphi_0, \varphi_1]$.

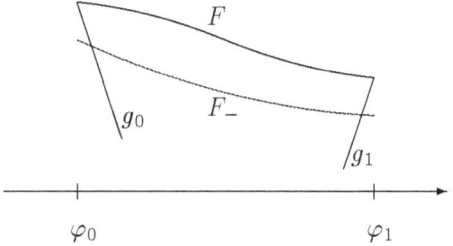

Figure 5: Overlay of geometrical and Lipschitz bounds over $[\varphi_0, \varphi_1]$.

2. While $\mathcal{U} \neq \emptyset$ and $\max_{[\varphi_0, \varphi_1] \in \mathcal{U}} \varphi_1 - \varphi_0 \geq \delta_0$ do

   (a) Selection of maximum length interval $[\varphi_0, \varphi_1] \in \mathcal{U}, \mathcal{U} = \mathcal{U} - \{[\varphi_0, \varphi_1]\}$.

   (b) If $H([\varphi_0, \varphi_1]) < M$, then $\mathcal{U} = \mathcal{U} \cup \{[\varphi_0, \varphi_{0,1}], [\varphi_{0,1}, \varphi_1]\}$ for

$$\varphi_{0,1} = \begin{cases} \frac{1}{\mu} \sum_{j=1}^{\mu} \varphi_{j,0}, & \text{if } \frac{1}{\mu} \sum_{j=1}^{\mu} \neq \varphi_0, \varphi_1 \\ \frac{\varphi_0 + \varphi_1}{2}, & \text{else}, \end{cases}$$

where $\varphi_{j,0}$ is optimal rotation angle for elastic H_j over $[\varphi_0, \varphi_1]$ and
if $\min\{F(\varphi_0), F(\varphi_{0,1}), F(\varphi_1)\} = M$, then
$Li = Li \cup \{argmin\{F(\varphi_0), F(\varphi_{0,1}), F(\varphi_1)\}\}$, else

if $\min\{F(\varphi_0), F(\varphi_{0,1}), F(\varphi_1)\} < M$, then
$Li = \{argmin\{F(\varphi_0), F(\varphi_{0,1}), F(\varphi_1)\}\}$ and $M = \min\{F(\varphi_0),$
$F(\varphi_{0,1}), F(\varphi_1)\}$.

3. Output minimum value M and list Li of arguments attaining M.

4   Variable correspondences

The number of correspondences grows exponentially in the size of data set even
if the component number μ is fixed. This renders correspondence enumeration
intractable.

4.1   Local optimality

The notion of local optimality requires a neighbourhood relation on $\mathcal{C}$. The
dependency of the fitting objective from correspondences and rotation angles
is denoted by $F(\varphi, C)$.

Definition 1 *The correspondence neighbourhood $N(C)$ of some $C = (X_1, \ldots, X_\mu) \in C$ is the set $\overline{N(C)}$ of all correspondences which differ from C in the assignment of at most one point from X.*

Definition 2 *A local correspondence minimum (φ_0, C_0) is given by*

1. *$\min_{\varphi \in [0, 2\pi)} F(\varphi, C_0) = F(\varphi_0, C_0)$, i.e. φ_0 is a global minimum for the fixed correspondence C_0 and*

2. *$F(\varphi_0, C_0) \leq \min_{\varphi \in [0, 2\pi)} F(\varphi, C') \ \forall C' \in N(C_0)$.*

It can easily be shown that local correspondence minimum has the closest point property meaning that each point from X is assigned to a hyperplane that is closest in the position belonging to rotation angle φ_0. This property leads to the frequently applied iterative closest point ICP algorithm which constructs improvements of φ and C until the first condition of the previous definition is (approximately) satisfied. Each new correspondence is constructed from the current correspondence by assigning all data points to the currently closest hyperplane.

The ICP need not terminate with a local minimum, i.e. the second condition of local correspondence minima need not be satisfied.

Example 2 *Two orthogonal lines are to be fitted to $X = \{p_1 = (6.2, 0)^T, p_2 = (6.2, 2)^T, p_3 = (5, 1)^T, p_4 = (5, -1)^T, p_5 = (0, 0)^T, p_6 = (0.5, 0)^T, \ldots, p_{13} = (4, 0)^T\}$. The matching $C_0 = (X_1 = \{p_1, p_2\}, X_2 = X - X_1)$ leads to the optimal line positions given in figure 6 with fitting objective $F(\varphi_{opt}, C_0) = 1^2 + 1^2$ and closest point property being satisfied. The ICP algorithm initialized with C_0 would terminate with it.*

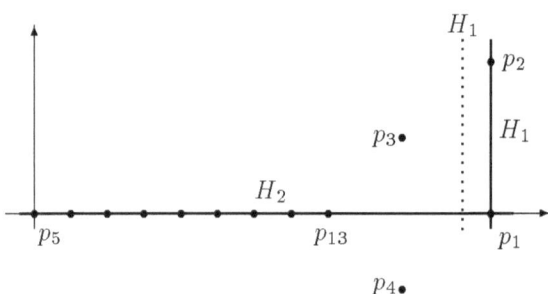

Figure 6: Uninterrupted lines show the optimal line positions for C_0. The dotted line shows an improved position for H_1 obtained from violating the closest point property.

However, the matching $C' = (X_1 = \{p_1, p_2, p_3\}, X_2 = X - X_1) \in N(C_0)$ leads to the objective $F(\varphi_{opt}, C') = (4/10)^2 + (4/10)^2 + (8/10)^2 + 1^2 = 1.96 < 2$ for $\varphi_{opt} = \varphi_{opt}(C_0)$. The optimal rotation for C' leads to an even better fit. ◇

An improvement of the ICP algorithm can be based on the notion of k-optimality which originally was developed for combinatorial optimization problems such as the traveling salesman problem [10].

Definition 3 *A correspondence C_0 is $\underline{k\text{-optimal}}$ for some $k \geq 1$ if no reassignment of up to k data points allows an improvement, i.e.*

$$\min_{\varphi \in [0,2\pi]} F(\varphi, C_0) \leq \min_{\varphi \in [0,2\pi]} F(\varphi, C)$$

$\forall C \in \mathcal{C}$ *which assign at most k points to other hyperplanes than C_0.*

The resulting algorithm is as follows.

IBP

1. Input initial correspondence C.

2. While $\exists C' \in \mathcal{C}$ with $\min_{\varphi \in [0,2\pi]} F(\varphi, C') < \min_{\varphi \in [0,2\pi]} F(\varphi, C)$ with C' and C differing in at most k assignments do

   (a) Select best C'
   (b) $C = C'$.

3. Output C and corresponding optimal rotation angle φ_{opt}.

Minimization in the condition of step 2 is perforemd by the algorithm **Afixcor**. In order to keep the combinatorial explosion to a moderate level, values for k in IBP are typically small such as $k = 1, 2, 3$. Whenever initialized with the same correspondence, IBP will result in an overall fit that is at least as good as that of ICP.

4.2   Complex fitting and mathematical programming

Finding a correspondence can be reduced to a conjoint assignment problem with binary variables over a complete bipartite graph with one vertex set corresponding to X and the other to $\{H_1, \ldots, H_\mu\}$.

$$\min \quad \sum_{j=1}^{\mu} f(X_j)$$

$$\text{s.t.} \quad \sum_{j=1}^{\mu} x_{ij} = 1 \ \forall \, i = 1, \ldots, n$$

$$x_{ij} \in \{0, 1\} \ \forall \, i = 1, \ldots, n \; j = 1, \ldots, \mu$$

where f is a real-valued function over $X_j = \{p_i \mid x_{ij} = 1\}$. The conjoint assignment problem generalizes the linear assignment problem. Another special case stems from codebook design [5, p. 360ff]. Also, certain clustering problems are comprised which implies the NP-hardness of the conjoint assignment problem. Efficient heuristics are currently under development.

5   Application

Algorithm **IBP** in the simple form of 1-optimality for correspondences was applied to laser scans. Data were collected by the Sick PLS 200 system which has a radial resolution of .5° and a longitudinal resolution of 4 *cm*. The laser scanner was mounted on a mobile indoor platform NOMAD 4000. The platform's odometry together with a particular visibilty criterion was used to generate an initial correspondence for **IBP**.

Figure 7 shows a hallway scene where the lower part shows the polygon in an arbitrary position and the upper part shows the estimated position. The latter was found within 2 *cm* and .5° which is as least as accurate as alternative measurements. Two more complex scenes are presented in figure 8.

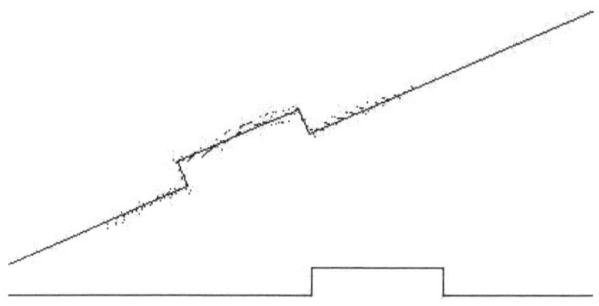

Figure 7: Hallway scene.

References

[1] Arras, K.O., Vestli, S.J., Tschichold-Gürmann, N.N. Echtzeitfähige Merkmalsextraktion und Situationsinterpretation von Laserscannerdaten. Proceedings Autonome Mobile Systeme, Springer Heidelberg, 1996:57-66

[2] Besl, P.J., McKay, N.D. A method for registration of 3-D shapes. IEEE Pattern Analysis and Machine Intelligence PAMI 1992; 14:239-252

[3] Cox, I.J. Blanche: position estimation for an autonomous robot vehicle. In: Cox, I.J., Wilfong, G.T. (eds.) Autonomous robot vehicles. Springer New York, 1990:221-228

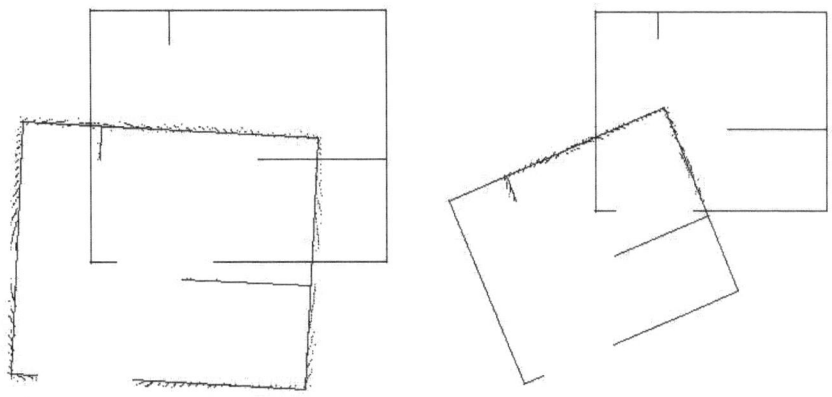

Figure 8: Position estimation based on 360° scan (left) and 180° scan (right).

[4] Faugeras, O.D., Hebert, M. The representation, recognition, and location of 3D objects. International Journal of Robotics Research 1986; 5:27-52

[5] Gersho, A., Gray, R.M. Vector quantization and signal compression. Kluver Boston, 1992

[6] Haralick, R.M. et al. Pose estimation from corresponding point data. IEEE Transactions on Systems, Man, and Cybernetics 1989; 19:1426-1446

[7] Hoover, A. et al. An experimental comparison of range image segmentation algorithms. IEEE Transactions on Pattern Analysis and Machine Intelligence, 1996; 18:673-689

[8] Horst, R., Tuy, H. Global optimization. Springer Berlin, 1990

[9] Kämpke, T., Strobel, M. Polygonal model fitting. Journal of Intelligent and Robotic Systems, 2000; to appear

[10] Lawler, E., Lenstra, J.K, Rinnooy Kan, A.H.G., Shmoys, D.B. The traveling salesman problem. Wiley New York, 1985

[11] Lu, F., Milios, E. Robot pose estimation in unknown environments by matching 2D range scans. Journal of Intelligent and Robotic Systems 1997; 18:249-275

[12] Schütz, C., Jost, T., Hügli, H. Free form 3D object reconstruction from range images. Proceedings International Conference on Virtual Systems and Multi Media VSMM'97, Geneva, IEEE Computer Society, 1997

[13] Wunsch, P., Hirzinger, G. Registration of CAD-models to images by iterative inverse perspective matching. Proceedings International Conference on Pattern Recognition ICPR, Vienna, 1996, 77-83

Application of adaptive committee classifiers in on-line character recognition

Matti Aksela[1], Jorma Laaksonen[1], Erkki Oja[1], and Jari Kangas[2]

[1] Helsinki University of Technology, Neural Networks Research Centre, P.O.Box 5400, Fin-02015 HUT, Finland
[2] Nokia Research Center, P.O.Box 100, Fin-33721 Tampere, Finland

Summary. There are two main approaches to classifier adaptation. A single adaptive classifier can be used, or an adaptive committee of classifiers whose members can be either adaptive or non-adaptive. We have experimented with some approaches to adaptive committee operations, including the Dynamically Expanding Context (DEC) and the Modified Current-Best-Learning (MCBL) approaches.

In the experiments of this paper the feasibility of using an adaptive committee classifier is explored and tested with on-line character recognition. The results clearly show that the use of adaptive committees can improve on the recognition results, both in comparison to the individual member classifiers and the non-adaptive reference committee.

Keywords. adaptive, committee, classifier combining, character recognition

1 Introduction

A common approach to any classification task is to use a set of reference samples, stored as prototypes or model coefficients, and match the input sample with them. In order to improve the classification performance in situations where a significant amount of variation in the input samples exists, classifier adaptation is an effective method.

Since the primary objective of any recognition system is to achieve the best attainable performance, it is viable to combine different classifiers in a committee formation to enhance overall performance. This is possible because in the outputs of several classifiers the errors are not necessarily overlapping and thus the committee can improve on its members' results [1].

Although the most common way of adaptation is to adapt a single recognizer to the given training data, it is also possible to construct a committee that as a whole is adaptive. The members of such a committee can be adaptive or non-adaptive themselves.

In on-line handwriting recognition the classifier or classifiers must be capable of dealing with natural handwriting. Because of the intrinsic variation

[1] Acknowledgement: This research was partly financed by the project New Information Processing Principles, Finnish Centre of Excellence Programme 2000-2005, Academy of Finland.

S. Singh, N. Murshed, and W. Kropatsch (Eds.): ICAPR 2001, LNCS 2013, pp. 270–279, 2001.

in writing styles adaptation is necessary for a user-dependent handwriting recognition application, as adopting the vast amount of variation into the initial models is usually impossible. With the continuous increase in computational power, the use of committee methods generally requiring more than one member classifier to recognize the input is no longer computationally too complex for even the smallest platforms performing on-line handwriting recognition, Personal Digital Assistants (PDAs).

In our research group, very positive results have been obtained with the Dynamic Time Warping (DTW) -based recognizer using single classifier adaptation [2–4]. Still, the question as to how these results could be improved further was left open. When searching for a suitable method of committee adaptation the idea of using the Dynamically Expanding Context (DEC) principle, previously mainly used for speech recognition [5,6], arose. The principle was modified somewhat to suit application in handwriting recognition [7].

Even though committee classification has been extensively researched, the use of adaptive committee classifiers is a much more novel approach. In this paper we present two examples of adaptive committee classifiers. In addition to the DEC committee, also a modification of the Current-Best-Learning (CBL) algorithm [8] will be examined and are explained below. We show that they outperform both a non-adaptive method and a simpler adaptive structure.

In Section 2 the principles for adaptive committee recognition are explored and the adaptive committees used later in the experiments are described. Section 3 explains the data sets and member classifiers used in our experiments and in Section 4 the obtained results are shown. Finally in Section 5 conclusions on the results are drawn and some future directions elaborated on.

2   Committee adaptation methods

The basic operation of a committee classifier is to take the results of the member classifiers and attempt to combine them in a way that improves performance. The member classifiers have a significant impact on the final performance of the committee. It can generally be said that the less the errors of the member classifiers are correlated, the more effective the committee can be in improving recognition accuracy.

Numerous committee structures have recently gained attention. Arguably the most widely known method of classifier combining, majority voting, has in spite of its simplicity been shown to be very effective [9]. Also Bayesian combination methods [10], multistage combinators [11], group-wise classification [12] and critic-driven combining [13] have been studied.

An adaptive committee can be thought of as consisting of two parts. First, every committee must have a base decision rule, which can be used when no adaptation has been performed. Then, some rule or set of rules for the adaptation must be included. The type of rules can vary from very simple weighting or preference adjusting schemes to the creation of complex lists of rules to determine the committee's behavior. Adaptive committee recognition methods found in the literature include, for instance, the Adaptive Integration of Multiple Experts (AIME) system [14].

2.1   Dynamically Expanding Context

The most effective adaptive committee used in our work in on-line handwritten character recognition is based on the Dynamically Expanding Context (DEC) algorithm. The algorithm was originally developed to create transformation rules that would correct typical coarticulation effects in phonemic speech recognition [5]. The notation for a DEC rule stands as $l(A)r \rightarrow B$, where A is a segment of the source string S, B is the corresponding segment in the transformed string T, and $l(\cdot)r$ is the context in string S where A occurs. In other words, A is replaced by B under the condition $l(\cdot)r$.

The main philosophy behind the approach is to determine just a sufficient amount of context for each individual segment A so that all conflicts in the set of training samples will be resolved [5]. Thus an optimal compromise between accuracy and generality is expected to be obtained. The central idea of the method is to always first try to find a production of the lowest contextual level to sufficiently separate contradictory cases. Starting with context level 0, or the context-free level, contexts of successively higher levels will be utilized until all conflicts are resolved.

The DEC principle has to be slightly modified to suit the setting of isolated handwritten character recognition [7]. The DEC committee consists of a number of classifiers, that are first initialized and then tested and ranked in the order of decreasing performance. The primary outputs and the second-ranking results of the member classifiers are used as a one-sided context for the creation of the DEC rules. The primary outputs and the second-ranking results of every member classifier are always different character classes. A schematic diagram of the DEC-based adaptive committee classifier is shown in Figure 1. In this example there are three member classifiers. The first-ranking results are denoted symbolically as a, b and c, and the second-ranking ones as d, e and f. For instance the rule "$abcd \rightarrow s$" means that if the first-ranking results for classifiers 1, 2 and 3 are a, b and c and the second-ranking result for classifier 1 is d, then the input character is classified in class s.

When training the DEC committee, characters of known classification are input one by one. Each time a character is input to the system, the member classifiers give the first- and second-ranking class. Then the existing rules are searched through and the first applicable rule gives the classification result. If no applicable rule is found, the default decision is applied. The classification result is compared to the correct class. If the recognition was incorrect, a new rule is created. Every new rule that is created employs more contextual knowledge, if at all possible, than the rule causing the conflict. Eventually the entire context available will be used and more precise rules can no longer be

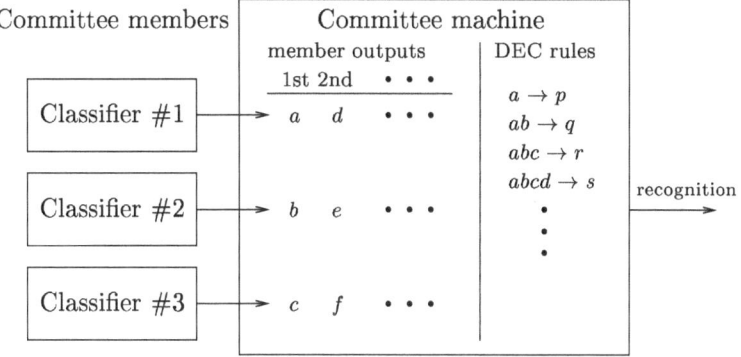

Fig. 1. A block diagram of the DEC-based adaptive committee classifier

written. For this situation a method for tracking the correctness of the rules can be used and the highest level rule most likely to be correct is applied.

The introduction of a new writer always results in the re-initialization of the rule base, as the adaptation is aimed to be user-dependent. With off-line training the training set could be reiterated until rule consistency is ensured. But with an on-line system storing all previous input samples and using them in an iterative manner would be too expensive in terms of both performance and storage space. Thus it is assumed that prior samples will not be available afterwards.

Several options were explored in the search for the best achievable recognition result using the DEC committee. These options included the following.

Default decision: The system's default decision rule is needed when no character-specific rules yet exist. Two methods for producing the default decision were experimented with. The first is to simply use the output of the best-ranked classifier. The alternative is to perform majority voting on the results obtained from the classifiers to make the default decision.

Requiring the inclusion of the output: Another variation implemented was the possibility to require that the output symbol B for a rule of the form $(A)r \rightarrow B$ must be included in the context $(A)r$. In other words, one of the classifiers must produce the result for it to be the output of the committee.

Use of second-ranking results: The committee can function either by using just the first-ranking results from its member classifiers or by also including the second-ranking results. The second-ranking results can be used in two ways, either horizontally or vertically.

The horizontal inclusion of the second-ranking results means that the first and second-ranking results from the best-performing member are used first. Then the two results from the second-best performing classifier are used in the same order, then the third classifier and so on. In Figure 1, this corresponds to the order 'a', 'd', 'b', 'e', 'c' and 'f'.

The vertical approach uses all first-ranked results prior to any second-ranked results from any classifier. So the first-ranked result of the best classifier is followed by the first-ranked results from the other classifiers until all primary outputs have been used. Then the second-ranked results are used in a similar fashion. This approach corresponds to the order 'a', 'b', 'c', 'd', 'e' and 'f' in Figure 1.

Conflict resolution: The initial version of the DEC implementation simply discarded rules as they resulted in an incorrect answer but this was quickly seen to be suboptimal. Hence three options were implemented to discriminate between conflicting high-level rules. These are 1) inactivation of the latest incorrect rule, 2) counting the correct applications and using the one with most correct results, or 3) counting both the correct and incorrect applications and making the decision based on their difference.

2.2   Modified Current-Best-Learning

The Current-Best-Learning (CBL) algorithm [8] strives for a consistent hypothesis for the entire set of samples by generalizing or specializing an initial hypothesis. The original algorithm uses backtracking to ensure that the hypothesis is also consistent with all prior samples. The specialization operation indicates that a unit, a location within the hypothesis space, that was previously positive must be deemed negative, and the generalization then refers to setting a previous negative to positive.

The algorithm used here has deviated quite far from that initial idea, but as the resemblance is still evident, it is here called Modified Current-Best-Learning (MCBL). As in the original version, the data space is a two-dimensional grid. The use of just a positive and negative value would require a separate class for each sample, which would not be practical. So the values used here are in a way estimates of the confidence in a particular decision, and are defined as

$$c_j(\overline{x}) = 1 - \frac{d_j(\overline{x})}{d_1(\overline{x}) + d_2(\overline{x})},\tag{1}$$

where $c_j(\overline{x})$ is the confidence output for the sample $\overline{x}$. $j \in \{1, 2\}$ is the index indicating whether the confidence value is being calculated for the first or second-ranking result, and $d_1(\overline{x})$ and $d_2(\overline{x})$ are the distances to the first and second-ranked prototypes, respectively.

By collecting the values and combining them into class-wise confidence values $p_k(\omega_j)$, where k is the number of the classifier and ω_j the class, a table containing the confidences of each classifier in the result for a particular class can be formed. The decision of the committee is simply that member classifier's result which has the largest confidence value. To modify the hypothesis, the values $p_k(\omega_j)$ are adjusted when the committee as a whole is incorrect. So when an individual classifier k is correct, the confidence of the

Table 1. Summary of the databases used in the experiments

Database	Subjects	Left-handed	Females	Characters	(a-z,0-9)
DB1	22	1	1	$\sim 10\,400$	8461
DB2	8	0	5	$\sim 8\,100$	4643

result for that classifier is added to the overall confidence of the class for that classifier. On the other hand, when a classifier produces an incorrect result, its total confidence is reduced by the corresponding amount, but not below zero. When the committee produces a correct result, no changes are made. The confidence values were initialized as the inverse of the ordering of the classifiers according to their decreasing recognition performance, ie. $p_k(\omega_j) = \frac{1}{k}$ for all k and j.

2.3 Selecting the currently best classifier

For the sake of comparison a very simple form of committee adaptation was also implemented. The main idea is to select the best classifier for each individual writer by evaluating each classifier's performance during operation and use the result from the classifier that has performed the best up to that point.

3 Experiments

All the committee experiments were run in batch mode simulating on-line operation by taking data in its original order and disallowing reiteration.

3.1 Description of the data sets

The data used in the experiments were isolated on-line characters collected on a Silicon Graphics workstation using a Wacom Artpad II tablet. The data was stored in UNIPEN format [15]. The preprocessing is covered in detail in [2]. The databases are summarized in Table 1, giving the total amount of writers and how many of them were female and left-handed, respectfully, as well as the total amount of characters and characters in the classes used for testing (a-z,0-9).

Database 1 consists of characters which were written without any visual feedback. The pressure level thresholding of the measured data into pen up and pen down movements was set individually for each writer. The distributions of the classes were according to their frequency in the Finnish language.

Database 2 was collected with a program that showed the pen trace on the screen and recognized the characters on-line. The minimum writing pressure for detecting pen down movements was the same for all writers. The distribution of the character classes was approximately even.

Table 2. Recognition error rates of the four committee member classifiers

Classifier	Distance measure	BBC	MC	Error %	Tail error %
1	PL		•	14.9	16.4
2	NPP		•	15.1	15.8
3	NPP	•		18.2	19.1
4	PL	•		19.6	20.9

The databases consisted of different writers. Only lower case letters and digits, a total of approximately 580 characters per writer, were used in the experiments. Database 1 was used for forming the initial user-independent prototype set which consisted of 7 prototypes per class and Database 2 was used as a test set.

3.2   Member classifiers

The experiments were performed using a committee consisting of four individual classifiers. All member classifiers are based on stroke-wise matching between the given character and prototypes. Dynamic Time Warping (DTW) was used to compute both the normalized point-to-point (NPP) and point-to-line (PL) distances [3], one of which was used by each classifier. The NPP distance simply uses the squared Euclidean distance between two data points as the cost function and the total sum is divided by the number of matchings performed. In the PL distance the points of a stroke are matched to lines interpolated between the successive points of the opposite stroke [16]. All samples were scaled so that the longer side of their bounding box was 1000 and the aspect ratio kept unchanged [3]. Also the centers of the character, defined by either the 'Mass center' as the input sample's mass center (MC) or by 'Bounding box' as the center of the sample's bounding box (BBC), is moved to the origin [3]. The configurations and error rates of the member classifiers are shown in Table 2.

In general a committee can be expected to perform the better the less the errors made by its members are correlated. Unfortunately uncorrelatedness is not the case here. As the DTW-based classifier was the only one capable of acceptable recognition performance, all the member classifiers are rather similar. This was confirmed by experiments. For all pair-wise combinations of the four classifiers, the occurrence of the same error is much more common (from 8.1% to 11.7%) than different errors (from 2.2% to 3.3%).

4   Results

Some averages of the effects of the different options on the DEC committee performance have been collected into Table 3. The tail error percentage in the

Table 3. Estimation of the effect of various individual options alone

Parameter	Total error %	Tail error %
default decision: best	12.8	13.2
default decision: majority	13.5	13.6
inclusion required	12.4	12.6
inclusion not required	14.0	14.2
vertical 2nd results	12.1	12.0
horizontal 2nd results	13.5	13.4
no 2nd results	14.1	14.7
just correct conflict resolution	12.9	12.9
correct and wrong conflict resolution	13.0	13.0
inactivate rule conflict resolution	13.8	14.3

Table 4. Comparison with reference classifiers

Combination method	Error %	Tail error %
DEC	11.1	11.3
MCBL	13.0	14.3
Selecting the currently best classifier	14.5	15.0
Non-adaptive Majority Voting	14.6	15.9
Best individual member classifier	14.9	16.4

tables corresponds to the error percentage calculated for the last 200 samples for each writer.

As a conclusion from Table 3, the following can be seen: 1) the default rule of the best classifier outperformed majority voting; 2) requiring the output symbol to be included in the input was in general preferable; 3) second-ranking results should be used in the vertical ordering; 4) the best conflict resolution of rules was based on correct results only.

The results of the adaptive committee classifiers and the non-adaptive majority voting reference as well as the result from the best member classifier are compared in Table 4. The DEC committee employed the best individual classifier base decision rule, vertical second results use and just correct tracking for conflict resolution to obtain this best result. All of the combination methods outperform the best member classifier. The DEC committee clearly outperforms all the other methods used. Also the MCBL committee provides a notable improvement and performs better than the two simpler committee classifiers. Selecting the currently best classifier provides an improvement especially in the tail error percentage in comparison with the majority voting approach.

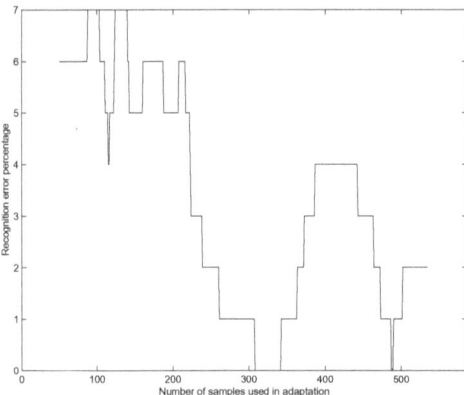

Fig. 2. The evolution of the recognition error rate for one writer from the DEC committee

The evolution of the recognition error rate, calculated within a sliding window of 100 characters, from the DEC committee for an example writer is shown in Figure 2. The average error rate for the writer was 3.2%, but the initial error rate is around 6-7%, and the final level is below 2%.

5   Conclusions

The experiments regarding adaptive committees have shown notable improvements in performance over any of the individual members for both the DEC and MCBL based committee combiners. The most effective combination for the DEC committee was to use the best individual classifier's result as the default rule, use the second results in the vertical manner and use either just the correct results or both correct and incorrect results for conflict resolution.

The next logical stage in the experiments with committee classifiers will be combining the adaptive committee with adaptive member classifiers. Perhaps the simplest way to combine member classifier adaptation and committee adaptation would be to simply first adapt the individual classifiers. The committee adaptation could be started when for example a certain accuracy level has been reached.

A notable problem with on-line adaptation in general is the difficulty of obtaining the correct labels for input samples. As in any real-world application the labeling will ultimately depend on how carefully the user corrects recognition mistakes. Labels can probably never be obtained with 100% correctness. So also the possibility of recovering from errors is something that must be taken into consideration when developing any adaptive on-line recognition system. Adaptive committees may be able to provide more effective error handling mechanisms for such situations and prove beneficial also in this respect.

References

1. Holmström L., Koistinen P., Laaksonen J., Oja E. Neural and statistical classifiers - taxonomy and two case studies. *IEEE Transactions on Neural Networks*, 8:5–17, 1997.
2. Vuori V. Adaptation in on-line recognition of handwriting. Master's thesis, Helsinki University of Technology, 1999.
3. Vuori V., Laaksonen J., Oja E., Kangas J. On-line adaptation in recognition of handwritten alphanumeric characters. In *Proceedings of International Conference on Document Analysis and Recognition*, pages 792–795, 1999.
4. Vuori V., Laaksonen J., Oja E., Kangas J. Experiments with adaptation strategies for a prototype-based recognition system of isolated handwritten characters. *International Journal of Document Analysis and Recognition*, Accepted to be published.
5. Kohonen T. Dynamically expanding context. *Journal of Intelligent Systems*, 1(1):79–95, 1987.
6. Torkkola K., Kohonen T. Correction of quasiphoneme strings by the dynamically expanding context. In *International Conference on Pattern Recognition*, volume 1, pages 487–489, 1988.
7. Laaksonen J., Aksela M., Oja E., Kangas J. Dynamically Expanding Context as committee adaptation method in on-line recognition of handwritten latin characters. In *Proceedings of International Conference on Document Analysis and Recognition*, pages 796–799, 1999.
8. Russell S. J., Norvig P. *Artificial Intelligence: A Modern Approach*. Prentice Hall, 1995.
9. Lam L., Suen C. Y. A theoretical analysis of the application of majority voting to pattern recognition. In *Proceedings of 12th International Conference on Pattern Recognition*, volume II, pages 418–420, Jerusalem, October 1994. IAPR.
10. Bouchaffra D., Govindaraju V. A methodology for mapping scores to probabilities. *IEEE Transactions on Pattern Analysis and Machine Intelligence*, 21(9):923–927, 1999.
11. Paik J., Cho S.b. , Lee K., Lee Y. Multiple recognizers system using two-stage combination. In *Proceedings of International Conference on Pattern Recognition*, pages 581–585. IEEE, 1996.
12. Rahman A., Fairhurst M. A comparative study of decision combination strategies for a novel multiple-expert classifier. In *International Conference on Image Processing and Its Applications*, volume 1, pages 131–135, 1997.
13. Miller D., Yan L. Ensemble classification by critic-driven combining. In *Proceedings of International Conference on Acoustics, Speech and Signal Processing*, volume 2, pages 1029–1032. IEEE, 1999.
14. Teow L.-N., Tan A.-H. Adaptive integration of multiple experts. In *Proceedings of International Conference on Neural Networks*, volume 3, pages 1215–1220, 1995.
15. Guyon I., Schomaker L., Plamondon R., Liberman M., Janet S. Unipen project of on-line data exchange and recognizer benchmark. In *Proceedings of International Conference on Pattern Recognition*, pages 29–33, 1994.
16. Sankoff D., Kruskal J. B. *Time warps, string edits, and macromolecules: the theory and practice of sequence comparison*. Addison-Wesley, 1983.

Learning Complex Action Patterns with CRG$_{ST}$

Walter F. Bischof and Terry Caelli

Department of Computing Science, University of Alberta, Edmonton, Alberta, T6G 2E8, Canada, Email: (wfb,tcaelli)@ualberta.ca

Abstract. This paper deals with the problem of automatically compiling rules which describe complex actions in terms of the spatio-temporal attributes of labeled parts. Of particular interest is the exploration of a model-based approach to induction of part attributes constrained by known properties of the generation process. The resultant algorithm is based on constraint propagation over spatio-temporal decision trees which produces Horn clause descriptions which depict the spatio-temporal properties of parts and their relations which satisfy training conditions.

Keywords: relational learning, spatio-temporal patterns, action learning, domain knowledge constraints, conditional rule generation

1 Introduction

Most current techniques for the encoding and recognition of actions use numerical machine learning models which are not relational in the sense that they typically induce rules over numerical attributes which are not linked via an underlying data structure (e.g. a relational structure description). Therefore, these models assume that the correspondence between candidate and model features is known *before* rule generation (learning) or rule evaluation (matching) occurs. This assumption is dangerous when large models or large test data are involved, as is the case in complex actions involving, for example, the tracking of multiple limb segments of humans. On the other hand, well known symbolic relational learners like Inductive Logic Programming (ILP) are not efficient for numerical data. So, although they are suited to induction over relational structures (e.g. Horn clauses), they typically generalize or specialize over the symbolic variables and not so much over numerical attributes. Further, it is very rare that symbolic representation *explicitly* constrain the types of permissible numerical learning or generalizations obtained from training data.

Over the past six years we have explored methods for combining the strengths of both sources of model structures [1–3] by combining the expressiveness of ILP with the generalization models of numerical machine learning. We have produced a system for numerical relational learning which induces

S. Singh, N. Murshed, and W. Kropatsch (Eds.): ICAPR 2001, LNCS 2013, pp. 280–289, 2001.
© Springer-Verlag Berlin Heidelberg 2001

over numerical attributes in ways which are constrained by relational patterns. Our approach, Conditional Rule Generation (CRG), generates rules for the recognition of pattern fragments that are linked via an underlying relational structure.

Since it induces over a relational structure it requires general model assumptions, the most important being that the models are defined by a labeled graph where relational attributes are defined only with respect to specific vertices. These can be defined in a general way (e.g. they might be defined only for adjacent image regions), or they can be defined *explicitly* through model definitions. It is often the case that the properties of one part are physically controlled by others (as we will see for the case of human body motion where one limb segment controls the range of another). These models constrain the types of unary and binary features which can be used to resolve uncertainties (Figure 1).

In the following, we first describe briefly CRG [1] and then CRG_{ST}, a spatio-temporal extension of CRG. We discuss representational issues, model constraints, rule generation and rule application, and then illustrate our approach with several examples.

2   Conditional Rule Generation

In Conditional Rule Generation [1], classification rules for patterns or pattern fragments are generated that include structural pattern information to the

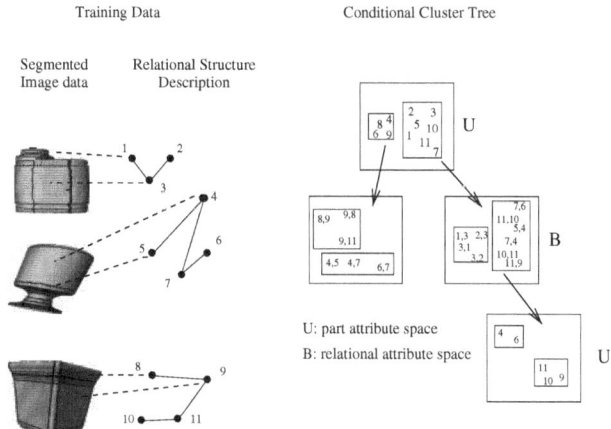

Fig. 1. Example of input data and conditional cluster tree generated by CRG method. The left panel shows segmented input data with a sketch of the relational structure descriptions generated for these data. The right panel shows a cluster tree generated for the data on the left. Classification rules are derived directly from this tree [5].

extent that is required for classifying correctly a set of training patterns. CRG analyzes unary and binary features of connected pattern components and creates a tree of hierarchically organized rules for classifying new patterns. Generation of a rule tree proceeds in the following manner (see Figure 1).

First, the unary features of all parts of all patterns are collected into a unary feature space U in which each point represents a single pattern part. The feature space U is partitioned into a number of clusters U_i. Some of these clusters may be unique with respect to class membership and provide a classification rule: If a pattern contains a part p_r whose unary features $\boldsymbol{u}(p_r)$ satisfy the bounds of a unique cluster U_i then the pattern can be assigned a unique classification. The non-unique clusters contain parts from multiple pattern classes and have to be analyzed further. For every part of a non-unique cluster we collect the binary features of this part with all adjacent parts in the pattern to form a (conditional) binary feature space UB_i. The binary feature space is clustered into a number of clusters UB_{ij}. Again, some clusters may be unique and provide a classification rule: If a pattern contains a part p_r whose unary features satisfy the bounds of cluster U_i, and there is an other part p_s, such that the binary features $\boldsymbol{b}(p_r, p_s)$ of the pair $\langle p_r, p_s \rangle$ satisfy the bounds of a unique cluster UB_{ij} then the pattern can be assigned a unique classification. For non-unique clusters, the unary features of the second part p_s are used to construct another unary feature space UBU_{ij} that is again clustered to produce clusters UBU_{ijk}. This expansion of the cluster tree continues until all classification rules are resolved or a maximum rule length has been reached.

If there remain unresolved rules at the end of the expansion procedure (which is normally the case), the generated rules are split into more discriminating rules using an entropy-based splitting procedure where the elements of a cluster are split along a feature dimension such that the normalized partition entropy $H_P(T) = (n_1 H(P_1) + n_2 H(P_2))/(n_1 + n_2)$ is minimized, where H is entropy. Rule splitting continues until all classification rules are unique or some termination criterion has been reached. This results in a tree of conditional feature spaces (Figure 1), and within each feature space, rules for cluster membership are developed in the form of a decision tree. Hence, CRG generates a tree of decision trees.

3   CRG$_{\text{ST}}$

We now turn to CRG$_{\text{ST}}$, the focus of this paper and a generalization of CRG from a purely spatial domain into a spatio-temporal domain. Data consist of time-indexed pattern descriptions, where pattern parts are described by unary features, part relations by (spatial) binary features, and changes of pattern parts by (temporal) binary features.

In contrast to other temporal learners like hidden Markov models [12] and recurrent neural networks [4], the temporal relations are not limited to first-order time differences but can involve more distant (lagged) temporal relations as a function of the data model and uncertainty resolution strategies. At the same time, CRG_{ST} allows for the generation of non-stationary rules, in contrast to stationary models like multivariate time series which also accommodate correlations beyond first-order time differences but do not allow for the use of different rules at different time periods.

3.1   Representation of Spatio-Temporal Patterns

A spatio-temporal pattern is defined by a set of labeled time-indexed attributed features, i.e. a pattern is defined as $P_i = \{p_{i1}(\boldsymbol{a} : t_{i1}), \ldots, p_{in}(\boldsymbol{a} : t_{in})\}$ where $p_{ij}(\boldsymbol{a} : t_{ij})$ corresponds to part j of pattern i with attributes $\boldsymbol{a}$ that are true at time j. The attributes $\boldsymbol{a}$ are defined with respect to specific labeled features, and consist of unary (i.e. single feature) attributes, spatial binary (i.e. spatial relational) and temporal binary (i.e. temporal relational) attributes, that is, $\boldsymbol{a} = \{\boldsymbol{u}, \boldsymbol{b}_s, \boldsymbol{b}_t\}$ (see Figure 2). Examples of unary attributes $\boldsymbol{u}$ include area, brightness, position; spatial binary attributes $\boldsymbol{b}_s$ include distance, relative size, and temporal binary attributes $\boldsymbol{b}_t$ include changes in unary attributes over time, such as size, orientation change, long range position change.

Our data model and consequently the rules generated are subject to several constraints, spatial and temporal adjacency (in the nearest neighbor sense) and temporal monotonicity, i.e. temporal indices for time must be monotonically increasing ("predictive" model) or decreasing ("causal" model). Further, we discuss additional constraints in Section 3.4, where induction over specific model-based relational structures is introduced. Although this limits the expressive power of our representation, it is still more general than strict first-order discrete time dynamical models such as hidden Markov models or Kalman filters.

For CRG_{ST} an "interpretation" then involves determining the smallest set of linked lists of attributed and labeled features, causally indexed (i.e. the starting times must be monotonically indexed) over time, which maximally index a given pattern, and it is defined by directed paths within the directed acyclic graph (DAG) which covers all examples and classes in the training set, as illustrated in Figure 2.

3.2   Rule Learning

CRG_{ST} generates classification rules for spatio-temporal patterns involving a small number of pattern parts subject to the following constraints: 1) The pattern fragments involve only pattern parts that are adjacent in space and time, 2) the pattern fragments involve only non-cyclic chains of parts, 3) temporal links are followed in the forward direction only to produce causal classification rules that can be used in classification and in prediction mode.

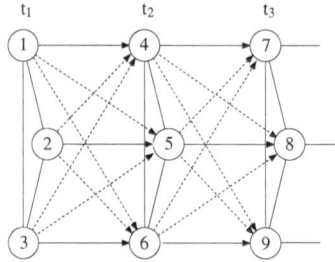

Fig. 2. Illustration of a spatio-temporal pattern consisting of three parts over three time-points. Undirected arcs indicate spatial binary connections, solid directed indicate temporal binary connections between the same part at different time-points, and dashed directed arcs indicate temporal binary connections between different parts at different time-points.

Rule learning proceeds in the following way: First, the unary features of all parts (of all patterns at all time points), $u(p_{it})$, $i = 1,\ldots,n$, $t = 1,\ldots,T$, are collected into a unary feature space U in which each each point represents a single pattern part at any time point $t = 1,\ldots,T$. From this unary feature space, cluster tree expansion can proceed in two directions, in the spatial domain and in the temporal domain. In the spatial domain cluster tree generation proceeds exactly as described in Section 2 following spatial binary relations, etc. In the temporal domain, binary relations can be followed only in strictly forward (predictive) or backward (causal) directions, analyzing recursively temporal changes of either the same part, $b_t(p_{it}, p_{it+1})$ (solid arrows in Figure 2), or of different pattern parts, $b_t(p_{it}, p_{jt+1})$ (dashed arrows in Figure 2) at subsequent time-points. This leads to a conditional cluster tree as shown in Figure 1, except that the relational attribute spaces B can be either spatial or temporal, in accordance with the usual Minimum Description Length (MDL) criterion for Decision Trees[10].

3.3   Rule Application

A set of classification rules is applied to a spatio-temporal pattern in the following way. Starting from each pattern part (at any time point), all possible sequences (chains) of parts are generated using parallel, iterative deepening, subject to the constraints the only adjacent parts are involved and no loops are generated. Note, again, that spatio-temporal adjacency and temporal monotonicity constraints are used for rule generation. Each chain is classified using the classification rules. Expansion of each chain $S_i = <p_{i1}, p_{i2}, \ldots, p_{in}>$ terminates if one of the following conditions occurs: 1) the chain cannot be expanded without creating a cycle, 2) all rules instantiated by S_i are completely resolved, or 3) the binary features $b_s(p_{ij}, p_{ij+1})$ or $b_t(p_{ij}, p_{ij+1})$ do not satisfy the features bounds of any rule.

If a chain S cannot be expanded, the evidence vectors of all rules instantiated by S are averaged to obtain the evidence vector $\boldsymbol{E}(S)$ of the chain S. Further, the set $\mathcal{S}_p$ of all chains that start at p is used to obtain an initial evidence vector for part p:

$$\boldsymbol{E}(p) = \frac{1}{\#(\mathcal{S}_p)} \sum_{S \in \mathcal{S}_p} \boldsymbol{E}(S). \tag{1}$$

where $\#(\mathcal{S})$ denotes the cardinality of the set $\mathcal{S}$. Evidence combination based on (1) is adequate if it is known that a single pattern is to be recognized. However, if the test pattern consists of multiple patterns then this simple scheme can easily produce incorrect results because some some part chains may not be contained completely within a single pattern but "cross" spatio-temporal boundaries between patterns. This occurs when actions corresponding to different types cross can intersect in time and/or space. These chains are likely to be classified in a arbitrary way. To the extent that they can be detected and eliminated, the part classification based on (1) can be improved.

We use general heuristics for detecting rule instantiations involving parts belonging to different patterns. They are based on measuring the compatibility of part evidence vectors and chain evidence vectors. More formally, the compatibility measure can be characterized as follows. For a chain $S_i = < p_{i1}, p_{i2}, ..., p_{in} >$,

$$\boldsymbol{w}(S_i) = \frac{1}{n} \sum_{k=1}^{n} \boldsymbol{E}(p_{ik}) \tag{2}$$

where $\boldsymbol{E}(p_{ik})$ refers to the evidence vector of part p_{ik}. Initially, this can be found by averaging the evidence vectors of the chains which begin with part p_{ik}. Then the compatibility measure is used for updating the part evidence vectors using an iterative relaxation scheme [7]:

$$\boldsymbol{F}^{(t+1)}(p) = \Phi \left(\frac{1}{Z} \sum_{S \in S_p} \boldsymbol{w}^{(t)}(S) \otimes \boldsymbol{E}(S) \right), \tag{3}$$

where Φ is the logistic function, Z a normalizing factor $Z = \sum_{S \in S_p} w^{(t)}(S)$, and the binary operator $\otimes$ is defined as a component-wise vector multiplication $[a\ b]^T \otimes [c\ d]^T = [ac\ bc]^T$. The updated part evidence vectors then reflect the partitioning of the test pattern into distinct subparts.

3.4   Rule Generation using Domain Model Constraints

The definition of spatio-temporal patterns introduced in Section 3.1 is very general and applies to situations where no domain knowledge is available. Learning of patterns may be made more efficient through introduction of relational constraints based on domain knowledge. For example, for the recognition of human body movements, the spatial relation between hand and elbow may be much more diagnostic than the relation between hand and knee, or, more generally, intra-limb spatial relations are more diagnostic than inter-limb spatial relations. For these reasons, arbitrary model-based constraints can be introduced into the underlying relational structure, thus covering the range from fully-connected non-directed relational models to specific directed relational models. Obviously, in situations where no domain knowledge is available, the most general model should be used, and learning is consequently slower and sub-optimal. Conversely, when sufficient domain knowledge is available, strong constraints can be imposed on the relational model, and learning is consequently more efficient.

4 Example

The CRG$_{\text{ST}}$ approach is illustrated in an example where the classification of four different variations of lifting movements were learned, two where a heavy object was lifted, and two where a light object was lifted. Both objects were either lifted with a knees bent and a straight back ("good lifting"), or with knees straight and the back bent ("bad lifting"). Thus there were four movement classes, 1) good lifting of heavy object, 2) good lifting of light object, 3) bad lifting of a heavy object, and 4) bad lifting of a light object. The movements are quite difficult to discriminate, even for human observers. This was done in order to test the limits of the movement learning system.

The movements were recorded using a Polhemus system [11] running at 120Hz for six sensors, located on the hip, above the knee, above the foot, on the upper arm, on the forearm, and on the hand of the left body side (see Figure 3). Each movement type was recorded five times. From the position data $(x(t), y(t), z(t))$ of these sensors, 3-D velocity $v(t)$ and acceleration $a(t)$ were extracted, both w.r.t. arc length $ds(t) = (dx^2(t) + dy^2(t) + dz^2(t))^{1/2}$, i.e. $v(t) = ds(t)/dt$ and $a(t) = d^2s(t)/dt^2$ [9]. Sample time-plots of these measurements are shown in Figure 4.

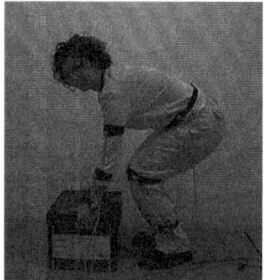

Fig. 3. Lifting a heavy object. The movement sensors were placed on the hip, above the knee, above the foot, on the upper arm, on the forearm, and on the hand of the left body side.

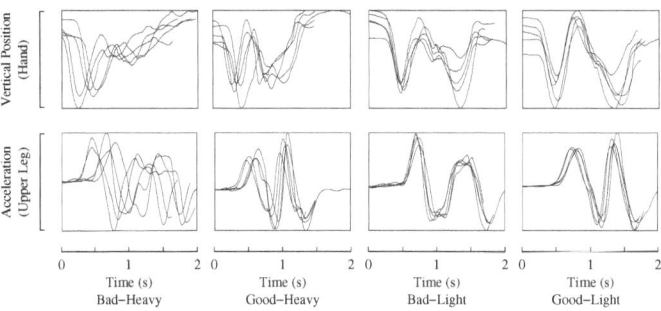

Fig. 4. Sample time-plots of the movement sequences illustrated in Figure 3. The first row shows time-plots for the vertical position of the sensor placed on the hand, the second row the acceleration of the sensor placed above the knee. The four columns show traces the four movement classes (see text for further details).

The spatio-temporal patterns were defined in the following way: At every time point, the patterns consisted of six parts, one for each sensor, each part being described by unary attributes $\boldsymbol{u} = [x, y, z, v, a]$. Binary attributes were defined by simple differences, i.e. the spatial attributes were defined as $\boldsymbol{b}_s(p_{it}, p_{jt}) = \boldsymbol{u}(p_{jt}) - \boldsymbol{u}(p_{it})$, and the temporal attributes were defined as $\boldsymbol{b}_t(p_{it}, p_{jt+1}) = \boldsymbol{u}(p_{jt+1}) - \boldsymbol{u}(p_{it})$.

Performance of CRG_{ST} was tested with a leave-one-out paradigm, i.e. in each test run, movement classes were learned using all but one sample, and the resulting rule system was used to classify the remaining pattern, as described in Section 3. The system was tested with three attribute combinations and four pattern models. The three attributes combinations were 1) $\boldsymbol{u} = [x, y, z]$, 2) $\boldsymbol{u} = [v, a]$ and 3) $\boldsymbol{u} = [x, y, z, v, a]$. The four pattern models were 1) a fully connected relational model (i.e. binary relations were defined between all six sensors), 2) a non-directional intra-limb model, i.e. binary relations were defined between hip - knee, knee - foot, upper arm - forearm, and forearm

Fig. 5. Sketch of the four pattern models used for the recognition of lifting movements. From left to right, the sketches show the fully connected relational model, the non-directional intra-limb model, the directional intra-limb model and an inter-limb model. See text for further explanations.

Model	xyz	va	$xyzva$
fully connected	48.7 (85)	24.6 (30)	45.7 (75)
intra-limb non-directional	46.2 (75)	32.4 (32)	46.2 (75)
intra-limb directional	52.7 (85)	24.1 (20)	63.3 (90)
inter-limb non-directional	41.4 (60)	22.1 (5)	42.1 (70)

Table 1. Performance of CRG$_{ST}$ for learning four different types of lifting actions. The first column indicates what relational model was used, and the three remaining columns give average performance for three different attributes combinations (xyz = position in 3D; v = velocity: a = acceleration). Each cell gives raw percentage correct for a model + feature set combination. The number in parentheses gives classification performance under the assumption that a single movement pattern is present and is obtained from the former using a simple winner-take-all criterion.

- hand, 3) a directional intra-limb model (i.e. binary relations were defined as in 2) but only in one direction), and finally 4) an inter-limb model (i.e. binary relations were defined between hip - upper arm, knee - forearm, and foot - hand) (see Figure 5).

Results of these tests are shown in Table 1, for the attribute subsets and the pattern models just described. The results show that performance is fairly high, in spite of the fact that the movement patterns are not easy to discriminate for human observers. Best performance is reached for the intra-limb directional model (see Figure 5) and the full feature combination $xyzva$. Even though performance for feature combination va is very low, the two features improve, not unexpectedly, performance for the xyz feature combination [6].

An example of the rules which demonstrate their higher-order spatio-temporal nature is the following, with V = velocity; A = acceleration, ΔV = velocity difference between different sensors or for the same sensor over different time points, ΔA = acceleration difference between different sensors or for the same sensor over different time points:

if $U_i(t)$ any value
and $B_{ij}(t)$ $-57 \leq \Delta V \leq 114$ and $-580 \leq \Delta A \leq 550$
and $U_j(t)$ $A \leq 180$
and $T_j(t, t+1)$ $-249 \leq \Delta V \leq 73$ and $181 \leq \Delta A \leq 2210$
and $U_j(t+1)$ $17 \leq V \leq 24$ and $132 \leq A \leq 301$
then   this is part of a good-heavy lifting action

In plain language, rules like the one above read something like the following: If the relative velocity between the upper and lower limb is in the range [-57,114] and that of the relative acceleration in the range [-580,550], and the lower limb has an acceleration less than 180, and to the next time step, velocity change of the lower limb is in the range [-249,73] and that of acceleration change is in the range [181,2210], and at the next time point velocity of the lower limb is in the range [17,24] and that of acceleration in the range [132,301], then this is part of a good lifting of a heavy object.

5   Conclusions

In this paper, we have considered a new type of spatio-temporal relational learner which, like explanation-based learning [8], uses domain knowledge constraints to control induction over training data. The results show that such constraints can indeed improve performance of decision-tree type learners. There are still many open questions to be solved. Of particular relevance is the ability of the spatio-temporal learners to incorporate multi-scaled interval temporal logic constraints and how the spatio-temporal domain modeling can be further used to generate rules which are generated to be robust, reliable and permit discovery of new relations while, at the same time, render valid interpretations.

References

1. W. F. Bischof and T. Caelli. Learning structural descriptions of patterns: A new technique for conditional clustering and rule generation. *Pattern Recognition*, 27:1231–1248, 1994.
2. W. F. Bischof and T. Caelli. Scene understanding by rule evaluation. *IEEE Transactions on Pattern Analysis and Machine Intelligence*, 19:1284–1288, 1997.
3. T. Caelli and W. F. Bischof, editors. *Machine Learning and Image Interpretation*. Plenum, New York, NY, 1997.
4. T. Caelli, L. Guan, and W. Wen. Modularity in neural computing. *Proceedings of the IEEE*, 87:1497–1518, 1999.
5. T. Caelli, G. West, M. Robey, and E. Osman. A relational learning method for pattern and object recognition. *Image and Vision Computing*, 17:391–401, 1999.
6. J. Kittler, R. P. W. Duin, and M. Hatef. Combining classifiers. In *Proceedings of the International Conference on Pattern Recognition*, 1996.
7. B. McCane and T. Caelli. Fuzzy conditional rule generation for the learning and recognition of 3d objects from 2d images. In T. Caelli and W. F. Bischof, editors, *Machine Learning and Image Interpretation*, pages 17–66. Plenum, New York, NY, 1997.
8. T. Mitchell. *Machine Learning*. McGraw-Hill, New York, 1997.
9. F. Mokhtarian. A theory of multiscale, torsion-based shape representation for space curves. *Computer Vision and Image Understanding*, 68:1–17, 1997.
10. J. R. Quinlan. MDL and categorical theories (continued). In *Proceedings of the 12th International Conference on Machine Learning*, pages 464–470, 1995.
11. F. H. Raab, E. B. Blood, T. O. Steiner, and H. R. Jones. Magnetic position and orientation tracking system. *IEEE Transactions on Aerospace and Electronic Systems*, AES-15:709–, 1979.
12. L. Rabiner and B.-H. Juang. *Fundamentals of Speech Recognition*. Prentice Hall, New York, NY, 1993.

Identification of electrical activity of the brain associated with changes in behavioural performance

A Salguero Beltran[1], M Petrou[1], G Barrett[2] and B Dickson[2]

(1)School of Electronic Engineering,
Information Technology and Mathematics,
University of Surrey, Guildford, GU2 7XH, UK
(2)Centre for Human Sciences,
DERA Farnborough, Farnborough, GU14 0LX, UK

Abstract

This paper presents an application of subspace projection techniques to the classification of some EEG data for cognitive psychology.

The data used come from an "odd ball" experiment, where the subject was shown targets to which they had to respond by pressing a button. The target was shown with frequency 1/10 of the frequency with which irrelevant targets (to which no response was necessary) were shown. The data used in this study concern only the recordings when the target of interest was actually shown. This means that we have the recordings of 20 EEG channels, from 1393 trials, concerning 11 different subjects. However, in the classification experiments presented, we use only a single channel at a time. The classes we try to disambiguate are those of fast and slow response. The signals in each class are further subdivided into two halves, one used for training and one for testing.

Our purpose is to predict as soon as possible after the visual stimulus whether the subject is likely to succeed (ie respond fast) or fail (ie respond slowly) in his task.

We show that if each subject is treated individually, and if we use parts of the signal that are identical for the two classes and parts that are maximally different, we obtain results that are significantly better than the pure chance level. The results presented are preliminary results of work in progress.

1 Introduction

There are two major approaches in understanding the functionality of the human brain and by extension human behaviour: trying to solve the inverse problem using the recordings of electroencephalograms (EEG) and magne-

S. Singh, N. Murshed, and W. Kropatsch (Eds.): ICAPR 2001, LNCS 2013, pp. 290–300, 2001.
© Springer-Verlag Berlin Heidelberg 2001

toencephalograms (MEG), and trying to find correlations between the observed recorded patterns and subsequent behaviour. In the first approach one tries to identify the electromagnetic state of the brain from the recorded values of the electric and/or the magnetic field outside the head, by postulating various dipole sources spatially distributed inside the head and trying to infer their degree of activation (eg [1, 4]). In the second approach one does not bother with the physical model that creates the observations, but instead tries to use various pattern recognition techniques to find phenomenological relationships between the patterns of behaviour observed and the patterns of the recorded signals (eg [5, 7]). Given that the number of recording channels used in such studies is limited to a few dozens at best, it is not possible to expect that one will ever establish an 1:1 correspondence between the recorded pattern and the thoughts of the subject. However, if one restricts the domain of behaviour to simple tasks, one may hope to be able to predict the expected behaviour of the subject from a limited number of observations.

Little attention has been devoted to the use of pattern recognition and signal processing techniques for predicting human performance. Only a few references were found in the literature. Trejo et al [9] used linear regression models to study the quantitative relationship between variations in the amplitude and latency of components of evoked responses and performance on a specific task across subjects as well as for individual subjects. Factor analysis of the reaction times, accuracy, and confidence of responses was used to create a global measurement of the performance. Using principal components analysis, factors were extracted from the correlation matrix of the single-trial performance measures for all subjects. The relation between the behavioural index and the variables of the tasks were studied by analysis of variance (ANOVA) and multivariate analysis of variance (MANOVA). The results depended on the signal to noise ratio. They concluded that linear combinations of single trial amplitudes of evoked responses and latency measures did not provide a useful real time index of task performance. However, models based on averaging of several adjacent trials produced more reliable prediction of the index of performance. It was suggested to include task relevant information for more accurate models of performance.

Trejo and Shensa in [8] reported a further development of evaluation models for human performance monitoring. They used the discrete wavelet transform (DWT) to extract features from the recorded EEG signals. The results were compared with models for which features were obtained by principal component analysis (PCA), and with results obtained with models using the raw EEG signals as features. Two types of classifiers were designed for every feature space. The first ones were based on neural networks. The second classifiers were developed by the linear regression model described in [9]. Both methods PCA and DWT yielded better results in both types of classifiers than the traditional latency and peak analysis. However the DWT method had better performance than PCA in all cases.

Other work concerned with single trial prediction reported results concerned with the relation between components of evoked responses and reaction time. Lange et al reported in [2] discriminatory effects of matched filters applied in the prediction of single trials. They presented sub-averages of trials which showed a direct relation between the latency of the P300 component and the reaction time. In [3] the same group used a statistical model of the firing instants of neuronal populations to decompose the P300 complex in subcomponents. Reciprocal changes in the amplitude of each sub P300 component were related with changes in the reaction time.

The objective of the paper is to use pattern recognition techniques to find correlations between the EEG recorded pattern after a stimulus has been presented to the subject and the subsequent performance of the subject, expressed by the subject's reaction time.

The data used come from an "odd ball" experiment, where the subject was shown targets to which they had to respond by pressing a button. The target was shown with frequency 1/10 of the frequency with which irrelevant targets (to which no response was necessary) were shown. The data used in this study concerned only the recordings when the target of interest was actually shown. This meant that we had the recordings of 20 EEG channels, from 1393 trials, concerning 11 different subjects. In most cases, the subjects had responded correctly by pressing the button. In some cases, however, they had not. The idea is to use the part of the signal soon after the target has been presented, in order to predict whether the subject is going to respond correctly or not. The result of the performance of the subject was binarised into two classes: "success" or "failure". Before we proceed, we must first decide what is meant by "success" and "failure". In many situations, pressing the button does not necessarily mean that the subject has succeeded. A delayed reaction, even if it is correct, it may be fatal. This is the case, for example, of a fighter pilot having to press a button when he sees an enemy target, or a train or car driver having to press the break when he sees a red light or a pedestrian on the line. In our experiments, only in 30 out of the 1393 trials the subject failed to press the button altogether. The reaction times, however, varied by as much as a factor of 4 or 5 (the shortest reaction time was 360ms, while the longest was 1932ms). So, we decided that the classes we would like to disambiguate would be those of fast and slow response. We divided therefore the data into two categories: Class "success" were the fastest half of the signals (ie signals with reaction times in the range $[360ms, 692ms]$), and class "failure" the slowest half (signals with reaction times in the range $(692ms, 1932ms]$). The signals in each class were further subdivided into two halves, one to be used for training and one for testing.

2   Methodology

Figure 1 shows a typical signal from channel C3 when the subject was performing the task. Time $t = 0$ corresponds to the time the stimulus is delivered. The vertical lines mark this time, as well as the time of the reaction of the

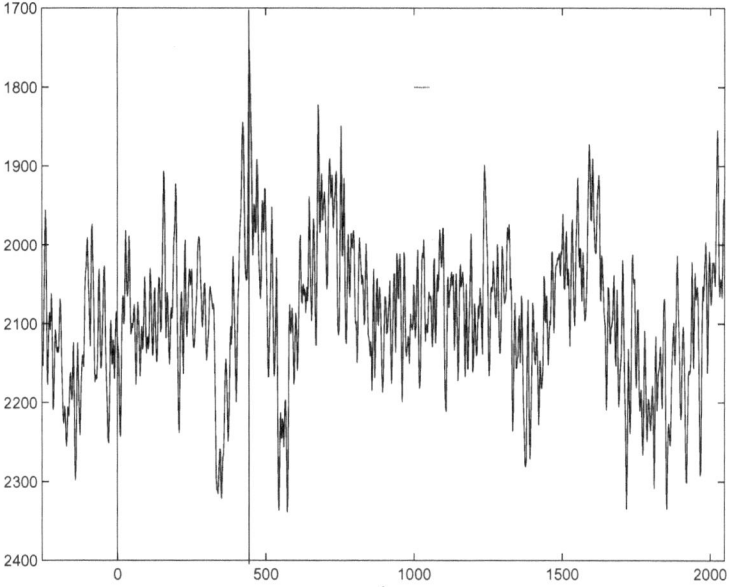

Figure 1: A typical signal recorded by channel C3. Time 0 is when the stimulus was shown. The vertical lines indicate the stimulus time (left line) and the time when the subject reacted (right line).

subject. The time span between the time of the stimulus and the time of the reaction is of interest to us. In what follows the word "signal" will refer to this segment of the recorded data, unless it is otherwise made clear by the context. Our purpose is to use the early part of each signal and check for correlations with the subsequent performance. The size (ie the duration) of the signal differs not only from subject to subject, but also between different trials performed by the same subject. The last $25ms$ or so correspond to the time taken for the signal indicating action to travel from the brain to the muscles of the hand of the subject. The earlier part, however, is the time taken by the brain to make the decision for action. As our purpose is early prediction, we can not a priori know the exact length of the signal. So, in our experiments we considered all signals we have for training, and identified the shortest of them. The length of this signal represents the shortest recorded reaction time over all subjects and all trials. We would like to be able to make our predictions at most in that length of time. So, for our analysis, all available signals were truncated to that length, which we shall call M_0. In other words, M_0 is the number of samples considered for all available signals. Perhaps not all of these samples are necessary for prediction. So, the number of samples used from each signal is $M_m < M_0$.

In this paper, we try to distinguish success or failure on the basis of the information we receive from a single recorded channel, and the issue of combining the information from more than one channels is left for future work.

In many pattern recognition tasks, what matters is the *relative* importance of the various components, as opposed to their absolute values. What matters then is not where the tip of the pattern vector in feature space is, but what is the *orientation* of the vector. As the magnitude of the pattern does not matter, people usually normalise all patterns to have the same magnitude, equal to 1, by dividing each one by its magnitude. This way they reduce the dimensionality of the problem by 1. To classify an unknown pattern on the basis of the *relative* values of its components, they compare then its orientation with the orientations of the vectors that represent the different classes. Measuring orientations amounts to measuring angles between vectors. Angles are found by taking the dot product of the vectors. As all vectors have length 1, the dot product is really the cosine of the angle between the two vectors. So, if we get 1 as an answer, the two vectors have the same orientation, and if we get 0 as an answer, the two vectors are orthogonal to each other. A result of -1 indicates totally opposite patterns.

Such methods are called **subspace projection** methods. They are most appropriate for pattern recognition tasks when non-parametric representations of the data are more acceptable, and when the absolute value of the response pattern is not important, but the *relative* values of the components in the pattern are important.

We found, however, that the amount of activation was also useful in our case, so the results presented here were obtained without normalising the patterns. The implication is that the measure we use to identify similarity between two patterns, is the component of the test pattern along the pattern that represents the class. The sign of the component is important as a negative sign implies anti-correlation and not similarity.

3   Practical considerations in applying subspace projection methods

When an unknown pattern vector is to be classified, we must project it on the vectors of each class to see where it has the highest projection. It is not efficient to use all training vectors that represent a class. Instead, we must use some representative vectors from each class. How we choose these representative vectors, is a matter of what criteria we use. The most common approach is to require that the components of the training patterns we have, when projected on these representative vectors, are decorrelated. Then it can be shown [6] that these representative vectors must be chosen to be the eigenvectors of the autocorrelation matrix of the class with non-zero eigenvalues.

When the two classes overlap, the common area is spanned by vectors of both classes. These vectors are not very useful and reliable for class discrimination. We would like, therefore, to omit them. There are techniques which allow us to identify only the eigenvectors that are outside the common area.

The way we achieve it is by identifying the eigenvectors which span all space that is not covered by class "failure", for example. Then we consider only the intersection of this space with the class "success".

To calculate the autocorrelation matrix of a class, we applied the following formula:

$$Q_{ij}^{(*)} = \frac{1}{N_*} \sum_{k=1}^{N_*} x_{ki}^{(*)} x_{kj}^{(*)} \tag{1}$$

where $*$ stands for s (for class "success"), or f (for class "failure"), and:

$Q_{ij}^{(*)}$: the (i, j) element of the autocorrelation matrix of the class;
N_* : the number of training patterns in the class;
$x_{ki}^{(*)}$: the ith component of the kth training pattern in the class.

To take into consideration the overlapping parts of the two classes, we need the definition of the *projection matrix*:

$$P^{(*)} = u_1^{(*)} u_1^{(*)T} + u_2^{(*)} u_2^{(*)T} + \ldots + u_{n_*}^{(*)} u_{n_*}^{(*)T} \tag{2}$$

where:

$P^{(*)}$: the projection matrix of the class;
n_* : the number of eigenvectors with non-zero eigenvalues of the autocorrelation matrix of the class;
$u_i^{(*)}$: the ith eigenvector of the class;
$u_i^{(*)T}$: the transpose of the ith eigenvector of the class.

Algorithm A: Training

1. Calculate the autocorrelation matrix of each class, using formula 1.

2. For each matrix calculate the eigenvectors and eigenvalues.

3. From each class keep all eigenvectors, with nonzero eigenvalues.

4. For each class compute the projection matrix using all eigenvectors and formula 2.

5. Compute matrix $\overline{P}^{(f)} \equiv I - P^{(f)}$ where I is the unit matrix.

6. Compute the eigenvectors of matrix Q defined by:

$$Q \equiv \frac{1}{2} P^{(s)} + \frac{1}{2} \overline{P}^{(f)} \tag{3}$$

7. For class "success" keep the eigenvectors of matrix Q that have eigenvalues 1 or near 1. For class "failure" keep the eigenvectors of matrix Q that have eigenvalues 0 or near 0.

Algorithm B: Testing

To classify an unknown signal follow the following steps:

1. Consider as pattern the same segment of the signal as that used for training.

2. Compute the projection of the pattern vector on each class by calculating its dot product with all the representative vectors of the class you identified during training.

3. Classify the signal according to the criterion:

$$\sum_i x^T u_i^s > \sum_j x^T u_j^f \qquad \text{to class "success"} \qquad (4)$$

$$\sum_j x^T u_j^f > \sum_i x^T u_i^s \qquad \text{to class "failure"} \qquad (5)$$

where:

x : the unknown vector
u_i^s : the ith eigenvector of class "success"
u_j^f : the jth eigenvector of class "failure"

4   Experiments

Each of the two classes ("success" and "failure") is characterised by large variability. This can be seen by averaging the signals of each class and calculating the standard deviation of the distribution of each sample. Figures 2 and 3 show the average signals of each class and the signals created by adding and subtracting one standard deviation from the mean signal, for one of the channels, namely channel Oz. In figure 2 the curves refer to the training data, and in figure 3 to the testing data. In both cases the class "success" is represented by the thick lines. It is interesting to observe that the two average signals show regions where they definitely diverge from each other, with these features being observed in both the training and the testing data. Given that the division of the data into training and testing was done at random, the fact that the same deviations are observed in both subsets, makes these differences significant. However, in all cases these differences are buried well inside

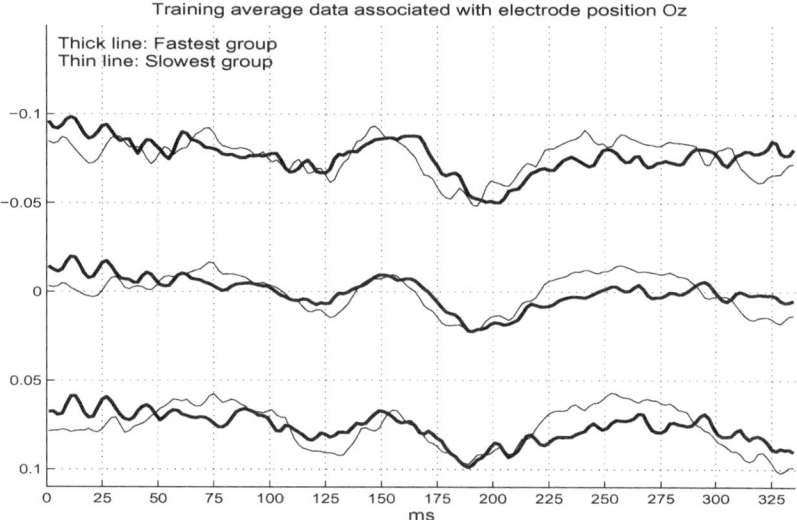

Figure 2: The mean signals for class "success" (thick line) and "failure" (thin line) and their counterparts plus and minus one standard deviation away. Class "success" means reaction time $\leq 692ms$. Class "failure" means reaction time $> 692ms$. Channel Oz. Training data only.

the one standard deviation limit. This means that disambiguation of the two classes on the basis of these samples will be very difficult if at all possible.

So, for each channel, we identified the promising ranges of samples, and used those as our patterns. If more than one range of samples appeared different in the two classes, all promising ranges were used. In addition, the full range consisting of 168 samples was also used. The classification results of these experiments were barely above the chance level. (Since we have only two classes, for the classification to be statistically significant, we expect to predict correctly with accuracy above 50% both successes and failures). The disappointing performance of this approach made us realise two important points:

- There is a large variation in the performance of individual subjects, as it can be judged from the range of their reaction times. The data we used concerned 11 different subjects. Better results should be expected if each subject was treated separately.

- The segment of the signal used was the one where the two average signals between success and failure were most distinct. However, the classifier we use is based on the calculation of correlation matrices which are second order statistics. The second order statistics are most distinct when each segment used contains a part which is similar to the signals for the other class and a part which is most dissimilar, so that the 2-point

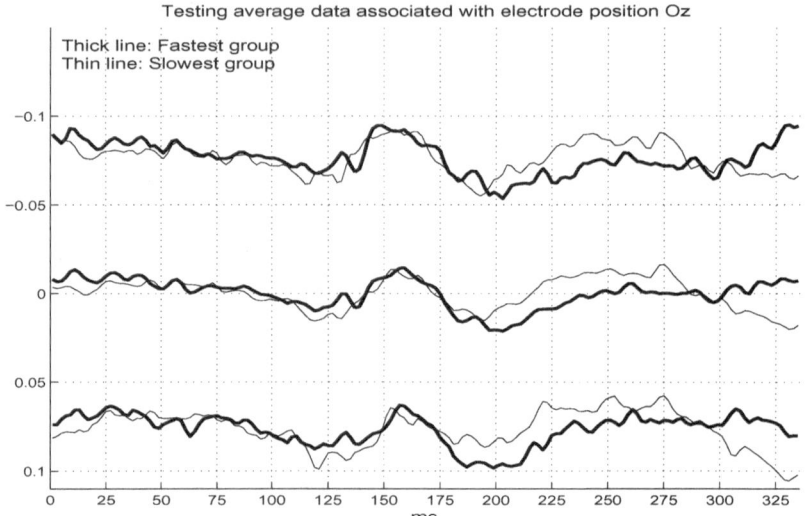

Figure 3: The mean signals for class "success" (thick line) and "failure" (thin line) and their counterparts plus and minus one standard deviation away. Class "success" means reaction time $\leq 692ms$. Class "failure" means reaction time $> 692ms$. Channel Oz. Testing data only.

difference between samples is most distinct between the two classes.

The final series of experiments we performed treated each subject separately, and used training data to train the classifier for each subject separately. In addition, during the training phase, a sliding window of the signal was used to identify the segment that would offer the maximum discrimination between success and failure. As predicted, the best windows were those which included the transition region at which the average signal of success from being very similar to the average signal of failure, becomes most dissimilar from it.

5   Results

Table 1 shows the best results obtained for each subject. The first column gives the identity of each subject. The second column gives the sample numbers that identify the segment of the signal used in the experiment with the results reported. These numbers are in msec after the presentation of the stimulus to the subject. The shortest reaction time of each subject is given in the next column. The fourth column shows the EEG recording channel from which these results were obtained. (The name of the channel is a recognised name by the practitioners of cognitive EEG studies, indicating the location of the corresponding electrode on the skull.) The final three columns give the percentages of correctly predicting the cases when the subject failed (under

"F") and when the subject succeeded (under "S"), as well as their average. All results are above the 50% limit which is the result of chance.

Table 1: **Results for channels Fz, Cz, and Pz considering each subject separately**

Subject	Window for best results	Fastest reaction time	Channel for best results	Best percentage of classification (%)		
				F	S	(Avg)
S1	244-304	360	Pz	69	58	64
S2	140-336	592	Cz	63	58	61
S3	124-254	432	Fz	61	83	72
S4	226-330	428	Fz	61	67	64
S5	220-300	412	Fz	72	55	64
S6	200-280	424	Fz	57	59	58
S7	116-182	368	Cz	65	65	65
S8	176-330	468	Fz	68	55	62
S9	284-336	436	Fz	68	58	63
S10	246-316	456	Fz	59	66	61
S11	144-240	540	Pz	83	58	71

6   Conclusions and future work

In this study only individual EEG channels were considered. The conclusions drawn therefore, cannot be final on the ability of pattern recognition to help predict success or failure. From the fact that the results were barely above chance when all subjects were treated together, one can conclude that a general purpose classifier of success or failure appropriate for all subjects is probably impossible. However, the results are significantly above the chance level when each subject is treated separately. It seems therefore, that as the patterns of success or failure are different for different individuals, it is necessary to develop custom-made decision systems for each individual.

Only 1/10 of the data were used, namely when the target was presented to the subject. Future work will make use of the recordings when the target was not presented to the subject. Studying how the patterns of success or failure for a certain individual differ when target is presented or target is not presented, may allow us to develop systems that tend to over-react or under-react to targets.

In addition, combinations of channels have to be used to see whether the prediction performance improves. If combinations of channels do not improve the results, then simpler systems may be designed which record the data from one channel only (or a small number of channels that are most relevant).

The development of such systems may be of very significant practical use, not only in military applications, but also in routine checks of baggage control at airports for example, or long distance driving.

References

[1] Baillet S and Garnero L, 1997. A Bayesian Approach to Introducing Anatomo-Functional Priors in the EEG/MEG inverse problem, IEEE Transactions on Biomedical Engineering, vol 44, pp 374–385.

[2] Lange D H, Pratt H and Inbar G F, 1995. Segmented matched filtering of single event related evoked potentials. IEEE Trans Biomed Eng, vol 42 No 3, pp 317–21.

[3] Lange D H, Pratt H and Inbar G F, 1997. Modelling and estimation of single evoked brain potential components. IEEE Trans Biomed Eng, vol 44 No 9, p 7

[4] Mosher J and Leahy R, 1998. Recursive MUSIC: A framework for EEG and MEG source localisation, IEEE Transactions on Biomedical Engineering, vol 45, pp 1342–1354.

[5] Jung T P, Makeig S, Stensmo M and Sejnowski T, 1997. Estimating alertness from the EEG power spectrum, IEEE Transactions on Biomedical Engineering, vol 44, pp 60–69.

[6] Oja E, 1983. Subspace Methods of Pattern Recognition, Research Studies Press, ISBN 0 86380 010 6.

[7] Roessgen M, Zoubir A and Boashash B, 1998. Seizure detection of newborn EEG using a model based approach, IEEE Transactions on Biomedical Engineering, vol 45, pp 673–685.

[8] Trejo L J and Shensa M J, 1999. Feature extraction of event-related potentials using wavelets: an application to human performance monitoring. Brain Lang, vol 66 No 1, pp 89–107.

[9] Trejo L J, Kramaer A and Arnold J, 1995. Event related potentials as indices of display monitoring performance. Biological Psychology, vol 40, pp 33–71.

Automatic Camera Calibration for Image Sequences of a Football Match

Flávio Szenberg[1], Paulo Cezar Pinto Carvalho[2], Marcelo Gattass[1]

[1]TeCGraf - Computer Science Department, PUC-Rio
Rua Marquês de São Vicente, 255, 22453-900, Rio de Janeiro, RJ, Brazil
{szenberg, gattass}@tecgraf.puc-rio.br

[2]IMPA - Institute of Pure and Applied Mathematics
Estrada Dona Castorina, 110, 22460-320, Rio de Janeiro, RJ, Brazil
pcezar@visgraf.impa.br

Abstract

In the broadcast of sports events one can commonly see adds or logos that are not actually there – instead, they are inserted into the image, with the appropriate perspective representation, by means of specialized computer graphics hardware. Such techniques involve camera calibration and the tracking of objects in the scene. This article introduces an automatic camera calibration algorithm for a smooth sequence of images of a football (soccer) match taken in the penalty area near one of the goals. The algorithm takes special steps for the first scene in the sequence and then uses coherence to efficiently update camera parameters for the remaining images. The algorithm is capable of treating in real-time a sequence of images obtained from a TV broadcast, without requiring any specialized hardware.

Keywords: camera calibration, automatic camera calibration, computer vision, tracking, object recognition, image processing.

1 Introduction

In the broadcast of sports events one can commonly see adds or logos that are not actually there – instead, they are inserted into the image, with the appropriate perspective representation, by means of specialized computer graphics hardware. Such techniques involve camera calibration and the tracking of objects in the scene.

In the present work, we describe an algorithm that, for a given broadcast image, is capable of calibrating the camera responsible for visualizing it and of tracking the field lines in the following scenes in the sequence. With this algorithm, the programs require minimal user intervention, thus performing what we call *automatic camera calibration*. Furthermore, we seek to develop efficient algorithms that can be used in widely available PC computers.

There are several works on camera calibration, such as [1], [2], [3], and the most

S. Singh, N. Murshed, and W. Kropatsch (Eds.): ICAPR 2001, LNCS 2013, pp. 301–310, 2001.

classical one, [4], which introduced the well-known Tsai method for camera calibration. All methods presented in these works require the user to specify reference points – that is, points in the image for which one knows the true position in the real world. In this work, our purpose is to obtain such data automatically.

The method for automatically obtaining reference points is based on object recognition. Some works related to this method include [5], [6], [7] and [8]. [9] discusses some limitations of model-based recognition.

In [10], a camera self-calibration method for video sequences is presented. Some points of interest in the images are tracked and, by using the Kruppa equations, the camera is calibrated. In the present work, we are interested in recognizing and tracking a model, based on the field lines, and only then calibrating the camera.

The scenes we are interested in tracking are those of a football (soccer) match, focused on the penalty area near one of the goals. There is where the events of the match that call more attention take place. In this article we restrict our scope to scene sequences that do not present cuts. That is, the camera's movement is smooth and the image sequence follows a coherent pattern.

The primary objective of our work was to develop an algorithm for a real-time system that works with television broadcast images. A major requirement for the algorithm is its ability to process at least 30 images per second.

2   General View of the Algorithm

The proposed algorithm is based on a sequence of steps, illustrated in the flowchart shown in Fig. 1. The first four steps are performed only for the first image in the scene. They include a segmentation step that supports the extraction of the field lines and the determination of a preliminary plane projective transformation. For the subsequent images of the sequence, the algorithm performs an adjustment of the camera parameters based on the lines obtained in the previous images and on the preliminary transformation.

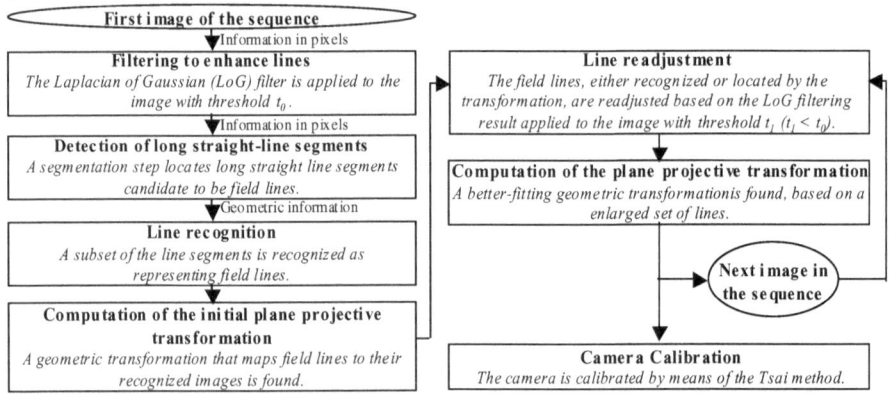

Fig. 1 - Algorithm flowchart.

3   Filtering

This step of the algorithm is responsible for improving the images obtained from the television broadcast. Our primary objective here is to enhance the image to support the extraction of straight-line segments corresponding to the markings on the field. To perform this step, we use classical image-processing tools [11]. In the present article, image processing is always done in grayscale. To transform color images into grayscale images, the image luminance is computed.

In order to extract pixels from the image that are candidate to lie on a straight-line segment, we apply the Laplacian filter. Because of noise, problems may arise if this filter is directly applied to the image. To minimize them, the Gaussian filter must first be applied to the image. Thus, the image is filtered by a composition of the above filters, usually called the *Laplacian of Gaussian (LoG)* filter.

The pixels in the image resulting from the *LoG* filtering with values greater than a specified threshold (black pixels) are candidate to be on one of the line segments. The remaining pixels (white pixels) are discarded.

Figs. 3, 4, and 5 show an example of this filtering step for the image given in Fig. 2. We will use this image to explain all the steps of the proposed algorithm. In these figures we can notice the improvement due to applying a Gaussian filter prior to the Laplacian filtering. The lines are much more noticeable in Fig. 5 than in Fig. 4.

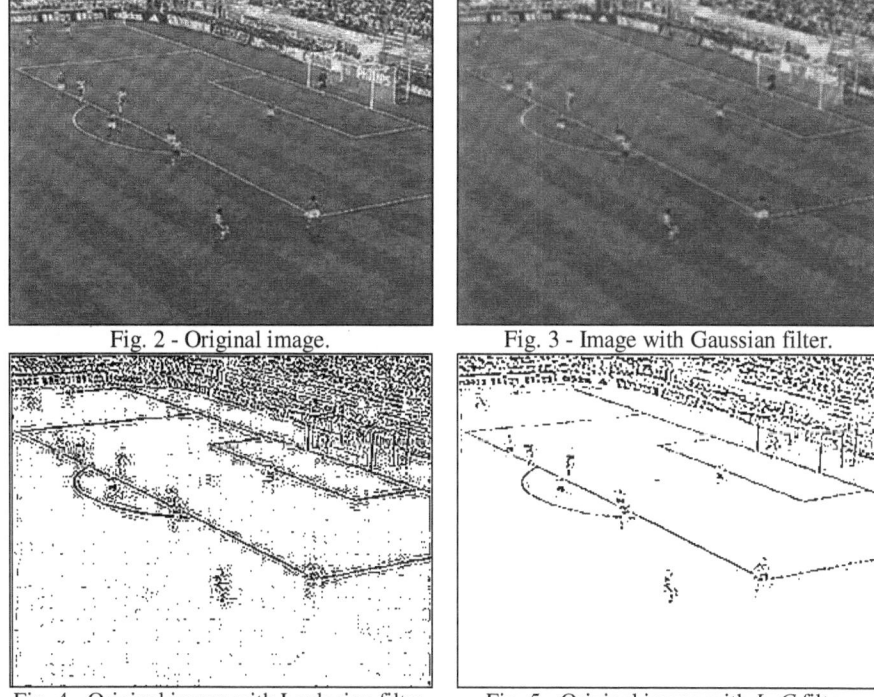

Fig. 2 - Original image.   Fig. 3 - Image with Gaussian filter.

Fig. 4 - Original image with Laplacian filter.   Fig. 5 - Original image with *LoG* filter.

4 Detecting Long Segments

Once the filtering step has roughly determined the pixels corresponding to the line segments, the next step consists in locating such segments. In our specific case, we are interested in long straight-line segments.

Up to now in the algorithm, we only have pixel information. The pixels that have passed through the *LoG* filtering are black; those that have not are white. The desired result, however, must be a geometric structure – more explicitly, parameters that define the straight-line segments.

The procedure proposed for detecting long segments is divided in two steps:

1.   Eliminating pixels that do not lie on line segments:

In this step, the image is divided into cells by a regular grid as shown in Fig. 6. For each of these cells, we compute the covariance matrix

$$\begin{bmatrix} \sum_{i=0}^{n}(x_i - x')^2 & \sum_{i=0}^{n}(x_i - x')(y_i - y') \\ \sum_{i=0}^{n}(x_i - x')(y_i - y') & \sum_{i=0}^{n}(y_i - y')^2 \end{bmatrix}$$

where n is the number of black pixels in the cell, x_i and y_i are the coordinates of each black pixel, and x' and y' are the corresponding averages. By computing the eigenvalues λ_1 and λ_2 of this matrix, we can determine to what extent the black pixels of each cell are positioned as a straight line. If one of such eigenvalues is null or if the ratio between the largest and the smallest eigenvalue is greater than a specified value, then the cell is selected and the eigenvector relative to the largest eigenvalue will provide the predominant direction for black pixel orientation. Otherwise, the cell is discarded. The result can be seen in Fig. 7.

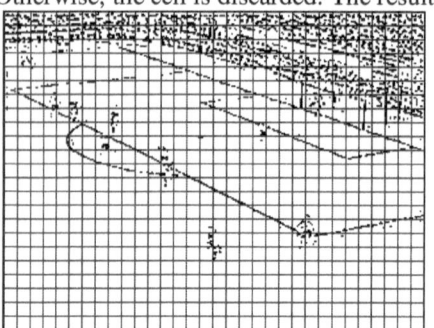
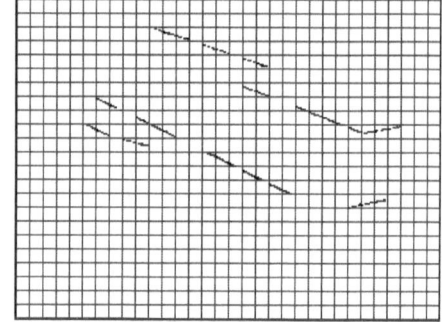

Fig. 6 - Image divided into cells.   Fig. 7 - Pixels forming straight-line segments.

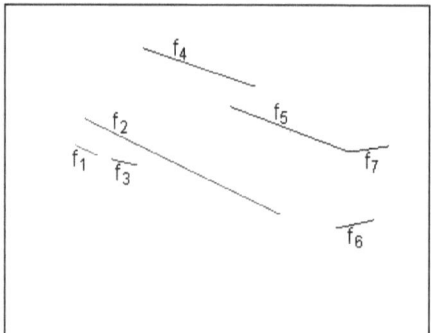

Fig. 8 - Extraction of straight-line segments.

2.   Determining line segments:

The described cells are traversed in such a way that columns are processed from left to right and the cells in each column are processed bottom-up. Each cell is given a label, which is a nonnegative integer. If there is no predominant direction in a cell, it is labeled 0. Otherwise the three neighboring cells to the left and the cell below the given cell are checked to verify whether they have a predominant direction similar to the one of the current cell. If any of them does, then the current cell receives its label; otherwise, a new label is used for the current cell. After this numbering scheme is performed, cells with the same label are grouped and, afterwards, groups that correspond to segments that lie on the same line are merged. At the end of the process, each group provides a line segment. The result is illustrated in Fig. 8.

5   Recognizing Field Lines

The information we have now is a collection of line segments, some of which correspond to field lines. Our current goal, then, is to recognize, among those segments, the ones that are indeed projections of a field line, and to identify that line.

For this purpose we use a model-based recognition method [5]. In our case, the model is the set of lines of a football field. This method is based on interpretations, that is, it interprets both data sets – the real model and the input data – and checks whether they are equivalent, according to certain restrictions

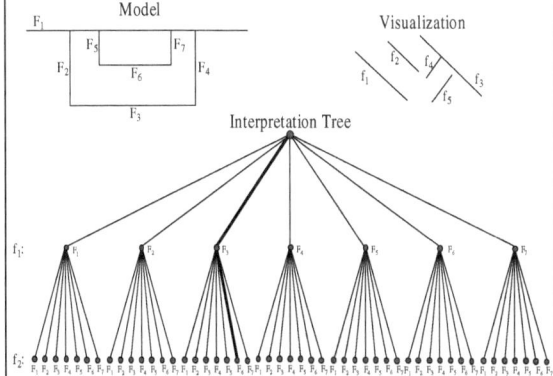

Fig. 9 - Example of an interpretation tree.

We use a tree structure, called *interpretation tree*, in which each leaf represents one possible solution. Fig. 9 illustrates the two first levels of an interpretation tree.

The line segments obtained in the previous step (f_1 through f_5) must be matched to the model given by the field lines F_1 through F_7. Each node of the tree represents a correspondence between a found segment f_x and a model segment F_v. The validity of a node is determined by a set of restrictions, some of which are given below.

1.   Two lines cannot have the same representation.
2.   Two lines are parallel (or almost parallel, due to the projective transformation) in the visualization only if their representatives in the model are also parallel.
3.   All lines must be in the same half-plane determined by the line representing F_1.
4.   All lines must be in the same half-plane determined by the line representing F_2, except for the one representing F_1.

An example of an application of these restrictions is the invalidation of the node shown in bold in Fig. 9; in this node, f_1 represents F_1 and f_2 represent F_2. The node is invalid because f_1 and f_2 are parallel, while F_1 and F_2 are orthogonal (thus contradicting restriction 2).

We do not require that all f_x lines correspond to some F_v model line. This leads to the existence of multiple feasible solutions. Therefore, a tie-breaking criterion must be applied: the chosen solution is the one with the largest sum of the lengths of the lines with representations. This, for instance, automatically discards the trivial solution (where none of the lines has a representation).

For the situation in Fig.9 we have: $f_1 : \varnothing$, $f_2 : F_3$, $f_3 : \varnothing$, $f_4 : F_1$, $f_5 : F_6$, $f_6 : F_4$, $f_7 : F_7$, where $f_x : F_y$ means that line f_x represents line F_y and $f_x : \varnothing$ indicates that f_x represents none of the model lines.

6   Computing the Planar Projective Transformation

In the previous section we discussed how to recognize visible field lines. However, some of the lines may not be clear in the image, and the algorithm may fail to detect them. In this section we shall discuss an algorithm for locating such lines.

We begin by using the pairs $f_x : F_y$ obtained in the previous step to compute a planar projective transformation that projects field lines onto the lines representing them. For that purpose, we find the intersection points of the recognized pairs of lines. This generates a set of points for which the position both in the field and in the image is known. We also compute, in the image, the vanishing points relative to the ox and oy directions of the model. Then, we use least squares to find a projective transformation – represented by a 3×3 matrix in homogeneous coordinates – that best maps field points to image points.

This initial transformation may not be very good due to errors in the location of the detected lines and because we may have a small number of points, since there may be field lines for which we have not found a representative. The transformation error is illustrated by Fig. 10, in which we can notice a considerable difference between a sideline of the penalty area and its reconstruction.

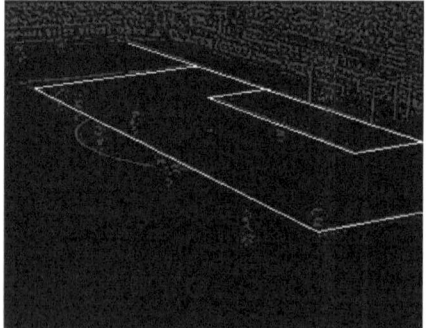

Fig. 10 - Initial transformation.   Fig. 11 - After line readjustment.

To improve this solution, we shall use the computed transformation to find the missing field lines. A field line may not have been correctly located by the previous step, especially if the line is faded in the image and most of its pixels are discarded by the LoG filter (for instance, the above mentioned sideline of the penalty area was not located in Fig. 8). However, once an approximate position for that line is known, these pixels may be retrieved by a LoG filter with a smaller threshold, but subject to be near the predicted position of one of the field lines.

The idea is to partition the pixels of the image resulting from the LoG filtering according to the nearest projected field line (computed by the initial projective transformation), discarding those pixels whose distance to all lines is larger than a certain value.

From each group of pixels, we use least squares to compute straight lines that best fit those pixels. Such lines will replace those that originated the groups. We call this step of the method *line readjustment*.

With this new set of lines, we compute a new planar projective transformation. This new transformation is expected to have better quality than the previous one, because the input points used to obtain the transformation are restricted to small regions in the vicinity of each line. Therefore, the noise introduced by the effect of other elements of the image is reduced.

With this new set of lines, we compute a new planar projective transformation, in the same way as done for the initial transformation. The result of this readjustment is illustrated in Fig. 11. These images are in negative to better highlight the extracted field lines, represented in white. The gray points in the images are the output of the *LoG* filter, and they are in the image only to provide an idea of the precision of the transformation. We can notice that the sideline of the penalty area in the upper part of the images is better located in Fig. 11 than in Fig. 10.

Some problems may arise in this readjustment due to the players. If there is a large number of them over a line – for instance, when there is a wall –, this line may not be well adjusted.

7 Camera Calibration

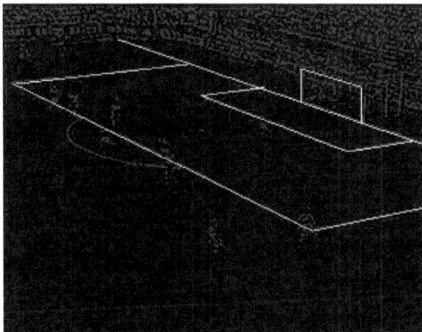

Fig. 12 - Result of the Tsai method.

The projective transformation computed in the previous section is planar, therefore it does not consider points outside the plane of the field, such as the top of the goal posts. In order to obtain a full three-dimensional reconstruction of the field, we must calibrate the camera used to capture the image, that is, we must find its intrinsic and extrinsic parameters. Tsai's algorithm [4] is employed for such purpose. A regular grid is generated inside the penalty area of the model, and pairs of the form (pc_i, pi_i), where pc_i are points of the model and pi_i are their images according to the last computed planar transformation, are passed to the calibration procedure. With this information the position, orientation and zoom factor of the camera can be recovered.

The result of the Tsai method is illustrated in Fig. 12. One can notice that it is now possible to appropriately reconstruct objects outside the field, such as the goal posts.

8 Working with a Sequence of Images

When there is a sequence of images (with no cuts), we are interested in calibrating the camera with the least possible computational effort, in order to obtain real-time processing. Since we are dealing with television images, this means that, for each image, we have 1/30 of a second to calibrate the camera.

For the first image, we apply the camera calibration process described above. In order to optimize the proposed algorithm from the second image on, we shall take advantage of the previous image. We can use its final plane projective transformation as an initial transformation for the current image, and go directly to the line readjusting method.

9   Results

To test the proposed algorithm we have analyzed two sequences of images. The first one is a synthetic sequence obtained from an OpenGL visualization of a football field aims at verifying if model. The second sequence was obtained by capturing real images from a TV broadcast using a video capture board. Each sequence has 27 frames with a resolution of 320x240. Figs. 13 and 14 show the first and the last images in each sequence, showing the reconstructed elements of the field.

In the first sequence of images the results from the algorithm reproduce the original model. The second sequence aims at verifying the behavior of the algorithm when working with real images. These should be harder for the algorithm, since they contain extraneous elements – such as the audience and marketing plates around the field – and feature curved field lines, due to lens distortion.

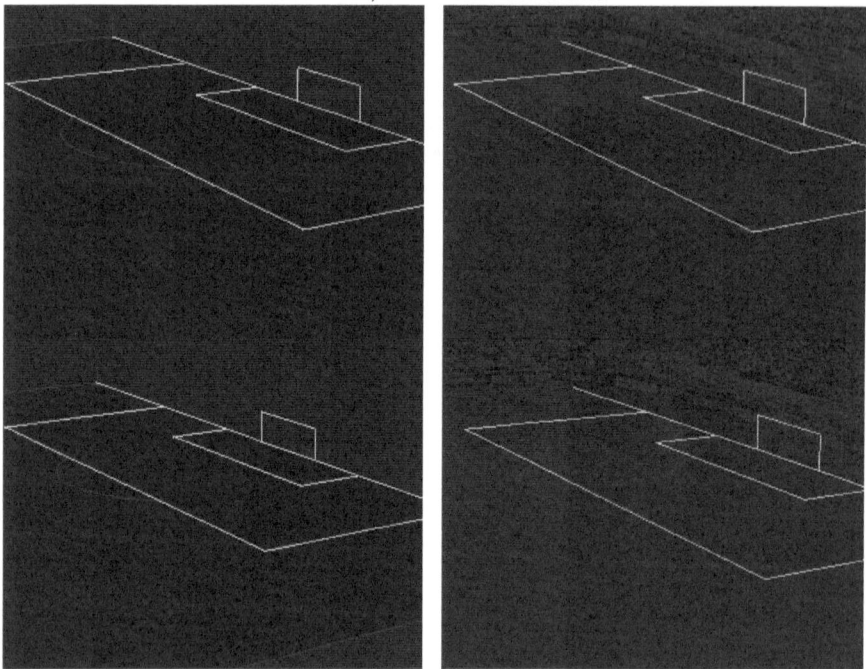

Fig. 13 - Artificial data.   Fig. 14 - Real data.

In the artificial sequence of images, visual errors cannot be noticed. In the real sequence, there are some small errors in the superposition of the reconstructed lines (white) over the image lines.

The numerical errors for the first sequence are shown in Tables 1 and 2. These tables present the correct projected coordinates and those resulting from our algorithm (reconstructed coordinates). The comparison shows that the error, for each point, is never greater than 2 pixels, with the typical average of about 0.5 pixel. These small errors result mainly from the discrete nature of the low-resolution image.

The tests were conducted in a Pentium III 600 MHz. The processing time was 380 milliseconds for the first sequence and 350 milliseconds for the second one. This difference results from the fact that the algorithm detected 10 line segments in the first image of the synthetic sequence and only 7 in the TV sequence, as we can see in Fig. 8 (the side lines and goal posts were not detected in the first TV image). This increase in the number of detected segments influences the processing time of the recognition step, increasing the depth of the interpretation tree. Both processing times are well below the time limit for real-time processing. If the desired frame rate is 30 fps, up to 900 milliseconds could be used for processing 27 frames.

10 Conclusions

The algorithm presented here has generated good results even when applied to noisy images extracted from TV. Our goal to obtain an efficient algorithm that could be used in widely available computers was reached. In the hardware platform where the tests were performed the processing time was well below the time needed for real-time processing. The extra time could be used, for example, to draw ads and logos on the field.

11 Future Works

Although the method presented here is capable of performing camera calibration in real time for an image sequence, the sequence resulting from the insertion of new elements in the scene suffers from some degree of jittery, due to fluctuations in the computed camera position and orientation. We intend to investigate processes for smoothing the sequence of cameras by applying Kalman filtering [12] or other related techniques.

Another interesting work is to develop techniques to track other objects moving on the field, such as the ball and the players. We also plan to investigate an efficient algorithm to draw objects on the field behind the players, thus giving the impression that the objects drawn are at grass level and the players seem to walk over them.

12 Acknowledgments

This work was developed in TeCGraf/PUC-Rio and Visgraf/IMPA, and was partially funded by CNPq. TeCGraf is a Laboratory mainly funded by PETROBRAS/CENPES. We are also grateful to Ralph Costa and Dibio Borges for their valuable suggestions.

References

1. Carvalho PCP, Szenberg F, Gattass M. Image-based Modeling Using a Two-step Camera Calibration Method. In: Proceedings of International Symposium on Computer Graphics, Image Processing and Vision, SIBGRAPI'98, Rio de Janeiro, 1998, pp 388-395
2. Faugeras O. Three-Dimensional Computer Vision: a Geometric ViewPoint. MIT

Press, 1993

3. Jain R, Kasturi R, Schunck BG. Machine Vision. McGraw-Hill, 1995

4. Tsai R. An Efficient and Accurate Camera Calibration Technique for 3D Machine Vision. In: Proceedings of IEEE Conference on Computer Vision and Pattern Recognition, Miami Beach, FL, 1986, pp 364-374

5. Grimson WEL. Object Recognition by Computer: The Role of Geometric Constraints. Massachusetts Institute of Technology, MIT Press, 1990

6. Munkelt O, Zierl C. Fast 3-D Object Recognition using Feature Based Aspect-Trees. Technishe Universität München, Institut für Informatik, Germany

7. Nagao K, Grimson WEL. Object Recognition by Alignment using Invariant Projections of Planar Surfaces. MIT, Artificial Intelligence Laboratory, A.I. Memo no. 1463, February, 1994

8. Pla F. Matching Features Points in Image Sequences through a Region-Based Method. In: Computer Vision and Image Understanding, vol. 66, no. 3, June, 1997, pp 271-285

9. Schweitzer H. Computational Limitations of Model Based Recognition. In: http://www.utdallas.edu/~haim/publications/html/modelnpc.html

10. Zeller C, Faugeras O. Camera Self-Calibration from Video Sequences: the Kruppa Equations Revisited, INRIA Sophia Antipolis, Programme 4, Rapport de Recherche no. 2793, Frévrier, 1996

11. Gonzalez RC, Woods RE. Digital Image Processing. Addison-Wesley Publishing Company, 1992

12. Welch G, Bishop G. An Introduction to the Kalman Filter. In: http://www.cs.unc.edu/~welch/media/ps/kalman.ps

Field's Points			Correct Coordinates		Reconstructed Coordinates		Error (Euclidean
x	y	z	u	v	u	v	Distance)
105.0	68.00	0.00	81.707	216.584	81.731	215.972	0.612
88.5	13.84	0.00	230.117	78.133	228.747	77.525	1.499
88.5	54.16	0.00	1.236	183.463	0.424	183.197	0.854
99.5	24.84	0.00	259.039	134.206	258.566	133.815	0.614
99.5	43.16	0.00	146.690	174.826	146.067	174.484	0.711
105.0	30.34	0.00	269.817	155.102	269.629	154.697	0.446
105.0	30.34	2.44	270.921	181.066	270.215	180.863	0.735
105.0	37.66	2.44	224.101	194.645	223.291	194.407	0.845
105.0	37.66	0.00	223.405	170.271	223.082	169.876	0.510
						Average Error	**0.696**

Tab. 1 - Comparison between the correct and reconstructed coordinates for the first scene.

Field's Points			Correct Coordinates		Reconstructed Coordinates		Error (Euclidean
x	y	z	u	v	u	v	Distance)
105.0	68.00	0.00	97.167	205.940	96.791	205.585	0.517
88.5	13.84	0.00	243.883	66.434	243.549	66.022	0.530
88.5	54.16	0.00	16.101	173.174	15.655	172.623	0.709
99.5	24.84	0.00	273.344	124.029	273.125	123.715	0.382
99.5	43.16	0.00	160.672	164.798	160.366	164.421	0.486
105.0	30.34	0.00	284.160	145.173	283.992	144.914	0.309
105.0	30.34	2.44	285.241	171.290	284.886	171.090	0.407
105.0	37.66	2.44	238.127	184.768	237.744	184.538	0.447
105.0	37.66	0.00	237.462	160.349	237.252	160.063	0.355
						Average Error	**0.452**

Tab. 2- Comparison between the correct and reconstructed coordinates for the last scene.

Locating and Tracking Facial Landmarks Using Gabor Wavelet Networks

Rogério S. Feris and Roberto M. Cesar Junior

Department of Computer Science, University of São Paulo,
Rua do Matão, 1010, 05508-900 São Paulo-SP, Brazil
{rferis,cesar}@ime.usp.br

Abstract. A new approach for locating and tracking facial landmarks in video sequences is introduced in this paper. Our method is based on Gabor wavelet networks, an effective technique that represents a discrete face template as a linear combination of 2D Gabor wavelet functions. This wavelet representation allows positioning of facial landmarks (e.g. eyes, nose and mouth), even in the presence of glasses, beard and different facial expressions. The feature tracking is robust to homogeneous illumination changes and affine deformations of the face image. Moreover, the tracking approach considers the overall geometry of the face, thus being robust to deformations such as eye blinking and smile, which is usually a critical situation to most local-based traditional methods.

Keywords: Computer Vision, Facial Feature Tracking, Gabor Wavelets.

1 Introduction

Computational face recognition is an important research problem in computer vision, presenting many applications such as in human-computer interaction, security systems and surveillance. There are two main approaches to face recognition by computers, namely, static and dynamic. While the former is related to recognizing people in still images, the latter addresses the problem of detecting, tracking, extracting information and recognizing moving people in digital video sequences. As far as the problem of tracking a face in a video sequence is concerned, there are three distinct approaches: (1) tracking the whole face region; (2) tracking the head outline (e.g. using active contour models); (3) tracking a set of feature points or facial landmarks, generally defined by the eyes, the nose and the mouth. The last approach presents, among its attractives, the potentiality for allowing faster recognition in real-time applications and the fact of presenting a psychophysical inspiration because of the well-known importance that these landmarks present to human perception. This paper introduces an approach for locating and tracking facial feature points, which has proven to be robust and even suitable for real-time applications.

The technique is based on a recent approach for face representation called Gabor wavelet network (GWN) [1]. The GWN represents the face as a linear combination of 2D Gabor wavelet functions, whose parameters (position,

S. Singh, N. Murshed, and W. Kropatsch (Eds.): ICAPR 2001, LNCS 2013, pp. 311–321, 2001.

scale and orientation) and weights are determined optimally so that the maximum of image information is preserved for a given number of wavelets.

Once that the GWN has been optimized, it can be repositioned with its wavelet parameters undergoing an affine transformation in order to match a target face image. The repositioning procedure is a key concept of this paper, being applied with two different purposes, namely, (1) for locating the facial feature points of the detected face-like blob in an initial frame and (2) for performing facial feature tracking.

Basically, our approach can be divided in three subsequent steps:

- *Face detection*, which is performed automatically by skin-color blob detection [2]. Once that a face-like blob is located, a simple correlation procedure is used to decide whether the blob actually corresponds or not to a true face.
- *Facial feature points positioning*, which is done automatically by matching a GWN,optimized considering a mean face, to the initial face-like blob;
- *Tracking of face and facial feature points* by the GWN. The tracking algorithm may be even executed in real-time. In this case, a suitable number of wavelets in the representation must be chosen with respect to to the available computational resources.

We show that our method is able to locate facial features points even in the presence of glasses, beard, and different facial expressions. The tracking approach is robust to homogeneous illumination changes and affine deformations of the face image. Moreover, since we consider the overall geometry of the face, it is robust to facial feature deformations such as eye blinking and smile.

The remainder of this paper is organized as follows. Section 2 reviews some techniques related to our work. Section 3 introduces the Gabor wavelet networks for face representation and advantages of this technique are discussed. Section 4 is concerned with the repositioning of a GWN, which allows face tracking. In section 5, the positioning of facial landmarks is presented. The facial feature tracking is described in section 6. Experimental results and some discussions are presented in section 7. Finally, section 8 concludes this paper with some remarks on further research directions.

2   Related Work

Many approaches have been proposed to locate and track faces and facial features in video sequences. Recently, color-based systems have been widely used to accomplish this task. For instance, we can cite the work of Jie Yang and Alex Waibel [3], which presents a real-time face tracker based on a statistical skin-color model [4]. Another example is the work of Stiefelhagen and Yang [5], that describes a color-based method for detection and tracking of specific facial features (pupils, nostrils and lipcorners). The use of color to track faces and facial features has advantages such as face pose invariance and real-time processing. On the other hand, this approach is, in general, not robust to illumination changes.

Liyanage Silva et. al. [6] used an edge-based approach to locate and track facial features in image sequences. This method is based on the fact that a higher edge concentration is observed in the center of facial features (eyes, nose and mouth), while slightly outside of such features a less edge concentration is observed. The method is simple but it fails in several situations, such as in the presence of cluttered backgrounds, glasses and hair covering the forehead.

Another different approach is presented in the work of Thomas Maurer and Christoph Malsburg [7], which describes a system for tracking facial features with the elastic graph matching technique. In this method, Gabor filters are applied in some facial feature locations (selected by hand), forming a feature vector, or a jet, for each face position. The face is then modeled as a graph, in which the nodes correspond to the jets and the edges encode face geometrical information. Facial feature tracking is performed by a graph matching procedure in each frame. The main disadvantage of this approach is the high computational cost required.

Our approach uses a wavelet representation for the face image that is even sparser than the Gabor jet representation. Also it differs from the one introduced by Mallat or Daubechies [8,9]. In fact, it is based on a wavelet network concept, which will be explained in the next section.

3   Face Representation Using GWN

Wavelet networks [10], or wavenets, were proposed as an alternative to feedforward neural networks for function approximation. In this section we will show, with basis on the recent work of Kruger and Sommer [1], that this mathematical tool may be used to approximate a discrete face template, providing an effective face representation.

To define a Gabor wavelet network, we start by taking a family of M 2D odd-Gabor wavelet functions $\Psi = \{\psi_{\mathbf{n}_1}, \ldots, \psi_{\mathbf{n}_M}\}$ of the form

$$
\begin{aligned}
\psi_{\mathbf{n}}(x, y) = \exp(-\frac{1}{2}&[s_x((x - c_x)cos\theta - (y - c_y)sin\theta)]^2 \\
&+ [s_y((x - c_x)sin\theta + (y - c_y)cos\theta]^2]) \\
\times\ & sin(s_x((x - c_x)cos\theta - (y - c_y)sin\theta))
\end{aligned}
\tag{1}
$$

with the parameter vector $\mathbf{n} = (c_x, c_y, \theta, s_x, s_y)$, where c_x, c_y denote the translation (position) of the Gabor wavelet, s_x, s_y denote the dilation (scale) and θ denotes the orientation.

In order to obtain a wavelet representation for a face image f, the weights and parameters of each wavelet are determined optimally, by means of a fitting technique, which minimizes the energy function

$$E = \min_{\mathbf{n}_i, w_i \forall i} ||f - (\sum_i w_i \psi_{\mathbf{n}_i} + \bar{f})||_2^2 \tag{2}$$

with respect to the weights $w_i \in R$ and wavelet parameters $\mathbf{n}_i \in R^5$. In the equation above, $\bar{f}$ is the DC-value of f. The Levenberg-Marquard gradient descent method [11] was employed to determine the optimal wavelet network for the face template. The method might get stuck in local minima and a careful selection of the initial parameters is important.

Then, we can say that the two optimized vectors $\mathbf{\Psi} = (\psi_{\mathbf{n}_1}, \dots, \psi_{\mathbf{n}_M})^T$ and $\mathbf{w} = (w_1, \dots, w_M)^T$ define an optimized Gabor Wavelet Network $(\mathbf{\Psi}, \mathbf{w})$ for a specific face image f. The wavelet representation for f may be considered as the reconstruction of the original image and it is given by:

$$\hat{f} = \sum_{i=1}^{M} w_i \psi_{\mathbf{n}_i} + \bar{f} \tag{3}$$

The precision of the face representation is determined by the number M of used wavelets. For instance, if we use a short number of wavelets, we obtain a coarse GWN, which may work well in different individuals and may be suitable for real-time applications. As we increase the number of wavelets, the representation becomes more specific, encoding more precise object information. Another aspect of the GWN representation is that it is invariant to some degree to affine deformations of the face image, as we will see in the next section. Furthermore, since the odd-Gabor Wavelets are DC-free, they are invariant to some degree to homogeneous illumination changes.

The Gabor functions are biologically motivated [12] and provide the best possible tradeoff between spatial and frequency resolution (Heisenberg principle). Besides, they act as good feature detectors, encoding texture and geometrical information in the representation.

Figure 1(a) shows a face template and its discretized representation is illustrated in figure 1(b), which we call the Gabor wavelet template (GWT). This representation was obtained by using a GWN of just $M = 52$ odd-Gabor wavelets, initialized in the inner face region. Figure 1(c) shows the position of the 16 largest wavelets, after optimization.

4   Face matching by the GWN

In the previous section, we have shown how a continuous wavelet representation for a face template is obtained based on a Gabor Wavelet Network. Now, we will see how this representation can match a new face image so that its wavelets are registered on the same facial features as in the original

Fig. 1. (a) The face template. (b) The wavelet representation obtained by the GWN. (c) Position of the 16 largest wavelets.

image. This process, which is called GWN repositioning, is done by applying a suitable affine deformation on the entire wavelet representation. It will be used both for positioning and for tracking the facial landmarks.

For instance, consider the face template shown in figure 1(a) and let G be its optimized GWN. Now, consider this face image in a different pose as shown in figure 2(a). In the repositioning process, the set of wavelets of G are positioned correctly on the same facial features in the distorted image. It is important to emphasize that the GWN repositioning may determine the parameters (translation, scale, rotation and shearing) of any affine deformation applied to the original image. Figure 2(b) shows the repositioned discrete face template representation (GWT), with 52 odd-Gabor wavelet functions. Figure 2(c) illustrates the position of the 16 largest wavelets of G in the image.

Fig. 2. (a) Face template in a different pose. (b) Repositioned wavelet representation. (c) Position of the 16 largest wavelets.

The repositioning of a GWN in a new image, i.e., the determination of the correct affine parameters, is established by using a superwavelet [13]. Let $\Psi = (\psi_{\mathbf{n}_1}, \ldots, \psi_{\mathbf{n}_M})$, $\mathbf{w} = (w_1, \ldots, w_M)$ be an optimized GWN. A Gabor superwavelet $\Psi_{\mathbf{n}}$ (GSW) may be defined as a linear combination of the wavelets $\psi_{\mathbf{n}_i}$ such that

$$\Psi_{\mathbf{n}}(\mathbf{x}) = \sum_i w_i \psi_{\mathbf{n}_i}(\mathbf{SR}(\mathbf{x} - \mathbf{c})) \tag{4}$$

where the parameters of vector $\mathbf{n}$ of the GSW Ψ define the dilation matrix $\mathbf{S}$, the rotation matrix $\mathbf{R}$ and the translation vector $\mathbf{c}$ with:

$$\mathbf{S} = \begin{pmatrix} s_x & 0 \\ 0 & s_y \end{pmatrix}, \mathbf{R} = \begin{pmatrix} cos\theta & -sin\theta \\ sin\theta & cos\theta \end{pmatrix}, \mathbf{c} = (c_x, c_y)^T.$$

Thus, a Gabor superwavelet $\Psi_{\mathbf{n}}$ is again a wavelet that has the typical parameters, i.e. dilation s_x, s_y, translation c_x, c_y and rotation θ. So, for a given new image g, we may arbitrarily deform the superwavelet by optimizing its parameter vector $\mathbf{n}$ so that the wavelet representation matches the face in image g. This is done by minimizing the energy function below, using the Levenberg-Marquard algorithm:

$$E = \min_{\mathbf{n}} ||g - \Psi_{\mathbf{n}}||_2^2 \tag{5}$$

It is important to note that the parameters of a wavelet include only translation, dilation and rotation. Even so, we may include shearing and thus allow any affine deformation of GSW $\Psi_{\mathbf{n}}$. For this, we add the parameter s_{xy} to vector $\mathbf{n}$ and rewrite the scaling matrix:

$$\mathbf{S} = \begin{pmatrix} s_x & s_{xy} \\ 0 & s_y \end{pmatrix}.$$

5   Locating Facial Landmarks

In this section, we address the problem of locating facial landmarks by using the GWN repositioning procedure described in the previous section. Our experiments were carried out on the Yale face database (http://cvc.yale.edu/projects/yalefaces/yalefaces.html), which consists of 15 different subjects with 11 images per person, showing different gestures. Because the database contains only grey-level images, we segmented the face region by hand. Experiments with color images and automatic face detection will be presented in the next section.

When we optimize a coarse GWN (with a short number of wavelets) on a face template, we obtain a wavelet representation that may be repositioned in different individuals. According to our experiments, the repositioning procedure never fails when the target face image is obtained from the same person with different facial expressions in which the GWN was optimized. However, we can not guarantee that a coarse GWN optimized considering a specific individual can always be repositioned in any person. The repositioning process depends heavily on the similarity between the person in which the GWN was optimized and the test person as well as on the number of used wavelets.

The solution that we propose for this problem is to optimize the GWN considering a mean face. We have normalized and averaged a set of 15 faces of the Yale database, corresponding each one to a different individual.

Using the GWN optimized considering this mean face, the repositioning worked well on all individual images of the Yale database. We are now investigating how to address the repositioning problem in any person considering very large face databases.

The proposed method for locating facial landmarks is now described. Initially, facial feature points are located in the mean face. We have considered the pupils, center of nose and center of mouth. Then, the GWN related to the mean face is repositioned in the target face image. In order to determine the facial landmarks in the test face image, we apply a suitable affine transformation to the initial facial feature points of the mean face. The correct parameters of this transformation are obtained from the superwavelet parameter vector $(s_x, s_y, s_{xy}, c_x, c_y, \theta)$, which is determined by equation (5) in the repositioning process.

The obtained results show the robustness of the method. Figure 3 illustrates the positioning of facial landmarks in three individuals of the Yale database. It is worth saying that the method may work even in the presence of glasses and beard. Furthermore, figure 4 illustrates the results considering face images of the same person under different expressions and illumination changes. Section 7 presents more discussions about this technique.

Fig. 3. Facial landmarks positioning in different individuals.

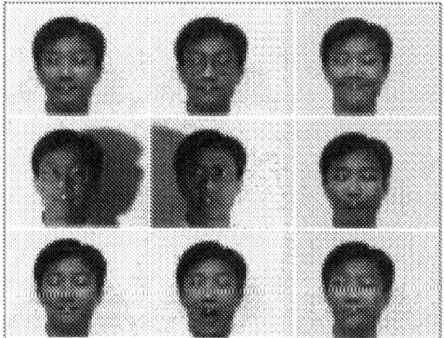

Fig. 4. Facial feature positioning under different expressions and illumination changes.

6   Tracking Facial Features

The GWN repositioning described in section 4 may be applied to an image sequence, allowing affine face tracking. Thus, for each frame J_t at time step t, the Gabor superwavelet $\Psi_{\mathbf{n}_t}$ is optimized according to the energy function:

$$E = \min_{\mathbf{n}_t} ||J_t - \Psi_{\mathbf{n}_t}||_2^2 \tag{6}$$

The parameter vector $\mathbf{n}_{t-1}$ is used as initial value for optimization in the frame J_t. As image changes are small from frame to frame, the optimization process converges quickly. Initial values for $\mathbf{n}_0$ in the first frame are derived from a color blob information.

Our tracking method assumes that the facial landmarks have been correctly determined in the first frame of the sequence, as described in the previous section. We then apply, in each frame, the suitable affine transformation to the located feature points, performing facial landmark tracking. The parameters of the affine transformation are obtained by means of the superwavelet parameter vector in each frame of the sequence.

It is important to emphasize that the procedure to track facial landmarks considers the overall face geometry, thus being robust to deformations such as eye blinking and smile, which is usually a critical situation to most local-based traditional approaches. It is also important to note that the introduced approach can be straighforwardly generalized in order to track additional feature points or even regions, such as arbitrary polygons around the eyes, nose and mouth.

7   Experiments and Discussion

As discussed in section 1, our approach can be divided in three subsequent steps: face detection, facial landmarks positioning and tracking of face and facial landmarks. The first step is performed by a skin-color approach as well as by a simple correlation procedure to verify the presence of a face in the located skin-blob [2]. Once the face was detected, its scale information is obtained and the color face region is converted to a grey-level image. Facial landmarks are then located by repositioning a GWN into the face region. The position and scale of the face-like blob are used as initial parameters in the repositioning procedure. Finally, face and facial landmarks are tracked along the video sequence as described in the previous section.

We have tested our method in different color video sequences, obtaining good results (http://www.ime.usp.br/~rferis). Figure 5 shows, in the left illustration, the detection of a face in the initial frame. The right illustration shows the facial landmarks positioning, which was achieved by repositioning the GWN optimized considering the mean face of the Yale database. Tracking of regions around the facial landmarks (eyes, nose and mouth) is illustrated in figure 6, which presents the frames 60, 98 and 221 of a specific video sequence. Note that the method is robust to eye blinking, homogeneous illumination changes and different facial expressions. We are still verifying the performance of the system so that future work will cover more experimental results as well as comparison with other systems.

Concerning facial landmarks positioning, our method has basically two limitations. The first one is related to GWN repositioning, for this procedure may fail when large databases are involved. The second limitation is derived from the fact that the distance among facial features varies from person to person. This may lead to imprecise facial landmarks location in some cases. So, it would be interesting to have another procedure that could adjust the position of the selected facial feature points after the GWN repositioning. These topics belong to our ongoing research work.

The tracking of facial landmarks may be imprecise under strong 3D face pose variation. On the other hand, it showed to be robust and even suitable for real-time applications, when a small number of wavelets is considered in the representation. We intend to use this approach for face recognition from video sequences.

Fig. 5. Locating a face and its facial landmarks.

Fig. 6. Tracking eyes, nose and mouth.

8   Conclusions

This paper described a method for locating and tracking facial landmarks using Gabor Wavelet Networks. The method is based on a continuous wavelet representation of a discrete face template, which is invariant to some degree to illumination changes and affine deformations of the face image.

The obtained results confirmed the robustness of the method. Positioning of facial landmarks in the initial frame may be accomplished even in the presence of glasses, beard and different facial expressions. The tracking approach considers the overall geometry of the face so that it is robust to facial feature deformations such as eye blinking and smile. As future work, we intend to use the GWN to perform face detection.

Acknowledgements

Roberto M. Cesar Junior is grateful to FAPESP for the financial support (98/07722-0 and 99/12765-2), to "pro-reitoria de pesquisa" and to "pro-reitoria de pós-graduação" - USP, as well as to CNPq (300722/ 98-2). Rogerio Feris is grateful to FAPESP (99/01487-1).

We are grateful to Volker Kruger for providing the source code of GWN technique and for discussions. Some images in the paper were derived from the Yale face database.

References

1. Kruger V. and Sommer G. (1999) Affine real-time face tracking using a wavelet network. Proceedings of ICCV'99 Workshop Recognition, Analysis, and Tracking of Faces and Gestures in Real-Time Systems, Corfu, Greece.
2. Feris R., Campos T. and Cesar R. (2000) Detection and tracking of facial features in video sequences. Lecture Notes in Artificial Intelligence, vol. 1793, pp. 127-135, Springer-Verlag.
3. Yang J. and Waibel A. (1996) A real-time face tracker. Proceedings of the Third IEEE Workshop on Applications of Computer Vision, pp. 142-147, Sarasota, Florida.
4. Yang J., Lu W. and Waibel A. (1997) Skin-color modeling and adaptation. CMU CS Technical Report, CMU-CS-97-146.
5. Stiefelhagen R. and Yang J. (1996) Gaze tracking for multimodal human computer interaction. University of Karlsruhe. Available at http://werner.ira.uka.de/ ISL.multimodal.publications.html
6. Silva L., Aizawa K. and Hatori M. (1995) Detection and tracking of facial features. Proceedings of SPIE Visual Communications and Image Processing, Taiwan.
7. Maurer T. and Malsburg C. (1996) Tracking and learning graphs and pose on image sequences of faces. Proceedings of Int. Conf. on Artificial Neural Networks, Bochum.
8. Mallat S. (1989) A theory for multiresolution signal decomposition: the wavelet representation. IEEE Trans. Pattern Analysis and Machine Intelligence, 11(7):674-693.
9. Daubechies I. (1990) The wavelet transform, time-frequency localization and signal analysis. IEEE Trans. Informat. Theory, 36(5):961-1004.
10. Zhang Q. and Benviste A. (1992) Wavelet networks. IEEE Trans. on Neural Networks, 3(6):889-898.
11. Press W., Flannery B., Teukolsky S. and Vetterling W. (1986) Numerical Recipes, The Art of Scientific Computing, Cambridge University Press, UK.
12. Daugman J. (1985) Uncertainty relation for resolution in space, spatial frequency, and orientation optimized two-dimensional visual cortical filters. Journal Opt. Soc. Am., 2(7):1160-1168.
13. Szu H., Telfer B. and Kadambe S. (1992) Neural network adaptive wavelets for signal representation and adaptation. Optical Engineering, 31(9):1907-1961.

Complex Images and Complex Filters: A Unified Model for Encoding and Matching Shape and Colour

Terry Caelli[1] and Andrew McCabe[1]

Department of Computing Science, The University of Alberta, Edmonton, Canada, T6G 2H1

Abstract. In many practical areas of visual pattern recognition the images are complex-valued. Examples include images generated from 2-dimensional colour, motion, radar and laser sensors. To this date the majority of encoding and matching schemes for such images do not treat the complex nature of the data in a unified way but, rather, separate the associated "channels" and combine them *after* processing each image attribute. In this paper we describe a technique which utilizes properties of the complex Fourier transform of complex images and develop new types of complex filters for colour and shape specific feature extraction and pattern matching. Results are encouraging particularly under quite noisy conditions.

Keywords: Spatio-chromatic filtering, colour encoding, complex Fourier transorm, complex images.

1 Introduction

Many current sensors generate complex-valued images in so far as the pixels have both an amplitude and a phase (angle) component. Examples include motion (velocity and direction), radar and laser (amplitude and phase properties of the received signal), and colour (hue and saturation). In this paper we focus on the area of colour vision though our results apply to any complex image. For colour, past approaches to encoding, filtering and matching features in such images have typically separated "colour" from "shape" or "texture" and more often than not treated the spatial characteristics of each colour channel separately. Examples abound in the image database retrieval areas where these attributes are typically treated separately: colour being a first-order (pixel) attribute and shape being second-order [1,2].

To overcome this limitation, in recent years a number of authors have proposed models for the extraction of features which encode specific types of spatial distributions and correlations of colours over space [3–6]. In this paper we extend this work to consider what we term the Spatio-Chromatic Fourier Transform (SCFT) whereby both colour and shape can be seamlessly encoded by one transform theory to result in a single class of filters and complex-valued correlation functions. What differentiates our approach from

S. Singh, N. Murshed, and W. Kropatsch (Eds.): ICAPR 2001, LNCS 2013, pp. 321–330, 2001.

previous ones (see, for example, [5]) is that we have derived an interpretation for the complex frequencies, filtering and correlations processes associated with such transforms [7].

To understand the SCFT it is necessary to understand how the complex-valued positive and negative frequencies actually contribute to the *generation* of the basis functions (gratings)[1]. For a real-valued input image, $f(p,q)$, the complex-valued Fourier transform is defined by:

$$F(P,Q) = \sum_{p=-\frac{N}{2}+1}^{\frac{N}{2}} \sum_{q=-\frac{N}{2}+1}^{\frac{N}{2}} f(p,q) \exp(-j2\pi(pP+qQ)/N) \tag{1}$$

where (P,Q) correspond to spatial frequencies, (p,q) to the complex image coordinates defined over an $N \times N$ grid. First, we note that each spatial frequency grating is generated with respect to an angle whose initial value is defined by the phase of the grating. We can then consider the positive frequency (P,Q) modulation to be generated by a clockwise rotation of angle, and the corresponding negative frequency $(F(-P,-Q))$ to be generated by an anticlockwise rotation. In general, then, the resultant of these two rotations is a harmonic motion which can be real, imaginary or, in general, complex. For real-valued input images, the resultant (harmonic motion) is real-valued as the amplitudes $(A(P,Q) = A(-P,-Q))$ are equal and phase angles are opposite $(\theta(P,Q) = -\theta(-P,-Q))$. However, for complex-valued inputs this is not the case and the resultant harmonic motion which describes how the positive and negative frequencies are combined is, in general, elliptical.

The key to applying this complex transformation to colour is that we can interpret these resultant elliptical harmonic motions in terms of the locus of hue and saturation changes (in complex colour space) along a given spatial frequency grating. Consequently, the Spatio-Chromatic Fourier transform (SCFT) requires a chromaticity model — for example the CIE 1976 $u'v'$ Chromaticity space [8]. Although the exact chromaticity model used is not critical to the theory, it should be chosen to suit the application and equipment (display) available. Again, the important aspect of this process is that chromaticity should be a two-dimensional quantity defined in a complex plane. A transformation into the CIE 1976 chromaticity $u'v'$ space is performed from the tri-stimulus values XYZ. These, in turn, are produced using a transformation matrix suitable for HDTV and the D_{65} white point. The $u'v'$ values are then rotated by $\pi/30$ radians in order to align the u' axis with the red-green orientation and the v' axis with the yellow-blue orientation in colour space.

---

[1] Since the lower part of the Fourier transform of real-valued inputs is redundant, we typically do not consider its role in generating the amplitude modulations for each component grating.

A 2D complex Fourier transform is then performed using the u' and v' components for the complex colour input image:

$$U(P,Q) + jV(P,Q) =$$

$$\sum_{p=-\frac{N}{2}+1}^{\frac{N}{2}} \sum_{q=-\frac{N}{2}+1}^{\frac{N}{2}} (u'(p,q) + jv'(p,q)) \exp(-2\pi j(Pp + Qq)/N). \qquad (2)$$

Here (p,q) corresponds to the spatial coordinates (pixels) of a square $(N \times N)$ image while $(u'(p,q), v'(p,q))$ represent the complex chromaticity coordinates at point (p,q) in the image. (P,Q) correspond to the spatial frequency gratings measured in picture cycles or cycles/pixel. The values of (U,V) correspond to the real and imaginary values occurring at the spatial frequency (P,Q) which, in this case, determines how the colour and saturation spatially change over the grating in the image forming basis functions which appear like "rainbow gratings". Figure 1 shows examples of different (opponent) colour paths which are straight line transitions at 0, $\pi/4$, $\pi/2$ and $3\pi/4$ to the u' axes, of which two are red-green and blue-yellow paths. That is, as the spatial frequency grating is generated over increments in angle, the colour positions generated by the vector sum of the motions in clockwise and anticlockwise directions result in harmonic motion between opponent colours in $u'v'$ colour.

Images are then constructed by the corresponding inverse Fourier transform defined by:

$$u'(p,q) + jv'(p,q) =$$

$$\sum_{P=-\frac{N}{2}+1}^{\frac{N}{2}} \sum_{Q=-\frac{N}{2}+1}^{\frac{N}{2}} (U(P,Q) + jV(P,Q)) \exp(2\pi j(Pp + Qq)/N). \qquad (3)$$

This representation allows us to generate spatial frequencies with modulations operating in either the red-green or yellow-blue colour opponency paths ("channels") in colour space. Again, it must be emphasized that the above discussion is solely focused on how to modulate the spatial frequency components with complex hue-saturation values. These amplitude (saturation) and phase (hue) values are independent of, but in addition to, the underlying spatial frequency amplitude and phase values. In all, then, the complete (hue, saturation) image is synthesized by sets of spatial frequency gratings, each of which is determined *spatially:* by frequency, orientation and phase and *chromatically:* by the four components of the two complex numbers corresponding to the positive and negative frequency values and resulting in the "rainbow" grating basis functions as illustrated in Fig. 1. All these properties are determined via one complex Fourier transform. These basis functions encode the distribution of colour over an image which, in turn, encodes shapes and textures by the attributes of the image colour contrasts.

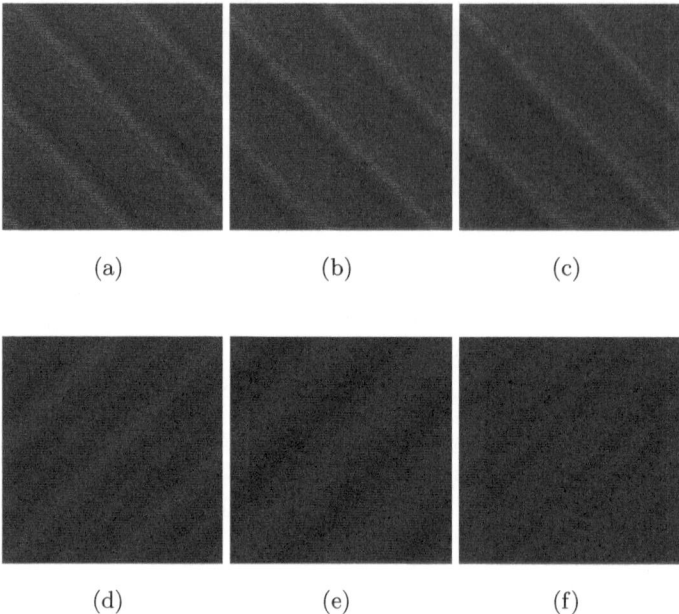

Fig. 1. Spatio-chromatic spatial frequency gratings defined at one spatial frequency (U, V two cycles/image: $2, 2$ top and $-2, 2$ bottom), with different values of $U(P,Q), V(P,Q), U(-P,-Q)$ and $V(-P,-Q)$. Top row shows rotation-type modulations in colour space while bottom row shows straight line composite rotations in the colour domain (see text for details)

Given this interpretation of the Fourier components for an input hue-saturation image, we can then consider how spatio-chromatic filtering and matching may apply.

2   Filtering complex images

Here we consider Gaussian filters, although all classes and filter profiles may be applied as well as equivalent wavelet formulations. For a complex input image f and filter h, and complex output g, let $g = f * h$, where $*$ denotes convolution. and H corresponds to its Fourier transform, we have:

$$H(P,Q) = A_{H(P,Q)} \exp(-j\theta_{H(P,Q)}). \tag{4}$$

Fully complex spatio-chromatic filters incorporate both real and imaginary values in the transfer function $H(P,Q)$. Such a filter can have many types of outputs ranging from purely real to purely imaginary resulting in chromatic rotations (phase alterations) from $\pi/2$ to $-\pi/2$ through to chromatic de-saturation (amplitude scaling).

An interesting property of these complex spatio-chromatic filters is that their point spread functions (PSF) can apply to both opponent colour dimensions — in this case red-green and blue-yellow axes of colour space. This is illustrated in Fig. 2. Here we have used red-green Gaussian bandpass filters at two differing orientations having the point spread functions (psf) shown in Figs. 2(b) and 2(f). The orientation of the vertical filter (Fig. 2(b)) only aligns with the top region of the input image (Fig. 2(a)). The real and imaginary filter responses in Figs. 2(c) and 2(d) demonstrate this dual opponency filter response property where the real output matches the filter in colour (red-green) and orientation while the imaginary matches the dual opponent colour (yellow-blue) and orientation. Identical dual (conjugate) responses occur with the oblique filter, as shown in Figs. 2(g) and 2(h).

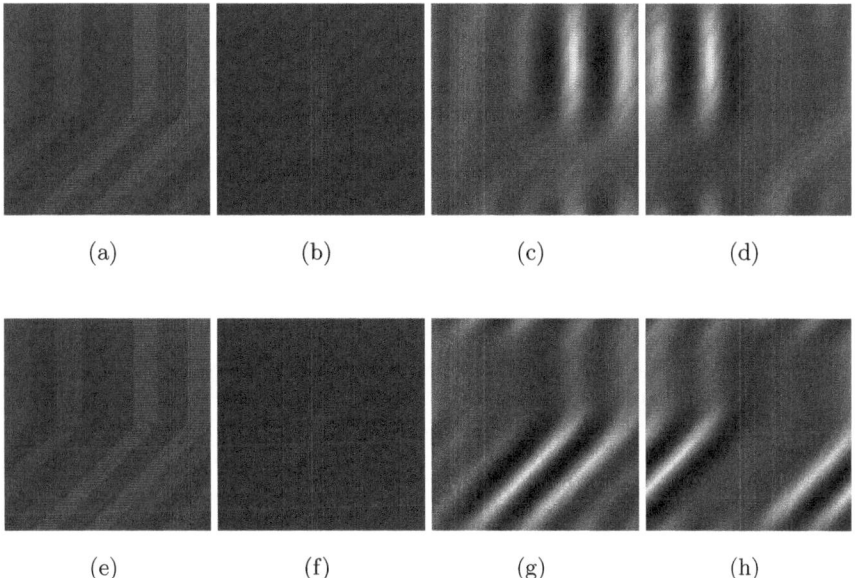

(a)	(b)	(c)	(d)
(e)	(f)	(g)	(h)

Fig. 2. Convolution-based filtering using oriented opponent filters. (a, e) input image; (b, f) oriented red-center green-surround point spread functions; convolution results: (c, g) real components, (d, h) imaginary components. Notice the response colour opponency relationship between real and imaginary outputs

From this example it is clear that this model allows us to create *linear filters* which are selectively sensitive to specific combinations of colour and shape: spatio-chromatic features defined by specific distributions of colour over space.

3   Spatio-Chromatic Correlation Functions

Cross-correlation is typically used for template matching [9,10]. The SCFT enables us to use one single cross-correlation operation to define and detect structures defined by shape and colour by employing a single complex cross-correlation operation. Again, it should be noted that in this context "colour" refers to properties of the spatial distribution of colour over the image and not just the properties of individual pixels.

Cross-correlation using Fourier methods involves the multiplication of the image by the complex conjugate of the template and then computing the inverse Fourier transform of this product to result in the cross-correlation (complex, in this case) image. Existing models and processes typically do not interpret or utilize the imaginary component of this output. We show that this imaginary output component from the cross-correlation can be interpreted as a (dual colour) conjugacy measure: the degree to which a given spatial distribution of colours in an image region are of dual opponent colour contrasts to a template. Two regions would be positively or negatively conjugate to a template if, for example, every occurrence of a given spatial distribution of red-green in the template had a corresponding blue-yellow or yellow-blue distribution in the image.

This results in four types of "matches":

- correlated — same shape and colours (+ similarity),
- negatively correlated — same shape and opposite colours, for example, red-green to green-red (- similarity),
- positive conjugacy — same spatial distributions as the template but with dual opponent colour contrasts, for example, red-green to yellow-blue (+ conjugacy) and
- negative conjugacy — same spatial distributions as the template but with dual opposite opponent colour contrasts, for example, red-green to blue-yellow (- conjugacy).

Zero matching values on both direct or conjugate colour dimensions indicate the lack of correlation between a template and an image region: the absence of a systematic relation with respect to shapes/textures and/or colour contrast distributions between the template and image region. (These relations are illustrated in Fig. 3(d)).

When summed over a large set of vector pairs, as occurs in the cross-correlation operation, these measures determine the degree to which the spatio-chromatic template is "parallel" (similar) and "orthogonal" (dual colour conjugates) to each region of the image which is being matched. This means that both measures can be somewhat reciprocal as the degree of colour densities lie on one of the two opponent colour axes. However, as the spatio-chromatic relationship between template and image region become less correlated in shape or colour (with respect to either opponent colour axes) these similarity measures converge to zero. As with the real-only case, these properties are derived from an extension of the Cauchy-Schwarz inequality (Equation 5) to both real and imaginary terms as:

$$\left(\sum_{k=1}^{n} a_k b_k \right)^2 \leq \left(\sum_{k=1}^{n} a_k^2 \right) \left(\sum_{k=1}^{n} b_k^2 \right) \tag{5}$$

where

$$|A \cdot B| \leq |A||B| \text{ with equality iff } A = \lambda B. \tag{6}$$

This is extended to the "conjugate matching" measure:

$$|A \times B^*| \leq |A||B^*| \text{ again, with equality iff } A = \lambda B^*. \tag{7}$$

3.1   Examples

The Mondrian test image (Fig. 3) demonstrates these measures at each pixel. The image (Fig. 3(a)) is cross-correlated with a central vertical orange-green patch (Fig. 3(b)) removed from the original. The results demonstrate that similar (correlated) oriented coloured regions only occur at two places within the original: a region at the top left, and also near the image center. The pseudo-coloured output image (Fig. 3(c)) provides a highlight in both these regions (in bright red). Fig. 3(d) shows the pseudo-colouring we have used to portray the results of such measures on the outputs of the cross-correlator. As can be seen there are no cases where there is a reversal of colour over the edge (green-orange as opposed to orange-green) and so there is no "green" in the pseudo-coloured output.

The next sequence of images has been produced as a practical example of spatio-chromatic pattern recognition. In this case we have considered the problem of matching the colour, shape and textures necessary to identify specific bank notes. Four bank notes have been combined into one image as shown in Fig. 4(a). As in the previous example, a template is selected by cutting out a region of this image (Fig. 4(b)) and using it as a template in a matching operation. The resultant pseudo-coloured cross-correlation image is shown in Fig. 4(c). Here it is clear that the removed template region results in the highest similarity match ("red"), and that other regions produce quite high conjugate similarity measures.

The second bank note example (Fig. 4(d)) uses uncorrelated (across colour channels) additive Gaussian noise to totally obscure the shapes embedded in the noise from human detection. That is, the Gaussian noise was independently generated and applied to each band of the original RGB image. The σ for each colour channel was set at 32 out of a total range of ± 128 grey-level values out of a dynamic range of 256 (8-bit) values. The success of this matched filtering (cross-correlation) operation can be seen in Fig. 5 where the template is detected.

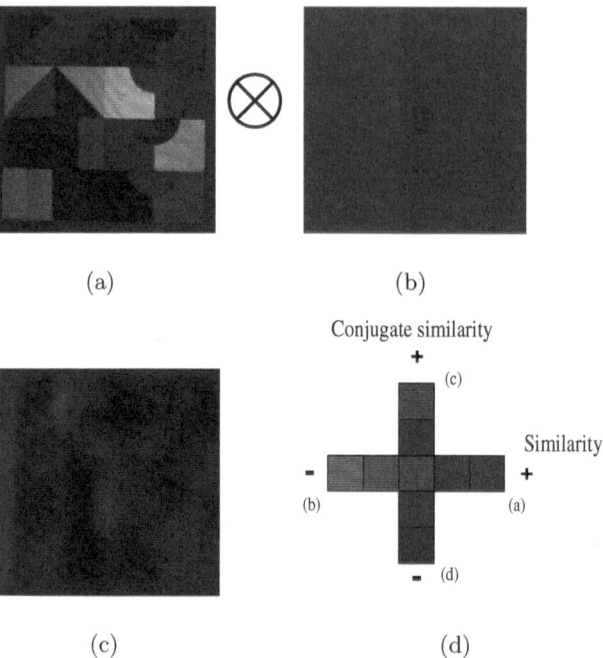

Fig. 3. Cross-correlation using the Mondrian test image. (a) input image, (b) small section of input image, (c) pseudo-coloured cross-correlation result and (d) pseudo-coloured indicator for types of complex correlations (see text for details)

4   Conclusions

We have shown how it is possible integrate colour and shape encoding into one singular Fourier transform, filter and matching model. In this theory images are decomposed into spatio-chromatic spatial frequency gratings ("rainbow gratings") which can include many different colour modulations over space as a function of their spatial frequencies and phase. A new type of image filtering was demonstrated using complex filters as well as traditional, purely real filters. Complex cross-correlation was also considered which produced a similarity measure in the real variable and a conjugate similarity measure in the imaginary variable. The robustness of the matching techniques was demonstrated with surprising success when applied to noisy images where the signal was not detectable by humans under normal observation conditions but easily found via the spatio-chromatic cross-correlation operation. Though not fully discussed here, it is clear that the theory can also be applied to the development of complex wavelets as a generalization of the oriented complex gaussian red-green point spread functions shown in Fig. 2. Such a unified

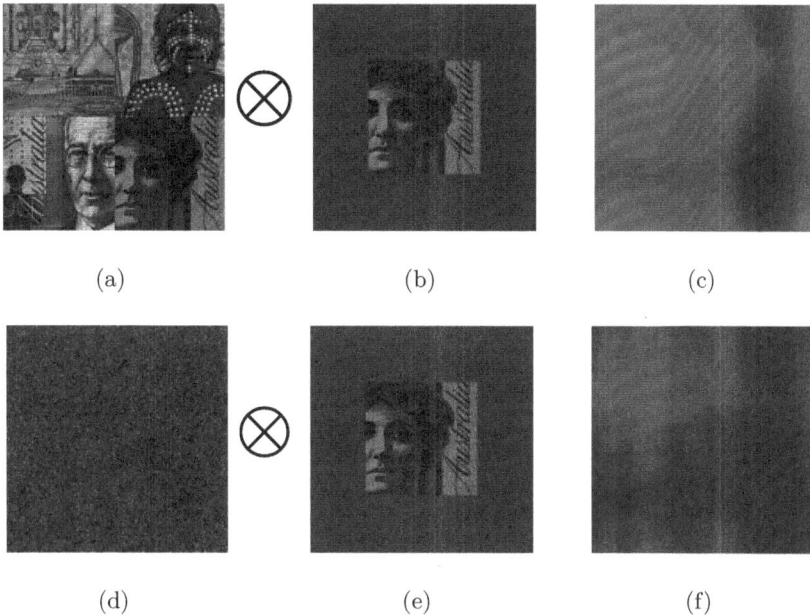

Fig. 4. Bank note examples showing (a) input template containing four images, (b) input image to be matched, (c) pseudo-coloured correlation result (d) input image (same as (a) with noise added), (e) input image to be matched and (f) pseudo-coloured correlation result (see Fig. 3(d) for pseudo-colour code)

approach to the encoding of shape and colour offers an alternative to the current practice of keeping both attributes of images separate for retrieval, recognition and identification of structures.

The theory can also be applied to many other complex signals like motion (flow) fields, orientation-edge maps and other types of complex images such as radar, laser and ultrasound. Finally, what is interesting to note is that although what is being coded and detected here is quite relational and multi-dimensional it can be performed using standard FFT algorithms and hardware.

References

1. M. Das, E. M. Riseman, and B. A. Draper. Focus: Searching for multi-colored objects in a diverse image. In *Compter Vision and Pattern Recognition 97*, pages 756–761, 1997.
2. J. Huang, S. R. Kumar, M. Mitra, W. Zhu, and R. Zabih. Image indexing using color correlograms. In *Computer Vision and Pattern Recognition 97*, pages 762–768, 1997.

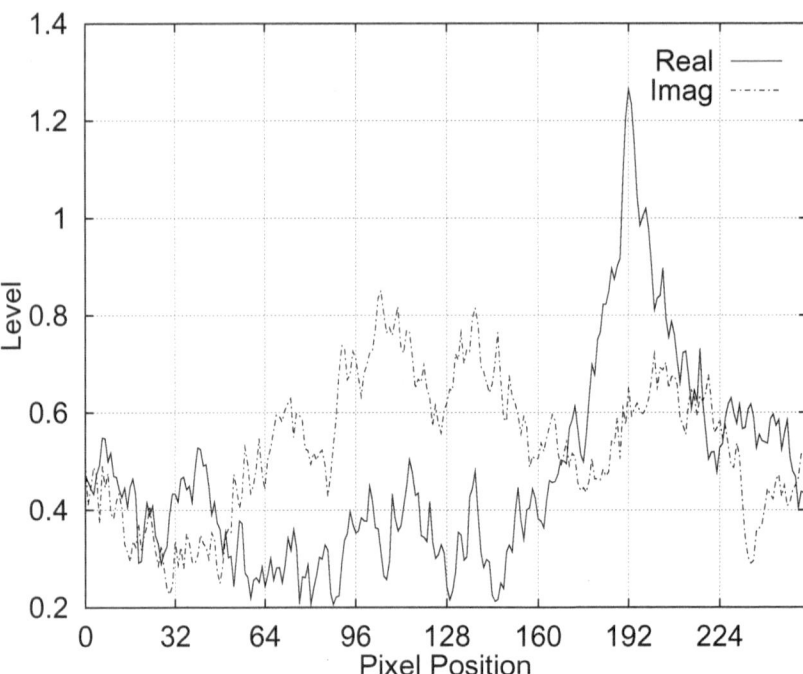

Fig. 5. Bank note detection under significant additive noise (Figs. 4(d & e)). Matching results showing cross-sectional plot through resultant image showing real component peak

3. C. J. Evans, S. J. Sangwine, and T. A. Ell. Hypercomplex color-sensitive smoothing filters. In *IEEE International Conference on Image Processing*, volume 1, pages 541–544, September 2000.
4. D. Carevic and T. Caelli. Region-based coding of colour images using Karhunen-Loève transform. *Graphical Models and Image Processing*, 59(1):27–38, 1997.
5. S. J. Sangwine. Fourier transforms of colour images using quaternion or hypercomplex numbers. *Electronics Letters*, 32(21):1979–1980, 1996.
6. T. Caelli and D. Reye. On the classification of image regions by colour, texture and shape. *Pattern Recognition*, 26(4):461–470, 1993.
7. A. McCabe, T. Caelli, G. West, and A. Reeves. A theory of spatio-chromatic image encoding and feature extraction. *The Journal of the Optical Society of America A.*, 2000. In Press.
8. CIE. Colorimetry. Technical Report 15.2 - 1986, CIE - International Commission on Illumination, Vienna, 1986. Second edition 1996.
9. J. D. Gaskill. *Linear Systems, Fourier Transforms and Optics*. John Wiley & Sons, New York, 1978.
10. Jae S. Lim. *Two-dimensional Signal and Image Processing*. Prentice-Hall Inc., New Jersey, 1990.

White Matter/Gray Matter Boundary Segmentation Using Geometric Snakes: A Fuzzy Deformable Model

Jasjit S. Suri

Magnetic Resonance Clinical Science Division, Marconi Medical Systems, Inc., Cleveland, OH 44143, USA

Abstract

This paper presents a fast region-based level set approach for extraction of white matter (WM), gray matter (GM) and cerebrospinal fluid (CSF) boundaries from two dimensional magnetic resonance slices of the human brain. The raw contour was placed inside the image, which was later pushed or pulled towards the convoluted brain topology. The forces in the level set approach used three kinds of speed control functions based on region, edge and curvature. Regional speed functions were determined based on the fuzzy membership function computed using the fuzzy clustering technique, while the edge and curvature speed functions were based on gradient and signed distance transform functions, respectively. The level set algorithm was implemented to run in the "narrow band" using a "fast marching method." The system was tested on synthetic convoluted shapes, and real magnetic resonance images of the human brain. The entire system took around a minute to estimate the WM/GM boundaries on XP1000 running Linux Operating System, when the raw contour was placed half way from its goal. The system took a few seconds if the raw contour was placed closed to the goal boundary which resulted with one hundred percent accuracy.

1 Introduction

The role of shape recovery has always been a critical component in 2-D and 3-D medical imagery since it assists largely in medical therapy (see the recent book by Suri *et al.* [1] and references therein). The applications of shape recovery have been increasing since scanning methods became faster, more accurate, and less artifacted (see the Chapter 4 by Suri *et al.* in [1]). Shape recovery of medical organs is more difficult compared to other computer vision and imaging fields. This is primarily due to the large shape variability, structure complexity, several kinds of artifacts and restrictive (scanning ability limited to acquiring in three orthogonal and oblique directions only) body scanning methods. In spite of the above complications, we have started to explore faster and more accurate software tools for shape recovery in 2-D and 3-D applications.

Deformations play a critical role in shape representation and this paper uses level sets as its tool to capture deforming shapes in medical imagery. In fact, the research in deformation started in the late 1980's when the paper called "snakes" (first class of deformable models) was published by Terzopoulous and co-workers (see Kass *et al.* [2]). Since then, there has been an extensive burst of publications in the area of parametric deformable models and their improvements. For details on the majority of the parametric deformable model papers, see the recently published paper by Suri [3] and the references there in. The discussions of these references are out of the scope in this paper. The second class of deformable models is level sets. These deformable models were begun by Osher and Sethian [4] which started from Sethian's Ph.D. thesis [5]. The

S. Singh, N. Murshed, and W. Kropatsch (Eds.): ICAPR 2001, LNCS 2013, pp. 331–338, 2001.
© Springer-Verlag Berlin Heidelberg 2001

fundamental difference between these two classes is: Parametric methods are based on energy minimization, while level sets methods are based on curvature dependent speeds of curves/fronts. Those familiar in the field of deformable models using parametric models will appreciate the major advantages and superiority of level sets compared to classical deformable models. We will, however, cover these briefly in this paper also.

The application of level sets in medical imaging was attempted by Sethian and his coworkers (see the works by Malladi *et al.* [6], [7]). The work done above uses a non-robust method of computing the speed at which the curve propagation happens. The earlier methods do not take advantage of the regional based statistics in the level set framework for curve propagation for WM/GM boundary estimation. This paper presents a fast region-based level set system (so-called geometric snakes[1] based on regions) for extraction of white matter (WM), gray matter (GM) and cerebrospinal fluid (CSF) boundaries from the two dimensional magnetic resonance images of the human brain.

The layout of this paper is as follows: Section 2 presents the derivation of geometric snakes from parametric models. The methodology and the segmentation system are presented in section 3. The same section also contains the numerical implementation of geometric snakes. The results are presented in section 4. Finally, the paper concludes by discussing the advantages and superiority of this method in section 5.

2   Derivation of the Regional Geometric Active Contour Model From the Classical Parametric Deformable Model

Parametric Snake Model: In this section, we derive the level set equation by embedding the region statistics into the parametric classical energy model. This method is in the spirit of Xu's *et al.* [8] attempt. We will discuss part of that derivation here. To start with, the standard dynamic classical energy model as given by Kass *et al.* [2] was:

$$\gamma \frac{\partial X}{\partial t} = \underbrace{\frac{\partial}{\partial s}(\alpha \frac{\partial X}{\partial s}) - \frac{\partial^2}{\partial s^2}(\beta \frac{\partial^2 X}{\partial s^2})}_{internal-energy} + \underbrace{F_{ext}(X)}_{external-energy} \quad , \tag{1}$$

where X is the parametric contour and γ was the damping coefficient. As seen in Eq. 1, the classical energy model constitutes an energy-minimizing spline guided by external and image forces that pulled the spline towards features such as lines and edges in the image. The energy-minimizing spline was named "snakes" because the spline softly and quietly moved while minimizing the energy term. The internal energy is composed of two terms: the first term was the first order derivative of the parametric curve which acts like a membrane, and the second term was the second derivative of the parametric curve which acts as a thin plate (so-called the pressure force). These terms were controlled by the elastic constants α and β. The second part of the classical energy model constitutes the external force given by $F_{ext}(X)$. This external energy term depended upon image forces which was a function of image gradient. Parametric snakes had flexibility to dynamically control the movements, but there were inherent drawbacks when they were applied to highly convoluted structures, sharp bends and corners, or on images with a large amount of noise. We therefore try to preserve the classical properties of the parametric contours but also bring the geometric properties which could capture the topology of the convoluted brain. Next, we show the derivation of the geometric snake from the above model in the level set framework.

---

[1] called as geometric active contour

Derivation of the Geometric Snake: Since the second derivative term in Eq. 1 did not affect significantly the performance of the active geometric snakes (see Caselles *et al.* [9]), we dropped that term and replaced it with a new pressure force term given as: $F_p(\mathbf{X})$. This pressure force is an outward force which is a function of the unit normal, $\mathcal{N}$ of the deforming curve. Thus defining the pressure force as: $F_p(\mathbf{X}) = w_p(\mathbf{X})\mathcal{N}(\mathbf{X})$, the new parametric active contour could be written as:

$$\gamma\frac{\partial \mathbf{X}}{\partial t} = \frac{\partial}{\partial s}(\alpha\frac{\partial \mathbf{X}}{\partial s}) - w_p(\mathbf{X})\mathcal{N}(\mathbf{X}) + F_{ext}(\mathbf{X}). \tag{2}$$

Bringing the Eq. 2 in terms of the curvature of the deformable curve by defining $\frac{\partial}{\partial s}(\frac{\partial \mathbf{X}}{\partial s})$ to be the curvature κ, and readjusting the terms by defining the constant $\epsilon = \frac{\alpha}{\gamma}$, $V_p = \frac{w_p(X)}{\gamma}\mathcal{N}(X)$, and $V_{ext} = \frac{F_{ext}}{\gamma}$, Eq. 2 can be rewritten as:

$$\frac{\partial \mathbf{X}}{\partial t} = (\epsilon\kappa + V_p + V_{ext}.\mathcal{N})\mathcal{N}. \tag{3}$$

The above Eq. is analogus to Sethian's [4] Eq. of curve evolution, given as: $\frac{\partial \phi}{\partial t} = V(\kappa)\mathcal{N}$, where $\mathcal{N} = -\frac{\nabla\phi}{|\nabla\phi|}$. Note, ϕ was the level set function, and $V(\kappa)$ was the curvature dependent speed with which the front (or zero-level-curve) propagates. The Eq. $\frac{\partial \phi}{\partial t} = V(\kappa)\mathcal{N}$ described the time evolution of the level set function (ϕ) in such a way that the zero-level-curve of this evolving function was always identified with the propagating interface. We will interchangably use the term "level set function" with the term "flow field" or simply "field" during the course of this paper. Comparing Eq. 3 and $\frac{\partial \phi}{\partial t} = V(\kappa)\mathcal{N}$, and using the geometric property of the curve's normal $\mathcal{N}$, and considering only the normal components of internal and external forces,

$$\frac{\partial}{\partial s}(\alpha\frac{\partial \mathbf{X}}{\partial s}).\mathcal{N} = (\alpha\kappa), \tag{4}$$

we obtain the level set function (ϕ) in the form of the partial differential equation (PDE) as:

$$\frac{\partial \phi}{\partial t} = (\epsilon\kappa + V_p)|\nabla\phi| - V_{ext}.\nabla\phi. \tag{5}$$

Note, V_p can be considered as a regional force term and and can be mathematically expressed as a combination of inside-outside regional area of the propagating curve. This can be defined as $\frac{w_R}{\gamma R}$, where R is the region indicator term that lies between 0 and 1. An example of such a region indicator could come from a membership function of the fuzzy classifier (see Bezdek *et al.* [11]). Thus, we see that regional information is one of the factors which controls the speed of the geometric snake or propagating curve in the level set framework. A framework in which a snake propagates by capturing the topology of the WM/GM, navigated by the regional, curvature, edge and gradient forces is called as geometric snakes. Also note that Eq. 5 has three terms: $(\epsilon\kappa)$, V_p and V_{ext}. These three terms are the speed functions which control the propagation of the curve. These three speed functions are known as curvature, regional and gradient speed functions, i they contribute towards the three kinds of forces occurring during the curve propagation. In the next section we used the numerical implementation to show how we solved such a PDE using diffusion propagation.

3   Methodology: Fast Brain Segmentation System

This section presents the entire system for computing WM/GM boundaries given the MR brain image and the initial user-placed raw contour. This system can be seen in Fig. 1. The system consists of three major stages. The first stage is the initial field computation, given the raw contour and the image; the second stage is the computation of the new flow field deformed by the three speed functions derived in section 2. The last stage is the re-initialization stage, which implements the isocontour extraction and the recomputation of the flow field. This recomputation is done in the narrow band using the fast marching method. Stage three and stage one are similar in the way that they compute the level set function over time using optimization techniques like narrow band and fast marching methods. It is a method of propagating the new field in the narrow band. The crux of the whole system lies in the computation of the integrated speed functions: regional, curvature and gradient, which are inputs to stage two for computation of the deformed level set function. Thus, we will spend more time in the three speed functions and their integration. Next, sub-section 3.1 presents the computation of the three speed functions (stage-II), while sub-section 3.2 presents the flow field computation in the narrow band using the fast marching method (stage I and stage III).

3.1   Numerical Implementation of the Three Speed Functions in the Level Set Framework for Geometric Snake Propagation: Stage II

In this sub-section, we mathematically present the speed control functions in terms of the level set function ϕ and integrating them to estimate ϕ over time. Let $I(x, y)$ represent the pixel intensity at image location (x, y), while $V_{reg}(x, y)$, $V_{grad}(x, y)$ and $V_{cur}(x, y)$ represent the regional, gradient and curvature speed terms at pixel location (x, y). Then, using the finite difference methods as discussed by Sethian [12] and Rouy et al. [10], the regional level set PDE Eq. 5 in time can be given as:

$$\phi_{x,y}^{n+1} = \phi_{x,y}^n - \Delta t \, \{ \, V_{reg}(x, y) + V_{grad}(x, y) - V_{cur}(x, y) \, \}, \tag{6}$$

where $\phi_{x,y}^n$ and $\phi_{x,y}^{n+1}$ were the level set functions at pixel location (x, y) at times n and $n + 1$, Δt was the time difference. The imporant thing to note here is that the curve is moving in the level set field, and the level set field is controlled by these three speed terms. In other words, these speeds are forces acting on the propagating contour. Mathematically, these speed terms can be given as under:

Regional Speed Term expressed in terms of level set function (ϕ): This is mathematically given as: $V_{reg}(x, y) = max\,(V_p(x, y), 0)\,\nabla^+ + min\,(V_p(x, y), 0)\,\nabla^-$, where $V_p(x, y)$, ∇^+ and ∇^- were given as: $V_p(x, y) = \frac{w_R}{\gamma\,R_{ind}(x,y)}$, $R_{ind} = 1 - 2\,u(x, y)$, $\nabla^+ = [\nabla_x^+ + \nabla_y^+]^{\frac{1}{2}}$, $\nabla^- = [\nabla_x^- + \nabla_y^-]^{\frac{1}{2}}$, $\nabla_x^+ = [max\,(D^{-x}(x, y), 0))^2 + min\,(D^{+x}(x, y), 0))^2]$, $\nabla_y^- = [max\,(D^{-y}(x, y), 0))^2 + min\,(D^{+y}(x, y), 0))^2]$, where $u(x, y)$ was the fuzzy membership function which had the value between 0 to 1 for a given input image I. R_{ind} was the region indicator function that falls in the range between -1 to +1. The fuzzy membership computation and pixel classification were done using fuzzy clustering to compute the fuzzy membership values for each pixel location (x, y). The number of classes taken were four corresponding to WM, GM and CSF and background (for details on fuzzy clustering, see Bezdek et al. [11]). Note, ∇_x^+ and ∇_y^+ are the forward level set gradients in the x and y directions. Similarly, ∇_x^- and ∇_y^- are the backward level set gradients in the x and y directions. Also note, ∇_x^-, ∇_y^+, ∇_x^- and ∇_y^- are expressed in terms of $D^{-x}(x, y)$, $D^{+x}(x, y)$, $D^{-y}(x, y)$, $D^{+y}(x, y)$ which are the forward and backward difference operators defined in terms of the level set function ϕ given in Eq. 7.

Gradient Speed Term expressed in terms of the level set function (ϕ): Here we compute the edge strength of the brain boundaries. The x and y components of the gradient speed terms are computed as: $V_{grad}(x, y) = V_{gradx}(x, y) + V_{grady}(x, y)$, $V_{gradx}(x, y) = max(p^n(x, y), 0)\,D^{-x}(x, y) + min(q^n(x, y), 0)\,D^{+x}(x, y)$, $V_{grady}(x, y) = max(q^n(x, y), 0)\,D^{-y}(x, y) + min(q^n(x, y), 0)\,D^{+y}(x, y)$, $p^n(x, y) = \nabla_x(w_e\,\nabla(G_\sigma * I))$ and $q^n(x, y) = \nabla_y(w_e\,\nabla(G_\sigma * I))$, where w_e was the weight of the edge and was a fixed constant. $p^n(x, y)$, and $q^n(x, y)$ were defined as the x and y components of the gradient strength at a pixel location (x, y). Note, G_σ is the Gaussian operator with a known standard deviation σ and I is the original gray scale image. Again, note that the edge speed term is dependent upon the forward and backward difference operators which were defined in terms of the level set function ϕ given in Eq. 7.

$$\begin{cases} D^{-x}(x,y) = \frac{(\phi(x,y)-\phi(x-1,y))}{\Delta x} \ \& \ D^{+x}(x,y) = \frac{(\phi(x+1,y)-\phi(x,y))}{\Delta x} \\ D^{-y}(x,y) = \frac{(\phi(x,y)-\phi(x,y-1))}{\Delta y} \ \& \ D^{-y}(x,y) = \frac{(\phi(x,y+1)-\phi(x,y))}{\Delta y} \end{cases} \tag{7}$$

where $\phi(x,y)$, $\phi(x-1,y)$, $\phi(x+1,y)$, $\phi(x,y-1)$, $\phi(x,y+1)$ were the level set functions at pixel locations (x,y), $(x-1,y)$, $(x+1,y)$, $(x,y-1)$, $(x,y+1)$, the four neighbours of (x,y).

Curvature Speed Term expressed in terms of level set function (ϕ): This is mathematically expressed in terms of the signed distance transform of the contour as:

$$V_{cur}(x,y) = \epsilon \kappa^n(x,y)[(D^{0x}(x,y))^2 + ((D^{0y}(x,y))^2]^{\frac{1}{2}}, \tag{8}$$

where ϵ was a fixed constant. $\kappa^n(x,y)$ was the curvature at a pixel location (x,y) at n^{th} iteration, given as: $\kappa^n(x,y) = \frac{\phi_{xx}^2 \phi_y^2 - \phi_x^2 \phi_y^2 \phi_{xy} + \phi_{yy}^2 \phi_x^2}{(\phi_x^2 + \phi_y^2)^{\frac{3}{2}}}$ and $D^{0x}(x,y)$ and $D^{0y}(x,y)$ were defined as: $D^{0x}(x,y) = \frac{(\phi(x+1,y)-\phi(x-1,y))}{2\Delta x}$ and $D^{0y}(x,y) = \frac{(\phi(x,y+1)-\phi(x,y-1))}{2\Delta y}$. To numerically solve Eq. 6, all we needed were the gradient speed values (p,q), and the curvature speed κ at pixel location (x,y) and the membership function $u(x,y)$. These speeds are integrated to compute the new flow field (level set function, ϕ). The integrated speed term helps in the computation of the new flow field for the next iteration $n+1$, given the flow field of the previous iteration n. So far, we discussed the flow field computation at every pixel location (x,y), but to speed up these computations, we compute the speeds only in a narrow band using the fast marching method, so-called optimization (used in stage I and III), which is discussed next.

3.2 Level Set Method in Narrow Band and Re-initialization: Stage I and III

Stage-I is a two step process, while stage-III is a three step process. Two steps (1 and 2) are common to both stages, while step 3 is an additional step for stage III. For details on these stages see Sethian et al. [12] and Suri et al. [1]. At the end of the process, a new zero-level curve was estimated which represented the final WM/GM boundary. Note this technique used all the global information integrated into the system. We will discuss the major advantages and superiority of this technique in section 5, but first we will present the results on sample gray scale brain images and some synthetic simulation on convoluted shapes like flowers.

4 MR Segmentation Results and Data Analysis

Data Preparation: We ran our system over the sagittal, coronal and transverse slices of several normal volunteers. The data was 256 cubed data using the following parameters: T_E=12.1 msec, BW=15.6 Hzs, T_R=500 msec, FOV=22.0 cm, Phase Sampling Ratio (PSR) =0.812, flip angle=90°, with slice thickness=5.0 using the Picker scanner. This data was converted to an isotropic volume using the internal Picker software. Then the MR brain images were ready for processing.

Variation in the Level Set Parameters: The following sets of parameters were chosen for all the real experiments. The major parameters which affect the performance of the region-based level set approach were w_R and the error threshold for the fuzzy clustering. We kept the value of the w_R=0.5 but its range falls between 0.0 and 1.0. This is the factor which controls the speed of convergence in the inner loop. Another factor which controls the accuracy of the system is the error threshold for computing the fuzzy membership values which we took as 0.5. The number of classes taken were four. A typical value of the narrow band-width (W)

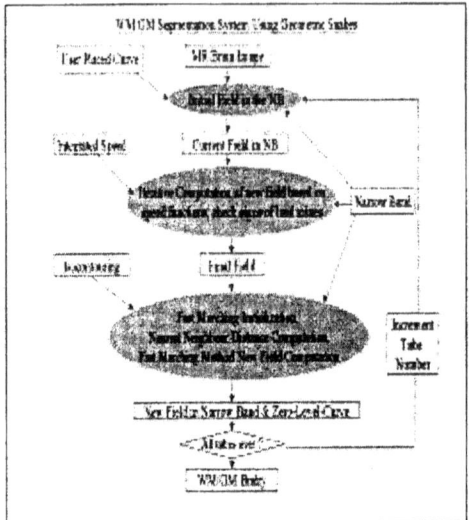

Figure 1: Brain segmentation system.

was, say, from 10 to 25, with the total land mine width ($\triangle_l$) ranging from 2 to 5. The level set constants α and γ and ϵ were fixed to 0.5, 1 and 1 for all experiments, respectively.

Results: The inputs to the system (see Fig. 1) were the gray scale image and the hand-draw contour points. The speed model was first activated by computing three types of speed: curvature, gradient and region-based. The level set function was solved in the narrow band using the fast marching method using these speed functions. Figure 2 shows all the major steps for estimating the WM/GM boundaries of the MR brain images. We also ran the fast marching and narrow band algorithms over synthetic convoluted shapes such as the flower as shown in Fig. 2 (see caption).

5   Discussions and Conclusions

Advantages of the current technique: The brain segmentation system has two major loops, one for external tubing (called the narrow band) and the second for the internal loop for estimating the final flow field in the narrow band. These two kinds of iterations were responsible for controlling the speed of the entire system. The outer loop speed was controlled by how fast the re-initialization of the signed distance transformation could be estimated given the zero-level-curve. This was done by the fast marching method using Sethian's approach. The second kind of speed was controlled by how fast the flow field was converged. This was controlled by the weighting factor w_R. Overall, the following are the key advantages of this brain segmentation system: The greatest advantage of this technique was its high *capture range* of the flow field (see Fig. 2). This increases the robustness of the initial contour placement. Even if the contour was placed anywhere in the image, it would find the object to segment itself. For all complete list of advantages, see Suri *et al.* [1].

Numerical Stability and signed distance transformation computation:

The numerical implementation needs a very careful design and all the variables should be float or double. This is because the finite difference comparisons are done with with respect to zero. Also, the re-initialization stage and the isocontour extraction depend upon the sign of the level set function which need to be tracked

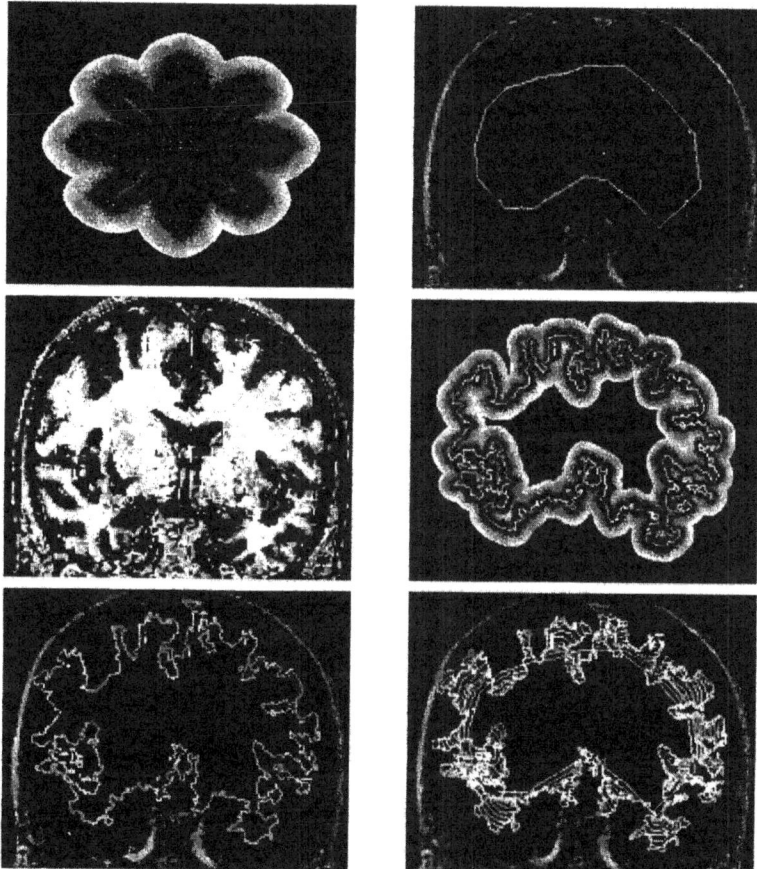

Figure 2: **Top Left**: Fast marching results over the synthetic flower image with 8 petals convoluted. **Top Right**: The raw contour with the MR gray scale coronal brain image. **Middle Left**: The pixel classification results. **Middle Right**: The narrow band flow field with the ZLC (5th iteration). **Bottom Left**: Final white matter segmented. **Bottom Right**: The level set growth of the zero level curves (a total of 6 iterations).

as well. During the signed distance transform computation, all distances for the inside region are made positive and after the computation of all the distances of the grid points, the distances are made negative. *Conclusions*: We have successfully demonstrated a system to segment the WM/GM boundaries in the level set framework whose speed functions are fuzzy in nature. The results are very encouraging and in the future we would like to extend this to 3-D. We also feel that we need to use some tools for the quantification of WM/GM boundaries and compare the results with ground truth using some distance computation schemes, such as the polyline methods as presented by Suri *et al.* [14] previously.

References

[1] Jasjit S. Suri, S. Kamaledin Setarehdan, Sameer Singh, Advanced Algorithmic Approaches to Medical Image Segmentation: State-of-the-Art Applications in Cardiology, Neurology, Mammography and Pathology, First Eds. In Press.

[2] Kass Wikins, Terzapolous, D., Snakes: Active Contour Models, International J. of Computer Vision, Vol. 1, No. 4, pp. 321-331, 1988.

[3] Jasjit S. Suri, Computer Vision. Image Processing and Pattern Recognition in Left Ventricle Segmentation: Last 50 Years, J. of Pattern Analysis and Applications, Vol. 3, No. 3, pp. 209-244, Sep. 2000.

[4] S. Osher and James A. Sethian, Fronts propagating with curvature-dependent speed: algorithms based on Hamiltons-Jacobi formulations, J. Computational Physics, Vol. 79, No. 1, pp. 12-49, 1988.

[5] James A. Sethian, An Analysis of Flame Propagation, Ph.D. thesis, Department of Mathematics, University of California, Berkeley, CA, 1982.

[6] Malladi R, Ron Kimmel, D. Adalsteinsson, G. Sapiro, V. Caselles and J. A. Sethian, A Geometric Approach to Segmentation and Analysis of 3-D Medical Images, Proc. of IEEE/SIAM workshop on Mathematical Morphology and Biomedical Image Analysis (MMBIA), San Francisco, California, pp. 244-252, June 1996.

[7] Malladi, R., Sethian, J.A., A Unified Approach to Noise Removal, Image-Enhancement, and Shape Recovery, IEEE Trans. in Image Processing, Vol. 5, No. 11, pp. 1554-1568, Nov. 1996.

[8] Chenyang Xu, On the relationship between the parametric and geometric active contours, Internal Tech. report, Johns Hopkins University, 1999.

[9] V. Caselles, R. Kimmel and G. Shapiro, Geodesic active contours, Int. J. of Computer Vision, Vol. 22, pp. 61-79, 1997.

[10] Elisabeth Rouy and Agnes Tourin, A viscosity solutions approach to shape-from-shading, SIAM J. of Numerical Analysis, Vol. 23, pp. 867-884, 1992.

[11] Bezdek, J.C, Hall, L.O., Review of MR image segmentation techniques using pattern recognition, Medical Physics, Vol. 20, pp. 1033-1048, March 1993.

[12] James A. Sethian, A fast marching level set method for monotonically advancing fronts, Proc. Natl. Acad. Science, Applied Mathematics, Vol. 93, pp. 1591-1595, 1996.

[13] D. Adalsteinsson, J. A. Sethian, The fast construction of extension velocities in level set methods, J. Computational Physics, Vol. 148, No. 1, pp. 2-22, 1999.

[14] Jasjit S. Suri, Robert M. Haralick and F. H. Sheehan, Greedy Algorithm for Error Correction in Automatically Produced Boundaries from Low Contrast Ventriculograms, Int. J. of Pattern Applications and Analysis, Vol. 1, No. 1, pp. 39-60, Jan. 2000.

Multiseeded Fuzzy Segmentation on the Face Centered Cubic Grid

Carvalho, B. M.[1]*, Garduño, E.[1], and Herman, G. T.[2]

[1] University of Pennsylvania, Philadelphia PA 19104, USA
[2] Temple University, Philadelphia PA 19122, USA

Summary. Fuzzy connectedness has been effectively used to segment out objects in volumes containing noise and/or shading. Multiseeded fuzzy segmentation is a generalized approach that produces a unique simultaneous segmentation of multiple objects. Fcc (face centered cubic) grids are grids formed by rhombic dodecahedral voxels that can be used to represent volumes with fewer elements than a normal cubic grid. Tomographic reconstructions (PET and CT) are used to evaluate the accuracy and speed of the algorithm.

keywords: multisegmentation, fuzzy conectedness, fuzzy graph, FCC grid, PET, CT.

1 Introduction

Segmentation is the process of recognizing objects in an image. If the image in question is corrupted by noise or the objects to be recognized are defined not only by the intensity assigned to the pixels belonging to them (i.e., they are defined by some textural property), then thresholding is not an appropriate method of segmentation but the concept of fuzzy connectedness can be successfully used to segment images [1–4]. The concept of fuzzy connectedness was introduced by Rosenfeld [5]. Our approach (introduced in [6]) is based on [7], but is generalized to arbitrary digital spaces [8].

In the fuzzy connectedness context we define a *chain* as a sequence of voxels (short for volume elements) and its *links* as the pairs of consecutive voxels. The *strength* of any link is automatically determined according to statistical properties of the links selected by the user as connecting two voxels within the object of interest. The strength of a chain is equal to the strength of its weakest link. The *fuzzy connectedness* between any pair of voxels is the

---

* This research is supported by NIH Grant HL28438 (BMC, EG and GTH), NFS Grant DMS96122077 (GTH), CAPES-BRASÍLIA-BRAZIL (BMC) and CONACyT-Mexico (EG).

S. Singh, N. Murshed, and W. Kropatsch (Eds.): ICAPR 2001, LNCS 2013, pp. 339–348, 2001.
© Springer-Verlag Berlin Heidelberg 2001

strength of the strongest chain between them. In multiseeded segmentation we generalize this approach by allowing each object to have its own definition of strength for the links and its own set of seed voxels. Then, each object is defined as the set of voxels that are connected in a stronger way to one of the seeds of that object than to any of the seeds of the other objects.

As this high-level description of the method suggests, the most computationally expensive task in determining these objects based on the pre-selected seeds is the calculation of the multiple fuzzy connectedness of all the voxels to the seed voxels. This involves finding the strongest chain between a voxel and one or more seed voxels. We make use of the greedy algorithm presented in [6] to efficiently achieve the segmentation of PET (Positron Emission Tomography) and CT (Computed Tomography) volumes on the fcc grid.

In Section 2 we describe in detail the theory and the algorithm which performs the multiseeded fuzzy segmentation. Section 3 describes the fcc grid and its advantages in volume representation when compared to the simple cubic grid. In Section 4 we describe the experiments used to evaluate the multiseeded fuzzy segmentation algorithm. Finally, in Section 5 we present our conclusions.

2   Multiseeded Fuzzy Segmentation

For a positive integer M, an M-*semisegmentation* of a set V (of *spels*, short for spatial element) is a function σ which maps each $c \in V$ into an $(M+1)$-dimensional vector $\sigma^c = (\sigma_0^c, \sigma_1^c, \cdots, \sigma_M^c)$, such that $\sigma_0^c \in [0,1]$ (i.e., it is nonnegative but not greater than 1) and for at least one m, in the range $1 \leq m \leq M$, $\sigma_m^c = \sigma_0^c$ and for all other m it is either 0 or σ_0^c. We say that σ is an M-segmentation if, for every spel c, σ_0^c is positive.

A *fuzzy spel affinity* on V is a function $\psi : V^2 \to [0,1]$. We think of (c,d) as a *link* and of $\psi(c,d)$ as its ψ-*strength*. (In some of the previous literature it was also assumed that $\psi(c,d) = \psi(d,c)$; we do not need this restriction.) We define a chain in $U(\subseteq V)$ from $c^{(0)}$ to $c^{(K)}$ to be a sequence $\langle c^{(0)}, \cdots, c^{(K)} \rangle$ of spels in U and the ψ-strength of this chain as the ψ-strength of its weakest link $(c^{(k-1)}, c^{(k)})$, $1 \leq k \leq K$. (In case $K = 0$, the ψ-strength is defined to be 1.) We say that U is ψ-*connected* if for every pair of distinct spels in U there is a chain in U of positive ψ-strength from the first spel of the pair to the second.

If there are multiple objects to be segmented, it is reasonable that each should have its own fuzzy spel affinity [9], which leads to the following. An M-*fuzzy graph* is a pair (V, Ψ), where V is a nonempty finite set and $\Psi = (\psi_1, \cdots, \psi_M)$ and ψ_m (for $1 \leq m \leq M$) is a fuzzy spel affinity such that

V is $(min_{1\leq m\leq M}\psi_m)$-connected. (This is defined by $(min_{1\leq m\leq M}\psi_m)(c,d) = min_{1\leq m\leq M}\psi_m(c,d)$.) For an M-semisegmentation σ of V and for $1 \leq m \leq M$, the chain $\langle c^{(0)},\cdots,c^{(K)}\rangle$ is said to be a σm-chain if $\sigma_m^{c^{(k)}} > 0$, for $0 \leq k \leq K$. Further, for $U \subseteq V$, $W \subseteq V$ and $c \in V$, we use $\mu_{\sigma,m,U,W}(c)$ to denote the maximal ψ-strength of a σm-chain in U from a spel in W to c. (This is equal to 0 if there is no such chain.)

Theorem. If (V,Ψ) is an M-fuzzy graph and, for $1 \leq m \leq M$, V_m is a subset (of *seed spels*) of V such that at least one of these subsets is nonempty, then there exists a unique M-semisegmentation (which is, in fact, an M-segmentation) σ of V with the following property. For every $c \in V$, if for $1 \leq n \leq M$

$$s_n^c = \begin{cases} 1, & \text{if } c \in V_n, \\ max_{d\in V}(min(\mu_{\sigma,n,V,V_n}(d), \psi_n(d,c))), & \text{otherwise,} \end{cases} \tag{1}$$

then for $1 \leq m \leq M$

$$\sigma_m^c = \begin{cases} s_m^c, & \text{if } s_m^c \geq s_n^c \text{ for } 1 \leq n \leq M, \\ 0, & \text{otherwise.} \end{cases} \tag{2}$$

The fact that if σ is a M-semisegmentation that has this property, then σ is in fact unique and a M-segmentation is proved in [6]. In the same paper a greedy algorithm is provided which receives as input M sets of spels (V_m, for $1 \leq m \leq M$) and updates, during its execution, the current M-semisegmentation σ; producing, at the end, an M-semisegmentation that satisfies the property of the Theorem.

An intuitive picture of our algorithm is the following. There are M competing armies (one corresponding to each object). Initially they each have full strength and they occupy their respective seed spels. All armies try to increase their respective territories, but the moving from a spel to another one reduces the strength of the soldiers to be the minimum of their strength on the previous spel and the affinity (for that army or object) between the spels. At any given time, a spel will be occupied by the soldiers of the armies which were not weaker than any other soldiers who reached that spel by that time. Eventually a steady state is reached; this steady state satisfies the property of the Theorem. The sequential algorithm simulates this intuitively described parallel behaviour of the M armies.

A priority queue H of spels c is used by the algorithm. This queue, with associated keys σ_0^c, is a *max-queue*, meaning that the "first" element of the queue is the element with the maximal key (we denote this value by Maximum-Key(H), that returns 0 if H is empty). The algorithm keeps inserting spels into the queue (each spel is inserted exactly once using the operation $H \leftarrow H \cup \{c\}$) and will eventually be extracted from the queue (using the operation Remove-Max(H) that removes the element at the top of the queue), at which time, this spel c already has the final value for the vector σ^c. The real variable l holds the current value of Maximum-Key(H) and the spels are removed from H in a non-increasing order of their keys σ_0^c.

In the initialization phase (steps 1-9 of algorithm), all spels have the values σ_m^c set to 0 for $0 \le m \le M$. Then, for every spel c belonging to one of the seed spel sets V_m, c is inserted into H and both σ_0^c and σ_m^c are set to 1. After this step, l is also set to 1.

After the initialization, the following conditions are satisfied:
1. σ is an M-semisegmentation of V.
2. A spel c is in H if, and only if, $\sigma_0^c > 0$.
3. $l = \text{Maximum-Key}(H)$.
4. For $1 \le m \le M$, $V_m = \{c \in H \mid \sigma_m^c = l\}$.

At the beginning of the main loop (steps 10-28), conditions 1 to 4 are satisfied, and this loop is executed for decreasing values of l until this variable is set to 0, at which point the priority queue is empty and the algorithm terminates.

The first part of the main loop (steps 10-23) is responsible for updating the values of σ_m^c. A value is updated when a σm-chain with a ψ_m-strength greater than the old value from an element of the seed spels in the initial V_m to c is found, and the value σ_m^c is set to 0 if it is found, for an $n \ne m$, that there is a σn-chain from an element of the seed spels in the initial V_n to c with a ψ_n-strength greater than the old value of σ_m^c. The second part of the loop (steps 24-28) is responsible for removing the spels c with maximum keys ($\sigma_0^c = l$), assigning to l the value of the new maximum key and setting V_m to be the set of spels c with $\sigma_m^c = l$, for $1 \le m \le M$, thus satisfying the conditions 3 and 4. The algorithm, using the conventions adopted in [10], is described on the next page.

3   The Fcc Grid

Now we explain why we use the fcc grid, by comparing it to the cubic grid and showing the advantages of the former.

Let G be a set of points defined in $\mathbb{Z}^N$. The *Voronoi neighborhood in G* of any element g of G is defined as

$$N_G(g) = \{v \in \mathbb{R}^N \mid \text{for all } h \in G, \|v - g\| \le \|v - h\|\}, \tag{3}$$

i.e., the Voronoi neighborhood of g consists of all points that are not nearer to any other point of G than they are to g. *Voxels* are the Voronoi neighborhoods associated with a grid in three-dimensional space.

Algorithm 1 Multiseeded segmentation algorithm.

```
1              for c ∈ V
2                  do for m ← 0 to M
3                      do σ_m^c ← 0
4              H ← ∅
5              for m ← 1 to M
6                  do for c ∈ V_m
7                      do if σ_0^c = 0 then H ← H ∪ {c}
8                          σ_0^c ← σ_m^c ← 1
9              l ← 1
10             while l > 0
11                 for m ← 1 to M
12                     do while V_m ≠ ∅
13                         do remove a spel d from V_m
14                             C ← {c ∈ V | σ_m^c < min(l, ψ_m(d,c))}
15                             while C ≠ ∅
16                                 do remove a spel c from C
17                                     t ← min(l, ψ_m(d,c))
18                                     if l = t and σ_m^c < l then V_m ← V_m ∪ {c}
19                                     if σ_0^c < t then
20                                         if σ_0^c = 0 then H ← H ∪ {c}
21                                         for n ← 1 to M
22                                             do σ_n^c ← 0
23                                         if σ_0^c ≤ t then σ_0^c ← σ_m^c ← t
24                 while Maximum-Key(H) = l
25                 Remove-Max(H)
26                 l ← Maximum-Key(H)
27                 for m ← 1 to M
28                     V_m ← {c ∈ H | σ_m^c = l}
```

The cubic grid G is $G = \{(c_1, c_2, c_3) \mid c_1, c_2, c_3 \in \mathbb{Z}\}$, (where Z is the set of integers). The voxels of G are cubes of unit volume. The fcc grid F is $F = \{(c_1, c_2, c_3) \mid c_1, c_2, c_3 \in \mathbb{Z} \text{ and } c_1 + c_2 + c_3 \equiv 0 \pmod{2}\}$. The voxels of F are rhombic dodecahedra (polyhedra with 12 identical rhombic faces) of twice unit volume. We define the *adjacency* β for the grid F by: for any pair (c, d) of grid points in F, $(c, d) \in \beta \Leftrightarrow \|c - d\| = \sqrt{2}$.

A grid point c has 12 β-adjacent grid points in F. In fact, two grid points in F are adjacent if, and only if, the associated voxels share a face. This fact points to the first advantage of the fcc grid: only a single adjacency relation β need to be used in computing the fuzzy connectedness. If we were using the cubic grid, then, for a grid point c, we may need to use several fuzzy affinity functions: ψ_{mf} for grid points whose voxels share a face, ψ_{me} for grid points whose voxels share an edge and ψ_{mc} for grid points whose voxels share a corner.

The fcc grid with the adjacency β forms a 1-*simply connected* digital space and boundaries in such digital spaces are automatically *Jordan surfaces* [8]; i.e., there is no path from a voxel $a \in A$ to a voxel $b \in B$ (where A and B are two different digitally connected objects) without crossing the boundary between A and B. The reader should consult [11] for a description of an efficient algorithm for boundary tracking in the fcc grid.

Another advantage of the fcc grid is that if we have an object made up from voxels on this grid, for any two boundary faces that share an edge, the normals of these faces make an angle of 60° with each other, resulting in a less blocky image than if we used a surface based on the cubic grid with voxels of the same size. This can be seen in Fig. 1, where we display approximations to a sphere based on different grids. Note that the display based on the fcc grid (b) has a better representation than the one based on cubic grid with the same voxel volume (a) and is comparable with the representation based on cubic grid with voxel volume equal to one eighth of the fcc voxel volume (c). This points to another advantage of fcc grids when compared to cubic grids: fewer grid points are necessary to obtain a comparable digital representation of a volume [11].

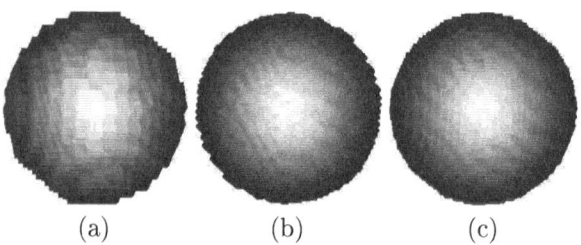

(a)   (b)   (c)

Fig. 1. Computer graphic display of a sphere using different grids. (a) is the display based on a cubic grid with voxels of the same volume as the display based on a fcc used for (b). The image (c) corresponds to a display based on a cubic grid with voxels of volume equal to one eight of the voxel volume in the other two images.

One might argue that the example of Fig. 1 is not general. In fact, we can choose a cube whose size is a multiple of the cubic grid voxel size and get a perfect representation of it as a collection of cubic voxels, but the same cannot be done with the fcc grid. However it is this latter example that is misleading, one can prove the general superiority of the fcc grid over the cubic grid for digital approximations of continuous functions (the fcc grid is said to be more *efficient* than the cubic grid). For a more detailed discussion of fcc and cubic grid efficiencies, the reader should consult [12] and [13].

4   Experimental Results and Discussion

In this section we show experiments that demonstrate the applicability of using the multiseeded fuzzy segmentation algorithm on the face centered cubic grid. For accuracy results and comparisons with other segmentation techniques for two-dimensional images, the reader can refer to [6].

The volumes used in the first segmentation experiments are PET reconstructions (with approximately 5,500,000 voxels) obtained using real data collected from a HEAD PENN-PET scanner, and the RAMLA algorithm for 2.5D [14] was used for reconstruction. The spatial resolution of the scanner used is $3.5 \times 3.5 \times 3.5\, mm$ FWHM. The phantom consists of 6 spheres with walls $1mm$ thick, where 2 are filled with cold (non-radioactive) and 4 are filled with hot (radioactive) water immersed in warm water (the concentration ratio between the hot spheres and the background is 8:1). The two cold spheres have diameters of 28 and $37mm$ and the hot spheres have diameters of 10, 13, 17 and $22mm$. In order to determine the robustness of the segmentation algorithm on this volume two of the authors and another user independently selected seeds for six fuzzy objects: one representing the two cold spheres, one for each one of the four hot spheres and one for the material in which they are immersed. The reason why we selected seeds for the hot spheres as separate fuzzy objects is that, although they have the same physical activity inside them, the reconstructed activity for each one is different due to inaccuracies in the data collection and reconstruction. The results were compared based on the volumes of the detected objects (Table 1).

Table 1. Comparison of actual and detected fuzzy object volumes (in cm^3) corresponding to seed selection by three users. (The first two columns correspond to the two cold objects and the last four columns correspond to the hot objects)

	Cold		Hot			
Actual	24.9	10.8	5.2	2.4	1.1	0.5
User 1	14.3	4.0	13.6	6.8	4.6	1.2
User 2	13.8	4.6	15.0	7.8	5.0	1.1
User 3	12.6	3.3	13.7	6.7	3.8	0.6

In this experiment we are measuring the robustness of the algorithm when receiving inputs from different users. The volume to be segmented is noisy and has low contrast, thus when we compare the volumes of the detected spheres with their actual sizes we are measuring the accuracy of the whole process, from scanning through reconstruction to segmentation. The detected volumes of cold and hot spheres have to be interpreted differently because of the physical properties [15] of the imaging device used. In PET, a positron generated in a hotter region often migrates to a neighboring colder region before annihilation, but the reverse is less likely to happen. For this reason, we should expect an increase in the apparent volume of the hot spheres and a decrease in the apparent volume of the cold spheres in a reconstruction.

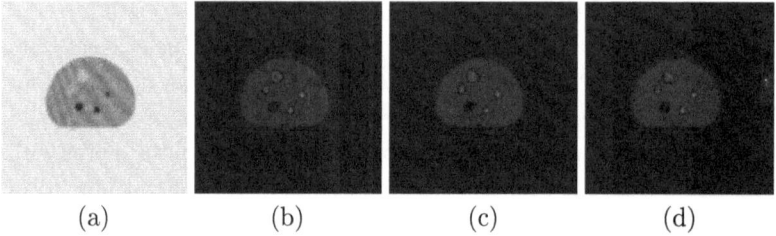

(a)   (b)   (c)   (d)

Fig. 2. Central slice of reconstructed phantom (**a**) and of the segmentations by the three users ((**b**), (**c**) and (**d**))

In Fig. 2 we show the central slice of the reconstructed phantom (a) and of the segmentation by the three users (b, c and d). In the cases of (b), (c) and (d), the hue indicates the object to which the voxel belongs (i.e., the m such that $\sigma_m^c = \sigma_0^c > 0$) and the intensity indicates the grade of membership (i.e., it is proportional to σ_0^c. The phantom slice showed in Fig. 2(a) had its gray levels inverted and adjusted in order to make all objects of interest visible. The average CPU time needed for segmenting the volume consisting of approximately 5,500,000 voxels using a Pentium III (450 MHz) was 7.5 minutes.

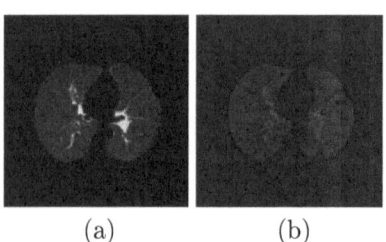

Fig. 3. Slice of CT volume (**a**) and of the segmentation (**b**)

(a)   (b)

In the second experiment we make use of the algorithm to segment the blood vessels inside the lungs, dividing the volume in three objects, the spels belonging to lung tissue (colored as red), blood vessels (green) and backgroud (blue). The user identified some points inside the three objects, providing the algorithm with the input needed. Since there is no ground truth, the quality of the segmentation is subjective and has to be assessed by a specialist.

The volume used for this experiment was collected using a CT (Computerized Tomography) scanner, with a spatial resolution of $1.0 \times 1.0 \times 5.0\,mm$ and interpolated to the FCC grid.

In Fig. 4 we show a slice of the reconstructed volume (a) and of the segmentation (b). Again, in the case of (b), the hue indicates the object to which the voxel belongs (i.e., the m such that $\sigma_m^c = \sigma_0^c > 0$) and the intensity indicates the grade of membership (i.e., it is proportional to σ_0^c). The volume slice showed in Fig. 4(a) also had its gray levels inverted and adjusted in order to make all objects of interest visible. The segmentation was evaluated by a pulmonary radiologist who judged it to be accurate except for some overestimation of blood vessels that can be removed by thresholding the conectedness map. The CPU time needed for segmenting the volume consisting of approximately 3,500,000 voxels using a Pentium III (450 MHz) was slightly under 3 minutes.

5   Conclusion

Multiseeded fuzzy segmentation is a semi-automatic method that allows the segmentation of multiple objects in images/volumes containing noise and/or shading. If the user chooses one of the objects to be the background in the volume (as in Fig. 2), then the fuzzy segmentation is achieved without any thresholding.

In this paper we showed that this method can be used to, within a reasonable time, perform segmentation on a poor contrast volume produced by PET reconstructions or on CT data using the fcc grid. The CPU time needed to perform the segmentation is especially important since our technique is semi-automatic, thus the user may wish to add, delete or change seeds after a first segmentation to achieve a better result.

The choice of the fcc grid was based on the facts that fewer grid elements have to be used to represent the same volume with similar accuracy than using a cubic grid and that only one adjacency (the face adjacency) is involved in the computation of the fuzzy affinity function values ,while in a cubic grid we may have as many as three different adjacencies involved at the same time (face, edge and corner adjacencies).

The results of the experiments shows that even when applied to a volume with very poor contrast, the volumes of the segmented fuzzy objects based on inputs from three different users are similar, and, when applied to a lung volume, it was able to segment blood vessels from lung tissue.

The selection of the seeds is a very important step of the process, it is there that the user gives the algorithm her/his high-level knowledge about the volume to be segmented. Our current work includes experiments whose intent is the determination of the best way to automatically select the seeds for the objects. This has to be application specific, in order to incorporate the high-level knowledge about the properties of the objects.

References

1. Dellepiane S.G., Fontana F., and Vernazza G.L. Nonlinear image labeling for multivalued segmentation. IEEE Trans. Image Process. 1996; 5:429–446
2. Udupa J.K., Wei L., Samarasekera S., Miki Y., van Buchem M.A., and Grossman R.I. Multiple sclerosis lesion quantification using fuzzy-connectedness principles. IEEE Trans. Med. Imag. 1997; 16:598–609
3. Moghaddam H.A. and Lerallut J.F. Volume visualization of the heart using MRI 4D cardiac images. J. Comput. Inform. Tech. 1998; 6:215–228
4. Carvalho B.M., Gau C.J., Herman G.T., and Kong T.Y. Algorithms for fuzzy segmentation. Pattern Anal. Appl. 1999; 2:73–81
5. Rosenfeld A. Fuzzy digital topology. Inform. and Control 1979; 40:76–87
6. Herman G.T. and Carvalho B.M. Multiseeded segmentation using fuzzy connectedness. IEEE Trans. Pattern Anal. Mach. Intell., to appear
7. Udupa J.K. and Samarasekera S. Fuzzy connectedness and object definition: Theory, algorithms and applications in image segmentation. Graph. Models Image Proc. 1996; 58:246–261
8. Herman G.T. Geometry of Digital Spaces. Birkhäuser, Boston, MA, 1998
9. Udupa J.K., Saha P.K., and Lotufo R.A. Fuzzy connected object definition in images with respect to co-objects. In: K.M. Hanson (ed) Image Processing, volume 3661 of Proc. SPIE, 1999, pp 236–245
10. Cormen T.H., Leiserson C.E., and Rivest R.L. Introduction to Algorithms. MIT Press, Cambridge, MA, 1990
11. Garduño E., Herman G.T., and Katz H. Boundary tracking in 3-D binary images to produce rhombic faces for a dodecahedral model. IEEE Trans. Med. Imag. 1998; 17:1097–1100
12. Matej S. and Lewitt R.M. Efficient 3D grids for image reconstruction using spherically-symmetric volume elements. IEEE Trans. Nucl. Sci. 1995; 42:1361–1370
13. Natterer F. The Mathematics of Computerized Tomography. John Wiley & Sons, Chichester, England, 1986
14. Obi T., Matej S., Lewitt R.M., and Herman G.T. 2.5D simultaneous multislice reconstruction by series expansion methods from Fourier-rebinned PET data. IEEE Trans. on Med. Imag. 2000; 19:474–484
15. Bendriem B. and Townsend D.W., editors. The Theory and Practice of 3D PET. Kluwer Academic Publishers, Dordrecht, The Netherlands, 1998

3D Wavelet based Video Retrieval

A. Del Bimbo, P. Pala, L. Tanganelli
Dipartimento Sistemi e Informatica – Università di Firenze
Firenze, Italy

Abstract

Content based video retrieval is particularly challenging because the huge amount of data associated with videos complicates the extraction of salient information content descriptors. Commercials are a video category where large part of the content depends on low level perceptual features such as colors and color dynamics. These are related to the evolution —in terms of shrinking, growth and translation— of colored regions along consecutive frames. Each colored region, during its evolution, defines a 3D volume: a *color flow*. In this paper, a system is presented that supports description of color flows based on 3D wavelet decomposition and retrieval of commercials based on color flow similarity.

1 Introduction

In the context of digital libraries of images and videos a key problem is the developement of efficient techniques for description and retrieval of visual information based on their content.

Retrieval of videos is particularly challenging because the huge amount of data involved complicates the extraction of salient information content descriptors. Several recent papers have addressed aspects and problems related to the access and retrieval by content of video streams. Research on automatic segmentation of a video into shots has been presented by several authors [1], [2], [3], [4], [5]. Once the video is segmented, video shots can be clustered into higher level aggregates. In [10], a set of rules to identify macro segments of a video is proposed. Algorithms to extract story units from video are described in [11]. In [12], [13] the specific characteristics of a video type are exploited to build higher level aggregates of shots.

Commercials are a video category where the link between low level perceptual features and high level semantics is stressed. Commercials convey information through a multiplicity of planes of communication which encompass what is represented in the frames, how frames are linked together, how the subject is imaged and so on. Hence, the effectiveness of commercials is mainly related

S. Singh, N. Murshed, and W. Kropatsch (Eds.): ICAPR 2001, LNCS 2013, pp. 349–358, 2001.

to its perceptual impact than to its mere content or explicit message: the way colors are chosen and modified throughout a spot, characters are coupled and shooting techniques are selected create a large part of the message in a commercial, while the extraction of canonical contents (e.g. imaged objects) has less conceptual relevance than in other contexts.

Quite recently, some works have been presented explicitly addressing commercials. They investigate the possibility of detecting and describing advertising content from a stream of video data. In [6] a system is presented for identification and recognition of commercials from TV broadcaster channels. In [14], commercials are analyzed under the semiotic perspective.

A common trait of commercials is the frequent use of colors and color dynamics to convey information. Colors and color dynamics are related to the evolution —in terms of shrinking, growth and translation— of colored regions along consecutive frames. During this evolution, a colored region defines a 3D volume: a *color flow* (Fig. 1). The 3D shape of the color flow retains information about dynamics of the region that generated it and can be used to represent relevant information associated with the commercial content.

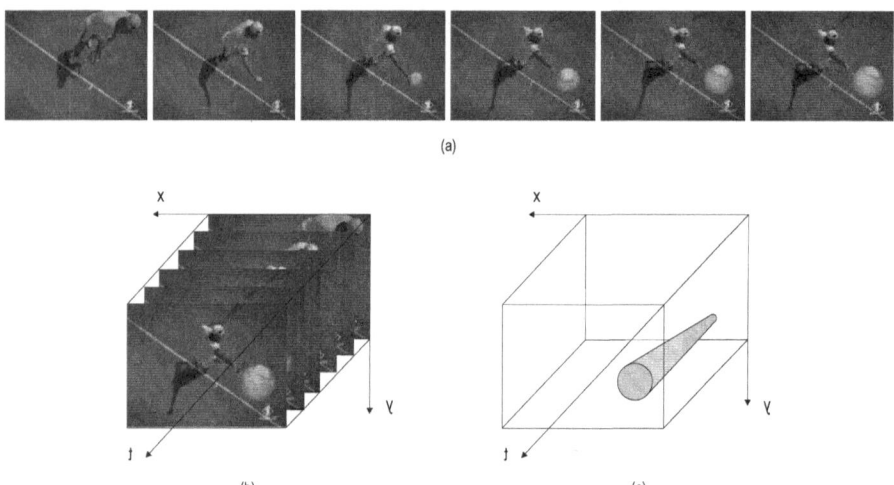

Figure 1: (a) A sequence of video frames. (b) Original color flows. (c) Extraction of one color flow.

In this paper, a system is presented that supports retrieval of commercials based on dynamics of color flows. The system is composed of three main modules: a video content analysis subsystem that performs video segmentation into shots, color segmentation of shot frames and extraction of color flows (described in Sect.2). A video content description subsystem that performs color flows description based on 3D wavelet decomposition (described in Sect.3). A retrieval engine that supports querying of commercials based on color flow similarity (described in Sect.4).

2   Video Segmentation and Color Flow Extraction

The primary task of video analysis is its segmentation, i.e. the identification of the start and end points of each shot that has been edited, in order to characterize the entire shot through its most representative *keyframes*. The automatic recognition of the beginning and end of each shot implies solving two problems: *i)* avoiding incorrect identification of shot changes due to rapid motion or sudden lighting change in the scene; *ii)* identification of sharp transitions (*cuts*) as well as gradual transitions (*dissolves*). For a detailed description of the techniques used for cut and dissolve detection the interested reader can refer to [14].

Video segmentation partitions a video into shots. Each shot is processed in order to extract relevant color flows. This requires that each shot frame is segmented so as to identify regions characterized by homogeneous colors. Then, regions are tracked over shot frames so as to reconstruct color flows.

2.1   Frame Segmentation

Image regions characterized by uniform color distribution are identified through a color image segmentation process. This is obtained by looking for clusters in the color space and then back–projecting cluster centroids onto the image [7]. To guarantee that small distances in the color space correspond to perceptually similar colors, colors are represented in the CIE $L^*u^*v^*$ (*extended chromaticity*) space.

Clustering in the 3-dimensional feature space is obtained using an improved version of the standard K-means algorithm [8], which avoids convergence to non–optimal solutions. *Competitive learning* has been adopted as the basic technique for grouping points in the color space as in [9].

In more detail, the clustering issue can be set as the problem of minimizing a functional $\mathcal{S}_W$ of *within cluster distance*, which penalizes the spread of a cluster and the distance between cluster centers. Let $\mathbf{x_i} \in \mathcal{X}$ ($\mathcal{X} = L^*u^*v^*$) be one of n points in the 3-dimensional color space, projection of an image pixel. If the n points are grouped into d clusters $\mathcal{C}_i$ of centers $\omega_\mathbf{i}$, then the within cluster distance is defined as:

$$\mathcal{S}_W = \frac{1}{n} \sum_{i=1}^{d} \sum_{\mathbf{x_k} \in \mathcal{C}_i} ||\mathbf{x_k} - \omega_\mathbf{i}||^2 \tag{1}$$

To achieve global minimization of (1), competitive learning repetitively compares the color coordinates $\mathbf{c} =< L, u, v >$ of a randomly chosen image pixel against the center $\omega_\mathbf{i}$ of each cluster $\mathcal{C}_i$ in the feature space; the image pixel is aggregated with the nearest cluster ($\mathbf{c}$ *votes* for cluster $\mathcal{C}_i$), which, in turn, modifies its centroid towards $\mathbf{c}$. The following stepwise *delta rule* implements cluster update:

$$\omega_\mathbf{c}(t+1) \quad = \quad \omega_\mathbf{c}(t) + \alpha[\mathbf{c}(t) - \omega_\mathbf{c}(t)]$$

$$\omega_i(t+1) \;=\; \omega_i(t) \quad \text{for} \;\; i \ne c \tag{2}$$

At the beginning, the entire image is associated with a single cluster, whose centroid is positioned on the global color average. During learning, clusters are recursively split on reaching an assigned number of votes until the pre-defined final number d of clusters is achieved, which imposes the number of distinct colors that will be present in the segmented image. The algorithm requires that the number of colors be preset during the initialization step, which may affect the overall segmentation process. A large value for d may result into an over-segmented image, where regions with similar colors have been split. On the other side a small value for d leads to relevant region missing, since it forces the learning to blend very different colors into their average in order to satisfy the constraint d. To evaluate a feasible estimate for the final number of color clusters, a rough estimate of color distribution over the image is performed, which exploits the cluster detection technique described by A. K. Jain in [8].

Once that the d "winning" $\{c_1, c_2, \ldots, c_d\}$ colors have been identified, each color pixel $c(x, y)$ is associated with its closest neighbor c_i such that

$$||c(x,y) - c_i||_{L_2} < ||c(x,y) - c_j||_{L_2} \quad \forall j \ne i \in [1, d]$$

and the pixel is labeled as an i-pixel. As a result, the segmented image will be a d-reduced color image.

2.2   Region Tracking

In order to extract color flows, homogeneous color regions identified in shot frames must be tracked. Region tracking is subject to the following constraints:

- a generic region in frame i is mapped into a region in frame $i + 1$ only if the two regions are characterized by similar colors and similar positions in the two frames.

- it is not necessary that every region of a generic frame is mapped into a region of the next frame. This allows the length of a color flow to be less than the length of the shot.

The similarity between region R_i^k in frame k and region R_j^{k+1} in frame $k+1$ is measured as:

$$S(R_i^k, R_j^{k+1}) := F(R_i^k, R_j^{k+1}) \cdot \frac{1}{C(R_i^k, R_j^{k+1})} \tag{3}$$

The first term in Eq. (3) is the Fisher distance between two color regions, that is:

$$F_h(R_i^k, R_j^{k+1}) := \frac{\sqrt{A(R_i^k) + A(R_j^{k+1})}\,|\mu_h(R_i^k) - \mu_h(R_j^{k+1})|}{\sqrt{A(R_i^k)\sigma_h^2(R_i^k) + A(R_j^{k+1})\sigma_h^2(R_j^{k+1})}}$$

where h identifies one of the three color components in the CIE $L^*u^*v^*$ color space ($h = 1$ for L*, $h = 2$ for u* and $h = 3$ for v*), $A(\cdot)$ is a measure of region area, $\mu_h(\cdot)$ the average value of the h-th color component and $\sigma_h(\cdot)$ its variance.

The second term of Eq.(3) accounts for the spatial location similarity between the two regions. It is based on projection of region R_j^{k+1} into frame k and measurement of the number of pixels that overlap with region R_i^k. Thus, the spatial location similarity between regions R_i^k and R_j^{k+1} is measured as:

$$C(, R_i^k, R_j^{k+1}) := \frac{4 \cdot Ovrl(R_i^k, R_j^{k+1})}{min(A(R_i^k), A(R_j^{k+1}))} \tag{4}$$

Segmentation results of $i - th$ frame are represented through a list $\mathcal{L}_i$, each node in the list corresponding to one region identified by the segmentation process. Eq. (3) can be used to measure the similarity between two nodes. Thus, region tracking is equivalent to a minimum search path problem. Presently, this is resolved through a *heuristic search* approach that requires to associate with a generic region in frame i the most similar region in frame $i + 1$. To account for those cases where a region cannot be mapped in the next frame, a threshold τ_S is used. Let $\mathcal{N}(R_i^k) \in \{R_j^{k+1}\} \oplus \emptyset$ be the region in frame $k + 1$ where region R_i^k is mapped. If region R_i^k cannot be mapped in frame $k + 1$ then $\mathcal{N}(R_i^k) = \emptyset$. $\mathcal{N}(R_i^k)$ is computed as follows:

$$\mathcal{N}(R_i^k) = \begin{cases} \emptyset & if \quad s > \tau_S \\ Arg\left(\min_{R_j^{k+1}} (S(R_i^k, R_j^{k+1}))\right) & if \quad s \le \tau_S \end{cases} \tag{5}$$

being $s = \min_{R_j^{k+1}} (S(R_i^k, R_j^{k+1}))$. Eq. (5) is used to track regions over contiguous frames. This procedure is recursively applied to every frame of the shot so as to identify color flows. The i-th color flow $\mathcal{F}_i^k$ within the k-th shot is identified through a binary function $\Gamma_i^k(i,j,t)$ that returns 1 if pixel (i,j) of frame f_t belongs to the color flow, 0 otherwise.

3 Color Flow Representation

Functions $F_i^k(i,j,t)$ identify color flows within a shot. In order to support retrieval by visual similarity of color flows, the characterizing visual elements of color flows have to be described. In our approach these elements retain information about both static and dynamic features. Static features address representation of color flow average color and color flow volume. Dynamic features address representation of color flow 3D shape.

The volume of color flow $\mathcal{F}_i^k$ is measured as:

$$V_i^k = \sum_{i,j,t} F_i^k(i,j,t)$$

Color flow average color $(\bar{L}_i^k, \bar{u}_i^k, \bar{v}_i^k)$ is measured in the CIE $L^*u^*v^*$ color space:

$$\bar{L}_i^k = \sum_{i,j,t} \frac{L(i,j,t) * F_i^k(i,j,t)}{V_i^k}$$

$$\bar{u}_i^k = \sum_{i,j,t} \frac{u(i,j,t) * F_i^k(i,j,t)}{V_i^k} \qquad \bar{v}_i^k = \sum_{i,j,t} \frac{v(i,j,t) * F_i^k(i,j,t)}{V_i^k}$$

Description of color flow 3D shape is carried out through a 3D wavelet representation, as expounded in the following section.

3.1   3D Wavelet Analysis

Description of color flow $\mathcal{F}_i^k$ is carried out through a Haar wavelet decomposition of function $F_i^k(i,j,t)$. Haar wavelets have been used because they are fast to compute and they are best suited to model binary functions such as $F_i^k(i,j,t)$.

Coefficients of the wavelet decomposition are computed by processing each coordinate axis separately. Functions $F_i^k(i,j,t)$ are scaled so as to fit in a 3D box $D \times D \times D$. The three-dimensional Haar wavelet decomposition of function $F_i^k(i,j,t)$ involves D two-dimensional Haar decomposition on each axis of the 3D space. The wavelet decomposition of $F_i^k(i,j,t)$ returns D^3 coefficients $W_i^k = \{w_0, \ldots, w_{D^3-1}\}$ retaining information about the 3D shape of the color flow (presently, the wavelet decomposition is carried out for $D = 64$, which results in 262144 distinct coefficients). Actually, due to intrinsic and well known properties of the wavelet decomposition, only a few coefficients are relevant for representation of the color flow. Therefore, coefficients are subjected to truncation and quantization, so as to keep only the prominent characterizing elements of the wavelet decomposition. Truncation is performed by retaining only those coefficients whose magnitude exceed a predefined threshold τ_t:

$$\hat{W}_i^k = \{(n, w_n) | |w_n| > \tau_t\}$$

Coefficients $\hat{W}$ are further subjected to a quantization process that compresses their dynamics to $\{-1, 1\}$:

$$\tilde{W}_i^k = \{(n, sign(w_n)) | |w_n| > \tau_t\}$$

Each element of the set $\tilde{W}_i^k$ includes one index (n) and the sign of the contribution of the corresponding wavelet coefficient. Since the wavelet decomposition provides a multi-resolution representation of data, some coefficients model coarse features of color flow shape, other coefficients model finer details. The value n of the index is used to associate a *relevance* $Rel(n)$ with the contribution $sign(w_n)$. Information about the relevance of $\tilde{W}$ elements is necessary in order to define an effective similarity metric between color flows.

3.2   Similarity Metric

The description of a generic color flow $\mathcal{F}_i^k$ retains the following elements:

$$< V_i^k \quad \bar{L}_i^k \bar{u}_i^k \bar{v}_i^k \quad \tilde{W}_i^k >$$

The distance between two color flows $\mathcal{F}_i^k$ and $\mathcal{F}_j^h$ is a weighted combination of distances in the volume, color and shape features:

$$
\begin{aligned}
\mathcal{D}(\mathcal{F}_i^k, \mathcal{F}_j^h) &= w_v * d_v(V_i^k, V_j^h) + \\
w_c * d_c(\bar{L}_i^k \bar{u}_i^k \bar{v}_i^k, \bar{L}_j^h \bar{u}_j^h \bar{v}_j^h) &+ \quad w_s * d_s(\tilde{W}_i^k, \tilde{W}_j^h)
\end{aligned}
\tag{6}
$$

Volume and color distances conform to the Euclidean distance model. Computing the distance between wavelet descriptors according to the Euclidean distance model would be a too rigid scheme and wouldn't allow weighting of multi-resolution coefficients according to their relevance. Hence, the distance between wavelet descriptors is computed as follows:

$$d_s(\tilde{W}_i^k, \tilde{W}_j^h) = \sum_{n \in S} w_{Rel(n)}$$

being $S \equiv \{m | (m, \mu_m) \in \tilde{W}_i^k, (m, \nu_m) \in \tilde{W}_j^h, \mu_m \neq \nu_m\}$ and $w_{Rel(n)}$ a penalty score that depends on the relevance of the n-th coefficient.

Eq.(6) is used to compute the distance between two generic shots, based on the distance of their color flows. Since two distinct shots almost never feature the same color flows, the method used to compute the distance between two shots considers the similarity of the most relevant color flows. Given two generic shots, their color flows are ordered in decreasing values of volume: from the largest color flow to the smallest one. Only the first τ_r color flows are compared for computation of the shot distance. Let $\{\mathcal{F}_1^1, \ldots, \mathcal{F}_{\tau_r}^1\}$ be the largest color flows of the first shot (S_1) and $\{\mathcal{F}_1^2, \ldots, \mathcal{F}_{\tau_r}^2\}$ the largest color flows of the second one (S_2). Computing the distance between the two shots requires to find the best color flow correspondence function. This is defined as the permutation $p : \{1, \ldots, \tau_r\} \to \{1, \ldots, \tau_r\}$ that minimizes the distances between corresponding color flows, that is:

$$\mathcal{D}_{shot}((S_1), (S_2)) = \min_p \left\{ \sum_{i=1}^{\tau_r} \mathcal{D}(\mathcal{F}_i^1, \mathcal{F}_{p(i)}^2) \right\} \tag{7}$$

4   Video Retrieval

The retrieval system has been implemented on a stand-alone platform, featuring a Silicon Graphics MIPS R10000 processor, 128 MB Memory and IRIX 6.2 Operating System. At database population time, each commercial is automatically processed in order to segmented it into shots. Each shot is analyzed and its color flows are extracted and described. Color flow descriptions extracted from all the database videos are stored in an index signature file with the following form:

$$< video_{ID}, shot_{ID}, V_i^k, \bar{L}_i^k, \bar{u}_i^k, \bar{v}_i^k, \tilde{W}_i^k >$$

Presently the system includes over 150 commercial videos digitized from several Italian TV channels.

The graphic interface is designed to support video retrieval by color flow similarity: the user can select a color flow from one of database videos and query for videos featuring similar color flows. A result list-box is used to present matched videos in decreasing order of similarity. By selecting a video from the list, the video can be either viewed at full or in its most salient keyframes through a movie player application.

Fig. 2(a) shows some frames of a shot used to query for color flow similarity. The shot features three main color flows (shown in Fig. 2(b)): a black flow —subjected to shrinking— in the upper part of the frames; an orange flow — subjected to growth— in the lower part of the frames; a gray flow in between the first two. Fig. 3(a)(b) shows the two best ranked shots according to the query of Fig. 2(a). It can be noticed that both shots feature a yellow-orange region subjected to growth and a black one subjected to shrinking. Similarly to the commercial used for query (that advertises a brand of pasta) the first two retrieved commercials advertise food products (a brand of rice and a brand of chicken soup). This result confirms the general criterion according to which the kind of promoted product often drives the choice of the graphic elements that characterize the commercial.

5   Conclusion and Future Work

In this paper a system is presented that supports retrieval of commercials based on dynamics of color flows. Color flows capture changes of color regions over contiguous frames. They retain prominent features of the video content, due to the tight relationships between color and motion features and the video content in commercials.

A 3D Haar wavelet decomposition technique is used to represent color flows. Based on this representation a metric is defined to compute color flow similarity. The metric combines into a unified measure the similarity between two color flows in terms of color, volume and 3D shape. A measure of the similarity between two shots is computed based on the similarity between their color flows. This measure is used to support retrieval of commercials based on color flow similarity.

Future enhancements include the possibility to enrich the description of the video content by exploiting additional clues such as audio and textual captions included in the video.

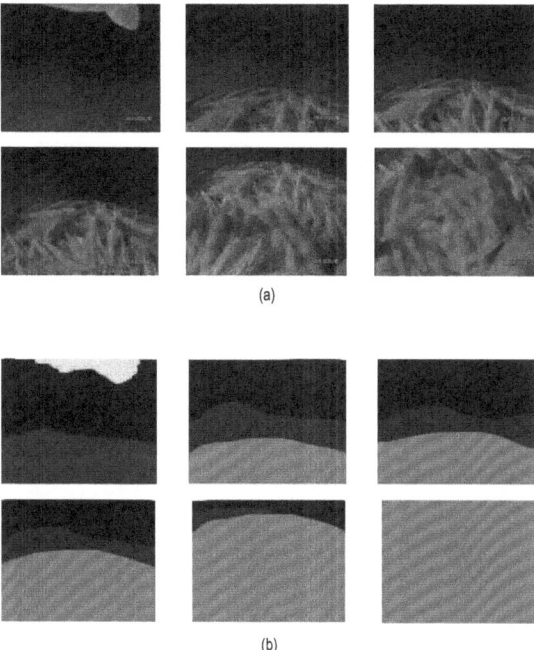

(a)

(b)

Figure 2: Original (a) and segmented (b) frames of a shot used to query based on color flow similarity.

References

[1] S. Smoliar and H. Zhang. Content-based video indexing and retrieval. *IEEE Multimedia*, 2(1):63–75, Summer 1994.

[2] Y. Tonomura, A. Akutsu, Y. Taniguchi, and G. Suzuki. Structured video computing. *IEEE Multimedia*, (3):35–43, Fall 1994.

[3] A. Nagasaka and Y. Tanaka. Automatic video indexing and full video search for object appearances. In W.E. Knuth, ed., *IFIP Trans., Visual Database Systems II*, pages 113–128, 1992.

[4] A. Hampapur, R. Jain, and T. Weymouth. Digital video segmentation. In 2nd *Annual ACM Multimedia Conference and Exposition*, San Francisco, CA, Oct. 1994.

[5] J.M. Corridoni and A. Del Bimbo. Film editing reconstruction and semantic analysis. In *Proc. CAIP'95*, Prague, Czech Republic, Sept. 1995.

[6] R. Lienhart, C. Kuhmünch, and W. Effelsberg. On the detection and recognition of television commercials. In *Proc. Int'l Conf. on Multimedia Computing and Systems*, pages 509–516, Ottawa, Canada, June 1997.

[7] J.M. Corridoni, A. Del Bimbo, P. Pala. Image Retrieval by Color Semantics. ACM Multimedia Systems Journal, Vol.7, n.3, pp.175-183, 1999.

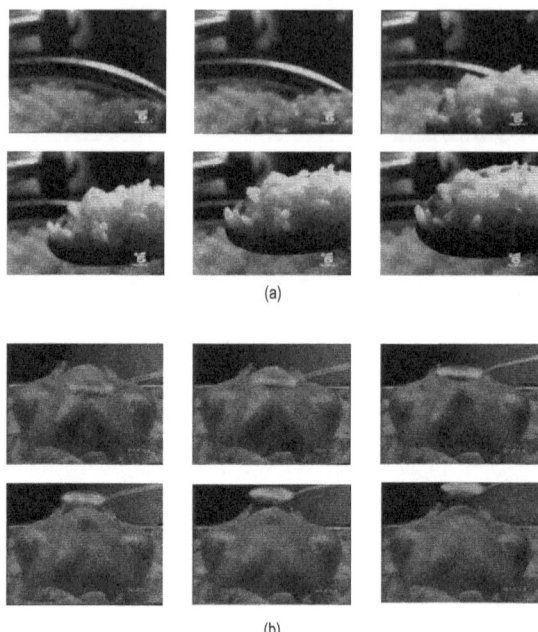

Figure 3: The first two retrieved shots according to the query of Fig. 2.

[8] A.K. Jain. *Algorithms for clustering data*. Prentice Hall, Englewood Cliffs (NJ), 1991.

[9] T. Uchiyama and M.A. Arbib. Color image segmentation using competitive learn-
     ing. *IEEE Trans. on Pattern Analysis and Machine Intelligence*, (16)12:1197–1206,
     Dec. 1994.

[10] P. Aigrain, P. Joly, P. Lepain, and V. Longueville. Medium knowledge-based macro seg-
     mentation of video sequences. In M. Maybury, ed., *Intelligent Multimedia Information
     Retrieval*, 1996.

[11] M. Yeung, B.L. Yeo, and B. Liu, Extracting story units from long programs for video
     browsing and navigation. In *Proc. IEEE Int'l Conf. on Multimedia Computing and
     Systems*, pages 296–305, Hiroshima, Japan, June 1996.

[12] D. Swanberg, C.F. Shu, and R. Jain. Knowledge guided parsing in video databases. In
     W. Niblack, ed., *Conf. on Storage and Retrieval for Image and Video Databases*, pages
     13–24, San Jose, CA, May 1993.

[13] J.M. Corridoni and A. Del Bimbo. Structured digital video indexing. In *Proc. 13th Int'l
     Conf. on Pattern Recognition ICPR'96*, pages (III):125–129, Wien, Austria. August
     1996.

[14] C. Colombo, A. Del Bimbo, and P. Pala. Retrieval by Semantic Content of Commercials:
     the Semiotic Perspective. To appear in Multimedia Tools and Application Journal 1999.

[15] J.M. Pike and C.G. Harris. A combined corner and edge detector. In *Proc. Fourth Alvey
     Vision Conference*, pages 147–151, 1988.

Combined Invariants to Convolution and Rotation and their Application to Image Registration

Jan Flusser and Barbara Zitová

Institute of Information Theory and Automation, Academy of Sciences of the Czech Republic, Pod vodárenskou věží 4, 182 08 Prague 8, Czech Republic
{flusser,zitova}@utia.cas.cz

Abstract. A new class of moment-based features invariant to image rotation, translation, and also to convolution with an unknown point-spread function is introduced in this paper. These features can be used for the recognition of objects captured by a nonideal imaging system of unknown position and blurring parameters. Practical applications to the registration of satellite images is presented.

Keywords: Complex moments, convolution invariants, rotation invariants, invariant basis, image registration.`

1 Introduction

In scene analysis, we often obtain the input information in the form of an image captured by a nonideal imaging system. Most real cameras and other sensors can be modeled as a *linear space-invariant* system, where the relationship between the input $f(x, y)$ and the acquired image $g(x, y)$ is described as

$$g(\tau(x, y)) = a(f * h)(x, y) + n(x, y). \tag{1}$$

In the above model, $h(x, y)$ is the point-spread function (PSF) of the system, $n(x, y)$ is an additive random noise, a is a constant describing the overall change of contrast, τ stands for a transform of spatial coordinates due to projective imaging geometry and $*$ denotes 2D convolution.

In many application areas, it is desirable to find a representation of the scene that does not depend on the imaging system without any prior knowledge of system parameters. Basically, there are two different approaches to this problem: image normalization or direct image description by invariants.

Image normalization consists of geometric registration, that eliminates the impact of imaging geometry and transforms the image into some "standard" form, and blind deconvolution, that removes or suppresses the blurring. Both steps have been extensively studied in the literature, we refer to the recent surveys on registration [3], [9] and on deconvolution/restoration techniques [11], [15]. Generally, image normalization is an ill-posed problem whose computing complexity can be extremely high.

S. Singh, N. Murshed, and W. Kropatsch (Eds.): ICAPR 2001, LNCS 2013, pp. 359–368, 2001.

In the *invariant approach* we look for image descriptors (features) that do not depend on $h(x, y)$, $\tau(x, y)$ and a. In this way we avoid a difficult inversion of eq. (1). In many applications, the invariant approach is much more effective than the normalization. Typical examples are the recognition of objects in the scene against a database, template matching, etc.

Much effort has been spent to find invariants to imaging geometry, particularly to linear and projective transformations. Moment invariants [10], [1], [17], [18], [7], Fourier-domain invariants [12], [2], differential invariants [19], [14], and point sets invariants [13], [16] are the most popular groups of them. On the other hand, only few invariants to convolution have been described in the literature. A consistent theory has been published recently in [8] where two sets of convolution invariants were constructed in spatial as well as Fourier domains. Unfortunately, those features are not invariant to rotation and therefore their practical utilization is limited.

This paper introduces *combined invariants* that are invariant both to convolution and linear transform of spatial coordinates.

The rest of the paper is organized as follows. In Section 2, basic definitions and propositions are given to build up the necessary mathematical background. In Section 3, the invariants to convolution composed of the complex moments are introduced and a derivation of the combined invariants is given. We also show how to select a complete and independent system of them. In Sections 4, an application of the combined invariants to satellite image registration is presented.

2   Mathematical background

In this Section, we introduce basic terms and propositions that will be used later in the paper.

Definition 1: By *image function* (or *image*) we understand any real function $f(x, y) \in L_1$ having a bounded support and nonzero integral.

Definition 2: *Complex moment* $c_{pq}^{(f)}$ of order $(p + q)$, where $p \geq 0$ and $q \geq 0$, of the image $f(x, y)$ is defined as

$$c_{pq}^{(f)} = \int_{-\infty}^{\infty} \int_{-\infty}^{\infty} (x + iy)^p (x - iy)^q f(x, y) dx dy, \tag{2}$$

where i denotes the imaginary unit.

In polar coordinates, (2) becomes the form

$$c_{pq}^{(f)} = \int_0^{\infty} \int_0^{2\pi} r^{p+q+1} e^{i(p-q)\theta} f(r, \theta) d\theta dr. \tag{3}$$

It follows immediately from (3) that $c_{pq} = c_{qp}^*$ (the asterix denotes a complex conjugate).

The following Lemmas describe an important rotation property of the complex moments and their behavior under convolution.

Lemma 1: Let f' be a rotated version (around the origin) of f, i. e. $f'(r,\theta) = f(r, \theta + \alpha)$ where α is the angle of rotation. Let us denote the complex moments of f' as c'_{pq}. Then

$$c'_{pq} = e^{-i(p-q)\alpha} \cdot c_{pq}. \tag{4}$$

Lemma 2: Let $f(x,y)$ and $h(x,y)$ be two image functions and let $g(x,y) = (f * h)(x,y)$. Then $g(x,y)$ is also an image function and we have, for its moments,

$$c_{pq}^{(g)} = \sum_{k=0}^{p} \sum_{j=0}^{q} \binom{p}{k} \binom{q}{j} c_{kj}^{(h)} c_{p-k,q-j}^{(f)}$$

for any p and q.

In the following text, we assume that the PSF $h(x,y)$ is centrally symmetric (i.e. $h(x,y) = h(-x,-y)$) and that the imaging system is energy preserving, i.e. $\int_{-\infty}^{\infty} \int_{-\infty}^{\infty} h(x,y)dxdy = 1$. The centrosymmetry implies that $c_{pq}^{(h)} = 0$ if $p+q$ is odd. The assumption of centrosymmetry is not a significant limitation of practical utilization of the method. Most real sensors and imaging systems, both optical and nonoptical ones, have the PSF with certain degree of symmetry. In many cases they have even higher symmetry than the central one, such as axial or radial symmetry. Thus, the central symmetry is general enough to describe almost all practical situations.

3   Invariants to convolution and rotation

In this Section, we introduce a new class of features, called *combined invariants*, invariant simultaneously to convolution with an arbitrary centrosymmetric PSF and rotation. Theorem 1 introduces invariants to convolution that are further used in Theorem 2 to define combined invariants.

Theorem 1: Let $f(x,y)$ be an image function. Let us define the following function $K^{(f)} : \mathcal{Z} \times \mathcal{Z} \to \mathcal{C}$, where $\mathcal{Z}$ is the set of non-negative integers and $\mathcal{C}$ is the set of complex numbers.
If $(p + q)$ is even then

$$K(p,q)^{(f)} = 0.$$

If $(p + q)$ is odd then

$$K(p,q)^{(f)} = c_{pq}^{(f)} - \frac{1}{c_{00}^{(f)}} \sum_{\substack{n=0 \\ 0<n+m<p+q}}^{p} \sum_{m=0}^{q} \binom{p}{n} \binom{q}{m} K(p-n,q-m)^{(f)} \cdot c_{nm}^{(f)}. \tag{5}$$

Then $K(p,q)^{(f*h)} = K(p,q)^{(f)}$ for any p and q and for any centrosymmetric $h(x,y)$.

For the proof of Theorem 1, we refer to our earlier paper [5], where a similar theorem is formulated and proven for standard moments. The proof in case of complex moments is analogous.

As can be easily proven by induction, the invariants $K(p, q)$ have the same rotation property as the complex moments themselves. Thus,

$$K'(p, q) = e^{-i(p-q)\alpha} \cdot K(p, q). \tag{6}$$

Theorem 2: Let $n \geq 1$ and let k_j, p_j and $q_j; j = 1, \cdots, n$, be non-negative integers such that $(p_j + q_j)$ is odd for each j and that

$$\sum_{j=1}^{n} k_j (p_j - q_j) = 0.$$

Then

$$I = \prod_{j=1}^{n} K(p_j, q_j)^{k_j} \tag{7}$$

is invariant to rotation around the origin and to convolution with a centrosymmetric PSF.

According to Theorem 2, simple examples of the combined invariants are $K(1,0)K(0,1)$, $K(1,0)K(1,2)$, $K(2,1)K(1,2)$, $K(2,1)^3 K(0,3)$, etc. Most invariants (7) are complex. If one prefers to have real-valued features, one can consider their real and imaginary parts separately.

Theorem 2 allows us to construct, for any order of the convolution invariants, an infinite number of the combined invariants, but only few of them are mutually independent. For the rest of this Section, the attention is paid to the construction of a basis of combined invariants. By the term *basis* we intuitively understand the smallest set of the combined invariants, by means of which all other invariants can be expressed. The knowledge of the basis is a crucial point in all object recognition tasks, because it provides the same discrimination power as the set of all invariants at minimum computational cost.

Definition 3: Let $k \geq 1$, let $\mathcal{I} = \{I_1, \cdots, I_k\}$ be a set of the combined invariants (7) and let J be an invariant of the same type. Invariant J is said to be *dependent on* $\mathcal{I}$ if and only if there exists a function F of k variables containing only the operations multiplication, involution with an integer (positive or negative) exponent and complex conjugation, such that

$$J = F(I_1, \cdots, I_k).$$

A set of invariants is said to be dependent if one of its elements depends on the rest of the set. Thus, $\{K(2,1)K(1,2), K(2,1)^2 K(1,2)^2\}$, $\{K(0,1)K(2,1), K(1,0)K(1,2)\}$ and $\{K(1,0)K(1,2), K(1,0)K(3,0)K(1,2)^4, K(3,0)K(1,2)^3\}$ are typical examples of dependent invariant sets.

Definition 4: Let $\mathcal{I}$ be a set of the combined invariants (7) and let $\mathcal{B}$ be its subset. $\mathcal{B}$ is a basis of $\mathcal{I}$ if and only if

- $\mathcal{B}$ is independent,
- Any element of $\mathcal{I} - \mathcal{B}$ depends on $\mathcal{B}$ (this property is called *completeness*).

Construction of the basis is solved by the following Theorem.

Theorem 3: Let $\mathcal{S}$ be a set of the convolution invariants (5) of any odd orders (not necessarily of all invariants), let $\mathcal{S}^*$ be a set of their complex conjugates and let $K(p_0, q_0) \in \mathcal{S} \cup \mathcal{S}^*$ such that $p_0 - q_0 = 1$ and $K(p_0, q_0) \neq 0$. Let $\mathcal{I}$ be a set of all combined invariants created from the elements of $\mathcal{S} \cup \mathcal{S}^*$ according to (7). Let $\mathcal{B} \subset \mathcal{I}$ be constructed as follows:

$$(\forall p, q | p > q \wedge K(p, q) \in \mathcal{S} \cup \mathcal{S}^*)(\varPhi(p, q) \equiv K(p, q)K(q_0, p_0)^{p-q} \in \mathcal{B}).$$

Then $\mathcal{B}$ is a basis of $\mathcal{I}$.

The proof of Theorem 3 can be found in our recent paper [6]. Using Theorem 3, we can set up for instance a basis of all combined invariants up to the fifth order $\mathcal{B}_5 = \{K(1,0)K(1,2), K(2,1)K(1,2), K(3,0)K(1,2)^3, K(5,0)K(1,2)^5, K(4,1)K(1,2)^3, K(3,2)K(1,2)\}$.

Note that Theorem 3 does not guarantee the uniqueness of the basis. Different choices of p_0 and q_0 lead to different bases. For practical reasons it is recommended to choose p_0 and q_0 as small as possible because low-order moments are more robust to noise than the higher-order ones.

4   Application to satellite image registration

Image registration is the process of overlaying two or more images of the same scene acquired from different viewpoints, by different sensors and/or at different times so that the pixels of the same coordinates in the images correspond to the same part of the scene. Image registration is required as a pre-processing stage in analysis of remotely sensed data, medical image analysis, image fusion, in automatic change detection and scene monitoring, among others. Here, the use of the combined invariants in satellite image registration is presented.

Regardless of the image data involved and of the particular application, image registration usually consists of the four major steps.

- *Detection of control point candidates.* CPCs are significant points or structures detected automatically (edge intersections, objects centroids, significant contour points, etc.) or manually by a domain expert.
- *Control point matching.* The correspondence between the CPCs in the reference and sensed images is established. Matching methods are based on the image content (cross-correlation, mutual information) or on symbolic description of the CPC sets (parameter clustering, graph matching, relaxation, invariant approaches).

Fig. 1. The detected CPCs in the reference image: real satellite data, SPOT subscene of the size 400×400 pixels, band 2. Numbered CPCs have the counterpart in the sensed image.

- *Estimation of the mapping model.* The type and parameters of spatial transform present between the reference and sensed images are estimated. The type of the mapping function can be global (linear, projective or quadratic transform model) or local (local triangular mapping, radial basis functions, thin-plate splines), depending on the type of the image distortions.
- *Resampling and transformation.* The sensed image is transformed over the reference one according to the above mapping model. Appropriate resampling technique (nearest neighbor, linear or cubic interpolation) is employed to find image values in non-integer coordinates.

The combined invariants enter the process of image registration in the second step, CP matching. They are calculated over a circular neighborhood of each CP candidate detected earlier in the first step. After that, the correspondence is established by minimum distance rule with thresholding in the Euclidean space of the invariants. Herein described application uses the combined invariants for registration of satellite images, that are rotated and shifted one another and differently blurred. In practice, the blurring function is often an unknown composite function describing the degradation effects of the sensor and the atmosphere. Thanks to the invariance of the combined invariants to rotation, translation and also to image blurring by any symmetric PSF, blurred images can be registered directly without any de-blurring. Most of the earlier matching methods fail in such a case.

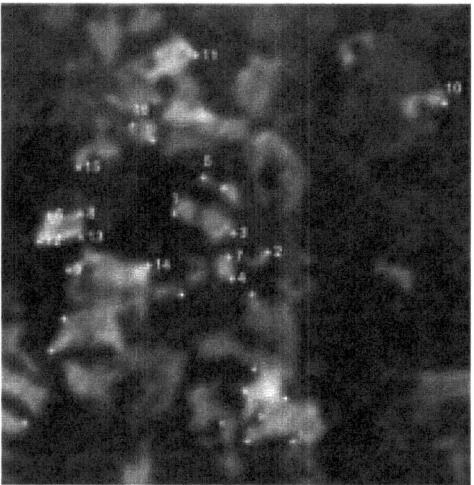

Fig. 2. The detected CPCs in the sensed image: real satellite data, different SPOT subscene of the size 325×325 pixels, band 2, from the same fly over covering approximately the same ground. The image was rotated by 15 degrees, the non-ideal acquisition was simulated by blurring with the 7×7 averaging mask. Numbered CPCs have the counterpart in the reference image.

The experiment was performed on real satellite data with simulated blurring and rotation. The reference image of the size 400×400 pixels was extracted from the SPOT subscene, Czech Republic, band 2 (see Fig. 1). The sensed image of the size 325×325 pixels was extracted from the different SPOT subscene, band 2, from the same flight covering approximately the same ground. It was then rotated by 15 degrees and the nonideal acquisition was simulated by blurring with the 7×7 averaging mask (see Fig. 2).

To find CPCs in the both frames, a method developed particularly for detection of corner-like dominant points in blurred images [20] was employed. 30 CPCs selected in the reference and sensed images are depicted in Figs. 1 and 2, respectively.

The CPC matching has been realized by the following algorithm.

Algorithm Match:

Input: Two sets of CPCs from the sensed and reference images. These sets may contain also some points having no counterparts in the other set.

1. *Invariant vector computation.* A vector of invariants is computed for each CPC over its circular neighborhood of the radius 60 pixels. The vector consist of the following blur-rotation invariants basic combined invariants: ($\Phi(2,1)$, $\Phi(3,0)$, $\Phi(5,0)$, $\Phi(4,1)$, $\Phi(3,2)$, $\Phi(7,0)$, $\Psi(6,1)$, $\Phi(5,2)$ and $\Phi(4,3)$, where $p_0 = 2$ and $q_0 = 1$).

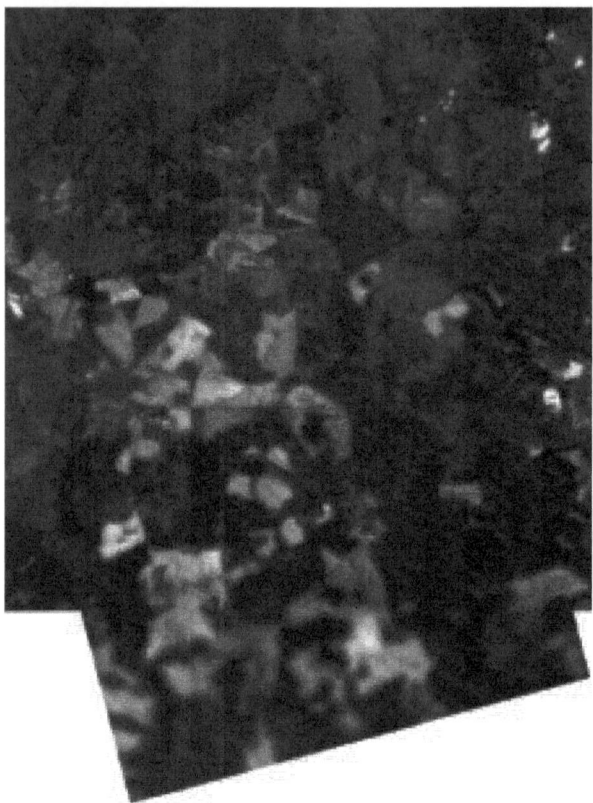

Fig. 3. The registered sensed image overlaid over the reference one. Intensity values in the overlapped area are calculated as the mean of the corresponding intensity values of the reference and sensed images.

2. *CPC correspondence.* The two most-likely matching CPC pairs can be found as the ones with the minimum distance of their invariant vectors. To gain higher robustness, the Matching Likelihood Coefficients [4] can be employed instead of the minimum distance criterion (as it was done in our experiments). CPCs from the sensed image are transformed using a similarity transform the coefficients of which are calculated by means of the two above mentioned CPC pairs. Correspondence between transformed CPCs from the sensed image and CPCs in the reference image is found via the thresholded nearest neighbor rule in the spatial domain (Figs. 1 and 2). Knowing the correspondence the set of matched control point (CP) pairs is established.

3. *Improvement of CP localization in the sensed image.* For each CP in the sensed image, its improved position is found in its local neighborhood. For every point from the neighborhood its invariant vector is computed according to Step 1. The point with the minimum distance between its invariant vector and the invariant vector of the CP counterpart is found and set as the improved position of the CP.

Algorithm Match has several user-defined parameters, namely the number of the invariants involved, the radius of the neighborhood the invariants are calculated from, the distance threshold used in Step 2 and the radius of the neighborhood used for localization improvement. The choice of the parameters is influenced by the type of the images and an extent of the blurring degradation, among others. The experiments we have performed indicate that from 3 to 9 invariants usually provide sufficient discriminative power. Furthermore, the more blurred the images are, the larger neighborhood for calculating the invariants should be. Common values range from 30 to 90 pixels. The neighborhood should be larger than the support of the PSF otherwise the robustness to the so-called "boundary effect" can be low. Along the boundary of the region of interest, gray level values are influenced by pixels from outside and convolution is not well defined within this region. The distance threshold in Step 2 should be low (typically less than 7 pixels), false matches could be found otherwise. The neighborhoods for position improvement should be small (2 or 3 pixel radius) because of high computational cost of this step and because the CPC detection algorithm should not produce higher deviations of the candidate positions.

The sensed image is transformed using the mapping function – similarity transform – whose coefficients were calculated via least-square technique by means of the matched CPs. Inter-pixel gray values are estimated via bilinear interpolation. The co-registered images are shown in Fig. 3. Intensity values in the overlapped area are calculated as the mean of the corresponding intensity values of the reference and sensed images.

5   Conclusion

In this paper, a consistent and well-developed theory of the invariants to image blurring and rotation is presented. Arbitrarily large independent and complete system of the combined invariants of any orders can be constructed by means of the method described in this paper. These invariants can be used for object recognition when an unknown rotation and blur are present. In that way, we avoid image deblurring and geometric normalization.

Practical applications of the presented theoretical results can be found in recognition of objects captured by a non-ideal imaging system, in medical and remote sensing image registration as well as in other tasks when dealing with non-ideal, blurred and geometrically distorted images.

5.1   Acknowledgment

This work has been supported by the grant No. 102/00/1711 of the Grant Agency of the Czech Republic.

References

[1] Y. S. Abu-Mostafa and D. Psaltis. Recognitive aspects of moment invariants. IEEE Trans. Pattern Analysis and Machine Intelligence, 6:698–706, 1984.

[2] K. Arbter, W. E. Snyder, H. Burkhardt, and G. Hirzinger. Application of affine-invariant Fourier descriptors to recognition of 3-D objects. IEEE Trans. Pattern Analysis and Machine Intelligence, 12:640–647, 1990.

[3] L. G. Brown. A survey of image registration techniques. ACM Computing Surveys, 24:325–376, 1992.

[4] J. Flusser. Object matching by means of matching likelihood coefficients. Pattern Recognition Letters, 16:893–900, 1995.

[5] J. Flusser and T. Suk. Degraded image analysis: An invariant approach. IEEE Transactions on Pattern Analysis and Machine Intelligence, 20(6):590–603, 1998.

[6] J. Flusser and B. Zitová. Combined invariants to linear filtering and rotation. Intl. J. Pattern Recognition Art. Intell., 13(8):1123–1136, 1999.

[7] J. Flusser and T. Suk. Pattern recognition by affine moment invariants. Pattern Recognition, 26:167–174, 1993.

[8] J. Flusser and T. Suk. Degraded image analysis: An invariant approach. IEEE Trans. Pattern Analysis and Machine Intelligence, 20:590–603, 1998.

[9] L. M. G. Fonseca and B. S. Manjunath. Registration techniques for multisensor remotely sensed imagery. Photogrammetric Eng. Remote Sensing, 62:1049–1056, 1996.

[10] M. K. Hu. Visual pattern recognition by moment invariants. IRE Trans. Information Theory, 8:179–187, 1962.

[11] D. Kundur and D. Hatzinakos. Blind image deconvolution. IEEE Signal Processing Magazine, 13(3):43–64, 1996.

[12] W. G. Lin and S. Wang. A note on the calculation of moments. Pattern Recognition Letters, 15:1065–1070, 1994.

[13] J. L. Mundy and A. Zisserman. Geometric Invariance in Computer Vision. MIT Press, 1992.

[14] C. A. Rothwell, A. Zisserman, D. A. Forsyth, and J. L. Mundy. Canonical frames for planar object recognition. Proc. 2nd European Conf. Computer Vision, pages 757–772, Springer, 1992.

[15] M. I. Sezan and A. M. Tekalp. Survey of recent developments in digital image restoration. Optical Engineering, 29:393–404, 1990.

[16] T. Suk and J. Flusser. Vertex-based features for recognition of projectively deformed polygons. Pattern Recognition, 29:361–367, 1996.

[17] M. R. Teague. Image analysis via the general theory of moments. J. Optical Soc. of America, 70:920–930, 1980.

[18] C. H. Teh and R. T. Chin. On image analysis by the method of moments. IEEE Trans. Pattern Analysis and Machine Intelligence, 10:496–513, 1988.

[19] I. Weiss. Projective invariants of shapes. Proc. Image Understanding Workshop, pages 1125–1134, Cambridge, Mass., 1988.

[20] B. Zitová, J. Kautsky, G. Peters, and J. Flusser. Robust detection of significant points in multiframe images. Pattern Recognition Letters, 20(2):199–206, 1999.

Modelling Plastic Distortion in Fingerprint Images

R. Cappelli, D. Maio and D. Maltoni

DEIS, CSITE - CNR, Università di Bologna, viale Risorgimento 2, 40136 Bologna - Italy.
E-mail: {rcappelli,dmaio,dmaltoni}@deis.unibo.it

Abstract

This paper introduces a plastic distortion model to cope with the non-linear deformations characterizing fingerprint images taken with on-line acquisition sensors. The problem has a great impact on several practical applications, ranging from the design of robust fingerprint matching algorithms to the generation of synthetic fingerprint images. The experimentation on real data validates the model and demonstrates its efficacy in registering minutiae data from highly distorted fingerprint samples.

Keywords: Biometric systems, Personal identification, Fingerprint matching, Fingerprint Deformation, Distortion Model.

1 Introduction

In the age of the new economy, the advent of a great number of applications requiring users to be securely authenticated (e-commerce, e-trading, personal computer protection) has revived the interest in biometric techniques [4] and, in particular, in fingerprint recognition [8].

Great progress has been made in the development of on-line fingerprint sensing techniques [4] and, as a consequence, several small and inexpensive sensing elements have overrun the market. Significant improvements have been achieved on the algorithmic side as well, but a great number of challenging problems still exist. In particular, a mass-adoption of such technologies requires the matching algorithms to become more tolerant with respect to some factors which prevent the false rejection rate (i.e. the percentage of users who are erroneously rejected by the system) from decreasing beyond a certain limit.

One of the main difficulties in matching two fingerprint samples of the same finger is to deal with the non linear distortions, often produced by an incorrect finger placement over the sensing element, which make a global rigid comparison unfeasible. Most of the existing matching techniques adopt strategies aimed at measuring local similarity (instead of global similarity) in order to improve their robustness with respect to the distortion affecting fingerprint patterns [6] [7] [8] [10]. To the best of our knowledge, none of these techniques explicitly attempts to model fingerprint distortion, but they tend to relax the definition of similarity to some extent in order to take into account small elastic deformations.

S. Singh, N. Murshed, and W. Kropatsch (Eds.): ICAPR 2001, LNCS 2013, pp. 369–376, 2001.
© Springer-Verlag Berlin Heidelberg 2001

The aim of this work is to introduce a plastic distortion model to describe how fingerprint images are deformed when the user improperly places his/her finger on the sensor plate. The motivation of this effort is twofold: first, a good comprehension of the distortion dynamics can be very useful in designing new robust (distortion tolerant) fingerprint matching algorithms; secondly in the context of synthetic fingerprint image generation [1], that we are promoting as a powerful and inexpensive way of generating large fingerprint databases for performance evaluation, the deformation model provides an effective way of producing different realistic impressions of the same finger.

2   The plastic distortion model

Pressing the finger tip against the plain surface of an on-line acquisition sensor produces, as the main effect, a 3d to 2d mapping of the finger skin. However, the aim of this work is not to investigate the characteristic of such a mapping; here we consider a fingerprint image as *non-distorted* when it is produced by a *correct* finger placement; a finger placement is correct when the user:

1. moves the finger towards the sensor in a direction which is perfectly orthogonal with respect to the sensor surface.
2. does not apply traction or torsion once the finger touches the sensor surface.

In fact, due to the skin plasticity, the application of forces, some of whose components are not orthogonal to the sensor surface, produces non-linear distortions (compression or stretching) in the acquired fingerprints.
In general, the finger pressure against the sensor plate is not uniform but decreases moving from the centre toward the borders, and it is possible to distinguish 3 distinct regions (see figure 1):

a) a close-contact region where the high pressure and the surface friction does not allow any skin slippage.

c) an external region, whose boundary delimits the fingerprint visible area, where the light pressure allows the finger skin to be dragged by the finger movement.

b) a transitional region where an elastic distortion is produced to smoothly combine regions *a* and *c*. The skin compression and stretching is restricted to region *b*, since points in *a* remain almost fixed and points in *c* rigidly move together with the rest of the finger.

Let $\mathbf{v} = [x, y]^T$ be a generic point on the fingerprint surface; we introduce the function $shapedist_a : \Re^2 \to \Re$ to model both:

- the shape of the close-contact region (*a*)
- the distance of a generic point $\mathbf{v}$ from the region *a*.

$$shapedist_a(\mathbf{v}) = \begin{cases} 0 & \text{within region } a \text{ (boundary included)} \\ dist_a(\mathbf{v}) & \text{outside region } a \end{cases}$$

$shapedist_a(\mathbf{v})$ indicates the position of $\mathbf{v}$ with respect to the region a; when $\mathbf{v}$ is outside a, this function returns a measure proportional to the distance between the point and the border of a ($dist_a(\mathbf{v})$ is here intentionally left undefined to confer a greater generality to the model).

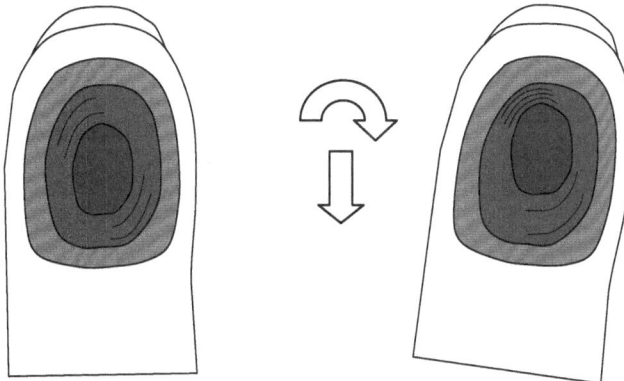

Fig. 1. Bottom view of a finger before and after the application of traction and torsion forces. In both cases the fingerprint area detected by the sensor (i.e. the finger touching area) is delimited by the external boundary of region c.

The torsion and traction forces applied to the finger move the points in region c by an amount $\Delta(\mathbf{v})$, which can be computed on the basis of a rotation angle θ and a displacement vector $\mathbf{d}$ (according to an affine transformation with no scale changes):

$$\Delta(\mathbf{v}) = (\mathbf{R}_\theta(\mathbf{v} - \mathbf{c}_0) + \mathbf{c}_0 + \mathbf{d}) - \mathbf{v}, \qquad \mathbf{d} = \begin{bmatrix} dx \\ dy \end{bmatrix}, \quad \mathbf{R}_\theta = \begin{bmatrix} \cos\theta & \sin\theta \\ -\sin\theta & \cos\theta \end{bmatrix}$$

where $\mathbf{c}_0$ is the centre of rotation.

The gradual transition occurring in region b, is described by the following function:

$$brake: \Re \times \Re \to \Re, \quad brake(t,k) = \begin{cases} 0 & \text{if } t \leq 0 \\ \dfrac{1}{2}\left(1 - \cos\left(\dfrac{t \cdot \pi}{k}\right)\right) & \text{if } 0 \leq t \leq k \\ 1 & \text{otherwise} \end{cases}$$

Figure 2 plots the *brake* function for a given *k*: this parameter denotes the width of the transition interval.

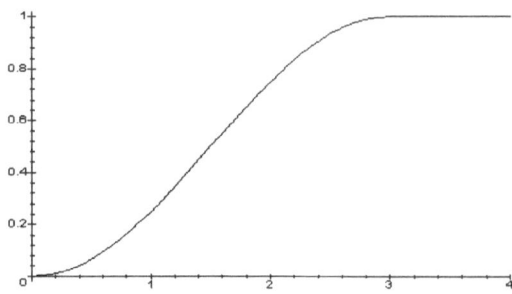

Fig. 2. The function *brake* plotted for $k=3$, $t=0..4$

The overall distortion transformation can then be expressed as:

$$distortion : \Re^2 \to \Re^2 , \quad distortion(\mathbf{v}) = \mathbf{v} + \Delta(\mathbf{v}) \cdot brake(shapedist_a(\mathbf{v}), k)$$

The shape and size of regions *b* and *c* are implicitly determined by *a*, $dist_a(\mathbf{v})$ and *k*; in fact, the internal *c* boundary is the locus of points where $brake(shapedist_a(\mathbf{v}), k) = 1$. The parameter *k* can be conceived as a skin plasticity coefficient, since using a higher *k* involves a larger *b* region and a smooth transition between *a* and *c*.

Intuitively, the mapping given by the above distortion formula can be viewed as an affine transformation (with no scale changes) which is progressively "braked" as it moves from *c* towards *a*.

During the experimentation (which will be discussed in the following section) we observed that the contact region is always near-elliptical; then a well-suited shape for the contact region is an ellipse (of centre $\mathbf{c}_e$ and semi-axes s_x and s_y) and a good definition of the $dist_a$ function is the Mahalanobis distance [3] decreased by one:

$$dist_{ell}(\mathbf{v}) = \sqrt{(\mathbf{v} - \mathbf{c}_e)^T \mathbf{A}^{-1}(\mathbf{v} - \mathbf{c}_e)} - 1, \quad \mathbf{c}_e = \begin{bmatrix} c_x \\ c_y \end{bmatrix} \text{ and } \mathbf{A} = \begin{bmatrix} s_x^2 & 0 \\ 0 & s_y^2 \end{bmatrix}$$

Summarizing, when an ellipse is used to model region *a*, the parameters controlling the distortion model are:

t	translation vector
$\theta, \mathbf{c}_0$	angle and centre of rotation
k	skin plasticity coefficient
$\mathbf{c}_e, \mathbf{A}$	ellipse

In figure 3 the distortion of a square mesh is shown for different parameter values.

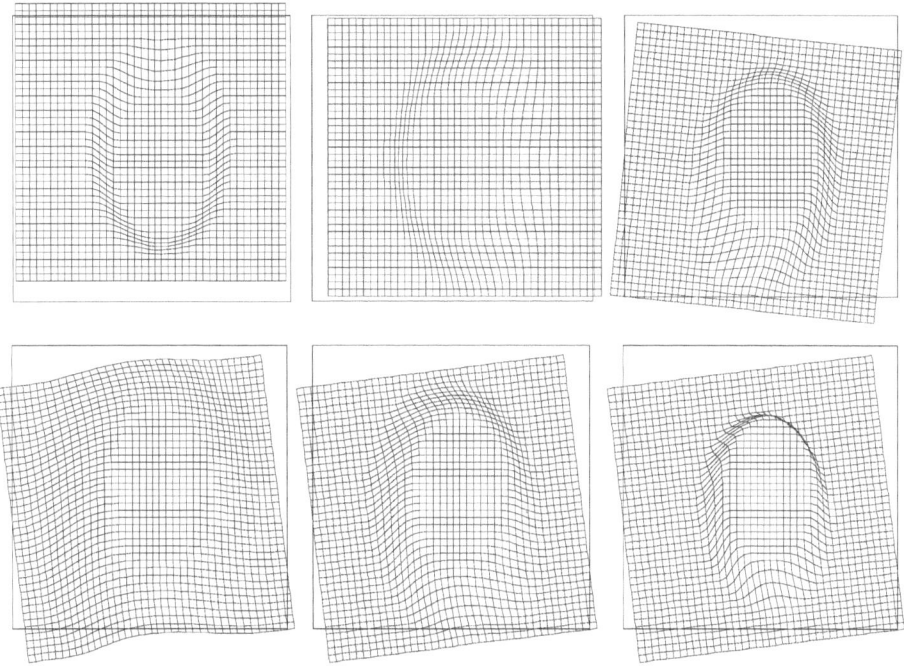

Fig. 3. Distortions of a square mesh obtained by applying the above model with different parameter settings. The black square denotes the initial mesh position and its movement with respect to the mesh boundary indicates the amount of displacement and rotation that occurred. In the first row different transformations are shown (from the left to the right: a vertical displacement (dy=-21), a horizontal displacement (dx=18) and a combined displacement + rotation (dx=-6, dy=27, θ =-6°)); the second row shows the effect of varying the skin plasticity coefficient k (2.0, 1.0 and 0.5 respectively) for a given transformation.

3   Model validation

In order to validate the distortion model discussed in section 2, we used two sets of distorted fingerprint images. The first set (A) of images was acquired in our laboratory by using a commercially available on-line fingerprint scanner; the second set (B) was extracted from NIST Special DB24 [2] [9] which contains 100 MPEG-2 Digital Video of Live-Scan Fingerprint Data. In both cases, users are required to place their finger on the sensor, and, once they have touched the surface, to intentionally move the finger without lifting it from the surface: doing this produces exaggerated plastic distortions which can be exploited for a better comprehension of the phenomenon.

Figure 4 contains two examples: one taken from set A (first row) and one from set B (second row); the first column shows non-distorted fingerprint images, the second column shows distorted impressions of the same fingers and the third column shows the pixel-by-pixel difference of the two images on the left. Some minutiae points [5] have been manually labelled on both the images for a better analysis of image correspondences.

In both cases, it is well evident (from the third column) that around a central region, where the image remains almost unchanged, significant differences exist. The shape of the constant region (corresponding to region a in our model) can be reasonably approximated by an ellipse.

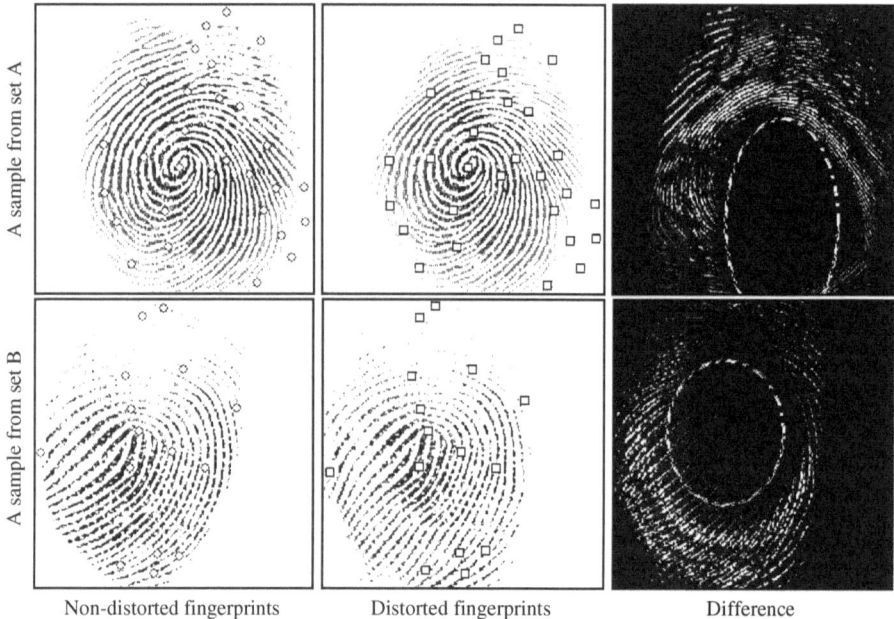

Fig. 4. Two examples of fingerprint distortion: the third column shows the pixel by pixel difference between the fingerprint pairs on the left.

In figure 5 (left column) the two distorted images in figure 4 (central column) are drawn together with their original minutiae (denoted by small squares) and the corresponding minutiae as located in the original images (denoted by small circles). Clearly evident displacements exist between pairs of corresponding minutiae, thus indicating the large amount of distortion affecting these images. In the central column, the same fingerprint images are shown, but now the minutiae from the non-distorted samples have been re-mapped by applying the distortion function introduced in section 2. The good spatial minutiae matching obtained proves that the model is capable of dealing with such deformations. The model parameters have been manually adjusted and not necessarily constitute the best choice. The corresponding mesh distortion is plotted in the third column and shows that in the former case the deformation is mainly caused by a vertical (downward) traction producing a compression at the top, whereas in the latter a (counter clockwise) torsion is the most evident cause.

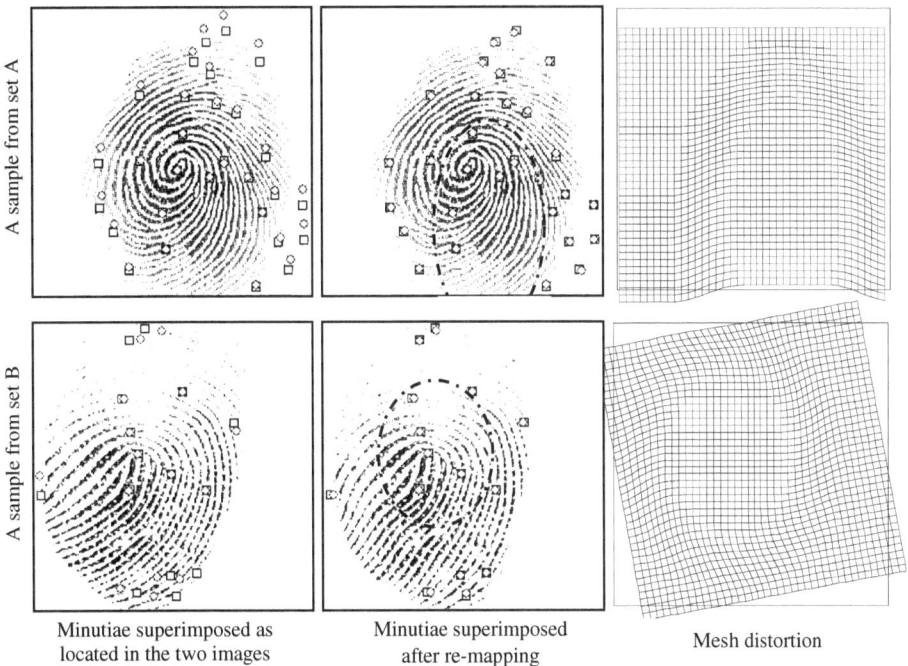

Minutiae superimposed as located in the two images   Minutiae superimposed after re-mapping   Mesh distortion

Fig. 5. Minutiae correspondence before (first column) and after (second column) the application of the distortion function. The third column shows the corresponding mesh deformation.

To numerically evaluate how much the distortion model fits real data, we manually labelled minutiae points in 10 image pairs (5 pairs from set A and 5 from set B); for each pair, we manually adjusted the model parameters and we measured the average distance between corresponding minutiae before and after applying the "normalizing" distortion function (table 1).

Table 1. Average distances between corresponding minutiae, before and after the application of the distortion function, respectively.

Set A		Set B	
Before	*After*	*Before*	*After*
10.37	3.82	12.14	1.98
10.83	2.24	24.60	2.56
10.04	2.88	24.74	5.10
9.30	2.23	17.11	2.76
5.77	2.32	26.96	3.00

Table 2 reports the average distances over all the fingerprints of the two sets: the results obtained are very good, thus proving that the distortion function here proposed is well-suited to model fingerprint plastic distortion.

Table 2. Average over all the experiments.

Average	
Before	*After*
15.19	2.89

4   Conclusions

This paper introduces a mathematical model for fingerprint plastic distortion, thus providing a valid instrument for developing new distortion-tolerant fingerprint matching algorithms. The experimental results prove that the problem, which was never adequately modelled to date, has been successfully addressed here.

The study of an effective and efficient optimisation technique which is capable of automatically extracting the deformation parameters (given a pair of fingerprint images) constitutes a very interesting challenge and is the target of our future efforts.

References

1. R. Cappelli, A. Erol, D. Maio and D. Maltoni, "Synthetic Fingerprint-image Generation", to appear on *proceedings International Conference on Pattern Recognition (ICPR2000)*, Barcelona, September 2000.
2. C. Dorai, N. K. Ratha and R. M. Bolle, "Detecting dynamic behaviour in compressed fingerprint videos: distortion", Proc. Of CVPR 2000, Hilton Head, Vol. II, pp. 320--326, June 2000.
3. R.O. Duda and P.E. Hart, *Pattern Classification and Scene Analysis*, Wiley, 1974.
4. A.K. Jain, R. Bolle and S. Pankanti, Biometrics, *Personal Identification in Networked Society*, Kluwer Academic Publisher, 1999.
5. H. C. Lee e R. E. Gaensslen, *Advances in Fingerprint Technology*, CRC Press, 1991.
6. D. Maio and D. Maltoni, "An efficient approach to on-line fingerprint verification", in *proceedings VIII International Symposium on Artificial Intelligence*, Mexico, pp.132-138, October 1995.
7. N. K. Ratha and R. M. Bolle, "Effect of controlled image acquisition on fingerprint matching", ICPR 98, Brisbane, Vol. II, pp. 1659-1661, Aug. 1998.
8. W. Shen and R. Khanna, *Proceedings of the IEEE (Special issue on Automated Biometric Systems)*, September 1997.
9. C.I. Watson, *NIST Special Database 24 Digital Video of Live-Scan Fingerprint Data*, U.S. National Institute of Standards and Technology, 1998.
10. C.L. Wilson, C.I. Watson and E.G. Paek, "Effect of Resolution and Image Quality on Combined Optical and Neural Network Fingerprint Matching", *Technical Report NISTIR 6184*, July 1998.

Image Retrieval Using a Hierarchy of Clusters

Daniela Stan & Ishwar K. Sethi
Intelligent Information Engineering Laboratory,
Department of Computer Science & Engineering, Oakland University,
Rochester, Michigan 48309-4478
dstan@oakland.edu & isethi@oakland.edu

Abstract

The goal of this paper is to describe an efficient procedure for color-based image retrieval. The proposed procedure consists of two stages. First, the image data set is hierarchically decomposed into disjoint subsets by applying an adaptation of the k-means clustering algorithm. Since Euclidean measure may not effectively reproduce human perception of a visual content, the adaptive algorithm uses a non-Euclidean similarity metric and clustroids as cluster prototypes. Second, the derived hierarchy is searched by a branch and bound method to facilitate rapid calculation of the k-nearest neighbors for retrieval in a ranked order. The proposed procedure has the advantage of handling high dimensional data, and dealing with non-Euclidean similarity metrics in order to explore the nature of the image feature vectors. The hierarchy also provides users with a tool for quick browsing.

1. Introduction

The increasing rate at which images are generated in many application areas, gives rise to the need of image retrieval systems to provide an effective and efficient access to image databases, based on their visual content. While it is perfectly feasible to identify a desired image from a small collection simply by browsing, techniques that are more effective are needed with collections containing thousands, or millions of items. The current image retrieval techniques can be classified according to the type and nature of the features used for indexing and retrieval. Keyword indexing techniques manually assign keywords or classification codes to each image when it is first added to the collection and use these descriptors as retrieval keys at search time. Their advantages consist of high expressive power, possibility to describe image content from the level of primitive features to the level of abstract features, involving a significant amount of reasoning about the meaning and purpose of the objects or scenes depicted.

On the other hand, manual indexing presents few drawbacks regarding the usefulness of the assigned keywords and the indexing time. Since the same picture can have different meanings for different people, different keywords could be associated with the same picture [1]. When the indexing time for every image takes few minutes, to index a collection of million images is an intensive and time consuming work.

Methods that permit image searching based on features automatically extracted from the images themselves are referred as content-based image retrieval (CBIR)

S. Singh, N. Murshed, and W. Kropatsch (Eds.): ICAPR 2001, LNCS 2013, pp. 377–386, 2001.

techniques [2]. Color retrieval yields the best results, in that the computer results of color similarity are similar to those derived by a human visual system [3]. The retrieval becomes more efficient when the spatial arrangement and coupling of colors over the image are taken into account or when one more low-level feature, such as texture or shape, is added to the system. The most notable example of querying by color is IBM's QBIC system [4] that has been applied successfully in color matching of items in electronic mail order catalogues. One drawback of the current content-based image retrieval systems is their limitation to the low level features even if some researchers have attempted to fill the gap between low-level features and semantic features, by deriving high-level semantic concepts (harmony, disharmony, calmness, excitement) from color arrangements [5]. Another problem with the existing image retrieval systems is that these systems do not provide a summary view of the images in their database to their users. The necessity of a summary view appears when the user has no specific query image at the beginning of the search process and wants to explore the image collection to locate images of interest [6]. The indexing structure is also a big issue for CBIR systems. Image features are often very high dimensional or the similarity metrics are too complex to have efficient indexing structures. The existing multi-dimensional indexing techniques concentrate only on how to identify and improve indexing techniques that are scalable to high dimensional feature vectors in image retrieval [7]. The other nature of feature vectors in Image Retrieval, i.e. non-Euclidean similarity measures, cannot be explored using structures that have been developed based on Euclidean distance metrics such as the k-d trees, the R-d trees and its variants.

The goal of this paper is to provide a CBIR system that is scalable to large size image collection and is based on an effective indexing module that solves both high dimensionality and non-Euclidean nature of some color feature spaces. The module is built using an adaptation of k-means clustering in which the metric is a non-Euclidean similarity metric and the cluster prototype is designed to summarize the cluster in a manner that is suited for quick human comprehension of its components. These prototypes give the system the capability of quick browsing through the entire image collection. The proposed system also uses a branch and bound tree-search module that applied to the hierarchy of the resultant clusters will facilitate rapid calculation of the nearest neighbors for retrieval.

The paper is organized as follows. Section 2 describes the color feature representation of the images from the database used in the proposed procedure. Section 3 explains how the hierarchy of similar groups is built by the adaptive k-means algorithm and Section 4 describes how the search is carried out by the branch and bound algorithm. Section 5 considers the effectiveness of the approach and how the user can browse elegantly through the image database; these considerations are expounded with experiments on a database of 2100 images. The paper concludes with some final comments and a note on future work.

2. Color feature representation

Color is one of the most widely used features for image similarity retrieval. This is not surprising given the facts that color is an easily recognizable element of an image and the human visual system is capable of differentiating between infinitely large numbers of colors.

In this paper, we use the Color-WISE representation for image retrieval described in detail in [8]. The representation is guided primarily on three factors. First, the representation must be closely related to human visual perception since a user determines whether a retrieval operation in response to an example query is successful or not. Color-WISE uses the HSV (hue, saturation, value) color coordinate system that correlates well with human color perception and is commonly used by artists to represent color information present in images. Second, the representation must encode the spatial distribution of color in an image. Because of this consideration, Color-WISE system relies on a fixed partitioning scheme. This is in contrast with several proposals in the literature [9] suggesting color-based segmentation to characterize the spatial distribution of color information. Although the color-based segmentation approach provides a more flexible representation and hence more powerful queries, we believe that these advantages are outweighed by the simplicity of the fixed partitioning approach. In the fixed partitioning scheme, each image is divided into M × N overlapping blocks as shown. The overlapping blocks allow a certain amount of 'fuzzy-ness' to be incorporated in the spatial distribution of color information, which helps in obtaining a better performance. Three separate local histograms (hue, saturation and value) for each block are computed. The third factor considered by the Color-WISE system is that fact that the representation should be as compact as possible to minimize storage and computation efforts. To obtain a compact representation, Color-Wise system extracts from each local histogram the location of its area-peak. Placing a fixed-sized window on the histogram at every possible location, the histogram area falling within the window is calculated. The location of the window yielding the highest area determines the histogram area-peak. This value represents the corresponding histogram. Thus, a more compact representation is obtained and each image is reduced to 3 × M × N numbers (3 represents the number of histograms for HSV).

3. Hierarchy of clusters

Clustering is a discovery process in data mining. It groups a set of data in a way that maximizes the similarity within clusters and minimizes the similarity between two different clusters. The discovered clusters can explain the characteristics of the underlying data distribution and serve as foundation for other analysis techniques [10]. Clustering is also useful in implementing the "divide and conquer" strategy to reduce the computational complexity of various decision-making algorithms in pattern recognition.

We use a variation of k-means clustering to build a hierarchy of clusters. At every level of the hierarchy, the variation of k-means clustering uses a non-Euclidean similarity metric and the cluster prototype is designed to summarize the cluster in a manner that is suited for quick human comprehension of its components. The resultant clusters are further divided into other disjoint sub-clusters performing organization of information at several levels, going for finer and finer distinctions.

The results of this hierarchy decomposition are represented by a tree structure in which each node of the tree represents a cluster prototype and at the last level, each leaf represents an image. The hierarchy of the cluster prototypes gives the system the capability of quick browsing through the entire image collection.

This adaptation of k-means algorithm is required since the color triplets (hue, saturation, and value) derived from RGB space by non-linear transformation, are not evenly distributed in the HSV space; the representative of a cluster calculated as a centroid also does not make much sense in such a space. Instead of using the Euclidean distance, we need to define a measure that is closer to the human perception in the sense that the distance between two color triplets is a better approximation to the difference perceived by human. We present below the used similarity metric that takes into account both the perceptual similarity between the different histograms bins and the fact that human perception is more sensitive to changes in hue values; we also present how the cluster representatives are calculated and what is the splitting criterion.

3.1 Color similarity metric

Clustering methods require that an index of proximity or associations be established between pairs of patterns [10]. A proximity index is either a similarity or dissimilarity. The more two images resemble each other, the larger a similarity index and the smaller a dissimilarity index will be.

Since our retrieval system is designed to retrieve the most similar images with a query image, the proximity index will be defined with respect to similarity. Different similarity measures have been suggested in the literature to compare images [3, 11].

We are using in our clustering algorithm the similarity measure that, besides the perceptual similarity between different bins of a color histogram, recognizes the fact that human perception is more sensitive to changes in hue values [8]. It also recognizes that human perception is not proportionally sensitive to changes in hue value.

Let q_i and t_i represent the block number i in a query Q and an image T, respectively. Let $(h_{q_i}, s_{q_i}, v_{q_i})$ and $(h_{t_i}, s_{t_i}, v_{t_i})$ represent the dominant hue-saturation pair of the selected block in the query image and in the image T, respectively. The block similarity is defined by the following relationship:

$$S(q_i, t_i) = \frac{1}{1 + a * D_h(h_{q_i}, h_{t_i}) + b * D_s(s_{q_i}, s_{t_i}) + c * D_v(v_{q_i}, v_{t_i})} \qquad (1)$$

Here D_h, D_s and D_v represent the functions that measure similarity in hue, saturation and value. The constants a, b and c define the relative importance of hue, saturation and value in similarity components. Since human perception is more sensitive to hue, a higher value is assigned to a than to b. The following function was used to calculate D_h:

$$D_h\left(h_{q_i}, h_{t_i}\right) = \frac{1 - \cos^k\left(\left\|h_{q_i} - h_{t_i}\right\| * \frac{2\pi}{256}\right)}{2} \tag{2}$$

The function D_h explicitly takes into account the fact that hue is measured as an angle. Through empirical evaluations, a value of k equal to two provides a good non-linearity in the similarity measure to approximate the subjective judgment of the hue similarity.

The saturation similarity is calculated by: $D_s\left(s_{q_i}, s_{t_i}\right) = \frac{\left\|s_{q_i} - s_{t_i}\right\|}{256}$ (3)

The value similarity is calculated by using the same formula as for saturation similarity. Using the similarities between the corresponding blocks from the query Q and image T, the similarity between a query and an image is calculated by the following expression: $S(Q,T) = \dfrac{\sum\limits_{i=1}^{M \times N} m_i S(q_i, t_i)}{\sum\limits_{i=1}^{M \times N} m_i}$ (4)

The quantity m_i in the above expression represents the masking bit for block i and $M \times N$ stands for the number of blocks.

3.2. Cluster prototypes

The cluster prototypes are designed to summarize the clusters in a manner that is suited for quick human comprehension of its components. They will inform the user about the approximate region in which clusters and their descendants are found. By building the hierarchical tree having the cluster prototypes as interior nodes, the system will allow users to browse the image collection at different levels of details.

We define the cluster prototype to be the most similar image to the other images from the corresponding cluster; in another words, the cluster representative is the *clustroid* point in the feature space, i.e., the point in the cluster that maximizes the sum of the squares of the similarity values to the other points of the cluster. If C is a cluster, its clustroid M is expressed as:

$$M = \arg\left(\max_{I \in C} \sum_{J \in C} S^2(I,J)\right) \tag{5}$$

Here I and J stand for any two images from the cluster C and $S(I,J)$ is their similarity value. We use $\arg$ to denote that the clustroid is the argument (image) for which the maximum of the sums is obtained.

3.3. Splitting criterion

To build a partition for a specified number of clusters K, a splitting criterion is necessary to be defined. Since the hierarchy aims to support similarity searches, we would like nearby feature vectors to be collected in the same or nearby nodes. Thus, the splitting criterion in our algorithm will try to find an optimal partition

$$J_e(K) = \sum_{k=1}^{K} w_k \sum_{I \in C_k} S^2(I, M_k), \text{where } w_k = \frac{1}{n_k} \tag{6}$$

that is defined as one that maximizes the criterion sum-of-squared-error function:

M_k and I stand for the clustroid and any image from cluster C_k, respectively; $S^2(I, M_k)$ represents the squared of the similarity value between I and M_k, and n_k represents the number of elements of cluster C_k.

The reason of maximizing the criterion function comes from the fact that the proximity index measures the similarity; that is, the larger a similarity index value is, the more two images resemble one another.

Once the partition is obtained, in order to validate the clusters, i.e. whether or not the samples form one more cluster, several steps are involved. First, we define the null hypothesis and the alternative hypothesis as follows: H_0: there are exactly K clusters for the n samples, and H_A: the samples form one more cluster. According to the Neyman-Pearson paradigm [12], a decision as to whether or not to reject H_0 in favor of H_A is made based on a statistics $T(n)$. The statistic is nothing else than the cluster validity index that is sensitive to the structure in the data:

$$T(n) = \frac{J_e(K)}{J_e(K+1)} \tag{7}$$

To obtain an approximate critical value for the statistic, that is the index is large enough to be 'unusual', we use a threshold that takes into account that, for large

n, $J_e(K)$ and $J_e(K+1)$ follow a normal distribution. Following these considerations, we consider the threshold τ defined in [13] as:

$$\tau = 1 - \frac{2}{\pi * d} - \alpha * \sqrt{\left[\frac{2 * \left(1 - \frac{8}{\pi^2 * d} \right)}{n * d} \right]} \tag{8}$$

The rejection region for the null hypothesis at the p-percent significance level is:

$$T(n) < \tau \tag{9}$$

The parameter α in (8) is determined from the probability p that the null hypothesis H_0 is rejected when it is true and d is the sample size. The last inequality provides us with a test for deciding whether the splitting of a cluster is justified.

4. The browsing and search strategy

The significant feature of our scheme is the possibility of quick browsing of the image set when no query image is specified. The user can browse first the highest level of the tree representing the hierarchy and get summary views of the entire image collection in the form of the prototypes of the clusters at that level. By traversing down the tree, the user gets finer and finer details from one level to another. Using an analogy with the view layers defined using a hierarchy of self-organization maps [6], we can consider the first level of the tree as a global view level of the entire image collection, the intermediate levels as regional levels and the last layer of the tree as a local layer giving the most detailed summary views for the images. Each node from the last layer points to a group of similar images named image layer.

When a query image is present, the second phase of our algorithm is involved. The search strategy implies a branch and bound algorithm in order to facilitate rapid calculation of the k-nearest neighbors for retrieval. We use the method defined in [14] which tests the nodes of the tree by two simple stopping rules that eliminates the necessity of calculating many distances. The first rule is meant to eliminate from consideration the node and its corresponding group of samples if the distance between the query and the node (clustroid) is greater than the sum between the current distance to the nearest neighbor and the farthest distance from the centroid to any sample from the cluster. The second rule reduces the number of calculations of distances between the query and the samples of the node that survived to rule 1. If the distance from the query to the clustroid is greater than the sum between the current distance to the nearest neighbor and the distance from the clustroid to a sample, do not calculate the distance between the sample and the query anymore.

To perform similarity search, the color representation of the query image is first matched at the first layer to determine the most similar cluster prototypes (nodes) that should be searched further. We eliminate from considerations each node from first layer for which rule 1 is satisfied. The matching is then repeated for the children of one of the nodes from the previous layer that survived to rule 1, and so on until the last layer is reached, which brings out a group of images that can be the most similar to the query image. We do not need to compare each one of these images with the query image since rule 2 filters out the images that not satisfy it. For the images that finally survive, the distances to the query image are calculated and ordered to find the current nearest neighbors. Then the algorithm is applied for the next node that was carried on after applying rule 1 and the table of the current nearest neighbors is updated as needed.

5. Experimental Results

We evaluate our algorithm for browsing and retrieval on an image database of 2100 images. The color vector representation of each image has 3*8*8 elements since each image is partitioned into 8*8 overlapping blocks and the image color content is characterized by three components: hue, saturation and intensity. To perform color-based similarity retrieval, the values of the constants (a, b and c) in formula (1) are experimentally chosen as being 2.5, 0.5 and 0, respectively. We rescale hue and saturation to values between 0 and 255. In order to obtain the first level (global layer) of the hierarchy, we apply k-means algorithm for k = 2, 3 … and at each consequent k, the cluster validity is checked, to ensure that the number of elements in every cluster is a moderate one and the sum-of-squared-error criterion to be satisfied. Comparing the values of the test statistic (7) and the values of the threshold (8) with respect to inequality (9), the possible number of clusters for different small values of the significance level is obtained. Since the value of the statistic for K = 31 is greater than the threshold for consecutive small values of p, we choose the value of K to be 30. Further, we split the nodes having at least 30 images (at least 2% out of the data set) by applying k-means algorithm again and so, a lower level (regional layer) of the hierarchy is obtained. The minimum number of elements in every cluster to go further with splitting is decided as a compromise between the size of the terminal nodes and the number of nodes in the tree. Fewer elements in the final groups produce fewer distance computations in the retrieval stage, but larger number of distance computation in the search stage. We end up with a search tree having 81 nodes, 4 levels and an average of 40 images per terminal node.

Fig. 2 shows a retrieval result for browsing mode. The user browses the first level (global layer) of the tree and hypothetically speaking, the user decides to look for images similar with the prototype of cluster 9. The image will be updated with the images (found in hierarchical clustering process) that are close to the centers of clusters at the next layer. Assuming that the user decides to see images similar with the first prototype of the second layer, the third layer (image layer) will display the group of images similar with the previous chosen prototype.

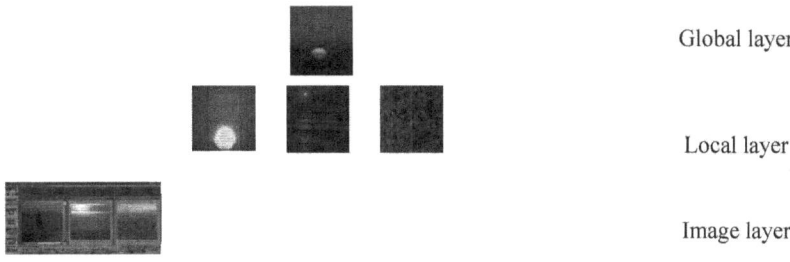

Global layer

Local layer

Image layer

Figure 2.

Fig. 3 shows a retrieval result for search mode. The image query is in the top left of the image. The user wants to retrieve the most three similar images with the image query. Applying the proposed scheme, the following nodes are reached in order to find the 3-nearest neighbors: node 5 at first level, node 28 at second layer, 76 at the final level. The nearest neighbors are picked up from the group of images pointed by node 76.

Query image

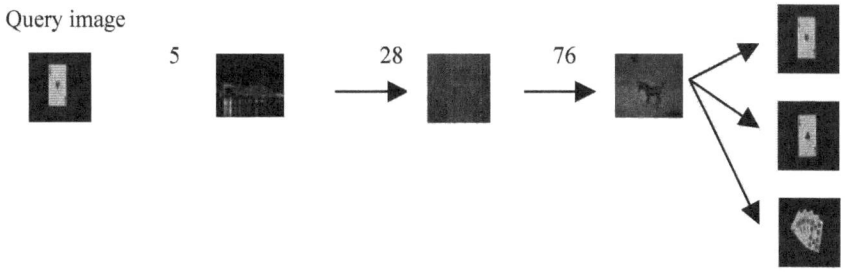

Figure 3.

For more results on color similarity retrieval visit our home page at http://iielab-secs.secs.oakland.edu

6. Conclusions and future work

This paper presented an efficient method for image retrieval. Since the proposed procedure organizes the color information as a hierarchy of different clusters, the user is provided with summary views of the entire image collection at different level of details. Fast calculation of the k-nearest neighbors is possible by using a branch and bound algorithm as a search strategy. As future work, we want to experiment our system with semantic features in addition to the low level ones. Since browsing computerized information has a social dimension, we will also develop an interface for better visualization of the information patterns being browsed and more effective means of communicating the browsing process.

References

1. Enser PGB. Pictorial information retrieval. Journal of Documentation, 51(2), pp. 126-170, 1995

2. Lew MS, Huijsmans DP, Denteneer D. Content based image retrieval: Optimal keys, Texture, Projections or Templates. Image Databases and Multi-Media Search, 1997; 8; 39-47

3. Faloutsos C, Equitz W, Flickner M. Efficient and Effective Querying by Image Content. Journal of Intelligent Information Systems 3, 1994; 231-262

4. Niblack W, Barber R, Equitz W. et al. The QBIC project: querying images by content using color, texture, shape. Proc. SPIE: Storage and Retrieval for Images and Video Databases 1993; 1908; 173-187

5. Corridoni J, Delbimbo A, Pala P. Image retrieval by color semantics. ACM Multimedia System Journal, 1998

6. Sethi IK, Coman I. Image retrieval using hierarchical self-organizing feature maps. Pattern Recognition Letters 20, 1999; 1337-1345

7. Rui Y, Huang TS, Chang SF. Image Retrieval: Past, Present, and Future. Journal of Visual Communication and Image Representation, 1999; 10; 1-23.

8. Sethi IK, Coman I, Day B et al. Color-WISE: A system for image similarity retrieval using color. Proc. SPIE: Storage and Retrieval for Image and Video Databases, 1998; 3312; 140-149

9. Smith JR and Chang SF. Tools and Techniques for Color Image Retrieval. Proceedings of the SPIE: Storage and Retrieval for Image and Video Databases IV, 1996; 2670; 381-392

10. Jain AK, Dubes RC. Algorithms for Clustering Data. Prentices Hall Advanced Reference Series, 1998

11. Swain MJ, Ballard DH. Color Indexing. International Journal of Computer Vision, 1991; 7(1); 11-32

12. Rice JA. Mathematical Statistics and Data Analysis. Duxbury Press, 1995.

13. Duda RO, Hart PE. Pattern classification and scene analysis. John Wiley & Sons, Inc., 1973.

14. Fukanaga K, Narendra PM. A branch and bound algorithm for computing k-nearest neighbors. IEEE Transactions on Computers, 1975; C-24; 750-753

Daniela Stan is a graduate student in Computer Science and Engineering at Oakland University. She received her M.A. in Computer Science in 1999 from Wayne State University and B.S. in Mathematics in 1993 from University of Bucharest, Romania. She is currently involved in the area of content-based image retrieval and data mining.

Ishwar K. Sethi is currently Professor and Chair of Computer Science and Engineering at Oakland University. His research interests include pattern recognition, data mining, and multimedia information processing and indexing. Professor Sethi serves on the editorial boards of several international journals including *IEEE Trans. Pattern Analysis and Machine Intelligence and IEEE Multimedia*.

Texture-adaptive active contour models

Thomas Lehmann, Jörg Bredno, and Klaus Spitzer
Institute of Medical Informatics,
Aachen University of Technology (RWTH),
D-52057 Aachen, Germany

Abstract

Unsupervised segmentation is a key challenge for automated quantification of medical images. Although a balloon model is able to detect arbitrarily shaped objects in images, it requires careful adjustment of parameters prior to segmentation.

Based on global texture analyses, our method allows to set these parameters automatically for heterogeneous images such as MRI, ultrasound, or microscopy. Cooccurrence matrices are extracted from prototype images and used as feature vectors to train a synergetic classifier. These matrices are computed likewise for all other images. To control segmentation, similarity measures for these features are applied to weight the linear combination of the prototype parameters.

The method was tested on 81 synthetic images and applied to a set of 1616 heterogeneous radiographs. Setting the parameters of active contour models by the proposed method improves the acceptance rate of unsupervised segmentation from 31% up to 71%.

Keywords: unsupervised segmentation, active contours, balloon model, parameterization, texture analysis

1 Introduction

In medical imaging, quantitative analyses require segmentation to identify objects of interest [1]. Since manual segmentation is tedious, automatic or semi-automatic segmentation methods have been examined [2]. Unsupervised segmentation of images is a key challenge for any automated analysis of images and major goal of research in bio-medical image processing.

So far, systems for automated quantification rely on reproducibly acquired images with similar appearance of considered objects. However, in medical imaging this assumption often is violated. Normalization and fixed units for image values are obtained from computed tomography but neither from magnetic resonance, ultrasound, radiographic, nor microscopic imaging. Furthermore, biological tissue often drastically varies in material properties the imaging is based on (e.g. radiometric density or sonographic reflection coefficients). Hence, the

S. Singh, N. Murshed, and W. Kropatsch (Eds.): ICAPR 2001, LNCS 2013, pp. 387–396, 2001.

appearance of medical images is not constant even if images are captured by identical devices.

When carefully adapted, active contours have been shown to result in reliable segmentation [2,3,4]. However, the adjustment of parameters is required for each task or application and still performed manually by technical experts. In our approach, the parameter adjustment is done automatically. Different sets of parameters are handled by texture-adaptive categorization of images.

Following a brief introduction to the balloon model that is used for segmentation (Sec. 2.1), we describe the training phase of a synergetic classifier for texture discrimination (Sec. 2.2) and the adaptive parameterization for individual images using this classifier (Sec. 2.3). In Section 2.4, our method is generalized to color images. The classification that is based on the logarithm of coocurrence matrices is evaluated in Section 3.1. Results are presented for a synthetic images (Sec. 3.2) as well as a heterogeneous archive of radiographs (Sec. 3.3).

2   Method

Our method combines a robust and well-known balloon model with an a-priori texture analysis that is used to determine the similarity of the current image with trained images. This allows to adapt the parameterization of the segmentation procedure.

2.1 Balloon model for segmentation

For segmentation of medical images, we apply a generalized balloon model [3] that is based on finite element meshes [4]. The edge elements of simplex meshes move under mechanical influences until they contact significant borders of objects in the

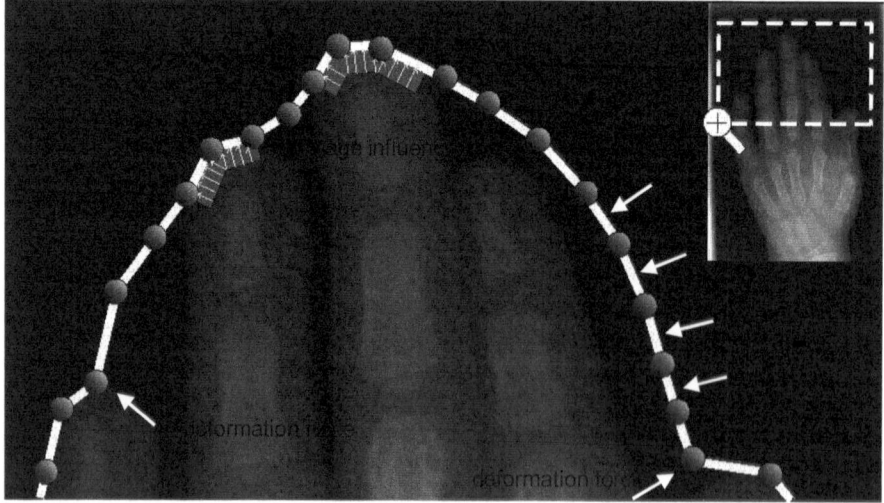

Figure 1: Influences acting on the balloon during iterative segmentation of a radiograph.

image. The edges of a polygon are moved iteratively by forces resulting from the pressure of the balloon, a deformation force that is reducing the 2nd order derivative of the polygons, and image influences (Fig. 1). The gray or color values are interpreted as image potentials resulting in region-based external forces and give local resistance to the movement of edges (Fig. 2).

Based on this model, the algorithm locates arbitrarily shaped structures in images without any initial contour. In comparison to classic snake approaches and all their variations [5], the balloon-based algorithm requires more careful consideration of the parameters controlling the segmentation. For our model, the following influences for the finite elements have to be adjusted according to the image:

- The maximal and minimal length of edges of the polygonal contour.
- The scale of gradients in the image occurring at the border or relevant objects.
- The appearance and intensity of these gradients, which are coded in the potentials of image values.
- The strength of the deformation force.
- The strength of the pressure force.

A unique set of segmentation parameters can be used for all images with similar appearance of objects of interest [6]. To enable automatic segmentation of arbitrary images, a training phase is needed prior to segmentation.

2.2 Training of texture

For unsupervised segmentation of heterogeneous image sets, the parameters have to be adjusted without a-priori knowledge on image contents. Therefore, global texture statistics are used to determine the similarity of appearances between

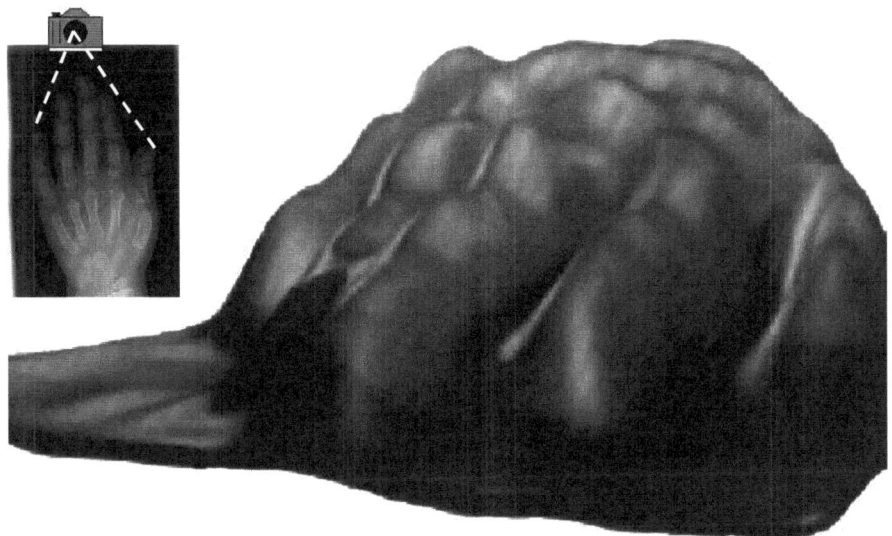

Figure 2: Visualization of image potentials for the radiograph in Figure 1.

images. In a training phase, we browse a representative subset of images to identify significant differences in appearance. For each class of appearance, a prototype image is chosen arbitrarily. The parameters for this prototype image are set using an automated method that employs an exemplary manual segmentation. Therefore, this initialization can be done easily by physicians [6]. Then, the appearance of those prototypes is described by their cooccurrence-matrix [7]. Such texture statistics are frequently used for texture classification [8,9].

All prototypes are downscaled to 256x256 pixels and the gray-scale is reduced to 64 using nearest-neighbor interpolation [10]. Cooccurrence matrices are extracted for these images with a displacement of 5. The segmentation parameters must be adjusted such that the balloon model is allowed to overcome irrelevant structures in the image but stops at the border of considered objects, where notable changes in the appearance of tissues occur. Therefore, the interesting entries in the cooccurrence matrix lay with distance to the main diagonal. Even for large displacements, the entries along the main diagonal significantly are larger than all others. Hence, mathematical operations that compute discriminative measures for these matrices face the danger of numerical instability. Therefore, the logarithm is applied to all entries of the cooccurrence matrix (Fig. 3). The resulting matrix is regarded as a high-dimensional feature vector $\vec{c}$ and normalized to mean zero and length one. For these features, we use the synergetic classifier proposed in [11] to achieve robust similarity measures.

This classifier relies on an orthonormal basis of adjoint vectors $\vec{c}_j^{\,+}$ for the prototype features $\vec{c}_i$. We demand

$$\vec{c}_i \cdot \vec{c}_j^{\,+} = \delta_{ij} \tag{1}$$

for all prototype feature vectors, where δ denotes the Kronecker delta symbol with $\delta_{ij} = 1 \,\forall\, i = j, 0$ else. The adjoint cooccurrence features $\vec{c}_j^{\,+}$ are build as a linear

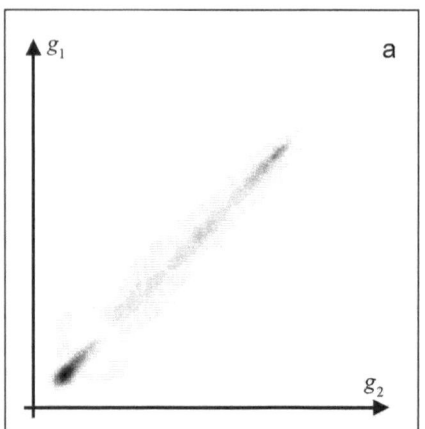
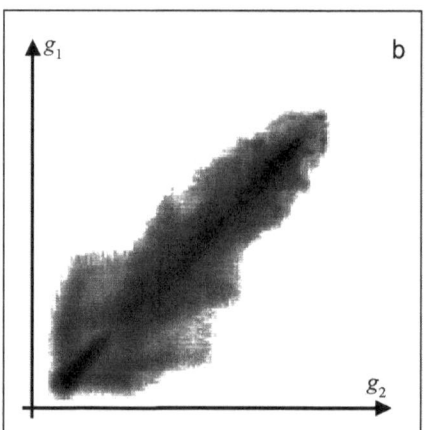

Figure 3: The cooccurrence matrix for gray values g_1 and g_2 of a radiograph are displayed without and with the logarithm of all values, (a) and (b), respectively. The histograms of both images have been stretched individually for contrast enhancement.

combination of all n prototype features $\vec{c}_k$:

$$\vec{c}_j^{\;+} = \sum_{k=1}^{n} a_{jk} \vec{c}_k \tag{2}$$

Multiplying (2) with the prototype vectors $\vec{c}_i$ and using (1) for the left side, we obtain a system of n^2 linear equations

$$I = \begin{pmatrix} 1 & \vec{c}_1 \cdot \vec{c}_2 & \cdots & \vec{c}_1 \cdot \vec{c}_n \\ \vec{c}_2 \cdot \vec{c}_1 & 1 & & \vec{c}_2 \cdot \vec{c}_n \\ \vdots & & \ddots & \vdots \\ \vec{c}_n \cdot \vec{c}_1 & \vec{c}_n \cdot \vec{c}_2 & \cdots & 1 \end{pmatrix} \cdot \begin{pmatrix} a_{11} & a_{12} & \cdots & a_{1n} \\ a_{21} & a_{22} & & a_{2n} \\ \vdots & & \ddots & \vdots \\ a_{n1} & a_{n2} & \cdots & a_{nn} \end{pmatrix} \tag{3}$$

with I denoting the identity matrix. The a_{jk} can be calculated by inverting the matrix of the scalar products of all prototype feature vectors

$$\begin{pmatrix} a_{11} & a_{12} & \cdots & a_{1n} \\ a_{21} & a_{22} & & a_{2n} \\ \vdots & & \ddots & \vdots \\ a_{n1} & a_{n2} & \cdots & a_{nn} \end{pmatrix} = \begin{pmatrix} 1 & \vec{c}_1 \cdot \vec{c}_2 & \cdots & \vec{c}_1 \cdot \vec{c}_n \\ \vec{c}_2 \cdot \vec{c}_1 & 1 & & \vec{c}_2 \cdot \vec{c}_n \\ \vdots & & \ddots & \vdots \\ \vec{c}_n \cdot \vec{c}_1 & \vec{c}_n \cdot \vec{c}_2 & \cdots & 1 \end{pmatrix}^{-1} \tag{4}$$

They are used to compute the adjoint prototype vectors $\vec{c}_j^{\;+}$ in (2).

2.3 Texture-adaptive parameterization

The parameter sets for prototype images resulting from training as well as the adjoint cooccurrence feature vectors $\vec{c}_j^{\;+}$ are used for the segmentation of heterogeneous images.

During segmentation, a cooccurrence feature vector is computed for each image. The scalar products of this vector with the adjoint vectors of all prototypes represent similarities. Therefore, these scalar products are used to automatically create an individual set of parameters for the image.

Let $\vec{c}_{\mathrm{image}}$ denote the cooccurrence matrix of an image that has to be segmented and $\vec{P}_j$ be a vector containing the parameters that are used for the segmentation of prototype image j. Then, the required parameters $\vec{P}_{\mathrm{image}}$ are calculated from the similarity of the cooccurrence feature $\vec{c}_{\mathrm{image}}$ and the adjoint prototype features $\vec{c}_j^{\;+}$

$$\vec{P}_{\mathrm{image}} = \frac{\sum_{j=1}^{n} w_j \vec{P}_j}{\sum_{j=1}^{n} w_j} \quad \text{with} \quad w_j = \begin{cases} \vec{c}_{\mathrm{image}} \cdot \vec{c}_j^{\;+} & \forall \quad 0 \le \vec{c}_{\mathrm{image}} \cdot \vec{c}_j^{\;+} \le 1 \\ 1 - \vec{c}_{\mathrm{image}} \cdot \vec{c}_j^{\;+} & \forall \quad 1 < \vec{c}_{\mathrm{image}} \cdot \vec{c}_j^{\;+} \le 2 \\ 0 & \text{else} \end{cases} \tag{5}$$

When segmenting an image, the parameters of the balloon model linearly are interpolated from all parameter sets of the prototypes using the weights w_j, which depend on the scalar products with the respective adjoint features. The balloon model detects significant contours in the image by a balance of all forces acting on an edge. Note that mechanical forces strictly are additive. This allows linear interpolation of their strengths.

2.4 Color images

For color images, the feature vector is composed by combining the within- and cross-cooccurrence matrices of the color channels [12]. The within-cooccurrence matrices contain separate entries for all color channels using the same displacement whereas the cross-cooccurrence matrices count the presence of image values at the same image position in different channels. For an RGB image, this results in a feature vector containing the cooccurrence matrices of the red, green, and blue channel as well as the cross-cooccurrence between red and green, red and blue, and green and blue. The dimension of this feature vector is six times the dimension of a grayscale feature vector. Since the complexity of similarity measures that are based on adjoint feature vectors only linearly depends on the dimension of the feature vectors, the method can be applied easily to color images.

External influences for the segmentation method are combined from all color channels and weighted according to the intensity of color gradients that occur at the border of objects of interest in the color channels. This gives also need to set appropriate parameters for each color channel separately. This setting is handled by the automated method described in [6].

3 Evaluation and Results

Numerical tests are performed to evaluate the stability of the adjoint vector computation, the segmentation of synthetic phantoms, and that of radiographs taken from diagnostic procedures in clinical routine.

3.1 Logarithm of cooccurrence matrix entries

So far, it has been postulated that the use of the logarithm increases the numerical stability of distance measures that are computed from the cooccurrence matrices. A test was performed to validate this supposition.

Four color images were extracted from an endoscopic video of vocal folds. Single frames do not contain textures of high contrast [12] and their histograms are compact. The numerical stability of the computation of adjoint feature vectors were assessed by the error measure

$$e = \max_{i,j=1}^{n} \left(\vec{c}_i \cdot \vec{c}_j^{\;+} - \delta_{ij} \right) \tag{6}$$

It determines the maximal deviation of the scalar products between all feature vectors and all corresponding vectors of prototypes.

In our test, we used single-precision floating point instructions of a Pentium II processor. The matrix inversion was taken from the image analysis tool Khoros 2 compiled under Linux with a standard GNU compiler. Using normalized cooccurrence matrices for the feature vectors, the error measure e reached unacceptable 0.78. It was reduced to 0.006 applying the logarithm to all entries in the cooccurrence matrices prior to normalization.

3.2 Evaluation using synthetic images

Gold-standards yielding a valid segmentation usually do not exist in medical imaging. Inter- as well as intra-observer variability hinder the quantification of segmentation quality. In order to give quantitative measures, 81 synthetic images have been created. These images of the size 128x128 pixel contain a centered object described by $r < r_0 + \Delta r \sin(k\varphi)$ with r_0=50, Δr=10 and k=5. Inside and outside are filled with Gaussian-distributed noise of mean μ_{in} and μ_{out}, respectively, and standard deviation σ. In order to prevent high gradients at the object's border, the gray values linearly are interpolated from inside to outside within a five pixel region (Fig. 4). Parameters for the creation of synthetic images were combined from $\mu_{in} \in \{130,140,150\}$, $\Delta\mu = \mu_{out} - \mu_{in} \in \{5,10,20\}$ and $\sigma \in \{2,6,10\}$. Each combination is based on three different images, giving an amplitude signal-to-noise ration of

$$SNR = 20\log\frac{\Delta\mu}{\sigma} \tag{7}$$

ranging from -6dB to 20dB. These images were segmented using either a fixed parameter set trained for the image with $\mu_{in} = 140$, $\mu_{out} = 150$, and $\sigma = 6$ (see the third example from the left in Fig. 4) or using an adaptive parameter set resulting from training of 4 or 8 prototype images from this set, respectively. The mean and Hausdorff (maximum) distances were calculated using the vertex positions in a Chamfer distance-transformed image of the original object. Additionally, the overlap measure

$$O = \frac{A \cap B}{A \cup B} \tag{8}$$

was calculated with A and B denoting the segmented and the original object, respectively. Segmentations were accepted for $O > 85\%$.

Segmentation using the balloon model fails if a fixed parameter set is used (Tab. 1). The contours either collapse or expand over the object towards the image border resulting in large distances and a small overlap measure. Only one third of all

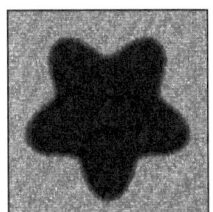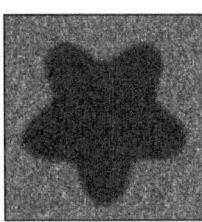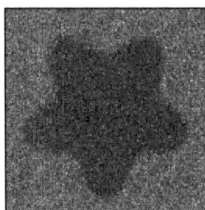

Figure 4: Synthetic images are used for evaluation. The parameters $(\Delta\mu,\sigma)$ that are used to create the displayed images are from left to right: (20,2), (20,6), (10,6), and (5,10). Note that the images have been histogram optimized for printing.

images is segmented sufficiently without parameter adaptation. Using 4 different images in training, nearly 80% of all segmentations are accepted. The mean difference reduces from about 20 down to 4.4. When 8 different prototypes are trained, the rate of acceptance raises to 89%. Now, the mean distance between all segmentations and the real contour is below 2 pixels. Nevertheless, the average Hausdorff distance about 7 still is notable. In many images, only parts of the contour are detected correctly due to the high amount of noise.

3.3 Segmentation of an heterogeneous image archive

The method was applied to a set of 1616 radiographs from the IRMA-project [13]. The images have been taken from daily routine at the Department of Diagnostic Radiology, Medical School, Aachen University of Technology. The radiographs were acquired by several modalities and partly scanned from film using different scanners. Aim of the IRMA-project is content-based access to medical image archives without manual indexing. Therefore, the main contours of imaged body regions have to be segmented automatically without user supervision. First, the balloon model was parameterized by an analysis of the images' histograms. Using the same model, all images were segmented again with the parameters automatically set by the method described above. All together, 19 different appearances have been identified. One of each class was used as a prototype.

All results were manually rated (Fig. 5). A physician either accepted or rejected the segmentation subjectively following his visual impression. Note that it is easier and less time consuming to decide whether a given segmentation result matches the expectation than to draw a manual segmentation. Furthermore, manual reference segmentations are not reproducible.

Using the heuristic histogram analysis, the relevant contours were detected sufficiently in only 496 out of 1616 images. Using the texture adaptation of the balloon model, the automatic segmentation was accepted for 1145 radiographs. The method improves the ratio of acceptance from 31% to 71%. As a main problem, the

parameter set	mean distance $\mu \pm \sigma$	Hausdorff distance $\mu \pm \sigma$	overlap $\mu \pm \sigma$ in %	# accepted / # total
fixed	19.9 ± 13,7	37.9 ± 24.7	45.1 ± 38.5	27 / 81
adaptive, 4 prototypes	4.4 ± 7.8	9.5 ± 12.8	83.7 ± 22.7	64 / 81
adaptive, 8 prototypes	2.0 ± 3.6	7.1 ± 10.2	90.9 ± 9.3	72 / 81

Table 1: Results for the segmentation of synthetic images with and without adaptive parameterization.

segmentation method was disturbed by collimator fields in the radiographs that were neither manually cut nor chosen according to image quality.

4. Discussion

Unsupervised segmentation of medical images can be done by balloon models. However, the parameterization of active contours is time consuming and requires expert knowledge on the model so far. Using global texture analysis, this parameterization is done automatically. Numerical robustness of texture calculations is increased by logarithm of cooccurrence matrices that are based on images with similar content and weak texture.

The IRMA archive that is used for evaluation of our method contains images of various regions of body, orientations, imaging modalities and scanning devices. The imaging parameters were not optimized to show contours but for the ability to perform findings in diagnostic regions of interest. Therefore, the increase of 31% to 71% and hence, acceptance of more than two thirds of all segmentations is absolutely reliable. Further improvement may result from optimizing both, texture feature extraction and similarity measures.

So far, the texture-adaptive parameterization method has been used for a balloon model. Note that this method of parameter adjustment is not bound to balloons and could be used for many other segmentation methods that require the choice of appropriate parameters. However, not all segmentation algorithms may be suitable for a linear interpolation of parameters according to the similarity to image prototypes.

References

1. Duncan JS, Ayache N. Medical Image Analysis: Progress over Two Decades and the Challenges Ahead. IEEE PAMI 2000; 22(1): 85-106
2. Mcinerney T, Terzopoulos D. Deformable models in medical image analysis: A survey. Medical Image Analysis 1996; 1: 91-108
3. Bredno J, Lehmann T, Spitzer K. A general finite element model for segmentation in 2, 3, and 4 dimensions. Proc. SPIE 2000; 3979: 1174-1184
4. Cohen LD, Cohen I. Finite-element methods for active contour models and balloons for 2-D and 3-D images. IEEE PAMI 1993; 15(11): 1131-1147

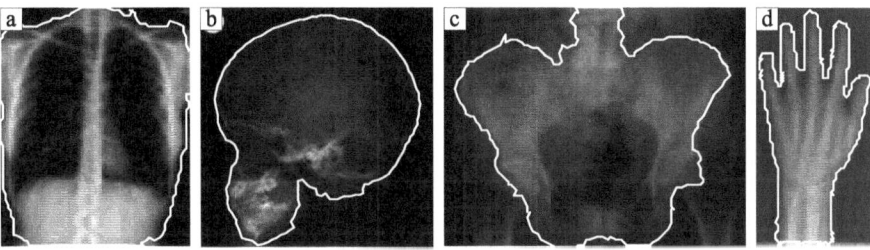

Figure 5: Exemplary segmentations of the categories chest (a), skull (b), pelvis (c), and extremities (d).

5. Kass M, Witkin A, Terzopoulos D. Snakes: Active contour models. International Journal of Computer Vision 1988; 1(4): 321-331
6. Bredno J, Lehmann T, Spitzer K: Automatic parameter setting for balloon models. Proc. SPIE 2000; 3979: 1185-1208
7. Haralick R, Shanmugam K, Dinstein I. Texture features for image classification. IEEE SMC 1973; 3: 610-621
8. Gotlieb C, Kreyszig H. Texture descriptors based on cooccurrence matrices. Computer Vision, Graphics and Image Processing 1990; 51: 70-86
9. Walker R, Jackway P, Longstaff I: Recent developments in the use of the co-occurrence matrix for texture recognition. In: Digital Signal Processing 1997, 63-65 (Proc. 13th International Conference Santorini, Greece)
10. Lehmann T, Gönner C, Spitzer K. Survey: Interpolation methods in medical image processing. IEEE MI 1999; 18(11): 1049-1075
11. Haken H. Synergetic Computers and Cognition. Springer Berlin Heidelberg New York, 1991
12. Palm C, Lehmann T, Spitzer K. Color texture analysis of vocal folds using approaches from statistics and signal theory. In: Braunschweig T, Hanson J, Schelhorn-Neise P, Witte H (eds) Advances in objective laryngoscopy, voice and speech research. 2000, 49-56 (Proc. 4th International Workshop, Jena, Friedrich-Schiller-University)
13. Lehmann T, Wein B, Dahmen J, Bredno J, Vogelsang F, Kohnen M. Content-based image retrieval in medical applications - a novel multi-step approach. Proc. SPIE 2000; 3972: 312-320

A Generalized Local Binary Pattern Operator for Multiresolution Gray Scale and Rotation Invariant Texture Classification

Timo Ojala, Matti Pietikäinen and Topi Mäenpää

Machine Vision and Media Processing Unit
Infotech Oulu, University of Oulu
P.O.Box 4500, FIN - 90014 University of Oulu, Finland
{skidi, mkp, topiolli}@ee.oulu.fi
http://www.ee.oulu.fi/research/imag/texture

Abstract. This paper presents generalizations to the gray scale and rotation invariant texture classification method based on local binary patterns that we have recently introduced. We derive a generalized presentation that allows for realizing a gray scale and rotation invariant LBP operator for any quantization of the angular space and for any spatial resolution, and present a method for combining multiple operators for multiresolution analysis. The proposed approach is very robust in terms of gray scale variations, since the operator is by definition invariant against any monotonic transformation of the gray scale. Another advantage is computational simplicity, as the operator can be realized with a few operations in a small neighborhood and a lookup table. Excellent experimental results obtained in a true problem of rotation invariance, where the classifier is trained at one particular rotation angle and tested with samples from other rotation angles, demonstrate that good discrimination can be achieved with the occurrence statistics of simple rotation invariant local binary patterns. These operators characterize the spatial configuration of local image texture and the performance can be further improved by combining them with rotation invariant variance measures that characterize the contrast of local image texture. The joint distributions of these orthogonal measures are shown to be very powerful tools for rotation invariant texture analysis.

nonparametric   texture analysis   distribution   histogram   Brodatz   contrast

1 Introduction

Most approaches to texture classification assume, either explicitly or implicitly, that the unknown samples to be classified are identical to the training samples with respect to spatial scale, orientation and gray scale properties. However, real world textures can occur at arbitrary spatial resolutions and rotations and they may be subjected to varying illumination conditions. This has inspired a collection of studies, which generally incorporate invariance with respect to one or at most two of the properties spatial scale, orientation and gray scale, among others [1,2,3,4,5,6,7,8,10,11,13,14].

This work focuses on gray scale and rotation invariant texture classification, which has been addressed by Chen and Kundu [2] and Wu and Wei [13]. Both studies approached gray scale invariance by assuming that the gray scale transformation is a linear function. This is a somewhat strong simplification, which may limit the usefulness of the proposed methods. Chen and Kundu realized gray scale invariance by glo-

S. Singh, N. Murshed, and W. Kropatsch (Eds.): ICAPR 2001, LNCS 2013, pp. 397–406, 2001.

bal normalization of the input image using histogram equalization. This is not a general solution, however, as global histogram equalization can not correct intraimage (local) gray scale variations.

Recently, we introduced a theoretically and computationally simple approach for gray scale and rotation invariant texture analysis based on Local Binary Patterns, which is robust in terms of gray scale variations and discriminated rotated textures efficiently [8,10]. A novel contribution of this paper is the generalized presentation of the operator that allows for realizing it for any quantization of the angular space and for any spatial resolution. We derive the operator for a general case based on a circularly symmetric neighbor set of P members on a circle of radius R. We call this operator $LBP_{P,R}^{riu2}$. P controls the quantization of the angular space, whereas R determines the spatial resolution of the operator. In addition to evaluating the performance of individual operators of a particular (P,R), we also propose a straightforward approach for multiresolution analysis, which combines the information provided by multiple operators.

The proposed operator $LBP_{P,R}^{riu2}$ is an excellent measure of the spatial structure of local image texture, but it by definition discards the other important property of local image texture, contrast, since it depends on the gray scale. If the stability of the gray scale is not a concern, the performance of $LBP_{P,R}^{riu2}$ can be further enhanced by combining it with a rotation invariant variance measure $VAR_{P,R}$ that characterizes the contrast of local image texture. We present the joint distribution of these two complementary operators, $LBP_{P,R}^{riu2}/VAR_{P,R}$, as a powerful tool for rotation invariant texture classification. The proposed operators are also computationally attractive, as they can be realized with a few operations in a small neighborhood and a lookup table.

The performance of the proposed approach is demonstrated with an image data used in a recent study on rotation invariant texture classification [11]. Excellent experimental results demonstrate that our texture representation learned at a specific rotation angle generalizes to other rotation angles.

The paper is organized as follows. The operators, the classification principle and a simple method for multiresolution analysis are described in Section 2. Experimental results are presented in Section 3 and Section 4 concludes the paper.

2 Methodology

2.1 Generalized Rotation Invariant LBP Operator

We start the derivation of our gray scale and rotation invariant texture operator by defining texture T in a local neighborhood of a monochrome texture image as the joint distribution of gray levels $\{g_c, g_0, ..., g_{P-1}\}$ ($P>1$). The gray value g_c corresponds to the gray value of the center pixel of the local neighborhood and g_p ($p=0,...,P-1$) correspond to the gray values of P equally spaced pixels on a circle of radius R ($R>0$) that form the circularly symmetric neighbor set $N(P,R)$. If the coordinates of g_c are $(0,0)$, then the coordinates of g_p are given by $(-R\sin(2\pi p/P), R\cos(2\pi p/P))$. For brevity we omit the derivation presented in [8], and obtain the following generalized operator for gray scale and rotation invariant texture description:

$$LBP_{P,R}^{riu2} = \begin{cases} \sum_{p=0}^{P-1} s(g_p - g_c) & \text{if } U(N(P,R)) \le 2 \\ P+1 & \text{otherwise} \end{cases} \tag{2}$$

where

$$s(x) = \begin{cases} 1, x \ge 0 \\ 0, x < 0 \end{cases} \tag{3}$$

and

$$U(N(P,R)) = \left| s(g_{P-1} - g_c) - s(g_0 - g_c) \right| + \sum_{p=1}^{P-1} \left| s(g_p - g_c) - s(g_{p-1} - g_c) \right| \tag{4}$$

Invariance against any monotonic transformation of the gray scale is achieved by considering the signs of the differences $s(g_p\text{-}g_c)$, which effectively corresponds to binary thresholding of the local neighborhood, hence the expression *Local Binary Pattern*. Rotation invariance is achieved by recognizing that a set of rotation variant patterns originates from a particular rotation invariant pattern upon rotation.

Uniformity measure U corresponds to the number of spatial transitions, i.e. bitwise 0/1 changes between successive bits in the circular representation of the *LBP*. We argue that the larger the uniformity value U is, i.e. the larger number of spatial transitions occurs in the pattern, the more likely the pattern is to change to a different pattern upon rotation in digital domain. Based on this argument we designate those rotation invariant patterns that have U value of at most 2 as 'uniform', and use the occurrence statistics of different 'uniform' patterns for texture discrimination.

By definition exactly $P+1$ 'uniform' binary patterns can occur in a circularly symmetric neighbor set of P pixels. Eq.(2) assigns an unique label to each of them, the label corresponding to the number of '1' bits in the pattern (0->P), while the 'nonuniform' patterns are grouped under the miscellaneous label $P+1$. The selection of 'uniform' patterns with the simultaneous compression of 'nonuniform' patterns is also supported by the fact that the former tend to dominate in deterministic textures [8]. In practice the computation of $LBP_{P,R}^{riu2}$, which has $P+2$ distinct output values, is best implemented with a lookup table of 2^P elements.

The expression in Eq.(2) allows generalizing the operator for any quantization of the angular space and for any spatial resolution. The quantization of the angular space is defined by $(360°/P)$. However, certain considerations have to be taken into account in the selection of P and R. First, they are related in the sense that for a given R, additional new elements placed on the circle are not likely to provide any useful information beyond a certain point. Second, an efficient implementation with a lookup table of 2^P elements sets a practical upper limit for P.

2.2 Rotation Invariant Variance Measures of Texture Contrast

The $LBP_{P,R}^{riu2}$ operator is a truly gray scale invariant measure, i.e. its output is not affected by any monotonic transformation of the gray scale. It is an excellent measure of the spatial pattern, but it by definition discards contrast. If we under stable lighting conditions wanted to incorporate the contrast of local image texture as well, we can measure it with a rotation invariant measure of local variance:

$$VAR_{P,R} = \frac{1}{P}\sum_{p=0}^{P-1}(g_p - \mu)^2 \quad , \text{ where } \mu = \frac{1}{P}\sum_{p=0}^{P-1}g_p \tag{5}$$

VAR_{PR} is by definition invariant against gray scale shifts. Since $LBP_{P,R}^{riu2}$ and VAR_{PR} are complementary, their joint distribution $LBP_{P,R}^{riu2}/VAR_{PR}$ is expected to be a very powerful rotation invariant measure of local image texture. Note that even though we in this study restrict ourselves to using only joint distributions of $LBP_{P,R}^{riu2}$ and VAR_{PR} operators that have the same (P,R) values, nothing would prevent us from using joint distributions of operators with different neighborhoods.

2.3 Nonparametric Classification Principle

In the classification phase a test sample S was assigned to the class of the model M that maximized the log-likelihood measure:

$$L(S, M) = \sum_{b=1}^{B}S_b\log M_b \tag{6}$$

where B is the number of bins, and S_b and M_b correspond to the sample and model probabilities at bin b, respectively. This nonparametric (pseudo-)metric measures likelihoods that samples are from alternative texture classes, based on exact probabilities of feature values of pre-classified texture prototypes. In the case of the joint distribution $LBP_{P,R}^{riu2}/VAR_{PR}$, the log-likelihood measure was extended in a straightforward manner to scan through the two-dimensional histograms.

Sample and model distributions were obtained by scanning the texture samples and prototypes with the chosen operator, and dividing the distributions of operator outputs into histograms having a fixed number of B bins. Since $LBP_{P,R}^{riu2}$ has a completely defined set of discrete output values $(0 \to P+1)$, no additional binning procedure is required, but the operator outputs are directly accumulated into a histogram of $P+2$ bins. Variance measure VAR_{PR} has a continuous-valued output, hence quantization of its feature space is needed, together with the selection of an appropriate value for B [9].

2.4 Multiresolution Analysis

By altering P and R we can realize our operators for any quantization of the angular space and for any spatial resolution. Multiresolution analysis can be accomplished by combining the information provided by multiple operators of different (P,R). In this study we perform straightforward multiresolution analysis by defining the aggregate (dis)similarity as the sum of individual log-likelihoods computed for individual operators:

$$L_O = \sum_{o=1}^{O} L(S^o, M^o) \qquad (7)$$

where O is the number of operators, and S^o and M^o correspond to the sample and model histograms extracted with operator o ($o=1,...,O$), respectively.

3 Experiments

We demonstrate the performance of our operators with imagery used in a recent study on rotation invariant texture classification by Porter and Canagarajah [11]. They presented three feature extraction schemes for rotation invariant texture classification, employing the wavelet transform, a circularly symmetric Gabor filter and a Gaussian Markov Random Field with a circularly symmetric neighbor set. They concluded that the wavelet-based approach was the most accurate and exhibited the best noise performance, having also the lowest computational complexity.

We first replicate the original experimental setup as carefully as possible, to get comparable results. Since in the original setup the training data included samples from several rotation angles, we also present results for a more challenging setup, where the samples of just one particular rotation angle are used for training the texture classifier, which is then tested with the samples of the other rotation angles. In each case we report as the result the error rate, i.e. the percentage of misclassified samples of all samples in the testing data, for the individual operators $LBP_{P,R}^{riu2}$ and $VAR_{P,R}$, and their joint distribution $LBP_{P,R}^{riu2}/VAR_{P,R}$.

Regarding the selection of P and R, in order to incorporate three different spatial resolutions and three different angular resolutions we chose to realize $LBP_{P,R}^{riu2}$ and $VAR_{P,R}$ with (P,R) values of (8,1), (16,2), and (24,3). In multiresolution analysis we use the three 2-resolution combinations and the one 3-resolution combination these three alternatives can form. Regarding the quantization of the continuous $VAR_{P,R}$ feature space, histograms contained 128 bins when $VAR_{P,R}$ operator was used by itself, and $(P+2)/16$ bins in the case of the joint $LBP_{P,R}^{riu2}/VAR_{P,R}$ operator.

3.1 Image Data and Experimental Setup

Image data included 16 texture classes from the Brodatz album shown in Fig. 1. For each texture class there were eight 256x256 images, of which the first was used for training the classifier, while the other seven images were used to test the classifier. Rotated textures had been created from these source images using a proprietary interpolation program that produced images of 180x180 pixels in size. If the rotation angle was a multiple of 90 degrees ($0°$ or $90°$ in the case of present ten rotation angles), a small amount of artificial blur had been added to the original images to simulate the effect of blurring on rotation at other angles [11].

In the original experimental setup the texture classifier was trained with several 16x16 subimages extracted from the training image. This fairly small size of training samples increases the difficulty of the problem nicely. The training set comprised rotation angles 0°, 30°, 45°, and 60°, while the textures for classification were presented at rotation angles 20°, 70°, 90°, 120°, 135°, and 150°. Consequently, the test data included 672 samples, 42 (6 angles x 7 images) for each of the 16 texture classes. Using a Mahalanobis distance classifier Porter and Canagarajah reported 95.8% accuracy for the rotation invariant wavelet-based features as the best result.

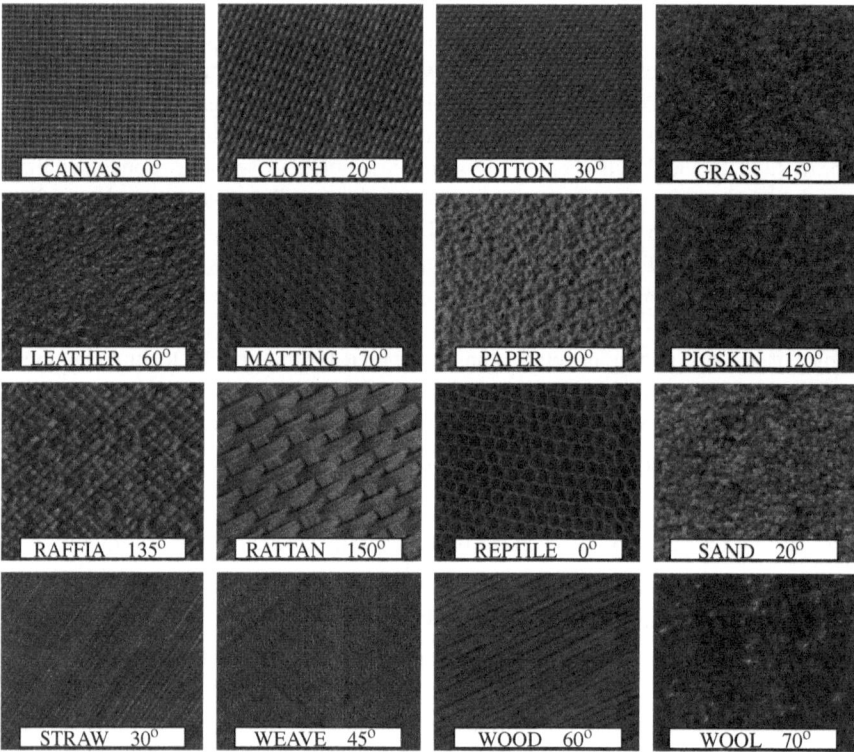

Fig. 1. Texture images printed at particular orientations.

3.2 Experimental Results

We started replicating the original experimental setup by dividing the 180x180 images of the four training angles (0°, 30°, 45°, and 60°) into 121 disjoint 16x16 subimages. In other words we had 7744 training samples, 484 (4 angles x 121 samples) in each of the 16 texture classes. We first computed the histogram of the chosen operator for each of the 16x16 samples. We then added the histograms of all samples belonging to a particular class into one big model histogram for this class, since the histograms of single 16x16 samples would have been too sparse to be reliable models. Also, using 7744 different models would have resulted in computational overhead, for in the classification phase the sample histograms were compared to every model histogram. Consequently, we obtained 16 reliable model histograms containing $484(16-2R)^2$ entries (the operators have a R pixel border). The performance of the operators was evaluated with the 672 testing images. Corresponding sample histograms contained $(180-2R)^2$ entries, hence we did not have to worry about their stability.

Table 1: Error rates (%) for the original experimental setup, where training is done with rotations $0°$, $30°$, $45°$, and $60°$.

P,R	$LBP_{P,R}^{riu2}$	$VAR_{P,R}$	$LBP_{P,R}^{riu2}/VAR_{P,R}$
8,1	11.76	4.46	1.64
16,2	1.49	11.61	0.15
24,3	0.89	13.39	3.57
8,1+16,2	1.04	1.34	0.30
8,1+24,3	0.45	1.64	0.00
16,2+24,3	1.04	12.05	0.89
8,1+16,2+24,3	0.89	3.42	0.00

Classification results are given in Table 1. As expected, $LBP_{16,2}^{riu2}$ and $LBP_{24,3}^{riu2}$ clearly outperformed their simpler counterpart $LBP_{8,1}^{riu2}$. $LBP_{8,1}^{riu2}$ had difficulties in discriminating strongly oriented textures, as misclassifications of *rattan*, *straw* and *wood* contributed 70 of the 79 misclassified samples. Interestingly, in all 79 cases the model of the true class ranked second right after the most similar model of a false class that led to misclassification. $LBP_{16,2}^{riu2}$ did much better, classifying all samples correctly except ten *grass* samples that were assigned to *leather*. Again, in all ten cases the model of the true class ranked second. $LBP_{24,3}^{riu2}$ provided further improvement by missing just five *grass* samples and a *matting* sample. In all six cases the model of the true class again ranked second. These results demonstrate that the $45°$ quantization of the angular space by $LBP_{8,1}^{riu2}$ is too crude.

Combining the $LBP_{P,R}^{riu2}$ operator with the $VAR_{P,R}$ operator, which did not too badly by itself, generally improved the performance. The lone exception was (24,3) where the addition of the poorly performing $VAR_{24,3}$ only hampered the excellent discrimination by $LBP_{24,3}^{riu2}$. We see that $LBP_{16,2}^{riu2}/VAR_{16,2}$ fell one sample short of a faultless result, as a *straw* sample at $90°$ angle was labeled as *grass*. The error rates for single resolutions are so low that there is not much room for improvement by the multiresolution analysis, though two alternatives of the joint distribution provided a perfect classification. The largest gain was achieved for the $VAR_{P,R}$ operator, especially when $VAR_{24,3}$ was excluded.

Even though a direct comparison to the results of Porter and Canagarajah may not be meaningful due to the different classification principle, the excellent results for our operators demonstrate their suitability for rotation invariant texture classification.

Table 2 presents results for a more challenging experimental setup, where the classifier was trained with samples of just one rotation angle and tested with samples of other nine rotation angles. We trained the classifier with the 121 16x16 samples extracted from the designated training image, again merging the histograms of the 16x16 samples of a particular texture class into one model histogram. The classifier was tested with the samples obtained from the other nine rotation angles of the seven source images reserved for testing purposes, totaling 1008 samples, 63 in each of the 16 texture classes. Note that in each texture class the seven testing images are physically different from the one designated training image, hence this setup is a true test for the texture operators' ability to produce a rotation invariant representation of local image texture that also generalizes to physically different samples.

Table 2: Error rates (%) when training is done at just one rotation angle, and the average error rate over the ten angles.

OPERATOR	P,R	TRAINING ANGLE										AVERAGE
		$0°$	$20°$	$30°$	$45°$	$60°$	$70°$	$90°$	$120°$	$135°$	$150°$	
$LBP_{P,R}^{riu2}$	8,1	31.3	13.6	15.3	23.6	15.0	15.7	30.6	15.6	23.7	15.2	19.94
	16,2	3.8	1.0	1.4	1.1	1.5	0.9	2.4	1.4	1.3	2.5	1.72
	24,3	1.3	1.1	0.9	2.4	0.8	1.8	0.0	1.3	3.3	2.0	1.48
	8,1+16,2	5.7	0.5	0.2	0.2	1.5	2.8	7.1	0.4	0.8	0.8	1.99
	8,1+24,3	3.8	0.4	0.6	1.4	0.6	1.1	2.8	0.5	1.7	0.6	1.34
	16,2+24,3	2.3	0.0	0.2	0.8	0.7	0.0	0.4	0.6	1.5	1.6	0.80
	8,1+16,2+24,3	2.4	0.0	0.0	0.8	0.0	0.0	1.5	0.0	1.4	0.2	0.63
$VAR_{P,R}$	8,1	7.3	3.4	5.4	6.0	4.4	3.1	6.1	5.8	5.4	4.4	5.10
	16,2	10.1	15.5	13.8	9.5	12.7	14.4	9.0	10.2	9.2	11.5	11.60
	24,3	14.6	13.6	14.3	15.6	14.6	14.4	14.0	13.3	13.7	14.1	14.21
	8,1+16,2	2.5	3.1	1.2	1.0	2.1	2.3	2.5	0.9	1.2	2.1	1.88
	8,1+24,3	4.8	3.0	1.3	1.1	2.5	1.5	3.9	0.5	1.0	2.1	2.15
	16,2+24,3	11.7	13.5	13.2	13.1	14.5	13.5	10.7	13.1	12.5	12.9	12.87
	8,1+16,2+24,3	5.1	5.4	3.0	1.7	3.8	3.8	5.0	1.8	1.9	2.7	3.39
$LBP^{riu2}_{P,R}/VAR_{P,R}$	8,1	0.9	5.8	4.3	2.7	4.8	5.6	0.7	4.0	2.7	4.4	3.56
	16,2	0.0	0.5	0.6	0.6	0.6	0.4	0.0	0.5	0.5	0.3	0.40
	24,3	4.2	5.0	3.8	2.6	4.0	4.5	4.4	2.8	2.1	2.1	3.52
	8,1+16,2	0.0	0.7	0.9	0.8	0.7	0.8	0.0	0.7	0.7	0.6	0.59
	8,1+24,3	0.2	0.2	0.4	0.2	0.4	0.2	0.4	0.3	0.2	0.1	0.26
	16,2+24,3	2.8	1.1	1.1	0.2	0.4	0.1	2.7	0.4	0.2	0.1	0.90
	8,1+16,2+24,3	0.0	0.3	0.5	0.2	0.4	0.3	0.2	0.4	0.2	0.1	0.26

Training with just one rotation angle allows a more conclusive analysis of the rotation invariance of our operators. For example, it is hardly surprising that $LBP_{8,1}^{riu2}$ provides highest error rates when the training angle is a multiple of 45°. Due to the crude quantization of the angular space the presentations learned at 0°, 45°, 90°, or 135° do not generalize that well to other angles. Again, the importance of the finer quantization of the angular space shows, as $LBP_{16,2}^{riu2}$ and $LBP_{24,3}^{riu2}$ provide a solid performance with average error rates of 1.72% and 1.48%, respectively. Even though the results for multiresolution analysis generally exhibit improved discrimination over single resolutions, they also serve as a welcome reminder that the addition of inferior operator does not necessarily enhance the performance.

4 Discussion

We presented a theoretically and computationally simple yet efficient multiresolution approach to gray scale and rotation invariant texture classification based on local binary patterns and nonparametric discrimination of sample and prototype distributions. We derived a generalized presentation that allows for realizing the gray scale and rotation invariant operator $LBP_{P,R}^{riu2}$ for any quantization of the angular space and for any spatial resolution, and proposed a method for multiresolution analysis.

The proposed approach is very robust in terms of gray scale variations, since the $LBP_{P,R}^{riu2}$ operator is by definition invariant against any monotonic transformation of the gray scale. This should make it very attractive in situations where varying illumination conditions are a concern, e.g. in visual inspection. Gray scale invariance is also necessary if the gray scale properties of the training and testing data differ. This was clearly demonstrated in our recent study [9] on supervised texture segmentation with the same the image set that was used by Randen and Husoy in their recent extensive comparative study [12]. However, real world textures with a large tactile dimension can also exhibit non-monotonic intensity changes, e.g. due to moving shadows, which neither our approach nor any other 2-D texture operator tolerates.

We achieved rotation invariance by recognizing that the LBP operator encodes a set of rotation invariant patterns. An interesting alternative to obtain rotation invariant features would be to carry out 1-D Fourier transform on the circularly symmetric neighbor set [1].

We showed that the performance can be further enhanced by multiresolution analysis. We presented a straightforward method for combining operators of different spatial resolutions for this purpose. Experimental results involving three different spatial resolutions showed that multiresolution analysis is beneficial, except in those cases where a single resolution was already sufficient for a very good discrimination. Ultimately, we would want to incorporate scale invariance, in addition to gray scale and rotation invariance.

We also reported that when there are classification errors, the model of the true class very often ranks second. This suggests that classification could be carried out in stages, by selecting features which best discriminate among remaining alternatives.

Acknowledgments

The authors wish to thank Dr. Nishan Canagarajah and Mr. Paul Hill from the University of Bristol for providing the texture images used in this study. The financial support provided by the Academy of Finland is gratefully acknowledged.

Note

The source code and the texture images used in this study, together with other imagery used in our published work, can be downloaded from *http://www.ee.oulu.fi/research/ imag/texture*.

References

1. Arof H and Deravi F. Circular neighbourhood and 1-D DFT features for texture classification and segmentation. IEE Proc. - Vision, Image and Signal Processing 1998; 145:167-172.
2. Chen J-L and Kundu A. Rotation and gray scale transform invariant texture identification using wavelet decomposition and hidden Markov model. IEEE Trans. Pattern Analysis and Machine Intelligence 1994; 16:208-214.
3. Cohen FS, Fan Z and Patel MA. Classification of rotated and scaled texture images using Gaussian Markov Random Field models. IEEE Trans. Pattern Analysis and Machine Intelligence 1991; 13:192-202.
4. Fountain SR and Tan TN. Efficient rotation invariant texture features for content-based image retrieval. Pattern Recognition 1998; 31:1725-1732.
5. Haley GM and Manjunath BS. Rotation-invariant texture classification using a complete space-frequency model. IEEE Trans. Image Processing 1999; 8:255-269.
6. Kashyap RL and Khotanzad A. A model-based method for rotation invariant texture classification. IEEE Trans. Pattern Analysis and Machine Intelligence 1986; 8:472-481.
7. Lam W-K and Li C-K. Rotated texture classification by improved iterative morphological decomposition. IEE Proc. - Vision, Image and Signal Processing 1997; 144:171-179.
8. Ojala T, Pietikäinen M & Mäenpää T. Gray scale and rotation invariant texture classification with Local Binary Patterns. Proc. Sixth European Conference on Computer Vision, Dublin, Ireland, 2000; 1:404-420.
9. Ojala T, Valkealahti K, Oja E and Pietikäinen M. Texture discrimination with multidimensional distributions of signed gray level differences. Pattern Recognition 2000; 34(3), in press.
10. Pietikäinen M, Ojala T and Xu Z. Rotation-invariant texture classification using feature distributions. Pattern Recognition 2000; 33:43-52.
11. Porter R and Canagarajah N. Robust rotation-invariant texture classification: wavelet, Gabor filter and GMRF based schemes. IEE Proc. - Vision, Image and Signal Processing 1997; 144:180-188.
12. Randen T and Husoy JH. Filtering for texture classification: a comparative study. IEEE Trans. Pattern Analysis and Machine Intelligence 1999; 21:291-310.
13. Wu W-R and Wei S-C. Rotation and gray-scale transform-invariant texture classification using spiral resampling, subband decomposition and Hidden Markov Model. IEEE Trans. Image Processing 1996; 5:1423-1434.
14. You J and Cohen HA. Classification and segmentation of rotated and scaled textured images using texture 'tuned' masks. Pattern Recognition 1993; 26:245-258.

Analysis of Curved Textured Surfaces Using Local Spectral Distortion

Eraldo Ribeiro and Edwin R. Hancock

Department of Computer Science,
University of York, York Y01 5DD, UK
erh@cs.york.ac.uk

Abstract. This paper presents a simple approach to the recovery of dense orientation estimates for curved textured surfaces. We make two contributions. Firstly, we show how pairs of spectral peaks can be used to make direct estimates of the slant and tilt angles for local tangent planes to the textured surface. We commence by computing the affine distortion matrices for pairs of corresponding spectral peaks. The key theoretical contribution is to show that the directions of the eigenvectors of the affine distortion matrices can be used to estimate local slant and tilt angles. In particular, the leading eigenvector points in the tilt direction. Although not as geometrically transparent, the direction of the second eigenvector can be used to estimate the slant direction. The main practical benefit furnished by our analysis is that it allows us to estimate the orientation angles in closed form without recourse to numerical optimisation. Based on these theoretical properties we present an algorithm for the analysis of regularly textured curved surfaces. We apply the method to a variety of real-world imagery.

Keywords: shape-from-texture, spectral analysis, shape analysis, needle map reconstruction, texture, surface shape.

1 Introduction

The recovery of surface shape using texture information is a process that is grounded in psychophysics [1]. Moreover, it has been identified by Marr [2] as being a potentially useful component of the $2\frac{1}{2}$D sketch. Stated succinctly the problem is as follows. Given a two dimensional image of a curved textured surface, how can the three dimensional shape of the viewed object be recovered? This is clearly an ill-posed problem. In order to be rendered tractable, restrictive simplifications must be made. These frequently hinge on the assumed periodicity, homogeneity [3] and isotropy of the underlying surface texture. When viewed from the standpoint of shape recovery, there are two distinct areas of activity in the literature. The first of these confines its attention to planar surfaces and focuses on the recovery of perspective geometry from texture gradient or vanishing point location [4–7]. The second problem is that of interpreting the geometry of curved surfaces [8–12]. Without detailed knowledge of the viewing geometry or camera optics, the latter problem involves recovering local surface orientation from texture gradient.

S. Singh, N. Murshed, and W. Kropatsch (Eds.): ICAPR 2001, LNCS 2013, pp. 407–416, 2001.

This second problem is perhaps the most interesting from the standpoint of shape perception and is the focus of this paper. The problem can be approached in two ways. The first of these is to use pre-segmented structural texture primitives and to measure texture gradient using the variation in the size of the primitives. This approach will clearly be sensitive to the process used to segment the required texture primitives. However, the method can be used with aperiodic textures. The second commonly used method is to adopt a frequency domain representation of the underlying texture distribution. The frequency domain approach can be applied more directly to the raw image data and is potentially less sensitive to the segmentation process. The applicability of the method is restricted to periodic textures.

2   Spectral distortion under perspectivity

This paper is concerned with recovering a dense map of surface orientations for surfaces which are uniformly painted with periodic textures. Our approach is a spectral one which is couched in the Fourier domain. We make use of an analysis of spectral distortion under perspective geometry extensively developed by Super and Bovik [5], Krumm and Shafer [13], and, by Malik and Rosenholtz [10] among others. This analysis simplifies the full perspective geometry of texture planes using a local affine approximation. Suppose that U_t represents the frequency vector associated with a spectral peak detected at the point with position-vector X_t on the texture plane. Further, let U_i and X_i represent the corresponding frequency vector and position vector when the texture plane undergoes perspective projection onto the image plane. If the perspective projection can be locally approximated by an affine distortion $T_A(X_i)$, then the relationship between the texture-plane and image-plane frequency vectors is $U_i = T_A(X_i)^{-T}U_t$. The affine distortion matrix is given by

$$T_A(X_i) = \frac{\Omega}{hf\cos\sigma}\begin{bmatrix} x_i\sin\sigma + f\cos\tau\cos\sigma & -f\sin\tau \\ y_i\sin\sigma + f\sin\tau\cos\sigma & f\cos\tau \end{bmatrix} \tag{1}$$

where f is the focal length of the camera, σ is the slant angle of the texture-plane, τ is the tilt angle of the texture-plane and $\Omega = f\cos\sigma + \sin\sigma \times (x_i\cos\tau + y_i\sin\tau)$.

In this paper we aim to show how an affine analysis of local spectral distortion can be used to recover the parameters of planar pose in closed form. Although affine analysis has previously been used by Krumm and Shafer in their work on shape-from-texture [13], the recovery of pose parameters has relied on exhaustive numerical search and spectral back-projection. In this paper, we demonstrate that the eigenvectors of the affine transformation matrix can be used to directly estimate the slant and tilt angles.

2.1   Spectral homographies

Our aim is to make local estimates of the slant and tilt angles using the observed distortions of the texture spectrum across the image plane. To do this we measure the affine distortion between corresponding spectral peaks. To commence, consider the point S on the texture plane. We sample the texture projection at two neighbouring points A and B laying on the image plane. The co-ordinates of the two points are respectively $\mathbf{X}_A = (x, y)^T$ and $\mathbf{X}_B = (x + \Delta x, y + \Delta y)^T$ where Δx and Δy are the image-plane displacements between the two points. Figure 1 illustrates the idea.

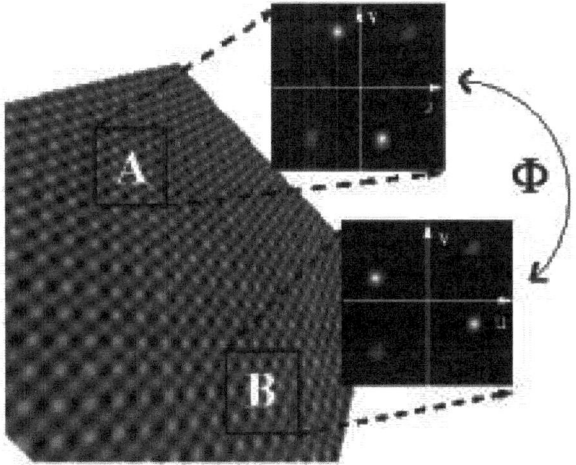

Fig. 1. Affine distortion between two neighbour local spectra

Consider a local-planar patch on the observed texture surface which has a spectral peak with frequency vector $U_S = (u_s, v_s)^T$. Suppose that we sample the corresponding image plane spectral peak at two distinct locations X_A and X_B where the measured frequency vectors are respectively $U_A = (u_A, v_A)^T$ and $U_B = (u_B, v_B)^T$. Provided that the two image-plane locations belong to the same planar region of the observed texture, then the image plane peak frequency vectors are related to the texture-surface frequency vector via the equations $U_A = (T_A(X_A)^{-1})^T U_S$ and $U_B = (T_A(X_B)^{-1})^T U_S$, where $T_A(X_A)$ is the local affine projection matrix of the planar surface patch at the point A and $T_A(X_B)$ is the corresponding affine projection matrix at the point B. As a result, the frequency vectors for the two corresponding spectral peaks on the image-plane are related to one-another via the local spectral distortion

$$U_B - \Phi U_A \tag{2}$$

where $\varPhi = (T_A(X_A)T_A(X_B)^{-1})^T$ is the texture-surface spectral distortion matrix. This 2×2 matrix relates the affine distortion of the image plane frequency vectors to the local planar pose parameters. Substituting for the affine approximation to the perspective transformation from Equation (2), the required matrix is given in terms of the slant and tilt angles as

$$\varPhi = \frac{\Omega\,(\mathbf{A})}{\Omega^2\,(\mathbf{B})} \begin{bmatrix} \Omega\,(\mathbf{A}) + \Delta y \sin\sigma \sin\tau & -\Delta y \sin\sigma \cos\tau \\ -\Delta x \sin\sigma \sin\tau & \Omega\,(\mathbf{A}) + \Delta x \sin\sigma \cos\tau \end{bmatrix} \tag{3}$$

where $\Omega(A) = f\cos\sigma + \sin\sigma\,(x\cos\tau + y\sin\tau)$ and $\Omega(B) = f\cos\sigma + \sin\sigma\,((x + \Delta x)\cos\tau + (y + \Delta y)\sin\tau)$. The above matrix represents the distortion of the spectrum sampled at the location B with respect to the sample at the location A.

2.2   Eigenstructure of the Affine Distortion Matrix

Let us consider the eigenvector equation for the distortion matrix $\varPhi$, i.e.

$$\varPhi \mathbf{w}_i = \lambda_i \mathbf{w}_i \tag{4}$$

where $\lambda_i, i = 1, 2$ are the eigenvalues of the distortion matrix $\varPhi$ and $\mathbf{w}_i$ are the corresponding eigenvectors. Since $\varPhi$ is a 2x2 matrix the two eigenvalues are found by solving the quadratic eigenvalue equation $det[\varPhi - \lambda I] = 0$ where I is the 2x2 identity matrix. The explicit eigenvalue equation is

$$\lambda^2 - Trace(\varPhi)\lambda + det(\varPhi) = 0 \tag{5}$$

where $Trace(\varPhi)$ and $det(\varPhi)$ are the trace and determinant of $\varPhi$. Substituting for the elements of the transformation matrix $\varPhi$, we have

$$\lambda^2 - \left[\frac{\Omega\,(\mathbf{A})}{\Omega\,(\mathbf{B})} + \frac{\Omega^2\,(\mathbf{A})}{\Omega^2\,(\mathbf{B})}\right]\lambda + \left[\frac{\Omega\,(\mathbf{A})}{\Omega\,(\mathbf{B})} \times \frac{\Omega^2\,(\mathbf{A})}{\Omega^2\,(\mathbf{B})}\right] = 0 \tag{6}$$

The two eigenvalue solutions of the above quadratic equation are

$$\lambda_1 = \frac{\Omega^2\,(\mathbf{A})}{\Omega^2\,(\mathbf{B})} \qquad and \qquad \lambda_2 = \frac{\Omega\,(\mathbf{A})}{\Omega\,(\mathbf{B})} \tag{7}$$

The eigenvectors depend on the quantities $\Omega(\mathbf{A})$ and $\Omega(\mathbf{B})$. These are just the lengths of the projections of the position-vectors of the two-points onto the z-axis after counterclockwise rotations by the slant angle and the tilt angle. The corresponding eigenvectors are $\mathbf{w}(\lambda_1) = [\mathbf{w}_x(\lambda_1), \mathbf{w}_y(\lambda_1)]^T$ and $\mathbf{w}(\lambda_2) = [\mathbf{w}_x(\lambda_2), \mathbf{w}_y(\lambda_2)]^T$. More explictly, the eigenvectors are

$$\mathbf{w}(\lambda_1) = [1, \tan\tau]^T \qquad and \qquad \mathbf{w}(\lambda_2) = \left[1, -\frac{\Delta x}{\Delta y}\right]^T \tag{8}$$

As a result we can directly determine the tilt angle from the vector components of the eigenvector associated with the eigenvalue λ_1. The tilt angle is given by

$$\tau = \arctan(\frac{\mathbf{w}_y\,(\lambda_1)}{\mathbf{w}_x\,(\lambda_1)}) \tag{9}$$

The intuitive justification for this result is that under perspective projection the only direction which remains invariant at all locations on the image plane is the tilt direction. As a result, a frequency vector which is aligned in the tilt direction will maintain a constant angle, but it will change in magnitude according to the position on the image plane. In other words, the tilt direction is an eigenvector of the local affine transformation.

Once the tilt angle has been obtained, we recover the slant angle by solving the equation

$$\lambda_2 = \frac{\Omega\,(\mathbf{A})}{\Omega\,(\mathbf{B})} = \frac{f\cos\sigma + \sin\sigma\,(x\cos\tau + y\sin\tau)}{f\cos\sigma + \sin\sigma\,(x + \Delta x)\cos\tau + (y + \Delta y)\sin\tau} \tag{10}$$

The solution is

$$\sigma = \arctan\left[\frac{f\,(\lambda_2 - 1)}{(y(1 - \lambda_2) - \lambda_2\Delta y)\sin\tau + (x(1 - \lambda_2) - \lambda_2\Delta x)\cos\tau}\right] \tag{11}$$

The complete derivation of the above equations is presented in the Appendix of this paper. With the slant and tilt angles to hand the surface normal $\mathbf{n}$ may be computed.

3   Computing local planar orientation

In this Section we explain how to recover local planar surface orientation using our affine distortion method. The first step in orientation recovery is to estimate the affine distortion matrix which represents the transformation between different local texture regions on the image plane. These image texture regions are assumed to belong to a single local planar patch on the curved texture surface. We do this by selecting pairs of neighbouring points on the image plane. At each point there may be several clear spectral peaks. Since the affine distortion matrix Φ has four elements that need to be estimated, we need to know the correspondences between at least two different spectral peaks at the different locations. Suppose that $U_1^{p_1} = (u_1^{p_1}, v_1^{p_1})^T$ and $U_1^{p_2} = (u_1^{p_2}, v_1^{p_2})^T$ represent the frequency vectors for two distinct spectral peaks located at the point with co-ordinates $\mathbf{X}_1 = (x_1, y_1)^T$ on the image plane. The frequency vectors are used to construct the columns of a 2x2 spectral measurement matrix $V_1 = (U_1^{p_1}|U_1^{p_2})$. Further, suppose that $U_2^{p_1} = (u_2^{p_1}, v_2^{p_1})^T$ and $U_2^{p_2} = (u_2^{p_2}, v_2^{p_2})^T$ represent the frequency vectors for the corresponding spectral peaks at the point $\mathbf{X}_2 = (x_2, y_2)^T$. The corresponding spectral measurement matrix is $V_2 = (U_2^{p_1}|U_2^{p_2})$. Under the affine model presented in Section 2, the spectral measurement matrices are related via the equation $V_2 = \Phi V_1$. As a result the local estimate of the spectral distortion matrix is $\Phi = (V_1^T)^{-1} V_2$.

In practice, we only make use of the most energetic peaks appearing in the power spectrum. That is to say we do not consider the detailed distribution of frequencies. Our method requires that we supply correspondences between spectral peaks so that the distortion matrices can be estimated. We use the energy amplitude of the peaks is establish the required correspondences. This is done by ordering the peaks according to their energy amplitude. The ordering of the amplitudes of peaks at different image locations establishes the required spectral correspondences.

In order to improve the orientation estimates returned by eigenvectors of the affine distortion matrix, we use the robust vector smoothing method developed by Worthington and Hancock [15] for shape-from-shading.

4   Experiments with Curved Surfaces

In this section we experiment with real world textured surfaces. We have generated the images used in this study by moulding regularly textured sheets into curved surfaces. The images used in this study are shown in the first column of Figure 2. There are two sets of images. The first four have been created by placing a table-cloth with a rectangular texture pattern on top of surfaces of various shapes. From top-to-bottom, the surface shapes are a ridge, a bulge, a series of ripples and a sphere (a balloon). The second group of images which appear in the fifth, sixth and seventh rows have been created by bending a regularly textured sheet of wrapping paper into various tubular shapes. The first of these is a cylinder, the second is a "wave" while the final example is an irregular tube. The textures in all seven images show strong perspective effects.

The remaining columns of Figure 2, from left to right, show the initial needle-map and the final smoothed needle-map. In the case of this real world data, the initial needle maps are more noisy and disorganised than their synthetic counterparts. However, there are clear regions of needle-map consistency. When robust smoothing is applied to the initial needle maps, then there is a significant improvement in the directional consistency of the needle directions. In the case of the ridge in the first image, the defining planes are uniform and the ridge-line is cleanly segmented. In the case of the bulge in the second image, the ridge or fold structure at the bottom of the picture is well identified. The ripples stand our clearly in the third image. The radial needle-map pattern emerges clearly in the case of the sphere. This radial pattern is also clear for the three "tubular" objects.

Finally, we illustrate how our method can be used to identify multiple texture planes. Here we use the Gustavson-Kessel [16] fuzzy clustering method to locate clusters in the distribution of needle-map directions after robust smoothing has been applied. Each cluster is taken to represent a distinct plane. The mean surface normal direction for the cluster represents the orientation of a distinct plane. Figure 3 show results obtained for real world images containing multiple texture-planes. In each figure panel a) is the original image, panel b) shows the initial distribution of needle-map directions, panel c) is the final needle-map distribution after robust smoothing and panel d) is the segmentation obtained by clustering the needle-map directions. The surface normal data is visualised on a unit sphere. The points indicate the positions where the surface normals intercept the sphere. In each case the initial distribution of needle-map direction is dispersed. After robust smoothing clear clusters develop corresponding to distinct planes. The cluster centres detected by Gustavson-Kessel method are indicated by circles, whose radius indicates the cluster-variance. The segmentations shown are obtained by labelling the smoothed surface normals according to the nearest cluster. In both cases the planar segmentation is in good subjective agreement with the image contents.

5   Conclusions

We have presented a new method for estimating the local orientation of tangent planes to curved textured surfaces. The method commences by finding affine spectral distortions between neighbouring points on the image plane. The directions of the eigenvalues of the local distortion matrices can be used to make closed form estimates of the slant and tilt directions. The initial orientation estimates returned by the new method are iteratively refined using a robust smoothing technique to produce a needle map of improved consistency.

The method is demonstrated on real-world images of man-made textured surfaces. The method proves useful in the analysis of both planar and curved surfaces.

There are a number of ways in which the ideas presented in this paper could be extended. Firstly, our texture measures are relatively crude and could be refined to allow us to analyse textures that are regular but not necessarily periodic. Secondly, there is scope for improving the quality of the needle map through measuring the back-projection error associated with the smoothed surface normal directions. Finally, we are investigating ways of utilising the extracted needle maps for recognising curved textured objects.

References

1. J. J. Gibson. *The perception of the visual world.* Houghton Miffin, Boston, 1950.
2. David Marr. *Vision: A computational investigation into the human representation and processing of visual information.* Freeman, 1982.

3. Andrew Blake and Constantinos Marinos. Shape from texture: estimation, isotropy and moments. *Artificial Intelligence*, 45(3):323–380, 1990.
4. John Krumm and Steve A. Shafer. Shape from periodic texture using spectrogram. In *IEEE Conference on Computer Vision and Pattern Recognition*, pages 284–289, 1992.
5. B.J. Super and A.C. Bovik. Planar surface orientation from texture spatial frequencies. *Pattern Recognition*, 28(5):729–743, 1995.
6. John R. Kender. Shape from texture: an aggregation transform that maps a class of texture into surface orientation. In *6th IJCAI, Tokyo*, pages 475–480, 1979.
7. J.S. Kwon, H.K. Hong, and J.S. Choi. Obtaining a 3-d orientation of projective textures using a morphological method. *Pattern Recognition*, 29:725–732, 1996.
8. Jonas Garding. Shape from texture for smooth curved surfaces. In *European Conference on Computer Vision*, pages 630–638, 1992.
9. Jonas Garding. Shape from texture for smooth curved surfaces in perspective projection. *J. of Mathematical Imaging and Vision*, 2:329–352, 1992.
10. J. Malik and R. Rosenholtz. A differential method for computing local shape-from-texture for planar and curved surfaces. In *IEEE Conference on Vision and Pattern Recognition*, pages 267–273, 1993.
11. J. Malik and R. Rosenholtz. Recovering surface curvature and orientation from texture distortion: a least squares algorithm and sensitive analysis. *Lectures Notes in Computer Science - ECCV'94*, 800:353–364, 1994.
12. B.J. Super and A.C. Bovik. Shape from texture using local spectral moments. *IEEE Trans. on Patt. Anal. and Mach. Intelligence*, 17(4):333–343, 1995.
13. John Krumm and Steve A. Shafer. Texture segmentation and shape in the same image. In *IEEE International Conference on Computer Vision*, pages 121–127, 1995.
14. Jonas Garding and Tony Lindeberg. Direct computation of shape cues using scale-adapted spatial derivatives operators. *International Journal of Computer Vision*, 17(2):163–191, 1994.
15. P.L. Worthington and E.R. Hancock. New constraints on data-closeness and needle map consistency for shape-from-shading. *IEEE Trans. on Pattern Analysis and Machine Intelligence*, 21(12):1250–1267, December 1999.
16. J. C. Bezdek. *Pattern Recognition with Fuzzy Objective Algorithms*. Plenum Press, 1981.

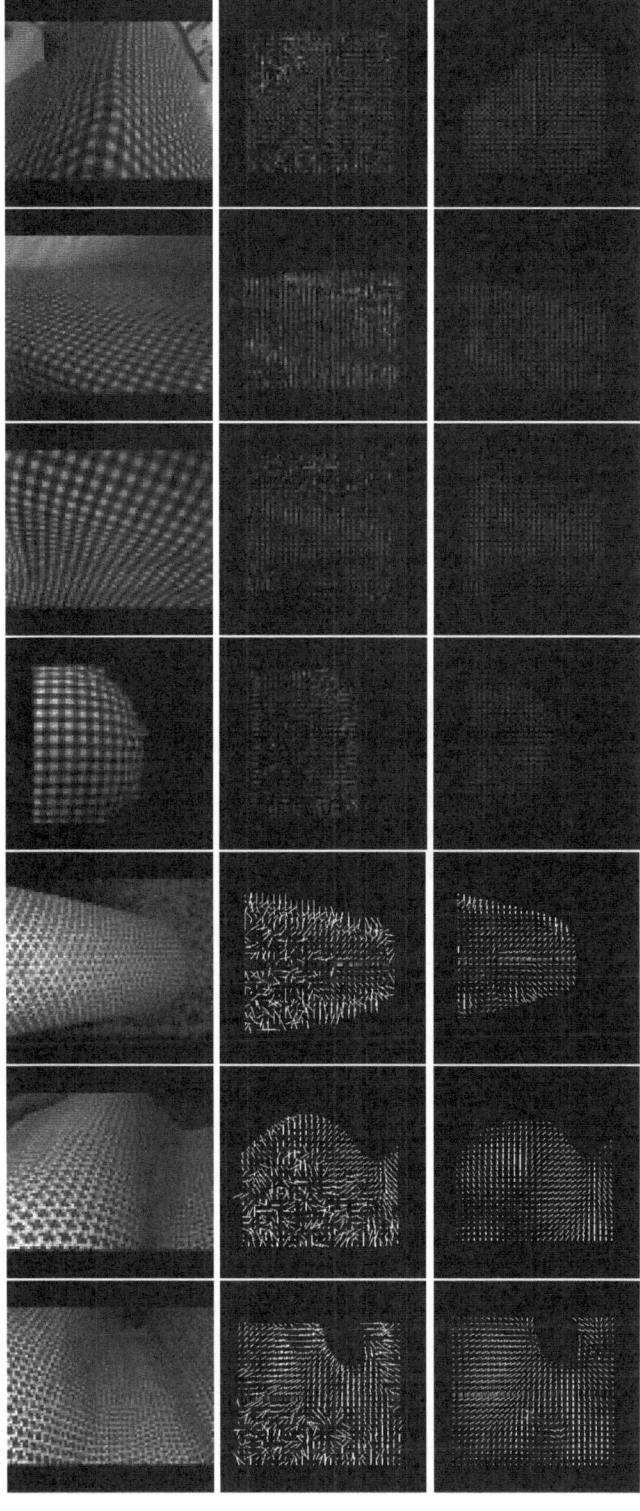

Fig. 2. Real curved surfaces. (a) original image; (b) recovered needle map; (c) Smoothed needle map

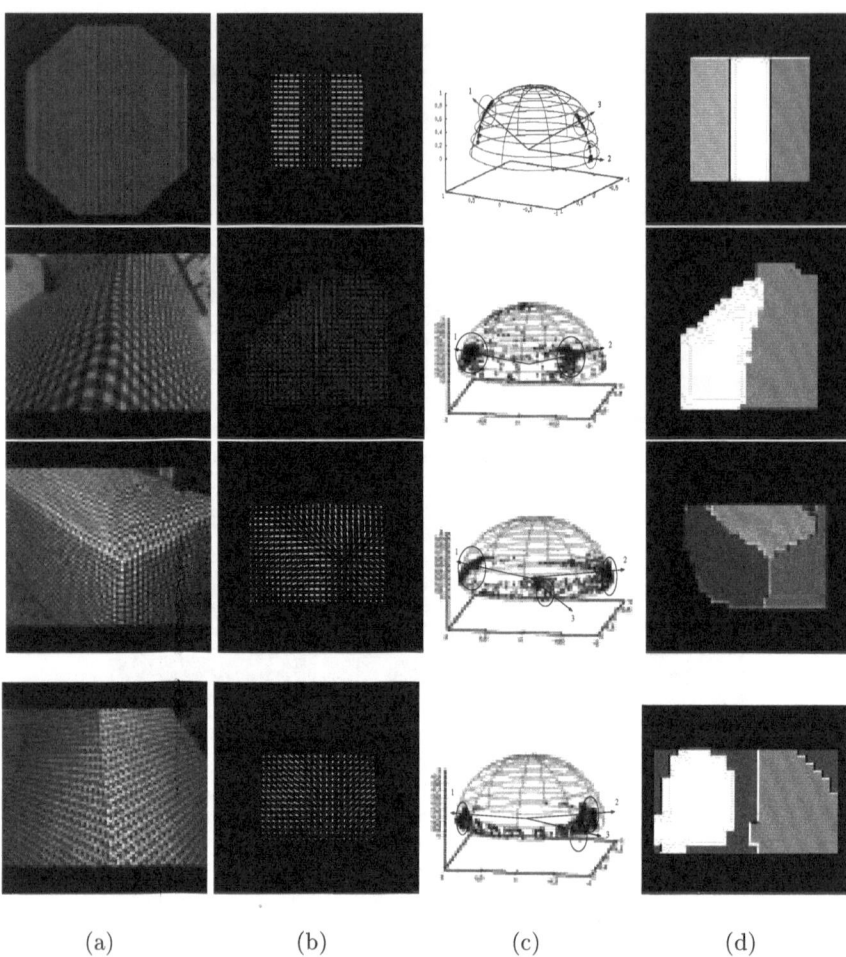

(a)   (b)   (c)   (d)

Fig. 3. 3D-plane segmentation. (a) original images; (b) estimated needle map; (c) spherical clusters; (d) segmented planes

Texture Analysis Experiments with Meastex and Vistex Benchmarks

S. Singh and M. Sharma

PANN Research, Department of Computer Science,
University of Exeter, Exeter, UK

Abstract. The analysis of texture in images is an important area of study. Image benchmarks such as Meastex and Vistex have been developed for researchers to compare their experiments on these texture benchmarks. In this paper we compare five different texture analysis methods on these benchmarks in terms of their recognition ability. Since these benchmarks are limited in terms of their content, we have divided each image into n images and performed our analysis on a larger data set. In this paper we investigate how well the following texture extraction methods perform: autocorrelation, co-occurrence matrices, edge frequency, Law's, and primitive length. We aim to determine if some of these methods outperform others by a significant margin and whether by combining them into a single feature set will have a significant impact on the overall recognition performance. For our analysis we have used the linear and nearest neighbour classifiers.

1. Texture Benchmarks

Performance evaluation of texture analysis algorithms is of fundamental importance in image analysis. The ability to rank algorithms based on how well they perform on recognising the surface properties of an image region is crucial to selecting optimal feature extraction methods. However, one must concede that a given texture analysis algorithm may have inherent strengths that are only evident when applied to a specific data set, i.e. no single algorithm is the best for all applications. This does not imply that benchmark evaluation studies are not useful. As synthetic benchmarks are generated to reflect naturally found textures, algorithm performances on these can be analysed to gain an understanding on where the algorithms are more likely to work better. For our study the objective is to compare texture algorithms from feature extraction perspective, and therefore the recognition rate of a classifier trained on these features is an appropriate measure of how well the texture algorithms perform.

Texture benchmark evaluation is not a new area of work, however previous work has either compared too few algorithms or used very small number of benchmark images that makes it difficult to generalise results (see [15] for a criticism of various studies on performance evaluation). Texture methods used can be categorised as: statistical, geometrical, structural, model-based and signal processing features [17]. Van Gool et al. [18] and Reed and Buf [13] present a detailed survey of the various texture

S. Singh, N. Murshed, and W. Kropatsch (Eds.): ICAPR 2001, LNCS 2013, pp. 417–424, 2001.
© Springer-Verlag Berlin Heidelberg 2001

methods used in image analysis studies. Randen and Husøy [12] conclude that most studies deal with statistical, model-based and signal processing techniques. Weszka et al. [20] compared the Fourier spectrum, second order gray level statistics, co-occurrence statistics and gray level run length statistics and found the co-occurrence were the best. Similarly, Ohanian and Dubes [8] compare Markov Random Field parameters, multi-channel filtering features, fractal based features and co-occurrence matrices features, and the co-occurrence method performed the best. The same conclusion was also drawn by Conners and Harlow [2] when comparing run-length difference, gray level difference density and power spectrum. Buf et al. [1] however report that several texture features have roughly the same performance when evaluating co-occurrence features, fractal dimension, transform and filter bank features, number of gray level extrema per unit area and curvilinear integration features. Compared to filtering features [12], co-occurrence based features were found better as reported by Strand and Taxt [14], however, some other studies have supported exactly the reverse. Pichler et al. [10] compare wavelet transforms with adaptive Gabor filtering feature extraction and report superior results using Gabor technique. However, the computational requirements are much larger than needed for wavelet transform, and in certain applications accuracy may be compromised for a faster algorithm. Ojala et al. [9] compared a range of texture methods using nearest neighbour classifiers including gray level difference method, Law's measures, center-symmetric covariance measures and local binary patterns applying them to Brodatz images. The best performance was achieved for the gray level difference method. Law's measures are criticised for not being rotationally invariant, for which reason other methods performed better.

In this paper we analyse the performance of five popular texture methods on the publicly available Meastex database [7,15] and Vistex database [19]. For each database we extract five feature sets and train a classifier. The performance of the classifier is evaluated using leave-one-out cross-validated method. The paper is organised as follows. We first present details of the Meastex and Vistex databases. Next, we describe our texture measures for data analysis and then present the experimental details. The results are discussed for the linear and nearest neighboour classifiers. Some conclusions are derived in the final section.

1.1 Meastex Benchmark

Meastex is a publicly available texture benchmark. Each image has a size of 512x512 pixels and is distributed in raw PGM format. We split each image into 16 sub-images to increase the number of samples available for each class. The textures are available for classes asphalt, concrete, grass and rock. Finally we get a total of 944 images from which texture features are extracted. Table 1 shows the number of features extracted for each texture method. Table 2 shows the composition of the Meastex database.

Table 1. The number of features for each texture algorithm

Feature extraction method	No. of features
Autocorrelation	99
Co-occurrence	14
Edge frequency	70
Law's	125
Primitive length	5

Table 2. Details of Meastex data

Label	Class	Samples
1	Asphalt	64
2	Concrete	192
3	Grass	288
4	Rock	400

We find that the data for these classes is overlapping no matter what feature extraction method is employed. Therefore, their classification is not a trivial task.

1.2 Vistex Benchmark

All images in the Vision Texture database are stored as raw ppm (P6) files with a resolution of 512x512 pixels. The analysis of Vistex data is more complicated than Meastex. There are several reasons for this. First, there is a larger number of classes involved. The increase in the number of classes does not always increase the complexity of the classification problem provided that the class data distributions are non-overlapping. However, in our case we find that Vistex class distributions are overlapping and the classification problem is by no means solvable using linear techniques alone. Second, Vistex data has much less number of samples for each class and it is expected that the imbalance between samples across different classes will make the classification more difficult. Third, and of most concern is the significant variability across samples of the same class in Vistex benchmark. The original Vistex database consists of 19 classes. Some of these classes have less than 5 sample images that have been removed from our analysis. We are finally left with 7classes that are: bark, fabric, food, metal, sand, tile, and water. Each image is divided into 4 images to increase the number of available samples.

Table 3. Details of Vistex data

Label	Class	Samples
1	Bark	36
2	Fabric	80
3	Food	48
4	Metal	24
5	Sand	28
6	Tile	32
7	Water	32

In Table 3 we summarise data details for Vistex analysis. Fig. 1 shows some of the samples of Meastex and Vistex benchmark data.

(a)

(b)

Fig. 1 (a) Samples of Meastex data including asphalt, concrete, grass and rock; (b) Samples of Vistex data inluding bark, fabric, food, metal, sand, tile and water

We next present the details of how our texture features are computed.

2. Texture Features

Each texture extraction algorithm is based on capturing the variability in gray scale images. The different methods capture how coarse or fine a texture is in their own ways. The textural character of an image depends on the spatial size of texture primitives [5]. Large primitives give rise to coarse texture (e.g. rock surface) and small primitives give fine texture (e.g. silk surface). To capture these characteristics, it has been suggested that spatial methods are superior than spectral approaches. The five feature extraction methods used as a part of this study are based on this spatial element rather than analysing the frequency domain information of the given images. The *autocorrelation* method is based on finding the linear spatial relationships between primitives. If the primitives are large, the function decreases slowly with increasing distance whereas it decreases rapidly if texture consists of small primitives. However, if the primitives are periodic, then the autocorrelation increases and decreases periodically with distance. The set of autocorrelation coefficients are computed by estimating the relationship between all pixel pairs $f(x,y)$ and $f(x+p, y+q)$, where the upper limit to the values of p and q is set by the user. The *co-occurrence* approach is based on the joint probability distribution of pixels in an image [3]. A co-occurrence matrix is the joint probability occurrence of gray levels i

and j for two pixels with a defined spatial relationship in an image. The spatial relationship is defined in terms of distance d and angle θ. If the texture is coarse and distance d is small compared to the size of the texture elements, the pairs of points at distance d should have similar gray levels. Conversely, for a fine texture, if distance d is comparable to the texture size, then the gray levels of points separated by distance d should often be quite different, so that the values in the co-occurrence matrix should be spread out relatively uniformly. Hence, a good way to analyse texture coarseness would be, for various values of distance d, some measure of scatter of the co-occurrence matrix around the main diagonal. Similarly, if the texture has some direction, i.e. is coarser in one direction than another, then the degree of spread of the values about the main diagonal in the co-occurrence matrix should vary with the direction θ. Thus texture directionality can be analysed by comparing spread measures of co-occurrence matrices constructed at various distances d. From co-occurrence matrices, a variety of features may be extracted. The original investigation into co-occurrence features was pioneered by Haralick et al. [4]. From each matrix, 14 statistical measures are extracted. For *edge frequency* method, we can compute the gradient difference between a pixel f(x,y) and its neighbours at a distance d. For a given value of distance, the gradient differences can be summed up over the whole image. For different values of d (in our case $1 \leq d \leq 70$), we obtain different feature measurements for the same image. For *Law's* method, a total of 25 masks are convolved with the image to detect different features such as linear elements, ripples, etc. These masks have been proposed by Law's [6]. . We compute five amplitude features for each convolution, namely mean, standard deviation, skewness, kurtosis, and energy measurement. Finally, for *primitive length* features, we evaluate the number of strings of pixels that have the same gray level. Coarse textures are represented by a large number of neighbouring pixels with the same gray level, whereas a small number represents fine texture. A primitive is a continuous set of maximum number of pixels in the same direction that have the same gray level. Each primitive is defined by its gray level, length and direction. Five statistical features defining the characteristics of these primitives are used as our features. The detailed algorithms for these methods are presented by Sonka et al. [16].

3. Experimental Details and Results

In this paper we present the experimental details of Meatex and Vistex separately. The texture feature sets have been derived from the above discussed methods. In addition, we also generate a combined feature set that contains all features from the five methods. There are total of 944 samples for Meastex data and 280 samples for Vistex data. We use leave-one-out method of cross-validation for exhaustively testing the data. In this method, for N samples, a total of N trials are conducted. In each trial a sample is taken out from the data set and kept for testing and the others are used for training. In each trial, therefore, we have a different set of training data and a different test data. The recognition performance is averaged across all trials. This methodology is superior to random partitioning of data to generate training and test sets as the resultant performance of the system may not reflect its true ability for texture recognition.

3.1 Meastex Results

The results for Meastex data are shown in Table 4.

Table 4. The performance of the linear and nearest neighbour classifier on Meastex

Texture Method	Linear Classifier	Best k	kNN Classifier on original data	Best k	kNN Classifier on PCA data
Autocorrelation	76.1%	5	79.4%	7	86.1%
Co-occurrence	79.2%	5	86.8%	5	93.5%
Edge Frequency	63.4%	3	70.7%	5	74.9%
Law's	82.8%	7	75.1%	7	69.3%
Primitive Length	43.1%	7	54.1%	7	55.9%
Combined	87.5%	5	83.3%	5	83.6%

We have used the classical linear discriminant analysis and the k nearest neighour method. For the nearest neighour method, the best performance has been selected for k=1, 3, 5 and 7 neighbours. We find that the best results have been produced by the linear classifier on the combined feature set. For individual feature sets, their performance with the linear classifier can be ranked as: Law's, co-occurrence, autocorrelation, edge frequency and primitive length. Similarly the performance with the linear classifier can be ranked as: co-occurrence, autocorrelation, Law's, edge frequency and primitive length. For the nearest neighour method, the combined feature set does not produce better results compared to the individual best performance of the co-occurrence method. We find that except for Law's and combined feature sets, the nearest neighbour classifier is a better classifier with an improvement of between nearly 3 to 10% better recognition. On the whole, most methods perform reasonably well on recognising this benchmark. A close evaluation of the confusion matrices shows that rock samples are by far the most difficult to classify. There is a considerable improvement in performance once PCA data is used. One of the reasons for this is that the PCA scores give low weight to features that are not too variable, thereby reducing their effect. As a result, nearest neighbour distance computations on the PCA data are more discriminatory across different class distributions than on original data. The improvements are for autocorrelation nearly 7% better, co-occurrence nearly 7% better, edge frequency nearly 4% better, primitive length 1% better and on combined features less than 1% better. The only inferior performance is that of Law's feature set where the recognition rate falls by nearly 6%.

3.2 Vistex Results

The results for Vistex data are shown in Table 5. On Vistex data, the nearest neighbour classifier is once again superior on all data sets except Law's and combined feature set with an improvement of up to 13% better performance. The most noticeable result using the linear classifier is with the combined feature set that gives a recognition performance of 94.6%. This is a considerable improvement on any single feature set performance. The same performance improvement is however not noticeable for nearest neighbour classifier. In ranked order of how well the feature sets perform with the linear classifier, we have: co-occurrence, Law's, autocorrelation, edge frequency and primitive length. For nearest neighbour, these ranks in descending order are: co-occurrence, autocorrelation, edge frequency, Law's and primitive length method.

Table 5. The performance of the linear and nearest neighbour classifier on Vistex

Texture Method	Linear Classifier	k	KNN Classifier	Best k	kNN Classifier on PCA data
Autocorrelation	66.7%	1	75.3%	1	91.4%
Co-occurrence	73.9%	1	80.7%	1	93.6%
Edge Frequency	53.2%	3	66.8%	3	76.1%
Law's	68.8%	7	56.1%	5	53.2%
Primitive Length	34.8%	7	42.4%	1	56.1%
Combined	94.6%	5	61.3%	3	85.0%

As before, PCA data gives a considerable amount of improvement on nearest neighbour classifier results. The results improve by nearly 16% on autocorrelation features, by nearly 13% on co-occurrence matrices, by nearly 10% on edge frequency features, by nearly 12% on Law's feature set and by nearly 24% on combined feature set. Once more, the results on law's feature set are slightly inferior by nearly 3%. On the whole, all methods demonstrate good performance on this database.

4. Conclusion

We find that for both Meastex and Vistex data excellent results are obtained with most of the texture analysis methods. The performance of the linear classifier is very good especially when we use a combined feature set for both benchmarks. For most feature sets, the performance can be further improved if we use a nearest neighbour classifier. Also, we find that for both Meastex and Vistex benchmarks, the ranked order of texture methods is similar. For example, co-occurrence matrix features are the best and primitive length features the worst for recognition. This ranked order is classifier dependent as we find that the order changes when we switch from a linear classifier to nearest neighbour method.

REFERENCES

[1] J.M.H. Buf, M. Kardan and M. Spann, Texture feature performance for image segmentation, *Pattern Recognition*, 23(3/4):291-309, 1990.
[2] R.W. Conners and C.A. Harlow, A theoretical comparison of texture algorithms, *IEEE Transactions on Pattern Analysis and Machine Intelligence*, 2(3):204-222, 1980.
[3] J.F. Haddon, J.F. Boyce, Co-occurrence matrices for image analysis, *IEE Electronics and Communications Engineering Journal*, 5(2):71-83, 1993.

[4] R. M. Haralick, K. Shanmugam and I. Dinstein, Textural features for image classification, *IEEE Transactions on System, Man, Cybernetics*, 3:610-621, 1973.

[5] K. Karu, A.K. Jain and R.M. Bolle, Is there any texture in the image? *Pattern Recognition*, 29(9):1437-1446, 1996.

[6] K.I. Laws, *Textured image segmentation*, PhD Thesis, University of Southern California, Electrical Engineering, January 1980.

[7] Meastex database: http://www.cssip.elec.uq.edu.au/~guy/meastex/meastex.html

[8] P.P. Ohanian and R.C. Dubes, Performance evaluation for four class of texture features, *Pattern Recognition*, 25(8):819-833, 1992.

[9] T. Ojala, M. Pietikainen, A comparative study of texture measures with classification based on feature distributions, *Pattern Recognition*, 29(1):51-59, 1996.

[10] O. Pichler, A. Teuner and B.J. Hosticka, A comparison of texture feature extraction using adaptive Gabor filter, pyramidal and tree structured wavelet transforms, *Pattern Recognition*, 29(5): 733-742, 1996.

[11] W.K. Pratt, *Digital image processing*, John Wiley, New York, 1991.

[12] T. Randen and J.H. Husøy, Filtering for texture classification: A comparative study, *IEEE Transactions on Pattern Analysis and Machine Intelligence*, 21(4):291-310, 1999.

[13] T. R. Reed and J.M.H. Buf, A review of recent texture segmentation and feature extraction techniques, *Computer Vision, Image Processing and Graphics*, 57(3):359-372, 1993.

[14] J. Strand and T. Taxt, Local frequency features for texture classification, *Pattern Recognition*, 27(10):1397-1406, 1994.

[15] G. Smith and I. Burns, Measuring texture classification algorithms, *Pattern Recognition Letters*, 18:1495-1501, 1997.

[16] M. Sonka, V. Hlavac and R. Boyle, *Image processing, analysis and machine vision*, PWS publishing, San Francisco, 1999.

[17] M. Tuceyran and A.K. Jain, Texture analysis, in Handbook of Pattern Recognition and Computer Vision, C.H. Chen, L.F. Pau and P.S.P. Wang (Eds.), chapter 2, 235-276, World Scientific, Singapore, 1993.

[18] L. vanGool, P. Dewaele and A. Oosterlinck, Texture analysis, *Computer Vision, Graphics and Image Processing*, 29:336-357, 1985.

[19] Vistex Database
http://www-white.media.mit.edu/vismod/imagery/VisionTexture/vistex.html

[20] J.S. Weszka, C. R. Dyer and A. Rosenfeld, A comparative study of texture measures for terrain classification, *IEEE Transactions on Systems, Man and Cybernetics*, 6:269-285, 1976.

Advances in Statistical Feature Selection

Josef Kittler*, Pavel Pudil and Petr Somol

Dept. of Pattern Recognition, Inst. of Information Theory and Automation,
Academy of Sciences of the Czech Republic, 182 08 Prague 8, Czech Republic
e-mail: {pudil,somol}@utia.cas.cz
*Centre for Vision, Speech and Signal Processing, University of Surrey, Guildford
GU2 7XH, UK
e-mail: J.Kittler@eim.surrey.ac.uk

Abstract. The problem of feature selection in statistical pattern recognition is addressed. After formulating feature selection as a combinatorial optimisation problem, a taxonomy of approaches to feature selection is introduced. The techniques available in the literature can be logically grouped into two main categories depending on the form of density functions involved. Recent advances in the methodology of feature selection are then overviewed in this taxonomical framework. The methods discussed include the latest variants of the Branch & Bound algorithm, enhanced Floating Search techniques and the simultaneous semiparametric pfd modelling and feature space selection method. [1]

1 Introduction

Traditionally, one of the key issues in pattern recognition system design has been the identification of a set of distinctive pattern properties, referred to as features, that can be used as a basis for pattern discrimination. Such features are selected from among a set of available measurements by mathematical tools which allow the designer to measure the discriminatory content of a feature set.

The early motivation for feature selection was largely of a pragmatic nature. Considering the constraints imposed by the primitive computing hardware of the time it was absolutely essential to reduce the dimensionality of pattern representation so as to minimise the complexity of the decision making process. However, later it was discovered that reducing the dimensionality of the feature space could also have a beneficial effect on the recognition performance. In fact, it was noted that adding features would initially enhance the system performance by virtue of the complementarity of the information made available to the classification stage. However, at some point the augmentation of the pattern representation space would start exhibiting the law of diminishing returns, resulting in a gradual performance degradation. This "peaking" phenomenon is a manifestation of an intricate relationship between

[1] This work was partially supported by EPSRC Grant GR/L61095 and Czech Ministry of Education Grants MŠMT No.VS96063, ME187, CEZ:J18/98:311600001

S. Singh, N. Murshed, and W. Kropatsch (Eds.): ICAPR 2001, LNCS 2013, pp. 425–434, 2001.

the dimensionality of the pattern space and the size of the training set. As the dimensionality of pattern representation increases, more degrees of freedom become available. Learning the decision rule of a classifier with many free parameters, using a finite training set, then gives a scope for over-fitting and therefore poor generalisation.

The peaking phenomenon has motivated the development of the methodology for feature selection for the last two decades. This motivation has been reinforced by the biological or psychophysical equivalent present in human decision making whereby pattern recognition carried out by the central nervous system appears to be based on the most significant attributes only. It also has a basis in logic as argued by Watanabe in his seminal text Knowing and Guessing [28]. Accordingly, any two objects would be equally similar or dissimilar unless one applied unequal weighting to the list of attributes that could potentially be observed. The feature selection process effectively imposes zero-one weights on the available attributes and therefore sharpens the distinctiveness of object classes.

The aim of this paper is to provide a concise overview of feature selection methods with the focus on the recent advances in this topic area. We acknowledge the arguments put forward by Vapnik [27] that the latest paradigm in classifier design based on the Support Vector concept avoids the problem of peaking. This would suggest that feature selection was not needed. While independent experimental research e.g. [9,10] supports Vapnik's theoretical predictions, it has been found that equally effective pattern recognition systems can be designed using conventional approaches. Such designs are likely to differ from and complement Support Vector Machines. They will help generate the necessary diversity of classifiers needed for multiple classifier systems which offer a path to improved performance.

The paper is organised as follows. The feature selection problem is formulated in the next section. Section 3 reviews optimal and suboptimal feature set search algorithms for classes assumed to be distributed normally. The feature selection methodology applicable to pattern recognition problems with classes characterised by general probability density distributions are discussed in Section 4. In Section 5 the paper is drawn to conclusion.

2   Formulation of the Feature Selection Problem

Following the statistical approach to pattern recognition, we assume that a pattern described by a real D-dimensional vector $X = (x_1, x_2, \cdots, x_D)^{\mathrm{T}} \in \mathcal{X} \subset \mathcal{R}^D$ is to be classified into one of a finite set of C different classes $\Omega = \{\omega_1, \omega_2, \cdots, \omega_C\}$. The patterns are supposed to occur randomly according to some true class conditional probability density functions (pdfs) $p^\star(X|\omega)$ and the respective a priori probabilities $P^\star(\omega)$. Since the class conditional pdfs and the a priori class probabilities are seldom specified in practice, it is necessary to estimate these functions from the training sets of samples with known classification.

The aim of dimensionality reduction is to find a set of d features, where $d < D$ (if possible $d \ll D$), so as to maximize an adopted criterion function. This goal requires:

- criterion for evaluating the quality of selected subset of features
- effective strategy of finding the optimal subset of cardinality d.

While the above named requirements are treated rather well in pattern recognition theory, it is fair to admit that the problem of determining how many features one should select (cardinality d) for the problem at hand is not yet satisfactorily solved. Usually our aim is to achieve the lowest misclassification rate with selected features. Thus if the probability of error or misclassification rate are used as the feature subset evaluation criterion, the optimal d is determined immediately when minimizing the criterion. However, in practice we often have to resort to some other criteria, only indirectly related to probability of error, and the optimal d has to be determined experimentally according to the results on an independent test set.

The set of d features can either be formed by a subset of the original set of D measured pattern vector components found by *feature selection* or alternatively derived from them by a certain transformation. The latter process is referred to as *feature extraction*. In this paper we concentrate on feature selection only. For the practical differences between feature selection and feature extraction see e.g. [14]

Assuming that a suitable criterion function has been chosen to evaluate the effectiveness of feature subsets, feature selection is reduced to a search for the optimal feature subset based on the selected measure.

2.1   Taxonomy of Feature Selection Approaches

There are perhaps two basic situations depending on the available *a priori* knowledge about the underlying probability structures:

a) Some apriori knowledge is available. If we can assume at least that pdfs are unimodal, we can implicitly approximate the class distributions by Gaussian densities. Under this assumption the use of probabilistic distance measures (like Mahalanobis, Bhattachaarya, etc.) as the evaluation criterion may be appropriate. The error rate may be even better provided it can reasonably be computed [22]. The feature set search algorithms available in the literature fall into two main categories: optimal, and suboptimal. The Branch & Bound strategy and its versions described in the sequel represent the category of optimal algorithms. Sequential selection algorithms typified by the Floating Search methods characterise the category of suboptimal search strategies. They are much more computationally efficient (facilitating FS in high dimensional problems). In a recent comparative study of currently available subset search strategies carried out by Jain and Zongker [8] the Floating Search algorithms were found superior to other techniques. Since then, other advances have been made in this area, most of which will be reviewed in Section 3 but for some novel approaches the reader is referred to [2,3,5,11].

b) No a priori knowledge is available. When we have no prior knowledge about the class conditional pdfs, the only source of available information is provided by the training data. Feature selection in such a case becomes a very challenging problem. The early solutions to this problem exhibited serious shortcomings(see [16]). Recently, a new approach which copes reasonably well in such circumstances has been developed. It is conceptually very different from those mentioned above. It is based on approximating the unknown conditional pdfs by finite mixtures of a special type as discussed in Section 4.

3   Gaussian Based Methods

In many practical problems a simplifying assumption about normality of underlying data structures may be accepted. Such an assumption offers the possibility to select features according to different criteria – probabilistic distance measures, dependence measures, entropy measures etc. It is then usually assumed that features yielding higher criterion values will also be better for the purpose of classification.

As it has been already stated, beside the criterion function a suitable search strategy has to be chosen. Ideally it should be able to find globally optimal results. However, all the known optimal search strategies exhibit combinatorial computational complexity which can be curtailed, to a certain degree, by incorporating intelligence into the search process. In any case, in the worst case scenario the optimum can be found only by exhaustive search which becomes computationally prohibitive even for lower-dimensional problems. The most important family of optimal algorithms which avoid the exhaustive search are the Branch & Bound algorithms [12]. They are applicable only in conjunction with monotonic feature selection criteria. That is why faster (polynomial) methods have been proposed, even if they cannot guarantee optimal results. A comprehensive list of optimal and suboptimal search procedures together with the corresponding formulas can be found e.g. in [4]. A very useful taxonomy of FS methods has been established in [8]. In the following we present a brief overview of these methods.

3.1   Optimal Search Methods

The only alternative to the exhaustive search is the Branch & Bound (BB) strategy. All the algorithms based on this strategy require criterion function fulfilling the *monotonicity condition*. Let $\bar{\chi}_j$ be the set of features obtained by removing j features $y_1, y_2, \cdots, y_j$ from the set Y of all D features, i.e.

$$\bar{\chi}_j = \{\xi_i | \xi_i \in Y, 1 \leq i \leq D; \xi_i \neq y_k, \forall k\} \qquad (1)$$

The *monotonicity condition* assumes that for feature subsets $\bar{\chi}_1, \bar{\chi}_2, \cdots, \bar{\chi}_j$, where $\bar{\chi}_1 \supset \bar{\chi}_2 \supset \cdots \supset \bar{\chi}_j$ the criterion function J fulfills

$$J(\bar{\chi}_1) \geq J(\bar{\chi}_2) \geq \cdots \geq J(\bar{\chi}_j). \tag{2}$$

The classical BB algorithm constructs a search tree where the root represents the set of all D features and leaves represent target subsets of d features. While tracking the tree down to leaves the algorithm removes successively single features from the current set of "candidates". The algorithm keeps the information about both the current best subset and the criterion value it yields (we denote this value the *bound*). Anytime the criterion value in some internal node is found to be lower than the current *bound*, due to condition (2) the whole sub-tree may be cut-off and many computations may be omitted. The course of the BB algorithm is illustrated on Fig. 1. For details see [12,7,4].

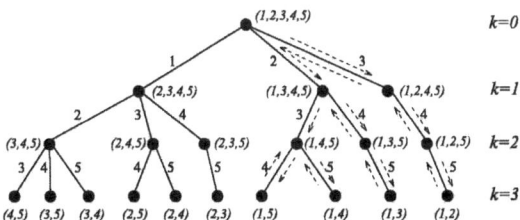

Fig. 1. Example of "branch & bound" problem solution, where $d = 2$ features are to be selected from the set of $D = 5$ features. The dashed arrows illustrate the way of tracking the search tree.

Several improvements of this scheme are known. The *"Improved" Branch & Bound Algorithm* [7] utilizes a heuristic for ordering search tree nodes so as to allow more effective sub-tree pruning. Moreover, any BB algorithm may be modified to construct the *"minimum solution tree"* [29].

The effectiveness of the Branch & Bound principle has been reinforced recently by introducing the prediction-based Branch & Bound algorithms [26,24], which operate several times faster than classical BB algorithms. By means of predicting the criterion value, the number of criterion computations can be reduced significantly. The prediction can be used in two different ways. In both cases the algorithm operates initially in a way similar to classical BB. Every time a feature is removed from the working set (while tracking the search tree down to leaves) the prediction mechanism records the difference of criterion values before and after the feature removal. Based on this information it is later (in different algorithm stages) possible to predict the effect of removing a particular feature. The information is stored individually for every feature; prediction may then start in different algorithm stages for different features.

The *Branch & Bound with Partial Prediction* [26] utilizes the prediction mechanism for ordering search tree nodes only. The idea of ordering tree nodes itself is the same as in the "Improved Branch & Bound". It has been experimentally proven that a slightly less effective heuristic tree node ordering caused by prediction inaccuracy is strongly outweighed by reducing the number of computationally expensive criterion value computations.

The *Fast Branch & Bound* [24] algorithm uses the prediction mechanism more extensively. It replaces criterion value computations by predictions whenever sufficient prediction information is available. In this way many criterion value computations are omitted in internal tree nodes. Whenever a subtree is to be cut-off according to the predicted criterion value (if it becomes lower than the current bound), the real criterion value must be computed first so as to preserve the optimality of the final result.

3.2   Sub-Optimal Search Methods

Most of sub-optimal search methods are based on step-wise adding and/or removing features from the current set so as to maximize (or minimize) the criterion function. A good example is the widely used SFS (Sequential Forward Search) (see e.g. [4]) or its backward counterpart SBS. The SFS starts with an empty set and adds repeatedly single features that increase the current criterion value maximally, until the required number of features is selected.

Simple methods operate fast, but may suffer from the "nesting problem" as a result of the failure to respect complicated statistical dependencies. They may spend a lot of time testing irrelevant subset sizes or may not be usable if a number of features are strongly correlated. The motivation to overcome such problems led to the development of new concepts.

A very practical novel concept has been introduced in the so-called *Floating Search* [17]. In contrast to the conventional sequential search methods the floating algorithms attempt to improve the feature subset after every step by means of backtracking. Consequently, the resulting dimensionality in respective intermediate stages of the algorithm is not changing monotonically but is actually "floating" up and down. Two different algorithms have been defined according to the dominant direction of the search: forward (SFFS) and backward (SBFS) one. The effectiveness of the floating search has been demonstrated on different problems [17,6,8]. The subsequent extension, the *Adaptive Floating Search* [23], is able to focus on the desired dimensionality and find a better solution but only at the cost of significantly increased computational time.

Unlike other methods, the *Oscillating Search* (OS) [25] repeatedly modifies the current subset of d features. This is achieved by alternating the so-called *down-* and *up-swings*. The *down-swing* removes o "bad" features from the current set to obtain a new set of $d - o$ features at first, then adds o "good" ones to obtain a renewed set of d features. A "good" feature may be defined as "a feature that being added increases the criterion value the most". The meaning of "bad" may be defined correspondingly. The *up-swing* is simply a counterpart to the *down-swing*. Two successive opposite swings form an *oscillation cycle*. Using this notion, the oscillating search consists of repeating oscillation cycles. The value of o is denoted the *oscillation cycle depth* and should be set to 1 initially. If the last oscillation cycle did improve the working subset of d features, the algorithm increases the oscillation cycle depth by setting $o = o + 1$. Whenever any swing results in finding better subset of d features, the depth value o is reset to 1. The algorithm stops after the value of o has exceeded a user-specified *limit*.

The flexible concept of oscillating search makes it possible to define a number of algorithms with different properties. It may be looked upon as a universal tuning mechanism which is able to improve solutions obtained in any other way. It can be used both in cases when the quality of solution is the most important goal, and in cases when on the contrary, the priority is given to the speed of finding a reasonable solution.

4   Gaussian-Mixtures Based Methods

When no simplifying assumptions can be made about the underlying class distributions we could in principle deploy nonparametric pdf estimation methods and use the estimated densities to evaluate a suitable feature selection criterion by numerical integration. However, such a procedure would abound in difficulties. A more promising approach is based on approximating the unknown class conditional distributions by finite mixtures of parametrized densities of a special type. In terms of the required computer storage this pfd estimation is considerably more efficient than nonparametric pdf estimation methods.

Denote the ωth class training set by $\mathbf{X}_\omega$ and let the cardinality of set $\mathbf{X}_\omega$ be N_ω. The modelling approach to feature selection taken here is to approximate the class densities by dividing each class $\omega \in \Omega$ into M_ω artificial subclasses. The choice of M_ω is discussed in e.g. [1,21,19,20]. The model assumes that each subclass m has a multivariate distribution $p_m(\mathbf{x}|\omega)$ with its own parameters. Let α_m^ω be the mixing probability for the mth subclass, $\sum_{m=1}^{M_\omega} \alpha_m^\omega = 1$. The following model for ωth class pdf of $\mathbf{x}$ is adopted [18,13]:

$$p(\mathbf{x}|\omega) = \sum_{m=1}^{M_\omega} \alpha_m^\omega p_m(\mathbf{x}|\omega) = \sum_{m=1}^{M_\omega} \alpha_m^\omega g_0(\mathbf{x}|\mathbf{b}_0) g(\mathbf{x}|\mathbf{b}_m^\omega, \mathbf{b}_0, \Phi), \quad \mathbf{x} \in \mathcal{X} \quad (3)$$

Each component density $p_m(\mathbf{x}|\omega)$ includes a nonzero "background" pdf g_0, common to all classes:

$$g_0(\mathbf{x}|\mathbf{b}_0) = \prod_{i=1}^{D} f_i(x_i|b_{0i}), \quad \mathbf{b}_0 = (b_{01}, b_{02}, \cdots, b_{0D}), \quad (4)$$

and a function g specific for each class of the form:

$$g(\mathbf{x}|\mathbf{b}_m^\omega, \mathbf{b}_0, \varPhi) = \prod_{i=1}^{D} \left[\frac{f_i(x_i|b_{mi}^\omega)}{f_i(x_i|b_{0i})} \right]^{\phi_i}, \quad \phi_i = \{0, 1\} \tag{5}$$

$$\mathbf{b}_m^\omega = (b_{m1}^\omega, b_{m2}^\omega, \cdots b_{mD}^\omega), \quad \varPhi = (\phi_1, \phi_2, \cdots, \phi_D) \in \{0, 1\}^D.$$

The univariate function f_i is assumed to be from a family of normal densities.

The model is based on the idea to identify a common "background" density for all the classes and to express each class density as a mixture of the product of this "background" density with a class-specific modulating function defined on a subspace of the feature vector space. This subspace is chosen by means of the nonzero binary parameters ϕ_i and the same subspace of $\mathcal{X}$ for each component density is used in all the classes. Any specific univariate function $f_i(x_i|b_{mi}^\omega)$ is substituted by the "background" density $f_i(x_i|b_{0i})$ whenever ϕ_i is zero. In this way the binary parameters ϕ_i can be looked upon as *control variables* as the complexity and the structure of the mixture (3) can be controlled by means of these parameters. For any choice of ϕ_i the finite mixture (3) can be rewritten by using (4) and (5) as

$$p(\mathbf{x}|\alpha_\omega, \mathbf{b}_\omega, \mathbf{b}_0, \varPhi) = \sum_{m=1}^{M_\omega} \alpha_m^\omega \prod_{i=1}^{D} [f_i(x_i|b_{0i})^{1-\phi_i} f_i(x_i|b_{mi}^\omega)^{\phi_i}] \tag{6}$$

$$\alpha_\omega = (\alpha_1^\omega, \alpha_2^\omega, \cdots, \alpha_{M_\omega}^\omega), \quad \mathbf{b}_\omega = (\mathbf{b}_1^\omega, \mathbf{b}_2^\omega, \cdots, \mathbf{b}_{M_\omega}^\omega).$$

The EM ("Expectation-Maximization") algorithm can be extended to allow a mixture of the form (6) to be fitted to the data. It should be emphasized that although the model looks rather *unfriendly*, its form leads to a tremendous simplification [18] when we use normal densities for functions f. The use of this model (6) makes the process of feature selection a simple task.

In order to select those features that are most useful in describing differences between two classes, it has been recommended to adopt as a criterion of discriminatory content the Kullback's J-divergence [13], defined in terms of the a posteriori probabilities (or equivalently the Kullback-Leibler measures of discriminatory information between two classes mixed in the proportions in which the classes truly occur). The goal of the method is to maximize the divergence discrimination, hence the name "divergence" method.

An important characteristic of this approach is that it effectively partitions the set X of all D features into two disjunct subsets X_d and $X - X_d$, where the joint distribution of the features from $X - X_d$ is common to all the classes and constitutes the background distribution, as opposed to the features forming X_d, which are significant for discriminating the classes. The joint distribution of these features constitutes the "specific" distribution defined in (5).

5   Conclusions

The problem of feature selection in statistical pattern recognition was addressed. After formulating feature selection as a combinatorial optimisation problem, a taxonomy of approaches to feature selection was introduced. Accordingly, the techniques available in the literature can be logically grouped into two main categories depending on the form of density functions involved. The feature selection methods in the first category are applicable under the assumption that the class distributions are Gaussian or at least can be adequately approximated by Gaussian densities. The second category comprises methods that can be used when no simplifying assumptions about the class distributions can be made. Recent advances in the methodology of feature selection were then overviewed in this taxonomical framework. The methods discussed included the latest variants of the Branch and Bound algorithm, enhanced Floating Search techniques and the simultaneous semiparametric pfd modelling and feature space selection method.

References

1. Akaike H. (1994) A New Look at Statistical Model Identification. *IEEE Trans. Automatic Control* **19**: 716–723.
2. Alkoot F.M. and Kittler J. (2000) Multiple Expert System Design by Combined Feature Selection and Probability Level Fusion. *Proc. Conf. Fusion 2000* , Paris.
3. Alkoot F.M. and Kittler J. (2000) Feature Selection for an Ensemble of Classifiers. *Proc. 4th World Multiconference on Systemics, Cybernetics and Informatics*, Orlando, Florida.
4. Devijver P. A. and Kittler J. (1982) *Pattern Recognition: A Statistical Approach.* Prentice-Hall.
5. Ferri F.J., Kadirkamanathan V. and Kittler J. (1993) Feature Subset Search Using Genetic Algorithms. *Proc. IEE Workshop on Natural Algorithms in Signal Processing*, 23/1-23/7.
6. Ferri F.J., Pudil P., Hatef M. and Kittler J. (1994) Comparative study of technique for large-scale features selection. *Proceedings Pattern Recognition in Practice IV: Multiple Paradigms, Comparative Studies and Hybrid Systems*, Elsevier, pp. 403–413.
7. Fukunaga K. (1990) *Introduction to Statistical Pattern Recognition: 2nd edition.* Academic Press, Inc.
8. Jain A. K. and Zongker D. (1997) Feature selection: Evaluation, application and small sample performance. *IEEE Transactions on PAMI*, **19**:153–158.
9. Jonsson K., Kittler J., Li Y.P. and Matas J. (1999) Support Vector Machine for Face Authentication. *Proceeding of BMVC'99*, pp.543–553.
10. Jonsson K., Kittler J. and Matas J. (2000) Learning Support Vectors for Face Authentication: Sensitivity to Mis-Registrations. *Proceeding of ACCV'00*, Taipei, 806–811.
11. Mayer H.A., Somol P., Huber R. and Pudil P. (2000) Improving Statistical Measures of Feature Subsets by Conventional and Evolutionary Approaches. *Proc. 3rd IAPR International Workshop on Statistical Techniques in Pattern Recognition*, Alicante.

12. Narendra P. M. and Fukunaga K. (1977) A branch and bound algorithm for feature subset selection. *IEEE Transactions on Computers*, C-**26**:917–922.
13. Novovičová J., Pudil P. and Kittler J. (1996) Divergence based feature selection for multimodal class densities. *IEEE Transactions on PAMI*, **18**(2): 218–223.
14. Pudil P., Novovičová J. (1988) Novel Methods for Subset Selection with Respect to Problem Knowledge. *IEEE Transactions on Intelligent Systems - Special Issue on Feature Transformation and Subset Selection*, pp.66–74.
15. Pudil P., Novovičová J., Choakjarernwanit N. and Kittler J. (1993) An analysis of the Max-Min approach to feature selection. *Pattern Recognition Letters*, **14** (11): 841–847.
16. Pudil P., Novovičová J. and Kittler J. (1994) Simultaneous learning of decision rules and important attributes for classification problems in image analysis. *Image and Vision Computing*, **12**(3): 193–198.
17. Pudil P., Novovičová J. and Kittler J. (1994) Floating search methods in feature selection. *Pattern Recognition Letters*, **15**:1119–1125.
18. Pudil P., Novovičová J., Choakjarerwanit N. and Kittler J. (1995) Feature selection based on the approximation of class densities by finite mixtures of special type. *Pattern Recognition*, **28**(9): 1389–1397.
19. Sardo L. and Kittler J. (1996) Minimum Complexity Estimator for RBF Networks Architecture Selection. *Proc. International Conference on Neural Networks*, Washington, pp.137–142.
20. Sardo L. and Kittler J. (1998) Model Complexity Validation for PDF Estimation Using Gaussian Mixtures. *Proc. 14th International Conference on Pattern Recognition*, Brisbane, pp.195–197.
21. Schwarz G. (1978) Estimating the Dimension of a Model. *The Annals of Statistics* **6**: 461–464.
22. Siedlecki W. and Sklansky J. (1988) On automatic feature selection. *International Journal of Pattern Recognition and Artificial Intelligence*, **2**(2):197–220.
23. Somol P., Pudil P., Novovičová J., Paclík P. (1999) Adaptive floating search methods in feature selection. *Pattern Recognition Letters*, **20**, 11/13, 1157-1163.
24. Somol P., Pudil P., Ferri F. J. and Kittler J. (2000) Fast Branch & Bound Algorithm in Feature Selection. *Proceedings of the SCI 2000 Conference*, Orlando, Florida, Vol. IIV: 646-651.
25. Somol P. and Pudil P. (2000) Oscillating search algorithms for feature selection. *Proceedings of the 15th International Conference on Pattern Recognition*, IEEE Computer Society, Los Alamitos, pp. 406-409.
26. Somol P., Pudil P. and Grim J. (2001) Branch & Bound Algorithm with Partial Prediction For Use with Recursive and Non-Recursive Criterion Forms. To appear in *Proceedings of the 2nd Int. Conf. on Advances in Pattern Recognition ICAPR 2001*, Rio de Janeiro.
27. Vapnik V.N. (1998) The Nature of Statistical Learning Theory. John Wiley, New York.
28. Watanabe S. (1969) *Knowing and Guessing.* John Wiley and Sons.
29. Yu B. and Yuan B. (1993) A more efficient branch and bound algorithm for feature selection. *Pattern Recognition*, **26**:883–889.

Learning-Based Detection, Segmentation and Matching of Objects

Nicolae Duta[1] and Anil K. Jain[2]

[1] Speech and Language Processing Department, BBN Technologies, Cambridge, USA
[2] Department of Computer Science and Engineering, Michigan State University, USA
dutanico@bbn.com, http://web.cse.msu.edu/~dutanico

1 Introduction

Object learning is an important problem in machine vision with direct implications on the ability of a computer to understand an image. The goal of this paper is to demonstrate an object *learning-detection-segmentation-matching* paradigm (Fig. 1) meant to facilitate image understanding by computers. We will show how various types of objects can be learned and subsequently retrieved from gray level images without attempting to completely partition and label the image.

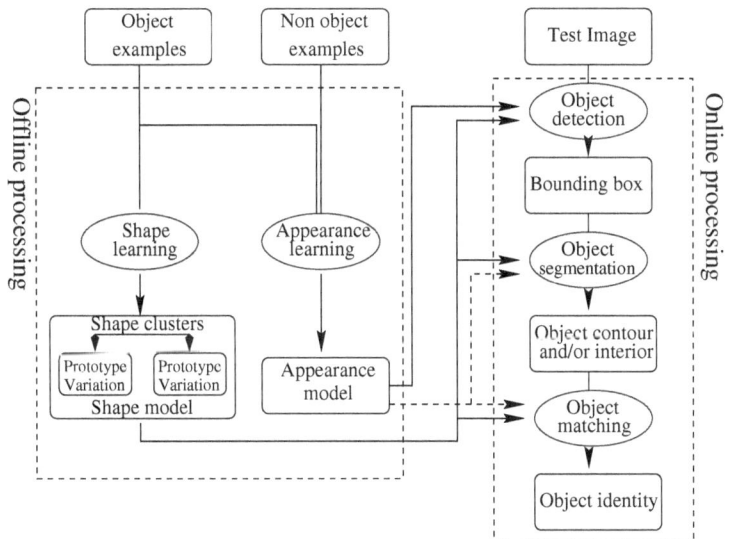

Fig. 1. Schematic diagram of the *learning-detection-segmentation-matching* paradigm for an object learning and retrieval system. The actions performed by the system are shown inside ellipsoidal boxes while the data involved in the process are shown inside rectangular boxes.

1. *Defining and training an object model.* A shape and/or appearance model is trained from several examples of the object of interest, and possibly, of the remaining pictorial universe (negative examples).

S. Singh, N. Murshed, and W. Kropatsch (Eds.): ICAPR 2001, LNCS 2013, pp. 435–444, 2001.

2. *Object detection.* We believe that in order to segment and recognize an object, we must first *detect* it [15]. In other words, we need to determine if the object we are looking for (or at least a part of it) is present in the image and if yes, then we determine a region of interest (or a bounding polygon) that contains it.
3. *Object segmentation.* After detection, an object may need to be segmented from the nearby background, either for computing some instance-specific properties (area, shape, etc.) or for verifying its identity.
4. *Object matching.* In some applications, after an object belonging to a general object class (e.g., human faces, hands, etc.) has been detected and segmented, the final goal is to assign/verify a precise identity (out of a set of possible identities).

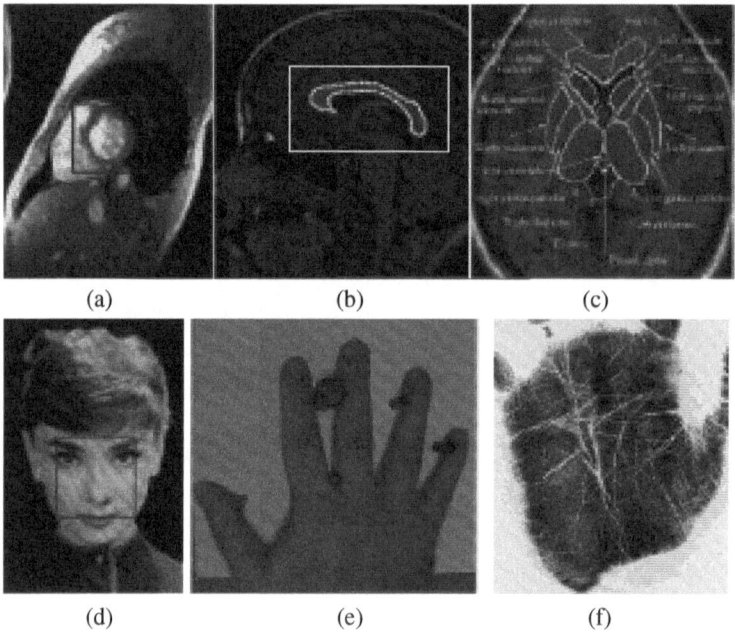

(a)   (b)   (c)

(d)   (e)   (f)

Fig. 2. Practical applications considered in this paper.

Our work addresses the following types of applications (Fig. 2):
1. *Medical* (i) Detection and segmentation of the left ventricle walls in MR cardiac images (Fig. 2a). The automatic segmentation is helping physicians diagnose heart diseases, but automatic diagnosis can be envisioned as a long term goal. (ii) Segmentation and shape analysis of Corpus Callosum in midsagittal MR brain images (Fig. 2b) of normal and dyslexic subjects for assessing if the disorder can be predicted by the Corpus Callosum shape. (iii) Segmentation and model design of neuroanatomic structures in coronal-viewed MR brain images (Fig. 2c).
2. *Human-computer interaction* Detection of human faces (Fig. 2d) is the first step towards a vision-based human-computer interaction system [14, 15].
3. *Biometric systems* Hand shapes [4] (Fig. 2e) and palmprints [7] (Fig. 2f) are some of the biometrics that can be used in applications that require some sort of user identity verification [10].

2   Object detection

Object detection can be defined as follows: given an object O and an arbitrary black and white, still image, find the pose (location and scale) of every instance of O contained in the image. Appearance-based object detectors have the advantage that their representation is less ambiguous than the representation which uses pure shape features or high level object specific features [1, 4].

Most appearance-based detection systems are inherently slow since for each window centered at a pixel in the test image, a feature vector with large dimensionality is extracted and classified. Two approaches have been proposed to speed up the detection process: (i) Amit *et al.* [1] employed an efficient focusing method during which a relatively small number of regions of interest is identified based on spatial arrangements of edge fragments. Only image patches centered at pixels that belong to the identified regions of interest are further classified into object or non-object. (ii) A fast way to perform the classification (*Information-based Maximum Discrimination*) was adapted by Colmenarez and Huang [3] for object detection. The object appearance is modeled as a Markov chain that maximizes the discrimination (Kullback distance) between positive and negative examples in a training set. The main advantage of the method is that the log-likelihood ratio of a test pattern can be computed extremely fast, only one addition operation per feature is needed.

Fig. 3. Face detection results produced by the maximum discrimination classifier on a group image. No arbitration has been performed; all patterns classified as faces are shown. 57 out of the 89 faces (64%) were successfully detected. About 35 background windows were misclassified as faces inducing a false accept rate of 1/49,000. The detection time was 362 secs.

A typical detection result produced by the MD classifier on a 620 × 1152 group image containing 89 faces from the CMU demo page is shown in Fig.

3. For complete details about training, testing, as well as a comparison of the results produced by 6 different classifiers on this problem see [4].

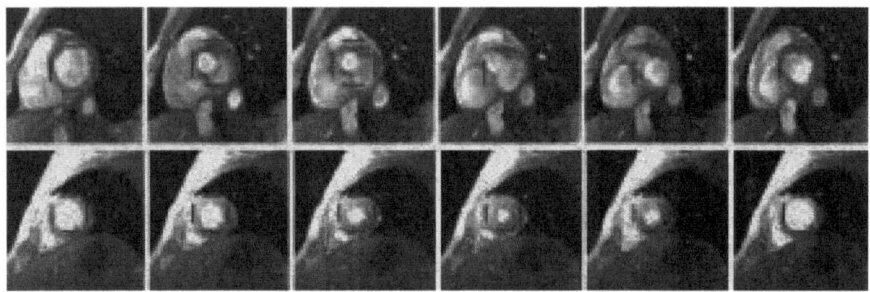

Fig. 4. Left ventricle detection results produced by the maximum discrimination classifier on a spatio-temporal study.

The cardiac ventricle detection system was tested on 1,350 MR cardiac images from 14 patients in a 2-way cross validation using the MD classifier and a signal warping-based arbitration (for details, including the ventricle walls segmentation procedure see the description of the commercial package Argus available on the Siemens MRI scanners [11]). For each patient, a number of slices (4 to 10) were acquired at different time instances (5 to 15) of the heart beat, thus producing a matrix of $2D$ images (in Fig. 4, slices are shown vertically and time instances are shown horizontally). For complete details about training and testing procedures see [6, 4, 11]. A typical detection result on a spatio-temporal (2 slice positions, 6 sampling times) sequence of one patient is shown in Fig. 4.

3   Automatic 2D shape model design

A current trend in automatic image interpretation is to use model-based methods. Shape models are especially useful when the object of interest has a homogeneous appearance and can be distinguished from other objects mostly by its shape (e.g. medical structures). Regardless of the shape representation used, the training data consists of a set of coordinates of some points along the contour of the object of interest from several images. It is usually desirable for a model to describe an *average object* (prototype), to contain information about shape variation within the training set and to be independent of the object pose. There have been few attempts to automate the shape alignment/averaging process in the least-squares framework: Bookstein [2] used thin-plate splines and Hill [9] used polygonal matching. However, none of these methods consider rejecting a training shape if it is significantly different from the majority in the training set.

We have developed a fully automated shape learning method (Fig. 5) which is based on a Procrustes analysis to obtain prototypes for sets of shapes. The main difference from previously reported methods is that the training set is first

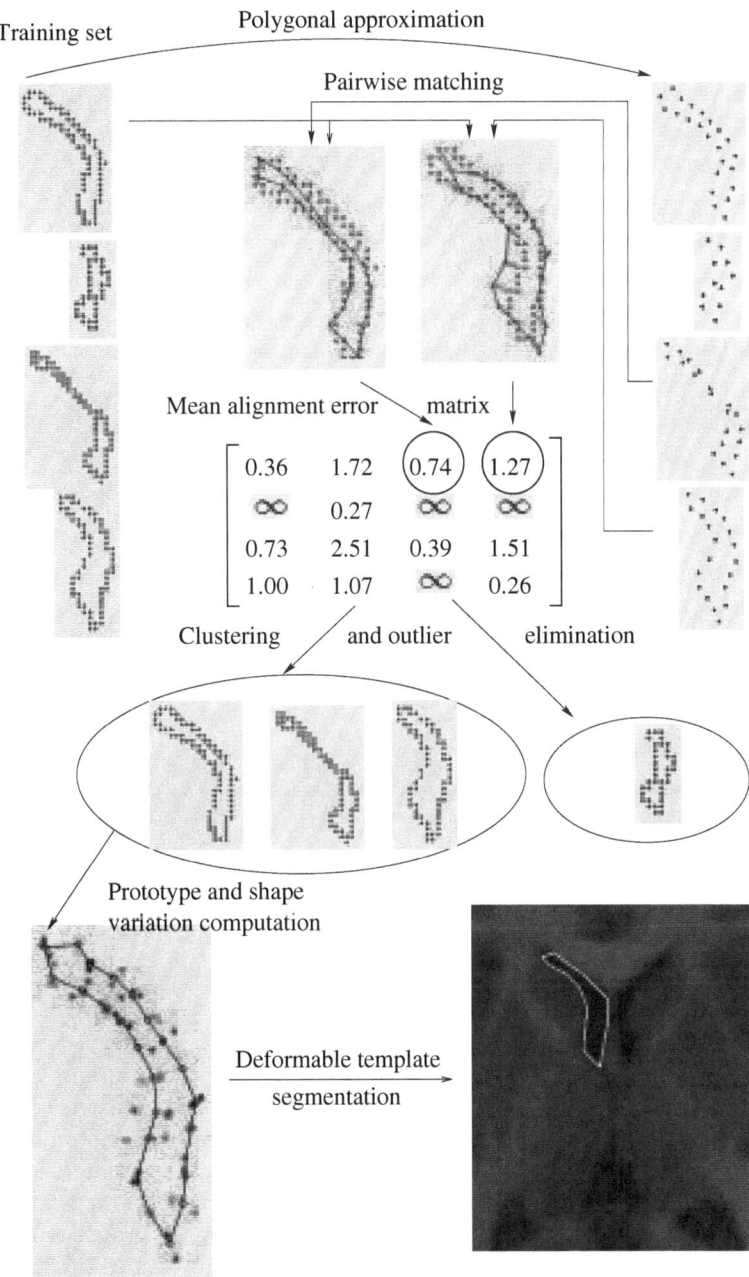

Fig. 5. The shape learning method.

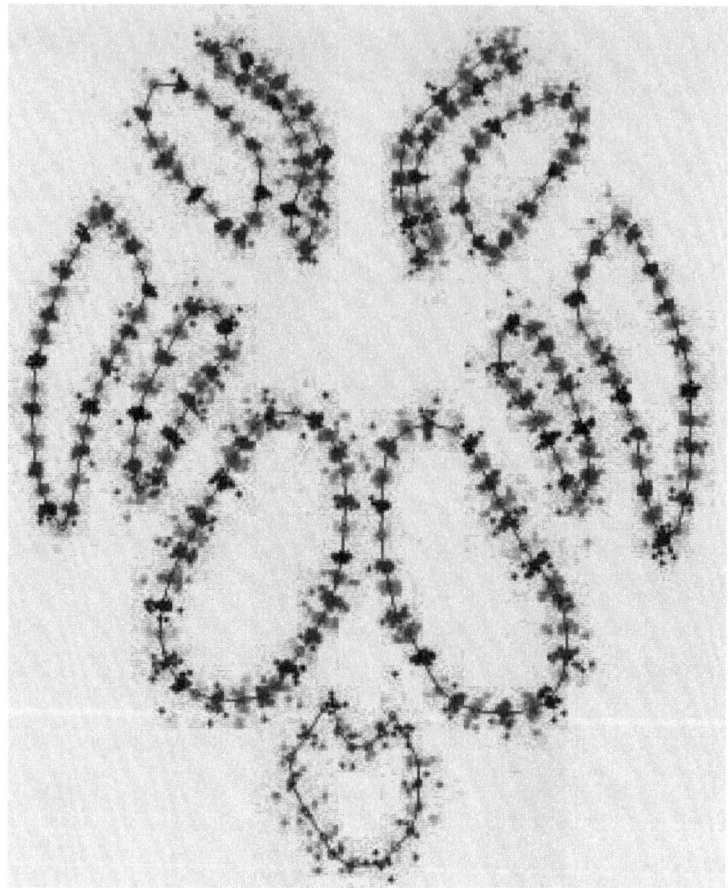

Fig. 6. Procrustes averages (prototypes) of the shapes in the main clusters for 11 brain structures with the aligned shape examples overlaid.

automatically clustered and those shapes considered to be outliers are discarded. The second difference is in the manner in which registered sets of points are extracted from each shape contour. We have proposed a flexible point matching technique that takes into account both pose/scale differences as well as non-linear shape differences between a pair of objects [5]. Our shape learning method was employed to design a shape model for 11 brain structures (results from several other applications are presented in Sections 4,5, [8] and at http://web.cse.msu.edu/~dutanico). The data set consisted of observer-defined contours identified by a neuroanatomist in 28 individual MR images of the human brain, imaged in the coronal plane with in-slice resolution of 256×256 pixels. Figure 6 shows the main cluster prototypes for 11 structures with the aligned shape examples overlaid.

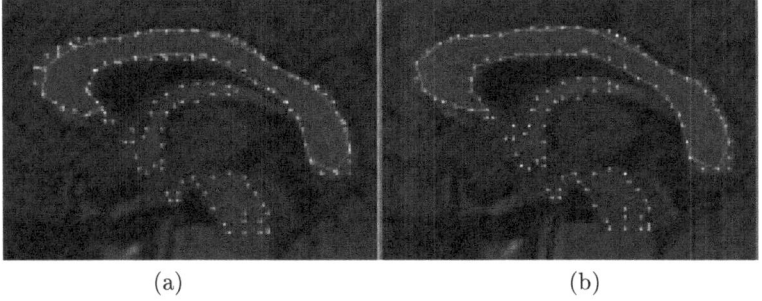

|(a)|(b)|

Fig. 7. a) Registration of an average CC to the edge map produced by a pixel clustering gray matter segmentation. b) Warping the average CC onto the edge image in (a).

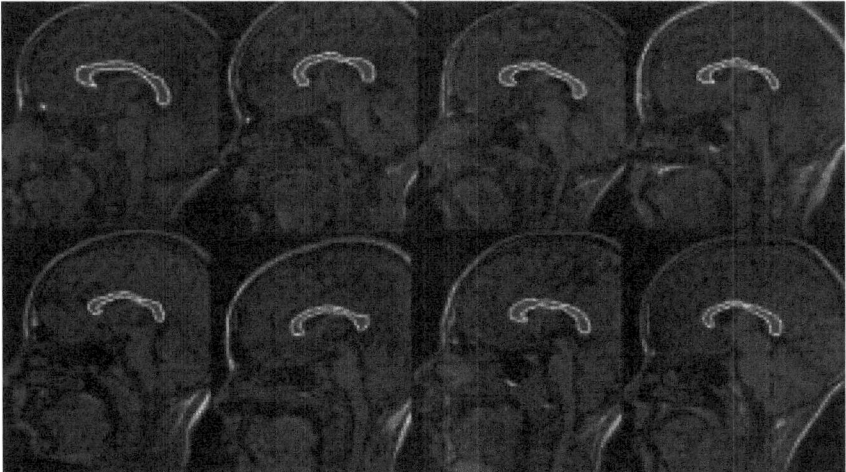

Fig. 8. Automatic segmentation of the Corpus Callosum in eight MR images using the warping-based paradigm.

4   Warping-based segmentation

When the object of interest is homogeneous and has a good contrast with respect to the immediate background, one can combine low-level with high-level segmentation methods. Low-level methods include edge detection and unsupervised segmentation followed by edge detection. High-level methods learn the shape and/or appearance of the object of interest and refine the low-level results using this additional information. For example, the main characteristic that makes the CC distinguishable from other structures in the brain is its shape. The CC shape can be learned from manual tracings (as shown in Section 3) and can be used in a model-based segmentation guided by a low-level edge map. The first stage of the warping-based segmentation is the alignment of a learned CC prototype to the edge image. Figure 7(a) shows the alignment of a CC prototype to an edge map obtained following a low-level pixel classification (for details on the CC detection and low-level gray matter segmentation see [12]). The second stage of the segmentation warps the CC prototype to the edge image: each vertex of the prototype moves towards its corresponding edge (Fig. 7(b)). If a vertex has no corresponding image edge, one can either keep the position of the model vertices with no corresponding image evidence after the alignment (if we are confident that the object of interest does not deviate significantly from the shape template) or one can simply exclude them from the template. Results of the automatic segmentation of the Corpus Callosum in eight MR images using the warping-based paradigm are shown in Fig. 8.

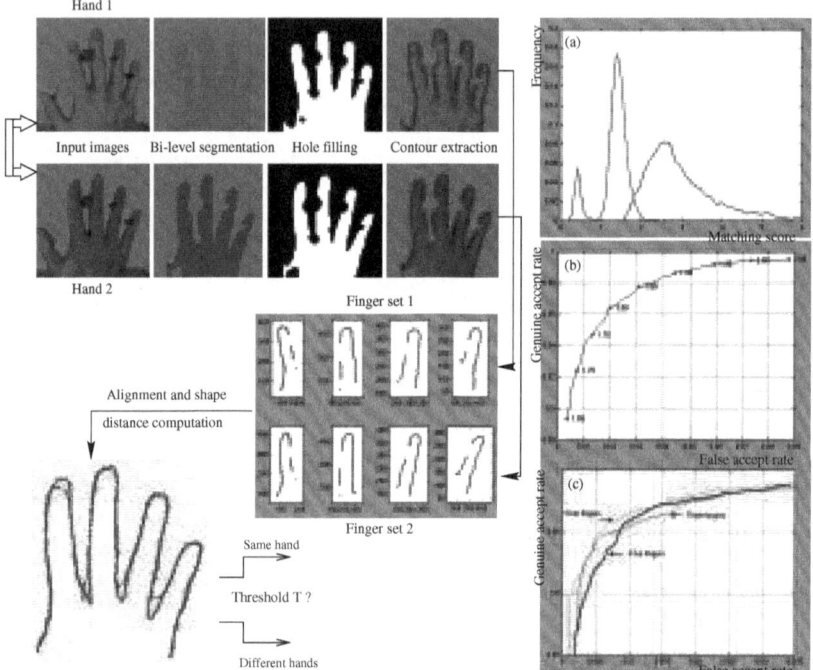

Fig. 9. Alignment-based hand verification system (left) and its performance. (a) Mean alignment error distributions for the genuine class (left) and imposter class (right). The distributions are derived based on a total of 353 hand images of 53 persons. (b) ROC curve for the hand shape-based verification system. The annotations on the curve represent different thresholds on the MAE distance. (c) ROC curves generated by taking into account three, four and five fingers in the alignment error computation.

5   Object matching

In many cases, after an object has been detected and segmented, one needs to classify it into one of several classes (assign it an "identity"). There are broadly two domains where visual object matching systems obeying the *verification paradigm* are currently employed: biometric-based personal identification [10] and medical image-based differentiation between healthy and sick patients [2]. We will now present an application from each of these domains.

Deformable matching of hand shapes for user verification Given a pair of top views of hand images acquired by a hand scanner, we propose the following hand shape matching paradigm (Fig. 9):

1. *Finger extraction and alignment.* The five pairs of corresponding fingers are extracted from each contour and aligned separately with respect to the rigid transformations group as described in [5].

2. *Pairwise distance computation.* Each alignment in Step 1 produces a set of point correspondences. The *Mean Alignment Error* (MAE) between the two hand shapes is defined as the average distance between the corresponding points.

3. *Verification.* A pair of hand shapes is said to belong to the same hand if their MAE is smaller than a threshold T. Usually, the Neymann-Pearson rule that minimizes the False Reject Rate (FRR) for a fixed False Accept Rate (FAR) is employed to compute T.

A data set of 353 hand images belonging to 53 persons was collected (the number of images per person varied between 2 and 15). To each pair of images of the same hand, we applied the algorithm presented above and obtained a complete set of 3,002 intra-class pairwise distances. We also randomly chose a set of 3,992 pairs of images of different hands and obtained a set of inter-class distances. Based on these distance sets, we computed genuine and imposter distributions (Fig. 9(a)). The *ROC* curve associated with the two distributions is shown in Fig. 9(b). One can see that the classification system is very accurate: e.g, for a threshold of $T = 1.80$, the genuine accept rate is 96.5% for a 2% false accept rate.

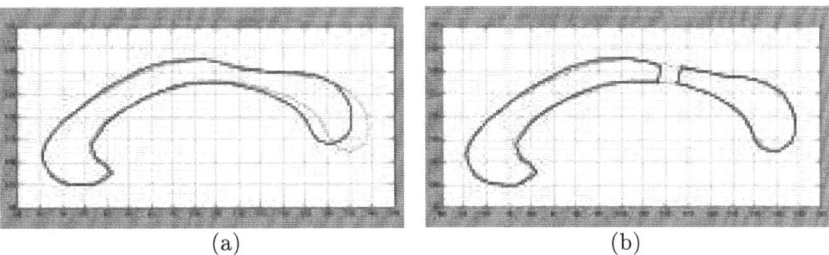

(a)   (b)

Fig. 10. Comparing the normal (light gray) and dyslexic (dark gray) group means of Corpus Callosum shapes. (a) *Rostrum* alignment. (b) Both *rostrum* and *splenium* alignment. The dyslexic prototype is actually cut into two parts which are aligned separately.

Corpus Callosum shape analysis We have investigated the possible differ ences in the Corpus Callosum shape associated with dyslexia by comparing the group means (prototypes) of CC shapes (for a description of the data set see

[13]). The choice of the group mean shapes was motivated by the fact that a simple visual inspection or set of features (e.g., perimeter, area, bounding box, etc.) did reveal any significant difference between the CC shapes belonging to different classes (e.g., dyslexic vs. normal). After aligning the *rostrum* of the two prototype shapes, one can notice a four-pixel length difference between them (Fig. 10(a)). Based on that fact, we have built a classification system which can distinguish a normal CC shape from dyslexic one about 80% of the time [4].

Acknowledgments

The authors would like to thank all those who kindly offered their data and/or code: Dr. Dorin Comaniciu, Dr. Mario Figueiredo, Dr. Arvid Lundervold, Dr. Kanti Mardia, Dr. Kerstin von Plessen, Dr. Milan Sonka and Dr. Torfinn Taxt. This work was supported by Siemens Corporate Research, Princeton, NJ.

References

1. Y. Amit, D. Geman, and B. Jedynak. Efficient focusing and face detection. In *Face Recognition: From Theory to Applications*, H. Wechsler *et al.* (*eds.*), 1997. NATO ASI Series F, Springer Verlag, Berlin.
2. F. L. Bookstein. Landmark methods for forms without landmarks: Morphometrics of group differences in outline shape. *Medical Image Analysis*, 1(3):225–244, 1997.
3. A. Colmenarez and T. Huang. Face detection with information-based maximum discrimination. In *Proceedings of CVPR-'97*, pages 782–787, San Juan, PR, 1997.
4. N. Duta. *Learning-based Detection, Segmentation and Matching of Objects*. Ph.D. thesis, Michigan State University, 2000.
5. N. Duta, A. K. Jain, and M. P. Jolly. Automatic construction of 2D shape models. *To appear in IEEE Trans. Pattern Anal. and Machine Intelligence*.
6. N. Duta, A. K. Jain, and M. P. Jolly. Learning-based object detection in cardiac MR images. In *Proceedings of ICCV '99*, pages 1210–1216, Corfu, Greece, 1999.
7. N. Duta, A. K. Jain, and K. V. Mardia. *Matching of palmprints*. Submitted, 2000.
8. R. Fisker, N. Schultz, N. Duta, and J. Carstensen. A general scheme for training and optimization of the Grenander deformable template model. In *Proceedings of CVPR 2000*, Hilton Head, SC, 2000.
9. A. Hill, C. J. Taylor, and A. D. Brett. A framework for automatic landmark identification using a new method of nonrigid correspondence. *IEEE Trans. Pattern Anal. and Machine Intelligence*, 22(3):241–251, 2000.
10. A. Jain, R. Bolle, and S. Pankanti. Introduction to biometrics. In *Biometrics: Personal Identification in Networked Society*, pages 1–41, A. Jain, R. Bolle and S. Pankanti (*eds.*). Kluwer Academic, Boston, 1999.
11. M-P. Jolly, N. Duta, and G. Funka-Lea *Segmentation of the left ventricle in cardiac MRI images*. Submitted to *IEEE Trans. Med. Imaging*, 2000.
12. A. Lundervold, N. Duta, T. Taxt, and A. K. Jain. Model-guided segmentation of Corpus Callosum in MR images. In *Proceedings of CVPR '99*, pages 231–237, Fort Collins, CO, 1999.
13. K. von Plessen, A. Lundervold, N. Duta, E. Heiervang, F. Klauschen, A. I. Smievoll, L. Ersland, and K. Hugdahl. *Size and shape of the Corpus Callosum in dyslexic boys - a structural MRI study*. Submitted, 2000.
14. H. Rowley, S. Baluja, and T. Kanade. Neural network-based face detection. *IEEE Trans. Pattern Anal. and Machine Intelligence*, 20(1):23–38, 1998.
15. H. Schneiderman. *A Statistical Approach to 3D Object Detection*. Ph.D. thesis, Carnegie Mellon University, 2000.

Automated Biometrics

Nalini K. Ratha, Andrew Senior and Ruud M. Bolle

IBM Thomas J. Watson Research Center

P. O. Box 704

Yorktown Heights, NY 10598

{ratha, aws, bolle}@us.ibm.com

Abstract

Identity verification becomes a challenging task when it has to be automated with high accuracy and non-repudiability. Existing automatic verification methods such as passwords and credit cards are vulnerable to misuse and fraud. Automated biometrics-based authentication methods solve these problems by providing a strong guarantee of the user's identity. In this tutorial, we present an overview of the fast-developing and exciting area of automated biometrics. Several popular biometrics including fingerprint, face and iris are reviewed, and an introduction to accuracy evaluation methods is presented.

1 Introduction

In the modern networked society, there is an ever-growing need to determine or verify the identity of a person. Where authorization is necessary for any action, be it picking up a child from daycare or boarding an aircraft, authorization is almost always vested in a single individual or a class of individuals. There are a number of methods to verify identity adopted by society or automated systems. These are summarized in Table 1. Traditional existing methods can be grouped into three classes [25]: (i) possessions; (ii) knowledge and (iii) biometrics. Biometrics is the science of identifying or verifying the identity of a person based on physiological or behavioral characteristics. Physiological characteristics include fingerprints and facial image. The behavioral characteristics are actions carried out by a person in a characteristic way and include signature and voice, though these are naturally dependent on physical characteristics. Often, the three identification methods are used in combination. The possession of a key is a physical conveyor of authorization; a password plus a user ID is a purely knowledge-based method of identification; an ATM card is a possession that requires knowledge to carry out a transaction; a passport is a possession that requires biometric verification.

Early automated authorization and authentication methods relied on possessions and knowledge, however, there are several well-known problems associated with these methods that restrict their use and the extent to which they can be trusted. These methods verify attributes which are usually assumed to imply the presence of a given person. The most important drawbacks of these methods are (i) possessions can be lost, forged or easily duplicated; (ii) knowledge can be forgotten; (iii) both knowledge and possessions can be shared or stolen. Consequently, repudiation is easy, that is, it is easy to deny that a given person carried out an action, because only the possessions or knowledge are checked, and these are only loosely coupled to the person's identity. Clearly, this cannot be tolerated in applications such as high security physical access control, bank account access and credit card authentication. The science of biometrics provides an elegant solution to these problems by truly verifying the identity of the individual. For contemporary applications, biometric authentication is automated to eliminate the need for human verification, and a number of new biometrics have been developed, taking advantage of improved understanding of the human body and advanced sensing techniques [17]. Newer physiological biometric

Method	Examples	Comments
What you know	userid, password, PIN	Forgotten Shared Many passwords are easy to guess
What you have	Cards, badges, keys	Lost or stolen Shared Can be duplicated
What you are	Fingerprint, face.....	Non-repudiable authentication

Table 1: Identification technologies.

S. Singh, N. Murshed, and W. Kropatsch (Eds.): ICAPR 2001, LNCS 2013, pp. 445–453, 2001.

authentication technologies that have been developed include iris patterns, retinal images and hand geometry; newer behavioral biometrics technologies, still very much in the research stage, are gait and key stroke patterns.

The behavioral characteristics must be insensitive to variations due to the state of health, mood of the user or passage of time. The physiological characteristics remain fairly constant over time. A biometrics system works with an enrolled biometric (identity) which is the first step. After enrolling, the user can be a verified many times.

1.1   Identification vs. authentication

Basically, there are two types of application scenarios: (i) identification and (ii) authentication. For identification, also known as $1 : N$ matching, the system uses the biometric to determine the corresponding person from a database containing many identities, or decides that a particular subject is not enrolled in the database. For authentication, also known as $1 : 1$ matching or identity verification, the system matches the input biometric against a single biometric record. The latter could be stored on a card presented at the transaction time, or retrieved from a database with the help of a key such as an account number or employee ID. The output of the match is either "Yes" if the two biometrics match or "No" otherwise. Often during the enrollment process, an identification system is employed to ensure that the subject is not already enrolled and that subsequent uses are authentication instances associated with the unique identifier assigned to the user during the enrollment.

1.2   Application characteristics

Several applications require biometrics. In general, wherever there is a password or PIN, one can replace these with biometrics. However, each application has a different set of requirements. For example, an ATM requires an unattended type of biometric authentication whereas a welfare disbursement center has a supervisor available. An application can be characterized by the following characteristics: (i) attended vs. unattended; (ii) overt vs. covert; (iii) cooperative vs. non-cooperative; (iv) scalable vs. non-scalable and (v) acceptable vs. non-acceptable. By scalable, we mean that the performance degrades slowly as the database size increases.

2   Pattern recognition-based biometrics systems

Biometric systems can be cast as a generic pattern recognition system as shown in Figure 1. The input subsystem consists of a special sensor needed to acquire the biometric signal. Reliable acquisition of the input signal is a challenge for sensor designers, especially in light of interpersonal and intrapersonal variations and varying environmental situations. The signal in its raw form contains the required identifying information hidden among much irrelevant information. Invariant features are extracted from the signal for representation purposes in the

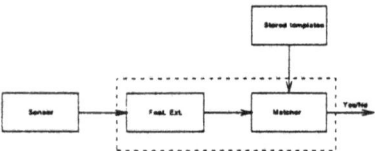

Figure 1: A generic biometrics system.

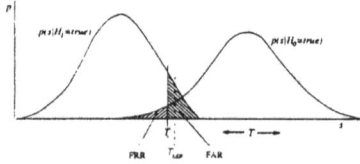

Figure 2: Impostor and genuine distributions with classification error definitions.

feature extraction subsystem. During the enrollment process, a representation (called template) of the biometrics in terms of these features is stored in the system. The matching subsystem accepts query and reference templates and returns the degree of match or mismatch as a score, i.e., a similarity measure. A final decision step compares the score to a decision threshold to deem the comparison a match or non-match. The overall performance of the system depends on the performance of all the subsystems. In addition, the system designer has to focus on efficient storage and retrieval, error free transmission and possible encryption and decryption of the result as well as intermediate signals.

2.1   Classification errors and performance evaluation

To assess the performance of a biometric system, we analyze it in a hypothesis testing framework. Let B' and B denote biometrics, e.g., two fingers. Further, let the stored biometric sample or template be pattern $P' = S(B')$ and the acquired one be pattern $P = S(B)$. Then, in terms of hypothesis testing, we have the null and alternative hypotheses:

$$H_0: \quad B = B', \quad \text{the claimed identity is correct} \tag{1}$$
$$H_1: \quad B \neq B', \quad \text{the claimed identity is } not \text{ correct.}$$

Often some similarity measure $s = Sim(P, P')$ is defined and H_0 is decided if $s \geq T_d$ and H_1 is decided if $s < T_d$, with T_d a decision threshold. (Some systems use a distance or dissimilarity measure. Without loss of generality we assume a similarity measure throughout.)

2.2   Measures of performance

The measure s is also referred to as a *score*. When $B = B'$, s is referred to as a *match score* and B and B' are called a *mated pair* or *matched pair*. When $P \neq P'$, s is referred to as a *non match score* and B and B' are called a *non-mated pair*.

For expression 1, deciding H_0 when H_1 is true gives a false acceptance; deciding H_1 when H_0 is true results in a false rejection. The False Accept Rate (FAR) (proportion of non-mated pairs resulting in false acceptance) and False Reject Rate (FRR) (proportion of mated pairs resulting in false rejection) together characterize the accuracy of a recognition system for a given decision threshold. Varying the threshold T_d trades FAR off against

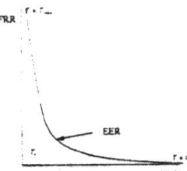

Figure 3: Receiver Operating Curve (ROC).

FRR. In Figure 2, the FAR is the area under the H_1 density function to the right of the threshold and the FRR is the area under the H_0 density function to the left of the threshold. More specifically for biometric systems, we can express the two errors as False Match Rate (FMR) and False Non-Match Rate (FNMR) [40].

The Equal Error Rate (EER) is the point at some threshold (T_{EER}) where FRR = FAR, *i.e.*, where the areas marked under the two curves in Fig. 2 are equal.

Rather than showing the error rates in terms of probability densities as in Figure 2, it is desirable to report system accuracy using a Receiver Operating Curve (ROC) [13, 27]. An ROC is a mapping $T_d \rightarrow$ (FAR, FRR),

$$\text{ROC}(T_d) = (\text{FAR}(T_d), \text{FRR}(T_d)),$$

as shown in Fig. 3.

Note that in a typical recognition system, all the information contained in the PDFs is also contained in the ROC. The ROC can be directly constructed from the probability density functions as

$$\text{FAR}(T_d) = Prob(s \geq T_d | H_1 = true) = [1 - \int_0^{T_d} p(s|H_1 = true)\,ds]$$
$$\text{FRR}(T_d) = Prob(s < T_d | H_0 = true) = \int_0^{T_d} p(s|H_0 = true)\,ds.$$

If we let T_d go to zero, the FAR goes to one and the FRR goes to zero; if we let T go to T_{max}, the FAR goes to zero and the FRR goes to one.

A measure of "goodness" d' (d-prime) can be defined in terms of parameters of the PDFs as [9]:

$$d' = \frac{\mu_1 - \mu_2}{\sqrt{(\sigma_1^2 + \sigma_2^2)}}. \tag{2}$$

This measure was originally developed to measure the separability of two normal (or at least symmetric) distributions.

3   Six most commonly used biometrics

We provide a brief description of the most widely used biometrics.

3.1   Fingerprint

Fingerprint is the mother biometric and the most widely used biometric. The advent of several inkless fingerprint scanning technologies coupled with the exponential increase in processor performance has taken fingerprint recognition beyond criminal identification applications to several civilian applications such as access control; time and attendance; and computer user login. Over the last decade, many novel techniques have been developed to acquire fingerprints without the use of ink. These scanners are known as "livescan" fingerprint scanners. The basic principle of these inkless methods is to sense the ridges on a finger, which are in contact with the surface of the scanner. The livescan image acquisition systems are based on four types of technology:

- Frustrated total internal reflection (FTIR) and other optical methods [14]: This technology is by far the oldest livescan method. A camera looks at the reflected signal from the prism as the subject touches a side of the prism. The typical image size of 1" × 1" is converted to 500 dpi images using a CCD or CMOS camera. Many variations of this principle, such as use of tactile sensors in place of a prism and the use of a holographic element [24], are also available. The main issue with these scanners is that the reflected light is a function of skin characteristics. If the skin is wet or dry, the fingerprint impression can be "saturated" or weak, respectively, and hard to process.

- CMOS capacitance [18]: The ridges and valleys of a finger create different charge accumulations when the finger touches a CMOS chip grid. With suitable electronics, the charge is converted to a pixel value. Normally at 500 dpi these scanners provide about 0.5" × 0.5" of scan area. This can be a problem as the two images acquired at two different times may have little overlap. They also tend to be affected by the skin dryness and wetness. In addition, these devices are sensitive to electrostatic discharge.

- Thermal [22]: The pyro-electric material in the sensor measures temperature changes as the finger is swiped over the scanner and produces an image. This technology is claimed to overcome the dry and wet skin issues in the optical scanners and can sustain higher static discharge. However, the images are not rich in gray values, i.e., dynamic range.

- Ultrasound [5]: An ultrasonic beam is scanned across the fingerprint surface to measure the ridge depth from the reflected signal. Skin conditions such as dry, wet and oil on the skin do not affect the imaging and the images better reflect the actual ridge topography. However, these units tend to very bulky and require larger scanning time than the optical scanners.

Recently, non-contact [2] fingerprint scanners have been announced that avoid problems related to touch-based sensing methods, including elastic distortion of the skin pattern.

The most commonly used fingerprint features are ridge bifurcations and ridge endings, collectively known as *minutiae*, which are extracted from the acquired image. The feature extraction process starts by examining the quality of the input gray-level image. Virtually every published method of feature extraction [23, 29] computes the orientation field of the fingerprint image which reflects the local ridge direction at every pixel. The local ridge orientation has been used to tune filter parameters for enhancement and ridge segmentation. From the segmented ridges, a thinned image is computed to locate the minutiae features. Usually, one has to go through a minutia post-processing stage to clean up several spurious minutiae resulting from either enhancement, ridge segmentation or thinning artifacts. The main goal of the fingerprint authentication module is to report some sort of distance between two fingerprint feature sets accurately and reliably. The authentication function has to compensate for (i) translation, (ii) rotation, (iii) missing features, (iv) additional features, (v) spurious features and, more importantly, (vi) elastic distortion between a pair of feature sets. Often storage and transmission of fingerprint images involves compression and decompression of the image. Standard compression techniques often remove the high frequency areas around the minutia features. Therefore, a novel fingerprint compression scheme called as Wavelet Scalar Quantization (WSQ) is recommended by the FBI. The main advantages of fingerprint as a biometric is the high accuracy and low cost of the system.

3.2 Iris

Although iris [41] is a relatively new biometric, it has been shown to be very accurate and stable. The colored part of the eye bounded by the pupil and sclera is the iris and is extremely rich in texture. Like fingerprints, this biometric results from the developmental process and is not dictated by genetics. So far, in the literature, there has been only a couple of iris recognition systems described. The primary reason being the difficulties in designing a reliable image acquisition stage. Often iris recognition is confused with the retinal recognition system which has a much harder-to-use input acquisition subsystem. In the Daugman system [8] for iris recognition, the texture of the iris is represented using Gabor wavelet responses and the matcher is an extremely simple and fast Hamming distance measure.

3.3 Hand geometry

Hand geometry based authentication is a limited scalable but extremely user-friendly biometric. The lengths of the fingers and other hand shape attributes are extracted from images of a hand and used in the representation. To derive such gross characteristics, a relatively inexpensive camera can be employed resulting in a overall low cost system. As the computation is also fairly light weight, a standalone system is easy to build. As this biometrics is not seen to compromise user privacy, it is quite widely accepted. However, hand geometry based authentication systems have relatively high FAR and FRR.

3.4 Face recognition

Face recognition [7, 31] is a particularly compelling biometric because it is one used every day by nearly everyone on earth. Since the advent of photography it has been institutionalized as a guarantor of identity in passports and identity cards. Because faces are easily captured by conventional optical imaging devices, there are large legacy databases (police mug-shots and television footage, for instance) that can be automatically searched. Because of its naturalness, face recognition is more acceptable than most biometrics, and the fact that cameras can acquire the biometric passively means that it can be very easy to use. Indeed, surveillance systems rely on capturing the face image without the cooperation of the person being imaged.

Despite these attractions, face recognition is not sufficiently accurate to accomplish the large-population identification tasks tackled with fingerprint or iris. One clear limit is the similarity of appearance of identical twins, but determining the identity of two photographs of the same person is hindered by all of the following problems, which can be divided into three classes.

- Physical changes: Expression change; aging; personal appearance (make-up, glasses, facial hair, hairstyle, disguise).

- Acquisition geometry changes: Change in scale, location and in-plane rotation of the face (facing the camera) as well as rotation in depth (facing the camera obliquely).

- Imaging changes: Lighting variation; camera variations; channel characteristics (especially in broadcast, or compressed images).

No current system can claim to handle all of these problems well. Indeed there has been little research on making face recognition robust to aging. In general, constraints on the problem definition and capture situation are used to limit the amount of invariance that needs to be afforded algorithmically.

The main challenges of face recognition today are handling rotation in depth and broad lighting changes, together with personal appearance changes. Even under good conditions, however, accuracy could be improved. There is interest in other acquisition modalities such as 3D shape through stereo or range-finders; near infrared or facial thermograms, all of which have attractions, but lack the compelling reasons for visible-light face recognition outlined above.

In general, face recognition systems proceed by detecting the face in the scene, thus estimating and normalizing for translation, scale and in-plane rotation. Approaches then divide [6] into appearance-based and geometric approaches, analyzing the appearance of the face and the distances between features respectively. In many systems these are combined, and indeed to apply appearance-based methods in the presence of facial expression changes requires generating an expressionless 'shape-free' face by image warping. Appearance based methods can be global [4, 12, 19, 34] where the whole face is considered as a single entity, or local, where many representations of separate areas of the face are created. [32, 33, 42].

Considerable progress has been made in recent years, with much commercialization of face recognition, but a lot remains to be done towards the 'general' face recognition problem.

3.5   Speaker identification

Like face, speaker identification [15] has attractions because of its prevalence in human communication. We expect to pick up the phone and be able to recognize someone by their voice after only a few words, although clearly the human brain is very good at exploiting context to narrow down the possibilities. Telephony is the main target of speaker identification, since it is a domain with ubiquitous existing hardware where no other biometric can be used. Increased security for applications such as telephone banking and 'm-commerce' means the potential for deployment is very large. Speaking solely in order to be identified can be somewhat unnatural, but in situations where the user is speaking anyway (e.g., a voice-controlled computer system, or when ordering something by phone) the biometric authentication becomes 'passive'. Physical and computer security by speaker ID have received some attention, but here it is less natural and poorer performing than other biometrics. Speaker ID is necessary for audio and video- indexing. Where a video signal is available lip-motion identification has also been used [11, 20, 21].

Speaker identification suffers considerably from any variations in the microphone [16, 30] and transmission channel, and performance deteriorates badly when enrollment and use conditions are mismatched This, of course, inevitably happens when a central server carries out speaker ID on telephone signals. Background noise can also be a considerable problem in some circumstances, and variations in voice due to illness, emotion or aging are further problems that have received little study.

Speaker verification is particularly vulnerable to replay attacks because of the ubiquity of sound recording and play-back devices. Consequently more thought has been given in this domain to avoiding such attacks. We can categorize speaker ID systems depending on the freedom in what is spoken, this taxonomy based on increasingly complex tasks also corresponds to the sophistication of algorithms used and the progress in the art over time.

- Fixed text: The speaker says a predetermined word or phrase, which was recorded at enrollment. The word may be secret, so acts as a password, but once recorded a replay attack is easy, and re-enrollment is necessary to change the password.

- Text dependent: The speaker is prompted by the system to say a specific thing. The machine aligns the utterance with the known text to determine the user. For this, enrollment is usually longer, but the prompted text can be changed at will. Limited systems (e.g., just using digit strings) are vulnerable to splicing-based replay attacks.

- Text independent: The speaker ID system processes any utterance of the speaker. Here the speech can be task-oriented, so it is hard to acquire speech that also accomplishes the impostor's goal. Monitoring can be continuous — the more that is said the greater the system's confidence in the identity of the user. The advent of trainable speech synthesis might enable attacks on this approach. Such systems can even identify a person when they switch language.

While traditionally used for verification, more recent technologies have started to address identification, one particular domain being in audio and video indexing [3].

3.6   Signature verification

Signature verification [26] is another biometric that has a long pedigree before the advent of computers, with considerable legal recognition and wide current usage in document authentication and transaction authorization in the form of checks and credit card receipts. Here the natural division is on-line vs. off-line, depending on the sensing modality. Off-line or 'static' signatures are scanned from paper documents where they were written in the conventional way [28]. On-line or 'dynamic' signatures are written with an electronically instrumented device and the dynamic information (pen tip location through time) is usually available at high resolution, even when the pen is not in contact with the paper. Some on-line signature capture systems can also measure pen angle and contact pressure [10]. These systems provide a much richer signal than is available in the on-line case, and making the identification problem correspondingly easier. These additional data make on-line signatures very robust to forgery. While forgery is a very difficult subject to research thoroughly, it is widely believed that most forgery is very simple and can be prevented with even relatively simple algorithms.

Because of the special hardware needed for the more robust on-line recognition, it seems unlikely that signature verification will spread beyond the domains where it is already used, but the volume of signature authorized transactions today is huge, making automation through signature verification very important.

Naturally, signature verification can be generalized to writer identification with the same categories (text dependent/independent) as speaker verification, but as a working biometric technology, attention has focussed on signature.

	Fingerprint	Speech	Face	Iris	Hand	Signature
Maturity	very high	high	medium	high	medium	medium
Best FAR	10^{-8}	10^{-2}	10^{-2}	10^{-10}	10^{-4}	10^{-4}
Best FRR	10^{-3}	10^{-3}	10^{-2}	10^{-4}	10^{-4}	10^{-4}
Scalability	high	medium	medium	very high	low	medium
Sensor cost	< $100	< $5	< $50	< $3000	< $500	<$300
Sensor type	contact	unobtrusive	unobtrusive	unobtrusive	contact	contact
Sensor size	small	very small	small	medium	large	medium
Template size	< 200 bytes	< 2K bytes	< 2k Bytes	256 bytes	< 10 bytes	< 200 bytes

Table 2: Comparison of six popular biometrics.

4   Standards, standard databases and interoperability issues

For wide acceptance of biometrics, standards for interfaces and performance evaluation are needed. Several standards are in the process of being developed and promoted. NIST is playing an important role in designing several fingerprint databases [35, 36, 37, 38, 39] and conducting speaker verification tests. The US Dept. of Defense runs the FERET face recognition test. The BioAPI [1] is a standard for the application programmer interface allowing the decoupling of biometrics-technologies from the applications that use them. At the hardware level, the devices for biometrics still remain non-interoperable except when sharing a common existing standard such as NTSC video.

4.1   Which biometric?

Table 2 compares the six biometrics. The comparison is based on the following factors: (i) maturity; (ii) accuracy; (iii) scalability; (iv) cost; (v) obtrusiveness; (vi) sensor size; and, (vii) representation (template) size. No single biometric really is appropriate for all the different applications.

5   Conclusions

The existing methods of automatic authentication involving knowledge or possessions have a number of limitations, particularly in that they can be transferred from one person to another. Automated biometrics can address that problem while overcoming other problems such as loss, sharing and forgery. Automated biometrics, by measuring hard-to-forge characteristics inherent in a person provide a non-repudiable guarantee of identity. Recent innovations in hardware and algorithms have meant that the field of biometrics has expanded tremendously, and many applications, not just in security, are being implemented with the use of biometric technology.

We have presented six popular biometrics with a comparison of their main attributes. We have also discussed how automated biometric systems can be modeled as pattern recognition systems, particularly when evaluating performance. While technologies continue to advance, and new biometrics will be pioneered, it seems clear that the complementary features of different biometrics will continue to mean that each finds its own domains of applicability, with no single biometric dominating the field.

References

[1] *BioAPI – http://www.bioapi.org*.

[2] *Non-contact fingerprint scanner: http://www.ddsi-cpc.com/pages/products/cscan300.html*.

[3] H. S. M. Beigi, S. H. Maes, U. V. Chaudhari, and J. S. Sorensen. IBM model-based and frame-by-frame speaker recognition. In *Speaker Recognition and its Commercial and Forensic Appications*, Avignon, April 1998.

[4] P. Belhumeur, J. Hespanha, and D. J. Kriegmand. Eigenfaces vs. Fisherfaces: Recognition using class specific linear projection. *IEEE Trans. on Pattern Analysis and Machine Intelligence*, 19(7):711–720, July 1997.

[5] W. Bicz, Z. Gurnienny, and M. Pluta. Ultrsound sensor for fingerprints recognition. In *Proc. of SPIE, Vol. 2634, Optoelectronic and electronic sensors*, pages 104–111, June 1995.

[6] R. Brunelli and T. Poggio. Face recognition: Features versus templates. *IEEE Trans. on Pattern Analysis and Machine Intelligence*, 15(10):1042–1052, October 1993.

[7] R. Chellappa, C. L. Wilson, and S. Sirohey. Human and machine recognition of faces: A survey. *Proceedings of the IEEE*, 83(5):705–740, May 1995.

[8] J. G. Daugman. High confidence visual recognition of persons by a test of statistical independence. *IEEE Trans. on Pattern Analysis and Machine Intelligence*, 15(11):1148–1161, Nov. 1993.

[9] J. G. Daugman and G. O. Williams. A proposed standard for biometric decidability. In *CardTechSecureTech*, pages 223–234, Atlanta, GA, 1996.

[10] J. G. A. Dolfing, E. H. L. Aarts, and v. J. J. G. M. On-line signature verification with hidden Markov models. In *Proceedings of the International Conference on Pattern Recognition*, pages 1309–12, August 1998.

[11] B. Duc, E. S. Bigün, J. Bigün, G. Maître, and S. Fischer. Fusion of audio and video information for multi modal person authentication. *Pattern Recognition Letters*, 18(9):835–843, 1997.

[12] G. J. Edwards, C. J. Taylor, and T. F. Cootes. Interpreting faces using active appearance models. In *International Conference on Face and Gesture Recognition*, number 3, pages 300–305, April 1998.

[13] B. G. et al. Issues in large scale automatic biometric identification. In *IEEE Workshop on Automatic Identification Advanced Technologies*, pages 43–46, Stony Brook, NY, Nov. 1996.

[14] D. T. Follette, E. B. Hultmark, and J. G. Jordan. *Direct optical input system for fingerprint verification*. IBM Technical Disclosure Bulletin: 04-74p3572, April 1974.

[15] S. Furui. Recent advances in speaker recognition. In B. Bigun, Chollet, editor, *Audio- and Video-based Biometric Person Authentication*, volume 1206 of *Lecture Notes in Computer Science*, pages 237–252. Springer, 1997.

[16] L. P. Heck and M. Weintraub. Handset-dependent background models for robust text-independent speaker recognition. In *Proceedings of the IEEE International Conference on Acoustics, Speech, and Signal Processing*, April 1997.

[17] A. Jain, R. Bolle, and S. Pankanti, editors. *Biometrics–Personal Identification in Networked Society*. Kluwer Academic Publishers, Boston, 1999.

[18] S. Jung, R. Thewes, T. Scheiter, K. F. Gooser, and W. Weber. A low-power and high-performance cmos fingerprint sensing and encoding architecture. *IEEE Journal of Solid-state Cicuits*, 34(7):978–984, July 1999.

[19] M. Kirby and L. Sirovich. Application of the Karhunen-Loève procedure for the characterization of human faces. *IEEE Trans. on Pattern Analysis and Machine Intelligence*, 12(1):103–108, 1990.

[20] J. Kittler, Y. Li, J. Matas, and M. Ramos Sánchez. Lip-shape dependent face verification. In J. Bigün, G. Chollet, and G. Borgefors, editors, *Audio- and Video-based Biometric Person Authentication*, volume 1206 of *Lecture Notes in Computer Science*, pages 61–68. Springer, March 1997.

[21] J. Luettin, N. A. Thacker, and S. W. Beet. Speaker identification by lipreading. In *Proceedings of the 4th International Conference on Spoken Language Processing (ICSLP'96)*, volume 1, pages 62–65, 1996.

[22] J.-F. Mainguet, M. Pegulu, and J. B. Harris. Fingerchip^{TM}: thermal imaging and finger sweeping in a silicon fingerprint sensor. In *Proc. of AutoID 99*, pages 91–94, October 99.

[23] D. Maio and D. Maltoni. Direct gray-scale minutiae detection in fingerprints. *IEEE Trans. on Pattern Analysis and Machine Intelligence*, 19(1):27–40, January 1997.

[24] M. H. Metz, Z. A. Coleman, N. J. Phillips, and C. Flatow. Holographic optical element for compact fingerprint imaging system. In *Proc. of SPIE, Vol. 2659, Optical security and counterfeit deterrance.techniques*, pages 141–151, 1996.

[25] B. Miller. Vital signs of identity. *IEEE Spectrum*, 31(2):22–30, February 1994.

[26] V. S. Nalwa. Automatic on-line signature verification. *Proceedings of the IEEE*, 85(2):215–239, February 1997.

[27] W. Peterson, T. Birdsall, and W. Fox. The theory of sigmal detectability. *Transactions of the IRE*, PGIT-4:171–212, April 1954.

[28] R. Plamondon and G. Lorette. Automatic signature verification and writer identification — The state of the art. *Pattern Recognition*, 22(2):107–129, 1989.

[29] N. K. Ratha, S. Chen, and A. K. Jain. Adaptive flow orientation based texture extraction in finger print images. *Pattern Recognition*, 28(11):1657–1672, November 1995.

[30] D. A. Reynolds. The effects of handset variability on speaker recognition performance: Experiments on the Switchboard Corpus. In *Proceedings of the IEEE International Conference on Acoustics, Speech, and Signal Processing*, May 1996.

[31] A. Samal and P. Iyengar. Automatic recognition and analysis of human faces and facial expressions: A survey. *Pattern Recognition*, 25(1):65–77, 1992.

[32] A. W. Senior. Recognizing faces in broadcast video. In *IEEE International Workshop on Recognition, Analysis, and Tracking of Faces and Gestures in Real-Time Systems*, pages 105–110, September 1999.

[33] D. L. Swets and J. J. Weng. Using discriminant eigenfeatures for image retrieval. *IEEE Trans. on Pattern Analysis and Machine Intelligence*, 18(8):831–836, Aug. 1996.

[34] M. Turk and A. Pentland. Eigenfaces for recognition. *Journal of Cognitive Neuro Science*, 3(1):71–86, 1991.

[35] C. I. Watson. *NIST special database 10: Supplemental Fingerprint Card Data for NIST Special Database 9*. Advanced Systems Division, Image Recognition Group , National Institute for Standards and Technology, February 1993.

[36] C. I. Watson. *NIST special database 14: Fingerprint Card Pairs 2*. Advanced Systems Division, Image Recognition Group , National Institute for Standards and Technology, February 1993.

[37] C. I. Watson. *NIST special database 4: 8-bit Gray scale Images of Fingerprint Image Groups*. Advanced Systems Division, Image Recognition Group , National Institute for Standards and Technology, February 1993.

[38] C. I. Watson. *NIST special database 9: Mated Fingerprint Card Pairs*. Advanced Systems Division, Image Recognition Group , National Institute for Standards and Technology, February 1993.

[39] C. I. Watson. *NIST special database 24: NIST Digital Video of Live-scan Fingerprint Database*. Advanced Systems Division, Image Recognition Group , National Institute for Standards and Technology, February 1998.

[40] J. L. Wayman. Error rate equations for the general biometrics system. *IEEE Automation and Robotics Magazine*, 6(1):35–48, March 1999.

[41] R. P. Wildes. Iris recognition: An emerging biometric technology. *Proc. of IEEE*, 85(9):1348–1363, Sept. 1997.

[42] L. Wiskott and C. von der Malsburg. Recognizing faces by dynamic link matching. In *Proceedings of the International Conference on Artificial Neural Networks*, pages 347–352, 1995.

Shigeru Akamatsu

Shigeru Akamatsu, Dr.Eng. received the B.E., M.E., and Dr. Eng. Degrees in Mathematical Engineering and Instrumentation Physics in 1975, 1977, and 1994, respectively, from the University of Tokyo, Japan. From 1977 through 1985, he engaged in research and development of optical character recognition systems for hand-written Chinese characters at the Electrical Communications Laboratories, Nippon Telegraph and Telephone Public Corporation. During the academic year 1985-86, he was a Visiting Researcher at the University of California Irvine, USA. Until 1992, he was a Senior Research Engineer, Supervisor, at NTT Human Interface Laboratories, and conducted the research on human image recognition. Since 1992, he has been Head of Department 2, ATR Human Information Processing Research Laboratories. Since 1999, he has been Guest Professor at Interdisciplinary Graduate School of Science and Engineering, Tokyo Institute of Technology. His research interests include computational and cognitive studies of high level vision, with a special interest in face recognition.

Matti Aksela

Matti Aksela received his M.Sc. degree in 2000 from Helsinki University of Technology, Finland, where he is currently working as a researcher in the Laboratory of Computer and Information Science and continuing his studies towards a doctoral degree. His research interest is in adaptive classification methods with application to on-line handwritten character recognition.

Adnan Amin

Adnan Amin received DEA in Electronics from the University of Paris XI (Orsay) in 1978 and presented his Doctorate D'Etat (D. Sc.) in computer Science to the University of Nancy I (CRIN), France, in 1985. From 1981 to 1985, Dr. Amin was Maitre Assistant at the University of Nancy II. Between 1985 and 1987 he worked in INTEGRO (Paris) as Head of Pattern Recognition Department. From 1987 to 1990, he was an Assistant Professor at Kuwait University and joined the School of Computer Science and Engineering at the University of New South Wales, Australia, in 1991 as a Senior Lecturer. His research interests include Pattern Recognition and Artificial Intelligence (Document Image understanding ranging from character / word recognition to integrating visual and linguistic information in document composition), Neural networks, Machine learning, and knowledge acquisition.

Marija Bacauskiene

Marija Bacauskiene is a senior researcher in the department of Applied Electronics at Kaunas University of Technology. She has published over 80 scientific papers in the fields of classification, image processing, fuzzy sets, and artificial neural networks.

Geoff Barrett

Geoff Barrett is a Principal Scientist in the Defence Evaluation and Research Agency (DERA) Centre for Human Sciences. He has almost 30 years experience in the design, performance, and analysis of electrophysiological studies relating to sensory, motor, and cognitive function. Geoff is the Senior Scientist for the UK Ministry of Defence's basic research programme on Human Sciences. Before joining DERA, Geoff spent 20 years as a member of the Medical Research Council team developing non-invasive tests of neurological function at the National Hospital for Neurology and Neurosurgery. The results of this work formed the basis of standard tests which are used in clinical neurophysiology laboratories throughout the world. Geoff is Editor-in-Chief of the Journal of Psychophysiology, and has published over 170 articles in scientific journals.

Christian Bauckhage

Christian Bauckhage studied computer science at the University of Bielefeld. After receiving his diploma in 1998 he joined the Applied Computer Science Group. He works in the collaborative research centre 360 "situated artificial communicators" (SFB 360). His research interest is the modeling of assembled objects for the purpose of image understanding and process monitoring.

Walter F. Bischof

He is Professor of Computing Science and Psychology at the University of Alberta. His interests lie in the areas of Machine Learning, Machine Vision and Human Vision. Within the area of Machine Vision, he is interested in systems for learning complex spatio-temporal patterns, such as human actions or man-machine interactions, and within Human Vision, he is interested in motion perception and attention-perception interactions.

Isabelle Bloch

Isabelle Bloch is Professor at ENST (Signal and Image Processing Department, Image Processing and Interpretation Group). She graduated from Ecole des Mines de Paris in 1986, received Ph.D. from ENST Paris in 1990, and the "Habilitation a Diriger des Recherches" from University Paris 5 in 1995. Her research interests include 3D image and object processing, 3D and fuzzy mathematical morphology, discrete 3D geometry and topology, decision theory, information fusion in image processing, fuzzy set theory, evidence theory, structural pattern recognition, spatial reasoning, medical imaging.

Flávio Bortolozzi

Flávio Bortolozzi received Ph.D. degree in Computer Vision from the *Université de Technologie de Compiégne*, France, in 1991. In the same year, he joined the Informatic Department of the *Pontifícia Universidade Católica do Paraná* (PUCPR, Curitiba, Brazil). In 1998, he was responsible for the implementation of the M.Sc. and Ph.D. Programs in Applied Informatic at PUCPR, where he is professor. Since 1999 he is the Pró-Rector of Research and Pos-Graduation of the same University. His research interests are in the areas of computer vision, document analysis and recognition, handwriting recognition and signature verification for banking and postal applications, multimedia and biomedical image processing.

Elke Braun

Elke Braun received the diploma in physics from the Technical University of Aachen, Germany, in 1997. Since October 1997 she is working in SFB 360 at the research group for Applied Computer Science at the University of Bielefeld. Her field of research is computer vision, especially the usage of hybrid systems in object recognition.

Jörg Bredno

Jörg Bredno received his MS degree in Mechanical Engineering from the Aachen University of Technology (RWTH) in 1999. In 1999 he was given the Springorum Medal from the Aachen University of Technology for his work on ceramic coatings of hip endoprosthesises. Currently, he holds a scholarship for his graduate studies at the Institute of Medical Informatics, RWTH Aachen. His research interests include active contour models, quantification of medical images in regard to diagnostic issues and image retrieval in medical applications. He co-authored a textbook on programming of graphical interfaces.

Horst Bunke

Horst Bunke received his M.S. and Ph.D. degrees in Computer Science from the University of Erlangen, Germany. In 1984, he joined the University of Bern, Switzerland, where he is a full professor in the Computer Science Department. Horst Bunke is a Fellow and has been Acting President of the International Association for Pattern Recognition (IAPR). He is an associate editor of the International Journal on Document Analysis and Recognition, Pattern Analysis and Applications, editor-in-charge of the International Journal of Pattern Recognition and Artificial Intelligence, and editor-in-chief of the book series on Machine Perception and Artificial Intelligence by World Scientific Publ. Co. He was on the program and organization committee of many conferences and served as a referee for numerous journals and scientific organizations.

Terry Caelli

His interests lie in Computer Vision, Pattern Recognition and Artificial Intelligence and their applications to image interpretation, the prototyping human perception-action and human-machine interactions. He is Professor of Computing Science and Director of the Research Institute for Multimedia Systems (RIMS) at the University of Alberta. He has many publications in these areas and is actively involved as an associate editor of a number of journals in the area, conference organizations and committees of the IEEE and International Association for Pattern Recognition.

Rui Ni Cao

Ruini Cao is a Ph.D. candidate in computer science at the School of Computing, National University of Singapore. She obtained her B. E. degree and M. Sc. Degree in computer science from Tsinghua University, P. R. China in 1994 and 1997 respectively. Her research interests include pattern recognition and document image analysis.

Raffaele Cappelli

Raffaele Cappelli received the degree in Computer Science from the University of Bologna, Italy, in 1998. Since November 1998 he is a Ph.D. student at DEIS, University of Bologna. His research interests include Biometric Systems, Pattern Recognition, Image Retrieval by Similarity.

Bruno M. Carvalho

Bruno M. Carvalho is a Ph.D. student in the Department of Computer and Information Science at the University of Pennsylvania since 1997. He received a B.Sc. in Computer Science from the Federal University of Rio Grande do Norte, Brazil in 1992, an M.Sc. in Computer Science from the Federal University of Pernambuco in 1995, and an M.Sc. in Engineering from the University of Pennsylvania in 1999. His main interests are medical imaging, computer vision and computer graphics.

Paulo Cezar Pinto Carvalho

Paulo Cezar Pinto Carvalho received a degree in Civil Engineering from the Instituto Militar de Engenharia (IME), in 1975. In 1980, he received a M.Sc. in Statistics from the Instituto de Matemática Pura e Aplicada (IMPA). In 1984, he received a Ph.D. degree in Operations Research from Cornell University. He is an Associate Researcher at IMPA, where he has been since 1979. He was a Visiting Professor at Cornell University from 1988 to 1989. He is a consultant to Tecgraf/PUC-Rio, to Fundação Cesgranrio and to Colégio Bahiense. His current research interests include Computational Geometry, Geometric Modeling, Geographical Information Systems, Image-based Modeling and Physically-based Modeling. He also has been involved with several activities related to the improvement of Mathematics education in Brazil.

Roberto Marcondes Cesar Junior

Roberto Marcondes Cesar Junior received a B.Sc. in Computer Science from the Universidade Estadual Paulista - UNESP, Brazil, a M.Sc. in Electrical Engineering from the Universidade de Campinas - UNICAMP, Brazil, and a PhD in Computational Physics at the Institute of Physics, Universidade de Sao Paulo at Sao Carlos, Brazil. He did his sandwich scholarship with the Departement de Physique of the Université Catholique de Louvain - Belgique. He held a post-doctoral position at the CVRG. He is currently a lecturer at DCC - IME - USP (http://www.vision.ime.usp.br/~creativision).

B. B. Chaudhuri

Professor B. B. Chaudhuri received his B.Sc. (Hons), B. Tech and M. Tech degrees from Calcutta University, India in 1969, 1972 and 1974, respectively and his Ph.D. degree from Indian Institute of Technology, Kanpur in 1980. He joined the Indian Statistical Institute in 1978 where he served as the Project Co-ordinator and Head of the National Nodal Center for Knowledge Based Computing funded by the United Nations Development Program and Dept. of Electronics, Govt. of India. Currently, he is the Head of the Computer Vision and Pattern Recognition Unit of the institute. His research interests include Pattern Recognition, Image Processing, Computer Vision, Natural Language Processing and Digital Document Processing. He developed the first workable OCR for Bangla and Devnagari, the major Indian scripts. Also, he has developed a speech synthesis and a spell-checker system in Bangla apart from doing many Computational linguistic studies on Indian languages. He has published about 200 research papers in reputed International Journals, conference proceedings and edited books. Also, he has authored two books entitled "Two Tone Image Processing and Recognition" (Wiley Eastern, 1993) and "Object Orientated Programming: Fundamentals and applications" (Prentice Hall, 1998). He was awarded Sir J. C. Bose Memorial Award for best engineering science orientated paper in 1986, M. N. Saha Memorial Award (twice) for best application orientated papers in 1989 and 1991, the Homi Bhabha Fellowship award in 1992 for OCR of the Indian Languages and computer orientation for the blind, Dr. Vikram Sarabhai Research Award in 1995 for his outstanding achievements in the fields of Electronics, Informatics and Telematics and C. Achuta Menon Prize in 1996 for computer based Indian language processing. He worked as a Leverhulme visiting fellow at Queen's University, U.K. in 1981-82, a visiting scientist at GSF, Munich and guest faculty at the Technical University of Hannover during 1986-88 and again in 1990-91. He is a Senior member of IEEE, member secretary (Indian Section) of International Academy of Sciences, Fellow of International Association of Pattern Recognition, Fellow of National Academy of Sciences (India), Fellow of Institution of Electronics and Telecommunication Engineering and Fellow of the Indian National Academy of Engineering. He is serving as associate editor of Pattern Recognition (Pergamon), Pattern Recognition Letters (Elsevier Sciences) and VIVEK. He also served as guest editor of the special issue of the Journal of Inst. Electronics & Telecom Engg. among others.

Teofilo Emidio de Campos
Teofilo Emidio de Campos received his Bachelor's degree in Computer Science from the Universidade Estadual Paulista - UNESP, Brazil, in 1998. Currently, he is a Master's degree student in Computer Science at Universidade de Sao Paulo - USP, Brazil, member of Creativision Group (http://www.vision.ime.usp.br/~creativision). His research interests include dimensionality reduction, face and gesture recognition, perceptual user interfaces, and wearable visual robotics. His Master's thesis is concerned with face recognition from video sequences.

Alberto Del Bimbo
Alberto Del Bimbo is Full Professor and Director of the Department of Sistemi e Informatica at the Universita degli Studi di Firenze, Italy. He is also the Director of the Master in Multimedia at the same University. His scientific interests and activity have addressed the subject of Image Technology and Multimedia, with particular reference to object recognition and image sequence analysis, content-based retrieval for image and video databases, visual languages and advanced man-machine interaction. Prof. Del Bimbo is the author of over 150 publications, appeared in the most distinguished international journals and conference proceedings and is the author of the monography "Visual Information Retrieval" edited by Morgan Kaufman in 1999. He has also been the Guest Editor of several special issues of International Journals and the Chairman of several conferences in the field of Image Processing, Image Databases and Multimedia. He is IAPR fellow and presently a Member of the Steering Committee of IEEE ICME, Int. Conference on Multimedia and Expo and of the VISUAL conference series. From 1996 to 2000 he was the President of the Italian Chapter of IAPR, the International Association for Pattern Recognition. Since 1999 he is a Member of the IEEE Publications Board. He presently serves as Associate Editor of IEEE Trans. on Multimedia, IEEE Trans. on Pattern Analysis and Machine Intelligence, Pattern Recognition, Journal of Visual Languages and Computing, and Multimedia Tools and Applications Journal.

Andreas Dengel
Andreas Dengel is a Professor of Computer Science at the University of Kaiserslautern and Scientific Director at the German Research Center for Artificial Intelligence (DFKI). From 1980 to 1986 he studied computer science and economics at the University of Kaiserslautern. In 1986 he joined Siemens R&D in Munich where he worked on pattern recognition. From 1987 to 1989 he worked as a research and teaching assistant at the University of Stuttgart where he also finished his Ph.D. in Computer Science. In 1989 he joined DFKI. In 1991 he worked for Xerox Parc as a visiting researcher. His major research activities are in document analysis, pattern recognition and knowledge management. In 1997 he received the ICDAR Young Investigator Award for outstanding contributions to the field of document analysis. He also received the Alcatel SEL Award For Technical Communication in the same year. Andreas Dengel is a member of IEEE, GI, and IAPR.

Massimo De Santo
Massimo De Santo received his Laurea degree (cum laude) in 1985 and Ph.D. in 1988 from the University of Naples. He has been Senior Researcher at the University of Salerno since 1990. He is Associate Professor of Computer Science in the Dipartimento di Ingegneria dell'Informazione ed Ingegneria Elettrica of the University of Salerno. Massimo De Santo participated to several research projects funded by the Ministry of University and by the Italian National Research Council. He is currently Coordinator of various Research Projects funded by the University of Salerno and Scientific Coordinator of the Web Area in the European Esprit Project EN 29.082 named "InTraSys". Massimo De Santo is author of over 60 scientific publications and of a Monography. He participated as Invited Speaker to several International Conferences and acted as a member of the Scientific Committee of International Workshops and Conferences. Since many years he gives his contribution as a Reviewer of well known International Journals. He is member of the IEEE, ACM and of the Italian Chapter of the IAPR.

Alceu de Souza Britto Jr
Alceu de Souza Britto Jr received M.Sc. degree in Industrial Informatic from the *Centro Federal de Educação Tecnológica do Paraná* (Brazil) in 1996. Since 1998, he is Ph.D. student in Document Analysis and Recognition at Pontifícia Universidade Católica do Paraná (PUCPR). In 1989, he joined the Informatic Department of the Universidade Estadual de Ponta Grossa (UEPG-Brazil). In 1995, he also joined the Informatic Department of the PUCPR. From July/1998 to July/2000 he worked on handwriting recognition area in Montreal (Canada) at the laboratories of the Centre for Pattern Recognition and Machine Intelligence (CENPARMI-Concordia University) and the *École de Technologie Supérieure (ÉTS-*

Université du Quebec). His research interests are in the areas of document analysis and handwriting recognition.

Michelangelo Diligenti

Michelangelo Diligenti received the M.Sc. degree in Telecommunication Engineering in 1998 at the University of Siena, Italy. Actually he is a Ph.D. student at the University of Florence, Italy. He has collaborated with the University of Wollongong and the Nec Reaserch Institute. His main research interests are in pattern recognition, visual databases and machine learning applied on the world wide web.

Ming Dong

Ming Dong received his B.S. in Electrical Engineering from Shanghai Jiao Tong University, China. He received a second B.S. in Industrial Management Engineering also from Shanghai Jiao Tong University, China. He is presently a Ph.D. candidate in the Department of Electrical & Computer Engineering & Computer Science at the University of Cincinnati

Nicolae Duta

Nicolae Duta is a staff scientist at BBN Technologies, Speech and Language Processing Department, Cambridge, Massachusetts. He received the BS degree in applied mathematics from the University of Bucharest (Romania) in 1991, the DEA degree in stochastic modeling from the University of Paris-Sud (France) in 1992, the MS degree in computer science from the University of Iowa in 1996 and the PhD degree in computer science and engineering with a concentration in computer vision and pattern recognition from Michigan State University in 2000. He held temporary research positions at INRIA-Rocquecourt (France) in 1993 and Siemens Corporate Research (Princeton, NJ) from 1997 to 1999. He is a member of IEEE and ACM and his current research interests include computer vision, pattern recognition, machine and biological learning.

Alexandr A. Ezhov

Alexandr A. Ezhov graduated from Moscow Engineering Physics Institute in 1976 and received his Ph.D. in theoretical and mathematical physics from the Kurchatov Institute of Atomic Energy in 1986. In 1979 he joined Affiliated Branch of this Institute in Troitsk (Moscow Region) – now Troitsk Institute of Innovation and Fusion Research (TRINITI). He is currently a Head of Laboratory of Neural Computing of the Center of Theoretical Physics and Computational Mathematics of TRINITI. His previous experience includes neutron transport theory and computational methods in physics. From 1983 his research interests include neural models of associative memory, pattern recognition (OCR) and quantum neural networks. He was a principal investigator of many international research projects in Optical Music Recognition, OCR of handwritten symbols, development of neural systems for DNA analysis and also of biomedical applications of neural technologies. A. Ezhov is author or co-author of 2 books and more than 50 scientific papers published, in particular, in international journals and conferences. He teaches neurocomputing in Moscow Engineering Physics Institute and also in Moscow Institute of Radio Engineering, Electronics and Automatics. As an active member of Russian Neural Networks Society he has been involved in organising different international conferences in neuroinformatics. He is an initiator and editor of recent international discussion about perspectives of neurocomputing in next decade *(Neural Network World*, 1999, v.9, pp. 103-174).

Rogério Schmidt Feris

Rogério Schmidt Feris received his Bachelor's degree in Computer Engineering from University of Rio Grande, Brazil, in 1998. Currently, he is a Master's degree student in Computer Science at University of São Paulo - USP, Brazil. His research interests include face and gesture recognition, vision-based interfaces, image analysis with wavelets and stereo vision. His Master's thesis is concerned with face detection and tracking in video sequences.

Jonathan Fieldsend

On leaving Truro College in 1995, Jonathan graduated with a BA (hons) degree in Economics from the University of Durham in 1998. Following this he completed an MSc in Computational Intelligence at the University of Plymouth, developing Neural Networks for estimating non-linear (G)ARCH asset volatility as part of his dissertation. In November 1999 Jonathan joined the PANN lab at Exeter University to undertake MPhil/PhD research in the area of financial forecasting using Neural Networks. Jonathan enjoys hiking, especially along the coastal paths of West Cornwall, and practising martial arts. His main research interests are in Neural Networks, Genetic Algorithms, Fractals and Econometric models relating to finance.

Jan Flusser

Jan Flusser was born in Prague, Czech Republic, on April 30, 1962. He received the M.Sc. degree in mathematical engineering from the Czech Technical University, Prague, Czech Republic in 1985 and the Ph.D. degree in computer science from the Czechoslovak Academy of Sciences in 1990. Since 1985 he has been with the Institute of Information Theory and Automation, Academy of Sciences of the Czech Republic, Prague. Since 1995 he has been holding the position of a head of Department of Image Processing. Since 1991 he has been also affiliated with the Faculty of Mathematics and Physics, Charles University, Prague and with the Czech Technical University, Prague, where he gives courses on Digital Image Processing and Pattern Recognition. Jan Flusser's current research interests include all aspects of image processing and pattern recognition, particularly image restoration, matching and invariants for object description. He is involved in applications in remote sensing, medicine and astronomy. He has authored and coauthored more about 100 scientific publications in these areas. He has been a leader/coordinator of seven national research projects. Jan Flusser is a member of the IEEE Computer Society, the IEEE Signal Processing Society, the IEEE Geoscience and Remote Sensing Society and the Pattern Recognition Society.

Paolo Frasconi

Paolo Frasconi received the M.Sc. degree in electronic engineering in 1990, and the Ph.D. degree in computer science in 1994, both from the University of Florence, Italy. He is an Associate Professor of Computer Science with the Department of Systems and Computer Science (DSI) at the University of Florence. His current research interests include learning in neural networks, Markovian models and belief networks, with particular emphasis on problems involving learning about sequential and structured information. Application fields of his interest include bioinformatics, natural language processing, and image document processing. Dr. Frasconi serves as an Associate Editor for the IEEE Transactions on Neural Networks and for the IEEE Transactions on Knowledge and Data Engineering. He is a member of the IEEE, the ICPR, and the AI*IA.

Toshio Fukuda

Toshio Fukuda graduated from Waseda University in 1971 and received the M.S. and Dr. Eng. from the University of Tokyo in 1973 and 1977, respectively. In 1977, he joined the National Mechanical Engineering Laboratory and became Visiting Research Fellow at the University of Stuttgart from 1979 to 1980. He joined the Science University of Tokyo in 1981, and then joined Nagoya University in 1989. Currently, he is Professor at Center for Cooperative Research in Advanced Science & Technology, Nagoya University, Japan, mainly engaging in the research fields of intelligent robotic system, mechatronics and micro robotics. He was awarded IEEE Fellow in 1995 and IEEE Eugene Mittlemann Award (1997). He is the VP of IEEE IES (1990~). IFSA Vice President (1997~). IEEE Robotics, Editor-in-Chief of the IEEE/ASME Trans. on Mechatronics and Director of IEEE Division X.

Gautam Garai

Gautam Garai received his B.E. degree in Computer Science & Technology from Calcutta University, Calcutta in 1987 and his M.E. degree in Computer Science and Engineering from Jadavpur University, Calcutta in 1991. He joined Saha Institute of Nuclear Physics, Calcutta in 1988 and is now Associate Professor of the Computer Division. His research interests include Pattern Recognition, Image Processing, Genetic Algorithms, Neural Networks, and Document Processing. He is a member of IEEE.

Edgar Garduno

Edgar Garduno is a Ph.D. student in the Department of Bioengineering at the University of Pennsylvania. He received a B.Sc. in Computer Engineering from the National Autonomous University of Mexico (U.N.A.M.), Mexico 1995, and an M.Sc. in Bioengineering from the University of Pennsylvania in 1998. From 1993 to 1996 he was affiliated with the Supercomputing Center and Instrumentation Center at U.N.A.M. His main interests are medical imaging, computer graphics, and computer vision.

Marcelo Gattass

B.Sc. Civil Engineering, PUC-Rio, 1975; M.Sc.: Structural Engineering, PUC-Rio, 1978; Ph.D.: Structural Eng. & Computer Graphics, Cornell U., USA, 1982. His research activities currently focus on Scientific Visualization, Geometric Modeling of Natural Objects and Geographical Information Systems. Professor at the Computer Science Department, PUC-Rio and Director of Tecgraf/PUC-Rio – Computer Graphics Technology Laboratory, where supervises several industry-cooperation projects in the areas of: 3D modeling and visualization, geographic information systems, user interfaces, and web-based applications. These contracts involve about 90 people including professors, researchers, Ph.D., M.Sc. and undergraduate students, system analysts, and administrative personnel both in PUC-Rio and in IMPA (Institute of Pure and Applied Mathematics). He has supervised 34 M.Sc. theses and 8 Ph.D. dissertations.

Adas Gelzinis

Adas Gelzinis received a Ph.D. degree in artificial neural networks at Kaunas University of Technology, Lithuania in 2000. He is a member of the Artificial Neural Networks and Image Processing research group at Kaunas University of Technology. His research interests include neural networks, image processing, unsupervised and partially supervised learning and stochastic optimisation.

Marco Gori

Marco Gori received the Laurea in electronic engineering from Universita di Firenze, Italy, in 1984, and the Ph.D. degree in 1990 from Universita di Bologna, Italy. From October 1988 to June 1989 he was a visiting student at the School of Computer Science (McGill University, Montreal). In 1992, he became an Associate Professor of Computer Science at Universita di Firenze and, in November 1995, he joined the University of Siena where he is currently full professor. His main research interests are in pattern recognition, web computing, and machine learning.

Dr. Gori served as a Program Committee member of several workshops and conferences mainly in his area of expertise. He acted as Guest Co-Editor of the Neurocomputing Journal for the special issue on recurrent neural networks (July 1997). He is an Associate Editor of a number of journals including the IEEE Trans. Neural Networks, Pattern Recognition, and Pattern Analysis and Applications. He is acting as the Italian chairman of the IEEE Neural Networks Council and as the co-chair of the TC3 Technical Committee of the IAPR on Neural Networks and Machine Learning.

Venu Govindaraju

Venu Govindaraju received his PhD in computer science from the State University of New York at Buffalo in 1992. He has coauthored more than 90 technical papers in various International journals and conferences and has one US patent. He is currently the associate director of CEDAR and concurrently holds the research associate professorship in the department of Computer Science and Engineering, State University of New York at Buffalo. He is the associate editor of the Journal of Pattern Recognition and the area chair of the IEEE SMC technical committee for pattern recognition. Dr. Govindaraju has been a co-principal investigator on several federally sponsored and industry sponsored projects. He is presently leading multiple projects on postal applications. He is a senior member of the IEEE.

Jiri Grim

Jiri Grim graduated in physical electronics from the Czech Technical University, Prague, in 1968. He received his C.Sc. (Ph.D.) in technical cybernetics from the Czechoslovak Academy of Sciences. Since 1968 he has been working in the field of statistical pattern recognition at the Institute of Information Theory and Automation of the Academy of Sciences of the Czech Republic, Prague. His present interest is the statistical pattern recognition and the probabilistic approach to neural networks.

Edwin Hancock

Edwin Hancock gained his B.Sc. in physics in 1977 and Ph.D. in high energy nuclear physics in 1981, both from the University of Durham, UK. After a period of postdoctoral research working on charm-photo-production experiments at the Stanford Linear Accelerator Centre, he moved into the fields of computer vision and pattern recognition in 1985. Between 1981 and 1991, he held posts at the Rutherford-Appleton Laboratory, the Open University and the University of Surrey. He joined the University of York as a lecturer in the Department of Computer Science in July 1991. After being promoted to Senior Lecturer in October 1997 and to Reader in October 1998, he was appointed Professor of Computer Vision in December 1998. He leads a group of some 15 researchers in the areas of computer vision and pattern recognition. He has published about 250 refereed papers in the fields of high energy nuclear physics, computer vision, image processing and pattern recognition. He was awarded the 1990 Pattern Recognition Society Medal and received an Outstanding Paper Award in 1997 for his contributions to the journal Pattern Recognition. Professor Hancock serves as an Associate Editor for the journals IEEE Transactions on Pattern Analysis and Machine Intelligence, and, Pattern Recognition. He has also been a guest editor for the Image and Vision Computing Journal and has been a co-guest editor for a special edition of the Pattern Recognition journal devoted to energy minimisation methods in computer vision and pattern recognition. He chaired the 1994 British Machine Vision Conference and has been a programme committee member for several national and international conferences. He is a fellow of the International Association for Pattern Recognition.

Yasuhisa Hasegawa
Yasuhisa Hasegawa received the B.Eng. and M.Eng. degrees from Nagoya University in 1994 and 1996, respectively. From 1996 to 1998, he was a designer at Mitsubishi Heavy Industries ltd., Japan. He joined Nagoya University in 1998. At present, he is Research Associate of Department of Micro System Engineering, Nagoya University, mainly engaging in the research fields of evolutionary computation, learning algorithm for motion control and intelligent robotic system.

Gunther Heidemann
Gunther Heidemann graduated in computer science at the University of Bielefeld in 1998. He is currently a member of the Neuroinformatics Group at the University of Bielefeld and is working in the SFB 360. His fields of research are in Computer Vision, Neural Networks and Hybrid Systems.

Gabor T. Herman
Gabor T. Herman received his Ph.D. in 1968. From 1969 to 1981, he was with the Department of Computer Science, SUNY at Buffalo, where he directed the Medical Image Processing Group. From 1981 till 2000, he was a Professor in the Medical Imaging Section of the Department of Radiology at the University of Pennsylvania, during which time he was Editor-in-Chief of the IEEE Transactions on Medical Imaging. Currently, he is the Director of the Center for Computer Science and Applied Mathematics at Temple University. His books include Image Reconstruction from Projections: The Fundamentals of Computerized Tomography (Academic, 1980), 3D Imaging in Medicine (CRC, 1991 and 2000), Geometry of Digital Spaces (Birkhauser, 1998) and Discrete Tomography: Foundations, Algorithms and Applications (Birkhauser, 1999).

Vaclav Hlavac
Vaclav Hlavac, born 1956, M.Sc. 1981, Ph.D. 1987 both from Czech Technical University, Associate Professor 1992, head of the Center for Machine Perception 1995 Faculty of Electrical Engineering, Prague, Czech Republic, Professor 1998. Main research interests: 3D computer vision, pattern recognition, genome informatics.

Anil Jain
Anil Jain is a University Distinguished Professor in the Department of Computer Science and Engineering at Michigan State University. His research interests include statistical pattern recognition, deformable models, texture analysis, document image analysis, fingerprint matching and 3D object recognition. He received the best paper awards in 1987 and 1991 and certificates for outstanding contributions in 1976, 1979, 1992, and 1997 from the Pattern Recognition Society. He also received the 1996 IEEE Trans. Neural Networks Outstanding Paper Award. He was the Editor-in-Chief of the IEEE Trans. on Pattern Analysis and Machine Intelligence (1990-94). He is the co-author of Algorithms for Clustering Data, Prentice-Hall, 1988, has edited the book Real-Time Object Measurement and Classification, Springer-Verlag, 1988, and co-edited the books, Analysis and Interpretation of Range Images, Springer-Verlag, 1989, Markov Random Fields, Academic Press, 1992, Artificial Neural Networks and Pattern Recognition, Elsevier, 1993, 3D Object Recognition, Elsevier, 1993, and BIOMETRICS: Personal Identification in Networked Society, Kluwer in 1999. He is a Fellow of the IEEE and IAPR. He received a Fulbright research award in 1998.

Xiaoyi Jiang

Xiaoyi Jiang received the B.S. degree in 1983 from Peking University, China, and the Ph.D. degree in 1989 from the University of Bern, Switzerland, both in Computer Science. In 1997 he received the Venia Docendi degree (Habilitation) from the University of Bern. Currently, he is a senior lecturer with the Department of Computer Science at the University of Bern. His research interests have focused on computer vision and pattern recognition. He has about seventy publications in these areas including a book on three-dimensional range image acquisition and analysis published by Springer-Verlag. He is co-organizer of a range image segmentation contest at the 15th International Conference on Pattern Recognition, Barcelona, 2000.

Markus Junker
Markus Junker is a research scientist and Ph.D. student at the German Research Center for Artificial Intelligence (DFKI GmbH). From 1989 to 1996 he studied Computer Science and Electrical Engineering at the University of Kaiserslautern. In 1995 he worked as a summer intern at Xerox Parc. After receiving his Master Degree in 1996, he joined DFKI in the Information Management and Document Analysis group of

Prof. Dengel. Since then he has been working on several research and industrial projects focusing on Information Retrieval and Machine Learning. He is currently in charge of a project on adaptive Information Retrieval systems.

Thomas Kaempke
Thomas Kaempke holds a diploma and a Ph.D. in mathematics from the University of Aachen, Germany. He had been visiting the University of California at Berkeley by a grant from the Humboldt foundation. Currently he is responsible for Autonomous Systems at the Research Institute for Applied Knowledge processing FAW, Ulm. His working areas are related to applied mathematics such as discrete and stochastic optimization, planning and control of autonomous mobile systems, signal analysis esp. image processing, processing of uncertain information, and bioinformatics.

Mohamed S. Kamel
Mohamed S. Kamel received the B.Sc. (Hons) degree in Electrical Engineering from the University of Alexandria, Egypt, M.Sc. degree in Computation from McMaster University, Hamilton, Canada, and Ph.D. degree in Computer Science from the University of Toronto, Canada. He is at present Professor and Co-Director of the Pattern Analysis and Machine Intelligence Laboratory at the Department of Systems Design Engineering, University of Waterloo, Canada. Dr. Kamel's research interests are in Machine Intelligence, Neural Networks and Pattern Recognition with applications in Robotics and Manufacturing. He has authored and co-authored over 130 papers in journals, and conference proceedings, 2 patents and numerous technical and industrial project reports. Under his supervision, 33 Ph.D. and M.A.SC students have completed their degrees. He is the Editor-in-Chief of the International Journal of Robotics and Automation, Associate Editor of the Intelligent Automation and Soft Computing, Simulation, the Journal of The Society for Computer Simulation, Pattern Recognition Letters, and member of the editorial board of the International Journal of Image and Graphics and Computers and Industrial Engineering Journal. Dr. Kamel is a member of ACM, AAAI, CIPS, APEO and a senior member of IEEE. He served as a consultant for General Motors, NCR, Diracto, IBM, Northern Telecom and Spar Aerospace. He is member of the board of directors and co-founder of Virtek Vision International in Waterloo.

Jari Kangas
Jari Kangas received his MSc degree in computer science from Helsinki University of Technology, Espoo, Finland, in 1988, and his PhD from the same university in 1994. He is currently a R&D manager and Principal Scientist at Nokia China R&D Center, Beijing, China. His research interests are in pattern recognition in general, emphasis being in methods and techniques to enhance the User Interface functions of mobile terminals by using, for example, handwriting recognition, speech recognition and image analysis.

Josef Kittler
Josef Kittler, Fellow of the Royal Academy of Engineering, graduated from the University of Cambridge in Electrical Engineering in 1971 where he also obtained his Ph.D. in Pattern Recognition in 1974 and the Sc.D. degree in 1991. He joined the University of Surrey in 1986 where he is Professor of Machine Intelligence, and Director of the Centre for Vision, Speech and Signal Processing. He has worked on various theoretical aspects of Pattern Recognition and Image Analysis, and on many applications including automatic inspection, ECG diagnosis, detection of microcalcifications in digital mammograms, video coding and retrieval, remote sensing, robot vision, speech recognition, and document processing. He has co-authored a book with the title "Pattern Recognition: A statistical approach" published by Prentice-Hall and published more than 400 papers. He is a member of the Editorial Boards of Pattern Recognition Journal, Image and Vision Computing, Pattern Recognition Letters, Pattern Recognition and Artificial Intelligence, Pattern Analysis and Applications, and Machine Vision and Applications.

Alessandro L. Koerich
Alessandro L. Koerich received the B.Sc. degree in electrical engineering from the Federal University of Santa Catarina (UFSC), Brazil in 1995, and the M.Sc. degree in electronics and communications from the University of Campinas (UNICAMP), Brazil, in 1997. He is currently a Ph.D. student in the Département de Génie de la Production Automatisée at the École de Technologie Supérieure (ETS), Université du Québec, Montréal, QC, Canada. He is also a visiting scientist at the Centre for Pattern Recognition and Machine Intelligence (CENPARMI). His research interests include pattern recognition and handwriting recognition.

Ravi Kothari
Ravi Kothari received his B.E. (with distinction) from Birla Institute of Technology, India, his M.S. from Louisiana State University and his Ph.D. from West Virginia University, all in Electrical Engineering. He is presently an Associate Professor in the Department of Electrical & Computer Engineering & Computer Science at the University of Cincinnati and Director of the Artificial Neural Systems Laboratory there. His areas of research include artificial neural networks, pattern recognition, and image analysis in which he has published more than 60 refereed papers.
Dr. Kothari received the William E. Restemeyer Teaching Excellence Award in 1994 and the Eta Kappa Nu Outstanding Professor of the Year award in 1995 from the Department of Electrical & Computer & Computer Science at the University of Cincinnati. He serves on the Editorial Board of the Journal Pattern Analysis and Applications (Springer-Verlag), and as an Associate Editor of the IEEE Transactions on Knowledge and Data Engineering. He is a Senior member of the IEEE, a member of the Sigma Xi, Eta Kappa Nu, Phi Kappa Phi, and Golden Key honor societies, and an Associate Member of the Imaging Research Center at the Childrens Hospital Medical Center in Cincinnati.

Victor Kulesh
Victor Kulesh is a graduate student in Computer Science and Engineering at Oakland Univeristy. He received his M.A. in Computer Science in 1999 from Wayne State University and B.S. in Mathematical Modeling in Economics in 1996 from National Technical University of Ukraine. He is currently involved in research in the area of multimedia information processing and indexing.

Franz Kummert
Franz Kummert received a Ph.D. (Dr.-Ing.) in computer science from the University of Erlangen-Nürnberg in 1991. From 1987 to 1990 he worked at the research group for Pattern Recognition at the University of Erlangen-Nürnberg. Since 1991, he is with the research group for Applied Computer Science at the University of Bielefeld. His fields of research are speech and image understanding.

Jorma Laaksonen
Jorma Laaksonen received his Dr. of Science in Technology degree in 1997 from Helsinki University of Technology, Finland, where he is presently Senior Research Scientist at the Laboratory of Computer and Information Science. He is an author of several journal and conference papers on pattern recognition, statistical classification, and neural networks. His research interests are in content-based image retrieval and recognition of handwriting. Dr. Laaksonen is a founding member of the SOM and LVQ Programming Teams, PicSOM Development Group, and a member of the International Association of Pattern Recognition (IAPR) Technical Committee 3: Neural Networks and Machine Learning.

Thomas Lehmann
Thomas Lehmann earned the MS degree in Electrical Engineering and the Ph.D. in Computer Science from the Aachen University of Technology (RWTH) in 1992 and 1998, respectively. He heads the Department of Medical Image Processing at the Institute of Medical Informatics, RWTH Aachen. In 1993 he was given the award from the German Association for Pattern Recognition (DAGM-Preis '93). In 1998 he received the Borcher's Medal from the RWTH Aachen. He is member of IEEE, SPIE and IADMFR. Since 1999, he serves on the International Editorial Board of Dentomaxillofacial Radiology. His research interests are discrete realizations of continuous image transforms, medical image processing applied to quantitative measurements for diagnoses, and content-based image retrieval from large medical databases. He has authored several papers and a textbook on medical image processing, which has been published by Springer-Verlag, Berlin.

Topi Mäenpää
Topi Mäenpää received the M.Sc. degree (with honors) in Electrical Engineering from the University of Oulu, Finland, in 1999. He is currently working with the Machine Vision and Media Processing Unit of Infotech Oulu and Department of Electrical Engineering as a postgraduate student of the national Graduate School in Electronics, Telecommunications and Automation. His current research area is combined color and texture analysis.

Dario Maio
Dario Maio is Full Professor at the Computer Science Department, University of Bologna, Italy. He has published in the fields of distributed computer systems, computer performance evaluation, database design, information systems, neural networks, biometric systems, autonomous agents. Before joining the Computer

Science Department, he received a fellowship from the C.N.R. (Italian National Research Council) for participation in the Air Traffic Control Project. He received the degree in Electronic Engineering from the University of Bologna in 1975. He is a IEEE member. He is with CSITE - C.N.R. and with DEIS; he teaches database and information systems at the Computer Science Dept., Cesena.

Kerstin Malmqvist

Kerstin Malmqvist received a Ph.D. degree in Applied Mathematics and Computer Science in 1980 at Umea University, Sweden. Her research is focused on methods and tools for color measurements in multicolor printing. She is a member of the board of VISIT, a national program for research in Visual Information Technology. She is also a member of TAPPI, Technical Association of the Pulp and Paper Industry.

Davide Maltoni

Davide Maltoni is an Associate Researcher at the Computer Science Department, University of Bologna, Italy. He received the degree in Computer Science from the University of Bologna, Italy, in 1993. In 1998 he received his Ph.D. in Computer Science and Electronic Engineering at DEIS, University of Bologna, with the research theme "Biometric Systems". His research interests also include autonomous agents, pattern recognition and neural nets. He is an IAPR member.

Andrew McCabe

Dr. Andrew McCabe is currently a research fellow with the Dept. of Computing Science at the University of Alberta, Canada. He is currently working in the area of modeling human action using temporal machine learning techniques. His current research interests include colour signal processing, spatio-temporal machine learning, and applied image processing. He received his B.Comp. in 1993 from Monash University in Melbourne, Australia, B.Sc. (Honors) in 1994 and Ph.D. in 1999 from Curtin University, Perth, Australia.

Daniel McReynolds

Daniel McReynolds received his Ph.D. in computer science from the University of British Columbia, Canada, in 1997. From 1997 to 1999, he was a post-doctoral researcher at the Université Laval, Canada. During the summer of 1999, he was an invited researcher at the Human Information Processing Laboratories at ATR, in Kyoto, Japan. Currently, he is a researcher with Imago Machine Vision, In Ottowa, Canada. His research interests include structure-for-motion, image matching, image stabilization, tracking, face detection, and feature representation.

Kieron Messer

Kieron Messer, graduated from Royal Holloway University of London in 1993 with a Bachelor of Science degree in Physics. In 1995 he obtained a Masters of Science degree in Machine Intelligence at the University of Surrey where he also obtained his Ph.D. in Image Database retrieval four years later. Presently, he is still based at the Centre for Vision, Speech and Signal Processing at the University of Surrey working as a research fellow.

Theo Moons

Theo Moons received a master's and a PhD degree in mathematics from the Katholieke Universiteit Leuven (Leuven, Belgium) in 1983 and 1990 respectively. He was a research assistant at the Limburgs Universitair Centrum (Diepenbeek, Belgium) between 1983 and 1990, after which he worked as a post-doctoral researcher within the Electrotechnical Engineering department of the Katholieke Universiteit Leuven. His research interests include invariance for object recognition and 3D reconstruction. In 1996 he became the head of the remote sensing group within the VISICS team at the K.U.Leuven; and in 2000, he also became professor of mathematics at the Faculty of Applied Economic Sciences of the Katholieke Universiteit Brussel (Brussels, Belgium).

Erkki Oja

Erkki Oja received his Dr.Sc. degree in 1977 from Helsinki University of Technology, Finland, where he is presently Professor of Computer Science and Director of the Neural Networks Research Centre. His research interests are in the study of principal components, independent components, self-organization, statistical pattern recognition, and applying artificial neural networks to computer vision and signal processing. Dr. Oja is an IEEE Fellow, IAPR Fellow, and President of the European Neural Network

Society. He is member of the editorial boards of several journals, including "Neural Computation", "IEEE Transactions on Neural Networks", and "Int. Journal of Pattern Recognition and Artificial Intelligence".

Timo Ojala

Timo Ojala received the M.Sc. (with honors) and Dr.Tech. degrees in Electrical Engineering from the University of Oulu, Finland, in 1992 and 1997, respectively. He currently serves as the Associate Director of MediaTeam Oulu research group in the University of Oulu. His research interests include computer vision, statistical pattern recognition, texture analysis and multimedia communications.

B. John Oommen

Dr. Oommen obtained his B.Tech. degree from the Indian Institute of Technology, Madras, India in 1975. He obtained his M.E. from the Indian Institute of Science in Bangalore, India in 1977. He then went on for his M.S. and Ph.D. which he obtained from Purdue University, in West Lafayettte, Indiana in 1979 and 1982 respectively. He joined the School of Computer Science at Carleton University in Ottawa, Canada, in the 1981-82 academic year. He is still at Carleton and holds the rank of a Full Professor. His research interests include Automata Learning, Adaptive Data Structures, Statistical and Syntactic Pattern Recognition, Stochastic Algorithms and Partitioning Algorithms. He is the author of over 165 refereed journal and conference publications, and is a Senior Member of the IEEE.

Tomas Pajdla

Tomas Pajdla, born 1969, MSc. Czech Technical University 1992, Assistant Professor n the Canter for Machine Perception, Faculty of Electrical Engineering, Prague, Czech Republic. Main research interests: 3D computer vision, scene reconstruction from uncalibrated images, range imaging, omni-directional vision, industrial applications of computer vision.

Pietro Pala

Pietro Pala graduated in Electronic Engineering at the Universita di Firenze, Italy, in 1994. In 1998, he received the Ph.D. in Information Science from the same University. Currently he is Assistant Professor at the Dipartimento di Sistemi e Informatica of the University of Florence. His current research interests include pattern recognition, image and video retrieval by content, and related applications.

Derek Partridge

Professor Derek Partridge is Professor of Computer Science at the University of Exeter, UK. Prior to his appointment to the chair at Exeter in 1986, he was professor of Computer Science at New Mexico State University, USA. He returned to the UK in 1987 having spent 15 years abroad, mostly in the USA but also at the University of Nairobi, Kenya (2 years), and The University of Queensland, Brisbane, Australia (8 months). In 1996 he was Visiting Professor at the Science University of Malaysia, Penang.

He was educated at London University: BSc Chemistry from University College in 1968, and a PhD in Computer Science from Imperial College in 1972. His research has ranged over Artificial Intelligence, Cognitive Science and Software Engineering. He is the author of many papers and a number of books on these subjects.

He is Head of Research for Computer Science within the School of Engineering and Computer Science. He has been the Principal Investigator of a number of projects that have been working towards the development of a multiversion software engineering methodology that is specifically designed for the exploitation of inductive programming technologies in software engineering and data mining. Currently, he leads an EPSRC-funded project exploring the uses of neural computing as a software technology for enhancement of air-traffic control software systems. This project involves both elucidation of the technology underlying neural computing and exploration of neural-net and decision-tree implementations of software modules as radically different (from conventionally programmed) versions in a multiversion approach to software reliability as well as a route to improving classical software specifications. Other current projects involve the prediction of medical outcomes (such as life or death in trauma cases, and risk of osteoporosis) and the prediction of likelihood of injury in basic training for army recruits.

Gennaro Percannella

Gennaro Percannella was born in Salerno, Italy, in 1973. He received a Laurea degree (cum laude) in Electronic Engineering from the University of Salerno, Italy, in 1998. He is currently a Ph.D. student at the same University. His research interests are in the area of visual and audio content analysis for advanced video-retrieval systems, with particular reference to the development of efficient video and audio segmentation techniques operating at different semantic level.

Maria Petrou
Maria Petrou received her B.Sc. in Physics from the Aristotle University of Thessaloniki, Greece, and her Ph.D. in Astronomy from the University of Cambridge, UK. She has published more than 200 papers, on Astronomy, Low Level Vision, Feature Extraction, Texture Analysis, Markov Random Fields, Multiresolution optimisation, Probabilistic Relaxation, Colour, Remote Sensing, Industrial Inspection, Medical Signal Processing, etc. She has co-authored a book "Image Processing: the fundamentals" published by John Wiley. She is Professor of Image Analysis at the School of Electronic Engineering, Information Technology and Mathematics of Surrey University, UK. She is a Chartered Engineer, member of IEEE, Fellow of IEE, Fellow of IAPR, the chairman of the Technical Committee for Remote Sensing of IAPR, and the chairman of the British Machine Vision Association (BMVA). She has served as an Associate Editor of IEEE Transactions on Image Processing and as the Newsletter Editor of IAPR from 1994-1998. She is on the editorial board of the journal Pattern Analysis and Applications and the magazine Image Processing Europe.

Matti Pietikäinen
Matti Pietikäinen received his Doctor of Technology degree in Electrical Engineering from the University of Oulu, Finland, in 1982. Currently he is Professor of Information Technology, Scientific Director of Infotech Oulu research center, and Head of Machine Vision and Media Processing Unit at the University of Oulu. From 1980 to 1981 and from 1984 to 1985 he was visiting the Computer Vision Laboratory at the University of Maryland, USA. His research interests cover wide aspects of machine vision, including texture analysis, color machine vision and document analysis. His research has been widely published in journals, books and conferences. He is Associate Editor of Pattern Recognition journal, and Editor of the books "Machine Vision for Advanced Production" (with L.F. Pau) and "Texture Analysis in Machine Vision" published by World Scientific in 1996 and 2000, respectively. Prof. Pietikäinen is a founding Fellow of International Association for Pattern Recognition (IAPR), past Chairman of Pattern Recognition Society of Finland, Senior Member of IEEE, and serves as Member of the Governing Board and Education Committee of IAPR. He has also served on committees of several international conferences.

Pavel Pudil
Pavel Pudil is currently the Head of Pattern Recognition Dept. at the Institute of Information Theory and Automation, Academy of Sciences of the Czech Republic. In 1996-2000 he was the Chairman of IAPR Technical Committee on "Statistical Techniques in Pattern Recognition". His primary research interests include statistical approach to pattern recognition, particularly the problem of dimensionality reduction and its applications in economics, management and medical diagnostics. He spent as a Research Fellow altogether 5 years at British universities (Cambridge, Surrey). After graduating from the Czech Technical University in Prague in 1964 he received a Ph.D. degree in Technical Cybernetics in 1970 and became Associate Professor in Prague University of Economics in 1998. He is a member of the Czech Society for Cybernetics and Informatics, Czech Pattern Recognition Society, Society for Biomedical Engineering, a member of IEEE and the IAPR Fellow.

Gopal Racherla
Dr. Gopal Racherla is presently a Network Architect at IOSPAN Wireless in San Jose, CA. He was previously a research engineer at SRI International in Menlo Park, CA. He received his Ph.D. and M.S. in Computer Science from the University of Oklahoma, Norman, and B.E. in Computer Engineering from Victoria Jubilee Technical Institute, Bombay. He has worked at the Indian Institute of Technology, Bombay and the Tata Electric Company (R&D Labs), Bombay. Dr. Racherla has over 30 publications in journals and conferences in the area of image processing, wireless networks, and parallel and distributed processing.

Sridhar Radhakrishan
Dr. Sridhar Radhakrishnan is an Associate Professor in the School of Computer Science at the University of Oklahoma, where he joined in 1990. He received his Ph.D. in Computer Science from Louisiana State University in 1990. His research interests are in the areas of protocol design for wireless and mobile computing, power aware protocols in mobile networks, algorithms for quality of service routing in broadband networks, and resource allocation problems in wireless networks. He has published over 50 research articles in journals, conference proceedings, and book chapters. His textbook on data structures titled *Object-oriented Data Structures Featuring C++* is currently under review for publication.

Eraldo Ribeiro

Eraldo Ribeiro has recently completed his D.Phil. degree in computer vision in the Department of Computer Science at the University of York. Prior to this Dr Ribeiro gained his Master of Science Degree with distinction in Computer Science (Image Processing) at the Federal University of Sao Carlos (UFSCar-SP), Brazil in 1995. His first degree is in Mathematics from the Catholic University of Salvador - Brazil (1992). His research interests are in shape from texture techniques and 3-D scene analysis. He has published some 25 papers in journals and refereed conferences.

Helge J. Ritter

Helge J. Ritter received a Ph.D. in Physics from the Technical University of Munich in 1988. After working at the Laboratory for Computer and Information Science at Helsinki University of Technology and at the Bockman Institute for Advanced Science and Technology and the Department of Physics at the University of Illinois at Urbana-Champaign he became Professor at the University of Bielefeld in 1990. His main interests are principles of neural computation, in particular self-organizing and learning systems, and their application to machine vision, robot control and interactive man-machine interfaces.

Robert Sabourin

Robert Sabourin received B.ing., M.Sc.A. and Ph.D. degrees in electrical engineering from the École Polytechnique de Montréal in 1977, 1980 and 1991 respectively. In 1977, he joined the physics department of the Université de Montréal where he was responsible for the design and development of scientific instrumentation for the Observatoire du Mont Mégantic. In 1983, he joined the staff of the École de Technologie Supérieure, Université du Québec, Montréal, P.Q., Canada, where he is currently a professeur titulaire in the Département de Génie de la Production Automatisée. In 1995, he joined also the Computer Science Department of the Pontifícia Universidade Católica do Paraná (PUCPR, Curitiba, Brazil) where he was co-responsible since 1998 for the implementation of a PhD program in applied informatics. Since 1996, he is a member of the Centre for Pattern Recognition and Machine Intelligence (CENPARMI). His research interests are in the areas of handwriting recognition and signature verification for banking and postal applications.

Mohammad T. Sadeghi

Mohammad T. Sadeghi received the B.Sc. degree in Electronic Engineering from Sharif University of Technology, Tehran, Iran in 1991 and the M.Sc. degree from Tarbiat-Modarres University, Tehran, Iran in 1994. Currently, he is working towards his Ph.D. in the Centre for Vision, Speech and Signal Processing at the University of Surrey. His research project is concerned with probability function modelling for adaptive and intelligent image analysis.

Mohamed Sadek

Mohamed Sadek was born in 1977 in Alexandria, Egypt. He just graduated from the École Nationale Supérieure des Télécommunications (ENST) in Paris, France, and is presently initiating a Diplôme d'Études Approfondies (DEA) in artificial intelligence at the University of Paris VI. In 1999, he was a research trainee at the Human Information Processing Research Laboratories (HIP) of ATR in Kyoto, Japan.

Gerhard Sagerer

Gerhard Sagerer received the Ph.D. (Dr.-Ing.) in computer science from the University of Erlangen-Nürnberg, Erlangen, Germany, in 1985. From 1980 to 1990 he was with the research group for pattern recognition at the University of Erlangen-Nürnberg. Since 1990 he is a professor of computer science at the University of Bielefeld, Germany, and head of the research group for Applied Computer Science. His research interests are in integrated speech and image understanding and bioinformatics.

Andres E. Salguero

Andres E. Salguero received his B.Sc. degree in electronic engineering from the Xavier University, Bogota, Colombia, in 1993. He worked as a Lecturer and as research fellow in the Department of Electronics Engineering at Xavier University between 1994 and 1998. His main research interests are associated with biomedical signal processing, in particular the study of EEG signals and their application to brain computer interfacing with neuroprosthetic devices. He is currently pursuing his Ph.D. degree at the Centre for Vision, Speech, and Signal Processing at the University of Surrey, UK. His current research is in the area of behaviour prediction based on event-related potentials.

Carlo Sansone
Carlo Sansone was born in Naples, Italy, in 1969. He received a Laurea degree (cum laude) in Electronic Engineering in 1993 and a Ph.D. Degree in Electronic and Computer Engineering in 1997, both from the University of Naples "Federico II". Since 1999 is Assistant Professor of Computer Science, and Neural Programming at the University of Naples "Federico II". His research interests are in the fields of Neural Networks Theory and Classification Methodologies, exploiting applications in different areas of Pattern Recognition as Optical Character Recognition, Document Processing and Signature Verification. Carlo Sansone is a member of the International Association for Pattern Recognition (IAPR).

Kevin Schaffer
Kevin Schaffer received his undergraduate degree in Computer Science from Michigan State University and is currently a software engineer with Mandala Sciences, Inc.

Daniel Schlüter
Daniel Schlüter received the diploma in computer science in 1995 from the University of Bielefeld. In 1996 he worked as a project and development engineer concerned with industrial applications of image processing. Since 1997 he is a member of the research group for Applied Computer Science at the University of Bielefeld. Currently he is working in the SFB 360. His interests are perceptual grouping/organization, image processing and computer vision.

Mark Schwartz
Mark Schwartz, PhD is the founder and CEO of Mandala Sciences, Inc. He received his PhD from UCLA and is currently involved in research in digital handwriting. He is a holder of two patents.

Ishwar K. Sethi
Ishwar K. Sethi is currently Professor and Chair of Computer Science and Engineering at Oakland University. His research interests include pattern recognition, data mining, and multimedia information processing and indexing. Professor Sethi serves on the editorial boards of several international journals including *IEEE Trans. Pattern Analysis and Machine Intelligence* and *IEEE Multimedia*.

Mona Sharma
Mona received her B.Sc. in Computer Science from Kurukshetra University, India in 1999 and Masters Diploma in Software Technology from IEC India in 1999. In early 2000 she finished writing her M.Phil. in the area of 'Performance evaluation of image segmentation and texture extraction methods for scene analysis' at the Department of Computer Science, University of Exeter. Her main research interests are in scene analysis, image processing and pattern recognition.

Pei Yi Shen
PeiYi Shen is a post doctoral research fellow in computer science at the School of Computing, National University of Singapore. He obtained his Ph.D. degree in computer science from Xidian University in 1999, P. R. China. His research interests include computer vision, real-time system and image processing.

Yunlong Sheng
Dr. Yunlong Sheng received his B.S. degree from the University of Sciences and Technology of China in 1964. He received the M.S., Doctor and Doctor d'Etat degrees in physics from the Université de Franche-Comté, Besançon, France in 1980, 1982 and 1986 respectively. Since 1985, he has joined the Centre d'Optique, Phonotique et Laser, University Laval and is now a full professor. Dr. Sheng has been author and co-author of more than 140 refereed journal papers, books and book chapters and conference papers. His research interests involve multisensor image processing, pattern recognition, neural networks, interconnects, diffractive optics and optical communication. Dr. Sheng is a Fellow of the SPIE-International society for optical engineering, am member of OSA and the International Neural Network Society. He serves as a member of programme committees and a chairperson of a number of international conferences and as a consultant for industrial companies in the USA and Canada. Since 1996 Dr. Yunlong Sheng has been the principal investigator in the project "Automatic stabilization, registration and fusion of multisensor images using wavelet transform" funded by the Department of National Defence (DND) Canada, the Natural Sciences and Engineering Research Council (NSERC) of Canada and Lockheed Martin Canada.

Mahadad Nouri Shirazi
Mahadad Nouri Shirazi was born in 1963 in Iran. He received his M.Sc. and Ph.D. degrees in Electrical Engineering from Tottori University and Kobe University, Japan, respectively. In 1993 he became a Post-Doctoral Research Fellow at the Communications Research Laboratory, funded by the Science and Technology Agency of Japan (STA). Since 1995 he has conducted research at the same laboratory, currently as a senior research scientist. His research interests include neural networks, pattern recognition, and image processing.

Sameer Singh
Sameer Singh was born in New Delhi, India and graduated from Birla Institute of Technology, India with a Bachelor of Engineering degree with distinction in Computer Engineering. He received his Master of Science degree in Information Technology for Manufacturing from the University of Warwick, UK and a Ph.D. in speech and language analysis of stroke patients from the University of the West of England, UK. His main research interests are in image processing, medical imaging, neural networks and pattern recognition. He is the Director of the Pattern Analysis and Neural Networks group at Exeter University. He serves as the Editor-in-Chief of the Pattern Analysis and Applications journal by Springer, Editor-in-Chief of the Springer book series on 'Advances in Pattern Recognition', Chairman of the British Computer Society Specialist group on Pattern Analysis and Robotics, Editorial Board member of Neural Computing and Applications journal, and Editorial Board member of the Perspectives in Neural Computing book series by Springer. He is a Fellow of the Royal Statistical Society, and a Member of BMVA-IAPR, IEE and IEEE.

Petr Somol
Petr Somol received his B.S., M.S., and Ph.D. degrees in 1993, 1995 and 2000, respectively, from the Faculty of Mathematics and Physics, Charles University, Prague, Czech Republic, all in computer science. He is currently with the Department of Pattern Recognition at the Institute of Information Theory and Automation, Academy of Sciences of the Czech Republic. His current activities include development of feature selection techniques, mixture modelling algorithms and decision support systems. He is particularly interested in statistical pattern recognition. His part-time interests include computer graphics application development.

Klaus Spitzer
Klaus Spitzer earned the MS degree in mathematics and Ph.D. in mathematics from the Friedrich-Wilhelms-University, Bonn, in 1983 and 1985, respectively. He earned the MD from the Friedrich-Wilhelms-University, Bonn, in 1983. From 1983 to 1993 he was physician and neurologist at the Department of Neurology, University Hospital of Hamburg. He was Professor of Neurology at the University of Hamburg from 1992 to 1994, and Associated Professor of Medical Informatics from 1993 to 1995 at the University of Heidelberg. Since 1995 he has been Professor of Medical Informatics and Chair of the Department of Medical Informatics and Biometry at the Aachen University of Technology (RWTH). His research fields are knowledge-based systems in medicine, computer-based training, digital patient records, hospital information systems, and management of IT-systems.

Daniela Stan
Daniela Stan is a graduate student in Computer Science and Engineering at Oakland University. She received her M.A. in Computer Science in 1999 from Wayne State University and B.S. in Mathematics in 1993 from University of Bucharest, Romania. She is currently involved in the area of content-based image retrieval and data mining.

Ching Y. Suen
Ching Y. Suen received an M.Sc. (Eng.) degree from the University of Hong Kong and a Ph.D. degree from the University of British Columbia, Canada. In 1972, he joined the Department of Computer Science of Concordia University where he became Professor in 1979 and served as Chairman from 1980 to 1984, and as Associate Dean for Research of the Faculty of Engineering and Computer Science from 1993 to 1997. Currently he is the Director of CENPARMI, the Centre for Pattern Recognition and Machine Intelligence. Prof. Suen is the author/editor of 11 books and more than 250 papers on subjects ranging from computer vision and handwriting recognition, to expert systems and computational linguistics. He is the founder and Editor-in-Chief of a journal and an Associate Editor of several journals related to pattern recognition. A Fellow of the IEEE, IAPR, and the Academy of Sciences of the Royal Society of Canada, he has served several professional societies as President, Vice-President, or Governor. He is also the founder

and chair of several conference series and is currently the General Chair of the International Conference on Pattern Recognition to be held in Quebec City in 2002. Dr. Suen is the recipient of several awards, including the ITAC/NSERC Award in 1992 and the Concordia "Research Fellow" award in 1998.

Jasjit Suri

Dr. Jasjit Suri received a Bachelor's degree in Electronics and Computer Engineering from MACT, Bhopal, a Master's degree in Computer Science from University of Illinois, Chicago and a Doctorate in Electrical Engineering from University of Washington, Seattle. Dr. Suri has been working in the area of Medical Image Segmentation for more than a decade and has published more than 60 publications in the area of Cardiac Imaging, Brain Magnetic Resonance, Abdomen Computed Tomography, Dental X-rays, Ultrasound and Pathology Imaging and has done more than 25 presentations/seminars at several international conferences in Europe, Australia and USA. He is on the editorial boards of IASTED and EMBS Journals. He has also served as a guest reviewer for Int. Journals of Pattern Analysis and Applications, Jour. of Computer Assisted Tomography, Radiology and several peer reviewed International Conferences. Dr. Suri has also served as associate editor for IEEE Information Technology in Biomedicine. His major interests are in Computer Vision, Graphics, Image Processing, Medical Imaging and applications of mathematical modeling for human body organs. During his career, Dr. Suri has received more than 45 scholarly, scientific, extra-curricular awards. Dr. Suri is a Senior member of IEEE, and holds membership of Sigma Xi, NYAS, EMBS, ACM, SPIE and Cleveland Engineering societies. Dr. Suri received the "Who's Who in the World" and is listed in Marquis Who's Who-18th Edition, and is also a recipient of the "International Executive Who's Who" award for the year 2000. He was honored with Indian President's Gold Medal in 1980.

Flávio Szenberg

Flávio Szenberg received a degree in Mathematics from the Fluminense Federal University (UFF) in 1993, in 1997 he received a M.Sc. in Computer Science from the Catholic University of Rio de Janeiro (PUC-Rio) where he is taking his Ph.D. He received an award from the Brazilian Society of Computer Science for his M.Sc. dissertation and an award from the Computer Graphics Symposium in 1998 for a technical video. He is currently a research assistant at Tecgraf/PUC-Rio where among other activities he developed the freeware JuizVirtual that implements some of the ideas of this paper. His current research interests include Computer Vision, Geometric Modeling, Image-based Modeling.

Chew Lim Tan

Chew Lim Tan is an associate professor in computer science at the School of Computing, National University of Singapore. His research interests are computer vision, document image analysis, intelligent text processing and neural networks. He obtained a B.Sc. (Hons) degree in Physics in 1971 from the University of Singapore, an M.Sc. degree in Radiation Studies in 1973 from the University of Surrey in UK, and a Ph.D. Degree in Computer Science in 1986 from the University of Virginia, USA.

Lorenzo Tanganelli

Lorenzo Tanganelli graduated in Electronic Engineering at the Universita di Firenze, Italy in 1998. His research interests include pattern video retrieval by content, and related applications.

Jean-Christophe Terrillon

Jean-Christophe Terrillon received a B.Sc. in physics from the University of Ottawa, an M.Sc. in plasma physics and biophysics from the Université de Montréal, and a Ph.D. in physics (optics) from the Université Laval, Canada, in 1983, 1987 and 1993 respectively. He is also an alumnus of the International Space University. He was awarded a post-doctoral fellowship by the Science and Technology Agency of Japan, which he held at the Communications Research Laboratory in Kobe, Japan, from 1994 to 1996. In 1996, he joined the Human Information Processing Research Laboratories (HIP) of the Advanced Telecommunications Research International (ATR) in Kyoto, Japan, as an invited researcher. He is presently a senior researcher at the Office of the Regional Intensive Research Project, Softopia Japan Foundation, in Gifu, Japan. His research interests include the development of computational models for human face detection in complex scene images by use of color and shape information, and more generally pattern recognition and image processing. He is a member of IEEE and of the Computer Society.

Andreas Turina
Andreas Turina received a master's degree in Electrical Engineering from the Swiss Federal Institute of Technology (ETH) in 1999. He works currently as a research assistant at the ETH Computer Vision Group in Zurich. His PhD thesis deals with the detection of repeated patterns and symmetries in images.

Tinne Tuytelaars
Tinne Tuytelaars graduated at the University of Leuven in 1996. Since then, she has been conducting research on computer vision at the same university, where she is about to finish her PhD. Her main research interests are invariance, object recognition and wide baseline stereo.

Luc Van Gool
Luc Van Gool is professor for computer vision at ETH Zurich, Switzerland, and the University of Leuven, Flanders, Belgium. His main interests include object recognition, 3D scene reconstruction, animation, grouping, and texture analysis and synthesis. He received several prizes, including a David Marr Prize, two TechArt Awards, a Golden Eye Award, a Henry Ford European Conservation Award, etc. He is co-founder of the company Eyetronics. He has served on the program committee of major vision conferences and has coordinated several European projects. With his teams, he also works on application oriented projects with industry, including inspection, surveillance, and precision agriculture.

Mario Vento
Mario Vento was born in Italy in 1960. In 1984 he received a Laurea degree (cum laude) in Electronic Engineering, and in 1988 a Ph.D. degree in Electronic and Computer Engineering, both from University of Naples "Federico II", where he is currently Associate Professor of Computer Science and Artificial Intelligence. His interests cover the areas of Artificial Intelligence, Image Analysis, Pattern Recognition, Machine Learning and Parallel Computing in Artificial Vision. He dedicated to Classification Techniques, either Statistical, Syntactic and Structural, giving contributions to Neural Network Theory, Statistical Learning, Graph Matching, Multi-Expert Classification and Symbolic Learning Methodologies. He participated to several projects in the areas of Handwritten Character Recognition, Document Processing, Car Plate Recognition, Signature Verification, Raster to Vector Conversion of Technical Drawings, and Automatic Interpretation of Biomedical Images. He authored over 70 research papers in International Journals and Conference Proceedings. Prof. Vento is a member of the IAPR, and of IAPR Technical Committee on "Graph Based Representations" (TC15).

Antanas Verikas
Antanas Verikas received a Ph.D. degree in pattern recognition at Kaunas University of Technology, Lithuania in 1981. Since 1975, he has been active in research in the fields of image processing, pattern recognition, neural networks and fuzzy logic. In 1992, he joined the Centre for Imaging Science and Technologies at Halmstad University, Sweden. He has published over 90 papers in the fields mentioned above. He is a member of the European Neural Network Society, International Pattern Recognition Society, and a member of the IEEE.

Nayer M. Wanas
Nayer M. Wanas received his B.Sc. and M.E. degree in Electronics and Communications Engineering from Cairo University, Egypt in 1992 and 1996 respectively. He currently is currently a research assistant working to- wards his Ph.D. degree in Systems Design Engineering at the University of Waterloo, Canada. His research is mainly focused on Decision Fusion. From 1992 till 1994 he was a research assistant at the National Research Center, Giza, Egypt. Since 1994 he has held a position of assistant researcher at the Electronics Research Institute, Giza, Egypt.

Qian Wang
Qian Wang is an analyst programmer at the Centre for Instructional Technology, National University of Singapore. He obtained his B.Sc. (Honours) degree in Computer Science from the National University of Singapore in 1999. His research interest is Document Image Analysis. He is currently pursuing an M.Sc. degree in Computer Science at the National University of Singapore.

Kazuhiko Yamamoto
Kazuhiko Yamamoto received the B.E. and M.E. in engineering from Tokyo Denki Univeristy in 1969 and 1971 respectively. From 1971 to 1995 he was with the Electro-technical laboratory (ETL), studying pattern recognition. He participated in the development of OCR from 1971 to 1979. From 1979 to 1980, he was a

visiting researcher in the Computer Vision Laboratory of the University of Maryland, where he worked on computer vision. He was a chief of the image understanding section of ETL from 1986 to 1995. He is a professor at Gifu University since 1995 and is the executive research leader of the office of joint-research for the regional intensive project at Softopia Japan since 1999. His research interests are pattern recognition and artificial intelligence. Dr. Yamamoto is a member of IEEE computer Society and IEICE Japan. He was awarded a fellow of IAPR.

Barbara Zitová

Barbara Zitová was born in Frýdek-Míystek, Czech Republic, on March 13, 1972. She received the M.Sc. degree in computer science from the Charles University, Prague, Czech Republic in 1995 and is currently a Ph.D. candidate in computer science at the Charles University, Prague, Czech Republic. Since 1995 she has been with the Institute of Information Theory and Automation, Academy of Sciences of the Czech Republic, Prague. Her current research interests include image processing, wavelets, geometric invariants and image registration.

Author Index

Lecture Notes in Computer Science

For information about Vols. 1–1926
please contact your bookseller or Springer-Verlag